★ ★

W9-BNP-920

WOMEN IN POLITICS:

OUTSIDERS OR INSIDERS?

A Collection of Readings

THIRD EDITION

Lois Duke Whitaker, Editor
Georgia Southern University

PRENTICE HALL
Upper Saddle River, New Jersey 07458

Library of Congress Cataloging-in-Publication Data

Women in politics : outsiders or insiders? : a collection of readings
/ Lois Duke Whitaker, editor. — 3rd ed.
    p.   cm.
  Includes bibliographical references.
  ISBN 0–13–096610-X
  1. Women in politics--United States.   2. Feminism--United States.
I. Whitaker, Lois Duke.
HQ1236.5.U6W663   1999
320.'.082—dc21

9820211
CIP

Editor-in-Chief: Nancy Roberts
Sr. Acquisition Editor: Beth Gillett
Associate Editor: Nicole Conforti
Managing Editor: Ann Marie McCarthy
Production Liaison: Fran Russello
Project Manager: Patty Donovan/Pine Tree Composition
Prepress and Manufacturing Buyer: Bob Anderson
Cover Director: Jayne Conte
Cover Design: Bruce Kenselaar
Cover Art: George Chan/Tony Stone Images
Marketing Manager: Christopher DeJohn

This book was set in *10/12 Garamond* by Pine Tree Composition, Inc.,
and was printed and bound by *Courier Companies.*
The cover was printed by *Phoenix Color Corp.*

 © 1999, 1996, 1993 by Prentice-Hall, Inc.
Simon & Schuster/A Viacom Company
Upper Saddle River, New Jersey 07458

Printed in the United States of America
10 9 8 7 6 5 4 3 2 1

ISBN: 0-13-096610-X

Prentice-Hall International (UK) Limited, *London*
Prentice-Hall of Australia Pty. Limited, *Sydney*
Prentice-Hall Canada Inc., *Toronto*
Prentice-Hall Hispanoamericana, S.A., *Mexico*
Prentice-Hall of India Private Limited, *New Delhi*
Prentice-Hall of Japan, Inc., *Tokyo*
Simon & Schuster Asia Pte. Ltd., *Singapore*
Editora Prentice-Hall do Brasil, Ltda., *Rio de Janeiro*

CONTENTS

PREFACE

What began as a much smaller project about nine years ago has now developed into a third edition. While the numbers of articles have increased somewhat, this third edition of this volume has attempted to maintain and merely update many of the pieces in the original edition. The basic thrust of the book is essentially unchanged. That is, this book is designed to provide a supplemental reader on the topic of women and politics to accompany texts for American government courses to aid in integrating the study of women in the political system, as well as for use in women and politics courses, and even as a supplement for graduate-level courses. This reader provides relevant research on women and politics across a spectrum of topics and perspectives; therefore, the book can provide merely a "snapshot." Each author has added a "Further Readings" section at the conclusion of his or her article to help in explaining more fully where the essays fit into the overall picture of other research.

We begin with a feminist theoretical framework, examine some gender differences in political attitudes and voting, look at gender cultural reflections in the mass media and group politics, and examine how women have fared in competing for public office. Next we look at the various branches of government and see how women are (and in some cases are not) participating in the functions of government. Then we explore women and national public policy, ending with women and empowerment and cultural expression.

ORGANIZATIONAL FRAMEWORK

The book is organized into nine chapters, which are arranged into four parts. Part I includes an analysis of "Women, Equality, and Feminist Theory." Part II explores the topic of "Women and Politics," including how women and men have changed in their opinions about women's roles in politics; gender differences in voting and attitudes; the concept of occupational stratification and how this affects political attitudes; women, the media, and movement politics; and women and elections. Part III, "Gender and Government," examines women and their role as policy makers in political institutions. This topic includes women as chief executives, females in the U.S. Congress and projections for their future role, females within the judicial system, and women's rights struggles and the U.S. Supreme Court's responses. Part IV looks at "Women's and National Policy" in such public policy areas as family and medical leave, sex at risk in insurance classifications, and affirmative action. We conclude with a chapter on "Women, Empowerment, and Cultural Expression." This includes an article on coffee drinking and the importance of free speech. Brief summaries of the chapters included in the book follow.

CHAPTER 1   THE STUDY OF WOMEN: THE NEW FRAMEWORK

Feminist Theory as Seeing   *Jennifer Ring*

Feminist theory is a way of seeing the world through the lens of gender, which is always present, but rarely recognized. In political science, as in most academic fields, gender is invisible, with the male gendered stance assumed to be neutral or objective. Here Jennifer Ring offers a feminist rereading of American slavery to demonstrate how the perspective of the most marginalized group in the social system, African American women, actually permits access to the deepest, most revealing insights. Viewing social and political systems from the margins permits greater insights into the "center", or the whole. A more general discussion of the nature of feminist theory along with a survey of well-known theorists follows the description and analysis of slavery. "Feminist-compatible" approaches to theory are identified as (1) liberalism and radicalism, (2) materialism, (3) a critique of objectivity, and (4) post-structuralist feminism, all of which presuppose a multicultural approach.

The Riddle of Consciousness: Racism and Identity in Feminist Theory   *Nancie E. Caraway*

Utilizing the political and epistemological contributions of contemporary black feminist theory, Nancie E. Caraway points up the intersections of gender, race, and class as determinants of oppression. She argues that the texts of black feminists teach us that feminist theory and politics should address this "multiple jeopardy." She cautions that feminists need to be wary of the damaging consequences of conceptions like identity and self, which have set up white norms. In her discussion of identity politics, Caraway questions many of the assumptions of mainstream white feminism. She proposes instead multicultural goals in which the themes of racism and identity come together in a configuration that can address the theoretical issues about the female subject. She argues that a critical identity politics cautions us not to become too comfortable too long in one spot with one identity lest we forget and stifle the ways in which we change, contradict, and grow in history.

CHAPTER 2   GENDER DIFFERENCES IN POLITICAL ATTITUDES AND VOTING

Changing Views about Gender Equality in Politics: Gradual Change and Lingering Doubts   *Linda L. M. Bennett and Stephen E. Bennett*

This article looks at how women and men have changed their opinions about women's roles in politics. Creating a Political Gender Roles Index from data in the National Opinion Research Center's (NORC) General Social Surveys between 1973 and 1996, the Bennett's find that while there are few gender differences about the role of women in politics, there are differences in the rate of change toward favoring more modern roles. The authors warn against assuming that there will be a natural progression in opinion favoring more modern roles, particularly among young, even well-educated, men.

The Generations of Feminism   *Elizabeth Adell Cook*

Previous research has found that younger women are more likely to hold feminist attitudes than are older women. There is also some evidence, however, that young women in the 1980s are less supportive of feminism than were older women. This suggests that there may be some generational influences at work. Cohort analysis of the 1972 to 1996 American National Election Studies indicates that women who came of age during the period of social activism of the 1960s and the growth of the women's movement in the 1970s exhibit higher levels of politicized feminist consciousness than do women of earlier generations; women who came of age during the anti-feminist Reagan administration are less feminist than those who reached adulthood during the women's liberation movement, or during the Clinton administration. In 1996, the Reagan or complacent cohort was not more conservative than earlier generations on policy issues such as child care and abortion—they were merely less supportive of the women's movement. This suggests that the name "complacent" may fit them well—they take for granted the successes of the movement while continuing to support gender equality and feminist policies. This is also confirmed by an item in the 1992 survey that revealed that the complacent cohort took less pride in the accomplishments of other women than did the women of the women's liberation cohort, but were more likely to express the belief that men and women ought to have equal power in society. Clear cohort differences persist over time, suggesting that generational effects are strong. Overall, the data show an increase in feminist consciousness over time. Younger generations of women tend to be more feminist than their predecessors.

Rethinking Pink and Blue: Gender, Occupational Stratification and Political Attitudes   *Gertrude A. Steuernagel, Maureen Rand Oakley, Thomas E. Yatsco, and Irene J. Barnett*

There have been revolutionary changes in the lives of twentieth-century American women. Foremost among these changes are those related to women's employment outside the home. In 1880, for example, by far the largest segment of working women were single. Today, a majority of married women are numbered in the ranks of working women, and women with children are a significant part of the labor force. An emphasis on these changes, however, obscures an important reality concerning American women's working lives, one that is not likely to change in the near future. The fact is that most American women work in so-called pink-collar ghettos, a condition known as occupational segregation. This study examines the effects of occupational segregation on political attitudes and behavior. Utilizing data from the National Election Study to measure political attitudes and behavior and data from the Department of Labor to measure occupational segregation, we first look at some basic differences in political attitudes and behavior between men and women. Specifically, we look at differences between men and women on items such as frequency of political discussions and response to an eight-issue liberalism-conservatism index. Advancing the position that useful as such analysis might be, we then argue and offer an empirical analysis that supports our contention—that studies of simple differences between men and women miss much of the complex dynamic surrounding gender, work, and political attitudes and behavior.

The Gender Gap in 1996: More Meaning Than a "Revenge of the Soccer Moms"   *Cal Clark and Janet Clark*

Probably the central explanation for the reelection of Democrat Bill Clinton as President in 1996 was the much noted "gender gap" in which Clinton received stronger support from women than from men. In popular imagery at least, Clinton was portrayed as benefiting from a "revenge of the soccer moms" against the less kinder and less gentler policies pushed by Republican Speaker of the House Newt Gingrich. This article seeks to go beyond the simple images in the headlines to provide a more sophisticated analysis of the extent and nature of the gender gap in the 1996 presidential election. The gender gap in which women disproportionately support Democratic candidates appears to have become a permanent fixture of the American political landscape. This gap first appeared in the 1980 presidential contest between Ronald Reagan and Jimmy Carter; and Clinton's gender gap of 11 percentage points (54 percent of women as opposed to 43 percent of men voted for him) is the largest gap that has occurred during the 1980s and 1990s. Still, the popular image of a new and dramatic gender gap is probably overblown. The 1996 gender gap was more a continuation of previous trends than a dramatic new development, and the size of the gender gap pales when compared to ideological and racial divisions in the electorate. Moreover, a complex set of factors reflecting the "three C's" of gender consciousness, compassion, the cost-bearing created by the feminization of poverty all contributed to the gender gap in voting. This indicates that the soccer moms (i.e., middle class, primarily working married mothers) were only one of a variety of types of women who made the gender gap in 1996 what it was. More broadly, the very different perspectives of some of these groups, especially between "economic" and "social" liberals, provides a strong but not necessarily fatal challenge to leaders promoting the coalescence of women's interests.

CHAPTER 3   WOMEN, MEDIA, AND GROUP POLITICS

Women and Sex Stereotypes: Cultural Reflections in the Mass Media   *Lois Duke Whitaker*

The editor explores some of the research that has been done concerning the manner in which the mass media have portrayed American political women in the news. Comparisons are drawn between the news about women and men in the American political environment. The editor considers influences on the newsmaking process, considers how specific agendas are passed through the media, looks at some of the myths and stereotypes about women that are portrayed in the media, and describes the white male domination of the news organization. She concludes that clearly the role of women in all facets of American political life is changing; these changes have been and are being reported by the mass media. However, the question then becomes, What is the content of this media coverage? What has been the role of the media in assessing the "reality" of some of these changes? Do women in politics not deserve a great deal more coverage than the media give them? She concludes that additional studies appear warranted as the number of female candidates increases in American politics. Studies especially are needed that would systematically compare the coverage about women who run for elective office with that of male candidates.

The Political Interests of Women: Movement Politics, Political Reform and Women's Organizations   *Denise L. Baer*

Scholars agree that there is no intrinsic or organic political interest that unites all women. Yet, in American history, three distinct women's movements have acted to mobilize and transform how women view themselves and their relationship to each and to their government. Each separate movement has built upon the advances of the preceding one. Denise L. Baer describes these movements: the Equal Rights Movement (1848–1869); the Suffrage Movement (1890–1920); today's Women's Rights Movement (1961–???). Baer shows the relationship of the women's movements to women's organizations and political parties. She finds that nearly all mainstream women's organizations have become feminist. Policy advocacy and reform, which have always been a central part of women's organizations, have brought about an increasing empowerment of women. However, in the contemporary era, lobbying by women's rights organizations has declined. Baer concludes that women remain outsiders in the interest group policy community; women still remain outsiders as leaders who can lay claim to group representation of women; women remain outsiders at the leadership levels in the Democratic and Republican Parties.

CHAPTER 4   WOMEN AND ELECTIONS: THE UPHILL STRUGGLE

Winning in My Own Backyard: "County Government, School Board Positions Steadily More Attractive to Women Candidates   *Susan A. MacManus, Charles S. Bullock III, Frances E. Akins, Laura Jane Hoffman, and Adam Newmark*

The Year of the Woman has been credited with producing sizable increases in the number of women serving in Congress. This chapter explores whether 1992 also marked a significant departure in the growth in the numbers of women holding elective county offices in Florida and Georgia. While the Year of the Woman did not accompany notable growth in Florida, women did become significantly more numerous in several Georgia offices. Rates of growth were most pronounced in rural and suburban counties, which are catching up with the greater shares of offices filled by women in urban counties.

On the Eve of Transition: Women in Southern Legislatures, 1946–1968   *Joanne V. Hawks and Carolyn Ellis Staton*

Many scholars considered the post–World War II era a quiescent time for white middle-class American women. After a period of wartime involvement, many women supposedly retreated into a more traditional lifestyle. Yet, between 1946 and 1968, almost 100 women entered legislatures in the South, a particularly traditional region. Data indicate that they were predominantly women who were already involved in the public sphere in one or more ways. Even though many were serious legislators, the press emphasized their domesticity and femininity instead of their legislative achievements.

The Impact of First Wives on Presidential Campaigns and Elections   *Charles Tien, Regan Checchio, Arthur H. Miller*

Using new public opinion data on first ladies, the authors explore their relationship with the public and their impact on presidential campaigns and elections. The authors show that the public still prefers a more traditional first lady, and that public evaluations of first wives influence public evaluations of their candidate husbands. Not only do first wives factor into their husband's popularity, they also appear to influence vote choice just as much as public assessments of economic performance.

CHAPTER 5   LEGISLATURES, WOMEN, AND POLICY MAKING

Women in Congress   *Marcia Lynn Whicker and Lois Duke Whitaker*

In recent years, women have made some inroads into elected political office. Those inroads, however, have not included gains in female representation in Congress. During the more than seventy-five years since women secured the right to participate politically with the passage of the Nineteen Amendment, female representation in Congress has increased from a minuscule 2 percent of total membership in 1922 to only 5.2 percent in 1988. At that rate of increase, women will not achieve equality in representation until the year 2582. By the 105th Congress, the percentage of women grew to 11 percent, a sizable increase but still much below the 50 percent proportion that representation by gender would entail. Women serve significantly fewer terms and are more likely to decline to seek reelection. The gap between democratic rhetoric and representational reality for women is great, despite a significant narrowing in the experiential backgrounds of men and women who are elected to Congress. Even though the number of women serving in the U.S. Congress roughly doubled with the 1992 election, many obstacles remain for women seeking congressional office.

Why Are More Women State Legislators?   *Wilma Rule*

This research analyzes why women's recruitment in the fifty state assemblies and senates increased 100 percent in the decade from 1974 to 1984 but has slipped over the past decade. Specifically, the author asks the following: (1) What were the reasons for women's steady advance from 1974 to 1984? (2) What has changed in 1994–1996? (3) What are the factors that were more favorable in the 1980s than in the 1970s? (4) How does 1994 compare with 1984? Analysis reveals that women's recruitment to state legislatures has almost tripled in the past twenty years. During the 1970s there was a building on the gains in the Republican-moralistic states most favorable to women in the 1960s. In the 1980s no political party or political culture was dominant in the states where women legislators had the most dramatic increases. States that led in the 1970s and 1980s continued to advance, with most of their state senates at least doubling the number of women members by the 1994 elections. Also, in 1994, the South broke out of its mold as the "solid Democratic South" for the first time in some 100 years. The author also finds that, at the same time, the Republican Party dominance was modified as a favorable factor for women's recruitment.

Women State Legislators: Three Decades of Gains in Representation
and Diversity   *Lynne E. Ford and Kathleen Dolan*

This article explores the question of whether there is a "new-style" contemporary female legislator serving in the 1990s. Literature assessing the relative paucity of women's representation up through the 1970s suggested that early female office seekers were different from men, but rather homogeneous as a group. Successful candidates of earlier decades fit a typology that limited a career in public service to a few women with the personal resources or familial connections to wage a campaign and without immediate family obligations to keep them in the home. Analyzing demographic, political, and legislative data from all women and a subsample of male legislators serving in fifteen states during 1972, 1982, and 1992, this chapter shows that women as a group have diversified their backgrounds and their interests over time. Data from a mail survey of 1372 female legislators serving in 1992 provides a more detailed description of the contemporary woman legislator's characteristics, legislative experience, and policy interests. Conclusions indicate that, if the launching role that state legislative experience has provided for men holds true for women, this diversity and greater numbers of women serving in elective office at the state level should ultimately mean a larger, more diverse pool of future candidates at the national level.

CHAPTER 6   THE EXECUTIVE BRANCH: WOMEN AND LEADERSHIP

The Maleness of the American Presidency   *Marcia Lynn Whicker*
and Hedy Leonie Isaacs

The authors explore why the U.S. presidency has historically been a bastion of maleness despite comments during the early Clinton administration that First Lady Hillary Rodham Clinton would be a "copresident." The authors identify factors that account for the unlevel presidential "playing field" that women candidates face; the presidential system of direct, popular election; the paucity of women who have gained experience in the three presidential "launching roles" of the vice presidency, the U.S. Senate, and governorships; the difficulty women face in securing campaign funding for national and subnational races; and long-standing public images of a conflict for women—but not for men—between familial and political roles.

The Governmental Status of the First Lady in Law and in Public Perception
Barbara C. Burrell

The first lady is a prominent figure in American political life. Her role as a policy adviser to the president is now both recognized and problematic. Public opinion and the legal system have influenced and conditioned her participation in public policy development within the White House. This piece brings together the legal conditioning of her formal governmental status with public perspectives on her roles. It considers the gendered nature of our response to the first lady as an actor in the White House advisory system and critiques limitations on her involvement as inconsistent with liberal political traditions. Laws, court decisions, and public opinion polls provide the "data" upon which this piece is built. This research brings together executive branch studies and issues evolving around the political equality of women in consideration of the presidential advisory system and the role of first lady. It shows that the first lady has been given a "quasi-governmental" status and that the public is ambivalent about her role in public policy making and her individualism.

The Feminist Face of State Executive Leadership: Women as Governors
Sara J. Weir

Focusing on the growing importance of the governorship in U.S. politics, Sara Weir explores a new era of scholarly inquiry—women as governors. From the 1925 election of Nellie Tayloe Ross (D-Wyoming) to the 1997 reelection of Christine Todd Whitman (R-New Jersey), fifteen women (twelve Democrats and three Republicans) have served as governors. While these numbers are small compared with the proportion of women elected to statewide offices or with men elected as governors, a growing number of women are running for and winning in gubernatorial contests and others are positioning themselves to run for governor by serving in other statewide elective offices. This article expands the study of gender and leadership to include the examination of the careers of the women who have served as governors, providing comparisons of their candidacies and administrations. Although the governorship has not served as the same avenue to the presidency for women as it has for men, the changing character of political ambition among women and the increased acceptance of women in high political office may change this.

CHAPTER 7   THE COURTS: WOMEN AND DECISIONS

Women's Rights and Legal Wrongs: The U.S. Supreme Court
and Sex Discrimination   *Karen O'Connor and Patricia Clark*

The authors trace the intertwined quest for expanded rights for women and the U.S. Supreme Court's responses to those actions. They begin with an overview of the colonial period, move to the Civil War years, address the suffrage movement litigation, review the press for state laws and for the Supreme Court to address the issue of gender, and explore the legal status of women at the workplace as well as more contemporary attempts to expand women's rights. They find that fewer and fewer constitutional cases involving sex discrimination are coming before the Supreme Court each year—perhaps because women's rights groups are using their time and money to fend off challenges to a series of decisions adverse to abortion rights. Also, the authors maintain that most of the "easy" constitutional cases have been decided, and there is fairly uniform application of the intermediate standard of review in the lower courts. Thus, most gender cases that the Supreme Court now chooses to hear involve employment discrimination and the scope of bona fide occupational qualifications permissible under Title VII of the Civil Rights Act of 1964. The authors conclude that, as the last decade of the 1990s draws to a close, the Supreme Court is expected to hand down decisions involving various kinds of sexual harassment. These decisions will be watched all the closer given Paula Jones' charges against Bill Clinton as well as the debate over Bill Clinton's relationship with White House intern, Monica Lewinsky. Thus, as most state practices that discriminate against women are found unconstitutional by lower courts applying recent Supreme Court decisions, the Court has largely moved on to deciding thornier issues of employment discrimination, especially, sexual harassment.

Women Judges: The New Generation   *Elaine Martin*

It has been even more difficult for women to attain judicial office than to attain other public office, but indications are that the rate of increase of women judges is on the rise. This article first presents data on the increase from 1976 to 1997 in the number of women judges, or numerical representation, and considers the eligible pool theory as an explanation for that increase. It then examines the potential impact of the increase in women judges on the diversification of gender perspectives on the judicial bench, or interest representation. Results from studies done in the 1970s and early 1980s suggested that men's and women's similar legal training and socialization as lawyers minimized any potential gender differences in judicial behavior. However, more recent studies indicate that, as women's numbers move beyond the token stage and as younger females educated after the women's movement become judges, differences based on gender emerge more clearly. Research on this new generation of women judges suggests that these gender-based differences in experience may contribute to a widening gap between the behavior of men and women judges with respect to decisions in cases raising issues of gender or minority discrimination, with respect to leadership of courtroom personnel, and with respect to judicial role conceptions of "acting for" women's perspectives.

CHAPTER 8   PUBLIC POLICY: THE FEMINIST PERSPECTIVE

The Handmaid's Tale and *The Birth Dearth:* Prophecy, Prescription, and Public Policy   *Diane D. Blair*

This article deals with the politics of reproduction. It compares and analyzes Margaret Atwood's novel *The Handmaid's Tale* (1986) and Ben Wattenberg's book *The Birth Dearth* (1987). Blair argues that Atwood, writing from a feminist perspective, posits a dystopia in which women have been reduced to the function of breeders. By contrast, Wattenberg, writing from what Blair describes as a "nationalistic perspective," deplores the current American "birth dearth," attributes it primarily to "working women," and proposes a variety of pro-natalist remedies. Blair maintains that among the significant implications of these two books, especially when they are read in tandem, are the following: that pro-natalism, justified by the United States' relatively low fertility rate, has climbed high on many conservative agendas; that this movement seriously jeopardizes many of the gains achieved by feminists in recent years; and that the contemporary pro-natalist drive has long and powerful historical precedents.

The Family and Medical Leave Act: A Policy for Families
Joan Hulse Thompson

The author examines the history of the Family and Medical Leave Act (FMLA) from initial draft through congressional enactment to executive and judicial interpretation. This legislation was passed by the House and Senate in 1990 and again in 1992, but President Bush vetoed the bill both times and Congress was unable to override. Both chambers passed the bill again early in 1993, and President Clinton signed it as his first major legislative accomplishment. The author describes the influence of the Congressional Caucus for Women's Issues (CCWI) in developing this legislation, building a bipartisan coalition across committee jurisdictions, and coordinating the efforts of outside advocacy groups. After the Republican victory in 1994, CCWI was able to survive only in a diminished, largely defensive role, but the FMLA represents a concrete achievement of the feminist movement for the benefit of working families.

Sex at Risk in Insurance Classifications? The Supreme Court as Shaper of Public Policy   *Ruth Bamberger*

Although numerous laws has been passed prohibiting sex discrimination in a variety of public policy areas, the insurance industry has retained the practice of discriminating by sex in determining prices of its products. The industry argues its position on cost-efficiency and actuarial grounds. Women's rights and civil rights groups have criticized such discrimination on grounds of fairness and prevailing social policy. Although they have pursued their cause through multiple channels of government, the Supreme Court is perceived to be a primary agent of policy change. The Court has signaled that sex may be at risk as an insurance classification, but its role as shaper of public policy on this issue has been incremental at best.

Affirmative Action and Women   *Roberta Ann Johnson*

Challenged from all sides, affirmative action, nevertheless, continues to live on as a highly charged issue. This chapter (1) defines affirmative action, (2) details the development of federal affirmative action guidelines, (3) describes Supreme Court decisions and congressional responses to affirmative action, (4) describes how the states and the lower courts have become battlegrounds on the issue of affirmative action, (5) considers the ways in which affirmative action is a woman's issue, and (6) considers the future of affirmative action.

CHAPTER 9   WOMEN, EMPOWERMENT AND CULTURAL EXPRESSION

Anarchist Feminism and Student Power: Is This Any Way to Run a Women's Studies Program?   *Kathleen P. Ianello*

This study analyzes systems of power within the framework of organizations. The author argues that it is from the notion of power as a type of energy or "empowerment" that a feminist framework for organizations emerges. Two feminist organizations were selected for in-depth study—the Feminist Peace Group and the Women's Health Collective. From the study of these two anarchist feminist groups, a modified consensual structure is identified. The most important defining element is the outward, not downward, delegation of routine decisions to the few and the reserving of critical decisions for the entire membership. Other important elements of the model include: (1) the recognition of ability or expertise rather than rank or position, (2) the notion of empowerment as a basis of consensual process, and (3) clarity of goals that are arrived at through this consensual process. The author uses a case study of the governing body of one women's studies program, the Women's Studies Program Advisory Council (WSPAC) at a small liberal arts college, to illustrate the challenges and benefits of organizing consensually in an academic environment. The implications for women in this modified consensual structure include experiences in an environment of trust and support as opposed to the more traditional hierarchical organizations in which only those at the top (all too often male figures) make critical policy with varying degrees of input from lower levels.

Grounds for Criticism: Coffee, Passion, and the Politics of Feminist Discourse
Elizabeth A. Kelly

This essay explores the relationship between coffee and political discourse, paying particular attention to the role of coffeehouses as alternative public spheres. It also examines the often-complex relationships between coffee, coffeehouse cultures, and gender, along with how these relationships have shifted historically. The author concludes with a look at the countercultural institutions that have emerged in the last two decades that draw on the traditions of free speech and cultural and political criticism that were integral to the coffeehouse cultures of centuries past. She describes the GI coffeehouse movement during the Vietnam Conflict and the feminist community organizing and cultural work since the late 1906s, which has often centered around coffeehouses, sometimes in tandem with feminist bookstores and other forms of cultural expression. Finally, the author describes two feminist coffeehouses and the political struggles attached to building alternative social and cultural institutions that prioritize the concerns or needs of women.

ACKNOWLEDGMENTS

This book is specifically dedicated to the women and men who have contributed to, supported, and been loyal to this project from its inception more than nine years ago. I would also like to thank the members of the Women's Caucus for Political Science for their encouragement and advice—even though you are too numerous to name here, you know who you are, and I value and appreciate you. A special word of thanks to the three reviewers commissioned by Prentice Hall to study the original essays in the first edition: Ellen Riggle, University of Kentucky; M. Margaret Conway, University of Florida; and Maureen Moakley, University of Rhode Island. Your suggestions and recommendations were of invaluable help.

Many thanks also go to Mary Phillips, Katherine Fitch, and Gay Wade at Georgia Southern University. I would also like to thank Beth Gillett, senior editor, and Nicole Conforti, Associate Editor, and the staff at Prentice Hall.

And, finally, a word of thanks to Louanne and Andy, my most supportive daughter and husband.

Lois Duke Whitaker

THE STUDY OF WOMEN: THE NEW FRAMEWORK

Until the 1960s, most of the research about movements for women's rights centered on women's suffrage in the nineteenth and early twentieth centuries. Since the 1960s, however, an enormous number of studies on women and politics have been added to the scholarly literature. Even a superficial review of the wealth of books, journal articles, and other publications analyzing the relationship between gender and politics reveals that the field of research in this area has grown substantially.

Over the past thirty years, scholars who wished to research the influence of women's political behavior in the American political process experienced numerous "growing pains." These included limited financial support for research on the topic, initial efforts to study a field that had established norms identified and defined from a male perspective and male-shaped understanding of the political world, and a tendency to view gender-related research as a "special-interest" focus, "outside" the normal theoretical framework. For all these reasons, many studies on women and politics turned out to be simply descriptive narratives drawn from traditional concepts, as opposed to empirically driven research studies.

The early pioneers of scholarly research on gender and politics, however, may currently reflect on a significant legacy of contributions. These include the present solid body of literature analyzing gender socialization, women's political behavior (at both the individual and the group level), and women's role (to include officeholding) in the political sector. As we enter the next century, however, it appears that the early scholars analyzing the issue of women in American politics have passed along to the next generation of researchers on this topic a clear challenge: to ascertain why it is that women are still represented in such small numbers in both elective and appointive political offices. Clearly there is a need to use the previously researched information to provide a new agenda in which findings on the role and performance of females in the public sector can be more conclusive. Why are more women not serving as elected and appointed officials in politics? Why are more issues of concern to women not being addressed in our public policies? Why are women still being discriminated against and still suffering sexual harassment and domestic violence? What are the political implications for women in the year 2000 as one looks at the congressional legislative agenda? Will the advances made during the women's rights movement of the 1960s be sustained some forty years later?

The next research agenda to explore further this issue of women and politics should address these questions. It would seem that only when women are able to mobilize support for continued advancement in the equal rights arena will the women's movement remain viable. We begin this book by considering the issue of equality for women from the perspective of feminist theory. We will then move to an examination of gender differences in political attitudes and voting and examine gender cultural reflections in the mass media. We will explore how women have competed for public office. We will look at women in U.S. government. We will then continue with an analysis of women and national policy. We will conclude with a look at female activism within an organization and the implications for political discourse among women centered around coffeehouses. Along the way we hope to provide some insight into the questions raised herein. First, however, let us consider several issues of concern to women from a theoretical feminist framework. For our purposes here, we define *feminist framework* as an overall analysis of the nature and causes of female inequality and an accompanying alternative or proposal for ending women's discrimination.

The first two articles analyze interlocking oppressions based on sex, gender, and race. In our first reading, Jennifer Ring critically argues that feminist theory is a way of seeing the world through the lens of gender, which is always present, but rarely recognized. In political science, as in most academic fields, gender is invisible, with the male gendered stance assumed to be neutral or objective. Ring offers a feminist re-reading of American slavery in order to demonstrate how the perspective of the most marginalized group in the social system, African American women, actually permits access to the deepest, most revealing insights. Viewing social and political systems from the margins permits greater insights into the "center" or the whole. A more general discussion of the nature of feminist theory along with a survey of well-known theorists follows the description and analysis of slavery. "Feminist-compatible" approaches to theory are identified as (1) liberalism and radicalism, (2) materialism, (3) a critique of objectivity, and (4) post-structuralist feminism, all of which presuppose a multicultural approach.

Nancie E. Caraway uses the political and epistemological contributions of contemporary Black feminist theory to point up the intersections of gender, race, and class as determinants of oppression. She argues that the texts of Black feminists teach us that feminist theory and politics should address this "multiple jeopardy." She cautions that feminists need to be wary of the damaging consequences of conceptions like *identity* and *self* that have set up white norms. In her discussion of identity politics, Caraway questions many of the assumptions of mainstream white feminism. She proposes instead multicultural goals in which the themes of racism and identity come together in a configuration that can address the theoretical issues about the female subject. She argues that a critical identity politics cautions us not to become too comfortable too long in one spot with one identity, lest we forget and stifle the ways in which we change, contradict, and grow in history. We begin with these two essays.

Feminist Theory as Seeing

Jennifer Ring

THE INVISIBILITY OF GENDER: CASE STUDIES

The most difficult problem feminist scholars of political science will encounter is the invisibility of gender. This may sound counterintuitive: Surely gender is highly visible. When political scientists wonder why women, despite having possessed the vote for seventy-five years, are not more highly represented in the arena of national political power, there is no ambiguity about who they mean. Women may be proportionally absent, or underrepresented, but few doubt that they know what gender is and can recognize it as an operative factor. So what can it mean to say that gender is invisible to political scientists? What I mean is that gender is omnipresent and pervasive, and yet its impact is all but denied by most political scientists. Feminist theory has as its task *seeing* gender at work when it is most often overlooked.

An eminent political scientist, a man of highly progressive political ideas, well acquainted with and respectful of a feminist perspective, recently lamented to me that so few women scholars seem attracted to the field of American political theory. He mused that perhaps the centrality of the "founding fathers" deterred women from pursuing the field. My response to him was that many women academics, although perhaps historians more than political scientists, were indeed teach-

Reprinted by permission.

ing American political theory. Rather than focusing their courses or scholarly research on the writings of Franklin, Paine, Adams, Jefferson, and Lincoln, they were teaching the same historical epoch from the standpoint of race and gender. They taught the Grimkes' writings on slavery and revolution, Stanton's, Anthony's and Sojourner Truth's responses to Lincoln on slavery, the debate over the fourteenth and fifteenth amendments from the standpoint of the conflict between race and gender, and the political writings of Elizabeth Cady Stanton, Frances Harper, Ida Wells Barnett, Frances Dana Gage, Alice Paul, and others on issues that range from the nature of liberal individualism, to treatises on direct political action, lynching, rape, racism, enfrancisement, and the rights of working people. My colleague had not been taught the works of these American political thinkers and activists, and so he, like many other academics, simply assumed that they were not central to the understanding of American political thought. They might belong in a course on "Women and American Politics," offered separately from "American Party Systems," "The Legislature," "State and Local Government," and so forth. But they were certainly not an essential component of "American Political Thought." He simply did not *see* that he was approaching the subject from his own gendered perspective. This is one example of the "invisibility of gender."

That the canon of American political science has survived as long as it has with so little impact from women's history and politics perpetuates the misconception that the traditional perspective is adequate, indeed complete, and that a course that omits the perspectives of the women who were also a part of history is not male-gendered but neutral. Women simply are not regarded as essential. In terms of the title of this volume, men are the insiders and women the outsiders.

But what do these terms mean? Feminist theory, as a way of *seeing*, must raise questions about the meaning of terms that are often used unthinkingly or uncritically. What does it mean to be an insider or an outsider in American politics? Is the presence of outsiders inevitable? Or, taking a cue again from the title of the book, can women achieve "insider" status in American politics without being interested in changing anything about the basic inequality of American society? In that case, is it necessary to demand that "women" as women be included as insiders? What difference does it make? Implicit in all these questions is the need to examine the nature of equality in the American polity. Why bother to distinguish between women and men elected to office if a feminist agenda plays no role in the politics of those elected? But these questions are all rather abstract. Let's take a look at what a feminist perspective might do to the standard reading of American political history.

In spite of caveats to the contrary, traditional views of political history adhere to an "add women and stir" perspective when it comes to women and politics. The "insiders" never doubt that they have the story right, or for the most part right. If they have left anybody out—blacks, women, and so forth—they can simply add their stories without fundamentally altering the traditional reading of American politics. But what happens to the traditional view when it is truly seen through the lens of gender, and race? For example, the phrase "blacks and women," which I used self-consciously above, has been standard throughout American history and became publicly problematic for the first time during the debate over the Fifteenth Amendment to the constitution in 1869, which enfranchised black men. The move was regarded as progressive, and the dire political necessity for blacks in the south after the Civil War. Angela Davis observes in *Women, Race and Class,* "As far as Black people in the postwar South were concerned, a state of emergency prevailed. Frederick Douglass' argument for Black suffrage was based on his insistence that the ballot was an emergency measure. . . . For Douglass, the ballot . . . was basically a survival measure—a means of guaranteeing the survival of the masses of his people."[1] Douglass, the eminent abolitionist, former slave, and early "women's rights man" insisted,

> When women, because they are women, are dragged from their homes and hung upon lamp-posts; when their children are torn from their arms and their brains dashed upon the pavement; when they are objects of insult and outrage at every turn; when they are in danger of having their homes burnt down over their heads; when their children are not allowed to enter schools; then they will have [the same] urgency to obtain the ballot.[2]

When nineteenth-century feminists attempted to include the term "sex" along with the term "race" in the wording of the Fifteenth Amendment, they were rebuked, reminded that it was "the Negroes' Hour," and told to withdraw their demands for women's suffrage, lest the enfranchisement of black men go down to defeat under the unreasonable burden of demanding votes for women.

But conceptualizing the debate over passage of the Fifteenth Amendment in these terms is only "reality" from one distorted perspective. Certainly the demand that American feminists in 1869 (both white and black) "get real" was not without some validity: There is little doubt that had the Fifteenth Amendment proposed extending the franchise to women as well as to black men, it would not have passed. The "political realists" who insisted that women suffragists take a back seat on this issue were indeed realistic. Even Angela Davis, who approvingly notes that Frederick Douglass' statement had an unmistakable lucidity about it, nonetheless fails to notice that his position did not acknowledge that black women and white were indeed the victims of specifically anti-female violence; that they were, and continue to be "the objects of insult and outrage at every turn" in the form of public belittlement, ridicule, silencing, pornography, and in the general devaluation of the feminine; that when their homes were not owned by their husbands and fathers in the colonial United States, there had been a history of burning both their homes and themselves, most dramatically during the witchcraft trials; and that neither women nor their female children were admitted to academic schools, colleges, or universities in America until well into the nineteenth century, and even then only very selectively. But even more outrageous and usually not even noticed when rights in America are treated as a finite sum to be divided between "blacks and women," is that the phrase itself renders black women invisible to history. "Blacks and women" signifies that all blacks are men and all women are white, which is fairly devastating if you happen to be an African American woman, or any woman of color for that matter. Uncritical use of the phrase is another example of the invisibility of gender.

Still, our mainstream but progressive political scientist might respond, "African American women constitute a tiny minority of the American population. Empirically speaking, it is not tremendously significant to exclude their perspective on an issue of national importance and vital significance to the African American people as a whole." But that response only confirms that truth is defined by insiders, and that women are marginal figures in American political history. The term "Blacks" is assumed to be sufficient to include black women, because women's distinct experiences are insignificant to those telling the story.

But if we compare the traditional and the black feminist perspectives, for example, on slavery, we get a sense of the price paid for excluding the perspective of the outsider. The traditional liberal reading of slavery treats it as a violation of the rights of individuals: Slaves were forced to labor, had no control over their own destiny or the destiny of their children, and were the victims of terrible violence and physical brutality. All of this is conceived in the American imagination primarily as overwork, whippings, and perhaps other less commonly remarked upon forms of physical torture: branding, mutilation, and so forth. An important component of slavery thus conceived was the "emasculation" of the male slaves, particularly evident in their inability to protect "their" women from white sexual predators. Sexual abuse seen from the women's perspective is seldom associated with racial slavery per se. Rape of the slave women is regarded as incidental: "Oh yeah, and the white masters and their sons sometimes raped the slave women. That was a part of slavery, too." In the traditional liberal reading, the origins of slavery are usually regarded as greed, propelled perhaps by capitalism, and a general lack of morality among southern whites, who used the Christian Bible to justify the inferiority of the black race. Northern slavery is rarely even considered in standard accounts of American slavery.

The Marxist account does add class analysis, but neglects to add sexual analysis as well. To Marxists, slavery was the result of historical contradictions between an outmoded feudal system (southern agriculture) and burgeoning northern capitalism. The two systems were bound to clash. From this perspective, slavery was less a violation of individual rights than a systematic violation of the rights of working people. Racism, or the institutional encouragement of a hierarchy of whites over people of color, simply keeps the working class battling among itself, rather than perceiving their exploitation in class terms, and directing their anger at the appropriate objects: owners of the means of production, either industrial or agricultural. To Marxist analysts racism, and certainly sexism, are by-products of class oppression.

What, then, does a feminist analysis do? How can the perspective of the feminist outsider yield more fundamental insight than the prevailing perspectives? Consider bell hooks' chapter, "Sexism and the Black Female Slave Experience," from her book *Ain't I a Woman: Black Women and Feminism.*[3] Hooks argues that racism and sexism may be separable, but slavery cannot be understood without understanding the centrality of sexism. She demonstrates that the abuse and exploitation of slave women, and the insistence upon dichotomizing female sexuality into entirely separate, hierarchically organized black and white experiences, kept not only slavery, but antebellum Southern society functioning. It was an exaggerated form of what has come to characterize much of American sexual dynamics. Slavery is understood as a template for understanding race and gender throughout American history. This should not be confused with a simplistic "all women are slaves" sort of reductionism.

According to hooks, sexual oppression of African women began on board the slave ships. The passage to America was regarded as a time for "socializing" the slaves in preparation for what awaited them. Since women were more likely to work in the household, in close proximity to the master's family, it was crucial that their spirits be broken. The women were kept naked, "allowed" to roam on shipboard (while the men were kept chained below), and raped at will by the ship's crew. Their babies were also the targets of extraordinary brutality at the hands of the crew.

Hooks debunks the more conventional reading of slavery, which suggests that the model of brutality was the mistreatment of male slaves, who were "emasculated."

> Sexist historians and sociologists have provided the American public with a perspective on slavery in which the most cruel and de-humanizing impact of slavery on the lives of black people was that black men were stripped of their masculinity, which they then argue resulted in the dissolution and overall disruption of any black familial structure. . . . Implicit in this assertion is the assumption that the worst that can happen to a man is that he be made to assume the social status of a woman. (hooks 20)

While not minimizing the sufferings of male slaves, hooks points to an overlooked dimension of slavery: the explicitly sexual abuse of female slaves. She suggests that black women were the objects of misogynistic treatment that *can* be understood as distinct from racial oppression, and that was also used as a means of keeping white women in line. While black men were *not* emasculated, "not forced to assume a role colonial American society regarded as 'feminine'" (hooks 22), black *women were* masculinized, made to do the same physical labor as men, and sometimes made to wear men's clothing, which was regarded as degrading. No such role changes were forced upon the male slaves. In addition, slave women were viewed as sexual animals, available and unobjecting to any man who chose to impose himself sexually, and the polar opposite of white women, who were "ladies," "belles," models of femininity, but defined by their *lack* of sexual desire. "The brutal treatment of enslaved black women by white men exposed the depths of male hatred of women and woman's body." (hooks 29) And the hatred was harbored against white as well as black women.

> Forcing white women to deny their physical beings was as much an expression of male hatred of woman as was regarding them as sex objects. Idealization of white women did not change the basic contempt white men felt towards them. . . . As American white men idealized white womanhood, they sexually assaulted and brutalized black women. The deep hatred of woman that had been embedded in the white colonizer's psyche by patriarchal ideology and anti-woman religious teachings both motivated and sanctioned white male brutality against black women. (hooks 32)

Bell hooks' reading is corroborated by other women scholars, including Jacqueline Jones, Patricia Hill Collins, and Shirley Abbott.[4] What is eye-opening about hooks' feminist reading is the presentation of sexual oppression as both distinguishable from racial oppression and as a central dynamic in the social organization of slave society. Slavery would not have been the same without the abuse of black women and the sequestering of white women. The antebellum Southern economy thrived on forced "production" of new "labor"—babies—that were the result of the systematic, institutionally condoned rape of black women, as well as the managerial role imposed upon white women.[5] Sexual abuse of female slaves and the control of the sexual lives of white women to ensure the "purity" of the white race is central to any understanding of the functioning of slave society. Indeed, it may be regarded as the essential template. Before this sort of feminist analysis, the rape of slave women could be written off as idiosyncratic misbehavior on the part of individual slave holders, or worse, an example of "boys will be boys." But feminist analysis permits us to see that sexual abuse was systematic, endemic, and *necessary* to the perpetuation of the slave order.

There are no innocent victims in this view: *All* elements of southern slave society are implicated. Bell hooks places responsibility not only on the shoulders of white men, who exhibited extraordinary violence against slaves of both sexes and did not even consider the impact of their rape of the slave women on the women, and also black men, black families in general, and the white women and girls who were the witnesses to the "infidelity" and brutality of their fathers, husbands, brothers, and sons. White women were also collusive. True, they were made to feel ashamed of their sexual feelings, and then accused of being cold and untouchable, enabling their menfolk to feel "compelled," and justified in turning to the "available" black women. But instead of confronting their men, white women, who had power over the blacks, but little over white men, blamed the slave women for seducing their husbands, and further punished them physically and emotionally, labeling them "prostitutes," and holding the black women responsible for the white men's infidelity. It was easier to cry "Whore!" than "Rape!"

Meanwhile, the black men, helpless to protect "their" women from the predatory slavers and feeling compromised by their ineffectiveness, were also likely to take out their frustration on the black women. It was easier, at least from time to time, instead of continually facing the reality of such complete oppression, to wonder if their own women hadn't in fact done something to bring on the sexual attentions of the master. Hooks regards this as identifying with a model of white patriarchy that encouraged maintenance of male sexual privilege rather than recognizing slavery as both racially and sexually oppressive. It divided black men from women and undermined any chance of political resistance.

But hooks is also critical of black women's participation in this travesty. She acknowledges that

> Most white women regarded black women who were the objects of their husbands' sexual assaults with hostility and rage. Having been taught by religious teachings that women were inherently sexual temptresses, mistresses often believed that the enslaved black woman was the culprit and their husbands the innocent victims. (hooks 36)

But she also observes, "This same sexual morality was adopted by slaves. Fellow slaves often pitied the lot of sexually exploited females but did not see them as blameless victims." (hooks 36)

> They did not advocate social equality between the sexes. Instead they bitterly resented that they were not considered "women" by the dominant culture and therefore were not the recipients of the considerations and privileges given white women. Modesty, sexual purity, innocence, and a submissive manner were the qualities associated with womanhood and femininity that enslaved black women endeavored to attain. . . . (hooks 49)

ANALYSIS

What we see from this example is that a feminist reading acts as a *lens* that permits us to see historical and political dynamics from a previously ignored perspective. We can see the interconnectedness of various systems of oppression, and to the extent that sexual hierarchies are a necessary part of racial oppression, we can understand the position expressed by black feminists, that the oppression of any one group in society inevitably involves the oppression of others. There either *is* equality or there is not: There can be no liberation of black people as long as women are regarded as inferior. Nor can women be "free and equal" so long as racial hierarchies exist.

The "standpoint," or the perspective, of the group conventionally regarded as "most oppressed" is the one that gives us access to what Patricia Hill Collins refers to as "the simultaneity of race, class and gender oppression" in a way that members of more privileged groups are less likely to see, because it would require acknowledging their own unequal access to privilege.[6] But, paradoxically, the perspective of the "most oppressed" also undermines the validity of quantitative degrees of oppression. To ask whether during slavery white or black women were "more" oppressed is to ask a question that is politically useless.

To be more specific: Jacqueline Jones tells of a teenage slave performing one of her assigned duties, cleaning the master's bedchamber. While performing her tasks, she was raped by the master, who appeared unexpectedly in the room. During the rape, the mistress entered the room, discovered her husband and the slave, and severely beat the girl for "seducing" her husband. A more complete and concrete picture of oppression is difficult to imagine. But what is the basis for comparing it to the exploitation of the mistress? The social structure of the ante-Bellum South insisted upon the white woman's silence about her husband's infidelity, drinking, and violence, in order to maintain the privilege of her class and race. In addition, the price she paid for her privilege included the denial of her own sexuality and her efficacy in the world, in the full knowledge that class and racial privilege were hers only so long as she behaved herself. She was forced to act in collusion with a society that publicly and systematically violated the bodies and spirits of women of color.[7] As bell hooks observes, "It takes little imagination to comprehend the significance of one oppressed black woman being brutally tortured while the more privileged white women look passively at her plight. . . . Surely, it must have occurred to white women that were enslaved black women not available to bear the brunt of such intense anti-women male aggression, they themselves might have been the victims." (hooks 38)

To protest, "But the black women *were* more oppressed! Physical oppression simply *is* worse than emotional oppression—if for no other reason than it is life-threatening!" is not entirely unproblematic. It offers only a distracting hierarchy, a rank ordering of suffering, that forecloses discussion by substituting blame rather than struggling to understand how similar problems plague us today. The enumeration of degrees of suffering is presumed to have objective validity, ignoring the subjective experience of oppression. It also patronizingly assumes that black women envy white women.

Rather than acknowledging the still existing sexual hierarchies lying at the core of racial—and economic—hierarchies, the conventional view avoids dealing with sexual oppression by defining sexual behavior in individual terms. In fact, while some masters were more brutal than others, the maintenance of sexual hierarchies lay at the heart of slavery. In order to understand the political and economic dynamics of slavery, we *must* understand the sexual dynamics. Feminist theory offers a perspective on how sexuality is usually rendered invisible by traditional political science approaches.

WHAT IS FEMINIST THEORY?

But what *is* feminist theory? Perhaps we have been able to see it "in action" as it were, from our feminist reinterpretation of American racial slavery. But can a theory be defined in the absence of an example of its practice? From one perspective, no theory possesses substantive content, nor can it influence content in a predictable way. If "feminist theory" always resulted in predictable political findings, it could not really be considered a theory: It would be more of an ideology, belonging in the realm of political action rather than scholarship. So how can there be a "feminist" theory, worthy of the title?

The word "theory" literally comes from the Greek, *theoreia,* "seeing." A theory is a way of seeing. But a theorist cannot approach the world believing that she knows what she is going to see. There are no inherent aspects to feminist theory that make it essentially feminist. However, there have emerged in the history of recent feminism several major identifiable tendencies that have been associated with a feminist approach. Perhaps it is most accurate to say that there is a way of theorizing that is *compatible* with feminist political concerns, but not limited to feminism, nor capable, like a heat-seeking missile, of arriving at inherently feminist perceptions. Let us consider the nature of these major "feminist-compatible" trends in theory. Although most lists are too formal and schematized to accurately reflect the fluidity of theory, consider the following four themes in feminist theory as handles to use to begin to get a grip on the subject: (1) liberalism and radicalism, (2) materialism, (3) critique of objectivity, and (4) post-structuralism. These descriptive titles are themselves both somewhat overlapping and somewhat contradictory.

Liberalism and Radicalism

The range of feminist theory parallels the range of more conventional "male" political theory in the sense that there are theories that view the world in a way that makes political reform the more "rational" outcome of analysis of the possibilities of change for women, and theories that lead us to the conclusion that change is possible only with more radical, pervasive change. Liberal or reform feminism accepts the framework of existing liberal capitalism and believes the system can be influenced to accept women into centers of political and economic power. This moderate feminism takes its cues from Anglo-American liberal individualist theory and views women as individuals fundamentally. "Idealist" notions such as the liberal profession of belief in freedom and equality are subject to persuasion from rational individuals who are capable of using the existing political structure to bring about a more inclusive society, which includes women and minorities in increasing numbers.

In contrast, various forms of radical feminism regard reform as illusory. Grounded in Marxist class analysis, radical feminism argues that the liberal capitalist state is moved only by what is profitable, and that hierarchies are necessary for capitalism's continued functioning. Women can "progress" in liberal capitalist society only by displacing others who in turn take their place as low-paid workers, or unpaid domestic workers and child-care providers. "Equality" for women is a chimera in liberal reform feminism, since it rests upon the inevitability of inequality for others, as well as lack of acknowledgement that women come from different class, racial, and ethnic backgrounds and do not necessarily share the same goals. From the perspective of radical feminism, change is possible only when the economic system has changed to ensure that no class or group of people is economically exploited for the benefit of others. For purposes of radical analysis, women are not viewed primarily as individuals, but as members of an economic class. When the class structure is abolished, when institutionally protected hierarchies no longer exist, then equality will be possible for women and others. As bell hooks remarks in *Killing Rage,* "There will be no feminist revolution without an end to racism and white supremacy. When all women and men engaged in feminist struggle understand the interlocking nature of systems of domination, of white supremacist capitalist patriarchy, the feminist movement will regain its revolutionary progressive momentum."[8]

The Marxist basis of radical feminist theory also lies at the heart of the black feminist contention that no freedom is possible so long as any one group is exploited or oppressed: what Collins refers to as the "simultaneity of oppression." Hierarchies are by definition incompatible with freedom and equality.

Materialism

Another aspect of radical feminist theory derived from Marxist is *materialism:* the belief that ideas are all grounded in concrete, economic reality. Nancy Hartsock coined the phrase "standpoint theory" derived from the Marxist contention that people who work with their hands and bodies have an essentially more complete view of the world than people who do not work with their hands and bodies, who do not mix their subjective human energy with the objective, material world.[9] Hartsock contends that since women do a disproportionate share of the manual and physical work of the world, including the physical experience of childbearing, their perspective, or "standpoint" is inherently more "essential" or complete than the view of others who give orders but have no direct experience of the hurly burly of daily life. The classic example is the wealthy corporate executive who may know how to maneuver in the world of high finance and politics, but who can't make his own dinner, buy socks or underwear, pick up his kids at school, or take them to the dentist or a music lesson without consulting his wife (or her maid). Patricia Hill Collins places this aspect at the center of her description of Black Feminism.

> Very different kinds of "thought" and "theories" emerge when abstract thought is joined with concrete action. Denied positions as scholars and writers which allow us to emphasize purely theoretical concerns, the work of most Black women intellectuals is influenced by the merger of action and theory. . . . Contemporary Black women intellectuals continue to draw on this tradition of using everyday actions and experiences in our theoretical work.[10]

Critique of Objectivity

But the centrality of materialism takes a different from in the legal theory of Catharine MacKinnon. Although her argument is more abstract, its applicability is perhaps most visible in terms of the impact of feminist theory on scholarship itself, specifically in political science. While the materialism of feminist theory is evident in the suggestion that a particularly acute perspective on reality is available to those who are most involved in the daily workings of life, MacKinnon challenges the privileging of objectivity itself. As she puts it,

> *Power to create the world from one's point of view is power in its male form.* The male epistemological stance, which corresponds to the world it creates, is objectivity: the ostensibly noninvolved stance, the view from a distance and from no particular perspective, apparently transparent to its reality. It does not comprehend its own perspectivity, does not recognize what it sees as subject like itself, or that the way it apprehends its world is a form of its subjugation and presupposes it.[11]

The implications of this position are more far-reaching than the "standpoint theory" that grants a privileged perspective to those who directly mix their labor with the mundane details of daily life, a theory that has the potential for creating an inverted hierarchy. Indeed, MacKinnon's challenge to the primacy of empirical reality goes to the heart of most social scientific methodology. It simply cuts off at the roots the traditional argument that the more tangible the suffering, the more oppressed is the "victim," which has been used to silence feminists whenever "more important" issues are at stake. The impulse to hierarchically organize oppression creates a sort of oppression sweepstakes, where the group who meets a certain externally defined conception of oppression wins the attention of whoever defines oppression. Thus, middle class white women rarely appear to have legitimate cause for making demands so long as poor and homeless people are more visibly distressed, or violent young male criminals frighten "respectable" middle-class citizens. Economic deprivation and violent criminal activity appear more urgent, because they are more empirically tangible and visible than the emotional deprivation and silencing suffered by many women. Even domestic violence is rendered invisible when it is regarded as a private, rather than a political problem.

Consider the difficulty of "proving" rape in a situation where no other visible violence occurred (such as beating or knifing), or the difficulty of "proving" sexual harrassment. Consider the fact that domestic battery has not, until very recently, been regarded as an issue appropriate to public policy, or that the prevalence of government-condoned mass rapes in parts of the world, sexual slavery, forced genital mutilation of females, or female infanticide are *not* considered violations of *human* rights. Human rights advocates often use the rubric of "cultural relativism" to prevent their intervention in cases of specifically sexual crimes against women. That the offending cultures are entirely male-defined is not noticed, hence once again gender is rendered invisible. Returning to our example of American racial slavery, the impact of rape and forced breeding upon slave women is less comprehensible to the empirically inclined who dominate the social sciences, because it *looks* just like consensual heterosexuality, pregnancy, and childbirth. Being beaten, wearing rags, and working long hours in backbreaking field labor *looks* more oppressive, from this point of view, and so it becomes the very model for slavery.

Post-Structuralist Feminism

With the ability to challenge the primacy of conventional stories about reality, we are close to the stance of "post-modern" or "deconstructionist" feminist theory. And this brings us right back to the question of outsiders or insiders. Deconstructionist theory replaces the authority of traditionally held views with radical perspectives from the margins, much as we have done in this chapter. Instead of proceeding as a numerically minded empiricist might, by assuming that the perspective of the most populous group, or the people with the most power, money or education provides the most reliable account, deconstructionist, or post-modern feminism begins with the most marginal and overlooked viewpoint—in the case of American slavery, from the viewpoint of African American women—assumes its validity, if not its universality, then employs it to gain access to truths not available to those whose reality is more "central." Obviously, implicit in the deconstructionist stance is the assumption that there can be no *one* central, legitimate perspective. Only through a dialogue, or actually a dialectic of multiple and often conflicting perspectives can a (still transitory) purchase on reality be achieved. This can be a rather never-wracking approach to truth, but it has the radical potential to undermine the legitimacy of conventionally accepted authorities. It is a learning tool, a lens, as is all theory.

We have explored several dominant approaches in feminist theory to see how they alter our way of looking at history and politics, at least according to the single example of American slavery. What are the questions feminist theory is likely to raise when exploring the issues in the remainder of this book, about women in contemporary politics, seeking access to conventional centers of power?

NOTES

1. Angela Davis, *Women, Race and Class* (New York: Vintage, 1983), p. 80.

2. From Elizabeth Cady Stanton, *History of Woman Suffrage,* Vol. 2, p. 382. Quoted in Davis, *op. cit.,* p. 82.

3. bell hooks, *Ain't I a Woman: Black Women and Feminism.* (Boston: South End Press, 1981). Page references follow in parentheses in text.

4. See Jacqueline Jones, *Labor of Love, Labor of Sorrow: Black Women, Work and the Family, From Slavery to the Present.* (New York: Vintage, 1985); Patricia Hill Collins: *Black Feminist Thought: Knowledge, Consciousness, and the Politics of Empowerment.* (New York: Routledge, 1990); Shirley Abbott, *Womenfolks: Growing Up Down South,* (New York: Ticknor and Fields, 1983).

5. "Willing or not, thousands of Southern women in the first half of the nineteenth century were confronted with this scenario. Ladies were no longer a luxury of upper-class life in the Tidewater. They were a managerial necessity, and a psychological and moral one as well. For if slavery was to be the foundation of economic life, and if one important crop on any large farm includes healthy black babies, a plantation becomes a complex domestic mechanism that can hardly be expected to function without a white woman around to figure out the endless de-

tails. Not only that, without her supposedly softening and mitigating influence around the place—or her mere cosmetic value—the whole operation quickly turns too rotten for a Christian to contemplate." (Shirley Abbott, *Womenfolks: Growing Up Down South.* [New York: Ticknor and Fields, 1983] pp. 88–89).

6. "Viewing the world through a both/and conceptual lens of the simultaneity of race, class, and gender oppression and of the need for a humanist vision of community creates new possibilities for empowering Afrocentric feminist knowledge. Many Black feminist intellectuals have long thought about the world in this way because this is the way we experience the world." Patricia Hill Collins, *Black Feminist Thought.* (New York: Routledge, 1990) pp. 221–222.

7. Jones offers this account of one white women's misery: "Divorce petitions provide one of the few sources that reveal white wives' outrage in response to their husbands' provocative behavior. For example, a witness in a Virginia divorce case in 1848 offered the following testimony: A master one morning told his favorite slave to sit down at the breakfast table, 'to which Mrs. N [his wife] objected, saying . . . that she (Mrs. N) would have her severely punished.' The husband then replied 'that in that event he would visit her (Mrs. N)

with a like punishment. Mrs. N then burst into tears and asked if it was not too much for her to stand.' Like at least some other masters, Mr. N freely admitted that his initial attraction to his future wife stemmed from her 'large Estate of land and negroes." (Thus a favorable marriage became one more consideration for the ambitious slaveholder.) However, this particular husband went out of his way to demonstrate his 'strong dislike and aversion to the company' of his bride by sleeping with the slave woman 'on a pallet in his wife's room' and by frequently embracing her in the presence of his wife. Mrs. N's first response was to lay 'her hands in an angry manner on the said servant.' Her husband, besides threatening his wife with bodily harm, 'told her if she did not like his course, to leave his house and take herself to some place she liked better.'" p. 26

8. bell hooks, *Killing Rage, Ending Racism.* (New York: Henry Holt and Company, 1995) See especially the chapters "Revolutionary Feminism" and "Teaching Resistance", e.g., "It should have come as no surprise to any of us that those white women who were mainly concerned with gaining equal access to domains of white male privilege quickly ceased to espouse a radical political agenda which included the dismantling of patriarchy as well as an anti-racist, anti-classist agenda. . . . Nor should it have surprised us that those individual white women who remained true to the radical and/or revolutionary vision of feminist politics . . . were soon marginalized as feminist politics entered the mainstream." (99) Also her discussion of the role of the mass media in "perpetuating and maintaining the values of white supremacy. Constantly and passively consuming white supremacist values both in educational systems and via prolonged engagement with mass media, contemporary black folks, and everyone else in this society, are vulnerable to a process of overt colonization that goes easily undetected. . . ." (111)

9. Nancy Hartsock, *Money, Sex and Power.* (New York: Longman, 1983) and "The Feminist Standpoint," in *Discovering Reality,* ed. Sandra Harding and Merrill B. Hintikka (Dordrecht, Holland: D. Reidel, 1983).

10. Collins, *op. cit.,* p. 29.

11. Catharine MacKinnon, "Feminism, Marxism, Method and the State" in *Feminist Theory: A Critique of Ideology,* ed. Nannerl O. Keohane, Michelle Z. Rosaldo, and Barbara C. Gelpi, (Chicago: University of Chicago Press, 1982). p. 23.

FURTHER READINGS

Collins, Patricia Hill, *Black Feminist Thought: Knowledge, Consciousness, and the Politics of Empowerment,* 1990. New York: Routledge.

Davis, Angela, *Women, Race and Class,* 1983. New York: Vintage.

Flax, Jane, *Thinking Fragments: Psychoanalysis, Feminism and Post-modernism in the Contemporary West,* 1990. Berkeley: University of California Press.

Hartsock, Nancy, *Money, Sex and Power,* 1983. New York: Longman.

hooks, bell, *Ain't I a woman: Black Women and Feminism,* 1981. Boston: South End Press.

hooks, bell, *Killing Rage, Ending Racism,* 1995. New York: Henry Holt and Company.

Keohane, Nannerl O., Michelle Z. Rosaldo, and Barbara Gelpi, *Feminist Theory: A Critique of Ideology.* 1982. Chicago: The University of Chicago Press.

MacKinnon, A. Catharine, *Towards a Feminist Theory of the State,* 1989. Cambridge: Harvard University Press.

Ring, Jennifer, *Modern Political Theory and Contemporary Feminism: A Dialectical Analysis,* 1991. Albany: State University of New York Press.

The Riddle of Consciousness: Racism and Identity in Feminist Theory

NANCIE E. CARAWAY

INTRODUCTION

Feminist scholarship offers both an intellectual and a political stimulus to undergraduate students in political science. It may fruitfully be called syncretic because it "brings together" so many threads about knowledge, political action, and power—and the implications of scholarship in general. Formally, it is akin to African American studies, gay studies, and other moments in ethnic studies (Chicano, Latino, Asian, Arab, Native American) because it crosses disciplines and introduces students to historical, theoretical, empirical, and interpretive modes of inquiry. And, importantly, these academic initiatives recognize their ties to grass-roots constituencies and movements for social justice. Being explicitly tied to social movements belies the claims of "neutrality" and "objectivity" professed by much social science conventional wisdom.

The increasing encounter of feminist scholarship with traditional concerns of political science (such as the Constitution, the judiciary, and electoral politics) has been challenging and revitalizing. It has displaced naturalized taboos (as in, "It's not natural for women/Blacks to participate in the nation's civil life") and exposed as riddles what were considered universal truths (as in, "We all know that politics is about state and national security, not sexual double standards, parenting, or housework"). It has resulted in the inclusion of courses in feminist theory in most political science departments at U.S. universities. This inclusion, however, carries with it the important caveat that one can't "just add women and stir."

The feminist imperative expands knowledge because it requires that we rethink old categories and accepted truths that have excluded women and women's experiences. What this means is that the concept of gender (the socially constructed "masculine" and "feminine" meanings attached to our biological plumbing) is now considered along with political authority, freedom, democracy, justice, race, and class as one of the important markers of political experience. The challenge requires as well new explanatory theories of "how things came to be this way" and new agendas for stimulating critical consciousness and accountability for oppression—whether oppression is practiced by the state, men, corporations, whites, *or* women.

The history of feminism itself is crucially a history of theory. Feminist scholarship has worked to demystify theory's abstractions by insisting, not only that the personal is political, but that the very meanings of the political and what counts as political experience are open to radical reinterpretation. This rethinking of traditional categories such as democracy, citizenship, and consciousness has enabled feminist theorists to ask subversive questions of the "canons" of political science: Which actions and experiences are considered political? How has the liberal public-private split rendered invisible women's contributions to culture? Who benefits from a social and political structure that subjugates women? What processes of identity and consciousness "produce" female and male political actors? And, importantly, how have traditional concepts of citizenship excluded women of all races?

So, although traditional concerns of political science remain legitimate, the perspectives from which they are examined are radicalized by feminist theory. Feminist political theorists have also turned to their own practices. They are attempting to examine the interlocking oppressions based on sex, gender, race, class, sexual preference, national origin, and ethnicity—and to devise strategies for overcoming those oppressions. Feminist theory describes (never unproblematically) the world from the perspectives of women by asking what kinds of political power and actions contribute to a more egalitarian society. This probing critique of traditional theories of citizenship and democracy has highlighted women's alternative political practices and the masculinist thought that has relegated women to inferior positions in the public world.

An analysis of grassroots activism of diverse women in the United States and other parts of the world historically has redefined the way "politics" is often thought of in our culture—as the actions of male elected officials. By making the activities of previously invisible women central, feminist scholars are helping to write both them and a new conception of democracy into the history of social change.

One of the most compelling turns in contemporary feminist theory is the emphasis on racism within feminism and the ways in which "women's oppression" has reflected the concerns of middle-class white women. This affords many new voices and feminisms the opportunity to negotiate community. Feminist women of color have insisted on articulating their own identities and experiences. In response, white feminists are working to contribute to this expanded understanding of "women" by interrogating their own racism, privilege, and the need for historical accountability for American apartheid and white supremacy. This is a painful but potentially liberating process that views racism and sexism not solely as "problems" but as textured ways of defining reality and living our lives. White feminists have learned that they too are "racialized."

The emphasis in feminist theory on identity politics, ethical commitments to creating coalitions of diverse women, and reflections on critical consciousness itself sets a new agenda for students of politics. These new configurations inhabit a challenging world of social theory to which I hope to introduce female and male political science students. A gentle warning to readers: Theoretical language provokes and often frustrates newcomers. But try to work with it. Think of theory's often technical terminology as an occasion for high-spirited translation (of the type required when we strain to "understand" the riffs of a Dylan concert)—and intellectual growth.

Multicultural feminist theory (the name for the dynamics I've been discussing) has its own mode of communicating—like rap, blues, jazz, or African American gospel testifying. The language of theory, however, does pose problems: It's dense, and it may ask that we read against the grain, follow the flow a bit while it teases us into a new coded way of thought. Much of these sentiments derive from something called *post-modernism* or *post-structuralism*—an intellectual attitude that offers skeptical insights, some of which are helpful to thoughtful feminists, some obfuscatory. This essay tries to sort out the criteria. Think of your frustration with theory-talk not as a declaration of verbal warfare, but as a meeting place of thought and spirit, a process of riddle solving.

As you travel the sometimes demanding terrain of this essay, remember the goal of creating a more robust "woman-friendly polity."[1] Toward this end, I employ two symbolic images of identity and consciousness in this essay as an entrée to these issues in current feminist theory: Toni Morrison's narrative in her novel of slavery, *Beloved,* and the autobiographical essay "Identity: Skin Blood Heart" by the white feminist Minnie Bruce Pratt.

KNOWING AND BEING: RACISM AND QUESTIONS OF FEMINIST THEORY

> Here, she said, in this place we flesh; flesh that weeps, laughs; flesh that dances on bare feet in grass. Love it. Love it hard. Yonder they do not love your flesh. They despise it. They don't love your eyes; they'd just as soon pick em out. No more do they love the skin on your back. Yonder they flay it. And O my people they do not love your hands. Those they only use, tie, bind, chop off and leave empty. Love your hands! Love them. Raise them up and kiss them. Touch others with them, pat them together, stroke them on your face 'cause they don't love that either. *You* got to love it, *you!*[2]

With this extraordinary declaration from her novel of enslavement,[3] Toni Morrison's "unchurched preacher" Baby Suggs articulates the passion of collective self-affirmation to her congregation of ex-slaves. Morrison's narrative speaks to the symbolic project that has defined the African American quest for agency and free space in the world the "whitethings" created.

This white world condemned by Morrison's text is a world in which African Americans have had their stories, identities, and very being defined by hegemonic white culture. I, as a white feminist, inhabit a similarly hegemonic terrain, that of the community of feminist scholars and activists whose legacy, too often, has been one of "whitethings" defining feminist life and aspirations for women of color. Fortunately, for our ethical health and our political direction, new stories, theories, and strategies voiced by feminist women of color are retooling feminist thought in penetrating and passionate modes to transform a deracinated "whitething" feminism. In this article, I want to chart some contours of this new multicultural direction, situate them within certain themes of identity politics, and provide a pedagogy about accountability for overcoming racism and developing critical consciousness, themes that come to us from Minnie Bruce Pratt.

As a political theorist, not a literary critic, I began to engage the coda of subjectivity and identity not through a technical philosophical discourse, but from the sheer emotional pull of Morrison's exhortation about the flesh of Black slaves—that is, the *identity* project of African Americans. The graphic physicality of Baby Suggs's statement concretizes for us that theory is truly never removed from the power-laden context of specific historical lives. When intellectuals consider utterances such as "deconstruction of the subject"—a provocative but often tediously hollow postmodernist challenge to certainties that we can truly "know" our "selves"—we need only return our thoughts to Morrison's prayerful *subjects* in the sun-dappled forest clearing to remember what social analysis is "about." This focus alerts us to the contributions of Black feminist theory to "our" (all women's) sense of the female subject. What can we learn about a revitalized polity and a newly committed series of feminisms if we look for the theoretical issues entangled within the arc narrated by Morrison?

Morrison's statement "*You* got to live it. *You!*" rejects the stigmas of otherness and difference inculcated by white supremacist culture, and validates, albeit tenuously, subjectivity and identity. This statement thus intersects in important ways with current epistemological debates—debates over "how we know what we know"—in feminist theory.[4] In particular, it demonstrates the creative challenges of Black feminism to feminist theory and politics.[5]

I have used Morrison's words to call attention to white racism within feminism and to validate feminist efforts at ending racist oppression as the central goal of feminist politics today. Let me note that the militant voices and courage of African American women were first to insist on the important task of decentering "whiteness" as the norm in feminist politics. In many historical moments, they have served as the conscience of feminist practice, the spirit that drives the movement back to the essential commitment feminist scholars ought to have toward enhancing the lives of marginalized women.

Contemporary Black feminist theory arises from the same spirit of affirmation and specificity reflected in Morrison's exhortation to the nineteenth-century Black community. The analysis that I will develop here characterizes such a project as "identity politics." But how do we reconcile this concern with agency and identity, given the red flags postmodernism sends up? The cultural power of our symbolic systems to seduce, delude, and encourage conceits about "self" and "authenticity" bear the footprints of metaphysics and take us away from the social and historical moorings in which such needs are produced. I want to think of identity politics as a contextual, not essentialist, process evolving out of political commitments and struggles for justice in multicultural feminist coalitions.[6] Identity is in the etched details of mediated lives and struggle. The reflective and reflexive political biography of the white feminist Minnie Bruce Pratt, to which I will return, is a luminous example of such a justice-seeking identity. Pratt's story is a chronicle of the fits and starts of seeking to know "how" one "is," a crucible of how a white feminist in a racist movement can be politicized through identity politics into a deeply personal interrogation of her own historical and racial roots.

What I hope to suggest in this essay is that questions about the self, about knowing and being, are not mutually exclusive. I am arguing that we must be able to articulate *some experiential foundation,* some notion of self, before we may act in the world. Rather than polarize antagonisms between feminists who "think" and feminists who "act," we need to see reflection and resistance as equally valid requirements of political and civic experience. Questions about and strategies for experiencing "identity" are crucial in this process. The perspectives derived from identity politics seek to emphasize the deep context, the "situated knowledges" (to use Donna Haraway's term), of our connected lives. Such a foundation is powerfully rendered in Morrison's preacher Baby Suggs's commentary: "In this place we flesh . . . *You* got to love it, *you!*" As Black feminist Cheryl Townsend Gilkes has pointed out, questions of identity have both historical and spiritual resonance for Black women *and* men. Black women's life experiences are grounded in a context that derives personal identity collectively, from a larger racially oppressed community "bound together by common interest, kinship, and tradition."[7] In charting the heroic and courageous activism of Black women in their struggle for dignity and equality ("uplift of the entire race") throughout American history, contemporary Black feminist historians *assume* the necessity of political agency, subjectivity, and identity as the very condition for social change.[8]

As a corollary to this understanding of the self as an entity that *is,* but is always in process, under seige, evolving as persons and events touch and change, African American women insist that for feminist discourse and politics to be relevant to their daily concerns, they must acknowledge the intersections of gender, race, and class as determinants of oppression, and not view gender as the *primary* form of oppression. This revolutionary paradigm shift is transforming feminism; we all are emerging from a new feminist "text" freshly educated about redefining the boundaries and connections of otherness. One need only observe the spectrum of contemporary feminist communities and activities to see the impact of such thinking. The writings of Black feminists are teaching us, in this regard, that feminist theory and politics should address the "multiple jeopardy" and "multiple consciousness" of Black women, in Deborah King's formulation.[9]

IDENTITY POLITICS: POSITIONAL RESISTANCE TO WHITE RACISM

As articulated by the Black feminist Combahee River Collective in a 1977 manifesto, "Our politics evolve from a healthy love for ourselves, our sisters, and our community. . . ." Their first commitment was to the cultural center they shared as women within the Black community.

> Even our Black women's style of talking, testifying in Black language about what we have experienced, has a resonance that is both cultural and political. We have spent a great deal of energy delving into the cultural and experiential nature of our oppression out of necessity because none of these matters have ever been looked at before. No one before has ever examined the multilayered texture of Black women's lives.[10]

The collective determined to align with progressive Black men in solidarity to resist racist oppression—struggling with them against sexism—and to frame their own oppression within the overlapping networks of family and community ties. More recently, Deborah King has spelled out these webbed commitments of Black feminists to the "special circumstances of our lives in the United States: the commonalities that we share with all women, as well as the bonds that connect us to the men of our race." King acknowledges the "distinctive context for Black womanhood," which she insists be defined and interpreted by Black women themselves: "While drawing on a rich tradition of struggle as blacks and as women, we continually establish and reestablish our own priorities."[11]

These statements argue for a politics of identity that is embodied in experiences and cultural spaces whose meanings are determined by those who live their daily lives in the tissue of interwoven contradictions. Alliances, priorities, and interpretations of self are relational and not responses to any set of given objective needs. Identity politics here finds affinity with a conceptualization of Donna Haraway in her explication of a feminist "objectivity" grounded in "partial local knowledges": "Feminism is about the sciences of the multiple subject with (at least) double vision. Feminism is about a critical vision consequent upon a critical positioning in unhomogeneous gendered social space."[12]

The operative phrase here is "critical positioning." For homophobes and chauvinists along with racists may well lay claim to a particular locus of cultural groundings and alliances that teach intolerance and racial and sexual revanchism. One might envision a mythologizing of David Duke as a southern populist, white male grass-roots expression of Arcadian-inspired public will, or even "white male, ex-Klansman and neo-Nazi"—that is to say, Duke's "identity." But it is not enough to issue a cultural-demographic schemata of one's identity-defining characteristics. In order to meet the politicized and justice-seeking criteria of identity politics, a fully articulated resistance and a critical positioning to oppression must be present. The multiple "subject" or shifting self that often comes to life in "nonfeminist" settings—as the women of the Combahee River Collective recognized—provides a more democratized terrain for feminist civic potential.

One colloquial way of stating this principle is to say that, as feminists, we need to "start where people are at," not insisting that feminist identity be based on shedding familial, regional, or religious local skins. How is it then that Black feminism's embodiment of identity politics demonstrates a *critical* and thus valorized stance?

One would be on dangerous ground in projecting a romanticized image of "the oppressed" as beyond criticism. We diminish our critical edge if we dismiss postmodernist admonitions about the human potential for culpability in projecting illusions, of adopting institutionalized discourses of truth, reason, and certainty as foundations for political life. At the same time, however, we can look to the political *knowledge* that comes from the oppositional worldview Black feminist bell hooks locates in living "on the edge" of white society.[13]

Such a critical and protean version of identity politics advances a space for political action and collective transformation. All feminists need to see value in the experience of those "on the edge" because such a vantage point embodies a negative moment, inherently attuned to flesh-and-blood deprivation and pain as central to political attention. As one feminist theorist has conceptualized such a stance, the knowledge gained by living "on the other side of the tracks" is justified by the critical positioning of those persons on the margins of societies.[14] The struggle against hierarchies of power is the substance that merits our allegiance to the practices and knowledge of the marginalized.

Toni Morrison in *Beloved* makes clear that "stories" and "identities" in America's apartheid have been far from reciprocal, far from the bridges of empathy and human understanding that ethical consciousness demands of human commerce. The "other" may indeed be alien and murderous. And one "identity" has not been as good as another. Morrison gives us a story about "subjects" struggling to wrest definition of what human beings are supposed to be from white masters. It is their *critical position* vis-à-vis the dominant racist society that must be endorsed, their determination to re-vision an "other" that does not annihilate, rather than their essence as "pure" petitioners.

BE THE RIGHT THING: POSITIONING WHITE FEMINIST IDENTITY AND RACIAL IMPERATIVES

This emerging portrait of identity politics tantalizes the theoretical imaginations of feminist scholars in its bonding of epistemological considerations with imperatives for historical political action. Feminist thinkers/activists may embrace knowledge about the "fluid" and unfixed construction of identity—albeit described in specific, historic local narratives. Such portraits need not be racially (or otherwise) specific; they surely fulfill the intertextual criteria of the most provocative multicultural feminist scholarship by speaking to "us all." Collectivities of multicultural, multiracial, sexually diverse feminists may find empowerment in the resources of identity politics about the shared and differentiated faces of female oppression.

Identity politics is the terrain of social outlaws.[15] It militantly asserts who "we" are and what "we" mean (this holds, especially so, for white feminists given the history of white assumptions in much feminist theory) and engages the potential for those explorations in coalition or affinity venues. It demands accountability for correcting the racism of everyday life which the expanded vision of multicultural feminism reveals to us. I want to briefly explore one of the most penetrating and transformative instances of identity politics work by a non-Black, non-person-of-color (to reverse the white solipsistic linguistic norm "non-white")—Minnie Bruce Pratt's 1984 essay "Identity: Skin Blood Heart."[16]

Pratt's text, an intensely probing mediation on her own shifting selves, is a powerful model for other white feminists to follow in order to question our own complicity in and accountability for correcting the myriad racist practices existing in the world around us—a precondition for successful coalition building. Pratt, a white, Southern-born, Christian-raised, lesbian woman, takes her reader inside an exploration of a divided consciousness, demonstrating the postmodernist feminist thesis that the "wholeness" of the self involves an inescapably protean encounter with others. The manner in which Pratt frames her experiential/political project of struggling to derive an "identity" from which the various layers of her life "fit," empowering her to act, foregrounds questions of otherness and accountability. Pratt uses her feminism, a politics of everyday life, as a springboard from which to investigate self-consciously those many "edges" on which she stands: ". . . I will try to be at the edge between my fear and outside, on the edge at my skin, listening, asking what new thing will I hear, will I see, will I let myself feel, beyond the fear."[17] Pratt is able to let her multiple experiences of otherness float in an uneasy alliance, allowing them to open her eyes to other scenarios of domination and oppression. Her own outsider status as a lesbian alerts her to the marginalization of others with whom she attempts to ally, without collapsing them all into one "grand polemics of oppression."[18]

Central to Pratt's articulation of her search for self and identity are two important metaprocesses that are important tools for white feminists' antiracist efforts. She has the ability to problematize, to evaluate reflectively, every encounter with another and to take nothing for granted in interracial relationships. These displacements provide a valuable corrective to status quo attitudes. Pratt encourages white women to scrutinize the historical and ideological layers attendant to encounters with "others"—paying particular attention to the concealments and exclusions, the buried "holes in the text,"[19] that submerge and mystify the violations of race, class, and gender.

Pratt is frustrated and doubtful of overcoming the chasm of racism. But Pratt keeps on keeping on. These painful incidents become challenges to overcome, not paralyzing dead ends in Pratt's story; they stand as markers of the quotidian signs of racism. As Pratt assays the cost to those whom her own protection and privilege as a southern white woman have disadvantaged, she is able to 'free' herself from the poisonous racism by acknowledging her own family's participation in its system. She is empowered to locate the harm, to identify the victims that the vision of the society of her white childhood excluded. By seeking the absences, she may now "gain truth" when she expands her constricted eye, "an eye that has only let in what I have been taught to see."[20]

Revelation and psychological unpeeling continue when Pratt's professor husband takes her and their children to a new town, a Southern "market town." Geography and history again stimulate her questioning of the town whose center, tellingly, is not a courthouse, but a market house. With complacent, middle-class white friends at dinner in a private club overlooking the town's central circle, she queries them about the marketplace. They chat about the fruits and vegetables, the auctioned tobacco that were sold at the market. "But not slaves," they said. It is left to the Black waiter—a silent figure who boldly breaks through "the anonymity of his red jacket"—to assume the role of educator, disrupting white historical amnesia to tell them of the men, women, and children who were sold at the market near where they now dine.

> What he told me was plain enough: This town was a place where some people had been used as livestock, chattel, slaves, cattle, capital, by other people; and this use had been justified by the physical fact of a different skin color and by the cultural fact of different ways of living. The white men and their families who had considered Black people to be animals with no right to their own children or to a home of their own still did not admit that they had done any wrong, nor that there had been any wrong, in *their* town. What he told me was plain enough: Be warned: they have not changed.[21]

The narrative of Pratt's identity journey is a useful feminist teaching precisely because her project does not become a study in narcissism, a withdrawing from political reality. Her newfound knowledge of racist history through a probing of her own personal history serves as a spur toward further inquiry and action. Her ability to approach the world and structures of domination as interlocked, as "overlapping circles," elicits knowledge of other traditions of struggle whose experiences she might draw upon. And importantly in the framework of coalition politics, Pratt perceives scenarios of persons in whose service she might present herself as an ally in their struggles.

> I knew nothing of these or other histories of struggle for equality and justice and one's own identity in the town I was living in: not a particularly big town, not liberal at all, not famous for anything: an almost rural eastern North Carolina town, in a region that you, perhaps, are used to thinking of as backward. Yet it was a place with so many resistances, so much creative challenge to the powers of the world: which is true of every county, town, or city in this country, each with its own buried history of struggle, of how people try to maintain their dignity within the restrictions placed around them, and how they struggle to break those restrictions.[22]

The potency of Pratt's story at this point in her account of the accumulated identities that she wrestles to incorporate has to do with her own connection to Southern racism. When she sought to find out what had been or was being done "in her name," the knowledge was shattering. "I had set out to make a new home with other women, only to find that the very ground I was building on was the grave of the people my kin had killed, and that my foundation, my birth culture, was mortared with blood."[23] The cracking and heaving and buckling Pratt experienced in what she describes as "the process of freeing myself" afforded no relief, no sanctimony. "This breaking through," she admits, "did not feel like liberation but like destruction." Her expanded sense of political accountability; her endeavors to locate a new "home," a chosen political community of women committed to justice; and her confession of loss are the flashpoints of Pratt's journey toward political conscience. This voice does not mute the pain and alienation such a process entails. Feel the drama in her telling:

> I think this is what happens, to a more or less extreme degree, every time we expand our limited being: it is upheaval, not catastrophe: more like a snake shedding its skin than like death: the old constriction is sloughed off with difficulty, but there is an expansion: not a change in basic shape or color, but an expansion, some growth, and some reward for struggle and curiosity. . . .
>
> As I try to strip away the layers of deceit that I have been taught, it is hard not to be afraid that these are like wrappings of a shroud and that what I will ultimately come to in myself is a disintegrating, rotting *nothing:* that the values that I have at my core, from my culture, will only be those of negativity, exclusion, fear, death. And my feeling is based in the reality that the group identity of my culture has been defined, often, not by positive qualities, but by negative characteristics: by the absence of: "no dogs, Negroes, or Jews"; we have gotten our jobs, bought our houses, borne and educated our children by the negative: no niggers, no kikes, no wops, no dagos, no spics, no A-rabs, no gooks, no queers [emphasis in original.][24]

Pratt's essay resonates in so many ways with wisdom and warnings vital to struggling antiracist feminists. The integrity with which she describes her story encourages our own probings. Her identity project can stand as a document of feminist politicization precisely because Pratt resists those self-destructive urges that are anathema to enacting social change: the reactionary extreme of abandoning her own complexly vexing Southern culture, the paralyzing guilt and fear that come with the knowledge of the enormity and barbarity of white privilege. Throughout this powerful essay, Pratt reveals herself determined to understand the volatile psychic hold of home, childhood, and patriarchal "protection" of white women in her class. There is no denouement in Pratt's search for "identity," only continued working-through. Hers, and ours, entails a long-term commitment, a meditation on consciousness that is grounded in daily actions that allow us to connect with or bypass the "others" with whom we seek community. This seeking is the riddle of consciousness to be grappled with through political struggle.

Pratt also shows her readers the psychic dangers of denial and its opposite, absorption into the other: the desire to cover her "naked, negative [self] with something from the positive traditions of identity which have served in part to help folks survive our people."[25] Finally Pratt can come to an awareness and acceptance of her own *whiteness*—while resisting the culture of white supremacy, on the one hand, and, on the other, avoiding the condescending trap of "cultural imperson-ation," of attempting to "become Black." We come to see such gestures for what they are—sentimental balms of political quietism.

In the language of postmodern thought, Pratt's essay provides a "genealogy," a deep sifting through the ideological and historical practices that render the tangle of "self." She asks how the contradictions that regulate her life came to be—in dis-course, in history, in region, in family. Pratt offers a response to the issues of racism within feminism that takes us to the other side of paralyzing white guilt. In the "knowing and being" philosophical frame of feminist thought, Pratt's example ties reflection with the crucial next step of political engagement and activism for justice. She offers us the gift of openness to begin again each day that struggle to turn our received "identities" upside down.

CONCLUSION

The concept of identity politics I have attempted to sketch questions many of the troubling assumptions of mainstream white feminism. It brings to life the need for white feminists not only to endorse a call for *inclusion* and *diversity* within femi-nist organizations, but to go "beyond the inclusion of persons and texts," as Sandra Harding has recently argued, and ask "what should *we* be doing in order to be de-sirable allies from *their* perspectives?"[26] Identity politics with a postmodern tilt, then, facilitates such a commitment by rejecting the possibility of a common "woman's experience" that can be objectively derived. This reading follows Minnie Bruce Pratt's example in cautioning against the tendency to substitute a critical consciousness, or therapy, or other premises that assume we have an unchanging "essence." We are encouraged to focus instead on strategic discourse, by asking under which conditions we may work together democratically, and on political ac-tion toward common goals.

Feminists interested in multicultural goals may employ these ideas with the model of political action in strategic coalitions of diverse women. The themes of racism and identity come together in a configuration that can address the theoreti-cal issues about the female subject so vital to current feminist thought. I hope my epigrammatic beginning, with Toni Morrison's searing accomplishment in *Beloved,* of textually imparting the criminal genealogy of Black flesh in America, reminds us all just what is at stake in questions of identity and racial memory.

We ought not forget how the construction of a "self" that sees its own reflec-tion to those "semiotic technologies"[27] created by the culture that creates us can still feel injustice and endure pain. At the same time, a critical identity politics cau-tions us not to become too comfortable too long in *that spot* with *that identity,* lest we forget and stifle the ways in which we change, contradict, and grow in history. The achievement of identity itself must be viewed as one moment of political strug-gle, a struggle that precludes our standing, innocent, on the other side of our cul-tural mediations.

Identity politics calls for practices of deep contextualization, with accounts of persons that are always explicitly described, colored, gendered, situated—that, to borrow from Louis Althusser, resist simplification in the last instance. And, more importantly, it gives us grounds for politics and coalitions in the renegade terrain of that "real" world of shared struggle in feminist community.

NOTES

1. Kathleen B. Jones, "Citizens in a Woman-Friendly Polity,"*Signs* 15 (4) (Summer 1990), pp. 781–812.

2. Toni Morrison, *Beloved* (New York: Knopf, 1987), pp. 88–89.

3. Although most critics have characterized Morrison's novel as a novel "of slavery," I wish to adopt the term *enslavement*. Black feminist and longtime civil rights activist Ruby Sales has made a strong case for rejecting the word *slavery* in favor of *enslavement*. In her analysis, the former term suggests a passivity and renders the process of enslavement benign. Using the word *slavery* diminishes the moral and political responsibility demanded of the one who enslaves. If there's enslavement, there's an enslaver and an enslaved person. The term *enslaved,* according to Sales, doesn't mean a person is passive; it implies coercive force was used against that person. Further, importantly, the term implies that the enslaved person is resisting. See Ruby Sales, "In Our Own Words: An Interview with Ruby Sales," *Woman's Review of Books,* 7 (5) (February 1990), p. 24.

4. The problematic has been identified in these debates as one of "subject-centered discourse" and is occasioned by currents in what is intellectually framed as "postmodernist skepticism" of the founding categories of Western Enlightenment thought—truth, objectivity, the coherent self, agency, identity—all constructs from which feminism itself derived. For lucid discussions of these issues and feminism's encounter with postmodernism, consult Kathy Ferguson, "Interpretation and Genealogy in Feminism," paper presented at the Western Political Science Association, San Francisco, March 1988; Kathy Ferguson, "Subject-Centeredness in Feminist Discourse," in Kathleen B. Jones and Anna G. Jonasdottir (Eds.), *The Political Interests of Gender* (London: Sage Publications, 1985), pp. 66–78. Linda J. Nicholson (Ed.), *Feminism/Postmodernism* (New York and London: Routledge, 1990); Jane Flax, "Postmodernism and Gender Relations in Feminist Theory," *Signs,* 12 (4) (Summer 1987), pp. 621–643; Linda Alcoff, "Cultural Feminism versus Post-Structuralism: The Identity Crisis in Feminist Theory," *Signs,* 13 (3) (Spring 1988), pp 406–436; Leslie Wahl Rabine, "A Feminist Politics of Non-Identity," *Feminist Studies,* 14 (2) (Spring 1988), pp. 11–31; the entire volume on "Feminism and Epistemology: Approaches to Research in Women and Politics," in *Women & Politics,* 7 (3) (Fall 1987); Donna Haraway, "A Manifesto for Cyborgs: Science, Technology, and Socialist Feminism in the 1980s," in Nicholson, *Feminism/Postmodernism,* pp. 190–233; Donna Haraway, "Situated Knowledges: The Science Question in Feminism and the Privilege of Partial Perspective," *Feminist Studies,* 14 (3) (Fall 1988), pp. 575–599.

5. See bell hooks, *Feminist Theory: From Margin to Center* (Boston: South End Press, 1984); bell hooks, *Ain't I a woman* (Boston: South End Press, 1989); bell hooks, *Yearning: Race, Gender, and Cultural Politics* (Boston: South End Press, 1990); Audre Lorde, *Sister Outsider* (Trumansburg, NY: Crossing Press, 1984).

6. I am persuaded by Judith Butler's reading of the identity problematic in postmodern thinking that the deconstruction of identity need not lead to the deconstruction of politics. Through the dynamic of political confrontation and coalition politics, we understand who we are and what we mean in our explication of feminist common differences. Butler argues the case "that there need not be a 'doer behind the deed,' but that the 'doer' is variably constructed in and through the deed." Butler does not, but I will, tip my voluntarist hat to Marx for the originary seeds of the insight about the self-defining character of political struggle. Judith Butler, *Gender Trouble: Feminism and the Subversion of Identity* (New York: Routledge, 1990), pp. 148, 142.

7. Cheryl Townsend Gilkes, "Dual Heroisms and Double Burdens: Interpreting Afro-American Women's Experience and History," *Feminist Studies,* 14 (3) (Fall 1989), pp. 573–590, esp. p. 573.

8. In reviewing Paula Giddings's excellent history of Black feminist activism, *When and Where I Enter: The Impact of Black Women on Race and Sex in America* (New York: William Morrow, 1984), Chery Townsend Gilkes states clearly that self-definition has historically been a major theme in Black feminist thought. Gilkes, "Dual Heroisms," p. 589, n. 4.

9. Deborah H. King, "Multiple Jeopardy, Multiple Consciousness: The Context of a Black Feminist Ideology," *Signs* 14, (3) (Autumn 1988), pp. 42–72.

10. "A Black Feminist Statement: The Combahee River Collective," in Gloria T. Hull, Patricia Bell Scott, and Barbara Smith (Eds.), *But Some of Us Are Brave* (Old Westbury, NY: Feminist Press, 1982), p. 17.

11. King, "Multiple Jeopardy," pp. 42, 72.

12. Haraway, "Situated Knowledges," p. 579.

13. hooks, *Feminist Theory,* preface.

14. Linda Alcoff has developed a related conceptual framework of positionality as a basis for feminist activism that does not depend on an identity that is "essentialized"—that is, on an identity that is idealized as "transcendent" and "pure," without fault. Positionality, as she defines it, is a contextual strategy of achieving one's subjectivity. Positionality views woman's identity "relative to a constantly shifting context, to a situation that includes a network of elements involving others, the objective economic conditions, cultural and political institutions and ideologies, and so on. . . . The position of woman is relative and not innate, and yet neither is it 'undecidable.'" *Alcoff,* "Cultural Feminism," pp. 433–434.

15. See Shane Phelan's highly original study of the political and theoretical dimensions of lesbian identity politics, *Identity Politics: Lesbian Feminism and the Limits of Community* (Philadelphia: Temple University Press, 1989).

16. Minnie Bruce Pratt, "Identity: Skin Blood Heart," in Elly Bulkin, Minnie Bruce Pratt, and Barbara Smith, (Eds.), *Yours in Struggle: Three Feminist Perspectives on Anti-Semitism and Racism* (Ithaca, NY: Firebrand Books, 1984).

17. *Ibid.,* p. 18.

18. I don't wish to replicate here the emphasis on the subjectivity question in Pratt's project taken up by Chandra Talpade Mohanty and Biddy Martin in their essay, "Feminist Politics: What's Home Got to Do with It?," in Teresa de Lauretis (Ed.), *Feminist Studies/Critical Studies* (Bloomington: Indiana University Press, 1986), p. 206. My approach in considering Pratt is to understand the powerful symbol of political transformation she represents vis-à-vis white racism and multicultural feminist politics. But I do want to acknowledge

Mohanty and Martin's skepticism about the potential of identity politics to be incorporated into feminist work for social change. The translation of discourses of self-revelation into strategic grassroots work is not axiomatic; we need to insist that the achievement of critical consciousness is a political, not solely a psychological, achievement. In this sense, a heightened consciousness leads to and requires moving from the local to the global, moving from psychic transformation to concrete acts in the material world to subvert systematic forms of oppression.

19. This is the phrase Friedrich Nietzsche employs in his critique of representation. Friedrich Nietzsche, *The Dawn of Day,* section 523, in Oscar Levy (Ed.), *The Complete Works of Friedrich Nietzsche,* Vol. 9 (New York: Gordon, 1974).

20. Pratt, "Identity: Skin Blood Heart," p. 17.

21. *Ibid.,* p. 21.

22. *Ibid.,* p. 29.

23. *Ibid.,* p. 35.

24. *Ibid.,* p. 39.

25. *Ibid.,* p. 40.

26. Sandra Harding, "The Permanent Revolution," *Women's Review of Books,* 7 (5) (February 1990), p. 17.

27. Eloise Buker offers an incisive path through the dense thicket of semiotic discourse. She argues that feminists need not be "put off" by its technical jargon nor should they fall into a depoliticized passivity in the face of its abstractions. "In Fact," Buker argues, "we may well find [postmodernism's skepticism of Enlightenment notions of truth] liberating because we do not have to pretend that we have found THE universal laws, or even patterns that characterize all persons for all times. We can figure out what we think best in our own limited worlds. We will not defer our decisions until we know for sure what to do since we will understand that we always act in the midst of both our knowledge and our ignorance. Putting-off politics is not possible." Eloise Buker, "Rhetoric in Postmodern Feminism: Put-offs, Put-ons and Political Plays," paper presented at the annual meeting of the American Political Science Association, San Francisco, August 30-September 2, 1990, p. 7.

FURTHER READINGS

Caraway, Nancie. *Segregated Sisterhood: Racism and the Politics of American Feminism*. Knoxville: University of Tennessee Press, 1991.

Bulkin, Elly, Minnie Bruce Pratt, and Barbara Smith. *Yours in Struggle: Three Feminist Perspectives on Anti-Semitism and Racism*. New York: Long Haul Press, 1984.

DuBois, E. C., and Vicki L. Ruiz, (Eds.), *Unequal Sisters*. New York: Routledge, 1990.

Nicholson, Linda (Ed.), *Feminism/Postmodernism*. New York: Routledge, 1990.

Flax, Jane. "Postmodernism and Gender Relations in Feminist Theory." *Signs* 12 (4) (1987), pp. 621–643.

Giddings, Paula. *When and Where I Enter: The Impact of Black Women on Race and Sex in America*. New York: William Morrow, 1984

GENDER DIFFERENCES IN POLITICAL ATTITUDES AND VOTING

Socialization partly explains our attitudes about politics and how politically active we later become as adults. For example, we know that women who have grown up in households in which their mothers took a relatively active role in politics are more likely themselves to vote and become active politically. Working under the assumption that political socialization can bring about ultimate political change, we first examine gender differences and similarities in political behavior and attitudes. Are younger Americans coming to greater agreement than their parents or grandparents on the issue of gender equality in the political arena? Linda L. M. Bennett and Stephen E. Bennett look at how women and men have changed in their opinions about women's roles in politics. Creating a Political Gender Roles Index from data in the National Opinion Research Center's (NORC) General Social Surveys between 1973 and 1996, the Bennetts find that there is increasing acceptance of modern political roles for women. Still, they also find intriguing evidence that the youngest Americans (aged 18–29) may not be as enthusiastic about modern roles for women as their parents. There remains significant gender differences, particularly among the college-educated, about women's roles in politics.

Previous research has found that younger women are more likely to hold feminist attitudes than are older women. There is also some evidence, however, that young women in the 1980s are less supportive of feminism than were older women. This suggests there may be some generational influences at work. Elizabeth Adell Cook explores this question using a technique called *cohort analysis*. Cohort (or generational) analysis of the 1972 to 1996 American National Election

Studies indicates that women who came of age during the period of social activism of the 1960s and the growth of the women's movement in the 1970s exhibit higher levels of politicized feminist consciousness than do women of earlier generations. Women who came of age during the anti-feminist Reagan administration are less feminist than those who reached adulthood during the women's liberation movement or during the Clinton administration. In 1996, the Reagan or complacent cohort was not more conservative than earlier generations on policy issues such as child care and abortion—they were merely less supportive of the women's movement. This suggest that the name "complacent" may fit them well—they take for granted the successes of the movement while continuing to support gender equality and feminist policies. This is also confirmed by an item in the 1992 survey, which revealed that the complacent cohort took less pride in the accomplishments of other women than did the women of the women's liberation cohort, but were more likely to express the belief that men and women ought to have equal power in society. Clear cohort differences persist over time, suggesting that generational effects are strong. Overall, the data show an increase in feminist consciousness over time. Younger generations of women tend to be more feminist than their predecessors.

There have been revolutionary changes in the lives of twentieth-century American women. Foremost among these changes are those related to women's employment outside the home. In 1880, for example, by far the largest segment of working women were single. Today, a majority of married women are numbered in the ranks of working women, and women with children are a significant part of the labor force. An emphasis on these changes, however, obscures an important reality concerning American women's working lives, one that is not likely to change in the near future. The fact is that most American women work in so-called pink-collar ghettos, a condition known as *occupational segregation.*

The next essay, by Gertrude A. Steuernagel, Maureen Rand Oakley, Thomas E. Yatsco, and Irene J. Barnett, examines the effects of occupational segregation on political attitudes and behavior. Utilizing data from the National Election Study to measure political attitudes and behavior and data from the Department of Labor to measure occupational segregation, the authors first look at some basic differences in political attitudes and behavior between men and women. Specifically, they look at differences between men and women on items such as frequency of political discussions and response to an eight-issue liberalism-conservatism index. Advancing the position that useful as such analysis might be, the authors then argue and offer an empirical analysis that supports their contention: studies of simple differences between men and women miss much of the complex dynamic surrounding gender, work, and political attitudes and behavior.

Are women more alike than they are different in certain aspects of political behavior? For example, some studies have shown that women tend to be more liberal on issues relating to social programs and economic security; that is, women have shown more humanitarian, social welfare–oriented attitudes. Women have also tended to be less supportive of militarist or aggressive action in foreign affairs.

What does the record show about gender differences in voting behavior? Why and when do women and men support different political candidates? Why might we expect (or not expect) differences in voting patterns based upon gender?

Janet Clark and Cal Clark explore the gender gap in the 1996 election; they note that probably the central explanation for the re-election of Democrat Bill Clinton as President in 1996 was the much noted "gender gap" in which Clinton received stronger support from women than from men. In popular imagery at least, Clinton was portrayed as benefitting from a "revenge of the soccer Moms" against the less kinder and less gentler policies pushed by Republican Speaker of the House Newt Gingrich. The authors seek to go beyond the simple images in the headlines to provide a more sophisticated analysis of the extent and nature of the gender gap in the 1996 presidential election.

The gender gap in which women disproportionately support Democratic candidates appears to have become a permanent fixture of the American political landscape. This gap first appeared in the 1980 presidential contest between Ronald Reagan and Jimmy Carter. Clinton's gender gap of 11 percentage points (54 percent of women as opposed to 43 percent of men voted for Clinton) is the largest gap that has occurred during the 1980s and 1990s. Still, the authors maintain, the popular image of a new and dramatic gender gap is probably overblown. They argue the 1996 gender gap was more a continuation of previous trends than a dramatic new development; and the size of the gender gap pales when compared to ideological and racial divisions in the electorate. Moreover, a complex set of factors reflecting the "three C's" of gender consciousness, compassion, the cost-bearing created by the feminization of poverty all contributed to the gender gap in voting.

This indicates that the Soccer Moms (that is, middle-class, primarily working married mothers) were only one of a variety of types of women who made the gender gap in 1996 what it was. More broadly, the very different perspectives of some of these groups, especially between "economic" and "social" liberals, provides a strong but not necessarily fatal challenge to leaders promoting the coalescence of women's interests.

Changing Views about Gender Equality in Politics: Gradual Change and Lingering Doubts

Linda L. M. Bennett and Stephen E. Bennett

INTRODUCTION

An important difference between women and men in the United States disappeared in the 1980s. Since ratification of the Nineteenth Amendment in 1920, women had voted in national elections in smaller proportions than men. But in the 1988 presidential election, the U.S. Census Bureau estimated that 58 percent of women 18 years old and older turned out, compared to 56 percent of similarly aged men. The Census Bureau reported that 62 percent of women 18 years old and older reported voting in the 1992 election, compared to 60 percent of men 18 years old and older. Finally, according to the Census Bureau, 55 percent of women 18 and older voted in the 1996 presidential election, compared to 53 percent of men aged 18 and older.[1] The turnout gap between women and men has also disappeared in local elections.[2]

Exercising the franchise is but one way a citizen can participate in this political system, and profound differences between women and men remain in other modes of participation (for example, running for political office). The end of turnout differences is significant, however, because it calls into question some of the ways researchers have explained gender differences in political behavior and attitudes. Do we need to revise our thinking about the different factors that affect women and men and their involvement in politics? Are women and men becoming more alike in how they view politics? And what is happening to opinions among younger Americans? For example, are the young coming to greater agreement than their parents or grandparents on the issue of gender equality in the political arena?

These are the questions we hope to answer in this essay. We begin with a review of explanations for gender differences in political behavior and attitudes. We will describe three basic explanations for gender differences: (1) *sex-role socialization* (how girls and boys learn "gender-appropriate" attitudes and behavior that affect how they view politics); (2) *structural* (the impact of education, occupation, income); and (3) *situational* (marital status, motherhood, homemaking). We create a way to measure what people think about political gender equality and describe those who still hold traditional conceptions of a "woman's place" in politics and society, as well as those who are taking on a more "modern" perspective that allows for full participation regardless of gender.

Even while some attitudes are changing, women are exhibiting far from full participation in the political arena. The sex-role socialization process continues to encourage political passivity among women, although its effects are clearly weakening in areas such as voting. Socialization remains an important factor that can help us to understand the lingering differences between women and men on a host of political attitudes and behaviors.

THREE EXPLANATIONS FOR GENDER DIFFERENCES

Sex-Role Socialization

In 1960 researchers defined sex-role socialization as "that portion of expectations about behavior proper for a male or female that involves political responses."[3] The authors went on to explain that the "role definitions" between women and men, and women's willingness to "leave politics to men," was the source of gender differences in attitudes during the 1950s. Socialization literature of the 1960s and early 1970s supported research from the 1950s and argued that the passive role learned by young girls was a significant reason they avoided politics later in life.[4] Studies in the 1980s asserted that girls were still learning passivity from their mothers and that this learning process accounted for their political passivity as adults.[5] Political roles are learned not only from parents, but also at school, in church, from peers, and from the media. By the late 1990s, with evidence that men and women still maintain differing levels of engagement in politics, researchers have called for a reinvigoration of political socialization research.[6] Four decades of research show that as a result of exposure to a number of socializing agents, many women and men grow up believing that politics is a "man's world."

The problem with sex-role socialization research is that much of it was developed from studies of children, with little evidence offered of a conclusive link between childhood experience and adult attitudes or behavior. Attempts to bridge the period between childhood and adult years depended on researchers eliminating the influence of as many other factors as possible (some of which are discussed under structural and situational factors) and then concluding that only socialization was left as a reasonable explanation for gender differences in political thought, feelings, and actions.[7]

Structural Factors

Socioeconomic factors such as education, occupation, and income have long been known to be important in shaping a variety of attitudes. Education has been one of the strongest predictors of women's involvement and participation. In a study comparing brothers and sisters differentiated only by college attendance, the sibling with college exposure was consistently more politically interested, informed, and participatory than the one without the benefit of a college education.[8]

Along with education, women's employment status has been found by some to have an impact on political participation. In a study from the early 1970s, Kristi Andersen found a combined effect of employment and holding feminist opinions on women's willingness to participate. Working women who were supportive of an equal role in society for their sex were more participatory than their working sisters who did not back gender equality in society.[9] Still others found no differences in voting turnout between working and nonworking women and attributed gender differences to the greater political passivity of older women, who were more likely to be socialized into the notion that politics was a "man's business."[10] Tapping into the paycheck reality of work, Ellen McDonagh emphasized that work is not "liberating" if it is low-paid drudgery.[11]

In addition to the impact of women's presence in the workforce as a possible stimulant to their political participation, Jeffrey Koch argues that the increasing presence of women in public office may also be an important goad to participation, under certain circumstances. He asserts that the mere presence of more women in public office may not be sufficient in itself. Rather, women politicians are more likely to trigger greater political interest among women in their constituencies when they articulate issues that are particularly important to those women.[12]

Situational Factors

The number of women who become wives and/or mothers or who remain at home in the traditional role of homemaker has changed tremendously in recent years.[13] For this reason, recent research on situational factors disputes the conclusions of earlier studies. Studies from the 1950s argued that the duties of motherhood depressed women's political participation. It was assumed that women adopted the political attitudes of their husbands and looked to them for guidance when voting.[14] Lower levels of participation were most evident among less educated, low-socioeconomic-status women. Women's absorption with the "private sphere" of the home supposedly created a major obstacle to their participation in the "public sphere" of politics.

Older, untested assumptions about women's political participation do not always hold up to empirical scrutiny. Later studies challenged the tendency of earlier studies to focus only on national elections and urged more attention to participation in state and local politics. More recent research offers more complex descriptions of the impact of motherhood and reveals an increased likelihood to participate in local politics among women with school-aged children.[15] Virginia Sapiro found that a complex joint effect of motherhood and education was linked to higher levels of community participation among women. She also argued that educational achievement is more important than marital status, homemaking, or motherhood in leading women to a general interest in politics.[16] On the other hand, Nancy Romer found that young women who were politically active in high school *expected* to be less politically active if they took on the roles of wife and mother.[17]

In reviewing the three explanations that have been offered for gender differences in political attitudes and participation, it should be evident that it is difficult to keep each explanation distinct. Researchers have tried to separate the effects of socialization from those of socioeconomic status and role choices such as being a wife and mother, but it is less clear that most women could separate them as easily. Even those who have argued for the impact of structural and situational factors find themselves returning to the key factor of how roles are learned, or socialization. As one group of researchers notes, "socialization into the traditional feminine role in our culture produces a sense of self which is relatively more dependent on the definitions of others and a concern with homes and families, and matters related to them, over more 'distant' matters."[18] In addition, structural and situational factors have been easier to study because there are clearer indicators by which their impact can be measured. Education, occupation, marital status, number of children—these are all simple questions on any public opinion survey, whereas socialization, a slow process of learning, is more difficult to uncover with surveys. Still, it remains a compelling explanation for how women and men view politics.

Having outlined the three explanations for gender differences, it is easy to see that socialization could be related to how much women strive to achieve in education and work, as well as their choices of marriage, motherhood, and whether they stay at home as caretakers to others.[19] Are there empirical indicators that can help us to measure attitudes developed from the socialization process? We find there are such indicators, although they are far from perfect, and we turn next to how sex-role socialization shows up in opinions about women's "proper place" in the political world. If socialization does have an impact on how interested and involved people are in politics, then we need to understand how those views are shaped. Have opinions about where women belong in the political arena changed in recent years?

MEASURING OPINIONS ABOUT GENDER ROLES IN POLITICS

The next section will present data on how much involvement in the political arena people feel is appropriate for women. Before presenting those data, we offer a brief section on where the data come from and how attitudes are being measured.

The seven time periods covered in this analysis are: 1974–1975, 1977–1978, 1982–1983, 1985–1986, 1988–1989, 1991–1993, and 1994–1996. Beginning in 1974, the National Opinion Research Center (NORC) at the University of Chicago included a series of questions on its General Social Survey asking a national sample of voting-age Americans about women's roles in business, industry, and politics. Several of these questions have been asked on most General Social Surveys since. Three of them focus on gender roles in politics:

1. Do you agree or disagree with this statement? Women should take care of running their homes and leave running the country up to men.
2. If your party nominated a woman for president, would you vote for her if she were qualified for the job?
3. Tell me if you agree or disagree with this statement: Most men are better suited emotionally for politics than are most women.

For this study, these items were combined to form a "Political Gender Roles Index."[20] An index allows the combination of several narrower items into a single indicator measuring a more general concept. The Political Gender Roles Index groups responses to the three items on a scale ranging from "very modern" (disagrees that women should leave running the country up to men, would vote for a woman for president, and disagrees that men are better suited emotionally for politics) to "very traditional" (agrees the country should be run by men, would not vote for a woman, and agrees that men are more emotionally suited for politics). Those with a mix of responses were labeled "slightly modern" or "slightly traditional." The few people who said they "didn't know" what to think about any of the questions were placed in a middle "neutral" category. As you will see, there are very few people who take a neutral position on what women's political roles should be.

TRENDS IN OPINIONS ABOUT GENDER ROLES IN POLITICS

We begin with a general overview of what people think about women's appropriate roles in politics. Table 2.1 shows how much change there has been from 1974–1975 to 1994–1996. There has been a sharp increase in the percentage of people adopting "very modern" responses to the three items comprising the Gender Roles Index. The largest increase occurs in the period from 1977–1978 to 1982–1983, though there was another sharp surge toward a modern orientation toward women's roles in politics from 1988–1989 to 1991–1993. By the time Representative Geraldine Ferraro (D-NY) was selected by Walter Mondale as his vice presidential running mate in the 1984 presidential election, a majority of Americans were claiming to have a very modern orientation towards gender roles in politics. Data from 1994–96 show the stability of these opinions, with the percentage of those with a "very modern" orientation increasingly slightly by the same percentage as the decline of "very traditional" respondents.

TABLE 2.1   Public Opinion about Political Gender Roles, for Selected Years, from 1974–75 to 1994–96, in Percentages

	1974–75	1977–78	1982–83	1985–86	1988–89	1991–93	1994–96
Very Modern	41	42	53	51	57	64	67
Slightly Modern	23	23	22	23	21	19	19
Neutral	3	3	3	2	3	3	2
Slightly Traditional	20	20	15	16	13	8	8
Very Traditional	13	12	8	8	6	6	3
(N=)	(2,237)	(3,053)	(2,498)	(2,980)	(1,975)	(2,087)	(3,912)

*Columns may total more or less to 100% due to rounding.
Source: NORC's General Social Surveys.

The percentage of those expressing a very traditional orientation towards gender roles has dropped by 10 percent from 1974–75 to 1994–96 (from 13% to 3%). Even those with a "slightly traditional" orientation towards women's roles fell from one in five respondents in 1974–75 to one in thirteen respondents by 1994–96.

Do women and men differ in their views about roles that are appropriate for women to take in the political arena? Figure 2.1 shows that there are more similarities than differences in what women and men think about gender roles in politics. There is a sizable gap between the percentage of women and that of men who hold modern views compared with those who hold traditional views. By 1994–96,

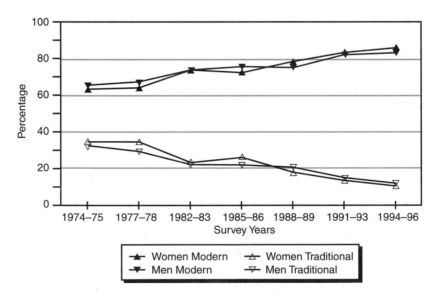

FIGURE 2.1   Political Gender Role Index Opinions by Gender and Survey Years

84 percent of women and 83 percent of men agree about a modern role for women in society. There was a 5 percent increase in modern views among women between 1991–93 and 1994–96, and a 7 percent increase in the same direction among men. By 1994–96 there were virtually no overall gender differences on the Political Gender Roles Index. If we are to understand why some people hold very modern views about political gender roles while others hold very traditional views, factors other than sex will have to be considered.

A MULTIVARIATE ANALYSIS OF THE SOURCES OF POLITICAL GENDER ROLE OPINIONS

A better understanding of who holds modern opinions about political gender roles and who holds traditional opinions is possible by using a statistical technique called *multiple regression,* which allows a researcher to gauge the relative impact of several factors, or variables, on a phenomenon—in this case, beliefs about women's proper roles in politics. Several variables were included in this analysis for each survey year. These included structural factors such as years of schooling (an imperfect but usable measure of education), family income, and occupational prestige (the social status connected with the respondent's occupation);[21] situational factors such as marital status and whether the respondent had children; socialization indicators that attempt to provide empirical links in experience between childhood and adult years such as whether the respondent's mother worked when the respondent was a child as well as the level of education achieved by the respondent's father and mother, and measures of religious fundamentalism. Finally, additional factors included those said to be related to how people view politics, such as race, age, political party identification, political ideology (liberal to conservative), region of the country where the respondent lived (the southern states are noted for harboring a more traditional culture), whether the respondent reads newspapers with any regularity, and the survey year to see if the passage of time had any impact on opinions.

From 1974–75 to 1994–96, what factors help to explain people's opinions about the appropriate roles for women in the political arena? The answer is largely structural and socialization factors (including region), with some help from some demographic factors such as age and gender. The region variable probably taps an important dimension of socialization into a more traditional culture. Even as the South is changing, the region's cultural conservatism continues to have an impact on its residents. Political influences (e.g., partisanship, ideology) complete the list of significant variables, listed in Table 2.2 in order of importance. The most important predictor of opinions about political gender roles is age. Younger people are far more likely to express modern views than are older people. In fact, younger women are slightly more likely than younger men to express modern views even when education, the third most important predictor in Table 2.2, is taken into consideration. Later in this chapter we will mention some recent findings that urge

TABLE 2.2 Significant Factors Affecting Opinions on the Political Gender Roles Index, in Rank Order, for all Survey Years from 1974–75 to 1994–96

Respondent's age	How often respondent reads a newspaper
Frequency of church attendance	Father's education
Respondent's education	Political party identification
Family income	Political ideology
Religious fundamentalism	Region of country where respondent lives
Mother's education	Year of survey
Mother worked after marriage/children	

Adjusted R^2 = .21

Source: NORC's General Social Surveys.

caution about assuming these differences between younger women and men will continue. The role of church attendance in shaping gender role orientations shows the resilience of this socialization factor in modern political life. Consider that among the fourteen indicators that were found to be important in predicting opinions about women's roles in politics, not a single situational indicator helped to explain opinions about gender roles. Gender enters as an important predictor because even though by 1994–96 there are no differences between women and men on gender roles, the adoption of those views has been slower among men than women. Although it would be risky to say that situational factors should be ignored in studies of gender and politics (as we will see in Table 2.3), they are clearly less important than previous literature would suggest.

Analyzing all the survey years together, as Table 2.2 does, can tell us about significant factors affecting opinions during that entire period, but it can hide changes that occur between the survey years included. Because the survey year does enter as a significant predictor of gender roles in politics, the passage of time is having an impact on the development of more modern orientations.

Gender does enter the overall regression model as a significant predictor, even though Figure 2.1 shows that by 1991–1993 women and men share the same opinions about women's roles in politics, at least as measured by our index. A closer look, using the same analysis technique as in Table 2.2, makes it possible to see if different forces work to shape women's and men's opinions on the Political Gender Roles Index. Table 2.3 lists in order of importance the factors that shape these opinions for both women and men. There are astoundingly few differences in the factors that shape women's and men's opinions. For men, the level of their mother's educational attainment and the race of the male respondent affects their inclination toward more modern views. And in a departure from Table 2.2, for both women and men, the situational factor of marital status does appear to affect opinions.

Items measuring religious fundamentalism, including the frequency of church attendance, appear in both Tables 2.2 and 2.3. This is consistent with the expectation that religious conservatism (be it Protestant, Catholic, or Jewish) holds to more

TABLE 2.3　**Significant Factors Affecting Women's and Men's Opinions on the Political Gender Roles Index, in Rank Order, for all Survey Years from 1974–75 to 1994–96**

Women	Men
Respondent's age	Respondent's age
Frequency of church attendance	Frequency of church attendance
Respondent's education	Respondent's education
Family income	Family income
Religious fundamentalism	Religious fundamentalism
Marital status	Mother's education
Mother worked after marriage/children	Marital status
How often respondent reads newspaper	Mother worked after marriage/children
Political party identification	How often respondent reads newspaper
Political ideology	Political party identification
Region where respondent lives	Political ideology
Year of survey	Respondent's race
	Region where respondent lives
	Year of survey
Adjusted R^2 = .26	*Adjusted* R^2 = .17

Source: NORC's General Social Surveys.

traditional roles for women in the private and public spheres of life. Although women are more frequent church attenders than men, the two items tapping this aspect of socialization enter all three regression models.

How successful are the regression models in explaining opinions about political gender roles? Success is defined as the cumulative ability of significant predictors to explain changing opinions on the Political Gender Roles Index. No social science model we know of is able to explain 100 percent of any phenomenon. Our models are able to explain from 17 to 26 percent—see the adjusted R^2 figures in Tables 2.2 and 2.3—of change on the index. Although we can point to previous studies that have relied on regression models of similar modest capacity,[22] that is cold comfort.

There are two reasons for the modest explanatory power of the regression models. First, given the limits of secondary survey analysis, the models probably leave out key factors accounting for opinions about gender roles in politics because there are not indicators in the data sets tapping respondent's relationships with parents and how parents passed on their political views. Recall that one reason some researchers have favored structural and situational factors to explain gender differences has been their ease of measurement. Second, the items making up our Political Gender Roles Index are too few and too imprecise to capture the entire range of opinions about political gender roles.

LINGERING DOUBTS

A separate percentage analysis of the most recent survey years (1991–1993 and 1994–96; data not shown here to save space revealed an intriguing trend: the impact of education and age on the opinions of women and men. Among the youngest respondents (aged 18–29) there is an increasing similarity in views about gender roles, but the reason is somewhat surprising. First, young men, even if they have completed a college education, are less likely to express a preference for very modern roles for women than are similarly educated young women. In 1991–93, young college-educated men lagged behind similarly educated young women in very modern views by 20 percent (92 percent of women, compared to 72 percent of young men). By 1994–96 that gap had narrowed to a difference of 12 percentage points, but this narrowing of the difference was because *young women were less likely to state very modern views* (82 percent of young women, compared to 70 percent of young men). Across those two survey years, young men show a relative stability in their opinions, whereas young women would appear to be retreating somewhat from a firm belief in very modern roles for women. In fact, the youngest age cohort, particularly men, reflect their grandparents' views more than their parents'. As if underscoring that the remnants of sex-role socialization remain strong, the 1997 survey of college freshmen by the Higher Education Research Institute at the University of California, Los Angeles, revealed that almost one-third of men and one-fifth of women entering college in the fall of 1997 believed that "the activities of married women are best confined to the home and family."[23]

These gender differences are echoed for every education level among the youngest respondents. There is a clear "gender gap" in views about gender roles with younger men lagging behind younger women in acceptance of very modern roles, but the dip in younger women's views should be watched as well. The number of cases in the 1991–93 and 1994–96 surveys are too small to make sweeping generalizations, but these are important differences to watch.

CONCLUSIONS

Does it make a difference for grassroots political behavior if people have traditional views of political gender roles? Yes, according to data from the 1993 GSS. There was a 10 percentage point difference in reported turnout in the 1992 presidential election among respondents depending upon whether they were "very modern" in their orientation towards women's roles (73 percent reported turning out to vote) compared to 63 percent of those with a "very traditional" view of women's political roles. A similar analysis for the 1996 presidential election is not possible because the 1996 GSS was conducted before the presidential election.

The disappearance of the turnout gap between women and men is only in part a result of increased voting among women. It is also the result of a sharp decline in turnout among men. Women remain less politically interested and less likely to follow media accounts of campaigns, even when education is taken into account.[24] Behind women's continuing tendency to be less politically interested is their greater likelihood to agree that "sometimes politics and government seem so complicated that a person like me can't really understand what's going on." According to data from the University of Michigan's Center for Political Studies' National Election Survey for 1996, 74 percent of women said they sometimes did not feel competent to understand public affairs, compared to 59 percent of men. Controlling for education does not eliminate gender differences on this item. If anything, differences between men and women are more pronounced among the college educated than among those whose formal schooling ended prior to graduation from high school. Among those with less than a high school education, 88 percent of women and 79 percent of men agree that politics and government "seem complicated." Compare that gender gap in opinion to the 61 percent of college-educated women and 36 percent of college-educated men who find politics and government too complicated and it is obvious that education is far more likely to enhance men's than women's understanding of the political world. The question that cannot be answered here is: Why?

The passage of time—allowing less educated, traditionally socialized Americans to leave the voting-age public, and increased exposure to higher education among the young—has significantly increased support for modern views of gender equality in politics. Still, the process will not be automatic. Recall that younger men, even those with a college education, are most likely to lag behind similarly educated young women in favoring modern roles, and that even young women show some signs of backing away from a modern role orientation. The differences may not yet signal a transformation in the opinion of the young, but they remind us that the momentum toward acceptance of gender equality in politics can be lost, including among the well-educated, unless continual effort is made to overcome older notions of where women "belong." The sex-role socialization process endures, even among our youngest citizens.

NOTES

1. U.S. Bureau of the Census, *Statistical Abstract of the United States: 1997,* 117th edition. (Washington, DC: U.S. Government Printing Office, 1997), p. 289.

2. Closure in the "turnout gap" is evident in data from the national Opinion Research Center (NORC). In 1967 NORC reported that 27 percent of women said they *never* voted, compared to 22 percent of men. Even this gap was smaller than it would have been in the 1920s and 1930s, immediately after the Nineteenth Amendment's ratification. By 1987 NORC data revealed women and men equally likely to report having voted (68 percent for both).

3. Angus Campbell, Philip Converse, Warren E. Miller, and Donald Stokes, *The American Voter* (New York: Wiley, 1960), p. 484.

4. Robert D. Hess and Judith V. Torney, *The Development of Political Attitudes in Children* (Chicago: Aldine, 1967); Fred I. Greenstein, *Children and Politics* (New Haven: Yale University Press, 1969).

5. Ronald B. Rapoport, "The Sex Gap in Political Persuading: Where the 'Structuring Principle' Works," *American Journal of Political Science,* 25 (1) (February 1981), pp. 32–48; "Sex Differences in Attitude Expression: A Generational Explanation," *Public Opinion*

Quarterly, 46 (1) (Spring 1982), pp. 86–96; "Like Mother, Like Daughter: Intergenerational Transmission of DK Response Rates," *Public Opinion Quarterly,* 49 (2) (Summer 1985), pp. 198–208.

6. Sidney Verba, Nancy Burns, and Kay Lehman Schlozman, "Knowing and Caring about Politics: Gender and Political Engagement," *Journal of Politics,* 59 (4) (November 1997), pp. 1051–72.

7. Anthony Orum, Roberta S. Cohen, Susan Grassmuck, and Amy W. Orum, "Sex, Socialization, and Politics," *American Sociological Review,* 39 (2) (April 1974), pp. 197–209.

8. Kent L. Tedin, David W. Brady, and Arnold Vedlitz, "Sex Differences in Political Attitudes and Behavior: The Case for Situational Factors," *Journal of Politics,* 39 (2) (May 1977), pp. 448–456; Ethel Klein, *Gender Politics* (Cambridge, MA: Harvard University Press, 1984).

9. Kristi Andersen, "Working Women and Political Participation," *American Journal of Political Science,* 19 (3) (August 1975), pp. 439–454.

10. Raymond E. Wolfinger and Steven J. Rosenstone, *Who Votes?* (New Haven: Yale University Press, 1980).

11. Ellen L. McDonagh, "To Work or Not to Work: The Differential Impact of Achieved and Derived Status upon the Political Participation of Women," *American Journal of Political Science,* 26 (2) (May 1982), pp. 280–297.

12. Jeffrey Koch, "Candidate Gender and Women's Psychological Engagement in Politics," *American Politics Quarterly,* 25 (1) (January 1997), pp. 118–133.

13. Klein, *Gender Politics.*

14. Robert E. Lane, *Political Life* (New York: Free Press, 1965); Campbell et al., *The American Voter.*

15. M. Kent Jennings, "Another Look at Politics and the Life Cycle," *American Journal of Political Science,* 23 (4) (November 1979), pp. 755–771.

16. Virginia Sapiro, *The Political Integration of Women* (Urbana: University of Illinois Press, 1983), pp. 89–90, 136–138.

17. Nancy Romer, "Is Political Activism Still a 'Masculine' Endeavor?" *Psychology of Women Quarterly,* 14 (2) (June 1990), pp. 229–243.

18. Kristi Andersen and Elizabeth Cook, "Women, Work, and Political Attitudes," *American Journal of Political Science,* 29 (3) (August 1985), pp. 606–622.

19. Cal Clark and Janet Clark, "Models of Gender and Political Participation in the United States," *Women and Politics,* 6 (1) (Spring 1986), pp. 5–25.

20. Before summing the three items, it was first determined if they belonged in a composite index. When all survey years were combined and the three items were fed into SPSS's RELIABILITY routine, the value of Cronbach's coefficient *alpha* was .70. The items have an average interitem correlation of r = .44. Although the Political Gender Roles Index contains some measurement error, it is a satisfactory device for tapping opinions about gender roles in politics.

21. The NORC codebook describes the occupational prestige rating process as one guided by the "respondents' estimation of the social standing of occupations." The respondents' ratings generally range along a nine-point scale and are useful in assigning some order to the thousands of occupation codes in U.S. Census Bureau data.

22. See especially Sapiro, *The Political Integration of Women.*

23. Ben Gose, "More Freshmen than Ever Appear Disengaged in Their Studies, Survey Finds," *The Chronicle of Higher Education,* XLIV (19) (16 January 1998), pp. A37–A39.

24. M. Margaret Conway, *Political Participation in the United States* (Washington, DC: Congressional Quarterly Press, 1985); Linda L. M. Bennett and Stephen E. Bennett, "Enduring Gender Differences in Political Interest: The Impact of Socialization and Political Dispositions," *American Politics Quarterly,* 17 (1) (January 1989), pp.105–122.

FURTHER READING

Bennett, Stephen Earl, and Eric W. Rademacher. 1997. "The 'Age of Indifference' Revisited: Patterns of Political Interest, Media Exposure, and Knowledge among generation X." In *After the Boom: The Politics of Generation X,* ed. Stephen C. Craig and Stephen Earl Bennett. Lanham, MD: Rowman & Littlefield.

Cook, Elizabeth Adell. 1994. "Voter Responses to Women Senate Candidates." In *The Year of the Woman,* ed. Elizabeth Adell Cook, Sue Thomas, and Clyde Wilcox. Boulder, CO: Westview.

Hansen, Susan B. 1997. "Talking about Politics: Gender and Contextual Effects on Proselytizing." *Journal of Politics,* 59 (February), pp. 73–104.

Schlozman, Kay Lehman, Nancy Elizabeth Burns, and Sidney Verba. 1994. "Gender and the Pathways to Participation." *Journal of Politics,* 56 (November), pp. 963–990.

Verba, Sidney, Nancy Burns, and Kay Lehman Schlozman. 1997. "Knowing and Caring about Politics: Gender and Political Engagement." *Journal of Politics,* 59 (November), pp. 1051–1072.

The Generations of Feminism

Elizabeth Adell Cook

It is often observed that young people have different political values and beliefs than older people. On many issues, including abortion, gay and lesbian rights, gender equality, and the willingness to allow atheists to teach in college, young people are more liberal than their parents, and much more liberal than their grandparents. Some of these differences will endure over time, and others will diminish. These differences can occur as the result of: (1) generational effects and (2) life cycle effects.

Generational effects refer to differences in the political values and behaviors of two different generations; these are the result of the different social and political context in which each generation grew up or came of age. Members of a generation bear the imprint of a particular period even as they age and times change. Think about the attitudes of Americans toward Japan. We would not expect Americans who grew up with the phrase "Remember Pearl Harbor" (and who in fact do) to feel as warmly toward Japan as Americans who learned about World War II in history class. Most likely, this younger generation of Americans grew up thinking of the United States and Japan as allies. Therefore, we would expect younger Americans to view Japan more warmly than the older generation, and we would not expect the views of younger Americans to change as a result of growing older.

Life cycle effects are defined as those differences in the political values and behaviors of two different generations resulting from different lifestyles and responsibilities as a function of age. When we compare the young to the middle aged, the young are less likely to be married, to have children, to own homes, to be saving for retirement, and to be concerned about elderly parents. Although a generation may marry later than preceding generations or have fewer children, eventually all young generations will become middle aged, and assume many of the trappings of middle age. ("Just wait until you have children of you own.") When a younger generation becomes more like an older generation as it ages and its lifestyle changes, we refer to this as the life cycle effect. The original differences observed between younger and older people were primarily the result of the differing life circumstances of the two generations. Thus, as the younger generation matures and experiences the changes in lifestyle usually associated with aging, it adopts the values and behaviors of the older generation. When generational effects occur, generations remain distinct over time. When life cycle effects occur, the younger generation becomes more like the older generation was as it ages.

A third kind of effect looks at changes affecting all generations. *Period effects* occur when the social and political context changes members of all generations. For example, intensive media coverage of crime problems during the early 1990s led Americans of all ages to express concern. In 1994, crime was listed as the most serious problem facing the country among all age groups in many polls.

GENERATIONS AND ATTITUDES ABOUT WOMEN

There have clearly been important changes in attitudes toward the role of women over the past few decades: for example, the public has become more supportive of working women. Although we take it for granted that women who do the same work as men ought to receive the same pay (even though they may in fact not), this view has not always been universally endorsed. And not all generations have responded similarly in how they view women's role.

Most studies have reported that age is a significant predictor of support for feminist programs and organizations. Studies in the 1970s and 1980s found that younger women were more supportive of egalitarian values, had higher levels of gender consciousness, and were more supportive of gender equality than were older women.

During the second half of the 1980s, however, controversy arose concerning the possibility of generational change in support for feminism. Bolotin reported the emergence of a post-feminist generation among young women—part of a general retreat from liberalism among the young.[1] Most of the scholarly research on this question has focused on the attitudes of college students. Studies have found that college women may support feminist ideals, but reject the collective efforts of the women's movement,[2] that there is support for equal rights but not for feminism,[3] and that the term feminist evokes negative connotations, even among students who support gender equality.[4]

Others have argued, however, that college students do not reject feminism per se, but want to redirect the movement to their own needs.[5] Research has suggested that college women become progressively more supportive of feminism during their academic years as they experience sex discrimination.[6]

All of these studies limit their analysis to college students. Although there is good theoretical reason to focus attention on the attitudes of college women (college education is a strong predictor of support for feminism), it is important to examine changing support for feminism among all women. Moreover, most research has not been conscious of its assumptions: Some studies assume that support for feminism among the young is related to life cycle, but others assume lasting generational differences. Finally, whatever the truth of arguments about the decline in feminism in the 1980s under the Reagan administration, it is possible that President Clinton's visible embrace of feminism and the active role played by Hillary Rodham Clinton in the administration may have led young women in the 1990s to greater support for feminism. This study, therefore, will examine the pattern of support among different generations of women over the period 1972–1996. The period covers the rise of feminism and through the re-election of Clinton. The data come from the American National Election Studies of 1972, 1976, 1980, 1984, 1988, 1992, and 1996.[7]

POLITICIZED FEMINIST CONSCIOUSNESS

Scholars who focus on the women's movement have argued that feminist support is best understood in terms of group consciousness. One of the earliest activities of the feminist movement was consciousness raising—attempting to develop a politicized feminist consciousness among women.[8] Klein suggested that individuals who acquire a feminist consciousness must go through three steps.[9] First, women must recognize their membership in a group (women) and that they share interests with that group. Second, women must reject the societal rationale for the situation of the group; that is, they must blame society and not women for the disadvantaged status of women. Finally, women must recognize the need for group solutions to problems.

Gurin, Miller and Gurin adopt a similar strategy, arguing that group consciousness consists of social group identification, power discontent, system blaming, and a collectivist orientation.[10] In other research, feminist consciousness has been defined as follows: non-feminists are defined as those women who do not believe that women should have an equal role with men in society; potential feminists are classified as those who believe in an equal role for women but do not support the women's liberation movement; and those who believe in an equal role and who support the movement are defined as having a politicized feminist consciousness.[11]

Support for the women's movement is measured by feeling thermometer items, which asked respondents in the 1972 to 1984 surveys to place the women's liberation movement (along with other social and political groups) on an imaginary scale which ranges from 0° (representing extreme coolness) to 100° (representing extreme warmth). Because individuals differ in the patterns of their responses to these items, responses were adjusted to account for individual differences.[12] In the 1988 survey, respondents were asked to place feminists on this thermometer, and the 1992 survey included feeling thermometers toward both feminists and the women's movement. The 1996 survey asked them to rate the women's movement. Because the public appears to be more negative toward feminists and more positive toward the women's movement than they are toward the women's liberation movement,[13] we should not make direct comparisons of the overall level of feminist support between the earlier surveys and the latter ones. However, within any given year, it is appropriate to compare the attitudes of different generations of women. Moreover, it is possible to compare the absolute levels of feminism across years using the same question—1972–1984, 1988–1992, and 1992–1996.

Table 2.4 presents the frequency distributions of the measures across the period of this study. Feminist consciousness increases from 1972 to 1976 and again in 1980, then declines somewhat in 1984. Although respondents respond less positively to the term "feminists" than the term "women's liberation movement," feminist consciousness increased from 1984 to 1988 (when the feeling thermometer changed) and again in 1992, when for the first time there were more feminists than non-feminists among American women. Table 2.4 shows two distinct values for 1992—one using a feeling thermometer toward "feminists" and the second toward the "women's movement." The latter item produces a more sympathetic response, and in 1996 this response is again quite positive.

Table 2.4 also contains the Percentage Difference Index (PDI) for each of the four studies. The PDI is a summary measure created by subtracting the percentage of women who are non-feminists from the percentage of women with a politicized feminist consciousness. The value is negative when there are more non-feminists than feminists, and positive when feminists outnumber non-feminists.

TABLE 2.4   Distribution of Feminist Consciousness

	Not Feminist	Potential Feminist	Feminist	N	PDI
Women's Liberation Movement					
1972	61	25	14	1224	−37
1976	51	23	26	1153	−25
1980	41	32	27	676	−14
1984	47	30	21	1024	−26
Feminists					
1988	36	43	21	933	−15
1992	28	44	29	1081	1
Women's Movement					
1992	26	28	45	1067	19
1996	25	30	45	760	20

Note: Because the feeling thermometer for the Women's Liberation Movement was used 1972–1984 and the feeling thermometer for Feminists was used for 1988 and 1992, and Women's Movement was used in 1992 and 1996, it is impossible to compare the frequencies of responses across years when the question wording changes. This is evident when the scores in 1992 for Feminists and the Women's Movement are compared.

POLITICIZED FEMINIST CONSCIOUSNESS AND GENERATIONS

Cohort, or generational, analysis allows us to compare women who came of age at different times across years. That is, instead of comparing samples of individuals of the same age group (which is forever in flux as individuals age into or out of the group), we can compare samples of a constant coming-of-age cohort. Cohort analysis allows us to start to sort out life cycle (or maturation) effects from generational (or cohort) effects.

In order for cohort analysis to be meaningful, the cohorts need to be defined according to eras. That is, the boundaries of each cohort should to the greatest extent possible represent transitions in the relevant social context. Fortunately, the task of defining cohorts relevant to the women's movement has already been taken on.

Sapiro defined seven coming-of-age cohorts relevant to women's history:

> The eras or transitions are marked by either events of particular importance to women or by the type of broad characterizations we often use to mark off historical periods. Thus, the ratification of the Nineteenth Amendment serves as a time marker, and the twenties, characterized by a post-suffrage flurry of recognition of women, is distinguished from the Depression era. Of particular interest is the transition from World War II, the era of Rosie the Riveter and national day care centers, to the thirteen-year period characterized by Betty Friedan as the time of the "Feminine Mystique," a "dark age" in women's history according to feminist observers. Although the entire post-1960 period saw the growth of social movements and policy-making aimed at equality, it is further divided by the birth of the Women's Liberation Movement.[14]

In addition to Sapiro's seven cohorts, two additional cohorts are defined in the 1984 and late studies, the Complacent or Reagan era cohort, and a post-Reagan cohort. It is possible that the anti-feminist rhetoric of the Reagan administration might have led young women coming of age during his presidency to be less supportive of feminism, and that the strong and explicitly feminist signals from Bill and Hillary Clinton led young women to become more supportive. Table 2.5 shows a

TABLE 2.5   Coming of Age Cohorts*

Pre-Suffrage	*Pre 1920*
Twenties	1921–1929
Depression	1930–1939
World War II	1940–1945
Mystique	1946–1959
Sixties	1960–1966
Women's Liberation	1967–1977
Complacent/Reagan	1978–1988
Post-Reagan	1989–1996

*The cohorts are defined according to periods in which the respondent turned 18.

breakdown of these cohorts. While Sapiro defined cohorts according to when respondents turned 21, for this analysis, respondents are placed in cohorts according to the year they turned 18. Sapiro chose 21 because it was for most of this century the legal age of majority, the age at which young people struck out on their own, and the average age of marriage for women. In this analysis, the younger age of 18 is used because individuals would seem to be more impressionable at this age—and will be making the choices in very early adulthood about education, careers, and forming their own families. These decisions will affect their life circumstances even three years into their futures when they turn 21.

COMING OF AGE COHORTS AND FEMINIST CONSCIOUSNESS

Table 2.6 shows politicized feminist consciousness by coming-of-age cohort. The oldest cohorts, women who came of age before women won the right to vote and during the 1920s, exhibited very low feminist consciousness in 1972 and by 1988 there were too few members of these cohorts left to analyze. The Depression cohort had very low levels of feminist consciousness in 1972, but gradually became more supportive of feminism. By 1996 there are too few women in this cohort to analyze.

The World War II cohort, like the older cohorts, exhibited very low levels of feminist consciousness in 1972—when these women were aged 45 to 50. The level of feminist consciousness increased in 1976, declined in 1984, and increased in 1988 and again in 1992 and 1996. Because the sample size for this cohort is so small after 1976, we need to be cautious in making estimates. Yet the steady increase in feminism in this cohort suggests an openness to adult learning.

TABLE 2.6 Coming of Age Cohorts and Feminist Consciousness

	1972	1976	1980	1984	1988	1992	1996
Pre-Suffrage							
Not	78	78	—	—	—	—	—
Potential	18	16	—	—	—	—	—
Feminist	4	7	—	—	—	—	—
PDI	[−74]	[−71]					
(N)	(124)	(83)	—	—	—	—	—
Twenties							
Not	73	74	63	74	—	—	—
Potential	22	15	25	16	—	—	—
Feminist	5	11	12	10	—	—	—
PDI	[−68]	[−63]	[−51]	[−64]			
(N)	(135)	(110)	(57)	(51)	—	—	—

TABLE 2.6 *Continued*

	1972	1976	1980	1984	1988	1992	1996
Depression							
Not	67	61	54	66	50	43	—
Potential	20	24	27	20	33	36	—
Feminist	13	15	19	14	17	21	—
PDI	[−54]	[−46]	[−35]	[−52]	[−33]	[−22]	—
(N)	(181)	(168)	(84)	(119)	(90)	(94)	—
World War II							
Not	69	50	46	67	37	35	28
Potential	25	29	38	20	44	39	26
Feminist	6	21	16	13	19	26	47
PDI	[−63]	[−29]	[−30]	[−54]	[−18]	[−9]	[19]
(N)	(128)	(103)	(50)	(75)	(73)	(75)	(58)
Mystique							
Not	57	48	38	46	45	36	34
Potential	29	25	38	27	39	40	33
Feminist	14	27	24	27	16	23	33
PDI	[−43]	[−21]	[−14]	[−19]	[−29]	[−13]	[−1]
(N)	(290)	(216)	(130)	(178)	(163)	(153)	(127)
Sixties							
Not	53	38	34	38	33	23	19
Potential	30	23	31	36	44	46	35
Feminist	17	39	35	26	24	32	46
PDI	[−36]	[1]	[1]	[−12]	[−9]	[−9]	[27]
(N)	(207)	(179)	(108)	(141)	(115)	(120)	(72)
*Women's Liberation**							
Not	45	40	34	35	23	24	15
Potential	23	24	33	36	48	41	29
Feminist	32	36	34	29	29	35	55
PDI	[−13]	[−4]	[0]	[−6]	[6]	[11]	[40]
(N)	(154)	(284)	(190)	(295)	(258)	(273)	
*Complacent***							
Not	—	—	—	40	28	20	18
Potential	—	—	—	36	50	51	33
Feminist	—	—	—	24	22	29	48
PDI	—	—	—	[−16]	[−6]	[9]	[30]
(N)	—	—	—	(136)	(181)	(279)	(186)
*Post Reagan****							
Not	—	—	—	—	—	—	19
Potential	—	—	—	—	—	—	23
Feminist	—	—	—	—	—	—	58
PDI	—	—	—	—	—	—	[39]
(N)	—	—	—	—	—	—	(79)

*Only part of the Women's Liberation cohort had turned 18 in 1972. The complete cohort did not come of age until 1977.

**Only part of the complacent cohort had turned 18 in 1980. The complete cohort did not come of age until 1992.

***There were too few members of the post-Reagan cohort in 1992 to include in the table.

The Mystique cohort, the mothers of the baby boom, in each year exhibit a higher level of feminist consciousness than the older cohorts until 1988, but are passed by the World War II cohort in the final three surveys. Feminist consciousness among this cohort seesawed; it increased from 1972 to 1976, declined in 1980 and increased again in 1984 and 1988 only to decline again in 1992 and 1996. That the World War II cohort was more feminist than this group of younger women fits with their life experiences: The World War II cohort entered the laborforce in large numbers while men were fighting the war, but were replaced by men after the war, perhaps creating an increased awareness of gender discrimination. In contrast, the Mystique cohort married earlier, and had more children than the World War II cohort in an era when "traditional" women's roles were emphasized.

The Sixties and Women's Liberation cohorts are both substantially more feminist than any cohort that came before. Both came of age during a time when social movements mobilized for equality, and the Women's Liberation cohort reached adulthood while the feminist movement was actively engaged in building feminist consciousness. The Women's Liberation movement cohort displays a higher level of feminist consciousness than the Sixties cohort in 1972. This suggests that the cohort was aptly named; these women responded more quickly to the women's movement than women who were older at its inception.

By 1984, the Complacent cohort was coming of age. While the overall trend had been for each successive cohort to exhibit a higher level of feminist consciousness than older cohorts, this youngest cohort reversed the trend, and in each year is slightly less feminist than the Women's Liberation cohort. This cohort closely resembles the Sixties cohort in its level of feminist consciousness.

But the post-Reagan cohort is substantially more feminist than the Complacent cohort in 1996 and indeed is the single most feminist cohort in that survey. We must be cautious because there are relatively few women in this survey who reached adulthood after 1988, and we have only observed them for a single election cycle. Nonetheless, it is interesting that among those women who came of age after the election of Clinton in 1992, the level of feminist consciousness is even higher: 69 percent of those who came of age during the Clinton administration exhibited feminist consciousness, compared with only 48 percent of those who came of age during Bush's presidency.

The data therefore show that life experiences shape women's reactions to feminism. The World War II generation, which entered the workplace in large numbers only to be displaced by men returning from the war, is somewhat more supportive of feminism than the Mystique cohort, which came of age during a period of unusual cultural conservatism that promoted Ozzie and Harriet as the ideal family type. Women who came of age during the anti-feminist Reagan administration are less feminist than those who reached adulthood during the women's liberation movement, or during the Clinton administration.

Interestingly, in 1996 the Reagan or Complacent cohort was not more conservative than earlier generations on policy issues such as child care and abortion—they were merely less supportive of the women's movement. This suggests that the name "complacent" may fit them well—they take for granted the successes of the movement while continuing to support gender equality and feminist policies. This is also confirmed by an item in the 1992 survey, which revealed that the Complacent cohort took less pride in the accomplishments of other women than did the women of the Women's Liberation cohort, but were more likely to express the belief that men and women ought to have equal power in society.

SUMMARY

A number of events occurred during the 1972 to 1996 time period that shaped attitudes: the mobilization of the women's movement, the passage by Congress of the Equal Rights Amendment (E.R.A.) and its early successes, the formation and mobilization of the anti-E.R.A. coalition, the strong anti-feminist platform of the Republicans in 1980, the Reagan presidency, the *Webster* decision, and the election of Bill Clinton and the visible feminism of Hillary Rodham Clinton. Moreover, the tenor of news coverage of the movement changed markedly over the course of this period, from strongly negative to even handed. Although the wording of the questions have changed over time, it appears that there has been a dramatic increase in the level of feminist consciousness over this period. This is evident in the responses to the one item in the feminist consciousness measure that remained unchanged: the equal role question.

Cohort analysis revealed that generational turnover helped to increase the level of feminist consciousness from 1972 to 1976, as more feminist younger women replaced more traditional older women. The most feminist women were those who came of age during the development of the women's movement in the 1970s. The youngest women, those who came of age in the late 1970s and 1980s, were less feminist than the Women's Liberation cohort, but more feminist than women overall. There is some evidence for a post-feminist cohort here, but the level of decline in support was not precipitous. Furthermore, in 1992 and 1996 these younger women were about as supportive of feminist issues as women of the Women's Liberation cohort. The post-Reagan cohort is much more feminist than those who came of age during the Reagan presidency, and indeed those who reached adulthood during the Clinton administration are more likely to exhibit a feminist consciousness than even the women's liberation cohort.

Although it is impossible to speak with certainty, there appear to have been both generational and period effects at work. Moreover, clear cohort differences persist over time, suggesting that generational effects are strong. Life experiences shape women's policy preferences, and also their support for collective policy action. The Complacent cohort is supportive of feminist policies, but does not have the politicized group identity that is an important component of feminist consciousness. When comparable measures are used, there is no increase in the level of feminist consciousness for the Complacent cohort from 1992 to 1996.

Although we need to be cautious in drawing conclusions about the youngest cohort, the post-Reagan generation, it appears to have a higher level of feminist consciousness than women of the complacent generation. Further, the youngest among this cohort—those who turned 18 during the Clinton administration—are more feminist still.

Overall, the data show an increase in feminist consciousness over time. Younger generations of women tend to be more feminist than their predecessors. However, there are clear differences between generations, with some generations exhibiting lower levels of feminist consciousness than the preceding one. Life experiences and the political climate and leadership do appear to have a socializing effect on generations. Those who turn 18 during eras of more public feminism are more likely to develop feminist consciousness—to support collective action to support feminist policies. Those who come of age during more conservative periods may support feminist policies but are less likely to develop the politicized group consciousness that leads to support of collective action.

NOTES

1. Susan Bolotin, "Views from the Post-Feminist Generation," *The New York Times Magazine* (October, 1982).

2. Mirra Komarovsky, *Women in College* (Basic Books, 1985)

3. M. Jacobson, "You Say Potato and I Say Potato: Attitudes Toward Feminism as a Function of Its Subject-Selected Labels," *Sex Roles,* 7 (1981), pp. 349–354.

4. M. Jacobson and W. Koch, "Attributed Reasons for Support of the Feminist Movement as a Function of Attractiveness," *Sex Roles,* 4, (1978), pp. 169–174.

5. Betty Friedan, *The Second State* (Summit Books, 1981).

6. Alan Bayer, "Sexist Students in American Colleges," *Journal of Marriage and the Family,* 37 (1975), pp. 391–397; Mirra Komarovsky, *Women in College* (Basic Books, 1985); C. Renzetti, "New Wave or Second Stage? Attitudes of College Women toward Feminism," *Sex Roles,* 16 (1987), pp. 265–277.

7. The data used in this article were made available by the Interuniversity Consortium for Political and Social Research. The data for the American National Election Studies were originally collected by the Center for Political Studies. Neither the collectors of the original data nor the Consortium bear any responsibility for the analyses or interpretations presented here.

8. C. Renzetti, "New Wave or Second Stage? Attitudes of College Women toward Feminism," *Sex Roles,* 16 (1987), pp. 265–277.

9. Ethel Klein, *Gender Politics* (Harvard University Press, 1984).

10. Patricia Gurin, Arthur Miller, and Gerald Gurin, "Stratum Identification and Consciousness," *Social Psychology Quarterly,* 43 (1980), pp. 30–47.

11. Elizabeth Adell cook, "Measuring Feminist Consciousness," *Women & Politics,* 9 (1989). The measure used here differs slightly from that described in the article cited above.

12. Support for the women's movement is based on the relative feeling thermometer for the "women's liberation movement" (1972 through 1984) and "feminists" (1988 and 1992). Because of changes in the question, the measure is not strictly comparable from the earlier period to the latter. This relative feeling thermometer is calculated as follows. First, a personal mean is calculated for each respondent across four social groups: liberals, conservatives, labor, and big business. These groups were used because they are common to all six studies and respondents' mean scores on this set of items is not correlated with their ideology. (See Clyde Wilcox, Lee Sigelman, and Elizabeth Cook. "Some Like it Hot: Individual Differences in Responses to Group Feeling Thermometers." *Public Opinion Quarterly,* 53 (1989) for a detailed discussion of using adjusted feeling thermometers.) This personal mean is subtracted from a respondent's rating of the women's liberation movement, and the remainder is divided by the personal mean [(score – mean)/mean]. The relative feeling thermometer thus represents percentage difference from the mean for the four groups. A score of 10 percent or more above their personal mean is defined here as support for the women's liberation movement.

13. Elizabeth Adell Cook and Clyde Wilcox. "A Rose by Any Other Name: Measuring Support for Organized Feminism using ANES Feeling Thermometers," *Women in Politics,* 12 (1992).

14. Virginia Sapiro, "News from the Front: Intersex and Intergenerational Conflict over the Status of Women" *Western Political Quarterly,* 33 (1980), p. 263.

FURTHER READING

Alan Bayer. "Sexist Students in American Colleges." *Journal of Marriage and the Family,* 37 (1975), pp. 391–397.

Susan Bolotin. "Views from the Post-Feminist Generation." *New York Times Magazine* (October, 1982).

Pamela Conover. "The Influence of Group Identifications on Political Perception and Evaluation." *Journal of Politics,* 46 (1984), pp. 760–785.

Pamela Conover. "Group Identification and Group Sympathy: Their Political Implications." Paper presented at the annual meeting of the Midwest Political Science Association, April 1986.

Elizabeth Cook and Clyde Wilcox, "A Rose by Any Other Name: Measuring Support for Organized Feminism." *Women & Politics,* 12 (1992), pp. 35–52.

Anne N. Costain. "Representing Women: The Transition from Social Movement to Interest Group." *Western Political Quarterly,* 34 (1981), pp. 100–113.

Anne N. Costain. *Inviting Women's Rebellion: A Political Process Interpretation of the Women's Movement.* (Baltimore: Johns Hopkins, 1992).

Betty Freidan. *The Second Stage.* (New York: Summit Books, 1981)

Patricia Gurin. "Women's Gender Consciousness." *Public Opinion Quarterly,* 49 (1986), pp. 143–163.

Patricia Gurin, Arthur Miller, and Gerald Gurin. "Stratum Identification and Consciousness." *Social Psychology Quarterly,* 43 (1980), pp. 30–47.

M. Jacobson. "You Say Potato and I Say Potato: Attitudes Toward Feminism as a Function of its Subject-Selected Labels." *Sex Roles,* 7 (1981), pp. 349–354.

Kent Jennings, and Richard Niemi. *Generations and Politics.* (Princeton, N.J.: Princeton University Press, 1981).

Kent Jennings, and Richard Niemi. "Continuity and Change in Political Orientations: A Longitudinal Study of Two Generations." In Dreyer and Rosenbaum (eds.), *Political Opinion and Behavior, 3rd ed.* Belmont, CA: Wadsworth, 1976.

Mirra Komarovsky. *Women in College.* New York: Basic Books, 1985.

Ethel Klein. *Gender Politics.* Cambridge, MA: Harvard University Press, 1984.

Richard Lau. "Reference Group Influence on Political Attitudes and Behavior: The Importance of the Social, Political, and Psychological Contexts." Paper presented at the annual meeting of the American Political Science Association, Chicago, September 1983.

Arthur Miller, Patricia Gurin, and Gerald Gurin. "Electoral Implications of Group Identification and Consciousness: The Reintroduction of a Concept." Paper presented at the annual meeting of the American Political Science Association, September 1978.

Arthur H. Miller, Anne M. Hildreth, and Grace I. Simmons. "The Political Implications of Gender Group Consciousness." Paper presented at the annual meeting of the Midwest Political Science Association, April 1986.

Arthur Miller, Grace L. Simmons, and Anne M. Hildreth. "Group Influences, Solidarity, and Electoral Outcomes." Paper presented at the annual meeting of the American Political Science Association, September 1986.

C. Renzetti. "New Wave or Second Stage? Attitudes of College Women Toward Feminism." *Sex Roles,* 16 (1987), pp. 265–277.

Sue Tolleson Rinehart. *Gender Consciousness and Politics.* New York: Routledge, 1992.

Virginia Sapiro. "News from the Front: Intersex and Intergenerational Conflict over the Status of Women." *Western Political Quarterly,* 33 (1980), pp. 260–277.

Verta Taylor. "The Future of Feminism in the 1980s." In L. Richardson and V. Taylor (eds.) *Feminist Frontiers.* Reading, MA: Addison-Wesley, 1983.

Arland Thornton and Deborah Freedman. "Changes in Sex Role Attitudes of Women, 1962–1977." *American Sociological Review,* 44 (1979), pp. 831–842.

Clyde Wilcox. "Popular Support for the Moral Majority in 1980: A Second Look." *Social Science Quarterly,* 68 (1987), pp. 157–166.

Rethinking Pink and Blue:
Gender, Occupational Stratification, and Political Attitudes

GERTRUDE A. STEUERNAGEL, MAUREEN RAND OAKLEY, THOMAS E. YATSCO, AND IRENE J. BARNETT

Revolutionary changes have dominated the lives of twentieth-century American women. Foremost among these changes are those related to women's employment outside the home. This is not to imply, of course, that prior to the 1900s, women were not involved in paid employment. African American women in particular have a history of combining family and work responsibilities. What is unprecedented about the current employment situation of American women are the numbers of married women and women with pre-school-age children who are employed as wage earners in a part-time or full-time capacity. A review of few statistics is useful in understanding the depth and scope of this major social restructuring. In 1880, women constituted 14 percent of this nation's workforce. One hundred years later, this figure had increased to 42.6 percent.[1] By 1995 it reached 46.1 percent.[2] During the same period, 1880 through 1980, the percent of all women who were employed outside the home increased from 16 percent to 51.5 percent.[3] By 1995 this figure increased to 58.9 percent.[4] Equally dramatic changes occurred in the demographic profile of working women. In 1880, by far the largest segment of working women were single. Today, a majority of married women are numbered among the ranks of working women; and women with children are a significant part of the labor force. As of 1995, 63.5 percent of married women with a child under the age of six participated in the labor force.[5]

WOMEN AND OCCUPATIONAL SEGREGATION

An emphasis on these changes, however, obscures an important reality concerning the lives of American working women. One significant characteristic of women's employment that has not radically changed in recent times and is not likely to be altered in the near future is that most American women work in what are commonly characterized as "pink collar ghettos." An employed American woman today is more likely than not to find herself in an occupationally segregated profession. She will work with other women in jobs traditionally held by women—jobs that reflect what society sees as appropriate to women's roles as wives, mothers, and care givers and that reflect women's supposed strengths as nurturers and helpmates. As of 1995, for example, women accounted for 98.5 percent of all dental assistants, 96.8 percent of all child care workers in private households, 82.9 percent of all data entry operators, 84.1 percent of all elementary school teachers, 83.9 percent of all librarians, and 93.1 percent of all registered nurses. In contrast, women accounted for 13.4 percent of all dentists, 4.5 percent of all carpenters, 29.5 percent of all computer programmers, 45.2 percent of all college and university professors, 21.4 percent of all lawyers and judges, and 24.4 percent of all physicians.[6]

Women, regardless of their race or ethnic group, are concentrated in low-paying and low-status jobs. Although certain factors such as changing attitudes concerning appropriate gender roles and legislation outlawing sex discrimination have led to a small decline in the degree of occupational segregation, there is reason to believe that occupational segregation will continue to affect the lives of working women well into the next century.[7]

Some of the consequences for women of occupational segregation are better documented than others. Occupational segregation is involved in the wage gap. That is to say, it is one of the factors, possibly the most important, in explaining why women on the whole earn less than men.[8] In 1995, for example, the median annual income for men who work year-round in a full-time capacity was $30,854. The income for comparable women was $22,205.[9]

In contrast, more information is needed on the impact of occupational segregation on women's conditions in the workplace. The area of workplace health hazards is a case in point. The risks to women in traditionally female occupations such as beautician and secretary, for example, are less obvious than the risks to men in fields such as construction and welding.[10]

Another area that merits exploration deals with the effects of occupational segregation on women's political attitudes. Although researchers have studied the effect of workforce involvement on women's political behavior—[11]and it is clear employment outside the home is associated with increased levels of political participation—little has been done on the specific effects of occupational segregation. If we want to understand the political behavior of American women, we need to understand the circumstances of their lives. Since there is considerable evidence that women's employment and their political behavior are related, we need to examine the relationship between the specific circumstances of that employment and their politics. Some research, for example, indicates that housewives and women employed in low-status, low-paying occupations (such as hairdresser and waitress) tend to show less support for feminism than women in higher-status, higher-paying jobs such as teacher and accountant.[12] Other research suggests women in male-dominated occupations display more feminist attitudes than women in other occupations.[13]

This study, therefore, will address questions concerning the effects of occupational segregation on women's political attitudes and will pay special attention to the intersection of occupational segregation and gender as it affects the political attitudes of women and men.

FINDINGS

Fortunately, there are available data that permit us to examine the effects of occupational segregation on political attitudes. We utilize data from the 1996 University of Michigan/Survey Research Center's National Election Study as well as statistics on occupational segregation from the U.S. Department of Labor. To give just one example of the selection process, consider the case of identifying women in female-dominated occupations at the managerial/professional level. Data from the Department of Labor reveal that the two professional occupations with the heaviest concentrations of women are dental hygienists (99.4 percent) and secretaries (98.5 percent). In the National Election Study (NES) those occupations are clustered together into categories 14 and 24, respectively, on Variable #960664: Respondent's Main Occupation, and contain totals of 27 and 42 women, respectively (and also 7 and 20 men, respectively). Thus, those 69 women comprise our subsample of women in female-segregated, professional occupations (and the 27 men our subsample of males in female-segregated, professional occupations). A similar pattern of identification was used for selecting the other subsamples, which then were aggregated across the different professional classifications to produce groups of men and women in male-dominated, integrated, and female-dominated occupations.[14]

In a preliminary review of the data, we examine in Tables 2.7 and 2.8 the differences between men and women generally in terms of their interest in and discussion of politics. Although the differences are not overwhelming, the data indicate that men tend to express more interest in following the events and issues of

TABLE 2.7   Attention to Campaign (V961001)

	Men	Women
Very Much Interested	33.6%	27.6%
Somewhat Interested	53.1	55.2
Not Very Interested	13.3	17.2

Chi square: $p = .014$; $n = 1519$

TABLE 2.8   Frequency of Political Discussion (V961005)

	Men	Women
Everyday	11.5%	11.1%
5–6 days per week	8.8	8.0
3–4 days per week	21.4	20.2
1–2 days per week	38.4	40.0
Less than once per week	19.9	20.8

Chi square: $p = .652$; $n = 1217$

the 1996 campaign, a finding consistent with research comparing men's and women's interest in campaigns and politics over the last four decades.[15] However, we find that no significant differences exist between men and women with regard to their frequency of political discussion during the campaign season. Other research has found, however, that, in general, women engage in fewer campaign activities than men.[16]

The fact that females follow politics less frequently than their male counterparts does not mean that women fail to perceive meaningful differences in social organization. Table 2.9 reveals that women are more likely than men to believe that their male counterparts possess more power than women in American society. The differences in perception among men and women are also reflected in their prescriptions concerning the exercise of societal power (Table 2.10). Not surprisingly, we find that men are more willing to say that they ought to exercise the greater power in society.[17]

Similar differences between men and women can be observed when we focus our attention on substantive policy issues. Rather than examine a long series of individual issues in search of policy-relevant differences between the sexes, we have simplified our investigation by combining seven separate issue areas into a single index that measures liberalism and conservatism. Responses to questions are measured in terms of the SRC's traditional seven-point scale, which ranges from most liberal to most conservative. The following issues comprise the liberalism/conservatism index: governmental spending and services (Variable #960450 in the

TABLE 2.9   Perceived Power of Men, Women in American Society (V6007, 1992)

	Men	Women
Men have more power	80.4%	84.0%
Women about equal	16.5	13.4
Women have more power	3.1	2.1

Chi square: $p = .059$; $n = 2.234$

TABLE 2.10   Desired Power for Men, women in American Society (V6008, 1992)

	Men	Women
Men should exercise more power	15.0%	11.2%
Men, women should exercise equal power	83.9	86.7
Women should exercise more power	1.1	2.1

Chi square: $p = .006$; $n = 2.212$

1996 NES), defense spending (V960463), government-provided health insurance (V960479), a government-guaranteed standard of living and job (V960483), governmental assistance for blacks (V961210), regulation of the environment (V960537), and women's role in society (V960543). Respondents were classified into three groups based upon the sums of their responses to the seven questions. As Table 2.11 illustrates, statistically significant differences between men and women exist on the overall liberalism-conservatism scale. As expected, women hold more liberal views than do men and, conversely, men hold more conservative views than do women. The majority of respondents do, however, fall into the moderate category.

A similar pattern emerges when we shift our attention from ideological-based issues to an assessment of differences among men and women in terms of their views on government spending. An index measuring preferences for governmental spending was constructed in much the same manner as the liberalism/conservatism index. For the spending index, the seven policy areas covered are Social Security (V960560), crime (V960563), child care (V960564), the environment (V960561), the poor (V960565), schools (V960562), and welfare (V960497). Based on their preferences, respondents were placed into one of three categories, as demonstrated in Table 2.12. Once again, statistically significant differences can be detected among men and women. Men are less likely to favor increased social spending and more likely to favor budget cuts, whereas women are more likely to exhibit the opposite tendencies.

The central argument of this analysis, however, is that concentrating on simple differences between men and women may draw attention away from the more

TABLE 2.11   Seven-Issue, Liberalism/Conservatism Index

	Men	Women
Liberal	11.8%	19.3%
Moderate	69.0	70.3
Conservative	19.2	10.4

Chi square: $p = .000$; $n = 971$

TABLE 2.12 Seven-Issue, Government Spending Index

	Men	Women
Increase spending	45.1%	54.1%
Maintain status quo	46.0	42.8
Decrease spending	9.0	3.1

Chi square: $p = .000$; $n = 1.650$

critical dynamics that drive attitude formation. Instead, we argue that social roles—in this case, the effects of gender-based segregation in the workplace—may influence the formation of political opinions. With that in mind, we reformulate the tables above by controlling for occupational segregation.[18]

We turn first to a reexamination of the political-interest and -discussion variables described in Tables 2.7 and 2.8. Table 2.13 reveals that men in female-segregated jobs (i.e., jobs where women make up 80 percent or more of the work force) are more interested in politics than are men in either integrated or male-dominated occupations (p [chi-square] = .001). Interestingly, we do not see a similar pattern for women. Based upon a review of the data we can conclude that the level of interest in politics among women does not differ by occupational segregation (p [chi square] = .936).

With respect to discussing politics, Table 2.14 reveals an opposite pattern. That is, females in male-dominated occupations are more engaged in political discussion than are women in the female-segregated and integrated occupations (p [chi-square] = .05). On the other hand, we discover that males' frequency of political discussion does not differ in relation to occupational segregation (p [chi square] = .190). We might speculate that, for women, being in the minority on the job serves as an inducement to keep one's political antennae attuned to their surroundings.

Next, we re-examine the findings depicted in Tables 2.9 and 2.10, which pertain to the perceived and prescribed power of women in our society. Although the simple breakdown by gender revealed statistically significant differences (but not

TABLE 2.13 Attention to Campaign

	Male-Dominated Occupations		Integrated Occupations		Female-Dominated Occupations	
	Men	*Women*	*Men*	*Women*	*Men*	*Women*
Very much interested	29.8%	23.1%	37.4%	26.2%	36.0%	24.2%
Somewhat interested	48.2	53.8	54.9	57.1	58.0	58.5
Not very interested	22.0	23.1	7.7	16.7	6.0	17.4
	n = 168	n = 26	n = 195	n = 168	n = 50	n = 207

TABLE 2.14   Frequency of Political Discussion

	Male-Dominated Occupations		Integrated Occupations		Female-Dominated Occupations	
	Men	*Women*	*Men*	*Women*	*Men*	*Women*
Everyday	11.3%	25.0%	11.6%	5.9%	12.2%	8.8%
5–6 days per week	6.8	5.0	9.4	11.0	7.3	5.7
3–4 days per week	18.0	15.0	23.8	26.5	17.12	21.4
1–2 days per week	35.3	25.0	38.7	35.3	51.2	44.0
Less often	28.6	30.0	16.6	21.3	12.2	20.1
	n = 133	n = 20	n = 181	n = 136	n = 41	n = 159

overwhelming in magnitude) in both cases, controlling for occupational segregation here demonstrates no significant distinctions between men and women.[19] Tables 2.15 and 2.16 reveal that all subgroups overwhelmingly perceive men to exercise the greater power in society. All subgroups also express support in favor of equal societal power for men and women.[20]

We also re-evaluate the issue-based ideology and spending indexes in Tables 2.17 and 2.18. Looking first at Table 2.17, we do not detect any ideological differences among men and women with regard to occupational segregation. While we find that women tend to be more liberal than men, no significant differences can be detected among men or women based upon their location within an occupational category. In other words, occupational segregation does not impact the ideology of men and women.

For the spending index, the significant differences are to be found among the men (p [chi-square] = .000). Those in traditionally female trades are markedly more likely to support government spending than are their counterparts in the male-dominated and integrated professions. Among women, however, any differences are not statistically significant (p [chi-square] = .682). Overall, our trends reveal that women, regardless of occupational segregation, tend to favor governmental spending.

TABLE 2.15   Perceived Power of Men, Women in American Society

	Male-Dominated Occupations		Integrated Occupations		Female-Dominated Occupations	
	Men	*Women*	*Men*	*Women*	*Men*	*Women*
Men have more power	78.8%	88.5%	86.5%	85.8%	90.7%	89.8%
Men, women about equal	18.2	11.5	10.8	12.3	7.4	7.3
Women have more power	3.0	—	2.7	1.9	1.92	2.9
	n = 269	n = 26	n = 111	n = 106	n = 54	n = 245

TABLE 2.16   Desired Power for Men, Women in American Society

	Male-Dominated Occupations		Integrated Occupations		Female-Dominated Occupations	
	Men	*Women*	*Men*	*Women*	*Men*	*Women*
Men should exercise more power	17.6%	8.0%	15.6%	6.6%	15.1%	9.0%
Men, women should exercise equal power	81.7	92.0	82.6	92.5	84.9	89.8
Women should exercise greater power	0.8	—	1.8	0.9	—	1.2
	n = 262	n = 25	n = 109	n = 106	n = 53	n = 244

Finally, we look at the degree of feminist consciousness found among men and women. Our main question is: Do men and women differ in their degree of identification with an active role for women in society? To begin, we measure feminist consciousness by constructing a feminist consciousness score.[21] We take the feeling thermometers of eight groups—big business (V961495), labor unions (961494), liberals (V961493), conservatives (V961492), whites (V961491), blacks (V961490), the military (V961488), and the poor (V961496)—and create a mean group rating for all groups. We then develop a measure of feminist consciousness based on the relationship of the individual's rating of the women's movement on the feeling thermometer (V961500), to the mean rating of all other groups. A second component of the feminist consciousness measure is based on the women's rights scale (V960543). This scale measures the degree to which individuals feel women should have an equal role in society (liberal), or should remain in the home (conservative). We have classified those who rate the women's movement 10 percent or more higher than the other groups combined, and who rate liberal on the women's rights scale, as feminists. Those who do not rate the women's movement 10 percent higher than other groups, but rate liberal on the women's rights scale are classified as potential feminists. Those who do not rate the women's movement 10 percent higher than other groups and rate

TABLE 2.17   Seven-Issue Liberalism/Conservatism Index

	Male-Dominated Occupations		Integrated Occupations		Female-Dominated Occupations	
	Men	*Women*	*Men*	*Women*	*Men*	*Women*
Liberal	8.4%	26.7%	11.3%	17.9%	11.1%	24.0%
Moderate	68.1	73.3	69.3	75.9	80.6	66.7
Conservative	23.5	—	19.3	6.3	8.3	9.3
	n = 119	n = 15	n = 150	n = 112	n = 36	n = 129

TABLE 2.18   Seven-Issue Government Spending Index

	Male-Dominated Occupations		Integrated Occupations		Female-Dominated Occupations	
	Men	*Women*	*Men*	*Women*	*Men*	*Women*
Increase Spending	41.5%	61.5%	37.0%	51.4%	60.0%	56.3%
Status Quo	51.9	38.5	47.1	44.8	40.0	40.6
Decrease Spending	6.6	—	15.9	3.9	8.3	3.1
	n = 183	n = 26	n = 208	n = 181	n = 60	n = 229

neutral or conservative on the women's rights scale are considered nonfeminists. The idea behind the potential feminist category is that while individuals may support an equal role for women, they may not have developed an identification with the women's movement.

Table 2.19 reveals that there are no differences between men and women in terms of levels of feminist consciousness (p [chi square] = .506). Our trends reveal that most men and women can be classified as potential feminists. The second highest group is the feminists. While men and women may not perceive themselves as being feminists, they nonetheless support an equal role for women in society.

In Table 2.20 we discover that no significant differences exist among men and women with regard to occupational segregation. Consistent with our earlier findings, the vast majority of both men and women across all three occupational categories can be classified as either feminists or potential feminists. Therefore, in this case men and women in general who not do not necessarily identify themselves with the women's movement nonetheless support an active role for women in society.

SUMMARY

Definitive answers to questions regarding gender attitudes are not possible with the given data. At this point, all we can do is reiterate the theme that emerges from our analysis here: Gender segregation in the workplace does, in some cases, appear to

TABLE 2.19   Degree of Feminist Consciousness Among Men and Women

	Men	Women
Presence of Feminist Consciousness	35.7%	38.7%
Potential Feminist	52.0	49.1
Lack of Feminist Consciousness	12.3	12.2

TABLE 2.20 Feminist Consciousness by Occupational Segregation

	Male-Dominated Occupations		Integrated Occupations		Female-Dominated Occupations	
	Men	*Women*	*Men*	*Women*	*Men*	*Women*
Presence of Feminist Consciousness	30.7%	45.5%	35.4%	38.1%	34.8%	32.4%
Potential Feminists	55.0	45.5	57.3	52.3	54.3	56.6
Lack of Feminist Consciousness	14.3	—	7.3	9.7	10.9	11.0
	n = 140	n = 22	n = 178	n = 155	n = 46	n = 182

play a role in the organization of various political attitudes. Although the simpler, broader distinction between men and women may be the more important influence on opinion formation; nevertheless, anyone seeking to understand the differences between the sexes must perform more advanced analysis and attempt to identify the constellation of factors that could interact with gender to influence political attitudes. In the end, it appears that biology is not solely determinative—to a large extent, culture matters. We found, for example, that the level of interest in politics among women does not differ by occupational segregation, but it does for men. In contrast, the data suggest the opposite relationship in respect to discussing politics. Males' frequency of political discussion is not related to occupational segregation, but it is for females. We also found that neither men's nor women's ideology is affected by where they work; but, ironically, although women's attitudes toward government spending are not affected by where they work, the same cannot be said for men. Men who work in traditionally female jobs are more likely than other men to support government spending.

The findings of this study are consistent with much of the current research in the field of gender and politics. Research has indicated, for example, that women and men differ on certain "humanitarian" issues.[22] The women in our study, through their liberal positions on issues and their positions on spending, did display a more consistent pattern of support for humanitarian positions than their male counterparts. Likewise, the women in our study, consistent with prior research, were not as interested in politics as were the men.

More important, however, our study suggests the need to look beyond the sex of the respondents if we want to understand the significance of gender and its relationship to political behavior. Biological males and females become gendered males and females in the context of particular cultures and particular historical periods. It is useful to think of gender in terms of what it represents for individuals. Gender viewed this way becomes for an individual a set of opportunity structures that a particular culture values. In the United States today, for example, gender is involved in the kinds of work experiences people choose or find themselves directed towards. As a result of gender role socialization, life-cycle demands, and discrimination, women tend to cluster in what we have referred to as female-segregated jobs. The data we have examined suggest the experiences they have in these jobs may affect some elements of their political attitudes and behavior. We can also speculate that since adult socialization appears to affect political attitudes,[23] the longer women remain in those positions the more their work experiences will affect their political attitudes. This is a subject for additional research. As the workplace changes so will American political life. The hows and whys of these changes present a challenge to citizens and political scientists alike.

NOTES

1. Lynn Weiner, *From Working Girl to Working Mother: The Female Labor Force in the United States, 1820–1980* (Chapel Hill, NC: The University of North Carolina Press, 1985), p. 4.

2. U.S. Bureau of the Census. *Statistical Abstract of the United States: 1996,* 11th edition (Washington, DC, 1996), Table 637, p. 405.

3. Weiner, *op. cit.,* p. 4.

4. *Statistical Abstract of the United States: 1996,* Table 615, p. 393.

5. *Statistical Abstract of the United States, 1996,* Table 625, p. 399 and Table 626, p. 400.

6. *Statistical Abstract of the United States: 1996,* Table 637, pp. 405–407.

7. Andrea H. Beller, "Occupational Segregation and the Earnings Gap." In *Comparable Worth: Issue for the 80's, Vol. 1* (Washington, DC: U.S. Commission on Civil Rights, 1984), p. 23.

8. Beller, *op. cit.* p. 32.

9. *Statistical Abstract of the United States: 1996,* Table 665, p. 428.

10. *Women's Health: Report of the Public Health Service Task Force on Women's Health Issues, Vol. II* (Washington, DC: U.S. Department of Health and Human Services), p. 16.

11. See, for example, Kristi Anderson and Elizabeth Cook, "Women, Work, and Political Attitudes," *American Journal of Political Science,* 29(3) (August 1985), p. 439–455; Kristi Anderson, "Working Women and Political Participation, 1952–1972," *American Journal of Political Science,* 19(3) (August 1975), p. 439–453.

12. Ethel Klein, *Gender Politics* (Cambridge, MA: Harvard University Press, 1984), p. 108.

13. Lee Ann Banaszak and Jan E. Leighley, "How Employment Affects Women's Gender Attitudes," *Political Geography Quarterly,* 10 (2) (April 1991), 174–185.

14. The SRC's method for classifying occupations does not allow for a precise identification of individual occupations. Rather than list the respondent's occupation by means of the Census Bureau's 1980 Standard Occupational Classification (SOC) code, the SRC collapses several SOC categories into a single category of similar occupations. In utilizing the more generic categorizations in the NES for selecting our subsamples, we have been careful not to do harm to the segregated nature of the occupational categories identified from the Labor Department's tables. In other words, if too many non-segregated occupations were included in an SRC-encoded category, we chose to exclude all those respondents from our analysis, rather than contaminate the results.

15. M. Margaret Conway, Gertrude A. Steuernagel, and David W. Ahern, *Women and Political Participation: Culture Change in the Political Arena* (Washington, DC: CQ Press, 1997), pp. 86–87.

16. Conway, Steuernagel, Ahern, *op. cit.,* 81.

17. For Tables 2.9 and 2.10, 1992 NES data were utilized. In 1996 the NES did not ask specific questions regarding the perceived and desired power of women in society.

18. In the discussion to follow, male-segregated occupations encompass jobs that are held by men at an 80 percent rate or higher; female-segregated jobs are those held by women at an 80 percent rate or higher; and integrated occupations generally fall into the 40–60 percent range.

19. p(chi-square, men, V6007) = 0.16195; p(chi-square, women, V6007 = 0.51387; p(chi-square, men, V6008) = 0.76506; p(chi-square, women, V6008) = 0.92027.

20. As with Tables 2.9 and 2.10, 1992 data were utilized due to the lack of availability of 1996 data on the perceived and desired power of women in society.

21. See Conway, Steuernagel, Ahern, *op. cit.,* Chapter 4.

22. See, for example, Sandra Baxter and Marjorie Lansing. *Women and Politics: The Invisible Majority* (University of Michigan Press, 1983); Cal Clark and Janet Clark, "The Gender Gap 1988: Comparison, Pacifism, and Indirect Feminism," in Lois Lovelace Duke, ed.,

Women in Politics: Outsiders or Insiders (Prentice Hall, 1993), pp. 32–45; Nancy E. McGlen and Karen O'Connor, *Women, Politics, and American Society* (Prentice Hall, 1995), pp. 71–72.

23. See, for example, Roberta Sigel, ed., *Political Learning in Adulthood* (Chicago: The University of Chicago Press, 1989).

FURTHER READING

Adler, Marina A. "Women's Work Values in Unified Germany: Regional Differences as Remnants of the Past." *Work and Occupations,* 241(2) (May 1997), 245–266.

Andes, Nancy. "Social Class and Gender: An Empirical Evaluation of Occupational Stratification." *Gender and Society,* 6(2) (June 1992), 231–251.

England, Paula. *Comparable Worth: Theories and Evidence.* New York: Aldine De Gruyter, 1992.

Gerschwender, James and Rita Carroll-Seguin. "Exploding the Myth of African American Progress." *Signs: Journal of Women in Culture and Society,* 15(2) (Winter 1990), 285–99.

Gurin, Patricia. "Women's Gender and Consciousness." *Public Opinion Quarterly,* 49(2) (Summer 1985), 143–63.

Jacobs, Jerry. "Long-Term Trends in Occupational Segregation by Sex." *American Journal of Sociology,* 95(1) (July 1989), 160–73.

Kelly, Rita Mae. *The Gendered Economy: Work, Careers and Success.* Newbury Park, CA: Sage Publications, 1991.

Kenney, Sally J., "New Research of Gendered Political Institutions." *Political Research Quarterly,* 49(2) (June 1996), 445–466.

Nelson, Barbara and Sara M. Evans. *Wage Justice: Comparable Worth and the Paradox of Technocratic Reform.* Chicago: University of Chicago Press, 1989.

Pollitt, Katha. "Thinking Pink." *Nation,* 263(18) (December 2, 1996), 9.

Sawa-Ozajka, Elzbieta. "International Trends: Are There Female Political Elites in Poland?" *Journal of Women's History,* 8(2) (Summer 1996), 103–110.

Welch, Susan and John Hibbing. "Financial Conditions, Gender and Volting in American National Elections." *The Journal of Politics,* 54(1) (February 1992), 197–213.

WEBSITES FOR FURTHER INFORMATION

Feminist Activist Resources on the Net, http://www.igc.apc.org/women/feminist.html

Feminist Gateway, http://feminist.org/gateway/sd__exec2.html#top

Internet Resources—Women's Rights, http://www.aclu.org/issues/women/irwo.html

National Organization for Women, http://www.now.org/web/whatsnew.html

U.S. Department of Labor, Labor Related Data, http://www.dol.gov/dol/welcome.htm

U.S. Department of Labor-Women's Bureau, http://www.dol.gov/dol/wb/

1996 Statistical Abstract of the United States, http://www.census.gov/prod/2/gen/96statab/96statab.html

AFL-CIO, http://www.aflcio.org/

National Election Study, http://www.umich.edu/~nes

The Gender Gap in 1996: More Meaning Than a "Revenge of the Soccer Moms"

CAL CLARK, JANET CLARK

Probably the most central explanation for the re-election of Democrat Bill Clinton as President in 1996 was the much noted "gender gap" in which Clinton received stronger support from women than from men. In popular imagery at least, Clinton was portrayed as benefiting from a "revenge of the soccer moms" against the less kinder and less gentler policies pushed by Republican Speaker of the House Newt Gingrich. Gingrich had gained power in the previous 1994 elections when Republicans rode a revolt of "the angry white male" to capture both Houses of Congress. While journalists seek to illuminate through such sharp images as soccer moms creating a gender gap at the polls, scholars tend to be far more measured in their evaluations. In fact, Richard Seltzer and his associates soon suggested that popular views of the gender gap were more than a little overdrawn—in research, incidentally, that was partially sponsored by the National Women's Political Caucus, which has a vested interest in emphasizing the gender gap.[1]

This chapter, therefore, seeks to provide a more balanced evaluation of the gender gap in the 1996 presidential elections. As will be seen, "the gap has not become a chasm, nor does it represent a war between the sexes."[2] In addition, the 1996 gender gap in voting was not a sudden eruption but, rather, part of a long-term and seemingly permanent trend. While these two themes suggest that the popular press may have overplayed it a bit, they should not be taken to imply that the gender gap is unimportant in American politics. Rather, we will argue the opposite: that the gender gap may be a harbinger of the future direction in which political contests are heading.

THE DIMENSIONS AND THE DEVELOPMENT OF THE GENDER GAP IN U.S. VOTING

For those like most of us who do not lovingly pore over voting and public opinion statistics, the very definition of the gender gap may be unclear. To help clarify the nature of the gender gap, Table 2.21 presents data on how men and women voted on the two major candidates for president in 1996. Part A calculates the gender gaps for the nominees of the two major parties according to the "traditional method." Women certainly preferred Clinton to his Republican challenger Robert Dole. The second column in the table shows that 54 percent of the women who voted pulled the lever, punched the computer card, or whatever for Clinton, while only 38 percent supported Dole (the rest voted for Ross Perot or minor party candidates). Thus, we can say that Clinton won among women by a convincing margin of 16 percentage points, that is, 54 percent − 38 percent = 16 percent. Some take this to represent the gender gap. It is not, however, as a moment's thought should indicate. The "gender gap" compares women's preferences to men's. Just because women prefer a candidate by a considerable margin does not necessarily mean that men do not share this opinion. In 1964, for example, Lyndon Johnson received a "landslide" 62 percent of women's vote, but he won almost as handily (60 percent) among men (see Table 2.22). Thus, it would be hard to say that there was much of a gender gap.

The 1996 results were much different, though, at least in the comparative political preferences of the two sexes. The first column in the table shows that men certainly did not share women's attraction to Clinton. In fact, Bob Dole narrowly carried

TABLE 2.21   Defining the Gender Gap in 1996

	Men	Women	Gender Gap Between Sexes
A. GENDER GAPS FOR MAJOR CANDIDATES			
Clinton	43%	54%	11%
Dole	44%	38%	−6%
B. CLINTON MARGIN OF VICTORY BY SEX			
	−1%	16%	17%
C. GENDER GAPS FOR OTHER CANDIDATES			
Perot	10%	7%	−3%
Other	3%	1%	−2%
D. SUM OF GENDER GAPS			22%

Source: New York Times. "Portrait of the Electorate: Gender." Nov. 10, 1996, p. 20.

TABLE 2.22   Development of the Gender Gap in Voting and Partisanship[6]

	Democratic Presidential Vote (%)			House Vote (%)			Party Identification Democrats (%)			Republicans (%)		
	Men	Women	Gap	Men	Women	Gap	Men	Women	Gap	Men	Women	Gap
1952	47	42	−5	48	49	1	48	49	1	26	30	4
1954	—	—	—	—	—	—	51	48	−3	25	31	6
1956	45	39	−6	58	48	−10	46	45	−1	26	34	8
1958	—	—	—	61	60	−1	49	53	4	28	30	2
1960	52	49	−3	55	56	1	43	49	6	28	32	4
1962	—	—	—	61	55	−6	50	47	−3	27	32	5
1964	60	62	2	65	65	0	51	54	3	24	26	2
1966	—	—	—	62	53	−9	46	47	1	24	26	2
1968	41	45	4	52	52	0	43	48	5	25	24	−1
1970	—	—	—	54	55	1	47	47	0	24	23	−1
1972	36	37	1	57	56	−1	37	44	7	23	24	1
1974	—	—	—	63	61	−2	35	43	8	23	23	0
1976	50	50	0	58	57	−1	37	42	5	21	26	5
1978	—	—	—	60	58	−2	38	42	4	19	23	4
1980	36	45	9	49	55	6	38	45	7	22	24	2
1982	—	—	—	55	58	3	39	50	11	26	23	−3
1984	37	44	7	48	54	6	34	41	7	28	28	0
1986	—	—	—	51	54	3	37	44	7	25	26	1
1988	41	49	8	52	57	5	30	40	10	29	28	−1
1990	—	—	—	52	55	3	36	43	7	27	23	−4
1992	41	45	4	52	55	3	32	40	8	28	23	−5
1994	—	—	—	42	53	11	28	38	10	33	29	−4
1996	43	54	11	45	54	9	34	43	6	32	24	−8

Source: New York Times. "Portrait of the Electorate: Gender." Nov. 10, 1996, p. 20. Richard A. Seltzer, Jody Newman, and Melissa Voorhees Leighton. *Sex as a Variable: Women Candidates and Voters in U.S. Elections.* Boulder, CO: Lynne Rienner, pp. 34–35, 37, 41, 131.

males by a 44 percent to 43 percent margin. In the days before the Nineteenth Amendment (which granted woman's suffrage), he would have gone to the White House instead of the talk show circuit. Thus, the "real" gender gap compares how well a candidate does among women to how well he or she does among men. As calculated in the last column, therefore, Clinton had a positive gender gap of 11 percentage points (54 percent − 43 percent = 11 percent), while Dole had a negative gender gap of 6 percentage points (38 percent − 44 percent = −6 percent). It is also worth noting that the size of the gender gaps for Clinton and Dole differed because there was a third candidate, Ross Perot, who had a negative gender gap. If there are only two candidates, the gender gaps for the two will be "mirror images" of each other—one will be positive and the other will be negative, but they will be equal in size.

Another facet of Table 2.21 concerns the way in which the gender gap was redefined in 1996. According to the cynical description of Seltzer and his associates:

> During the stampede by the media, pollsters, and pundits in 1996 to make the gap appear as new and dramatic as possible, the definition used to measure it was changed to one that made it look twice as large as the traditional definition. In the past . . . , the gender gap has been defined as the difference between the *percentage of the vote* that the candidate received among women and the percentage of vote he or she received among men. Over the last year, the pundits and press started defining it as the difference between the *margin of victory* that a candidate received among women and the margin of victory he or she received among men.[3]

Part B in Table 2.22 shows how this new definition of the gender gap inflates its value. The first step is to calculate Clinton's margin of victory separately for men and women. As indicated above this was 16 percentage points for women (54 percent − 38 percent). For men, in contrast, the margin of victory was actually negative (or a margin of loss): 43 percent − 44 percent = −1 percent. The difference between these two is: 16 percent − (−1 percent) = 17 percent. This figure is also, as the third column shows, equal to the sum of the absolute values (minuses are removed) of the individual gender gap for Clinton and for Dole: 11 percent + 6 percent = 17 percent. Finally, Part C of the table shows that adding in the votes for Perot and other candidates would indeed double the gender gap of 11 percent for Clinton to 22 percent.

All this mathematical manipulation may well leave the reader somewhat confused and in sympathy with Mark Twain's observation that there are two kinds of lies: "damn lies and statistics." This should turn our attention, though, to more profitable paths of inquiry concerning the extent of the 1996 gender gap in presidential voting. In particular, we will put the 1996 gender gap into perspective by making two comparisons that should show whether it was, in fact, "new and dramatic." The first is with previous gender gaps in voting and partisanship that indicate whether Clinton's advantage among women was new. Second, we will compare the size of the gender gap to other divisions among the electorate to assess whether it was dramatic.

Table 2.22 presents data on the gender gap from 1952 through 1996 in voting for president and for the House of Representatives, as well as for party identification. The table contains a horrendous and perhaps intimidating array of figures. Yet, its message can be summarized quite simply. In voting and, to a lesser extent, party identification, a key period of change can be identified in the gender gap. It is not 1996 or 1994, though, but the 1980 election contest between Ronald Reagan and Jimmy Carter.[4] Before 1980, the gender gap in voting was generally small and erratic; and, if anything, women supported Republicans more than Democrats. Beginning in 1980, though, women clearly began to support Democrats by the significant margin of 8 percentage points in presidential and 5 points in House elections. *Female and feminist Democratic candidates, in particular, were able to attract significantly more votes from women than from men.*[5] For party identification, the Democrats had gained an advantage of seven or eight percentage points among women a few years earlier in the 1970s, but the Republicans did not experience a negative gender gap for women until the 1990s (the gender gaps for the two parties are not mirror images of each other because there is a substantial number of independents).

The data in Table 2.22 also invalidate the popular image that the gender gap has resulted from a change in women's voting patterns. Women's support of House Democrats actually changed very little between the late 1950s and the mid 1990s, declining almost imperceptibly from slightly above to slightly below 55 percent, while men's support levels fell by about 15 percentage points with the early 1980s and mid-1990s being the two major points of change. Similarly, the decline in men's identification with the Democrats was about three times women's (15 percentage points to 5); and men's identification with the Republicans increased by about 5 percentage points, while women's fell by a similar amount.

The second perspective for assessing the significance of the 1996 gender gap compares it to the gaps or differences in support for Clinton between groups conventionally considered to define important divides in U.S. politics. Table 2.23 presents such data from the 1996 National Election Survey. The first line for the total population indicates that the respondents in this survey were slightly more pro-Clinton than the American people as a whole (53 percent versus 49 percent of the actual vote). The gender gap was also slightly larger than in the exit polls cited in Table 2.22 (13 percentage points versus 11). Yet, these differences are so small that there is no reason to doubt the overall comparison of the gender gap with the "gaps" that emerged in other areas.[7]

Certainly, the gender gap of 13 percentage points is no "chasm" when compared to the expected huge differences between Democrats and Republicans of 74 percentage points, or between liberals and conservatives of 66 points. The 1996 elections also evoked a stark racial divide with the almost unanimous support of blacks for Clinton being almost double the 49 percent of the vote that whites gave him. Yet, when the gender gap is compared to normal indicators of socioeconomic status (SES) that have traditionally divided Democrats and Republicans, it looks quite respectable. It does not differ much in magnitude from that produced by income and education, the two central indicators of SES, and appears significantly greater than the differences associated with age, region, and religion (excepting the

TABLE 2.23　Clinton's "Gaps" among Selected Voting Groups

	Anti-Group (%)	Pro-Group (%)	Group Gap (%)
Total Population	53	53	0
Gender (male/female)	47	60	13
Family Income (over/under $30,000)	48	65	17
Education (some college+/high school−)	49	62	13
Age (over/under 35)	53	55	2
Religion (Protestant/Catholic)	47	55	8
Religion (Born Again/Jewish)	44	92	48
Marital Status (married/unmarried)	48	63	15
Region (south–west/north east-midwest-pacific)	53	53	0
Race (white/black)	49	97	48
Ideology (conservative/liberal)	23	89	66
Party (Republican/Democrat)	14	88	74

After each characteristic, the two categories being compared are listed with the first one being the group less supportive of Clinton and the second the one more supportive. The first column then gives the percentage of the first group who voted for Clinton, while the second column gives the percentage of the second group who voted for him. The "group gap," thus, is the difference between these two figures.

Source: Computed from data from the 1996 National Election Study of the Survey Research Center, distributed by the International Consortium for Political and Social Research. Reprinted with permission.

highly Democratic Jewish vote). Interestingly, marital status also emerges as having a similar gap of 15 percentage points.

In sum, an evaluation of the importance of the gender gap in the 1996 elections produces a picture of the proverbial half a glass of water: Whether it is considered half full or half empty depends on the eye of the beholder. Certainly, a gender gap benefiting Democrats is not "new." This gender gap clearly started in 1980. Still, these gaps, especially in voting for House candidates, were somewhat higher than for 1980–1992, suggesting that the trends underlying them may be intensifying. Similarly, the gender gap is quite moderate compared to the extent that Americans are divided by ideology and race. However, the fact that it is now approaching the level of differences among income groups indicates that gender certainly cannot be dismissed out of hand as irrelevant to American politics. The next section, consequently, provides a much more detailed consideration of the nature of the gender gap in American politics.

EXPLORING EXPLANATIONS FOR THE GENDER GAP

The gender gap of the 1980s and 1990s has often been attributed to women's distinctive values and ways of thinking that emphasize interpersonal relationships more than power and community more than conflict.[8] These values, in turn, became increasingly salient politically during the 1970s and 1980s due to women's changing role in American society as denoted by the growth of the Women's Movement, women's increased entrance into higher education and the workplace, and the growing "feminization of poverty" that has resulted from a combination of a rising divorce rate and declining welfare expenditures.[9] Thus, the gender gap evidently has had several distinct elements or sources that may be summarized in terms of a set of what we like to call the "Three Cs":

1. Women's rising gender **consciousness** and feminism[10]
2. Women's greater (as opposed to men's) **compassion** for the less fortunate in society[11]
3. Women's **cost-bearing** that has been generated by the feminization of poverty and growing inequality in America[12]

These three elements of the gender gap, in turn, are consistent with two basic dimensions of issue cleavage in American politics: the traditional New Deal dimension on economic and welfare issues and the newer division on cultural and social issues. These dimensions are associated with different partisan and ideological alignments. On economic issues, those with lower socioeconomic status (SES) tend to be somewhat more liberal, while in contrast, people with higher education and, to a somewhat lesser extent, higher income tend to be more liberal on cultural issues. Thus, the growing importance of the second dimension in shaping public opinion helps explain the recent partisan flux in the United States.[13]

Compassion and cost-bearing clearly fit on the liberal end of the economic continuum, while feminist consciousness is one of the leading liberal positions on culture wars issues. Indeed, the gender gap in voting is undergirded and probably stimulated by a stable gender gap on a wide array of economic issues and several central cultural/social ones.[14] Nevertheless, the relationship of gender to a person's stance on cultural issues is somewhat ambiguous. Women have in the past been more supportive of moral issues that now are on the conservative side of the skirmishes in the culture wars. The split between feminists and traditional women can be seen, for example, in the fact that there has *not* been much of a gender gap on several issues central to the Women's Movement, such as the Equal Rights Amendment and abortion because of the anti-ERA and pro-Life positions that many women with traditional values have taken.[15]

Table 2.24, which presents the gender gap on voting and on a representative set of political attitudes, demonstrates that the gender differences outlined above certainly persisted in 1996. In addition to the largest gender gap in voting in the postwar era (and very probably in the history of U.S. elections), a gender gap of equal margins existed in which women were more Democratic in their party allegiance and more liberal in their ideological self-identification (or, more accurately, less conservative, since conservatives outnumber liberals by approximately two to one in contemporary America). A similar pattern of women's greater liberalism emerged for the traditional economic issues. The gap was greatest on the general

TABLE 2.24   Gender Gap in 1996 on Voting, Partisanship, and Selected Issues

	Men (%)	Women (%)	Gender Gap (%)
Voting			
Clinton for President	47	60	13
Democrat for House	44	52	8
Partisanship			
Democrat*	46*	58*	12
Republican*	46	33	−13
Liberal	21	30	9
Conservative	52	37	−15
Economic Issues			
Government should do more	44	63	19
Spend more on child care	46	56	10
Spend more on homeless	50	64	14
Spend more on social security	39	54	15
Culture Wars Issues			
Pro-choice	39	44	5
Like Women's Movement	59	71	12
Like gays & lesbians	17	29	12
Support gun laws	34	57	23
Like fundamentalists	41	45	4
Alienation from Government			
Trust fed govt most of time	29	29	0
Fed govt run for big interests	73	72	−1

*The percentages of Americans classified here as Democrats and Republicans are higher than in Table 2.22 because these data include as party identifiers a category of Independents leaning toward either of the parties that was excluded from the time series data in Table 2.22

Source: Computed from data from the 1996 National Election Study of the Survey Research Center, distributed by the International Consortium for Political and Social Research. Reprinted with permission.

issue of whether government should do more or less as women were more supportive of increasing government activism by nearly 20 percentage points. There were also gender gaps of about 15 percentage points on increasing spending for the homeless (probably the most disadvantaged group in the U.S.) and for social security (caring for the elderly tends to fall disproportionately on women). Interestingly, the gender gap was a little smaller (10 percentage points) for child care, an issue that taps the direct concerns of many women; and, despite women's much greater advocacy of activist government, they were just as alienated as men from the existing federal government.

As in previous years, the gender gap in the area of "culture wars" varied more across issues. Consequently, it may appear less pronounced than for economic concerns, but still should be considered quite significant because "normal" gender gaps of 10 to 15 percentage points existed on many issues. For issues of direct concern to women and feminists, the gender gap on reproductive rights remained surprisingly small, but for the first time since polling started in the 1970s women were significantly more likely to be pro-choice than men by a 44 percent to 39 percent margin. In addition, there was a gender gap of 12 percentage points for having a positive attitude toward both the Women's Movement and gays and lesbians. Moreover, a huge gender gap emerged on "macho issues" as 57 percent of women but only 34 percent of men favored gun control laws. Thus, women were considerably more liberal than men on many cultural issues in 1996. In contrast, women were slightly more favorably disposed towards Christian fundamentalists than men (45 percent to 41 percent viewed fundamentalists positively), suggesting the split between traditional women and feminists noted above.

Significant gender gaps can be found, therefore, on a wide variety of attitudes that tap all of our three Cs: consciousness, compassion, and cost-bearing. This raises the question of how much or little each of these attitudes explains the gender gap in voting. An estimate of such "explanatory power" can be made by calculating the gender gap on voting for Clinton separately for respondents who hold different positions on the attitude in question. For example, one might reasonably suppose that ideological self-identification explains the gender gap in voting. That is, the data in Table 2.24 show that women, compared to men, were more likely to call themselves liberals and less likely to consider themselves conservatives, while Table 2.23 indicated that liberals were quite likely to vote for Clinton and conservatives quite likely to vote against him. Thus, women's ideological differences from men might well explain their different pattern of voting. If this were the case, there would be little or no gender gap *within* the categories. Thus, a rough estimate of how greatly an attitude affects the gender gap is to see how much the gender gap of 13 percent for all Americans is reduced when the population is broken down into separate groups according to their positions on the attitude in question.

Table 2.25 presents these findings. Ideology, as expected, evidently explains most of the gender gap in voting for president in 1996. What is unexpected, however, is the lack of explanatory power displayed by almost all the other variables considered here. One would expect, for example, that party identification would be even more closely related to voting than ideology, but "controlling" for party allegiance only cut the voting gender gap in half,[16] suggesting that more ideologically driven party realignment might still be expected. In addition, views on the general role of government explained about half of the difference between the sexes in voting. However, none of the attitudes about helping individual groups (homeless people, the elderly, or working mothers) affected the gender gap at all. Even more surprisingly, feminist attitudes about abortion, the Women's Movement, and gays and lesbians did not influence the gender gap in voting a whit! Neither did views about fundamentalists.

Consciousness, compassion, and cost-bearing should all make women more Democratic, liberal, and supportive of an activist government than men.

TABLE 2.25 How Clinton's Gender Gap Was Affected by Voters' Attitudes and Characteristics***

	Men (%)	Women (%)	Gender Gap (%)
All Americans	47	60	13
Ideology			
Conservative	24	23	−1
Middle-of-Road	58	59	1
Liberal	86	91	5
Party			
Republican	11	17	6
Independent	36	43	7
Democrat	85	90	5
Government Role			
Less Government	25	34	9
More Government	74	78	4
Homeless Spending*			
Cut	19	32	13
Keep Same	39	49	10
Increase	63	71	8
Abortion**			
ProLife	33	47	14
ProChoice	61	73	12
Like Fundamentalists			
No	54	67	13
Neutral	46	65	19
Yes	38	52	15

*Similar results are produced by the other two spending items (child care and social security).

**Similar results are produced by attitudes about the Women's Movement and about gays and lesbians.

***The figures represent what percentages of men and women with a given characteristic voted for Clinton. For example, among Republicans 11% of the men and 17% of the women voted for Clinton.

Source: Computed from data from the 1996 National Election Study of the Survey Research Center, distributed by the International Consortium for Political and Social Research. Reprinted with permission.

Women's different views on these three items did indeed explain a good deal of Clinton's gender gap in 1996. The fact that direct indicators of each factor had little direct correlation with the voting gender gap is, therefore, quite surprising. What seemingly occurred, hence, is that the contributions that each set of factors made to general ideology were somewhat contradictory. For example, feminist consciousness and compassion make well educated and affluent women more liberal, while cost-bearing (and perhaps compassion) increase the liberalism of the less educated and less affluent, such as the "pink collar proletariat."[17]

CULTURE WARS AMONG WOMEN OR A MULTITUDE OF GENDER GAPS?

These contradictory tendencies highlight the differences in perspectives among women themselves that a focus on just the gender gap itself obscures. The nature of these difference, in turn, should have significant implications about the stability of the gender gap and of the special "women's position" that it presumably represents. In particular, a fundamental question for understanding the future dynamics of the gender gap concerns whether the presumed culture wars between traditional women and feminists are breaking women apart as a distinct interest group—in the 1992 elections, for example, this split was quite significant in determining which women supported women candidates.[18] Conversely, compassion and self-interest in reducing cost-bearing could bring women together. One method for assessing this is to examine how these subgroups of women differ or are similar on various sets of issues. If traditional women and feminists are fixed in solid opposition on a wide range of cultural and economic issues, the gender gap will probably decline over time due to the divisions among women. In contrast, if these issues create cross-cutting cleavages and overlapping groups, the right leadership of the Women's Movement (or even the drift of domestic politics) could bring the convergence rather than the clash of women's interests that would probably widen the gender gap, thereby increasing pressures for the increased representation of women among America's political leadership.

Thus, Table 2.26 examines how different or similar the views of the various subgroups of women were for a representative group of ten items concerning voting, culture wars issues, and traditional economic issues. The first line in the table gives the percentage of all women holding a specific attitude. In general, women were quite liberal on most, but not all, of these attitudes, although self-proclaimed conservatives actually outnumber liberals among American women by 37 percent to 30 percent (see the data in the first column for liberals and conservatives further down the table). Majorities voted for Clinton (60 percent), liked the Women's Movement (71 percent), wanted a more active government (63 percent), and favored more spending for child care, social security, and the poor (50 percent to 56 percent). *In addition, they were slightly liberal on reproduction rights with only 44 percent taking an unambiguously pro-choice position (versus 41 percent who were clearly pro-life).* On the other hand, while women were more liberal than men on these issues, they were quite conservative concerning affirmative action and welfare spending as less than a fifth favored each.

The rest of the table indicates what percentage of women within a variety of groups held these attitudes. To highlight this imposing array of data, figures that were 20 percent higher or lower than the average for all women are shown in bold to indicate groups that were especially liberal (above average) or conservative (below average). The first group in the table is formed by four paired items concerning partisanship: Democrats and Republicans; liberals and conservatives. Table 2.26 shows that both the cultural and economic issues evoked considerable and

TABLE 2.26 Attitudinal Divisions among Women

Grouping	Percent of All Women	Voted for Clinton	Pro Choice	Like Women's Movement	Pro Affirmative Action	Pro Big Government	More Child Care Spending	More Social Security Spending	More Poor Spending	More Welfare Spending
All Women	100	60	44	71	19	63	56	54	50	14
Partisanship										
Democrats	58	**90**	50	83	25	**76**	65	61	**61**	**18**
Republicans	33	**17**	35	53	**9**	**40**	**40**	**40**	**29**	**7**
Liberals	30	**91**	**71**	**87**	**27**	73	**76**	49	58	**20**
Conservatives	37	**23**	**26**	54	**6**	**38**	**33**	**40**	**38**	**5**
Culture Wars										
Feels Feminist	14	**81**	**64**	**94**	**33**	74	67	**40**	50	**21**
ProChoice	44	**73**	**100**	77	19	64	63	51	52	13
ProLife	41	47	**0**	61	20	62	51	57	52	14
Homemaker	13	46	**25**	70	20	57	49	47	43	16
ProFundamentalists	45	52	35	**36**	23	65	55	59	52	13
Listens to Rush	14	**33**	35	**51**	**9**	**37**	**39**	**37**	**30**	**5**
SES Splits										
Low Family Income*	26	70	**32**	76	**30**	72	65	64	**60**	**24**
High Family Income	16	48	**60**	67	**11**	**49**	**44**	**34**	**35**	**6**
Low Education	48	67	**33**	71	21	70	58	**67**	59	16
High Education	23	55	**62**	73	20	52	54	**32**	**39**	13
African-American	14	**100**	44	**87**	**58**	**91**	**82**	**83**	**86**	**30**
Under 30	17	64	50	82	17	67	68	48	55	**20**
Over 50	42	58	35	68	19	61	48	57	46	12

Percent of Group Holding Attitude

Boldfaced data are 20 percent higher or lower than the figures for "All Women."

*Low family income is under $15,000; high is over $60,000; low education is a high school degree or less; high is a college B.A. or more.

Source: Computed from data from the 1996 National Election Study of the Survey Research Center, distributed by the International Consortium for Political and Social Research. Reprinted with permission.

consistent partisan and ideological divisions among women. Liberals compared to conservatives and Democrats compared to Republicans were substantially more supportive of the liberal position, generally by margins of at least two-to-one, in all but one instance (liberals' slightly conservative stance on social security). Women, therefore, appear to be divided into fairly consistent ideological and partisan groups.

While there may be a stable ideological and partisan division among women, there does, however, appear to be alternative routes to their liberal and conservative positions, as indicated by the differing results that emerge for variables tapping the culture wars as opposed to the rich versus poor cleavages. Table 2.26 includes six groups who should split strongly over culture wars issues: women who felt close to feminists or were pro-choice, on the presumably liberal side, versus those who were pro-life or homemakers, liked fundamentalists, or listened to Rush Limbaugh on the presumably conservative side. These groups were split as expected on voting for Clinton, and, although the difference between them was not quite as great as for the partisanship items, the gap between liberals and conservatives could probably be called a chasm. On abortion, as expected, the liberal-conservative divide was even more pronounced, surpassing the partisanship splits.

There was a considerable divide between liberals and conservatives on the Women's Movement as well, but several exceptions are noteworthy. First, homemakers who had the lowest support for abortion rights among any of the groups in the table (except, of course, for the group defined by their pro-life position) were right at the average with 70 percent support for the Women's Movement. Second, the small group of women who listen to Rush Limbaugh even occasionally were superconservatives on all other issues; yet half of them expressed positive feelings toward the Women's Movement. Clearly, therefore, attitudes towards the Women's Movement turn upon more than the feminist-traditionalist division. Moreover, except for the strongly conservative Rush listeners and the feminist identifiers who were liberal on issues concerning women and blacks but not on other economic ones, most of these groups were fairly middle of the road on economic issues. Advocates of the pro-choice and pro-life positions both matched the average for all women quite closely on these issues with the ironic slight exception that those taking the pro-choice position were somewhat more supportive of increased spending for child care (63 percent to 51 percent). Homemakers and those who had a favorable impression of Christian fundamentalists also failed to appear very conservative on economic issues.

The reason for this lack of ideological consistency becomes clear in the bottom portion of the table, which provides breakdowns for the ten political attitudes by SES categories (education, income, and race) often associated with ideological conflicts over economic issues. There is a clear pattern for high SES women to have conservative attitudes on economic issues but liberal ones in the cultural/social area, while the reverse is true for those with low SES. Again, there is evidence that support for the Women's Movement is not entirely derivative from culture wars issues since, if anything, low SES women were slightly more supportive of the

Women's Movement than high SES ones. In terms of voting, economic interests were clearly more important than cultural ones since those with low SES were more likely to vote for Clinton. Finally, young people were generally somewhat more liberal than their elders with the difference being more pronounced on abortion and the Women's Movement than on the economic issues; in addition, the special concern of each group with "its own" issue (child care for the young and social security for the old) is clearly in evidence as well. Thus, the economic "cost-bearing" of presumed antifeminist groups evidently acts to mitigate the ideological division among women.

The nature and extent of these relationships, therefore, suggest that issue divisions among American women may be somewhat fluid. First, because different types of people are pushed in conservative and liberal directions by cultural issues, on the one hand, and economic issues on the other, many women are undoubtedly cross-pressured and, thus, more open to re-examining their loyalties than might otherwise be the case. Second, since the younger generation is more liberal on almost all these issues, unlike the flip-flop for socioeconomic status, the interacting effects of age and SES almost certainly create ideological cross-pressures as well. Finally, African American and poor women are much more liberal in their views of the Women's Movement than they are on other cultural issues. This suggests that many women facing financial hardships, whether personally feminists or not, appreciate the role of the Women's Movement in promoting more economic opportunities for them. *In fact, Patricia Misciagno has explicitly argued that postwar changes in the economic status of American women, particularly the feminization of poverty, created a large number of "de facto feminists" (i.e., women favoring feminist policies, despite not calling themselves feminists).*[19] Even homemakers and pro-life supporters are surprisingly supportive of the Women's Movement (70 percent and 61 percent respectively) for groups conventionally considered antifeminist. Thus, the Women's Movement could serve as a unifier of social and economic liberals, but only if both are willing to refrain from pushing "their" issue to the exclusion of the other's strong feelings.

THE GENDER GAP AS A CALL FOR A "NEW POLITICS"

The gender gap, therefore, does not appear to have been created by a monolithic group of women, either feminist or otherwise, with a wide range of similar issue positions. Rather, it is the cumulative result of a set of overlapping concerns. Several such chains of overlapping agreement can be discerned. For example, women of color and women in blue- and pink-collar occupations share common interests on and support for economic policies and welfare issues. While not as overwhelming liberal, perhaps, feminists are quite supportive of these issues due to their gender ideology. More surprisingly, the perspectives of homemakers and even pro-life and fundamentalist women differ in degree, rather than strong conservative opposition, on these economic issues. Conversely, in regard to cultural issues feminists find more agreement from younger and more highly educated women, whether feminist or not, reflecting the prevalent mechanisms of what has been called "countersocialization"[20] in the United States today. Given this complex set of interests and groups among women, the splintering of women into warring camps over cultural (or any other) issues is certainly not foreordained. In fact, the growing gender gap in the 1994 and 1996 elections suggests that a coalescence of women's interests may be coming to the fore in American politics.

Quite possibly, the presumed "women's perspective" has become more essential as turbulent economic change has swept over America in the last decade, threatening the security of both blue-collar workers and middle managers who fall victim to downsizing.[21] The "angry white male" response was to lash out at the nearest objects of blame. The women's perspective is to seek collaborative solutions to mitigate the damage. Gerald Pomper argues that this difference in perspective became a central factor in stimulating the gender gap on which Clinton's victory rested:

> Generally, women were more likely to emphasize the protective aspects of government, men more likely to emphasize its restrictions. . . . The protective aspects of government framed the particular issues of the 1996 campaign. . . . Matching gender stereotypes, men were more likely to emphasize foreign policy, taxes, and the deficit; women gave higher priority to Medicare and education. Men were more likely to focus on the candidates' general "view of government," women on whether or not the candidate "cares about people like you." These differences are grounded in real world experiences. Women are more likely to be involved in their children's education or in the care of elderly parents or in their families' health. More aware of these problems, "women are more likely to feel that it's important to preserve the social safety net of this country." Clinton's emphasis on these issues, and his perceived concern for their solution, brought him the unusual degree of support from women.[22]

For several reasons, therefore, the gender gap in the 1996 elections appears to be much more than a one-shot "revenge of the soccer moms" that will be forgotten when pundits come up with a new one-liner for the 1998 elections. First, the gap appears to be stable and ongoing; second, the *soccer moms* (i.e., middle class, primarily working married mothers) were only one of a variety of types of women who made the gender gap in 1996 what it was; third, as Pomper's analysis implies, the gender gap can be related to much deeper economic and social forces sweeping the nation. The impact of socioeconomic change upon American politics is still unforeseeable. Still, the shape of our public policy will almost certainly be influenced by the outcome of the current swirling of the various gender gaps—in particular, whether it will eventually bring a coalescence or fragmentation of women's positions.

NOTES

1. Richard A. Seltzer, Jody Newman, and Melissa Voorhees Leighton. *Sex as a Political Variable: Women as Candidates and Voters in U.S. Elections* (Boulder, CO: Lynne Rienner, 1997).

2. *Ibid.,* p. 2.

3. *Ibid,* pp. 128–129.

4. On the development of the gender gap, see Sandra Baxter and Marjorie Lansing, *Women and Politics: The Invisible Majority* (Ann Arbor: University of Michigan Press, 1980); R. Darcy, Susan Welch, and Janet Clark, *Women, Elections, and Representation,* 2nd ed. (Lincoln: University of Nebraska Press, 1994); Carol M. Mueller, Ed., *The Politics of the Gender Gap: The Social Construction of Political Influence* (Beverly Hills, CA.: Sage, 1988); Keith T. Poole and L. Harmon Zeigler, *Women, Public Opinion, and Politics: The Changing Political Attitudes of American Women* (New York: Longman, 1985); Robert Y. Shapiro and Harpreet Mahajan, "Gender Differences in Policy Preferences: A Summary of Trends from the 1960s to the 1980s." *Public Opinion Quarterly,* 50 (Spring 1986), pp. 42–61.

5. Barbara Burrell, *A Woman's Place Is in the House: Campaigning for Congress in the Feminist Era* (Ann Arbor: University of Michigan Press, 1994); Kathlee Dolan, "Voting for Women in the 'Year of the Woman,'" *American Journal of Political Science,* 42 (January 1998), pp. 272–293; Phillip Paolino, "Group-Salient Issues and Group Representation: Support for Women Candidates in the 1992 Senate Elections." *American Journal of Political Science,* 39 (May 1995), pp. 294–313; Eric Plutzer and John Zipp, "Identity Politics, Partisanship, and Voting for Women Candidates." *Public Opinion Quarterly,* 60 (Spring 1996) pp. 30–57.

6. All data on how men and women vote, of course, rely on polls since the identity of people casting secret ballots cannot be established. For this table we used, where possible, the huge exit polls of news media, such as the one conducted by the *New York Times,* which are probably the most reliable. For earlier dates when these data are not available, we used the poll with the most consistent data over time, usually the National Election Survey (NES) conducted by the University of Michigan. In particular, the polls used in this table are: President: Gallup 1952–1968, *New York Times,* 1970–1996; House: NES, 1952–1978; *New York Times,* 1980–1996 Party Identification: NES, 1952–1996.

7. For similar results based on exit poll data, see Seltzer et al., *Sex as a Political Variable,* pp. 131–133.

8. Carol Gilligan, *In a Different Voice: Psychological Theory and Women's Development* (Cambridge: Harvard University Press, 1982).

9. Baxter and Lansing, *Women and Politics;* Darcy et al., *Women, Elections, and Representation;* Diane Fowlkes, "Developing a Theory of Countersocialization: Gender, Race, and Politics in the Lives of Women Activists." *Micropolitics,* 3 (Number 2, 1983), pp. 181–225; Ethel Klein, *Gender Politics: From Consciousness to Mass Politics* (Cambridge: Harvard University Press, 1984); Mueller, *Politics of the Gender Gap;* Virginia Sapiro, *The Political Integration of Women: Roles, Socialization, and Politics* (Urbana: University of Illinois Press, 1983).

10. Burrell, *A Woman's Place Is in the House;* Susan J. Carroll, "Women's Autonomy and the Gender Gap: 1980 and 1982." pp. 236–257 in Carol M. Mueller, ed., *The Politics of the Gender Gap: The Social Construction of Political Influence* (Beverly Hills, CA: Sage, 1988); Pamela Johnston Conover, "Feminists and the Gender Gap." *Journal of Politics,* 50 (November 1988), pp. 985–1010; Klein, *Gender Politics;* Patricia S. Misciagno, *Rethinking Feminist Identification: The Case for De Facto Feminism* (Westport, CT: Praeger, 1997); Sue Tolleson Rinehart, *Gender Consciousness and Politics* (New York: Routledge, 1992).

11. Janet Clark and Cal Clark, "The Gender Gap: A Manifestation of Women's Dissatisfaction with the American Polity?" pp. 167–182 in Stephen C. Craig, ed., *Broken Contract? Changing Relationships between Citizens and their Government in the United States* (Boulder, CO: Westview, 1996); Shapiro and Mahajan, "Gender Differences in Policy Preference;" Emily Stoper, "The Gender Gap Concealed and Revealed: 1936–1984." *Journal of Political Science,* 17 (Spring 1989), pp. 50–62.

12. Gertrude Schiffner Goldberg and Eleanor Kremen, Eds., *The Feminization of Poverty: Only in America?* (New York: Greenwood Press, 1990), Chapters 1 & 2; Misciagno, *The Case for De Facto Feminism.*

13. Byron E. Shafer and William J.M. Claggett, *The Two Majorities: The Issue Context of Modern American Politics* (Baltimore: Johns Hopkins University Press, 1995).

14. Cal Clark and Janet Clark, "Whither the Gender Gap? Converging and Conflicting Attitudes among Women," pp. 78–99 in Lois Lovelace Duke, Ed., *Women in Politics: Outsiders or Insiders?* 2nd ed. (Upper Saddle River, NJ: Prentice Hall, 1996); Seltzer et al., *Sex as a Political Variable.*

15. David O. Sears, and Leonie Huddie, "On the Origins of Political Disunity Among Women," pp. 249–277 in Louise A. Tilly and Patricia Gurin, Eds., *Women, Politics, and Change* (New York: Russell Sage, 1990), pp. 249–277; Shapiro and Mahajan, "Gender Differences in Policy Preferences."

16. For similar findings, see Dolan, "Voting for Women."

17. Gertrude A. Steuernagel, Thomas A. Yantek, and Irene J. Barnett, "More than Pink and Blue: Gender, Occupational Stratification, and Political Attitudes," pp. 55–64 in Lois Lovelace Duke, Ed., *Women in Politics:*

Outsiders or Insiders? (Upper Saddle River, NJ: Prentice-Hall, 1996).

18. Dolan, "Voting for Women."

19. Misciagno, *The Case for De Facto Feminism.* Her economic analysis is based on the work of Barbara R. Bergman, *The Economic Emergence of Women* (New York: Basic Books, 1986).

20. Clark and Clark, "Whither the Gender Gap?" Fowlkes, "Countersocialization;" Sapiro, *The Political Integration of Women.*

21. William Greider, *One World, Ready or Not: The Manic Logic of Global Capitalism* (New York: Simon & Schuster, 1997).

22. Gerald M. Pomper, "The Presidential Election," pp. 173–204 in Gerald M. Pomper, Walter Dean Burnham, Anthony Corrado, Marjorie Randon Hershey, Marion R. Just, Scott Keeter, Wilson Carey McWilliams, and William G. Mayer, *The Election of 1996: Reports and Interpretations* (Chatham, NJ: Chatham House, 1997), quote is from p. 185.

FURTHER READING

Burrell, Barbara. *A Woman's Place Is in the House: Campaigning for Congress in the Feminist Era.* Ann Arbor: University Michigan Press, 1994.

Clark, Janet and Cal Clark. "The Gender Gap: A Manifestation of Women's Dissatisfaction with the American Polity?" In Stephen C. Craig (Ed.), *Broken Contract? Changing Relationships between Citizens and their Government in the United States* (pp. 167–182). Boulder, CO: Westview, 1996.

Darcy, R., Susan Welch, and Janet Clark. *Women, Elections, and Representation* (2nd ed.). Lincoln: University of Nebraska Press, 1994.

Dolan, Kathleen. "Voting for Women in the 'Year of the Woman.'" *American Journal of Political Science,* 42 (January 1998), 272–293.

Gilligan, Carol. *In a Different Voice: Psychological Theory and Women's Development.* Cambridge: Harvard University Press, 1982.

Klein, Ethel. *Gender Politics: From Consciousness to Mass Politics.* Cambridge: Harvard University Press, 1984.

Misciagno, Patricia S. *Rethinking Feminist Identification: The Case for De Facto Feminism.* Westport, CT: Praeger, 1997.

Mueller, Carol M. (Ed.). *The Politics of the Gender Gap: The Social Construction of Political Influence.* Beverly Hills, CA: Sage, 1988.

Poole, Keith T. and L. Harmon Zeigler. *Women, Public Opinion, and Politics: The Changing Political Attitudes of American Women.* New York: Longman, 1985.

Pomper, Gerald M. "The Presidential Election," In Gerald M. Pomper, Walter Dean Burnham, Anthony Corrado, Marjorie Randon Hershey, Marion R. Just, Scott Keeter, Wilson Carey McWilliams, and William G. Mayer. *The Election of 1996: Reports and Interpretations* (pp. 173–204). Chatham, NJ: Chatham House, 1997.

Sapiro, Virginia. *The Political Integration of Women: Roles, Socialization, and Politics.* Urbana: University of Illinois Press, 1983.

Seltzer, Richard A., Jody Newman, and Melissa Voorhees Leighton. *Sex as a Political Variable: Women as Candidates and Voters in U.S. Elections.* Boulder, CO: Lynne Reinner, 1997.

Stopper, Emily. "The Gender Gap Concealed and Revealed: 1936–1984." *Journal of Political Science,* 17 (Spring 1989), 50–62.

3

WOMEN, MEDIA,
AND GROUP POLITICS

The media serve as sex-role socialization agents for young women and men. How-ever, women are basically underrepresented in the top management positions within the mass media organizations; consequently, women have had less control in determining media content and in how women are depicted in the news. Does this influence how accurately and realistically the changing role of women in American political society is portrayed in the mass media? Do the media set an agenda that helps the general public better understand the political participation of American women within our society? The first essay in this chapter examines some of the research that has been done concerning the manner in which the mass media have reported news about American political women. Comparisons are drawn between the news about women and men in the U.S. political environment. The author concludes that clearly the role of women in all facets of American polit-ical life is changing; these changes have been and are being reported by the mass media. However, she cautions that additional studies appear warranted as the num-ber of female candidates increases in American politics to further determine the content of this media coverage, the "reality" of political gender roles, and how the media cover these, and to compare the coverage about women who run for elec-tive office with the coverage given male candidates.

　　We next move from news about women and men in the American political en-vironment to a review of the women's movement in this country and group politics.

　　Scholars agree that there is no intrinsic or organic political interest that unites all women. Yet, in American history, three distinct women's movements have acted to mobilize and transform how women view themselves and their relationship to each and to their government. Each separate movement has built upon the advances of the preceding one. Denise L. Baer describes these movements: the Equal Rights Movement (1848–1869); the Suffrage Movement (1890–1920); and today's Women's Rights Movement (1961–???). Baer shows the relationship of the women's movements to women's organizations and political parties. She finds that nearly all mainstream women's organizations have become feminist. Policy advocacy and reform, which have always been a central part of women's organizations, have brought about an increasing empowerment of women. However, in the contemporary era, lobbying by women's rights organizations has declined. Baer concludes that women remain outsiders in the interest group policy community; women still remain outsiders as leaders who can lay claim to group representation of women; women remain outsiders at the leadership levels in the Democratic and Republican parties.

Women and Sex Stereotypes: Cultural Reflections in the Mass Media

Lois Duke Whitaker

Walter Lippmann believed that people act on the basis of pictures they carry around in their heads, pictures of the way they think things are. These pictures constitute what is "real" for us, and, according to Lippmann, much of what we know about the world and our relationship to it reaches us indirectly. Lippman, who was analyzing public opinion more than seventy years ago, believed that what each person does is based not on direct observation or certain knowledge but on pictures made by the individual or given to her or him.[1] This is especially important when one considers how the mass media shape our perceptions by transmitting information.

Many images of what we interpret as real are conceived based on second-hand accounts provided by the mass media, or what Nimmo and Combs describe as "mediated" realities.[2] These mediated realities are perceptions, which are focused, filtered, and fantasized by the mass media. Because these perceived realities are shared with others, a group fantasy takes on an aura of truth that the private fantasies of individuals do not.[3]

All too often, the news about women is reported based on these "mediated" realities or on other myths driven by cultural norms and standards of what are deemed "appropriate" roles for women in American society; in some instances, it is

A previous version of this article was presented at the 1994 Western Political Science Association Meeting, Albuquerque, New Mexico, March 10–12. I would like to thank David L. Paletz and Doris A. Graber for reading and critiquing an earlier version of this article.

determined by institutionalized discrimination and common socialization within the news organization itself.

This article will explore some of the research that has been done concerning the manner in which the mass media have portrayed American political women in the news. Comparisons will be drawn between the news about women and men in the American political environment. For the purposes of this article, mass media will include newspapers, network television news, fiction and entertainment television programs, and political advertisements. Numerous other studies about women and the mass media have been done—far too many to cite here. For example, these studies include research into the various media cited earlier as well as analyses of movies, talk shows, music videos as shown on MTV and other stations, commercial advertisements, and magazines that explore many issues of concern to women (e.g., rape, sexual violence, aging, pornography, female health matters, sexual harassment, and the beauty myth).

INFLUENCES ON NEWS MAKING

Scholars, including Gaye Tuchman and Bernard Roshco, argue that journalists construct reality in deciding what's news rather than merely providing a "picture of reality." This portrayal of what is real is influenced by the journalists' interpretation of reality.[4] Tuchman further cites certain "strategic rituals" journalists follow in striving for "objectivity."[5] Included in these "rituals" is the process of presenting conflicting possibilities, as seen when "both sides" of a story are presented. Tuchman also explains how "topical chains of command" in the hierarchy of news organizations affect the news product and the events of day-to-day happenings that culminate as news.[6]

Other internal influences on news determination cited in previous research include recruitment, socialization, and control of the reporting staff. Lee Sigelman and Warren Breed, among others, argue that news is affected by organizational structure and relationships between reporters and editors.[7] Roshco maintains that news making is also affected by journalists' beats, sources, and organizational constraints of time and space.[8] Prior studies have also concluded that internal influences on the news from within the newspaper organization stem from the more liberal political ideology of reporters as compared with their generally more conservative editors or publishers.[9]

These internal factors have determined the construction of the news, but women, other minorities, and those less influential in our society also have not had equitable access to the news organization. Thus, in many instances, issues of concern to these groups have not been addressed in the mass media. For example, Edie N. Goldenberg researched the access of resource-poor groups to the metropolitan press in Boston.[10] Goldenberg discovered that sources rich in resources within the political system enjoy certain advantages that place them in a much stronger position to manage the news than do resource-poor interest groups. That is, the groups who maintain continuing interaction with the mass media will have much greater access than most resource-poor groups, who are unable to establish and maintain an ongoing exchange with news personnel.[11]

SPECIFIC AGENDAS PASSED THROUGH THE MEDIA

The mass media not only favor certain classes and races of news story subject matter; they also are selective in what they write about, how they play up or play down a story, the "saturation" coverage they can give, sources of their stories and how balanced these sources are, endorsement and legitimacy given to the status quo by the media, and other means of conveying information.[12]

McCombs and Shaw maintain that editors, newsroom staff, and broadcasters, in choosing and displaying news, play an important part in shaping political reality.[13] That is, readers learn not only about a given issue but also how much importance to attach to that issue from the amount of information in a news story and its position. Therefore, in reflecting what candidates are saying during a campaign, the mass media may well determine the important issues—that is, the media may set the "agenda" of the campaign.[14]

Even though women and other minorities have made recent strides into the public and governmental arena, for the most part the mass media still reflect a "cultural" lag in depicting these advances through realistic news portrayal. Lang argues the "news media are both potential agents of change and captives of their own assumptions."[15]

As but one example of the coverage given African Americans in the news, previous research into how newspapers reported on issues of race and southern politics over a thirty-year time frame revealed that four Carolina newspapers reflected more bias in the news content about issues of intense social conflict during the civil rights movement (*Brown v. Board of Education* decision and school desegregation) than in the news coverage about those issues less socially threatening to the white community (the 1964 Civil Rights Act, the 1965 Voting Rights Act, and Senate reapportionment of the South Carolina General Assembly).[16] The bias of the dominant white influence was significantly more negative in direction when the news coverage was about a more socially and politically threatening issue. Bias appeared to be directly related to the degree of the social and political threat to the White community.

As a result, a political culture was passed along for many years. This culture was spread from the politicians of the era to the populace and the mass media. The newspapers, in turn, further fanned the racism and stereotypes dominant in the times by catering to the white male establishment, while at the same time basically ignoring the viewpoints of the black community.

Thus, as politicians used the issue of race and fear of integration in their campaign rhetoric as they sought state and national office, this negativity toward blacks became an entrenched part of the culture. Newspapers picked up on this negativism, as reflected by their bias on the news pages and in their editorials against progressive change. The newspapers, in most instances, were basically a mouthpiece for the dominant social, cultural, and political views of the White southern community.[17]

MYTHS AND STEREOTYPES ABOUT WOMEN PORTRAYED IN THE MEDIA

Women also have been subjected to sex-role stereotypes, cultural standards, and myths established by societal norms and passed along through the news media. For example, Elizabeth Janeway points out that every society invents myths about itself and then proceeds to act on those myths as if they were fact.[18] The technology, format, economic costs, and journalistic presentation of the news products further lend themselves to stereotypes and myths. For example, it is much easier to package the "You've come a long way, baby" new woman in a cigarette advertisement than it is to portray the so-called liberated woman in a documentary film or in-depth news story.[19]

For example, some research into how the press covered the contemporary women's movement revealed evidence of sex stereotypes. David Broder explains that when the National Organization for Women (NOW) was formed in 1966, it was not considered news in the eyes of the *Washington Post*. Even though the *New York Times* reported the event, the news was reported on the "Food, Fashion, Family and Furnishings" page. According to Broder, this news was placed "down at the bottom of the page, under the recipes for the 'traditional Thanksgiving menu' and the picture of 'the culinary star of the day, the turkey, roasted, stuffed and surrounded by other festive Thanksgiving specialties.'"[20] Alger also points out that in assessing themes depicting women in the media, women's activities have most often been portrayed as concerned with the home or with men.[21]

Broder goes on to explain that the women's movement did not make the front pages of the *Post* or the *Times* until August 1970. This happened after Betty Friedan, a key figure in the women's movement and founder of NOW, organized a strike of women workers (housewives as well as office and factory workers) and protest marches in Washington, New York, and other cities throughout the United States. The tactic worked, the movement became news, and issues of concern (discrimination in pay and employment opportunities, passage of the Equal Rights Amendment, provision of child care and abortion facilities) were finally debated.[22] Kahn and Goldenberg also examined news coverage of the women's movement; they found that the early media coverage of the women's movement did not help the movement to grow. In fact, they argue that the press coverage of the women's movement—when there was any at all—was unflattering. Their findings indicate that the movement grew despite the media.[23]

Thirty years later, this media trend of stereotyping females by portraying women as primarily concerned with home and family is still in existence. According to Clara Bingham, forty female members of Congress met with Hillary Rodham Clinton in 1993 to discuss politics and policy. When the *Washington Post* published a story about the first meeting of the women's caucus with the First Lady, the story ran on the front page of "Style," the newspaper's section devoted to lifestyle features and cultural happenings. To contrast coverage along these same lines, the First Lady met several weeks before with a group of members of Congress (the black caucus and the Hispanic caucus) and the story appeared in the "A" section of the newspaper.[24]

Still other scholars have identified certain patterns in the manner in which women are portrayed in the mass media. For example, Lichter, Lichter, and Rothman reviewed and identified the social background, personal traits, and activities of over 7000 characters from a sample of television program episodes selected yearly from 1955 through 1985.[25] Themes, morals, and social commentary were also recorded and analyzed from a total of 620 episodes.

These researchers found that male roles greatly outnumbered female roles (although the gap has narrowed slightly since 1975). Two out of three men were involved in an occupation, whereas only two of five women were. From 1955 to 1985, 93 percent of all judges, 93 percent of all doctors, 86 percent of all corporate executives, 87 percent of all lawyers, and 87 percent of all college professors were played by men. More generally, nine of ten educated professionals were men. Perhaps even more significant, of those characters whose education was made known, men accounted for 85 percent of all college graduates and 89 percent of those with graduate school in the television shows.[26]

Vande Berg and Streckfuss studied 116 prime-time television program episodes that covered two weeks of programming for each of the three major U.S. commercial networks (CBS, NBC, and ABC).[27] One sample week was from the spring of 1986, and the other was from the spring of 1987. They found that male characters were found to outnumber female characters by a factor of about two to one. Females were seen far more frequently than males in household occupations and as students. The researchers also found that, proportionately, female characters were far more likely than male characters to be portrayed as enacting a humane, interpersonally focused, cooperative, concerned, information-sharing style of working and managing. Male characters, on the other hand, were far more likely to be seen fulfilling decisional, political, and operational functions in organizations. These studies concluded that relatively little has changed over forty years of prime-time television in terms of the portrayal of working women—that the overall image of women continues to be one in which they are defined primarily through stereotypical domestic roles.[28]

A recent study by Women, Men and Media, an organization that examines the treatment of women in the media, found men continue to receive more attention from the country's news organization. Men still dominated the news, receiving 85 percent of front-page references in February 1996, the period covered by the study, as against 15 percent for women.[29] When females were covered on key pages as the main figure of a story, more than half were victims or perpetrators of crimes or alleged misconduct, rather than persons of accomplishment and achievement. Fewer than 1 percent of the references in front-page political stories were about females. Males appeared in 67 percent of the front-page pictures, while females appeared in 33 percent; this was a significant decline from the high of 39 percent recorded in 1994.[30]

Recognizing that the role of women has changed in American society, one wonders how and why myths and stereotypes about contemporary American women continue to appear in the mass media. One explanation for this is the male control of the internal news organization. That is, the male viewpoint is still dominant in the hierarchy of the news organization and in the recruitment and socialization of media personnel.

WHITE MALE DOMINATION OF THE MEDIA

Parenti points out that the news media are largely an affluent white male domain. Women, blacks, Latinos, Asians, and the poor are accorded brief mention on special occasions. This coverage is determined by a news organization made up predominantly of white males.[31] Still other studies have demonstrated that news making is dominated by white males; as a result, more often than not the news reflects these social and cultural biases.[32]

As recently as February 1996, men continued to write the majority of the news and opinion articles published in American newspapers. The study, sponsored by Women, Men and Media, mentioned earlier, showed that men contributed 65 percent of the front-page articles and 74 percent of the opinion articles published on newspaper op-ed pages.[33]

Alger and others point out that women still constitute a much lower percentage of newspeople than they do in the general population.[34] Therefore, newspeople have values that correspond to their middle- or upper-middle-class status. Thus, according to Alger, socioeconomic status affects their "reality judgments" and their decisions about what is news and how news should be handled.[35]

Rivers describes the differences between male reality and female reality as viewed by reporters. She explains that many events as portrayed in the mass media are depictions of what is edited, filtered, preselected—usually through the mesh of the male perspective. According to Rivers, this reflects a universe in which women are too often totally invisible—or just barely so. She uses the example of Walter Cronkite and how he used to say, at the end of the CBS newscast, "And that's the way it is." According to Rivers, he should have said, " 'And that's the way it is—as decided by a very small group of people, nearly all of whom are white, male, who make more than thirty thousand dollars a year and never take their own clothes to the cleaners."[36]

What does this mean for the element of bias one might expect in news coverage of the contemporary American woman and her changing role? Generally, women and other minorities, the poor, those outside the power order, and those with differing ideological perspectives that clash with the system will, in all probability, continue to be subject to disparities in media coverage. There is a cultural, social, political, and economic redefinition of what is news and how it should be reported. Let us next look at the studies that have been completed about news coverage of women in political elections and campaigns.

WOMEN, POLITICS, AND THE MEDIA

As women advance in all political arenas, including elective and appointive offices, how do the mass media respond? Kahn analyzed newspaper coverage in forty-seven statewide campaigns between 1982 and 1988. Findings show that the media differentiated between male and female candidates in their campaign coverage. The differences were found to be more dramatic in U.S. Senate races, but the distinctions were evident in gubernatorial contests as well. In senatorial races, women received less campaign coverage than their male counterparts; the coverage they received was more negative—emphasizing their unlikely chances of winning. In both senatorial and gubernatorial races, women received consistently less issue attention than their male counterparts. Finally, the news media seemed more responsive to the messages sent by male candidates. The media's agenda more closely resembled the agenda issued by male candidates in their televised political advertisements.[37]

Mandel has argued that "female candidates must deal with how they present themselves as women. Whatever the particular circumstances, their sex is part of women's campaign consciousness."[38] Procter, Aden, and Japp confirmed Mandel's observation in their study of the television advertising in the 1986 Nebraska gubernatorial campaign that pitted Helen Boosalis against Kay Orr, the first time in American history that two women opposed each other in such an election. The study focused on the identity-building strategies of each candidate as revealed in their television ads. They found that there continue to be gender problems for women in political campaigns. Specifically, Orr was more effective in integrating traditional women's roles and stereotypes with perceptions of leadership in order to win.[39]

On the other hand, Kaid, Myers, Pipps, and Hunter used an experimental study to test reactions to both male and female candidates in each of six advertising settings.[40] Two of these were settings traditionally associated with females, two were settings traditionally associated with males, and two were neutral settings. The researchers found that female candidates can be just as successful in television advertisements as male candidates, and that females are particularly successful when performing in male settings. In fact, the female candidate received her highest overall rating on the semantic differential scales when she appeared in a male setting, the hard hat spot. The authors suggest one possible reason is that the appearance of a female in such a role would be somewhat novel to the audience.[41]

Still a more recent study of statewide campaigns in 1994 also indicates that portrayals of female candidates seem to have been more positive. Kevin B. Smith found much smaller coverage differences than in studies relying on pre-1990 data. Although systematic gender-based patterns are still detectable, they are not so glaring as reported in previous studies, and not always to the disadvantage of female candidates. Thus, one could conclude that this study indicates such a shift may be underway and that one could expect even more equal treatment of female candidates in the press in the future.[42]

Patty Murray (D-WA), the woman who ran for the U.S. Senate in 1992 as the "mom in tennis shoes," not only was successful in her bid for election; she also landed an assignment to the powerful Senate Appropriations Committee on her first day on the job. How did the *Seattle Times* report this committee assignment? The news was reported in the local pages instead of on the front page.[43] One has to question the placement decision by newspaper personnel, which unquestionably downplayed this news item. Would the same "news" have been subjugated to inside pages if the Washington senator had been male?

Analysis of the newspaper coverage given the nominations for attorney general of Zoe Baird and Kimba Wood revealed newspapers set an agenda that depicted typical female stereotypes. That is, the newspaper accounts tended to highlight and focus not just on the issue of lawbreaking but on the problems of female professionals and the issue of child care.[44] Of course, child care has traditionally been perceived to be a female responsibility. Our society and our government leaders have delegated the nurturing role to women, which, to many, means women are the prime caretakers of children.

To contrast perceptions of male and female roles in child care, twenty years ago it was learned that then–Deputy Attorney General William Ruckelshaus had an alien woman with an improper visa working in his home. Stories in the media attributed this arrangement to his wife, and the story quickly died.[45] Thus, even though the nominee in question had employed an alien woman, the basic issue of child care was linked to the wife's responsibility—and not that of the male nominee—and the issue was put to rest.

The nominations of Baird and Wood were withdrawn by the Clinton administration, and Janet Reno, a single woman without child care responsibility, was nominated and confirmed as the first female U.S. attorney general. Shortly thereafter, Commerce Secretary Ronald H. Brown reported that he had failed to pay Social Security taxes for a household worker. Newspaper accounts explained this double-standard in the following manner:

> What is the distinction between Mr. Brown and Judge Wood? In the screening process for Presidential nominees, Mr. Brown was not asked about his compliance with immigration and tax laws. By contrast, Judge Wood was asked several times and "she was not completely forthcoming," Mr. Stephanopoulos (Clinton spokesperson) said.
>
> Judge Wood said that she was asked if she had a 'Zoe Baird problem' and that she interpreted that to mean had she ever hired an illegal alien when it was against the law and not paid Social Security and other taxes for that worker, as Ms. Baird had. She said she had replied truthfully that she had not.[46]

Thus, we have a situation in which a woman was not confirmed although she had broken no law and a man who had not complied with the law avoided the same critical scrutiny by the press during the confirmation process. The mass media play into this double standard in other ways. The press provides not only information but the particular "spin" the public and our government officials associate with this news report or this issue.

The mass media interpret what is perceived as a "female" burden or problem and pass this along to the general populace. Public opinion coalesces around this issue, elected and other officials within government interpret this stereotypical role for women, and female professionals often are the losers.

CONCLUSION

The very nature of the news-making process dictates that reporters, journalists, editors, and/or publishers, by necessity, must make news decisions. Judgments as to what is news and what is not; decisions of how to "play" a story as far as importance; judgments regarding placement of news; the amount of coverage to be given a particular issue, event, or personality; and other internal decisions within the media organization will always be determined by institutional norms of what is and ought to be "news." These internal constraints of media organizations and personnel, by necessity, dictate the ultimate news product. As Paletz and Entman have observed, "Seeking neither to praise nor deplore, we have shown that much of the news is determined less by external 'reality' than by the internal logic of media organizations and personnel."[47]

In addition, mass media professionals bring their own culture, their own social norms, and their own political views and preferences to the news-making procedure. Despite the professionalism of the individual reporter and her or his news organization, the final news product will be influenced by any number of internal and external factors.

Thus, whether the issue is women seeking elective or appointive public office, ethnicity in the Northeast, the environment in the West, or religion or race in the Deep South, specific issues and events will be selected for coverage, while others will be ignored or downplayed. Still other issues will be addressed by giving the story a different "spin" in the newspapers' pages or in the nightly television news. And the sociological and cultural influences of the individuals making these decisions will always be a human determination.

It falls, then, to the American public to recognize media coverage for what it is and to work beyond the stereotypes that do end up in the news. The role of women in all facets of American life has changed significantly over the past four decades, and is continuing to change. Clearly, these changes have been and are being reported by the mass media. But, a number of questions remain: What is the content of this media coverage? What has been the role of the media in assessing the "reality" of some of these changes? How have these changes subsequently been reported by the mass media? Do women not deserve a great deal more coverage, even under the present constraints as outlined above, than the media give them?

And, should not the coverage focus on issues, opinions, assessments by female candidates and policymakers much as now given to men? Women have made strides in American politics. But much remains to be rectified such that we do not have newspaper columns as this one reported by Paula LaRocque: "At 36, she's still a knockout, her clear English skin and sparkling blue eyes set off by auburn curls . . . (column about a woman who had won political office)."[48]

Obviously, this is a preliminary article written to synthesize some of the research that has been done in the area of press coverage of women in American politics. As the number of female candidates increases and the number of women in other important positions within our government grows, further studies are indicated that will examine and analyze the media coverage given women by the press. Studies that would further explore how the news is reported about women who run for elective office and how this coverage compares with that of male candidates especially appear to be warranted. More longitudinal studies certainly appear to be needed; as more women seek and are elected to public office, one hopes that additional research can be done in this area.

NOTES

1. Walter Lippmann, "The World Outside and the Pictures in Our Heads," in *Public Opinion* (New York: Macmillan, 1922), chap. 1.

2. Dan Nimmo and James E. Combs, *Mediated Political Realities,* 2nd ed. (New York: Longman, 1990), p. 2.

3. *Ibid.,* pp. 1–20.

4. Gaye Tuchman, *Making News: A Study in the Construction of Reality* (New York: Free Press, 1978), p. 23; Bernard Roshco, *Newsmaking* (Chicago: University of Chicago Press, 1975), p. 4.

5. Tuchman, *Making News,* p. 667.

6. *Ibid.,* p. 12.

7. Lee Sigelman, "Reporting the News: An Organizational Analysis," *American Journal of Sociology, 79* (July–November 1973), pp. 132–151; Warren Breed, "Social Control in the Newsroom: A Functional Analysis," *Social Forces, 33* (May 1955), pp. 326–335.

8. Roshco, *Newsmaking,* pp. 4–5.

9. Bob Schulman, "The Liberal Tilt of Our Newsroom," *Bulletin of the American Society of Newspaper Editors,* 654 (October 1982), pp. 3–7; Joseph Kraft, "The Imperial Media," *Commentary, 71* (May 1981), p. 36; Robert S. Lichter and Stanley Rothman, "Media and Business Elites," *Public Opinion* 4 (5) (October/November 1981), pp. 43–44.

10. Edie N. Goldenberg, *Making the Papers* (Lexington, MA: Lexington Books, 1975), pp. 1–6.

11. *Ibid.,* pp. 145–146, 148.

12. Among others, see Michael Parenti, *Inventing Reality: The Politics of News Media,* 2nd ed. (New York: St.

Martin's Press, 1993), pp. 191–210. Also see Mark Fishman, *Manufacturing the News* (Austin: University of Texas Press, 1980); Daniel C. Hallin, "Sound Bite News," in Gary Orren (Ed.), *Blurring the Lines.* (New York: Free Press, 1990); Martin A. Lee and Norman Solomon, *Unreliable Sources* (New York: Carol Publishing Group, 1991); and Martin Linskey, *Impact: How the Press Affects Federal Policymaking* (New York: Norton, 1986).

13. Maxwell E. McCombs and Donald L. Shaw, "The Agenda-Setting Function of Mass Media," *Public Opinion Quarterly, 36* (Summer 1972), pp. 176–187. Also see Everett M. Rogers and James W. Dearing, "Agenda-Setting Research: Where Has It Been and Where Is It Going?" in James A. Anderson (Ed.), *Communication Yearbook,* vol. 2 (Beverly Hills, CA: Sage, 1988).

14. Maxwell E. McCombs and Donald L. Shaw, "The Agenda-Setting Function of Mass Media," *Public Opinion Quarterly, 36* (Summer 1972), p. 177.

15. Gladys Engel Lang, "The Most Admired Women: Image-Making in the News," in Gaye Tuchman, Arlene Kaplan Daniels, and James Benet (Eds.), *Hearth and Home* (New York: Oxford University Press, 1978), p. 147.

16. Lois Lovelace Duke, "Cultural Redefinition of News: Racial Issues in South Carolina, 1954–1984," Ph.D. diss., University of South Carolina, 1986.

17. Among others who discuss basic distortions in the media, see Parenti, *Inventing Reality,* p. 8; Bernard Rubin, "Visualizing Stereotypes: Updating Walter Lippmann," in Bernard Rubin (Ed.), *When Information*

Counts: Grading the Media (Lexington, MA: D. C. Heath, 1985) pp. 29–58; and Kathleen Hall Jamieson and Karlyn Kohrs Campbell, *The Interplay of Influence* (Belmont, CA: Wadsworth, 1992); especially pp. 98–124.

18. Elizabeth Janeway, *Man's World, Woman's Place* (New York: Dell, 1971); and Caryl Rivers, "Women, Myth, and the Media," in Rubin (Ed.), *When Information Counts,* p. 4.

19. Rubin, "Visualizing Stereotypes: Updating Walter Lippman," in Rubin (Ed.), *When Information Counts,* p. 34.

20. David S. Broder, *Behind the Front Page* (New York: Simon and Schuster, 1987), p. 126.

21. Dean E. Alger, *The Media and Politics* (Englewood Cliffs, NJ: Prentice-Hall, 1989), p. 26.

22. Broder, *Behind the Front Page,* pp. 125–127.

23. Kim Fridkin Kahn and Edie N. Goldenberg, "The Media: Obstacle or Ally of Feminists?" *Annals of the American Academy of Political and Social Science,* 515 (1991), pp. 104–113.

24. Clara Bingham, *Women on the Hill* (New York: Times Books, 1997), p. 82.

25. Robert Lichter, Linda S. Lichter, and Stanley Rothman, "From Lucy to Lacy: TV's Dream Girls, *Public Opinion,* 9 (3) (September/October 1986), pp. 16–19; and Alger, *The Media and Politics,* p. 26.

26. *Ibid.*

27. Leah R. Vande Berg and Diane Streckfuss, "Prime-Time Television's Portrayal of Women and the World of Work: A Demographic Profile," *Journal of Broadcasting and Electronic Media,* 36 (Spring 1992), pp. 195–208.

28. *Ibid.*

29. Debra Gersh Hernandez, "Women and Front-page News," *Editor and Publisher,* 129 (36) (September 7, 1996), pp. 18, 37.

30. *Ibid.*

31. Parenti, *Inventing Reality,* p. 8.

32. Among others, see J. P. Henningham, "Ethnic Minorities in Australian Media," in Y. Atal (Ed.), *Mass Media and the Minorities* (Bangkok: UNESCO Regional Office, 1986); Lee Becker, Gerald Kosicki, and Felecia Jones "Racial Differences in Evaluations of the Mass Media," *Journalism Quarterly,* 69 (1) (1992), pp. 124–134; and Diana Owen and Jack Dennis, "Sex Differences in Politicization: The Influence of Mass Media," *Women and Politics,* 12 (4) (1992), pp. 19–41.

33. Hernandez, "Women and Front-page News," pp. 18, 37.

34. Alger, *The Media and Politics,* pp. 104–105; Clint C. Wilson II and Felix Gutierrez, *Minorities and Media Diversity and the End of Mass Communication* (Newbury Park, CA: Sage, 1985), pp. 159–163.

35. Alger, *The Media and Politics,* pp. 104–105; Herbert Gans, *Deciding What's News* (New York: Vintage Books, 1980), pp. 208–209.

36. Rivers, "Women, Myth, and the Media," p. 4.

37. Kim Fridkin Kahn, "The Distorted Mirror: Press Coverage of Women Candidates for Statewide Office," *Journal of Politics,* 56 (1) (February 1994), pp. 154–173; also see Kahn and Goldenberg, "Women Candidates in the News: An Examination of Gender Differences in U.S. Senate Campaign Coverage," *Public Opinion Quarterly* 55 (Summer 1991), pp. 180–199; Kahn, "Does Being Male Help? An Investigation of the Effect of Candidate Gender and Campaign Coverage on Evaluations of U.S. Senate Candidates," Ph.D. diss., University of Michigan, 1989.

38. Ruth B. Mandel, *In the Running: The New Woman Candidate* (New York: Ticknor and Fields, 1981), pp. 33–62.

39. David E. Procter, Roger C. Aden, and Phyllis Japp, "Gender/Issue Interaction in Political Identity Making: Nebraska's Woman vs. Woman Gubernatorial Campaign," *Central State Speech Journal,* 39 (Fall/Winter 1988), pp. 190–203.

40. Lynda Lee Kaid, Sandra L. Myers, Val Pipps, and Jan Hunter, "Sex Role Perceptions and Televised Political Advertising: Comparing Male and Female Candidates," *Women and Politics,* 4 (Winter 1984), pp. 41–53.

41. *Ibid.*

42. Kevin B. Smith, "When All's Fair, Signs of Parity in Media Coverage of Female Candidates," *Political Communication* 14 (1997), pp. 71–82.

43. Junior Bridge, "The Media Mirror: Reading between the (News) Lines," *Quill,* January/February 1994, pp. 18–19.

44. See numerous accounts in major newspapers during the period January–February 1993. In particular, see Anna Quindlen, "The Sins of Zoe Baird," *New York Times,* January 20, 1993, p. A23.

45. "It's Gender Stupid," *New York Times,* February 8, 1993, p. A17.

46. "Nominees Are Screened for Illegal Hiring," *New York Times,* February 9, 1993, p. A1.

47. David L. Paletz and Robert M. Entman, *Media Power Politics* (New York: Free Press, 1981), p. 24.

48. Paula LaRocque, "Political Correctness has its Roots in Cultural Condition," *Quill* 84 (4) (May 1996), p. 34.

FURTHER READINGS

Bagdikian, Ben H. *The Media Monopoly.* 5th ed. Boston: Beacon Press, 1997.

Braden, Maria. "Women Politicians and the Media." Lexington, Kentucky: University Press of Kentucky, 1996.

Broder, David S. *Behind the Front Page: A Candid Look at How the News is Made.* Simon and Schuster, 1987.

Bennett, W. Lance. *News: The Politics of Illusion*. 3rd ed. White Plains, NY: Longman, 1996.

Epstein, Edward J. *News from Nowhere*. New York: Random House, 1973.

Gans, Herbert. *Deciding What's News*. New York: Pantheon Books, 1979.

Graber, Doris A. *Mass Media and American Politics*. 5th ed. Washington, DC: Congressional Quarterly Press, 1997.

Iyengar, Shanto. *Is Anyone Responsible? How Television Frames Political Issues*. Chicago: University of Chicago Press, 1991.

Iyengar, Shanto, and Donald R. Kinder. *News That Matters*. Chicago: University of Chicago Press, 1987.

Kahn, Kim Fridkin, *The Political Consequences of Being a Woman*. New York: Columbia University Press, 1996.

Nesbit, Dorothy D. *Videostyle in Senate Campaigns*. Knoxville: University of Tennessee Press, 1988.

Neuman, W. Russell. *The Paradox of Mass Politics: Knowledge and Opinion in the American Electorate*. Cambridge, MA: Harvard University Press, 1986.

Rivers, Caryl. *Slick Spins & Fractured Facts: How Cultural Myths Distort the News*. New York: Columbia University Press, 1996.

Tuchman, Gaye. *Making News: A Study in the Construction of Reality*. New York: Free Press, 1978.

Tuchman, Gaye, Arlene Kaplan Daniels, and James Benet (Eds.). *Hearth and Home Images of Women in the Mass Media*. New York: Oxford University Press, 1978.

The Political Interests of Women:
Movement Politics, Political Reform, and Women's Organizations

Denise L. Baer

Scholars agree that there is no intrinsic or organic political interest that unites all women. Yet in American history, three distinct women's movements have acted to mobilize and transform how women view themselves and their relationship to each and to their government. Each separate movement has built upon the advances of the preceding one in a cyclical (perhaps dialectical) fashion such that we can refer to an overarching women's movement with both active and latent phases. Social movement theory points out that it is only when women's interests are politically segregated or else coalesce due to an outside stimulus that women become a distinctive political force. Movements do not develop out of a vacuum. While some now view the women's movement as in decline, the contemporary women's rights movement has been a major factor in reforming American politics and advancing the status and role of women in American life. This is a remarkable set of events that to understand requires a focus on organizational structure as well as movement politics.

THE RESEARCH GAP ON WOMEN'S ORGANIZATIONS

Each movement has developed new organizations and re-energized existing women's groups. Unfortunately, the distinct theoretical emphases of the Women and Politics Research (W&PR) and Mainstream Political Science Research (MPSR) have conspired to leave a research gap on women's organizations. W&PR scholarship has accepted as its basic operating premise that the contemporary women's movement is a genuine, new social movement arising from a common political identity.[1] This, for most, has meant emphasizing movement politics over organized or group-based politics,[2] which, in turn, slights the contributions of older or "traditional" organizations such as the League of Women Voters (LWV), the American Association of University Women (AAUW), and the General Federation of Women's Clubs (GFWC) in favor of 1960s and 1970s movement organizations such as the National Organization of Women (NOW), and the National Women's Political Caucus (NWPC).

MPSR, on the other hand, treats all movements—including the women's movement—as irrational and unconventional.[3] The highly developed body of MPSR interest group theory is based upon the twin pillars of rational choice and pluralist/mass society theories. According to pluralist and mass society theory, all other types of groups, particularly movement groups, are an aberration. Because pluralists view all participation in politics "irrational," "normal" participation is limited to traditional roles and groups organized around immediate social (familial, neighborhood) or economic (work and profession) needs. When movements do develop, they arise from the scarier elements of society: the irrational and dangerous participation of the rootless and alienated urged on by unscrupulous elites during periods characterized by a social breakdown of values.[4]

Rational choice theorists tell us it is impossible for movement style organizations even to form because of the "free rider" problem that states that without a direct personal financial gain or personal friendship, no one will work for a group for public policy changes (or purposive goals).[5] The "free ride" is taken by individual citizens when they rationalize that they would gain the benefit of a new public policy without the work since public policy is written for all citizens. "While not denying that these [purposive] incentives do attract many activists, the logic indicates that such incentives, unreinforced by private benefits, have little staying power."[6] For rational choice theorists, all mass movements are unusual events in that they can occur only through outside sponsorship,[7] or the singlehanded actions of an entrepreneur[8] who seeks personal and professional gain. Both sets of MPSR theories ignore the validity of purposive goals: MPSR scholars view mass movements as irrational, extremist and demagogic in nature. This has meant that MPSR scholarship has ranged from treating the women's movement as illegitimate and potentially destructive of democracy[9] to treating it merely as a trivial exception that proves the rule.[10]

Outside the W&PR literature, the women's movement is commonly treated as *not* originating in the widespread autonomous and spontaneous development of a variety of different organizations responding to genuine discrimination, but rather the unscrupulous actions of irresponsible and self-interested elites. W&PR scholars have turned to other theories to explain how the women's movement developed: classical social movement theory, resource mobilization theory, and political process theory. All three theories agree that movements develop based on discrimination against an outgroup; they differ in terms of the factors used to explain organization of the movement.[11] Classic social movement theory[12] stresses collective group consciousness and the creation of new elites from within the group, while resource mobilization theory[13] traces the origins of movements to resources external to the group (e.g., charitable foundations and trusts, activists such as college students and middle-class social reform professionals). The political process theory[14] de-emphasizes organizational factors, instead stressing the use of political leverage, public opinion, and the structure of political opportunities.

Classic social movement theory, based upon the civil rights model, posits the development of a social movement as based in four stages: elite networks of interaction, out-group organizational resources, group consciousness and a felt need for government action, and a critical mobilizing event.[15] New work by Belinda Robnett[16] on the leadership of African American women in the civil rights movement suggests women provided a unique and critical leadership tier within the civil rights movement itself: excluded from formal leadership positions, African American women nonetheless made essential contributions as *bridge leaders*. Bridge leaders were informal leaders who connected the movement to the masses through personal efforts drawing upon either their professional position in civil rights organizations, local community groups, mainstream national organizations, or their role as "floaters" active in several movement organizations.

This might explain the paradox of the women's movement: As women's rights organizations age, they tend to lose their focus as a group whose primary mission is to advance the interests of women. The contemporary women's movement differs from the civil rights movement because women, unlike blacks, had no preexisting group like the NAACP to lay the groundwork for a grassroots movement or to work for constitutional change (e.g., *Brown v. Board of Education* 1954).[17] Despite growing ferment among activists in the 1960s, existing women's organizations, like the National Federation of Business and Professional Women (BPW), and the American Association of University Women (AAUW) and women's colleges were uninterested in initiating the movement. The contemporary women's rights movement depended upon the formation of *new* organizations to lead the movement—the National Organization for Women (NOW) in 1966, Women's Equity Action League (WEAL) in 1968, the Women's Lobby in 1970, and the National Women's Political Caucus (NWPC) in 1971.

Robnett's work helps us to understand what steps are necessary to take a latent social movement to the active phase—not only expanded mass involvement, but also new informal leaders—which even in other movements are often women—who bridge between existing organizations and leaders and the masses.[18] Many of the women's groups generated in the 1960s and early 1970s started as leadership or cadre groups, but did later develop a mass base.[19] For this reason, the supposed 1970s gulf between what is known as the "older" established and the "younger" informal movement of the New Left may be less than previously thought. Feminist group consciousness has been found to increase political participation.[20] Within some powerless groups, such as blacks, women were still ex-

cluded from formal leadership positions during the critical formative years, yet
made critical contributions as women bridge leaders.[21] Unlike some other powerless groups (children, the handicapped, etc.) women differ because they did organize on their own:

> The women's movement would undoubtedly have made an important mark upon
> American life without leadership and financial support from the government in its
> early years, but the organizations representing it almost certainly would have been
> more narrowly focused, smaller, and more parochial . . . [and] they would have found
> it much more difficult to attract the attention of the communications media or the po-
> litical leadership.[22]

Despite its use by some to denigrate the legitimacy of the women's movement, the "free rider" concept highlights the great difficulty with which women—or
any other disadvantaged group—can organize for change. Historians list not one,
but three distinct, organized movements for women: the *Equal Rights Movement,*
arising from the 1848 Seneca Falls Declaration of Sentiments; the *Suffrage Movement,* developing in 1890 out of the merger of the two rival woman suffrage
groups; and the contemporary *Women's Rights Movement,* originating in 1966
when the National Organization for Women was formed to lobby the Equal Employment Opportunity Commission. These movements are compared using the
Group Mobilization Model in using classic social movement theory in Box 3.1.

EMPOWERING WOMEN

Social movements are a new mechanism by which *nonelites* can influence elites.
Regardless of the specific movement theory, all assume that women *do* comprise a
discriminated group who do share interests in common. Unlike traditional methods
of participation and action (e.g., voting, campaigning, volunteering for an existing
group), social movements are not constrained by alternatives already determined
by existing elites. Social movements create new elites, and they expand the public
policy agenda in unique ways. Women's organizations represent women: They are
based in movement politics that seek to empower women and advocate in policy
to benefit women.

Women's Organizations Represent Women

While most interest groups represent economic interests, this is not true of
women's organizations. A 1980 survey of women's organizations found that seven
of ten women's organizations were citizens' groups as opposed to nonprofit organizations or profit business groups.[23] This is also true of the women's political action committees (PACs). Women's organizations are diverse. They vary from those
whose mission serves women or girls (Girl Scouts, AAUW), to those whose membership is primarily women but whose mission is not primarily women or girl-

BOX 3.1 Organization of the Three Women's Movements Compared[1]

Factor	Equal Rights (1848–1869)	Suffrage (1890–1920)	Women's Rights (1961–????)
Critical Mobilizing Event	*Mass:* 1848 Seneca Falls Declaration *Leadership:* Refusal to seat women as part of delegates to 1840 World Anti-Slavery Convention in London	*Mass:* 1913 Washington March *Leadership:* 1890 Merger of AWSA and NWSA; 1879 endorsement of suffrage by Women's Christian Temperance Union (WCTU)	*Mass:* 1970 event and media-driven "Mushroom Effect" *Leadership:* 1961 Presidential Commission on Status of Women 1963 publication of *Feminine Mystique;* 1966 refusal of EEOC to enforce on behalf of women; 1966 formation of NOW; 1968 Sandy Springs meeting of New Left women's leaders
Initial Leadership Networks	Abolition movement & conventions Female Anti-Slavery Societies	Settlement house movement Temperance/anti-domestic violence movement Child & women's labor movement Women's club movement	Washington community of women Civil rights movement Anti-War movement
Group Organizational Resources	Churches Abolitionist newspapers	Women's colleges WCTU (1874) Women's Trade Union League National Consumers League	Women's colleges Women's party organizations & clubs National Student Association Student Mobilization Committee to End the War in Vietnam Student Nonviolent Coordinating Committee (SNCC)
New Organizations	American Equal Rights Association (1866) National Woman Suffrage Association (1869) American Woman Suffrage Association (1869)	National American Woman Suffrage Association (1890) General Federation of Women's Clubs (GFWC) (1890) National Association of Colored Women (NACW) (1896) National Pan-Hellenic Association (1891)	NOW (1966) NWPC (1971) WEAL (1968) Women's Campaign Fund (WCF) NPCBW (1984) EMILY's List (1988)
Major Leaders	Elizabeth Cady Stanton Lucretia Mott Susan B. Anthony. Lucy Stone Sojourner Truth	Anna Howard Shaw Carrie Chapman Catt Jane Addams Alice Paul Ida B. Wells	Betty Friedan Gloria Steinem Eleanor Smeal C. DeLores Tucker
Major Actions	Lecture circuit Petition drives Direct action (voting)	Meetings Petition drives / referenda Marches (1913 D.C. March Greeting Pres.	Organized protest through marches, sit-ins, strikes, pickets, boycotts Legal challenges; new legislation/policy

BOX 3.1 *Continued*

Factor	Equal Rights (1848–1869)	Suffrage (1890–1920)	Women's Rights (1961–????)
		Wilson's inauguration; Direct action (protests/arrests/hunger strikes launched from Sewell-Belmont House)	Organized new groups including within major professional organizations; Symbolic efforts (take back the night marches)
Major Achievements	Right of women to speak in public; Married Women's Property Act(s); Founding of Women's Colleges; Admission of Women to Major Universities; 1867 Kansas Referendum on suffrage; 1868–69 Federal Suffrage Amendment introduced in Senate and House; 19 states granted limited suffrage by 1890 (plus 3 tax and bond)	Suffrage Amendment Ratified (1920); Women accepted as delegates at major party conventions beginning in 1900; Equal Division Rule for national Democratic and Republican party Committees (1920–24); First women elected to state legislatures (1894)	Equal Pay (1963); Equal Employment (1964/1972/1991); Equal Education (Title IX, 1972); Equal Credit (1974); Pregnancy Nondiscrimination (1978); Affirmative Action Plans; Party Reform (increase in women delegates; Equal Division for Democratic Party Delegates in 1980)
Partisan Alignment	Third Party Activity; Whigs cease to exist; Republicans formed in 1860; Democrats continue in an era of Republican dominance	Third-party activity; Progressive Party endorses Suffrage (1912); Democrats and Republicans both include women via 50/50 Rule	Democratic party reform from within; Republican party responds without making rules changes; development of Christian Right within GOP drives out many feminist women
End of Active Phase	Split of AERA into two rival woman suffrage organizations (NWSA and AWSA)	Ratification of 19th Amendment August 18, 1920	No one event; some facts contradict decline (e.g., 1992 mobilized women candidates and voters following widespread reaction to sexual harassment charges lodged against Supreme Court nominee Clarence Thomas by Anita Hill
Post Movement Activities	State referenda in Michigan (1974); Colorado (1877); Nebraska (1882); Oregon (1884); Rhode Island (1887); Washington (1889); International movement develops direct action: between 1871 and 1872, 150 women tried to vote in DC and in 10 states; Continued growth of national women's organizations: AAUW (1881); YWCA (1881)	Increased 50/50 movement efforts; Introduction of Equal Rights Amendment; Removal of last legal restrictions on election of women to office (1928); Election of women to state legislatures in all 48 states (1936); continued slow progress; NAWSA becomes League of Women Voters (LWV); Formation of National Council of Negro Women (NCNW) (1929)	????

¹This chart is not meant to be comprehensive: It is a selective, summary listing stressing major highlights of the three women's movements.

serving (e.g., the National Education Association), to those that are the women or girl-serving affiliate of a larger non-women's organization (e.g., National Baptist Women's Division), and those that are women-led, but whose mission is not primarily woman or girl-serving (e.g., Children's Defense Fund). The variety of women's organizations includes women's rights groups, religious groups, Greek letter, social and fraternal orders, community organizations, children and youth, women's clubs, labor, international affairs, women elected officials and support groups, business, health professionals, partisan groups, media, and senior citizens.

Even women lobbyists have more often been less associated with business interests. According to Schlozman, in 1985, 61 percent of male representatives compared to only 49 percent of women lobbyists represented business organizations.[24] The Heinz and colleagues economic policy domain study found that women lobbyists were much more common in government affairs offices (a staff position) than as higher status executives of Washington organizations, and only 7 percent of women were executives in business organizations and 17 percent were business government affairs representatives.[25] While citizen and good government associations were a small portion of the economic policy domain study, women lobbyists were most prevalent as citizen group executives (29 percent) and government affairs representatives (19 percent).[26]

The Movement Basis of Both Traditional and Women's Rights Organizations

What are considered traditional women's organizations today had their start as movement organizations. National women's organizations of all types seem to have been formed during one of two major "waves"[27] of group organization: the 1890s to the early 1900s, and the 1960s–70s.[28] Prior to the Civil War, there were two distinct phases of local organization: religiously based benevolent societies during the early 1800s and reform organizations springing from religious values during the mid-1800s. As Harriet Martineau noted in 1827, during this era, religion was the only "occupation" open to women besides marriage. And historically, it has been found that women's organizations and "clubs held a more significant place in women's lives than men's clubs and organizations did for men."[29]

REACTIVATING THE EXISTING COMMUNITY OF WOMEN

Traditional first-wave women's organizations were, in turn, affected by the 1960s contemporary movement organizations, as well as the expanding women's movement. Anne Costain finds that ratification of the Equal Rights Amendment, while led by the newer women's rights organizations, received significant resources from mainstream women's groups from the 1970s on.[30] The reform basis of today's traditional organizations could not help being reactivated by the growth spurt in women's coalitional activity from 1988 to 1992, particularly with the change in focus after the Equal Rights Amendment failed to be ratified in 1983, which allowed attention to turn from legal equality to broader and substantive policy issues.

A key transition point occurred with the adoption of the Women's Agenda in Des Moines, Iowa in January 1988. Forty-two women's organizations (including occupational, labor union, civic, ethnic, and church groups as well as the new women's rights organizations) adopted the Women's Agenda. The Agenda encompassed family policies, economic opportunity for women, comprehensive health care, women's rights, and a federal budget that balanced global human and economic development with defense. The conference represented a new level of formal coalition-building because all declared presidential candidates were invited to speak, and traditional groups have since embraced an increased activism between 1988 and 1992.

Since 1988, the growth of what interest group scholars call "issue networks" has expanded among women's groups.[31] Women's organizations interact formally through an organization called the Presidents' Council, comprised of the presidents of the now over 100 women's organizations. Lead influential groups within the Presidents' Council include such traditional first wave groups as the General Federation of Women's Clubs (GFWC) and the Young Women's Christian Association (YWCA) as well as the AAUW and BPW. Other informal associations include the Women's Network of progressive and women's organizations. Other informal groups come together on an issue-by-issue basis, such as the reauthorization of the Violence Against Women Act or the effort to get Congress to commission a new woman suffrage statue to replace the Portrait Monument. Organized labor, which was an opponent of the women's movement in the early 1970s, is now an ally. Labor actively supports women's issues and influences progressive groups through weekly meetings.

BPW, previously a predominantly Republican-leaning group, now has a political action committee that endorsed Bill Clinton in 1996 and has embraced comparable worth and pay equity. AAUW supports reproductive rights and the Equal Rights Amendment (ERA) and has made child care, family leave, pay equity, and education funding priority issues. Similarly, occupational groups like the American Nurses Association (ANA), the National Association of Social Workers (NASW), and the National Educational Association (NEA) have adopted formal positions advocating pay equity, family leave, civil rights, and affirmative action.

Nearly all mainstream women's organizations have become feminist. Of 89 women's organizations surveyed in 1985, only 4 did not express support for "feminist goals," while another 6 offered only "passive" support.[32] According to Schlozman, this indicates a high level of "sisterhood" and feminist activity in their organized activity.[33] Further, Schlozman found that women's organizations, while sophisticated in working with any group that shared their goals, often made special efforts to work with other women's organizations, and women's rights organizations were central in developing coalitions among women's organizations in the early 1980s.[34] Exceptions to sisterhood are few and include the new right and Christian organizations (e.g., the Concerned Women of America, which has selected Beverly LeHaye "President for Life"; the conservative-sponsored Independent Women's Forum) that were not originated as primarily women's organizations and whose policy agendas are structured by "male" organizations.

The convergence of "traditional" versus "feminist" organizations deserves more recognition and analysis among W&PR scholars, who continue to focus almost exclusively on the latter. Suffrage organizations defeated the anti-suffrage organizations—they did not join forces with them. What this seems to demonstrate is that traditional women's organizations also respond to the same dynamics as the women who organized the newer feminist organizations. Women's activity in organized groups of all types is structured around the changing fabric of family and work. For example, even the exclusive Junior League—probably the most prototypical middle- and upper-class leisure service organization among women's groups—has become more "feminist." The Junior League did not stagnate in response to the women's movement in the 1970s and the increasing labor force participation of women. Instead, Kaminer points out that an increasing number of Junior League members worked (about one-third), and that half either worked or attended graduate school.[35]

Movement-Based Policy Advocacy

Policy advocacy and reform have always been a central part of women's organizations. The history of women's clubs finds them moving issues from the private sphere to the public sphere. Pendleton Herring found that women's lobby groups only second in number to trade associations in the 1920s, and that the women's suffrage associations introduced new techniques of lobbying in their systematic campaign to gain suffrage.[36]

In the contemporary era, lobbying by women's rights organizations has declined.[37] WEAL has ceased to exist, and both NOW and the NWPC no longer have full-time lobbyists on staff. But the slack has been taken up by the more "traditional" organizations, as well as new organizations. The AAUW in 1992–1994, for example, embarked upon a study of girls and self-esteem, a high profile project that produced a research report and prompted congressional hearings.

Changes in Empowerment of Women

The most fundamental change has been the increasing empowerment of women. Schlozman, for example, found that in terms of ideology, the policy agenda, and their willingness to work in coalition with other women's organizations, organizations of women represented by men were less feminist than those represented by women.[38] Alan Rosenthal, in his analysis of lobbyists and lobbying in the states, believes that the increase in the 1980s among women lobbyists is tied directly to the increase in women state legislators, which has changed the legislative culture.[39]

Take Colorado, where one-third of the legislators are women. The "good ol' boy atmosphere is practically gone in Colorado and is no longer as pervasive even in Florida and Texas, which now has a female governor.[40]

The *1996 Women's Vote Project,* chaired by Irene Natividad, involved a large coordinated effort by 110 women's organizations. The 1996 Project utilized grassroots efforts to identify and register previously inactive women, and targeted ten states[41] where women's voting had been historically low.

Empowerment has also come from the women's funding community, organized as free-standing political action committees (PACs). PACs usually only donate funds,[42] while the goal of the women's funding community is to elect more women, not to lobby for economic profit for a business. But women's PACs and women candidates have mobilized women as donor and activist pools in ways that had not been done before—they do not rely upon the existing candidate pool recruited through "male" organizations. Women's PACs actively recruit and train women candidates; they work in coalition with other women's groups by sharing information, commissioning polls, conducting research on women candidates and campaign strategy,[43] and developing a long-term strategy to advance empowerment of women. Among major PACs, only GOPAC has engaged in such broadbased recruitment.

Prior to 1982, federal women candidates were only able to raise about three-fourths of what equivalent men were able to raise (since federal disclosure was established in 1974). While there was an increase in the number of women major party candidates for Congress in the 1970s, their success rates decreased from 48 percent in 1970 to figures ranging from 33 percent in 1976 to 38 percent in 1982 and 36 percent in 1986. It was not until the women's funding community began expanding its support of women in the late 1980s that the success rate of women candidates returned to the 40 percent range. Women candidates now raise comparable amounts to similar male candidates (after accounting for incumbency), and women's PACs have played a unique role in producing this recent parity. This has made it attractive for party leaders to support women candidates as a "seat-maximizing" strategy, an important advance when they remain reluctant to do so as an "equity" commitment.[44]

TRANSFORMING THE RULES OF THE POLITICAL GAME

The women's movement has from its inception sought to reform the rules of the game. The Democratic Party, founded in 1796, and the Republican Party, formed in 1860, both predate the three identified women's movements, a fact that greatly limited opportunities for forming a political party for women. While there have been many third-party efforts in American history, "suffrage activism normally institutionalized itself in interest group activism"[45] rather than in forming a new party.[46] Parity means transforming male institutions—a quite different objective than creating separate women's organizations. The Equal Rights Movement sought to give women legal existence and rights; the Suffrage Movement political rights and identity; today's Women's Rights Movement focused on parity in political representation in both formal and informal political institutions.

Gender Parity and the Campaign for the 50/50 Rule

Suffrage leaders were aware of the need to include women in party leadership roles. The 50/50 campaign was chosen to achieve parity. Adopted in Colorado in 1910 by state statute, the 50/50 Rule gained momentum at the state level after adoption of the Nineteenth Amendment on August 18, 1920 guaranteeing women the right to vote. Nationally, the Democratic Party adopted the 50/50 rule in 1920, the Republicans in 1924. In 1940, the Republican Convention passed Rule 29, providing for equal representation of women on all committees of the RNC. These were major advances. But the decline of movement politics meant that, increasingly, women found the inner circles of party power closed to them in the immediate post-suffrage era.[47] As a consequence, the representation of women rested more heavily upon party culture and traditions.

In the absence of organized pressure, the Republican party was relatively more open to including Republican women based on their contributions to the party than was true of the Democratic party, with its machine politics and ethnic and blue-collar supporters. When Alice Paul sought a partisan strategy to get suffrage adopted, it was the Democratic party that she targeted as the opposition party. The Republican party took the lead in adding the Equal Rights Amendment to its party platform in 1940, followed by the Democrats in 1944. By the 1960s, Cotter and Hennessy found as many as half of Democratic national committeewomen, but only one-third of Republican committeewomen were rated quite unimportant by their peers.[48] The 50/50 balance on the RNC (but not RNC committees) ended in 1952 with the addition of Republican state chairs to the RNC—an overwhelmingly male group. Today, the RNC has a minimum of one-third female representation. In 1960, Republican women gained a significant advance when the Convention adopted a rule providing for 50/50 representation of women delegates with men on all Convention committees.

The new political cleavages developing with the Women's Rights Movement reversed the Republican partisan advantage in 1972. The watershed event was the demand for parity at the conventions—the Democrats reformed and the Republicans refused. Prior to the 1970s, there had been no organized efforts to demand parity in convention delegate selection. This meant that the nominating conventions—where control of the party by a dominant faction and the selection of party leaders as well as recruitment and vetting of cabinet and subcabinet appointees were determined—remained in the control of the informal but closed "old boy" network.

Party Reform and Party Conventions

Political opportunities expanded for women in 1968 when the Democratic Convention authorized the appointment of a reform commission (later known as the

McGovern-Fraser Commission) to study Democratic party rules.[49] The newly organized NWPC took the lead and chose as its inaugural initiative the reform of the Democratic and Republican parties. This was an important political battle—still under-appreciated by the W&PR—that succeeded in doubling and tripling women's representation in the post-party reform era (Figure 3–1).

The dominance of the Democratic party by the southern wing (traditionally least supportive of women's rights) and by organized labor (then quite hostile to the women's movement) meant no change would come easily. It was McGovern-Fraser, under pressure from NWPC (and other groups) in 1971–1972, that *mandated* proportional representation for women, blacks, and youth (those under 30) for the 1972 Democratic convention. As a result, the proportion of women tripled from 13 percent in 1968 to 40 percent in 1972. Following McGovern's defeat, party reform came under attack by dominant party forces. In response, the Mikulski Commission rewrote delegate selection rules, banning "quotas" in favor of affirmative action efforts. Since states that filed an affirmative action plan were granted immunity from credentials challenges, efforts to include women depended upon local party culture and traditions. The proportion of women dropped sharply in 1976 to 34 percent.

In 1974, Democratic women gained a significant advance by using the historical precedent of the 50/50 Rule. First, the 1974 Democratic Party Charter established the supremacy of national party law, a move that permanently reduced the power of sectional and local interests to oppose inclusion of women. Second, while the McGovern-Fraser quotas were "banned," the Charter expressly exempted

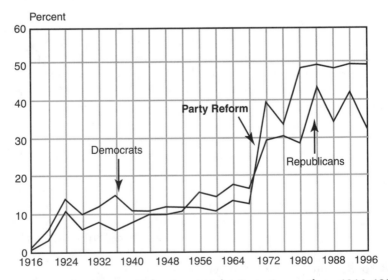

FIGURE 3–1   Proportion Women Delegates at Major Party Conventions, 1916–1996. (*Source:* Data for 1988–1996 calculated by the author from official lists of delegates provided by the national parties: data for earlier years from the Center for the American Woman and Politics, Rutgers University: Eagleton Institute.)

equal division of men and women from the ban (Article Ten, Section 11). This was done at the behest of women delegates to the 1974 Mid-Term Convention following a contentious session in which both black and women delegates walked out, protesting efforts to undermine party reform. In 1980, the Democratic National Committee, acting under the Charter exemption, adopted the 50/50 Rule for delegates.[50] In 1988, at the behest of presidential candidate Jesse Jackson, the 1988 Convention amended the Charter to extend the 50/50 Rule from the final statewide delegation to each candidate's delegation within each state.

The Republican party has traditionally regarded the selection of delegates as a state matter. While there were two reform commissions appointed (DO—Delegates and Organization—and Rule 29 committees), party traditions prevailed. The Republican party, adamantly refusing to mandate parity, remains unreformed. However, following the dramatic upsurge of Democratic women delegates in 1972, the proportion of Republican women delegates also rose in the years in 1972 to 1980 to about one-third of the delegates.

After discovery that the new gender gap in voting threatened the prospects of Republican presidential candidates, Republican leaders have grown more concerned about the low proportion of women at Republican conventions making the party look unresponsive. In the absence of official rules, however, efforts to include women rest with the traditional mechanism of personal intervention by influential leaders[51]—which is affected by whether an incumbent is running for reelection. In 1984, the proportion of Republican women increased to a record 44 percent largely through the intervention of President Reagan's campaign manager, Ed Rollins, who personally called each state party. In 1988, however, when the race involved a contested primary and no incumbent, the proportion of women delegates returned to one-third. With an incumbent president, Republican women delegates increased to 41 percent in 1992, only to drop in 1996 to 33 percent following a contested primary campaign. Without extraordinary efforts, there seems to be an informal "glass ceiling" for Republican women of about one-third of the delegates (Figure 3–2). These party differences are structured by partisan culture. Despite the lack of parity, Republican women have achieved considerable influence at the leadership levels—an achievement without parallel in the Democratic party. In 1985, the DNC under Chair Paul Kirk disestablished the DNC Women's Caucus. In contrast, in 1988, the NFRW was granted a voting seat on the 28-member Council that governs the RNC between its quadrennial meetings. A key question is whether Democratic party culture has advanced to the point that women have equal influence, not just parity—and mandated rules are no longer necessary to break the "glass ceiling."

Parity has different meanings for Republican women than for Democratic women. Within the Republican party, the feminist and anti-feminist forces have been "at war" since 1980 when anti-feminist forces were able to remove the pro-choice plank from the Republican party platform.[52] The key question for Republicans, beyond mere numbers of women, is What kind of woman?[53] The two parties have provided entirely different and culturally distinct arenas for women's partici-

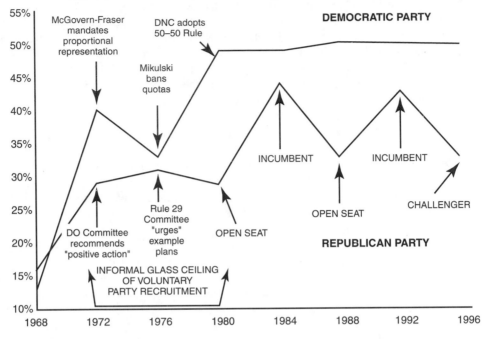

FIGURE 3–2   Party Reform vs. The Glass Ceiling. (*Source:* Data for 1988–1996 calculated by the author from offi-cial lists of delegates provided by the national parties: data for earlier years from the Center for the American Woman and Politics. Rutgers University: Eagleton Institute.)

pation.[54] Participation of Republican women occurs through the large network of local Republican women's clubs, the state federations, and the National Federation of Republican Women (NFRW). Apart from the Ripon Society, which attracts but a small part of the Republican party, the NFRW monopolizes the organized factional participation of Republican women. While NFRW members are more likely than non-members to be active in traditional as well as newer feminist groups, the pro-portions remain quite low.[55]

THE PARTISAN CLEAVAGE OVER WOMEN'S ISSUES

Women's organizations have by and large employed a bipartisan strategy. Based on research at successive Democratic and Republican conventions since 1976, Jo Freeman has concluded that the parties are in the early stages of a realignment over gender and culture.[56] These realigning issues include "gender roles, sexual be-havior, reproduction, care of children, family structure, intersection of work and family obligations, military service," while traditional issues like race, welfare, and education have been transformed by this cleavage.[57] Quoting Pat Buchanan's fears of a "cultural war" in his speech before the 1992 Republican convention, Freeman speculates that "the realignment of the next 20 years will transform the nature of party competition from a mere fight for office to a surrogate civil war."[58] Republican Tanya Melich has concluded that the Republican war against women has stemmed in part from its alliance with the Christian right.[59]

This split is obvious among the party coalitions, their platforms, and their activists.[60] Republican Party elites are much more married and living in traditional families.[61] Over four-fifths of Republicans are married, and of these, 28 percent of the women identify themselves as housewives and 44 percent of the Republican men say their wife is a housewife.[62] By contrast, only 7 percent of Democratic women are housewives, and only 28 percent of Democratic men so identify their wives.[63] To the extent that more Republican women are housewives, this becomes an identity that structures their participation as well as affecting male/female status differentials.

The more traditional roles among Republican activist women are reinforced by their lesser achieved status. Less than half of Republican women (42 percent) are employed full-time, compared to two-thirds (66 percent) of Democratic women. By contrast, a similar proportion of Republican men (82 percent) and Democratic men (85 percent) are employed full-time. Only 37 percent of Republican women are employed in professional or technical occupations, compared to at least three-fifths of Republican men (60 percent), Democratic women (62 percent), and Democratic men (70 percent). In comparison, 38 percent of Democratic men and 29 percent of Republican men in professional or technical fields are lawyers.[64]

In the pre-reform party system, women were recruited to political activism and office holding primarily outside of the party system via women's organizations. The significance of factional conflict is that the advent of true factions within the institutionalized party system in the 1970s enhances the impact of informal associations, apprenticeships, and recruitment among party activists within the parties. Therefore, the more active women are within the party, the more opportunity they have to be recruited via party-linked factions and groups—a fundamentally decentralized and "privatized" process beyond the reach of party rules. No longer is recruitment in the hands of a few party bosses. *This means that women are increasingly dependent on the extent to which they have organized clout as a movement within the party—a more difficult hurdle.*

It is this fundamental fact that explains why Republican women have achieved such power within the national party despite the lack of formal parity. Those studies that find that the parties treat announced men and women candidates about the same[65] do not address the actual recruitment process whereby party activists garner the appropriate apprenticeship for waging competitive campaigns, only how parties treat those who have *already* gained that experience.

WOMEN: OUTSIDERS OR INSIDERS TO POLITICAL POWER?

The contemporary women's movement is no longer young. An analysis of women in the 1990s must begin with the fact that, as Anne Costain points out,

The peak period has now passed. . . . Political opportunities have narrowed, consciousness has diminished, and organizations . . . are now preoccupied with just maintaining themselves.[66]

Despite the growing excitement over women's growing political power at elite levels following the media proclaimed "Year of the Woman" in 1992,[67] the organizing potential for women's groups in the 1990s is decidedly less than it was thirty years ago. Younger women today are less supportive of feminism than those who came of age during the peak period of the women's movement.[68] However, this point must be tempered by the fact that the two prior women's movements (1869–1875 and 1890–1920) developed out of organizational foundations laid by earlier leaders. The advance of women as a movement is cyclical and much remains to be done even as the mass mobilization has declined.

Therefore, women remain outsiders in the interest group policy community. Among *all* organizations with representation in Washington, women's organizations remain vastly underrepresented, comprising only about 1 or 2 percent of these groups as recently as the 1980s.[69] Women lobbyists have also greatly increased in number, but still remain underrepresented. In the late 1950s, women were only 7 percent of a sample of all Washington lobbyists.[70] By 1985, women comprised as many as 22 percent of all Washington lobbyists.[71] In a more selective sample of four economic policy domains (agriculture, energy, health, labor), women comprised only 12 percent of lobbyists in 1982–1983.[72] In recent years, groups like NOW and NWPC that formerly had in-house lobbyists, no longer lobby.

Women still remain outsiders as leaders who can lay claim to group representation of women. The decline of active movement politics means that continued advances must rely on inside access during an era when inside access in the new institutionalized parties is more difficult. The issue is *incorporation* of a group rather than mere representation of individuals within the group.[73] Put another way: Are *women and women's organizations able to choose their own leaders within male-dominated organizations and male-dominated parties?*

Women's organizations do not monopolize the definition of the gender gap and are limited in the ability to lead on gender gap issues. While most women's organizations are in agreement on issues that are usually found within the Democratic party platform—and increasingly, most national women's organizations (whether organized as a nonpartisan or as a Democratic partisan group) do work with the Democratic party—women leaders are just as prominent in both party caucuses and conventions. While the Democratic party provides more compatible policies, these policies are not defined by women's leaders. This lessens the degree to which "gender bloc" voting could develop, leaving the gender gap an ill-understood secular phenomenon that no candidate can target.

Women also remain outsiders at the leadership levels. While parity is a realized objective (or nearly so) among the activists' ranks, top party leadership posts remain rare for women. In the post-reform party system, the post of state party chair now serves as a stepping stone to elective office for both men[74] and women. This is important because a major avenue of political recruitment remains relatively closed to women. Current House members Nancy Pelosi (D-CA)(elected in 1987) and Jennifer Dunn (R-WA)(elected in 1992) served as chairs of their state parties. But women have but a fraction of the state party posts: In 1996, women served as state chairs in ten Democratic parties (20 percent of the total),[75] and in six Republican parties (10 percent of the total).[76]

The Democratic and Republican parties have each had only one woman national party chair—Jean Westwood and Mary Louise Smith, respectively. Neither Westwood or Smith gained the usual perks of office granted to former national party leaders,[77] and neither served as the elected Chair of a party out-of-power during the critical party-building years (i.e., outside of the immediate election year). *This means that women have not yet gained power as a dominant faction within either major party with enough clout to take control without endorsement or support from an established male leader.* Further, since both Westwood and Smith served during the early years of the women's movement and were associated with ascendant reform forces, their selection occurred during unique circumstances not likely to be recreated in today's conservative environment.

Congressional party leadership positions also leave women as outsiders. No woman in either party has ever served in the upper ranks of elected formal party leadership, including Speaker of the House, Majority Leader, Whip, or Caucus or Conference Chair. With the singular exception of the Congressional Black Caucus (CBC),[78] women have made few inroads in leadership of influential informal groups, like the Republican Wednesday Group or the Democratic Study Group. The Congressional Caucus for Women's Issues, organized in 1977, might have offered an alternate route to leadership for women. But it did not for several reasons. First, it was formed late—after many other congressional caucuses and such women's groups were organized in state and local legislative bodies.[79] Second, it was bipartisan and therefore ineffective during an era when congressional parties were gaining in importance. Third, the Caucus co-chairs posts were not term-limited, unlike all other congressional caucuses.[80] The Caucus has since declined further as a leadership vehicle (all caucuses were defunded by the Republican Majority in the 104th Congress).

Considerable gains have been made by the contemporary movement. Women increasingly sit at the table, but without an institutionalized women's constituency, they will never sit at the head of the table as leaders of women rather than just as women leaders. No longer outsiders, women do not yet qualify as insiders. The irony is that as women were instrumental in party reform, the new institutionalized parties that resulted are now less permeable to influence by women. Each of the three distinct women's movements has left undone issues taken up by the next active phase of the movement to develop and achieve. For the coming fourth movement, women's leaders and W&PR scholars must lay the groundwork for a movement based in the mass mobilization of women as a distinctive policy constituency represented by women leaders.

NOTES

1. Denise L. Baer and David A. Bositis, *Elite Cadres and Party Coalitions: Representing the Public in Party Politics* (Westport, CT: Greenwood Press, 1988), pp. 106–112; Denise L. Baer and David A. Bositis, *Politics and Linkage in a Democratic Society* (Westport, CT: Prentice Hall, 1993), pp. 176–182; Jo Freeman, *The Politics of Women's Liberation* (New York: Longman, 1975), pp. 44–70; Jo Freeman, "On the Origins of Social Movements," in Jo Freeman (Ed.), *Social Movements of the Sixties and Seventies* (New York: Longman, 1983), pp. 8–32; Nancy E. McGlen and Karen O'Connor, *Women's Rights: The Struggle for Equality in the 19th and 20th Century* (New York: Praeger, 1983), pp. 3–15.

2. Denise L. Baer, "Political Parties: The Missing Variable in Women and Politics Research," *Political Research Quarterly,* 46 (1993) pp. 547–576; Kay Lehman Schlozman, "Representing Women in Washington: Sisterhood and Pressure Politics," paper presented at the annual meeting of the American Political Science Association, Washington, DC, 1986.

3. Joseph R. Gusfield, "Mass Society and Extremist Politics," *American Sociological Review* 27 (1962), pp. 19–30.

4. William Kornhauser, *The Politics of Mass Society* (Glencoe, IL: The Free Press, 1959), pp. 59–65; Nelson Polsby, *Consequences of Party Reform* (New York: Oxford University Press, 1983), pp. 130–145.

5. Mancur Olson, *The Logic of Collective Action* (Cambridge, MA: Harvard University Press, 1965), pp. 160–164.

6. Joseph A. Schlesinger, "On the Theory of Party Organization." *Journal of Politics* 46 (1984) pp. 369–400.

7. John D. McCarthy and Mayer N. Zald, *The Trends of Social Movements in America: Professionalization and Resource Mobilization* (Morristown, NJ: General Learning Press, 1973).

8. Robert H. Salisbury, "An Exchange Theory of Interest Groups," *Midwest Journal of Political Science,* 13 (1969), pp. 1–32.

9. Nelson Polsby, "The News Media as an Alternative to Party in the Presidential Selection Process," in Robert M. Goldwin (Ed.), *Consequences of Party Reform* (Washington, DC: American Enterprise Institute, 1980), p. 133.

10. Jack H. Nagel, *Participation* (Englewood Cliffs, NJ: Prentice Hall, 1987) p. 127.

11. Resource mobilization, classic social movement, and political process theories differ on the emphasis they place on the primary factor driving women as a social movement. While some would reserve the resource mobilization theory as a distinctive mobilization of a group which *cannot* organize for itself by outside social service professionals or ambitious leaders seeking personal or professional gain. See Jack L. Walker, Jr., *Mobilizing Interest Groups in America: Patrons, Professions, and Social Movements* (Ann Arobr: University of Michigan Press, 1991) pp. 31–32 and Baer and Bositis *Politics and Linkage in a Democratic Society.*

12. Freeman, *The Politics of Women's Liberation;* McGlen and O'Connor, *Women's Rights: The Struggle for Equality in the 19th and 20th Century;* Baer and Bositis, *Politics and Linkage in a Democratic Society.*

13. McCarthy and Zald, *The Trends of Social Movements in America: Professionalization and Resource Mobilization;* Pamela J. Conover and Virginia Gray, *Feminism and the New Right: Conflict Over the American Family* (New York: Praeger, 1983).

14. Doug McAdam, *Political Process and the Development of Black Insurgency, 1930–1970* (Chicago: University of Chicago Press, 1982), pp. 36–59; Anne N. Costain, *Inviting Women's Rebellion: A Political Process Interpretation of the Women's Movement* (Baltimore, MD: Johns Hopkins University Press, 1992), pp. xi–xx and pp. 1–25.

15. Baer and Bositis, *Politics and Linkage in a Democratic Society,* pp. 165–170.

16. Belinda Robnett, *How Long? How Long? African-American Women in the Struggle for Civil Rights* (New York: Oxford University Press, 1997), pp. 12–35.

17. Freeman, "On the Origins of Social Movements."

18. Robnett, *How Long? How Long?,* pp. 12–35.

19. Joyce Gelb and Marian Palley, *Women and Public Policies* (Princeton: Princeton University Press, 1982), p. 25.

20. Ethel Klein, *Gender Politics: From Consciousness to Mass Politics* (Cambridge, MA: Harvard University Press, 1984) pp. 1–8; Claire Knoche Fulenwider, *Feminism in American Politics: A Study of Ideological Influence* (New York: Praeger, 1980) pp. 1–7 and pp. 127–141; Elizabeth Adell Cook, "Generations of Feminism," in Lois Lovelace Duke, *Women in Politics: Insiders or Outsiders?* (Englewood Cliffs, NJ: Prentice-Hall 1993), pp. 57–66.

21. Robnett, *How Long? How Long?*

22. Jack L. Walker, Jr., *Mobilizing Interest Groups in America: Patrons, Professions and Social Movements* (Ann Arbor: University of Michigan Press, 1991), pp. 31–32.

23. *Ibid.,* p. 188.

24. Schlozman, "Representing Women in Washington: Sisterhood and Pressure Politics."

25. John P. Heinz, Edward O. Laumann, Robert L. Nelson, and Robert H. Salisbury, *The Hollow Core: Private Interests in National Policy Making* (Cambridge, MA: Harvard University Press, 1993), pp. 222–224.

26. *Ibid.*

27. David Truman, *Governmental Process: Political Interests and Public Opinion,* 2nd Edition (New York: Alfred Knopf, 1971).

28. McGlen and O'Connor, *Women's Rights: The Struggle for Equality in the 19th and 20th Century.*

29. Karen J. Blair, *History of American Women's Voluntary Organizations, 1810–1960: A Guide to Sources* (Boston, MA: G. K. Hall, 1989), p. x.

30. Costain, *Inviting Women's Rebellion: A Political Process Interpretation of the Women's Movement,* p. 52.

31. Hugh Heclo, "Issue Networks and the Executive Establishment," in Anthony King (Ed.), *The New American Political System* (Washington, DC: American Enterprise Institute, 1978), pp. 103; Jeffrey M. Berry, "Subgovernments, Issue Networks and Political Conflict," in Richard A. Harris and Sidney M. Milkis (Eds.), *Remaking American Politics* (Boulder, CO: Westview Press, 1989), pp. 239–60.

32. Kay Lehman Schlozman, "Representing Women in Washington: Sisterhood and Pressure Politics." Paper delivered at the 1986 annual meeting of the American Political Science Association, Washington, DC, August 28–31.

33. *Ibid.*

34. *Ibid.*

35. Wendy Kaminer, *Women Volunteering: The Pleasure, Pain and Politics of Unpaid Work from 1930 to the Present* (Garden City, NY: Anchor, 1984).

36. E. Pendleton Herring, *Group Representation Before Congress* (Baltimore, MD: Johns Hopkins Press, 1941), pp. 34–36, 186.

37. One of the few studies of women's organizations in lobbying has found that many if not most of the advances in federal law occurred in advance of significant lobbying by women's organizations (Costain 1994).

38. Schlozman, "Representing Women in Washington."

39. Alan Rosenthal, *The Third House: Lobbyists and Lobbying in the States* (Washington, DC: CQ Press, 1993).

40. *Ibid.,* p. 85.

41. These included Arkansas, Colorado, Georgia, Massachusetts, Minnesota, Missouri, North Carolina, Pennsylvania, Tennessee, and Texas.

42. Even the more influential mainstream PACs limit their influence to other similar PACs (e.g., the so-called "lead PACs" like BIPAC and the AFL-CIO handicap upcoming races and make recommendations to other organizations).

43. For example, in 1996, EMILY's List produced a series of polling reports in their *Monitor,* and in 1989 published *Campaigning in a Different Voice,* which studied women's campaigns. In 1994 and 1995, NWPC published 5 research reports on how women vote, a survey of potential women candidates, and two studies of the success rates of women candidates.

44. Robert Biersak and Paul Herrnson, "Political Parties and the Year of the Woman," in Elizabeth Adell Cook, Sue Thomas, and Clyde Wilcox, (eds.), *The Year of the WOMAN: Myths and Realities* (Boulder, CO: Westview Press, 1993), pp. 161–180.

45. David J. Gillespie, *Politics at the Periphery: Third Parties in Two-Party America* (Columbia, SC: University of South Carolina Press, 1993), p. 143.

46. Rare exceptions include the Equal Rights Party which ran Belva Lockwood for president in 1884 and 1888; Alice Paul's National Women's Party (organized in 1916) which did not formally nominate candidates, and the 21st Century Party, launched by NOW in August 1992 and has yet to run candidates under its own label.

47. Cornelius P. Cotter and Bernard Hennessy, *Politics Without Power* (New York: Atherton Press, 1964).

48. *Ibid.,* p. 58.

49. Bella Abzug with Mim Kelber, *Gender Gap* (Boston, MA: Houghton Mifflin, 1984); Baer and Bositis, *Elite Cadres and Party Coalitions.*

50. The Charter was also amended in 1980 to provide equal division *for all party groups*—namely "the Democratic National Committee, the Executive Committee, Democratic state central committees, commissions, and like bodies" (Article eleven, Section 16). Interestingly, the DNC has not tried to demand compliance with this rule since an early and incomplete effort in 1981–82.

51. At the state level, some state parties have voluntarily chosen to employ equal division (e.g., the California Republican delegation in 1988).

52. Tanya Melich, *The Republican War Against Women,* 2nd Edition, (New York: Bantam Books, 1998).

53. Baer, "Political Parties: This Missing Variable."

54. Jo Freeman, "The Political Culture of the Democratic and Republican Parties," *Political Science Quarterly,* 101 (1986), pp. 327–356.

55. Denise L. Baer and Julie A. Dolan, "Intimate Connections: Political Interests and Group Activity in State and Local Parties," *American Review of Politics,* 15, (1994) pp. 257–289.

56. Jo Freeman, "Feminism vs. Family Values: Women at the 1992 Democratic and Republican Conventions," *P.S.* 26 (1993), pp. 21–28.

57. *Ibid.*

58. *Ibid.*

59. Melich, *The Republican War Against Women.*

60. Jo Freeman, "Women at the 1992 Democratic and Republican Conventions."

61. Denise Baer and Julie A. Dolan, "Choice and Change for Women in American Political Parties: Just How High is the Glass Ceiling?" Paper presented at the 1994 Midwest Political Science Association Annual Meeting in Chicago, April 14–16.

62. *Ibid.*

63. *Ibid.*

64. Interestingly, similarly low proportions of Democratic and Republican women are lawyers—6 to 11% depending upon the base used for calculation. *Ibid.*

65. Robert Biersak and Paul S. Herrnson, "Political Parties and the Year of the Woman," in Elizabeth Adell Cook, Sue Thomas and Clyde Wilcox, (Eds.), *The Year*

of the WOMAN: Myths and Realities (Boulder, CO: Westview Press, 1994), pp. 161–80; Barbara C. Burrell, "Money and Women's Candidacies for Public Office." Paper prepared for a conference on "Research on Women and American Politics: Agenda Setting for the 21st Century." Center for the American Women and Politics, Eagleton Institute of Politics, Rutgers University, April 22–24, 1994; Robert M. Darcy, Susan Welch, and Janet Clark, Women, Elections and Representation (New York: Longman, 1987).

66. Costain, Inviting Women's Rebellion, p. 141.

67. Clyde Wilcox, "Why Was 1992 the 'Year of the Woman'? Explaining Women's Gains in 1992," in Elizabeth Adell Cook, Sue Thomas and Clyde Wilcox (eds.), The Year of the WOMAN: Myths and Realities (Boulder, CO: Westview press, 1993), pp. 1–24.

68. Cook, "Generations of Feminism."

69. Schlozman, "Representing Women in Washington."

70. Lester Milbrath, The Washington Lobbyists, 2nd edition (Chicago: Rand McNally, 1961), pp. 61–67.

71. Schlozman, "Representing Women in Washington."

72. Heinz, Laumann, Nelson and Salisbury, The Hollow Core, p. 70.

73. Rufus P. Browning, Dale Rogers Marshall and David H. Tabb, "Has Political Incorporation Been Achieved? Is It Enough?" in Rufus P. Browning, Dale Rogers Marshall and David H. Tabb (Eds.), Racial Politics in American Cities (New York: Longman, 1990), pp. 212–30.

74. This has been true, for example, for Representatives Bart Gordon (D-TN) (elected in 1984) and David Price (D-NC) (elected in 1986–1994; reelected in 1996); and Senator Spencer Abraham (R-MI) (elected in 1994).

75. These include Florida, Maine, Nebraska, Nevada, New York, North Carolina, Oklahoma, Oregon, Virginia, and Wyoming.

76. Arizona, Hawaii, Maryland, Michigan, Montana, and Oklahoma.

77. After the McGovern defeat, Westwood was challenged, and was ultimately replaced by Robert Strauss as DNC Chair in 1973. Smith, while appointed to the U.S. Civil Rights Commission by Ronald Reagan 1981, was ousted two years later after controversy developed over her views on civil rights.

78. There have been three women chairs of the CBC since its founding in 1971: Maxine Waters in the 105th Congress, Cardiss Collins in the 96th Congress, and Yvonne Braithwaite Burke in the 94th Congress.

79. Irwin Gertzog, Congressional Women (New York: Praeger, 1984).

80. The long tenure of former Representatives Pat Schroeder (D-CO) (now retired), Olympia Snowe (R-ME) (later elected to the U.S. Senate) as co-chairs blocked other congressional women from this leadership post, which also limited the Women's Caucus as a stepping stone to party leadership.

FURTHER READINGS

Baer, Denise L. "Political Parties: The Missing Variable in Women and Politics Research." Political Research Quarterly, 46 (1993), pp. 547–576.

Daniels, Arlene Kaplan. Invisible Careers: Women Civic Leaders from the Volunteer World. Chicago: University of Chicago Press, 1988.

Giddings, Paula. When and Where I Enter: The Impact of Black Women on Race and Sex in America. New York: William Morrow, 1984.

Giddings, Paula. In Search of Sisterhood: Delta Sigma Theta and the Challenge of the Black Sorority Movement. New York: William Morrow, 1988.

Hooks, Bell. Ain't I a Woman?: Black Women and Feminism. Boston, MA: South End Press, 1981.

Kraditor, Aileen S. The Ideas of the Woman Suffrage Movement: 1890–1920. New York: W.W. Norton, 1971.

Malveaux, Julianne, Ed. African American Women on the Issues. Washington, DC: National Council of Negro Women, 1996.

Muncy, Robyn. Creating a Female Dominion in American Reform, 1890–1935. New York: Oxford University Press, 1994.

Pateman, Carole. Political Participation and Workplace Democracy. Cambridge, UK: Cambridge University Press, 1970.

Rosenstone, Steven J. and John Mark Hansen. Mobilization, Participation and Democracy in America. New York: Macmillan, 1993.

Schattschneider, E. E. The Semisovereign People. Hinsdale, IL: The Dryden Press, 1975 [Reissue].

Scott, Anne Firor. "Women's Voluntary Associations: From Charity to Reform." In Kathleen D. McCarthy (Ed.), Lady Bountiful Revisited: Women's Philanthropy and Power. New Brunswick, NJ: Rutgers University Press, 1990, pp. 35–54.

Shafer, Byron. Quiet Revolution: The Struggle for the Democratic Party and the Shaping of Post-Reform Politics. New York: Russell Sage, 1983.

Sommers, Christina Hoff. Who Stole Feminism? New York: Simon and Schuster, 1994.

Wells, Mildred. Unity in Diversity: The History of the General Federation of Women's Clubs. Washington, DC: General Federation of Women's Clubs, 1975.

4

WOMEN AND ELECTIONS:
THE UPHILL STRUGGLE

Even though the political role of women is changing when one examines the history of women in politics over the last two centuries, women still are stifled in their attempts to seek elective and appointive office in the United States. For example, while breaking into this new arena, women have had to deal with establishing fund raising networks, proving to the voters that women have qualifications to seek office, handling campaign strategy to deal with potential bias of women by voters (that is, "Who will take care of your children if you should win?"), the effect of fewer women in "launching roles" in the recruitment of qualified women for public office, women's limited roles in party organizations, and the effect of family responsibilities on women seeking careers in politics.

The following three articles examine women and elections at three levels of government: local/country, women in Southern legislatures in the post-World War II era, and the impact of first wives on presidential campaigns and elections. We begin with an article that explores whether 1992 (dubbed the Year of the Woman with sizable increases in the number of women serving in Congress) also marked a significant departure in the growth in the numbers of women holding elective county offices in Florida and Georgia. Charles S. Bullock, III, Susan A. MacManus, Frances E. Akins, Laura Jane Hoffman, and Adam Newmark find that, while the Year of the Woman did not accompany notable growth in Florida, women did become significantly more numerous in several Georgia offices. Rates of growth were most pronounced in rural and suburban counties, which are catching up with the greater shares of offices filled by women in urban counties.

Next, Joanne V. Hawks and Carolyn Ellis Staton provide a critique of women in Southern legislatures during the period 1946–1968. Many scholars considered the post-World War II era a quiescent time for white, middle-class American women. After a period of wartime involvement, women supposedly retreated into a more traditional lifestyle. Between 1946 and 1968, however, almost 100 women entered legislatures in the South, a particularly traditional region. Data indicate that they were predominantly women who were already involved in the public sphere in one or more ways. Even though many were serious legislators, the press emphasized their domesticity and femininity instead of their legislative achievements. The authors critique this period of transition—and reflect on the political environment for these Southern women.

Finally, Charles Tien, Regan Checchio, and Arthur H. Miller examine the impact of first wives on presidential campaigns and elections. Using new public opinion data on first ladies, the authors explore their relationship with the public and their influence on election outcomes. They show that the public still prefers a more traditional first lady, and that public evaluations of "first wives" influence public evaluations of their candidate husbands. Not only do first wives factor into their husbands' popularity, they also appear to influence vote choice just as much as public assessments of economic performance.

"Winning in My Own Back Yard": County Government, School Board Positions Steadily More Attractive to Women Candidates

Charles S. Bullock III, Susan A. MacManus, Frances E. Akins, Laura Jane Hoffman, and Adam Newmark

The "Year of the Woman," 1992, focused attention on efforts to increase the numbers of females winning national and state offices.[1] More women ran and the ranks of officeholders rose. But did this effort prompt a spurt in women running and winning "in their own back yards," that is, for local offices? If so, was the spurt sustained? Our data show that more women are winning county and school district posts but that there may also be a glass ceiling phenomenon. We find that during the 1990s, female representation levels fluctuated across offices and that women officials became more numerous in types of counties in which they had traditionally been most seriously underrepresented.

MORE ATTRACTIVE OFFICES

The 1992 Census of Governments identified more than 3000 counties and 14,422 school districts in the United States,[2] yet studies of local women officials have focused more on successes capturing municipal offices (mayor, city council)[3] than county[4] or school district[5] posts. As we approach the third millennium, there are powerful reasons to believe that counties and school districts may be increasingly attractive venues for women interested in public office.

We appreciate the help given in the preparation of this manuscript by Keith Gaddie. Reprinted by permission.

County, rather than city, elective positions are likely to be the local government of choice for many, since in recent years county governments have acquired responsibilities far beyond the traditional tasks of paving roads and law enforcement.[6] Term limits that many states have imposed on state legislative service may make county offices more attractive as launching pads for legislative slots that will come open on a fairly regular basis. Women, like some of those we profile, may hold multiple local offices, a pattern encouraged if term limits circumscribe service at the local level.

Women have become more interested in running for school board or school superintendent posts (where elected) but for different reasons. For years, more women than men have taught in the elementary and secondary grades; more recently, female teachers have made in-roads into school administrator positions. The percentage of women principals jumped from 16 percent in 1982 to 34 percent in 1993.[7] Experience in these posts has given some women more confidence in their ability to manage a school system and served as the impetus to run for office.

Not all women serving on boards of education come from the classroom. Today, more women are charged with almost singular responsibility for their children's education, often as single parents. The more interaction mothers have with the school system, the more concerned some become. Although little empirical research has been done on the topic, cursory looks at the backgrounds of school board members show that a high percentage first ran when they had school-age children.

Finally, the 1990s emphasis on grassroots governance, decentralization, and devolution has thrust local governments into the limelight. National polls consistently show that Americans give higher marks to their local officials than to state or national politicos. Citizens regard local officials as more approachable and better capable of resolving problems that matter to the average person in the street. The typical American cares more about property taxes, potholes, traffic congestion, and local schools than about U.S. policy toward Bosnia, the space program, or fast track authority for the president. More voters now realize that *local* offices impact their lives in more direct ways than do the higher profile decisions rendered in the U.S. Capitol or the state legislature.

NATIONAL TRENDS: WOMEN IN COUNTY ELECTED OFFICES[8]

Counties are often called "the forgotten governments."[9] As if to bear out that assessment, data on female county office-holding have been sparse until recently (see Table 4–1). Even now, most studies focus on women on county commissions rather than on executive or judicial posts.

County Commissions

Between 1975 and 1988, the number of women serving on county governing boards rose from 456 to 1,653, or from 3 percent of all county commission seats to

TABLE 4.1 National Trends: County, School District Offices

Elective Position		Year/% Women Office-Holders				
		1975		*1988*		*1998*
County Commission		3%		9%		24%
	1971	1975	1980	1985	1990	1993
School Superintendent*	0.6%	0.5%	1.0%	2.7%	6.0%	7.1%
		1978		1986/87	1992	1997
School Board*		25.7%		36.6%	39.9%	44.0%

*These data include both elected and appointed positions.

Sources: International City/County Management Association (1975, 1988 county commission data); National Association of Counties (1998 county commission data); American Association of School Administrators (school superintendent data); National Association of School Boards (school board data).

9 percent.[10] By the end of 1997, the percentage had risen to 24 percent, a remarkable increase in eleven years.

Women have made greatest progress in large, urban, cosmopolitan areas.[11] For example, a 1993 survey of the nation's largest counties (1990 populations over 423,000) found that the percentage of women on these boards was 27.5 percent—above the national average.[12] Within metropolitan areas, there are more women's groups (professional, social, political) that may provide critical support and more women professionals willing to run.[13]

Few studies have focused on the backgrounds of women commissioners. The first, and perhaps most, extensive study (in the 1970s) found that women commissioners were most likely to be 40 to 59 years old (68 percent), with some college (75 percent), and in professional or technical occupations (50 percent).[14] A high proportion belonged to a political organization (65 percent) while over half (53 percent) had held a political party position at one time or another.

Other Elective County Offices

A variety of other county officers are elected, such as the sheriff, probate judge, clerk of the court, some type of revenue officer (tax collector, tax commissioner, property appraiser), and the supervisor of elections, to name the most common. Because of the wide variation in the number and type of county elective posts, there are no national aggregate statistics available for these positions.

Research has shown that women are more likely to capture some of these positions than others. A 1989 study of women county officeholders in Georgia and South Carolina found that the positions most frequently held by women have a record-keeping or bookkeeping component.[15] Positions that have the greatest discretion (sheriff and solicitor) have largely been beyond the reach of women.

The 1989 study found that approximately three of every five clerks of court in these states were female. Women also held approximately half of the revenue-related elected positions in the two states and about 40 percent of the probate judgeships. On the other hand, neither state had a female sheriff in 1989 and women coroners, solicitors and surveyors were extremely rare. In summary, the administrative positions to which women are most frequently elected are ones that bear some similarity to traditional female occupations.

NATIONAL TRENDS: WOMEN IN SCHOOL DISTRICT POSITIONS

Women have been more successful at winning seats on school boards than at capturing school superintendent positions. Data reported by the National School Boards Association show that between 1978 and 1992, the percentage of women school board members jumped from 25.7 percent to 39.9 percent and by 1997, it had risen to 44 percent.

Several theories suggest why women occupy a much higher proportion of school board seats than of any other legislative body. The first involves desirability theory, which posits that because school boards have traditionally been viewed as "lower in the prestige order" than other elective positions, women are more likely to run for them.[16] More recent research, however, suggests that "increased attention to all facets of education by the media and the public at-large and the higher stakes attached to controlling educational policy and expenditures have suddenly weakened the 'lower prestige' or 'occupational segregation' explanation for increases in female school board representation."[17] The second theory is that women are more successful at winning school board seats because their service on school boards is not threatening to men since it is consistent with the traditional roles of motherhood and child-rearing.[18]

Descriptive data on school board members are collected annually by the *American School Board Journal* and the Virginia Polytechnic Institute. A longitudinal look at these data showed that between 1982 and 1992, the most dramatic increase in the proportion of women serving on school boards occurred in the South (22.3 percent to 40.2 percent).[19] Studies focusing on *elected* school boards in several southern states have concluded that women do better in larger, urban, and more cosmopolitan settings.[20]

TESTING THE THEORY IN TWO LARGE STATES

In this chapter, we look at changes in women's successes at the county and school district levels using data collected from Florida and Georgia, the nation's fourth and tenth largest states. A full descriptive analysis of women officeholders in all U.S. counties and school districts would be a massive undertaking and well beyond the scope of our efforts here. Even the National Association of Counties does not have longitudinal data on the number and percent of women commissioners, county executives, sheriffs, clerks, supervisors of election, and so on.

The wide variance in which posts are elected at the county and school district levels makes national comparisons difficult. For example, the American Association of School Administrators does not distinguish between elected and appointed school superintendents. Even within the same state, counties and school districts may vary in which positions are elective and which are appointive under their separate charters.

Florida and Georgia: Rapidly Changing Population Profiles

At first blush, there may be the temptation to discount any patterns observed in these two southern states as being "aberrant." However, the changing demographics of Florida and Georgia due to tremendous growth in the 1980s and 1990s[21] have made them much less southern. (The 1990 Census showed that two-thirds of Florida's residents were not born in the state.) In-migrants from other regions of the country and, in the case of Florida, from other countries have also changed their political profiles considerably. At the close of the twentieth century, Florida and Georgia now mirror the nation much more closely in terms of partisan identification, party competitiveness, and race/ethnicity.[22]

County and School District Offices Examined

We have collected information on a wide range of county-level offices. Each has a four-year term but not all counties choose local officers on the same cycle, with some electing officials in presidential years, a number electing officials in off-years, while still others stagger the terms of county commissioners and school board members.

All Florida (67) and Georgia (159) counties have county commissions although the number of commissioners varies considerably. In Georgia, they range from ten members down to one as thirteen counties retain the sole commissioner form of government.[23] In Florida, most commissions have five members, several have six or seven, and two counties have at least ten (Miami-Dade, 10; Jacksonville-Duval, 19).

Each Georgia county has an elected sheriff, probate judge, clerk of the court, and all but five a tax commissioner. Most Georgia counties also elect a coroner and/or a surveyor. In Florida, county-level elected "constitutional officers" are the sheriff,[24] clerk of the circuit court,[25] supervisor of elections,[26] tax collector,[27] and property appraiser.[28] (One county has an appointed tax collector or revenue officer.)

In both states, all school board members are elected. Ninety percent of Florida's school boards have five members, six counties have seven, and one (Miami-Dade) has nine. In Florida, 42 of 67 (63 percent) counties elect their school superintendent while in the remaining counties the superintendent is selected by the school board. Georgia school boards usually have five or seven members although the range is from four to nine. Since 1992 all school superintendents have been elected.[29]

SHARP OR INCREMENTAL CHANGE IN THE 1990s?

In 1992, unprecedented numbers of women ran for Congress and met with historically high levels of success. The number of women in the U.S. Senate, which had never before exceeded 3, went to 7 and California became the first state to have an all-female Senate delegation. The ranks of women in the House jumped from 29 to 48. After two more rounds of elections, women now hold 9 seats in the Senate and 51 in the House.

The percentage of women also became more numerous in state legislatures, jumping from 18.3 percent in 1991 to 20.5 percent in 1993.[30] The 2.2 percentage point increase was the largest since 1975 and has not been duplicated since. The increase following the 1992 election was the second largest since 1969 and probably the second largest ever.

But was "the Year of the Woman" phenomenon, so clearly observable at the national and state levels, fact or fiction at the local level? Is there any evidence of the same sharp increase in women holding county and school district offices after 1992?

Georgia

In Georgia, we have biennial data on the percent of females in various offices at nine specific times from 1981 to 1997 (see Table 4.2). A look at the data for all county offices indicates the presence of a "Year of the Woman" bump—a 4.7 percent rise in female officeholders. This increase was more than three times greater than the second largest, a rise of 1.5 points produced by the 1988 election.

TABLE 4.2 Percentage Female in Various Georgia County Offices

	1981	1983	1985	1987	1989	1991	1993	1995	1997
Summary of eight Local Offices	14.2	15.5	16.6	17.8	19.3	19.2	23.9	24.2	24.9
County Commission	5.1	5.5	5.2	5.1	5.8	6.3	7.8	10.0	10.4
Clerk of Court	45.9	47.8	51.6	53.5	59.1	57.2	68.6	66.7	68.6
Probate Judge	42.1	37.3	39.6	39.0	39.6	39.6	49.1	50.3	48.4
Coroner	2.6	3.2	3.8	3.8	6.5	7.2	9.3	8.8	9.9
Sheriff	0	0	0	0	0	0	.6	.6	.6
Tax Commissioner	36.7	39.2	43.7	47.5	49.1	47.7	54.5	52.8	61.7
Surveyor	1.1	1.1	2.0	1.9	2.3	2.3	1.3	1.3	2.7
School Board	12.5	15.0	17.8	21.2	22.9	21.6	27.9	27.7	28.1

The 1992 upsurge was not constant across offices. As Table 4.2 shows, the most dramatic gain came among women serving as clerk of court, which rose from 57.2 percent in 1991 to 68.6 percent two years later. The Year of the Woman also coincided with the largest increases up until that time in women serving as probate judge (+9.5 percentage points), tax collector (+6.8 points), and school board member (+6.3 points). The percentage of female coroners rose by 2.1 points after the 1992 election, which may prove significant since that constitutes an increase of more than 25 percent over the 1991 election although women increased by 2.7 points in 1989. The 1992 election also saw the first woman elected sheriff in many years.

The number of women county commissioners also increased (+1.5 points), but since that gain was outpaced in the next election, the 1992 elections do not constitute a unique rise in female officials. Surveyor is the only office in which the share of women declined following the 1992 election, and this is one of the offices that women have rarely held.

Difficulty in sustaining the 1993 momentum is evident when one looks at data after the next two elections (1995, 1997). Four of the offices that saw increases in the percentage of women in 1993 actually had fewer women in place after the next election, while probate judges, which saw a continued increase in 1995, experienced a decline in 1997 (the glass ceiling effect). In only two offices (tax commissioner and county commissioner) did women register non-negligible gains after the Year of the Woman. After a slight drop in 1995, the growth in female tax commissioners in 1997 actually outpaced the increment that accompanied the Year of the Woman. The 1.5 point increase in women county commissioners in 1993, which was the most impressive advance until that point, was eclipsed in the next election. The growth subsided in the 1996 election with the 0.4 increment being more in the range observed during the previous decade.

A distinguishing feature between offices in which women made sizable gains and those that lagged was the extent to which women already served in an office before 1992. Women made unprecedented gains in each of the four offices in which they were already relatively numerous while not scoring major breakthroughs in offices that heretofore eluded them. The Year of the Woman phenomenon had less impact on posts that have proven most elusive for women. Thus, the number of women serving as chief law enforcement officers in their county rose from zero to one but the number of female surveyors actually dropped slightly.

A final test of whether the gains registered in 1992 were unique involves the use of times series analysis. This analytic technique is appropriate when a researcher has collected data from multiple points in time (a longitudinal data set). Using this technique, the year 1992 is coded as 1 and the other years as 0 so that the Year of the Woman is a "pulse" variable. In addition to the "pulse" variable the model includes a "counter" variable in which the first election (1980) is coded zero and each successive year is coded one greater so that 1982 is coded 1, 1984 is coded 2, and so forth. Both the pulse and counter variables are entered as independent variables into a model to predict the proportion of women in the position being analyzed. If the Year of the Woman had a unique impact, the pulse variable will be statistically significant in the model. A separate model is estimated for each office in Table 4.2.

The clearest evidence that the 1992 elections made a significant difference in the numbers of women officials shows up in three models: one in which the dependent variable is the proportion of all eight county offices filled by women, another is the model for coroners, and the third is the model for clerks of court. For these three models, the pulse variable (1992) is a statistically significant predictor (at the .05 level) of female representation. The Year of the Woman had an impact on school board elections although the pulse variable just misses statistical significance at the .05 level. Overall, women became substantially more visible in Georgia courthouses at the same time they made historic gains in Congress and state legislatures.

Evidence of the uniqueness of 1992 is unimpressive for two of the three offices most often filled by women. While the sign for the pulse variable is positive, it does not turn out to be a statistically significant predictor of female representation among tax commissioners or probate judges. The Year of the Woman was not significant for tax commissioners because of the increase in female incumbents after the 1996 election, an increase that exceeds 1992. Of offices to which women gravitate, only that of clerk of the superior court experienced a major jump in 1992.

Florida

Data for Florida's county officials are more limited and to the extent that longitudinal comparisons are possible, they suggest incremental, rather than sharp, increases during the 1990s for most county posts (see Table 4.3). However, Florida

TABLE 4.3   Percent Female in Florida County, School District Offices

Elective Position	%Females in Office	
	1991	1997
COUNTY		
County Commission	19.5	20.6
Sheriff	0	0
Clerk of the Court	23.9	31.3
Tax Collector	35.8	37.3
Property Appraiser	4.5	10.4
Supervisor of Elections	76% (1988)	68.7
SCHOOL DISTRICT		
Superintendent	NA	11.6
School Board	38.1	40.7

Note: NA = not available.

Sources: 1991 data are from telephone surveys by Susan A. MacManus, 1991 data; 1997 figures were calculated from data reported in Tom Fiedler and Lance deHaven-Smith, *Almanac of Florida Politics 1998* (Dubuque, IA: Kendall/Hunt Publishing Company, 1998 and from telephone surveys by Susan A. MacManus.)

already had larger shares of women officeholders than a number of other states due to increases that occurred in the 1980s. In 1950, there were only 2 female county commissioners. The number rose to 18 by 1976, still a small percentage of all commissioners.[31] By 1991, the number had increased to 72 (19.5 percent), more than three times the rate in Georgia. The next survey data available, 1997, show that 20.6 percent of all Florida county commissioners are female—only an incremental shift. Women have also been much more likely to serve on Florida than Georgia school boards. Florida's earlier and more extensive urbanization may help account for these inter-state differences.

Another pattern similar to Georgia's is that the Florida administrative positions most frequently held by women bear some similarity to traditional female occupations. Over two-thirds of Florida's supervisors of elections are female, as are 37 percent of its tax collectors and 31 percent of its clerks of the courts. Unlike in Georgia, however, Florida women do not dominate the clerk of court and tax administration jobs. Another difference is that only one administrative position has a larger share of women than do school boards while in Georgia, women served in higher percentages in three administrative offices than on school boards. Florida has had no female sheriffs since the 1950s. All 11 women who served as sheriff between 1938 and 1959 "secured the position after their husband, the then incumbent sheriff, died in office."[32] Most served only a few months, usually just until the next election.

BIGGEST GAINS IN THE 1990s: URBAN, SUBURBAN, OR RURAL AREAS?

Prior to the Year of the Woman, women were more successful at capturing county and school district offices in large urban areas (see Tables 4.4 and 4.5.) The question we wish to examine is whether the Year of the Woman had a diffusion effect. Did the attention on women running for national and state office spark increases in the percentages of women office-holders in suburban and rural areas? Students of women in politics have long described rural and suburban areas as having more traditional patriarchal cultures inhibiting female candidacies and victories.

TABLE 4.4 Incidence of Female Officeholding by Level of Urbanization, 1991–1997 (All numbers are percentages)

	Rural		Suburban		Urban	
	1991	*1997*	*1991*	*1997*	*1991*	*1997*
Commission	4.6	8.4	11.5	13.7	23.0	18.2
School Board	19.6	25.4	28.7	34.6	39.1	37.3
All Offices	17.5	23.1	23.8	29.0	29.1	30.3
N	120		31		8	

TABLE 4.5   Incidence of Female Officeholding in Florida by Level of Urbanization
1991–1997 (All numbers are mean percentages)

Office	Rural		Suburban		Urban	
	1991	*1997*	*1991*	*1997*	*1991*	*1997*
Commission	9.7	7.3	21.7	25.7	33.7	34.6
School Board	27.3	32.7	50.5	41.7	48.7	50.5
N		35		15		19

Georgia

To test whether the degree of urbanization is associated with the incidence of women in county office, we divided counties into three groups: rural, suburban, and urban. Georgia's 8 urban counties are ones that contain the central city of a metropolitan area. The 31 suburban counties are in metropolitan areas but do not contain the central city while the 120 rural counties lie outside a metropolitan area.

Table 4.4 compares the presence of women across three types of counties in 1991, just before the Year of the Woman, and again in 1997. This analysis will shed light on whether women made more inroads in rural and suburban than in urban areas. Comparisons of the level of female representation on the two collegial bodies (county commissions and school boards) are made along with a comparison across time of a summary measure that includes the collegial bodies and the various administrative and executive offices, such as sheriff and probate judge.

The female percentage in each of the three office categories rose from 1991 to 1997 in rural and suburban counties. However, in urban counties, the percentage of women commissioners and school board members dropped, resulting in a negligible 1.2 percentage point increase across all local offices.

With the rate of increase in women elected officials falling in urban counties, the disparity between women in offices in these counties and in suburban counties largely disappeared for school boards and for all county offices, while shrinking to less than 5 percentage points for commissioners. Is it possible that there is a glass ceiling for the incidence of women holding local office that kicks in somewhere between 30 and 40 percent?

A more detailed comparison of shifts in school board representation helps us address the question posed above.[33] For example, as early as 1991, women constituted majorities on ten school boards and had half the seats on another two. Six years later, twenty-one counties had school boards dominated by women and on another three, women held half the seats. In 1991, two of the twelve counties having boards at least 50 percent female were urban, four were suburban, and half were rural. The pattern for 1997 is similar. Two of the 24 counties with boards 50 percent or more female are urban and seven are suburban. But what is perhaps most interesting is that while the distribution of counties with concentrations of women in more urbanized areas were similar in 1991 and 1997, only four of the twelve 1991 counties showed up on the 1997 list. The growing numbers of school boards dominated by women and the four counties (including Georgia's most populous) in which women outnumber men in elected office, suggest that if there is a glass ceiling it is not at a constant level in all counties.

Florida

Collegial bodies in Florida's urban counties, like those in Georgia, have higher levels of female representation than in rural counties (see Table 4.5). The fact that a much higher proportion of Floridians than Georgians live in metropolitan areas (93 percent v. 67 percent)[34] helps account for generally higher levels of female representation in Florida across all county and school district positions.

There is a much more uneven pattern to female representation gains in Florida's rural, suburban, and urban counties. Between 1991 and 1997, female representation on rural school boards went up 5.4 points, more than in either urban (+ 1.8 points) or suburban (−8.8 points) counties. But on county commissions, rural counties experienced a slight decline (−2.4 points), while female representation went up four points in suburban counties and inched up in urban counties.

The percentage of counties with a majority female county commission remained stable in urban and rural counties, but dipped 3.3 percentage points in suburban counties. The percentage of counties with majority female school boards increased in all three categories, but increased most sharply in urban counties (up 21.1 percentage points, compared to an increase of 3 points in rural counties and 1 point in suburban counties). As in Georgia, the counties with majority female commissions and school boards shifted across time. Undoubtedly, changing partisan politics and term limits in the case of county commissioners prompted some of the fluctuations.

In summary, both the Florida and Georgia data show there is volatility in the levels of female representation. There is no guarantee that once a county has a large number of women in office, the number will remain stable even six years later. In other words, gains in female representation on individual collegial boards are not necessarily permanent.

CONCLUSION

Both states examined have experienced growth in the numbers of female county officials during the 1990s. As the profiles of women officials indicate, there is no single type who wins local office. Women serving in Georgia and Florida have had a variety of political experiences and backgrounds and as women become more numerous in leadership positions, we expect that still greater variation will become apparent.

PROFILES OF WOMEN COUNTY OFFICIALS

Nancy Denson, Tax Commissioner

Nancy Denson grew up in a political environment as her father was a deputy sheriff who had to support the incumbent to retain his position. This childhood exposure coupled with unhappiness about zoning policy prompted her to take on an incumbent and become Athens' first city councilwoman. Despite having been around politicians as a child, Denson jokes that, "If I had known what you need to do to get elected, I'd have never run for office." This points up the learning curve that many local officeholders experience both in campaigning and governing.

After five years on the council, a part-time post, Denson challenged another incumbent and won election as tax commissioner, the position she has held for thirteen years. County tax commissioners in Georgia prepare the statements sent to property holders each fall that indicate the assessed value of land and buildings, the rate at which those holdings are taxed and the amount owed. The position becomes controversial when tax bills go up—as they often do. Denson has tried to reduce the pain of paying taxes by getting the homestead exemption increased from $2,000 to $10,000 for home owners.

Denson has passed her interest in politics on to her daughter, who was her initial campaign manager and now serves as village manager in Waterford, Wisconsin.

Perla Tabares Hantman, School board

Perla Hantman, a Republican, is a member of the Miami-Dade County School Board. She was first elected to the School Board in November 1996 from District 4, although she is voted upon countywide.

Perla was born in Havana, Cuba in 1941. She completed high school in Cuba, then attended the University of Havana before entering Barry University in Miami. She began her professional life as a first-grade teacher at St. George's School, her alma mater. Forced to emigrate to the United States as a young woman due to political circumstances, Ms. Tabares Hantman began a new career of public service, helping her fellow Cubans as a member of the Cuban Refugee Program. She later worked for the U.S. Department of State as a United States Foreign Service Officer at the American Embassy in Mexico City.

Perla learned many of her lessons about politics from years of service on some prominent state boards. From 1987–1990, she served on the Florida Board of Medicine. From 1990–1996 she was a member of the Florida Board of Regents—the body that governs the state university system—the first Hispanic woman in the United States to hold such a position. She has served as a Trustee of the Florida International University Foundation Board and is an Honorary Life Member of the National PTA.

She has been extremely active in numerous community service organizations and a strong advocate for the rights of women, students, and minorities. Ms. Hantman has been named the American Cancer Society's "Most Dynamic Woman in Miami-Dade County," the Stephen P. Clark Children's "Outstanding Miami-Dade County Educator," and the Cuban Women's Club's "Floridian of the Year."

Married and the mother of three children, Hantman entered school board politics after her children were grown. She still says her greatest achievement has been building a strong family and raising her children.

Edith Ingram, Probate Judge

In 1968, Edith Ingram defeated the incumbent in the Democratic primary to become the first African American probate judge in America. Ingram's election was part of the takeover of county government in hancock County, which with an almost 80 percent African American population, is one of the most heavily black counties in the United States. Ingram's election came two years after her father became the first black member of the county school board.

Ingram had returned home after earning a teaching degree at Fort Valley State College. Her motivation for seeking the post of probate judge was the unwillingness of her predecessor to appoint black poll workers. With conducting elections one of the responsibilities of the probate judge, Ingram achieved a critical position during the civil rights revolution when African Americans, long denied the vote, were often hesitant about entering a polling place filled with hostile whites.

Even now after three decades in office, Ingram finds few other African American county officials in Georgia, although she has been joined in Hancock County by a virtually all-black set of elected government leaders.

Pam Iorio, Supervisor of Elections

Pam Iorio, Democrat, is the Supervisor of Elections for Hillsborough County (Tampa), Florida. She served two terms on the Hillsborough County Commission before term limits drove her to run for another county post. While on the County Commission, she served as its Chair.

When asked why she chooses to run for county-level offices, she replies: "I believe that service at the local level can most directly affect the quality of life in a community. To register an 18-year-old to vote for the first time, to see a new library opened, a roadway widened, a flooding problem solved—these are the deeds, both large and small, that collectively result in a better community. To be even a small part of that process, to know at the end of the day your community might be better off because you served, comes a satisfaction and fulfillment that is the very essence of public service."

Iorio and her husband, Mark Woodward (a budget director for a Florida city) have two children. This two-career family is very active in community affairs—living the life they preach. Iorio is a member of Leadership Florida, Class XV, and volunteers her time in the community on the Board of Trustees of the Tampa Bay History Center, the Board of Directors of the United Way, and the Board of Directors of the Head Start Community Foundation, Inc.

Iorio was born in Waterville, Maine in 1959. Her family moved to Florida in 1963. She attended Hillsborough County Public Schools. She graduated from the American University in Washington, DC, with a bachelor's degree in Political Science.

E. Denise Lee, Commissioner

Denise Lee, Democrat, is an African American and a single parent. She was appointed to the Council Jacksonville Duval County Council (a consolidated government) in 1982, then ran for the post in 1983 and has been re-elected to the position ever since. Prior to her tenure on the Council, she was employed by the City of Jacksonville.

On the Council, she chairs the Public Health and Safety Committee and is a member of the Public Services and Rules committees. Lee served as Vice Chair of a Florida League of Cities Committee, which authored the Youth Corps Act. She also

(continued)

sponsored legislation in 1986 that made Jacksonville the first Florida city with an official holiday commemorating Dr. Martin Luther King's birthday.

Lee attended Florida A & M University and Edward Waters College. Florida A & M University has honored her with the African American Heritage Award in Government.

She is quite active in Democratic Party politics and serves on the Duval County Democratic Executive Committee.

Gwen O'Looney, Chief Executive Officer

Gwen O'Looney has been the only person to serve as the chief executive officer of the consolidated government of Clarke County, Georgia. O'Looney, who had been on the Athens city council for six years, worked to unify the college town and the surrounding county and succeeded in making Clarke County the second such consolidated government in the state.

This county government leader has proven an adept campaigner, having won two hard-fought elections. Despite a claim in some quarters that majority-vote requirements discriminate against women, O'Looney won runoffs in each of her campaigns to head up the county. Her campaigns have been relatively inexpensive affairs and she has relied on her gregarious personality to fuel a far-flung grassroots campaigns.

O'Looney came to electoral politics in 1985 after a career working in the nonprofit sector. Listed on her resume are stints with the YWCA and Boys Clubs, along with work as an independent consultant. She prepared for this career with a double undergraduate major in sociology and psychology.

In offices for which longitudinal comparisons can be made, Florida had more women on collegial bodies at the beginning of the decade and after the 1996 elections. The advantages women enjoy on Florida collegial bodies do not extend to administrative posts; yet in Georgia, women dominate the clerk of court and tax commissioner jobs and serve as probate judge in half the counties. While women officials continue to be more common in urban counties, the growth produced in the 1990s has not been in big city counties. Particularly in Georgia, the ranks of women have expanded in rural and suburban counties where, if there is a glass ceiling, greater opportunity for growth remains.

Evidence on the impact of the Year of the Woman is mixed; the strongest support is found in Georgia for clerk of court, coroner, the full set of county offices and weaker support for school board. Of three Florida offices for which we have longitudinal data, female representation increased only slightly on the collegial bodies and dropped by seven points for supervisor of elections. The absence of a Year of the Woman effect in Florida may be due to the greater presence of women before 1992 coupled with a possible glass ceiling in some, but not all, counties. The jump in percent for women in Congress and in some state legislatures after the 1992 election shares an important characteristic with three of the Georgia models where a Year of the Woman effect was found—there were not many women before 1992. Going into that election, women were less frequent in the U.S. Congress than coroners in Georgia and the proportion of female state legislators was on par with the proportion of women in county office. Contributing to the Year of the Woman phenomenon in some offices may have been the relative absence of women prior to 1992.

NOTES

1. See Elizabeth Adell Cook, Sue Thomas, and Clyde Wilcox, eds. *The Year of the Woman: Myths & Realities.* (Boulder, CO: Westview Press, 1994).

2. U.S. Department of Commerce, Bureau of the Census, *Statistical Abstract of the United States, 1996.* (Washington, DC: Government Printing Office, 1996), p. 295.

3. See for example: Denise Antolini, "Women in Local Government: An Overview," in Janet Flammang, ed., *Political Women* (Beverly Hills, CA: Sage, 1984); Susan Abrams Beck, "Rethinking Municipal Governance: Gender Distinctions on Local Councils," in Debra L. Dodson, ed., *Gender and Policymaking: Studies of Women in Office.* (New Brunswick, NJ: Center for the American Woman and Politics, Eagleton Institute of Politics, Rutgers University, 1991), pp. 103–113; Timothy Bledsoe, *Careers in City Politics: The Case for Urban Democracy* (Pittsburgh, PA: University of Pittsburgh Press, 1993); Janet K. Boles, "Advancing the Women's Agenda Within Local Legislatures: The Role of Female Elected Officials," in Debra L. Dodson, ed., *Gender and Policymaking: Studies of Women in Office* (New Brunswick, NJ: Center for the American Woman and Politics, Eagleton Institute of Politics, Rutgers University, 1991), pp. 39–48; Charles S. Bullock, III and Susan A. MacManus, "Municipal Electoral Structure and the Election of Councilwomen," *Journal of Politics* 53 (February) 1991: 75–89; Janet A. Flammang, "Filling the Party Vacuum: Women at the Grass-Roots Level in Local Politics," in Janet A. Flammang, ed., *Political Women: Current Roles in State and Local Government* (Beverly Hills, CA: Sage, 1984), pp. 87–114; Arnold Fleischman and Lana Stein, "Minority and Female Success in Municipal Runoff Elections," *Social Science Quarterly* 68 (June). 1987: 378–385; Joyce Gelb, "Seeking Equality: The Role of Activist Women in Cities," in Janet K. Boles, ed., *The Egalitarian City* (New York: Praeger, 1986), pp. 93–109; Jeanette Jennings, "Black Women Mayors: Reflections on Race and Gender," in Debra L. Dodson, ed., *Gender and Policymaking: Studies of Women in Office* (New Brunswick, NJ: Center for the American Woman and Politics, Eagleton Institute of Politics, Rutgers University, 1991), pp. 73–79; Albert Karnig and B. Oliver Walter, "Election of Women to City Councils," *Social Science Quarterly* 56 (March), 1976: 605–613; Albert K. Karnig and Susan Welch, "Sex and Ethnic Differences in Municipal Representation," *Social Science Quarterly* 60 (December) 1979: 465–481; Susan A. MacManus, "How to Get More Women in Office: The Perspectives of Local Elected Officials (Mayors and City Councilors)," *Urban Affairs Quarterly* 28 (September), 1992: 159–170; Susan A. MacManus and Charles S. Bullock III, "Women on Southern City Councils: A Decade of Change," *Journal of Political Science* 17 (Spring), 1989: 32–49; Susan A. MacManus and Charles S. Bullock III, "Electing Women to City Council: A Focus on Small cities in Florida," in Wilma Rule and Joseph F. Zimmerman, eds., *United States Electoral Systems: Their Impact on Women and Minorities* (New York: Greenwood Press, 1992), pp. 167–181; Susan A. MacManus and Charles S. Bullock III, "Women on Southern City Councils: Does Structure Matter?" in Lois Lovelace Duke, ed., *Women and Politics: Outsiders or Insiders?* (Englewood Cliffs, NJ: Prentice-Hall, 1993), pp. 107–122; Susan A. MacManus and Charles S. Bullock III, "Women and Racial/Ethnic Minorities in Mayoral and Council Positions," in International City/County Management Association, *The Municipal Year Book 1993* (Washington, DC: ICMA, 1993), pp. 70–84; Sharyne Merritt, "Winners and Losers: Sex Differences in Municipal Elections," *American Journal of Political Science,* 21 (November), 1977: 731–744; Susan Welch and Rebekah Herrick, "The Impact of At-Large Elections on the Representation of Minority Women," in Wilma Rule and Joseph F. Zimmerman, eds., *United States Electoral Systems: Their Impact on Women and Minorities* (New York: Greenwood Press, 1992), pp. 153–166; Susan Welch and Albert K. Karnig, "Correlates of Female Office-Holding in City Politics," *Journal of Politics* 41 (May), 1979: 478–491; Susan A. MacManus and Charles S. Bullock III, "Second Best? Women Mayors and Council Members: A New Test of the Desirability Thesis," in Lois Lovelace Duke, ed., *Women and Politics: Outsiders or Insiders?,* 2nd ed. (Englewood Cliffs, NJ: Prentice-Hall, 1996), pps. 590–610.

4. Susan A. MacManus and Charles S. Bullock III, "Electing Women to Local Office," in Judith A. Garber and Robyne S. Turner, eds. *Gender in Urban Research* (Thousand Oaks, CA: Sage, 1995), pp. 155–177; Charles S. Bullock III, "Women Candidates and Success at the County Level." Paper presented at the Annual Meeting of the Southern Political Science Association, Atlanta, GA, November 8–10, 1990; Victor DeSantis and Tari Renner, "Minority and Gender

Representation in American County Legislatures: The Effect of Election Systems," in Wilma Rule and Joseph F. Zimmerman, eds., *United States Electoral Systems: Their Impact on Women and Minorities* (New York: Greenwood Press, 1992), pp. 143–152; Susan A. Mac-Manus, "Representation at the Local Level in Florida: County Commissions, School Boards, and City Councils," in Susan A. MacManus, ed., *Reapportionment and Representation in Florida: A Historical Collection* (Tampa, FL: Intrabay Innovation Institute, University of South Florida, 1991), pp. 489–538; Susan A. Mac-Manus, "Politics, Partisanship, and Board Elections," in Donald C. Menzel, ed., *The American County: Frontiers of Knowledge,* Tuscaloosa, AL: University of Alabama Press, 1996. pps. 53–79.

5. Trudy Haffrom Bers, "Local Political Elites: Men and Women on Boards of Education," *Western Political Quarterly* 31 (September), 1978: 381–391; Peter J. Cistone, "The Recruitment and Socialization of School Board Members," in Peter J. Cistone, ed., *Understanding School Boards: Problems and Prospects* (Lexington, MA: Lexington Books, 1975), pp. 47–61; Kenneth Greene, "School Board Members' Responsiveness to Constituents," *Urban Education* 24 (January), 1990: 363–375; Marilyn Johnson and Kathy Stanwick, "Local Office Holding and the Community: The Case of Local School Boards," in Bernice Cummings and Victoria Schuck, eds., *Women Organizing* (Metuchen, NJ: Scarecrow Press, 1979), pp. 61–81; Rebecca Luckett, Kenneth E. Underwood, and Jimmy C. Fortune, "Men and Women Make Discernibly Different Contributions to Their Boards," *The American School Board Journal,* 174 (January), 1987: 21–41; Susan A. MacManus, "Representation at the Local Level in Florida: County Commissions, School Boards, and City Councils," in Susan A. MacManus, ed., *Reapportionment and Representation in Florida: A Historical Collection* (Tampa, FL: Intrabay Innovation Institute, University of South Florida, 1991), pp. 489–538; Susan A. MacManus and Rayme Suarez, "Female Representation on School Boards: Supportive Constituency Characteristics," *The Political Chronicle* 4 (Fall/Winter), 1992: 1–8; National School Boards Association, "School Boards: The Past Ten Years" (Alexandria, VA: National School Boards Association, 1993); Ted Robinson and Robert E. England, "Black Representation on Central City School Boards Revisited," *Social Science Quarterly* 62 (September), 1981: 495–502; Joseph Stewart, Jr., Robert E. England, and Kenneth J. Meier, "Black Representatives in Urban School Districts: From School Board to Office to Classroom," *Western Political Quarterly* 42 (June), 1989: 287–305. Leon Weaver and Judith Baum, "Proportional Representation on New York City Community School Boards," in Wilma Rule and Joseph F. Zimmerman, eds., *United States Electoral Systems: Their Impact on Women and Minorities* (New York: Greenwood Press, 1992), pp. 197–205; Frederick M. Wirt, "Social Diversity and School Board Responsiveness in Urban Schools," in Peter J. Cistone, ed., *Understanding School Boards: Problems and Prospects* (Lexington, MA: Lexington Books, 1975); pp. 189–216. Harmon L. Zeigler, M. Kent Jennings, and Wayne G. Peak, *Governing American Schools: Political Interaction in Local School Districts* (North Scituate, MA: Duxbury, 1974).

6. Donald C. Menzel, ed. *The American County: Frontiers of Knowledge* (Tuscaloosa, AL: University of Alabama Press, 1996).

7. See Xenia Montenegro, *Women and Racial Minority Representation in School Administration* (Arlington, VA: American Association of School Administrators, 1993).

8. Much of the following discussion of trends is from MacManus and Bullock, "Electing Women to Local Office."

9. Vincent Marando and Robert D. Thomas, *The Forgotten Governments: County Commissioners as Policy Makers* (Gainesville: University Presses of Florida, 1977).

10. Center for the American Woman and Politics (CAWP). "Fact Sheet: Women in Elective Office 1992" (New Brunswick, NJ: CAWP, Eagleton Institute of Politics, Rutgers University, 1992).

11. For a review of this literature, see MacManus and Bullock, "Electing Women to Local Office."

12. Susan A. MacManus, "Politics, Partisanship, and Board Elections," in Donald C. Menzel, ed., *The American County,* 1993, pps. 53–79.

13. Robert Darcy, Susan Welch, and Janet Clark, *Women, Elections, and Representation* (New York: Longman, 1987).

14. Marilyn Johnson and Susan Carroll. "Statistical Report: Profile of Women Holding Offices, 1977," in Center for the American Woman and Politics, *Women in Public Office,* 2nd ed. (Metuchen, NJ: The Scarecrow Press, 1978), pp. 1A–65A.

15. Charles S. Bullock III, "Women Candidates and Success at the County Level." Paper presented at the Annual Meeting of the Southern Political Science Association, Atlanta, GA, November 8–10, 1990.

16. Roger D. Rada, "A Public Choice Theory of School Board Member Behavior," *Educational Evaluation and Policy Analysis,* 10 (Fall), 1988: 225–236.

17. Susan A. MacManus and Rayme Suarez, "Female Representation on School Boards: Supportive Constituency Characteristics," *The Political Chronicle* 4 (Fall/Winter), 1992: 1–8.

18. Trudy Haffrom Bers, "Local Political Elites: Men and Women on Boards of Education,"*Western Political Quarterly* 31 (September), 1978: 381–391.

19. Unfortunately, the study does not distinguish between elective and appointive positions.

20. MacManus and Bullock, "Electing Women to Local Office."

21. The percent change in Georgia's population from 1980–1990 was 18.6%; from 1990–1995, 11.2%. For Florida, the percent change from 1980–1990 was 32.7%; 9.5% from 1990–95. Source: *Statistical Abstract of the United States 1996*, p. 29.

22. Susan A. MacManus, "Florida: An American Microcosm," *The World & I*, August, 1996, 36–41.

23. Georgia is the only state to have a sole commissioner local government and the number of counties using this format is declining, although the U.S. Supreme Court upheld this system in the face of a challenge brought under Section 2 of the Voting Rights Act (*Holder v. Hall*, 512 U.S. 874, 1994).

24. The sheriff is the chief law enforcement officer and executive officer of the courts. The sheriff is responsible for the execution of all process, writs, warrants, and other papers issued by the state and county courts; maintaining law and order; apprehending violators of the law; and operating the county jail.

25. The clerk is responsible for all circuit and county court records. Other duties include: serving as ex officio clerk of the Board of County Commissioners, auditor, recorder, custodian of all county funds, recording documents such as deeds, mortgages, and satisfaction of liens; disbursing of court-ordered alimony and child support payments; and issuing of marriage licenses.

26. The supervisor administers all elections, conducts voter registration, issues voter identification cards, updates voter registration lists, and handles absentee registration and voting. The supervisor is also responsible for qualifying candidates for local offices, receiving candidate campaign finance reports, maintaining election equipment, hiring and training poll workers, and keeping registration and election statistics.

27. The collector bills, collects, and disburses the annual property taxes levied by all governments in the county. The office also collects other types of taxes and issues various types of licenses.

28. The appraiser is responsible for identifying, locating, and fairly valuing real and tangible personal property within the county for ad valorem tax purposes.

29. Some counties used to elect their school superintendent. In 1992, legislation was passed making all school district superintendents appointive posts.

30. Center for the American Woman and Politics, "Fact Sheet." (New Brunswick, NJ: author, 1997).

31. Joan Carver, "Women in Florida," *Journal of Politics* 41 (August), 1979: 941–955.

32. Tom Berlinger, Director of Operational Services, Florida Sheriffs Association, faxed document sent January 27, 1998.

33. We recognize that this question cannot be fully answered here but we raise it to prompt other researchers to test the proposition with data from their counties and school districts.

34. *Statistical Abstract of the United States 1996*, p. 39.

FURTHER READINGS

Carroll, Susan J. *Women as Candidates in American Politics*, 2nd ed. Bloomington, IN: Indiana University Press, 1994.

Cohen, Cathy J., Kathleen B. Jones, and Joan C. Tronto (Eds.). *Women Transforming Politics: An Alternative Reader*. New York: New York University Press, 1997.

Darcy, R., Susan Welch, and Janet Clark. *Women, Elections, & Representation,* 2nd ed. Lincoln: University of Nebraska Press, 1994.

Gruber, Susan. *How To Win Your First Election,* 2nd ed. Boca Raton, FL: St. Lucie Press, 1997.

Seltzer, Richard A., Jody Newman, and Melissa Voorhees Leighton, *Sex as a Political Variable: Women as Candidates and Voters in U.S. Elections.* Boulder, CO: Lynne Rienner Publishers, 1997.

Witt, Linda, Karen M. Paget, and Glenna Matthews. *Running as a Woman: Gender and Power in American Politics*. New York: Macmillan, 1994.

On the Eve of Transition: Women in Southern Legislatures, 1946–1968

Joanne V. Hawks
Carolyn Ellis Staton

This study focuses on women who served in southern legislatures in the period following World War II, beginning with the election of 1946 and culminating in 1968. During this period—especially in the earlier years—middle-class women received many signals that their proper sphere encompassed home, family, and related activities. The willingness of women to enter the legislature against society's traditional expectations of them may have been a mild form of rebellion, but it was nonetheless real. To some extent the women serving between 1946 and 1968 were transitional figures, standing between an earlier group of legislative women whose mere presence made them important and a later group of more activist women. They set the stage for the political women of the 1970s and 1980s, the activist women who benefited directly or indirectly from the women's movement.

The postwar legislators followed a group of trailblazers, women who had emerged from the suffrage movement with new rights and imperatives. These earlier women had begun moving into southern legislatures in a slow but steady stream in the decade of the 1920s.[1] Most were short-term legislators; few served more than one or two terms. For the most part, they could be characterized as southern progressives, people who wanted to use state government as a means of ameliorating conditions in their communities.[2] Many of them were especially con-

Part of the research for this paper was supported by a Basic Research Grant from the National Endowment for the Humanities.

cerned with the needs of women, children, and persons with mental, physical, and moral handicaps. Even though much of their proposed legislation did not pass, they brought certain needs into focus as matters of public concern. Just as importantly, they established the right and ability of women to serve competently as state legislators.

In the Great Depression and World War II years, a slightly larger group of women were elected. By 1936 all eleven of the former Confederate states had female as well as male legislators.

After a period of wartime involvement in paid employment or volunteer services, many women in the late 1940s and early 1950s supposedly retreated into a more traditional lifestyle.[3] According to many historical and sociological treatises, the post-World War II era was a quiescent time for U.S. women, especially middle-class white women. Andrew Sinclair has called the postwar attitude New Victorianism because of its emphasis on sharp distinctions between male and female roles and proper behavior by women.[4] The prescription for the times called upon women to immerse themselves in private concerns surrounding their families and homes and to surrender activity in the public realm to the returning veterans.

In light of these generally observed patterns, it is interesting to consider the movement of women into southern legislatures in the years following the war. In a region of the nation considered to be particularly traditional, where proper sex roles had been carefully defined and political participation had long been regarded as a white male preserve, women began entering southern legislatures in increasing numbers. Although the incidence varied from a low of one person in Alabama to a high of nineteen in the neighboring state of Mississippi, a total of ninety-three women were seated in the legislatures of the eleven former Confederate states between 1946 and 1968.

HOW WOMEN ENTERED THE LEGISLATURE

One means by which women entered legislatures was what has been termed "the widow's route," a method whereby a wife succeeded to a seat formerly held by her deceased husband. During this period, twenty-four women from the eleven states in this study entered via succession. Twenty-one were widows elected or appointed to complete their husbands' legislative terms. Two were wives who ran when their husbands resigned before their terms were completed. One, Maud Isaacks, was a daughter who succeeded her father. Most were elected to office, although a few were appointed. Of the entire group of successors, only Maud Isaacks of Texas served for an extended period of time.[5] Most finished the husband's unexpired term and then retired from office. A few ran for reelection, but most of those who were reelected served only one additional term before retiring or being defeated. Their positions seemed to be regarded by many voters as a gesture of courtesy. For instance, when Governor Earl Long of Louisiana appointed Mrs. E. D. Gleason to complete her husband's term, he expressed doubt about his authority to make the appointment, but he assured his audience that she was a nice lady and had promised not to run again.[6]

Thus, approximately 25.5 percent of the total group of women serving between 1946 and 1968 were "fill-ins" for seats that were deemed to "belong" to their predecessors. But what of the remaining 74.5 percent? Who were they, and what motivated them to seek office?

Data indicated that they were predominantly women who were already involved in the public sphere in one way or another, as professional or business women, local officeholders, political party workers, or active members of women's organizations. Fifty-four had a profession or business in which they were contemporaneously engaged or which they had previously practiced. By far the largest single group—twenty women—were teachers. Nine women were attorneys. Ten were owners or co-owners of businesses. Two were farmers, two journalists, two physicians, and two government workers. The remainder held various other positions in the business world.

At least six women had held local political office before running for the legislature, most of them as city or county council members. Even more had served on local and state executive committees of their party, worked with the women's division, or helped in the campaigns of others before seeking office themselves. Of the nine Republican women elected during this period, most had been heavily involved in Republican party politics and were committed to strengthening two-party politics in their states. Several of the women were from political families.

In addition to these two groups—professional and business women and those with political activity of one kind or another—most of the other women were involved significantly in one or more women's organizations. At least two women became interested in politics as a result of their participation in Parent–Teacher Associations (PTAs). Other women were involved in Federated Women's Clubs, Business and Professional Women, the League of Women Voters, the American Association of University Women, the Farm Bureau (or related Home Demonstration groups), garden clubs, and other groups. Through these organizations they became aware of issues and gained a sense of how to accomplish things through their club work. In many cases, their legislative interests mirrored the concerns of the organized groups in which they had worked or held leadership positions. Maxine Baker of Florida (1963–1973) said, "I wanted to serve in the Legislature to try to accomplish some of the things I had been working for during my years as member and President of the Florida League of Women Voters. . . ."[7] Others, like Carolyn Frederick of South Carolina (1964–1976), a member of the American Association of University Women, had lobbied legislators in behalf of interests supported by their organizations, only to find that legislators tended to be longer on promises than on favorable action. Kathryn Stone of Virginia (1954–1966), a national vice president of the League of Women voters, admonished women to join service and civic organizations to learn skills and to move on to the political arena from there.[8] She believed that women should not confine themselves to any one civic group but should become involved in party politics.[9]

Stone's comments were closely echoed by Grace Hamilton of Georgia:

> If you are concerned about working in the legislative branch of government, you had better get some experience in working other than in the legislature on the matters that concern you. . . . If you look at people who have been effective legislators, they usually have been effective in something that was non-political, related to issues before them. I personally think that the League of Women Voters is a good training, very good training to have, but I think sometimes you need to graduate from the League.[10]

Some of the women worked primarily with one particular organization; many were active in several and held membership in many more. At least eighteen women appeared to be heavily involved in club work. A few of these could also be grouped with one or both of the categories previously discussed. In fact, women who had several connections with the public sphere seemed to be especially likely at some point to consider public office.

LEGISLATIVE ISSUES

A survey of the issues in which the female legislators expressed interest leads to rather predictable findings. Many issues came readily to their attention as mothers and community volunteers. Education was a key interest, with many in favor of strengthening the public schools, providing child care and kindergartens, and raising teachers' pay. Other concerns included health, mental health, aid to the handicapped, problems of children and youth, care of the aged, alcohol and drug abuse, consumer and environmental protection, and election reform. Rural legislators often focused on agricultural problems while those elected from urban districts concentrated their efforts on urban problems, including the need for adequate representation in the legislature and better services in their areas.

A few of the women expressed concern for the so-called women's issues of the day. Jury service for women appeared to be the most generally supported proposal. A federal equal rights amendment was a more problematic issue. The few who were outspoken supporters of equal rights for women were balanced by a similar number who opposed the concept. Many women preferred to equivocate or to avoid the issue altogether.

Middle-class, mature women, long trained to be conciliatory persons—peacemakers—often seemed reluctant to take on highly controversial issues. In a period when civil rights, women's rights, youth protest, and antiwar and antiestablishment issues were eroding society's postwar complacency, most of the southern legislative women avoided identification with any of these divisive movements. They concentrated instead on gradual elimination of community problems and provision of government services to segments of the society who had unmet needs.

Civil Rights Issues

Of all the contemporary issues, the civil rights issue struck nearest to home. Clearly, the easiest way to deal with the problems of the day was to ignore them, and it is amazing how many of the legislators during this period managed to do just that. But for others the issues had to be confronted, and women, like their male counterparts, lined up on both sides of the civil rights question.

In Virginia, in particular, women could not avoid the issue. In the aftermath of the United States Supreme Court's decision in *Brown v. Board of Education*, Virginia almost immediately sought to forestall school integration by a number of measures, some as extreme as closing whole school systems. One is struck by the courage of the moderates and liberals during this time in Virginia politics. Most of the women legislators favored compliance with the law and opposed massive resistance. The usually ultrachivalrous male-dominated assembly proved that it had its raw side; it could behave rudely toward them when they tried to keep the Virginia schools open.[11]

Although most of the Virginia women delegates supported compliance, such was not the case everywhere. In Mississippi, for instance, just the opposite situation prevailed. The segregation establishment reigned supreme. As Jack Bass and Walter DeVries have stated,

> These were not ordinary times. The executive director of the Citizens Council . . . had begun preparing [Governor] Barnett's speeches. Citizens Council members were named to the State Sovereignty Commission, the official state segregation committee and a propaganda arm of the Citizens Council. . . . The Citizens Council claimed 80,000 members in the state. . . .[12]

The female legislators seemed to oppose attempts to integrate the schools as stridently as most of the male delegates. At least two women were part of the segregaton establishment, the White Citizens Council and the State Sovereignty Commission. Occasionally, a legislator who proclaimed that she was a segregationist would, however, champion the rights of others. A notable example occurred in Mississippi when Senator Orene Farese argued vehemently against passage of a bill that would have eliminated the property tax exemption for churches that used their facilities on an integrated basis.[13]

Because of these stands, Farese felt compelled in her next senatorial campaign to proclaim staunchly her segregationist views. In her campaign literature she maintained that her purpose in opposing the removal of tax exemptions for integrated churches was to keep segregation intact and preserve tax exemptions for churches.[14] Perhaps, like many other politicians of the day, Farese maintained a certain façade of segregation that did not always conform to other ideas that she held.

By 1967, the civil rights movement had begun to have a significant impact on portions of the South, legislative resistance notwithstanding. Because of the movement and *Baker v. Carr*, the United States Supreme Court decision that mandated "one man, one vote," legislative redistricting was required. One result of redistricting was to increase voting strength in urban areas—places where there might be a large population of Blacks. It is not surprising, then, that in 1967 three Black women in the South entered their state legislatures: Barbara Jordan of Texas, Dorothy Brown of Tennessee, and Grace Hamilton of Georgia. The civil rights movement, by changing both the social climate and the laws, gave them opportunities for political office that they had previously lacked.

PRESS IMAGES

The times were changing, but the public's image of women in politics was not changing at the same pace. This was best indicated by contemporary press coverage, which emphasized femininity. The renewed emphasis on femininity may have been a result of a convert campaign to force women out of the traditionally male jobs that many had held during the war years. It may also have been an effort to glamorize the homemaker so that she, as consumer, might aid in the improving economy. Moreover, as the country recovered from the difficult war period, some people longed to return to a less confused, less complicated world.

In the postwar period, press treatment of female legislators primarily covered personal rather than political aspects of their lives. Articles on these women tended to focus on specific female roles. A prevalent form of feature article was the portrait of the lady legislator as family member, either wife, mother, homemaker, or grandmother. Orene Farese, who served along with her husband in the Mississippi legislature during the 1950s, was consistently spotlighted in her domestic roles. The following excerpt from a feature story about her is characteristic of the coverage she received:

> Mrs. Farese, though public minded, is a very domestic and home loving person. . . .
> She is a capable housekeeper and a wonderful homemaker. With the help of a full time maid she cares for their four bedroom, two bathroom home. . . .[15]

Farese discussed her cooking, sewing, and home decorating abilities.[16] The article proceeded to describe her to the readers:

> When you see this lovely senator-elect . . . she will most likely be wearing a stunning tailored dress or suit in one of her favorite colors, the blues, aqua or yellow in medium tone.[17]

The newspaper account contained virtually no mention of Farese's legislative and political interests. She was treated primarily as a housewife who went to the legislature.

A somewhat more muted example of the lady legislator as homemaker occurred with Grace Rodenbough of North Carolina. Although Rodenbough, who served in the legislature from 1953 to 1966, was a woman of considerable stature, the press on several different occasions focused on her fondness for her antebellum home.[18] Rodenbough might play a significant role in the legislature, but she was still seen as the southern aristocratic lady.

Rodenbough's fellow North Carolinian, Mary Faye Brumby, was subjected to similar treatment. When Brumby went to the legislature, she took her eleven-year-old son along. Her child care arrangements were highlighted in the press.[19] By taking her son with her to the capital rather than leaving him at home, she avoided being seen as the abandoning mother who pursued her own interests.

Although some accounts were brief in their mention of the legislators' children, comment was usually made. For instance, Iris Blitch of Georgia, who later went to Congress, was simply described as devoted to her children.[20]

The epitome of the legislator-as-wife stories involves Lillian Neblett Scott of Tennessee. Scott, always referred to as Mrs. Scott, was being routinely interviewed by a reporter from the Nashville *Banner* when her husband entered the room. The spotlight of the article immediately became *Mr.* Scott and his stories of marital harmony: "Somebody asked me how I made out with Lillian so active in politics, I just tole 'em that I still have my hot biscuits 365 days a year."[21] Scott continued his antics: "As the couple exchanged a look of deep affection and long understanding, 'I've never had to spank her.'"[22] Throughout the article, Lillian Scott is seen not as the incredibly active woman she was, but as a wife who knew her place. As is true of all of these features, there is an implicit statement that these women legislators were all right because, first and foremost, their principal roles were as wives and mothers.

Domesticity, Femininity, and Beauty

When they were viewed primarily as domestic creatures, female legislators lost their "strangeness." The same principle applied if the emphasis was on their femininity rather than their domesticity. Moreover, by their being pigeonholed as either a domestic or a feminine type, these women, working in a nontraditional forum, threatened no one. For example, articles such as the following 1954 feature in the *Jackson Daily News* made the idea of female legislators more palatable to the public:

> The universal feminine preoccupation with weddings, babies, and bringing up children reaches strongly into the Mississippi legislature. . . .
> Far from being a sentimental interest, confined to cooing over the newlywedded or recently born, theirs is an informed concern aimed at changes in the laws. . . .[23]

The article went on to provide an apologia for these women:

> . . . it is, perhaps, to the state's advantage to number among its lawmakers those whose beliefs are conditioned by the previous primary experience of wife, mother, and frequently teacher.[24]

Since the days of Scarlett O'Hara, femininity and gracious beauty have been part of the mystique of southern womanhood. The beauty queen has been a consistent southern type, one with which southern society felt comfortable. In many instances, by emphasizing pulchritude, southern society was able to accept women on its own terms, and by doing so, could avoid accepting them as serious legislators. Ruth Williams of South Carolina was linked with "the rustle of silk and the faint scent of perfume" and managed "somehow, to cling to her femininity and still compete with men. . . ."[25]

Mary Shadow of Tennessee, like Williams, was young and single when she entered the legislature. Shadow, however, married during her legislative stint. News of the marriage was widely featured. Shadow, a college teacher, was quoted as saying that in her forthcoming marriage she wanted to cook, keep house, and raise a large family. One article was captioned "Miss Shadow Plans to Keep House, Raise Family."[26] Upon Shadow's marriage it was assumed that she would become a traditional housewife.

Because of the emphasis on femininity, there was a never-ending discussion of physical appearance. To some extent this focus suggested to the public that, after all, these female legislators were more female than legislator. Blitch was often described as "an attractive brunette"[27] with "a perfect size 12 figure."[28] Shadow was described as a "pretty, charming legislator";[29] and Betty Jane Long of Mississippi was depicted as "lovely."[30] Mississippi's Mary Lou Godbold and Orene Farese "add[ed] much to the lustre of [the legislature]. And the men [were] all in favor of the ladies."[31]

Kathryn Stone of Virginia, in particular, was the topic of much publicity about her physical appearance. The press found it noteworthy that one Virginia senator said to another upon seeing Stone presiding in the senate," 'Have you ever seen a lovelier creature presiding from the chair of the president of the Senate?' whereupon the other senator then responded, 'I yield to the lovely creature. . . .'"[32] On another occasion, the press claimed that "Mrs. Stone . . . is the prettiest thing to hit the General Assembly since Sarong Siren Dorothy Lamour dropped in at the Capitol one day a few years ago. Besides looks . . . she has brains."[33] Another feature described her clothing and home decor.[34] No matter how significant these women were as legislators and politicians, their colleagues and the press trivialized them in many instances by focusing on irrelevant considerations.

As if to stereotype them even further, the press played up the emotional nature of these women. Blitch is depicted as on the verge of tears when an adverse amendment was added to her original bill.[35] When Orene Farese opposed taxing churches that did not practice segregation, she was choked with tearful emotion.[36] Although the situation may have warranted tears, no comment is made in the coverage of the heated senate debate about the emotions of her male colleagues.

How Women Legislators Were Treated

During this period when there was an emphasis on the female attributes of the women politicians, several of them were singled out for what was then considered a chivalrous tribute. When only one woman served in a legislative body, she might be entitled sweetheart of the senate or house or some honorific variation. Blitch was named queen of the Georgia General Assembly,[37] Collins was elected sweetheart of the Alabama house,[38] and Berta Lee White of Mississippi was designated sweetheart of the senate.[39] In Collins's case, this meant that the house members might on occasion be addressed as "Mister Speaker, gentlemen of the House and sweetheart of the House."[40] In some instances the chivalry was rather overdone.

For example, in making seat assignments at the beginning of the session, the speaker of the Georgia house announced that "the Lady of the House [Blitch] and the physically handicapped will get their first choice of seats."[41] Sometimes the chivalry became quite time-consuming. When the speaker of the Virginia house instructed Kathryn Stone, the sole female legislator, to make a communiqué to the senate, Stone was accompanied by the entire Virginia house delegation to the senate chambers. The newspaper described the event as a "chivalry safari."[42]

When the female legislators occasionally acted out of character from the role in which the public had cast them, it was definitely noted. Thus, when the women were perceived as politicians rather than as ladies, they were likened to males. For instance, the newspaper remarked that "Mrs. Blitch had to fight like a man."[43] Perhaps it was her ability to fight like a man that won Blitch the sobriquet "the wench from Clinch."[44] In Mississippi when three women were elected to the legislature in the same term, it was noted that they could fare well against strong male opposition.[45] The tenacity of Clara Collins was editorialized as "stubbornness, albeit justified."[46] It was with Martha Evans of North Carolina that the press had a field day. Practically every story about Evans mentioned that she was a redhead with a temper to match. For instance, in one article she was referred to as "a red-headed pepperpot."[47] Evans, who was held in a certain amount of esteem for her work, was excused by the press from stepping out of the traditional role of southern womanhood:

> In Raleigh she'll stand on her own small feet. . . . That's because she's always felt she is the equal of the male politician. And she's "been around," as the saying goes among office seekers.[48]

The women were newsworthy. When they conformed to the stereotyped version of southern womanhood, they were viewed as nonthreatening. When they did not conform to the standard image, the media nevertheless tried to force them into that mold. When they were not susceptible to being molded, they were excused, as was Evans, on the basis of being an "outsider." They were less novel than the women who preceded them in the earlier decades, but the public was still not quite comfortable with them and still regarded them as curiosities.

SUMMARY

Female legislators of the post-World War II era tried to live up to societal expectations of them as women while they practiced their political skills. For some, the substance of lawmaking was secondary to their role as lady legislator. For most, the legislature was not a stepping stone to greater political heights but it was a forum for public service. By their service these women set the stage for the more activist, more ambitious, and more political women who succeeded them.

NOTES

1. Anne Firor Scott, *The Southern Lady: From Pedestal to Politics, 1830–1930* (Chicago: University of Chicago Press, 1970), pp. 186–211.

2. Dewey W. Grantham, *Southern Progressivism: The Reconciliation of Progress and Tradition* (Knoxville: University of Tennessee Press, 1983), pp. 410–422.

3. William H. Chafe, *The American Woman, Her Changing Social, Economic, and Political Roles, 1920–1970* (New York: Oxford University Press, 1972), pp. 176–178, 199–212. Chafe's bibliography includes many other treatises on the subject.

4. Andrew Sinclair, *The Emancipation of the American Woman* (New York: Harper & Row, 1965), pp. 354–367.

5. Mary Beth Rogers (Ed.), *Texas Women: A Celebration of History* (Austin: Texas Foundation for Women's Resources, 1981), p. 100.

6. Baton Rouge *State-Times,* August 5, 1959, Sec. A, p. 11.

7. Questionnaire completed by Maxine Baker, January 21, 1986, in possession of the authors.

8. Richmond *Times-Dispatch,* March 23, 1954.

9. *Ibid.*

10. Taped interview with Grace Hamilton, conducted by the authors, August 8, 1984, in possession of the authors.

11. See, e.g., Richmond *Times-Dispatch,* February 23, 1958.

12. Jack Bass and Walter DeVries, *The Transformation of Southern Politics: Social Change and Political Consequence since 1945* (New York: Basic Books, 1976), p. 196.

13. Unnamed, undated clipping in possession of the authors.

14. *The Southern Advocate,* July 23, 1959.

15. *Jackson Advertiser—TV News,* September 15, 1955, p. 6.

16. *Ibid.*

17. *Ibid.*

18. *The News and the Observer* (Raleigh), January 17, 1963, p. 8.

19. Unnamed clipping, February 14, 1965.

20. *Atlanta Constitution,* October 6, 1949, p. 26.

21. Nashville *Banner,* January 10, 1957, p. 8.

22. *Ibid.*

23. *Jackson Daily News,* January 24, 1954.

24. *Ibid.*

25. *The State* (Columbia), November 6, 1964, Sec. A, p. 1.

26. *The Nashville Tennessean,* November 19, 1950, Society Section, p. 1.

27. *Atlanta Constitution,* October 6, 1949, p. 27.

28. *Ibid.,* October 24, 1954.

29. *The Nashville Tennessean,* January 7, 1948, p. 8.

30. *Jackson Daily News,* August 29, 1955, p. 2.

31. Unnamed clipping, January 12, 1958.

32. Richmond *Times-Dispatch,* March 15, 1954, p. 4.

33. *Ibid.,* January 13, 1954, p. 16.

34. *Ibid.,* November 11, 1953.

35. *Atlanta Constitution,* January 27, 1953, p. 1.

36. Jackson *Clarion-Ledger,* March 27, 1956, p. 1.

37. *Atlanta Constitution,* October 6, 1949, p. 26.

38. *Advertiser-Journal* (Montgomery), Alabama Sunday Magazine, August 16, 1965, p. 12.

39. Questionnaire completed by Berta Lee White, in possession of the authors.

40. *Advertiser-Journal* (Montgomery), Alabama Sunday Magazine, August 15, 1965, p. 12.

41. *Atlanta Constitution,* January 11, 1949, p. 1.

42. Richmond *News Leader,* March 9, 1954.

43. *Atlanta Constitution,* October 24, 1954.

44. Ibid., December 28, 1970.

45. *Jackson Daily News,* August 29, 1955, p. 2.

46. *Montgomery Advertiser,* August 13, 1967.

47. *Durham Morning Herald,* November 18, 1962, Sec. C, p. 9.

48. *Ibid.*

FURTHER READINGS

Baxter, Sandra, and Marjorie Lansing. *Women and Politics.* Rev. ed. Ann Arbor: University of Michigan Press, 1983.

Carroll, Susan J. *Women as Candidates in American Politics.* Bloomington: Indiana University Press, 1985.

Chafe, William H. *Paradox of Change: American Women in the Twentieth Century.* New York: Oxford University Press, 1991.

Diamond, Irene. *Sex Roles in the State House.* New Haven, CT: Yale University Press, 1977.

Dodson, Debra L., and Susan J. Carroll. *Reshaping the Agenda: Women in State Legislatures.* New Brunswick, NJ: Eagleton Institute of Politics, Rutgers, State University of New Jersey, 1991.

Fowlkes, Diane. *White Political Women: Paths from Privilege to Empowerment.* Knoxville: University of Tennessee Press, 1992.

Githens, Marianne, and Jewel L. Prestage (Eds.). *A Portrait of Marginality: The Political Behavior of the American Woman.* New York: David McKay, 1977.

Jewel, Malcolm Edwin, and Marcia Lynn Whicker. "The Feminization of Leadership in State Legislatures." *Quarterly of American Political Science Association,* 26 (4) (December 1993), pp. 705–712.

Johnson, Louise B. *Women of the Louisiana Legislature.* Farmerville, LA: Greenbay Publishing, 1986.

Jones, Leslie Ellen. "The Relationship between Home Styles and Legislative Styles and Its Implication for Representation: A Comparison of Women and Men in a Southern State Legislature." Ph.D. diss., Georgia State University, 1990.

Kirkpatrick, Jeane J. *Political Woman.* New York: Basic Books, 1974.

Klein, Ethel. *Gender Politics.* Cambridge, MA: Harvard University Press, 1984.

Mandel, Ruth B. *In the Running: The New Woman Candidate.* Boston: Beacon Press, 1981.

Nelson, Albert J. *Emerging Influentials in State Legislatures: Women, Blacks, and Hispanics.* New York: Praeger, 1991.

Thomas, Sue. *How Women Legislate.* New York: Oxford University Press, 1994.

The Impact of First Wives on Presidential Campaigns and Elections

CHARLES TIEN, REGAN CHECCHIO, AND ARTHUR H. MILLER

INTRODUCTION

The attention that Hillary Rodham Clinton, Barbara Bush, and Elizabeth Dole received in the 1992 and 1996 presidential elections has motivated research that looks at the influence of the candidates' spouses, or "First Wives," on campaigns and elections. There is disagreement in this research over the importance of first wives in election outcomes.[1] In this chapter, we explore the relationship between first ladies and the public, and argue that first wives have had an independent effect on presidential elections and should continue to be a force in presidential elections in the future. We argue with and support public opinion data that each candidate's popularity is influenced by the popularity of the candidate's spouse, and that evaluations of both the candidates and their spouses are independent determinants of vote choice.

The presence of first wives in presidential campaigns has been noticeable for years. There is nothing new to candidates using their spouses as campaign surrogates. Voters seem to enjoy meeting the spouses and it essentially allows the candi-

A previous version of this paper was presented at the 1997 Annual American Political Science Association Meetings, Washington, DC. We thank Chia-Hsing Lu for technical assistance; John McIver, Andrew J. Polsky, and Kenneth S. Sherrill for helpful comments; and all the telephone interviewers and interviewing staff at the University of Iowa Social Science Institute who participated in the Institute's 1996 Heartland Poll. All errors remain our own. Reprinted by permission.

dates to be at two places at one time. In the 1992 campaign Elizabeth Dole apologized to Iowans for "accepting the pinch-hitter" role when her husband Bob Dole was stuck in Washington handling Senate business. No one appeared to mind, and Bob Dole said that "somebody wrote me a note and said, 'Send her to Iowa and you stay home.'"[2] Campaigns often employ first wives because spouses potentially benefit their husbands by appealing to undecided voters, to potential party defectors, and possibly across party lines. Their enhanced appeal may stem from first wives possibly being either less polarizing politically or more acceptable to different wings of the party. For example, the Johnson campaign in 1964 sent Lady Bird Johnson to campaign in the south, where voters opposed Johnson's stand on civil rights, hoping that she would soften the opposition towards the administration. Lady Bird Johnson "enticed local politicos to join her (although many of them would have balked at being photographed with the president). Because they could pass off the appearance at Lady Bird's side as simple chivalry, one after another recalcitrant Democrat climbed aboard [her campaign train]. Some of the holdouts sent their wives."[3]

Hillary Clinton went beyond the surrogate role in 1992 when she appeared with then-candidate Bill Clinton on *60 Minutes* to address infidelity charges against him. Her prominence and importance in the 1992 and 1996 campaigns have coincided with the trend of increased campaigning by spouses in recent years. The 1996 Republican primary campaign highlights this trend. Leslee Alexander appeared in campaign commercials for her husband Lamar Alexander; Wendy Gramm attempted to rollerskate across Maryland; and Char Lugar held rallies in New Hampshire bowling allies.[4] This development of more active first wives in campaigns, combined with Hillary Clinton's prominent role in the White House during her husband's first term and Elizabeth Dole's impressive career in government led *Time* to write that it is first ladies who are really the ones that are just a heartbeat away.[5] Understanding the impact of first wives on presidential campaigns and elections, however, requires an understanding of first ladies and their relationships to the American public. This is because first wives in presidential campaigns are often sitting first ladies, since incumbent presidents rarely step down before they are constitutionally required. Table 4.6 lists the Democratic and Republican first wives in each presidential election since 1948 and highlights the number of first ladies. Nine of the last thirteen elections have included an incumbent first lady. We begin our analyses of the impact of first wives on presidential elections by first looking at first ladies and the public.

PUBLIC ROLE OF THE FIRST LADY

While at least a few of the duties of the President of the United States are outlined in the Constitution, the duties of their spouses are not formalized at all. As the office of the first lady has gradually become institutionalized, the role and functions of the office differ greatly according to the woman filling the position and the time

TABLE 4.6   Spouses in Presidential Campaigns

Year	Democratic Candidate's Spouse	Republican Candidate's Spouse
1996	Hillary Clinton*	Elizabeth Dole
1992	Hillary Clinton	Barbara Bush*
1988	Kitty Dukakis	Barbara Bush
1984	Joan Mondale	Nancy Reagan*
1980	Rosalynn Carter*	Nancy Reagan
1976	Rosalynn Carter	Betty Ford*
1972	Eleanor McGovern	Pat Nixon*
1968	Muriel Humphrey	Pat Nixon
1964	Lady Bird Johnson*	Margaret Goldwater
1960	Jackie Kennedy	Pat Nixon
1956	—**	Mamie Eisenhower*
1952	—**	Mamie Eisenhower
1948	Bess Truman*	Frances Dewey

*Incumbent first Lady.

**Adlai Stevenson was divorced.

in which she lived. Not only does the first lady's own personality influence her public role, but public expectations and perceptions can greatly enlarge or constrict the functions of the office. This tension between public and private life exists for every first lady. As Margaret Truman[6] asks pointedly, "How much can a first lady be herself—pursuing and enjoying what comes naturally to her—and remain this public person who has suddenly become a symbol for American womanhood in all its myriad guises?" Not only do these women have to find a comfortable role for themselves, they have to fulfill public expectations.

Truman[7] argues that the American public has always expected and wanted the first lady to be a traditional wife and mother first. Any other interests, especially political ones, have usually been greeted with criticism. For example, when her husband took office in 1797, Abigail Adams was criticized for "playing politics" and being partisan.[8] Nearly two hundred years later, Rosalynn Carter expressed interest in being her husband's public partner when her husband became president in 1977. However, during Carter's re-election campaign she declared that "she never told Jimmy what to do, he was a strong person and he made up his own mind."[9] This may have been a strategy to appeal to the public that may not have wanted a public partner for the president. This strategy may have been appropriate as our data, which we turn to next, suggest that the public still prefers a more traditional first lady over an activist first lady.

Gutin[10] argues convincingly that modern first ladies can be divided into three major types—based upon the role they sought for themselves and the time in which they lived (see Table 4.7). The first group includes the first ladies who treated the office largely as "ceremonial," such as Florence Harding, Grace

TABLE 4.7   A Typology of First Ladies*

Ceremonial	Spokeswoman	Political Surrogate and Independent Advocate
Florence Harding	Lou Hoover	Eleanor Roosevelt
Grace Coolidge	Jacqueline Kennedy	Lady Bird Johnson
Bess Truman	Pat Nixon	Betty Ford
Mamie Eisenhower	Nancy Reagan	Rosalynn Carter
Nancy Reagan	Barbara Bush	Nancy Reagan
	Hillary Clinton	Hillary Clinton

*This typology is based on Gutin's work. We essentially agree with her classification of first ladies that ended with Nancy Reagan. We added Barbara Bush and Hillary Clinton to the table.
Source: Gutin, Myra G. 1989. *The President's Partner.* New York: Greenwood Press.

Coolidge, Bess Truman, and Mamie Eisenhower. We characterize this group as "hostess." The second group is the "spokeswoman." The women in this category (Lou Hoover, Jacqueline Kennedy, Pat Nixon) tended to adopt specific projects upon which to spend their time working.[11] The final group is the "political surrogates and independent advocates," including Eleanor Roosevelt, Lady Bird Johnson, Betty Ford, and Rosalynn Carter.[12] This final category could be characterized more loosely as first lady as "politico."

First Lady as Hostess

First ladies have historically played the role of White House hostess, which was established by Martha Washington. Caroli[13] writes that Martha Washington "gave no evidence of playing anything other than the hostess role" and describes how Martha spent a considerable amount of time returning visits of ladies who left calling cards, as was customary at the time; she also regularly held "drawing room" parties; and she entertained dinner guests that the president invited home without warning. More recent examples of first ladies as hostesses include Jacqueline Kennedy's working to furnish the White House with antiques, and Nancy Reagan's raising money to refurbish the White House.

Gutin[14] argues that the first ladies who adopted the more traditional, ceremonial role had limited public contact and gave little thought about taking ideas to the country through the media. Arguably, Florence Harding and Grace Coolidge were simply following the nineteenth-century norm (although Abigail Adams, Sarah Polk, and Helen Taft had broken from tradition). Bess Truman and Mamie Eisenhower, however, consciously rejected the example of Eleanor Roosevelt and adopted the more accepted, traditional role.

Data from the 1996 Iowa Social Science Institute (ISSI) Heartland Poll[15] suggest that Americans still prefer a more traditional approach to the job of first lady. The traditional first lady generally plays a supportive role—looks after the health and well-being of the president, focuses on being a good White House hostess, makes occasional goodwill visits to other countries, and most important, keeps out of policy decisions (or at least downplays her influence in them). When asked whether it is fully acceptable, somewhat acceptable, or not at all acceptable for first ladies to serve their country by making goodwill visits to other countries as representatives of the United States, 90 percent of respondents from the national ISSI poll answered that it was fully or somewhat acceptable, yet 48 percent said it was unacceptable for the first lady to influence decisions the president makes on policy issues.

First Lady as Advocate

Although taking a strong political role does not generate popularity for most first ladies, many modern first ladies have embraced certain social issues. These projects could be characterized as "feminine" and publicly acceptable, with little impact on foreign and domestic policy.[16] Despite this limited role, the "advocate" is a more public figure than the "hostess." With this publicity comes more controversy than is associated with the hostess role.

Pat Nixon provides an interesting example demonstrating the tensions inherent in adopting this role. Living in Washington during the 1950s, Pat Nixon watched Bess Truman and Mamie Eisenhower play the hostess role of first lady, but she recognized that Jackie Kennedy and Lady Bird Johnson had generated public interest by being more activist first ladies. Although uncomfortable with a more public role, Pat Nixon resolved to change with the times. "Showing that she understood the shift, Pat Nixon tried to attach herself to a cause that would complement her husband's agenda for social welfare measures."[17] She was unsuccessful. First, she tried adult education and job training, then volunteerism, then "Right to Read," then the environment, and finally "improvement of the quality of life." Her inability to find a single cause with which she could be identified was a source of criticism for some observers.[18] Although she modeled her behavior after them, she did not have the skill of Kennedy or Johnson in her public appearances.

While Betty Ford, Rosalynn Carter, and Nancy Reagan further enlarged the public role of first lady (as politico), Barbara Bush returned to the advocate role. She felt that the projects a first lady adopted "should help the most people possible, but not cost the government more money and not be controversial."[19] Barbara Bush had a clear conception of the limits she placed upon herself as first lady.

First Lady as Politico

Some first ladies have not shied away from being involved in making government policy, either openly or discreetly. Examples of first ladies influencing policy are well-known. Rosalynn Carter sat in on cabinet meetings and testified before the Senate for increased appropriations for mental health programs. Betty Ford campaigned for the Equal Rights Amendment, and admitted that she often used "pillow talk" to persuade the president of her point of view. Nancy Reagan held considerable influence in personnel and scheduling decisions in the Reagan administration. And Hillary Clinton directed the President's most ambitious policy project in his first term—health-care reform.

This type of modern first lady actively exploits the power of the White House to promote her causes in the media. In contrast to many first ladies, Eleanor Roosevelt was unique in the scope and variety of issues she embraced. She also differed from the advocacy model because she never hesitated to use all the communication outlets provided by the White House whenever she was trying to build public support for a policy. She, unlike previous first ladies—even those with friendly relationships with the press—gave overwhelming access to the Washington media. She established her own press corps of women, and the practice of Monday morning press conferences became firmly established.[20] Yet, although Eleanor Roosevelt was seen as a proponent of many issues, she never got publicly involved in the legislative process. Betty Ford, in fact, was the first first lady to publicly support a piece of legislation, the Equal Rights Amendment.[21] Her efforts, while not successful, expanded the perceived role of a first lady, and she was invited on to *60 Minutes* to express her political views.

Despite the long record of first ladies influencing government policy, either directly and openly or behind the scenes, public opinion for the most part regards helping make government policy as inappropriate behavior for a first lady. When asked about the appropriateness of first ladies helping to make government decisions, 54 percent of the 1996 respondents in the ISSI survey answered not at all acceptable. Even when abroad, for first ladies to engage in anything beyond goodwill diplomacy would apparently be regarded as inappropriate. The data indicate that trips like Rosalynn Carter's to Central and South America in 1977 (controversial at the time), described as substantive where policy decisions were made, would still be frowned upon today. Despite candidate Bill Clinton's proclamation in 1992 that voters would be getting two-for-one if he won the election, the aversion to first ladies influencing or making national policy may be because the public does not see them as elected government officials who are held accountable by the public. When health-care reform meetings chaired by Hillary Clinton were closed to the public on the grounds that the commission was comprised of government officials, doctors claimed that Hillary did not deserve such status—that she was not a government official. The doctors filed a suit claiming that the public (and thus doctors) should be allowed to attend the meetings.[22]

Some first ladies, however, have managed to avoid public censure and still retain a political role for themselves. Unlike many of the other nineteenth century first ladies, Sarah Polk (1845–1849) did not seek anonymity and maintained a close working relationship with her husband. Self-confident and well-educated for her time, Sarah Polk usually rejected traditional domesticity in order to spend time with her husband—a choice endorsed by her husband. After the first year of James Polk's congressional term, she followed him to Washington. "James reportedly supported his wife's view of her role, because she explained that she had volunteered to stay in Tennessee and take care of the house but that he had chided her, 'Why? If it burns down, we can live without it.'"[23] Instead of concentrating on domestic and social chores, Sarah Polk spent her early time in Washington cultivating friend-ships with strong, opinionated women—some of whom were political enemies of James Polk. She had strong political interests, but unlike Abigail Adams was not criticized for her views. As Caroli[24] points out, though, "[t]he affability that cloaked Sarah Polk's remarkably political interest satisfied observers who expected women to be merely pretty, social creatures. Had she broken the rules and dressed eccen-trically or entertained inappropriately, she might have been criticized, but she did not." Obviously, it has not only been the modern first ladies who are placed under a microscope for their actions.

Changing social forces, though, have made it more publicly acceptable for first ladies to have their own careers. For example, Marilyn Quayle, Ruth Harkin, Jeanne Simon, and Hillary Clinton were accomplished lawyers in their own rights before their husbands ran for president; Wendy Gramm had served as head of the Commodity Futures Trading Commission. Elizabeth Dole had held two cabinet posts, and was head of the American Red Cross; her pronouncements that she would resume her job as head of the American Red Cross if her husband won did not create an uproar. Though no first lady has yet to be employed while her hus-band served as president, public opinion is not averse to the idea of it. Only 15 percent of ISSI respondents answered that it is not at all acceptable for a first lady to have a career outside of government.[25] As expected, younger respondents were more accepting of first ladies having their own careers outside of government. Sev-enty-one percent of respondents 35 years old or younger said that it was fully ac-ceptable for first lady to have an outside career, while only 58 percent of respon-dents over 35 thought the same.

So, what does the public consider as appropriate roles for a first lady to play? In short, it is acceptable to be a full-time wife and mother, hostess of the White House, supporter of feel-good causes, and goodwill ambassador to the world who stays out of policy—like Barbara Bush. It is also acceptable to have an outside ca-reer—as Elizabeth Dole said she would have had. What seems unacceptable is to exert an inordinate amount of influence on national policy decisions, whether it is chairing the Health Care Reform Committee as Hillary Clinton did or whispering into the president's ear at night to influence his decisions as Betty Ford did.

Many influential and outwardly active first ladies, however, have been quite popular—most notably Eleanor Roosevelt. The next section will show that first ladies who do not fit the mold of the public's ideal first lady can remain popular because first ladies are evaluated on multiple dimensions, as other determinants can overcome the negative reactions to their participation in policy making.

CANDIDATES AND SPOUSES: THE DETERMINANTS OF AFFECT

We hypothesize that first wives have become a force in electoral politics. They are strong determinants of affect towards their candidate husbands, and more impor-tant, they influence voter decisions as well. This contrasts from previous work on first wives. Mughan and Burden[26] write that first wives, in general, do not play a large role in electoral politics: There is no

> guarantee that future aspirants to the position, even if they model themselves after Hillary Clinton, will be players of the same magnitude in the presidential election game. She was an electoral asset to her husband less because she commanded the affection of liberated progressives and more because she was the pole around which their collected affect for a particular individual of passing importance in American politics, Anita Hill. Had it not been for the Clarence Thomas confirmation hearings and the controversy they generated, Hillary Clinton would likely not have been the electoral force she was in the 1992 contest.

Simonton[27] also argues that the first lady has a limited influence on the success of the president. He uses a 1982 reputational survey of first ladies by historians, among other data sources, to argue that "[t]he President's reputation contributes directly to the first lady's reputation, but in the absence of any reciprocal influence." He goes on to write that, "[m]oreover, we found no evidence that the women may influence the President's standing in more subtle ways."[28]

To empirically test the supposition that first wives have no impact on their husbands' fortunes, we examine the impact of first wives on presidential elections by looking at how they influence affect towards the candidates and the individual vote choice. We believe that to accurately capture the effect of first wives on candidate affect, the reciprocal causal link between attitudes toward the husband and wife must be considered. Mughan's and Burden's[29] evaluations of the sources of affect for the candidates and their spouses did not incorporate the two-way causality that we believe exists between the husband's and the wife's popularity. Simonton[30] does not find evidence of reciprocal causality between each spouse's rating. He, however, used stepwise regression in the first ladies' reputation model and does not use any instrumental variables for the endogenous independent variables in his models.[31] Thus, respectively, variables that enter the first-ladies' model do so purely for statistical reasons rather than theoretical, and the ordinary least squares (OLS) estimates of effect of the first ladies' reputation on each president's greatness measure calculated by Simonton are biased.

We believe that two stage least squares (2SLS) must be used to accurately capture the reciprocal influence of candidates and spouses. Evaluations of first wives are strongly influenced by evaluations of their candidate husbands, and vice versa. The causal arrow for evaluating spouses is two-way, primarily because candidates and wives since the 1960s are often considered intense partnerships. Troy[32] supports this conclusion by suggesting that in the 1960s, the image of the First Couple became prevalent in the media:

> The revolutions in feminism, media technology, and journalism that would build the American obsession with its First Couple had begun. Nearly one-third of America's married women was in the work force. Television was in 87 percent of all homes. Print reporters were trying to justify their jobs by jazzing up stories and bringing their

readers behind the scenes. Democrats marketed 'Jack and Jackie' aggressively to these anxious journalists and a willing public. As America moved toward a public-relations presidency, the First Lady became the president's most important PR flack.

What people think about a husband often colors their perception of the wife, and vice versa. This has implications for the proper statistical analysis necessary to test for the relative size of the impact that perceptions of each spouse has on evaluations of the other spouse. When there is reciprocal causality in a model, estimation methods must take into consideration the correlation between the error term and the endogenous regressors.[33] Two stage least squares (2SLS), the method we employ, corrects for this correlation, and produces more accurate estimates of the effect one spouse's ratings has on the other spouse's ratings.

Our simultaneous equations model examines the thermometer ratings of each presidential candidate and his spouse for 1996.[34] We include the standard demographic control variables and build the instruments for each husband's and each wife's feeling thermometer by separately regressing each person's feeling thermometer on all the exogenous variables in the system.[35] Each equation in the system meets the requirement of being identified—the number of exogenous variables in the model excluded from each equation is greater than or equal to the number of endogenous independent variables included in each equation. The predicted values from the first stage regressions were then used in the second stage regressions to determine the unbiased influence of each person's affect on his or her spouse's rating.

Table 4.8 presents the results of the second stage regressions where missing data were deleted pairwise from the 1996 ISSI Heartland Poll. The first column under each person lists the unstandardized regression coefficients and their t-scores. The reported coefficients indicate how much each candidate's or each wife's thermometer score would change, on average, with a one unit change in the independent variable. The second column reports the beta weights to compare the relative importance of the independent variables to each other. The table provides a further look at how first ladies are evaluated by the public, and a first look at how first wives influence campaigns. We start with a discussion on the evaluations of first ladies and then look at how they influence public attitudes towards the candidates.

Looking at Hillary Clinton's and Elizabeth Dole's results in Table 4.8 provides two insights into the public's evaluations of first wives. First, how well first wives are perceived to fit into the roles that the public considers as appropriate for first ladies to play influences affect towards them. The more the public believes that the spouse has spent (or will spend) time doing the type of things "a first lady should do," the more warmly they feel towards her (see Table 4.8). For Hillary Clinton, respondents who believed that she spent her time as first ladies should rated her 17 points higher, on average, than respondents who believed that she did not spend her time as first ladies should. In the previous section we found that the public still prefers a traditional first lady—goodwill visits to foreign countries and hosting

TABLE 4.8   Determinants of Affect toward Candidates and Their Spouses, 1996.

	Bill		Hillary		Bob		Elizabeth	
Age	.02	.01	.01	.00	.02	.01	.18**	.12
	(.27)		(.16)		(.20)		(1.95)	
Education	−.39	−.04	.47	.05	−.01	−.00	.55	.07
	(−.94)		(1.21)		(−.03)		(1.15)	
Income	.19	.02	.10	.01	−.37	−.04	.95**	.11
	(.44)		(.24)		(−.04)		(1.79)	
Party ID	−3.24*	−.24	−1.59**	−.12	2.57*	.22	1.31	.12
	(−4.05)		(−1.68)		(3.04)		(1.23)	
Race	−3.68	−.04	3.39	.04	.05	.00	−3.00	−.04
	(−.98)		(.91)		(.01)		(−.66)	
Sex	−.27	−.00	−.08	.00	−4.04***	−.08	2.23	.05
	(−.12)		(−.04)		(−1.45)		(.77)	
Economy	−2.61	−.07			1.93	.06		
	(−1.55)				(1.00)			
Traits	−6.63*	−.43	−2.80**	−.19	−5.38*	−.36	−4.92*	−.31
	(-6.17)		(−2.07)		(−3.83)		(−3.61)	
Spouse	.23**	.18	.38*	.31	.33***	.19	.25***	.18
	(1.94)		(2.59)		(1.63)		(1.50)	
Spend Time as should			−8.50*	−.21			−4.92**	−.13
			(−4.01)				(−2.02)	
Policy influence	2.18	.04	7.32*	.14	2.84	.07	3.09	.08
	(.82)		(3.07)		(1.17)		(1.26)	
Constant	90.45*		35.47**				31.74**	
	(7.23)		(1.77)				(1.99)	
R-squared	.64		.67		.48		.40	
N	251		250		197		193	

Figure in parentheses are t-scores.

*statistical significance at .01 one-tail.

**statistical significance at .05 one-tail.

***statistical significance at .10 one-tail.

White House functions are considered appropriate behavior, whereas wielding too much influence in the White House is considered inappropriate behavior. Table 4.8 suggests that first wives are partially judged by how well they are perceived to meet these public preferences.

The perception of Hillary Clinton's influence in the White House also had a strong impact on her public ratings. Respondents who believed that Hillary Clinton had too much influence felt colder towards her than respondents who felt otherwise. This may be because the Clintons widely publicized Hillary's influence on policy decisions during the first term. President Clinton often publicly acknowledged Hillary's influence and appeared to have encouraged it. He brought recognition to her work on health care during his State of the Union address—his most public act. Even after health-care reform failed, he said in a nationally televised interview that he was considering having Hillary coordinate welfare reform implementation. The public's reaction, however, was that it saw Hillary Clinton as having too much influence on White House policy making. Forty-eight percent of respondents answered that Hillary has too much influence when asked whether Hillary has too much, too little, or just about the right amount of influence on President Clinton's decisions. This is more than double the percent of respondents who thought that Elizabeth Dole would have too much influence if she were to become First Lady (20 percent). Hillary Clinton's amount of influence was considered inappropriate behavior for first ladies, and her ratings suffered for it. Hillary received ratings that were 7.32 points lower among those who think she had too much influence in the White House relative to those who think she had the right amount of influence.

The second insight about first wives suggested by Table 4.8 is that they are somewhat detached from partisan politics. For Hillary Clinton the party identification variable is borderline significant at .05 one-tail, and the beta weight reveals that party identification is less important than her personal traits (moral and caring), how well she fits the public's "ideal" First Lady, and affect towards Bill Clinton (see Table 4.8). For Elizabeth Dole the party variable is statistically insignificant. The respondents' party identification had no bearing on their affect towards her. Her perceived personal traits and how well people believe she would fit the "ideal" first lady are both stronger predictors of affect towards her than is party identification.

A third result from Table 4.8 that is worth noting is somewhat counterintuitive. The results suggest that first wives may be as equally as important to their husbands' ratings as husbands are to their wives' ratings. One would expect that given the prominence of presidents and presidential aspirants that their effect on their wives' public popularity would have a much stronger impact than their wives would have on their popularity. However, the results in Table 4.8 suggest otherwise. The results indicate that first wives can develop individual personalities separate from their candidate husbands and can be judged on their own merits outside of their husbands' long shadows. The Clintons appear close to being integrally connected—the beta weight from Hillary's analysis shows that her husband's popularity is the most important predictor of her popularity. Public ratings of Bob and Elizabeth Dole, however, are more independent of each other. Affect towards Bob Dole is barely significant at the .10 one-tail level in explaining affect towards Elizabeth Dole. This result probably stems from the fact that Elizabeth Dole was as much a player in national politics in her own right as was her husband. She served in cabinet positions in two separate administrations, and has probably sat in on more cabinet meetings than Bill Clinton, Hillary Clinton, and Bob Dole combined.[36] She is one of the most accomplished first wives ever, and her independent career and successes gave her her own identity in the 1996 campaign. The importance of first wives in the candidates ratings is further supported by a recent Gallup Poll that found Hillary Clinton as America's most admired woman.[37] Voters have strong opinions about the first wives, and their opinions seem to influence how voters evaluate the candidates.

Juxtaposed to the husbands' influence on the wives' ratings in Table 4.8 are the wives' influence towards the husband's ratings. The results provide evidence that first wives do influence affect towards their husbands, and vice versa—the spouse variable is significant in all four equations. Public affect towards Bill Clinton and Bob Dole are both influenced by affect towards their wives. Only party identification and personal traits (moral and caring) were stronger predictors of affect towards both candidates (see beta weights). It appears that presidential candidates are judged by the people they marry. The next section suggests that campaign strategists are aware of this influence that the first wife can have on the popularity of her husband and take it into account during the general election campaign.

FIRST LADIES AND CAMPAIGNS

While it seems very conventional for a presidential candidate's wife to campaign for her husband, this phenomenon is very recent and still potentially risky. Eleanor Roosevelt, known for breaking taboos with the office of the first lady, felt it "unseemly" for a wife to campaign for her husband. As recently as 1976, Rosalynn Carter encountered much hostility for her strong campaigning for Jimmy Carter. Like Mrs. Roosevelt, some thought it "unseemly"; others felt she should be spending her time taking care of her ten-year-old daughter.[38] Rosalynn traveled separately, made speeches, and even graduated to having her own private plane to keep up with her hectic schedule. Her press secretary noted in a *New York Times* article that Rosalynn had traveled to 34 states in a mere fourteen months to campaign for her husband.[39] Caroli[40] writes that Rosalynn's fourteen months on the road before her husband won the 1976 nomination was "a campaign unequaled among politicians' wives." Still, Carter had her campaigning predecessors.

Sarah Polk was the first wife of a presidential candidate to contrast herself with the wife of her husband's challenger. Also, unlike many nineteenth- and even twentieth-century women, Sarah Polk was unafraid to express her rejection of domesticity publicly. She reportedly boasted that "If I get to the White House, I expect to live on $25,000 a year and I will neither keep house nor make butter."[41] Her remark about not keeping house or making butter was intended to contrast her with Henry Clay's wife, perceived as a model of domesticity.[42] When one considers the fervor that greeted Hillary Clinton's cookie-baking comment in 1992, it is conceivable that a modern first lady is treated more harshly during the contemporary campaign season than during the nineteenth century. For example, although not as vigorous a campaigner as Carter, an impromptu remark made by Jackie Kennedy during the 1960 campaign season all but eliminated her public role. Following Kennedy into the ladies room, Nan Robertson of the *New York Times* quoted her as saying she "couldn't spend as much on clothes as Pat Nixon did unless I wore sable underwear." It was the last interview she was allowed to give until after the election.

A recent article in *Newsweek*[43] reporting on the 1996 British elections, wondered why when voting women are increasingly important to election outcomes, the two candidates' wives kept such a low profile. The answer was characterized as a "Hillary problem"—referring to the difficulties Hillary Rodham Clinton encountered in 1992 by seeming to belittle stay-at-home mothers and her subsequent low profile in 1996.

Figure 4.1 demonstrates the remarkable difference between Hillary Clinton's visibility in the 1992 and 1996 elections in the major news markets. In all the major

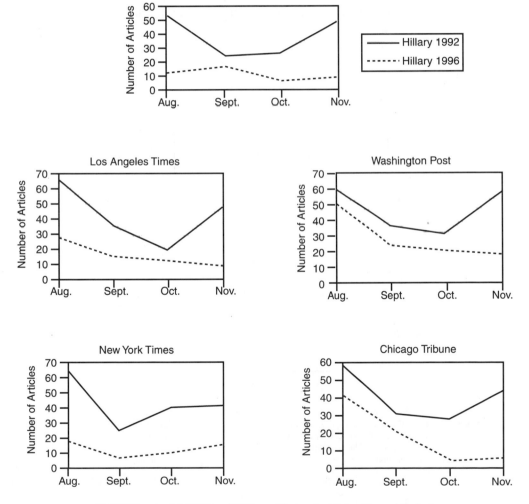

FIGURE 4.1   Visibility of Hillary Clinton in Major News Markets

news markets, Hillary Clinton was much less visible in 1996 than in 1992.[44] In fact, with the exception of the *Chicago Tribune* and the *Washington Post* in 1996, her average visibility per month in the general election was the lowest seen by any first wife in 1992 *or* 1996.[45] For example, the average number of stories written about Hillary Clinton per month in the *Los Angeles Times* during the 1992 general election was 42.5; in 1996, it was only 17.

Comparing coverage in the major and minor news markets also demonstrates that Hillary Clinton was not spending any more time in the minor news markets in 1996 than she was in 1992, so that does not explain her relative absence in the major news markets (Figure 4.2). Further comparing news markets by region (see Figure 4.3), it is apparent that although Hillary Clinton had some increased visibility in the South, the 1996 levels were lower in general across all regions of the country.

Of course, Hillary Clinton's relative lower visibility in 1996 may have been caused by her familiarity to both the press and public.[46] Still, many hypothesize that the Clinton campaign kept her role to a minimum because she was perceived

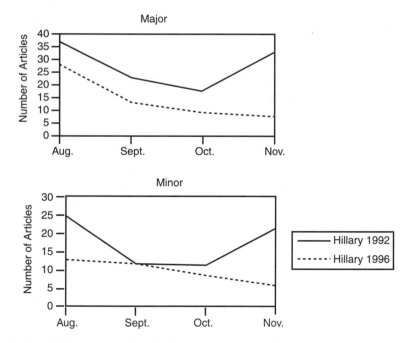

Note: Data is compiled from averages of number of articles mentioning First Ladies.

Major papers: Wall Street Journal, USA Today, New York Times, Los Angeles Times, Washington Post, Chicago Tribune, Houston Chronicle, Boston Globe, Chicago Sun-Times, Minneapolis Star Tribune

Minor Papers: St. Petersburg Times, St. Louis Post-Dispatch, Atlanta Constitution, Orlando Sentinel, Seattle Times, Hartford Courant, Washington Times, Lewiston Morning Tribune, Christian Science Monitor

FIGURE 4.2   Visibility of Hillary Clinton in Major and Minor News Markets (*Source:* Leading U.S. Daily Newspapers, 1995. World Almanac Book of Facts, 1997)

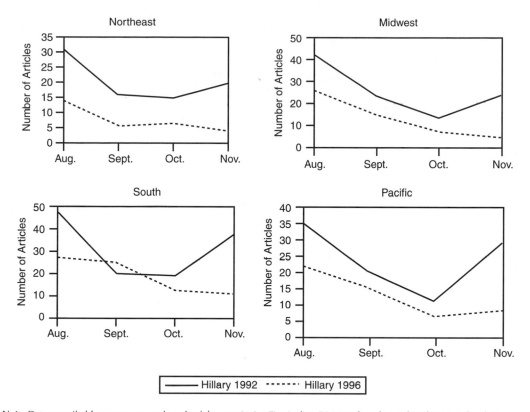

FIGURE 4.3 Visibility of Hillary Clinton in Regional News Markets

Note: Data compiled from average number of articles mentioning First Ladies. Divisions based on Political-Geographical Divisions, Bureau of Census, 1991.
Northeast: Boston Globe, Hartford Courant, Lewiston Morning Tribune, New York Times
Midwest: Chicago Sun-Times, Chicago Tribune, Minneapolis Star Tribune, St. Louis Post-Dispatch
South: Atlanta Journal, Houston Chronicle, Orlando Sentinel Times, St. Petersburg Times, Washington Post
Pacific: Los Angeles Times, San Francisco Chronicle, Seattle Times, Washington Times

as a liability to the President's reelection efforts. As noted earlier, if this was the case, Hillary Clinton was not the first political spouse to be forced off the campaign trail.

FIRST WIVES AND THE VOTE

The previous sections suggested that first wives have a strong impact on affect towards their candidate husbands, and presidential campaigns are structured to emphasize (or de-emphasize) this. How voters feel towards Hillary Clinton can influence how they feel towards Bill Clinton. Attitudes towards Elizabeth Dole also colored voters' perceptions of Bob Dole. But did this impact on the popularity of these candidates also influence the vote decision? Mughan and Burden[47] argue that Hillary Clinton was able to influence the vote in 1992, but only because of the negative feelings the Clarence Thomas–Anita Hill hearings produced within the electorate. Did Hillary Clinton impact the vote in 1996, despite the Clinton strategists' attempt to hide her from the press during the campaign? If she did, and if Elizabeth Dole was also a factor in the 1996 vote, then it would suggest that first wives are becoming a new force in American politics that demands greater attention from serious political analysts.

Table 4.9 shows the result of our analysis of the 1996 presidential vote. The dependent variable is the respondent's vote (0 = Clinton, .5 = Perot, 1 = Dole), and missing data were deleted pairwise. The unstandardized coefficients and beta

TABLE 4.9   First Wives and the 1996 Vote

	Unstandardized Coefficient	Beta Weight
Age	.001** (1.84)	.04
Education	.002 (.63)	.01
Income	.008** (1.97)	.05
Party ID	.06* (8.74)	.29
Race	.02 (.65)	.02
Sex	.00 (.02)	.001
Economy	.04* (2.69)	.06
Bill Clinton Thermometer	−.006* (−9.83)	−.39
Bob Dole Thermometer	.004* (7.33)	.24
Hillary Clinton Thermometer	−.001*** (1.58)	−.06
Elizabeth Dole Thermometer	.001** (1.77)	.05
R-squared	.76	
N	618	

Figures in parentheses are t-scores.

*statistical significance at .01 one-tail.

**statistical significance at .05 one-tail.

***statistical significance at .10 one-tail.

weights are both reported. The former indicates the increased likelihood of voting for Dole, and the latter indicates the comparative importance of the variable compared to the others in the model. As the table indicates, there are many significant determinants of the 1996 vote. Party identification and affect towards both candidates are all statistically significant at the .01, one-tail level. Their beta weights indicate that they are the three most important determinants of the vote. This is no surprise. According to the beta weights, however, the next group of important explanatory variables includes affect towards Hillary Clinton and Elizabeth Dole and evaluations of the economy within the last year. First wives appear to influence vote choice just as much as public assessments of economic performance, even in a year where one campaign tried to keep the spouse out of the press.

The 1996 vote analysis shows that first wives played an important role in the election. First wives, especially Hillary Clinton, had a strong impact on the public popularity of their husbands, and they also influenced the vote (on the same magnitude that evaluations of the economy did). The results suggest that first wives are important players in national politics. Even in a year that wasn't dubbed "The Year of the Woman," they seemed to make a difference.

CONCLUSION

A new era of influence for first wives is upon us. In the 1992 campaign the first wives were an issue because of their contrasts. Each of the first wives represented the generation in which they grew up. Barbara Bush was the domestic, support your husband, "June Cleaver" type of first lady, while Hillary Rodham Clinton typified the progressive, feminist, working mom. In 1996 debates centered around who would be the "better" full partner as first lady. Hillary Clinton, who had been quite policy-oriented during her husband's first term, was being "challenged" by Elizabeth Dole. In comparison on paper, Elizabeth Dole made Hillary look like the stay-at-home mom. Elizabeth put off marriage and motherhood to pursue her career in Washington, DC. Hillary, on the other hand, had given up her Washington career, followed her husband to Arkansas, and became a working mom. In both Democratic and Republican campaigns in 1996, the first wives influenced their husbands' public popularity, and factored into the vote as strongly as did public perceptions of economic performance.

Previous work by Simonton[48] and biographers who suggest that there is no spillover effect from evaluations of first ladies onto their husbands is clearly called into question by our data above. This is due to the differences in research approaches. We did not go to "experts" for their evaluations of first ladies and presidents, nor did we use biographers' interpretations of their characteristics. We went to the public to get its evaluations of first wives. From the point of view of the voting public, there is a strong connection between presidential candidates and their spouses. The popularity of first wives does influence the popularity of the presidential candidates.

While we find a connection between spouses, this does not mean that other explanatory factors of the popularity of the first lady are overshadowed by the president's presence. We find that the public does have an "ideal" first lady, and that first ladies are partially judged by how well they match the public's ideal. The public's ideal first lady is still a traditional one—White House hostess, goodwill ambassador to the world, supportive of her husband, and more important, one who stays out of White House policy decisions. This certainly benefited Barbara Bush, but can be a negative for women who do not want to play this role. Women, like Hillary Clinton in 1992, who are independent and career oriented are potentially a political liability to their husbands. The Clintons apparently realized this, as Hillary's role in the 1996 campaign was downplayed, and she appears to have transformed herself as first lady as well. She has done a fair amount of international travel during the second term instead of chairing important policy committees. And her schedule for the fall of 1997 included far away destinations such as Panama, Brazil, Venezuela, Argentina, Kazakstan, Turkmenistan, Uzbekistan, Kyrgz, and even Siberia[49] rather than Capitol Hill.

Past analyses of elections have paid scant attention to the influence of first wives. Mughan and Burden[50] analyzed the 1992 election and concluded that Hillary's influence in 1992 was an aberration due to the Anita Hill–Clarence Thomas hearings, which sparked the mobilization of women that generated the "Year of the Woman." Our finding that first wives mattered again in 1996 disputes Mughan's and Burden's[51] first conclusion and agrees with their revised one.[52] First wives are a new force in presidential elections that analysts must grant attention to in the future.

NOTES

1. See for example Anthony Mughan and Barry C. Burden, "Hillary Clinton and the President's Reelection," (Presented at the American Political Science Association meeting, Washington, DC, 1997); Anthony Mughan and Barry C. Burden, "The Candidates' Wives" in *Democracy's Feast,* edited by Herbert F. Weisberg (New Jersey: Chatham House Publishers, Inc., 1995); Dean Keith Simonton, "Presidents' Wives and First Ladies: On Achieving Eminence Within a Traditional Gender Role," *Sex Roles,* 35, 1996, pp. 309–336.

2. Paul Tolme, "GOP candidates call on wives to help campaign," *The Daily Iowan,* 6 (February 1996), section A, 8A.

3. Betty Boyd Caroli, *First Ladies,* Expanded Edition (New York: Oxford University Press, 1995), p. 237.

4. Paul Tolme, "GOP candidates call on wives to help campaign," *The Daily Iowan,* 6 February 1996, section A, 8A.

5. Nancy Gibbs and Michael Duffy, "Just Heartbeats Away," *Time,* July 1, 1996, p. 24.

6. Margaret Truman, *First Ladies* (New York: Random House, 1995), p. 10.

7. Ibid., pp. 3–15.

8. Betty Boyd Caroli, *First Ladies,* Expanded Edition (New York: Oxford University Press, 1995), p. 8.

9. Margaret Truman, *First Ladies* (New York: Random House, 1995), p. 14.

10. Myra G. Gutin, *The President's Partner* (New York: Greenwood Press, 1989), pp. 2–3.

11. Barbara Bush could be added to this category due to her work with literacy programs.

12. Hillary Rodham Clinton could be added to this category for her work in shaping White House policy, most notably the preparation of a universal health-care bill. Gutin places Nancy Reagan in all three categories—evolving from ceremonial during the first term to independent advocate by the end of her husband's second term.

13. Betty Boyd Caroli, *First Ladies,* Expanded Edition (New York: Oxford University Press, 1995), pp. 6–8.

14. Myra G. Gutin, *The President's Partner* (New York: Greenwood Press, 1989), p. 276.

15. The data used in our analyses are made available by the University of Iowa Social Science Institute. The

data for the Heartland Poll "1996", were originally collected under the overall direction of Arthur H. Miller. The Poll included a national sample of 1,000 respondents. Interviews were conducted between October 9 and October 30 for the pre-election survey ($N = 632$). And between November 5 and November 23 for the post-election survey (remainder of sample).

16. Myra G. Gutin, *The President's Partner* (New York: Greenwood Press, 1989), p. 176.

17. Betty Boyd Caroli, *First Ladies,* Expanded Edition (New York: Oxford University Press, 1995), p. 244.

18. Betty Boyd Caroli, *First Ladies,* Expanded Edition (New York: Oxford University Press, 1995), p. 244.

19. As quoted in Gil Troy, *Affairs of State* (New York: The Free Press, 1997), p. 320.

20. Ishbel Ross, *Ladies of the Press* (New York: Harper and Brothers, 1936), pp. 317–318.

21. Margaret Truman, *First Ladies* (New York: Random House, 1995), p. 135.

22. A district federal court ruled that Hillary was not a government official, and required that the meetings be opened to the public. However, a federal appeals court overruled the lower court's decision and said that "a long standing tradition of public service by First Ladies" existed (as quoted in Caroli 1995, p. 304).

23. Betty Boyd Caroli, *First Ladies,* Expanded Edition (New York: Oxford University Press, 1995), p, 62.

24. Betty Boyd Caroli, *First Ladies,* Expanded Edition (New York: Oxford University Press, 1995), p. 62.

25. It is reasonable to speculate, however, that should a First Lady be employed outside of government that conflict of interest questions would arise. For example, if a First Lady were a practicing physician, it would be easy for critics to claim that any favorable policy taken by the administration towards the medical profession would benefit the president's spouse.

26. Anthony Mughan and Barry C. Burden, "The Candidates' Wives" in *Democracy's Feast,* edited by Herbert F. Weisberg (New Jersey: Chatham House Publishers, Inc., 1995), p. 149.

27. Dean Keith Simonton, "Presidents' Wives and First Ladies: On Achieving Eminence Within a Traditional Gender Role," *Sex Roles,* 35, 1996, pp. 309–336.

28. Ibid, p. 330.

29. Anthony Mughan and Barry C. Burden, "The Candidates' Wives" in *Democracy's Feast,* edited by Herbert F. Weisberg (New Jersey: Chatham House Publishers, Inc., 1995), p. 144.

30. Dean Keith Simonton, "Presidents' Wives and First Ladies: On Achieving Eminence Within a Traditional Gender Role," *Sex Roles,* 35, 1996, pp. 309–336.

31. An instrumental variable is uncorrelated with the error term, and is a proxy for the independent variable that is correlated with the error term. In the footnote 34, notice that in Eq. 1 the First Wife's popularity is partially a function of the error term (e). Therefore, in Eq. 2 where the First Wife's popularity is now an independent variable, it is an independent variable that is correlated with the error term. The instrumental variable for the First Wife's popularity is needed to purge this correlation from the equation.

32. Gil Troy, *Affairs of State* (New York: The Free Press, 1997), p. 15.

33. The correlation between the error term and endogenous regressors causes ordinary multivariate analysis (OLS) coefficient estimates to be biased. By building an instrumental variable, which 2SLS does, the correlation between the error term and the endogenous regressor is purged, and resulting estimated coefficients are unbiased.

34. Mathematically, the 2SLS model looks like this:

$$\text{First Wife}_i = a + b_1\text{Candidate} + b_2\text{Party} + b_3\text{Sex} + b_4\text{Educ} + b_5\text{Income} + b_6\text{Race} + b_7\text{Age}_i + b_8\text{Traits}_i + b_9\text{Influence}_i + b_{10}\text{Time}_i + e \quad \text{(Eq.1)}$$

$$\text{Candidate}_i = a + b_1\text{First Wife} + b_2\text{Party} + b_3\text{Sex} + b_4\text{Educ} + b_5\text{Income} + b_6\text{Race} + b_7\text{Age}_i + b_8\text{Traits}_i + b_9\text{Influence}_i + b_{10}\text{Econ} + e \quad \text{(Eq.2)}$$

where First Wife = feeling thermometer for each "First Wife" (range is from 0 to 100 where scores closer to 0 indicate coldness and scores closer to 100 indicate warmth towards the "First Wife").

Candidate = feeling thermometer for each candidate (range is from 0 to 100 where scores closer to 0 indicate coldness and scores closer to 100 indicate warmth towards the candidate).

i = each of the spouses and candidates.

Party = respondent's party identification (1 = strong Democrat and 7 = strong Republican).

Sex = respondent's sex (1 = male, 2 = female).

Educ = respondent's education in years (1 to 16).

Income = respondent's income (1 to 12 where higher numbers represent higher income).

Race = respondent's race (1 = white, 2 = black). The data are weighted such that blacks make up 13% of the sample.

Age = respondent's age in years. Age was missing for approximately 30 percent of respondents. We predicted these ages with a model based on length of time in community, education, income, marital status, number of children, age of youngest child, and home owner/renter status.

Traits = index of character traits of each wife or candidate (moral + cares about people like you, range is from 1 to 7 where higher scores indicate less moral and less caring).

Influence = amount of influence first lady has or would have in administration (1 to 3 where lower numbers indicate too much influence).

Time = spending or would spend time as a first lady should (1 to 3 where lower numbers indicate agreement with the statement).

Econ = respondent's evaluation of the national economy in the past year (range is from 1 to 3 where higher scores indicate economy performed worse).

35. For a review of 2SLS see Peter Kennedy, *A Guide to Econometrics,* Thlrd Edition (Cambridge, MA: The MIT Press, 1993), pp. 151–175.

36. Nancy Gibbs and Michael Duffy, "Just Heartbeats Away," *Time,* July 1, 1996.

37. Gallup Poll, "Most Admired Poll Finds Americans Lack Major Heroes," http://www/gallup.com/poll/news/980101.html, 1997.

38. Margaret Truman, *First Ladies* (New York: Random House, 1995), p. 146.

39. Judy Klemesrud, "For Mrs. Carter, a Rest at Last," *The New York Times,* 11 June 1976, p. A1.

40. Betty Boyd Caroli, *First Ladies,* Expanded Edition (New York: Oxford University Press, 1995), p. 265.

41. Ibid, p. 62.

42. Margaret Truman, *First Ladies* (New York: Random House, 1995), pp. 98–99.

43. Stryker McGuire, "Norma and Cherie Who?" *Newsweek,* 5 (May 1997), p. 40.

44. A Lexis search was conducted, counting the number of mentions each of the "First Wives" generated in these news markets during the 1992 and 1996 general elections (months of August, September, October, November).

45. Average number of stories for the "First Wives" in the major newspapers was (see table below). Hillary's coverage in the *Chicago Tribune* in 1996 is probably because the Democratic National Convention was held in her hometown, Chicago, in 1996.

46. To test this, the election visibility of First Ladies was compared with their visibility when their husband first ran for the presidency. The data used are from the *New York Times* coverage of the elections from 1932 to 1996. With the exception of Nancy Reagan in 1984, all incumbent First Ladies received more press attention than when they were the wives of first-time challengers.

47. Anthony Mughan and Barry C. Burden, "The Candidates' Wives" in *Democracy's Feast,* edited by Herbert F. Weisberg (New Jersey: Chatham House Publishers, Inc., 1995), pp. 149–150.

48. Dean Keith Simonton, "Presidents' Wives and First Ladies: On Achieving Eminence Within a Traditional Gender Role," *Sex Roles,* 35, 1996, pp. 309–336.

49. *Newsweek,* "On the Road, Again," 18 (August 1997), p. 6.

50. Anthony Mughan and Barry C. Burden, "The Candidates' Wives" in *Democracy's Feast,* edited by Herbert F. Weisberg (New Jersey: Chatham House Publishers, Inc., 1995).

51. Anthony Mughan and Barry C. Burden, "The Candidates' Wives" in *Democracy's Feast,* edited by Herbert F. Weisberg (New Jersey: Chatham House Publishers, Inc., 1995), p. 149.

52. Anthony Mughan and Barry C. Burden, "Hillary Clinton and the President's Reelection." (Presented at the American Political Science Association meeting, Washington, DC, 1997), p. 13.

Paper	Hillary 1996	Elizabeth 1996	Hillary 1992	Barbara 1992
The Los Angeles Times	17	21.25	42.5	36.25
The Chicago Tribune	18.75	13.75	40.25	32.25
The Washington Post	29	21	46.75	34.75
The New York Times	12.75	24.75	42.75	37.25
The Atlanta Journal	10.75	20	37.5	37.25

LEGISLATURES, WOMEN, AND POLICY MAKING

Do female legislators make a difference in their impact on public policy? If we have greater numbers of women in our legislative bodies, can we expect a shift in issues that deal explicitly with women's concerns? For example, Michelle A. Saint-Germain in her article, "Does Their Difference Make a Difference? The Impact of Women on Public Policy in the Arizona Legislature" published in *Social Science Quarterly* (70, 4, December 1989, pps. 956–968) found that women legislators generally initiated more proposals than men in traditional women's interest areas and on feminist issues. Thus, one could argue that female legislators can make a difference in the public policy decisions about such matters as child care, health benefits, sex discrimination, and steps to curtail bombings at abortion clinics across the nation. (The Freedom of Access to Clinic Entrances Act [FACE] guided through Congress in 1994 by legislators including former Rep. Patricia Schroeder [D-CO], Senator Barbara Boxer [D-CA], and Rep. Louise Slaughter [D-NY] has resulted in a decrease in bombings at abortion clinics across the nation.)

How then have women fared in running for Congress and state legislative bodies? Marcia Lynn Whicker and the editor find that there is an unequal representation of women in the Congress. These researchers find that, across the more than 70 years since women secured the right to participate politically with the passage of the Nineteenth Amendment, female representation in Congress has increased from a minuscule 0.2 percent of total membership in 1922 to only 5.2 percent in 1988. At that rate of increase, women will not achieve equality in representation until the year 2582. By the 105th Congress, the percentage of women grew to 11 percent, a sizable increase, but still much below the 50 percent proportion that representation by gender would entail. This study also shows that women who do obtain congressional office do so at an older age than their male counterparts, serve significantly fewer terms, and are less likely to seek reelection. Thus, the gap between democratic rhetoric and representational reality for women is great, despite a significant narrowing in the experiential backgrounds of men and women who are elected to Congress.

On the other hand, we find that women's election to state assemblies and senates has increased 100 percent from 1974 to 1984. However, Wilma Rule finds recruitment to state assemblies and senates has slipped over the past decade. Her analysis reveals that, for the 1970s, there was a building on the gains in the Republican-moralistic states most favorable to women in the 1960s. In the 1980s no political party or political culture was dominant in the states where women legislators had the most dramatic increase. Rule finds that states that led in the 1970s and 1980s continued to advance, with most of their state senates at least doubling the number of women members by the 1994 elections. In 1994 the South broke out of its mold as the "solid Democratic South" for the first time in some 100 years. The author also concludes that, at the same time, the Republican Party dominance was modified as a favorable factor for women's recruitment.

We next move from recruitment of women to state assemblies and senates to an article that explores the question of whether there is a "new style" contemporary female legislator serving in the 1990s. Literature assessing the relative paucity of women's representation up through the 1970s suggested that early female office seekers were different in kind from men, but rather homogeneous as a group. Successful candidates of earlier decades fit a typology that limited a career in public service to a few women with the personal resources or familial connections to wage a campaign and without immediate family obligations to keep them in the home. Analyzing demographic, political, and legislative data from all women and a sub-sample of male legislators serving in fifteen states during 1972, 1982, and 1992, this article shows that women as a group have diversified their backgrounds and their interests over time. Data from a mail survey of 1372 female legislators serving in 1992 provides a more detailed description of the contemporary women legislator's characteristics, legislative experience, and policy interests. Conclusions indicate that, if the launching role that state legislative experience has provided for men holds true for women, this diversity and the greater numbers of women serving in elective office at the state level should ultimately mean a larger more diverse pool of future candidates at the national level.

We turn our attention next to women and legislative bodies

Women in Congress

Marcia Lynn Whicker

Lois Duke Whitaker

EXPLANATIONS OF THE PARADOX OF FEMALE VOTING STRENGTH AND REPRESENTATIONAL WEAKNESS

At one level, a paradox surrounds women in politics. While constituting about 51 percent of the population, women have held only a fraction of elected offices at all levels of government.[1] As a political group, women exhibit considerable voting strength but, simultaneously, representational weakness, especially at the national level. In 1988 women held only 28 of the 535 total seats in Congress (5.2 percent). At least partially because of the Anita Hill–Clarence Thomas controversy in late 1991, more women ran for the U.S. Congress in 1992. As a result, the 103rd Congress included seven female senators and forty-seven women in the U.S. House of Representatives (about 11 percent). The representation of women in the U.S. Congress after the 1994 GOP sweep left the numbers of women in the U.S. House at forty-seven, but included five more Republican women for a total of seventeen. After the 1994 election, women in the U.S. Senate increased to eight (five Democrats and three Republicans). After the 1996 election, women held 59 or 11 percent of the 535 seats in the 105th U.S. Congress; there were 50 women in the U.S. House of Representatives or 11.5 per-

This article originally appeared in *Free Inquiry in Creative Sociology,* Vol. 19. No. 2, 1991, Reprinted with permission.

cent and nine women were elected to the U.S. Senate or 9 percent of the 100 seats. These small numbers of women as a proportion of total national representation contrast with still small but nonetheless, in some instances, more than double percentages of female representation at subnational levels of government. Women held eighty-two statewide elected executive positions in state government (25.3 percent) and 1604 of the total 7424 state legislative seats (21.6 percent) in 1997. Since 1969 the number of women serving in state legislatures has increased fivefold.[2]

Women who attempt to enter the political elite continue experiencing considerable difficulty.[3] One study of women in three midwestern state legislatures found that they polled significantly fewer votes and won significantly fewer elections than men.[4] Further, women held fewer seats in professionally developed legislatures and city councils, in part due to stiffer male opposition in states and communities where the compensation is higher, the tenure is longer, and the prestige of office-holding is greater.[5]

The weakened political position of women in elected politics has been tied to their weakened economic condition in the marketplace. Rossi anticipates that as female participation and success in the labor force increase, so will the electoral potency of women candidates.[6] Other factors offered to explain the discrepancy between female voting strength and elected legislative representation include personality differences,[7] situational factors,[8] and sex-role socialization.[9]

Situational Explanations of the Paradox

Situational factors include a lower socioeconomic status for many women, little free time, less occupational experience than men have, and lower educational status. These factors have contributed to the absence of women in state legislatures, which have frequently been "launching roles" for men elected to Congress. Yet these factors alone explain only part of the political paradox for women. According to one study using 1970s data, if women had attained the same occupational and educational status as men, they would have constituted about 25 percent of state legislatures, rather than the 5 percent of the upper houses and 8 percent of the lower houses they then constituted.[10]

Socialization Explanations of the Paradox

Socialization includes the development of stereotypical attitudes that only a restricted range of behaviors are appropriate for women, and that politics is typically a male domain.[11] "Female values" of nurturing and caretaking are viewed by both men and women as incompatible with the rough-and-tumble action and toughness that politics and effective leadership require.[12] Women have also had to deal with conflicting roles as mother and wife and political roles. Thus, women have not as readily perceived politics as a viable option for themselves.

Voter Stereotypes as Explanations of the Paradox

Women candidates have faced considerable hurdles in winning voter approval, since voters, as well as potential female candidates, have been influenced by sex-role stereotyping.[13] While men have been viewed by voters in terms of occupational roles, women have been perceived in terms of domestic roles.[14] Stereotypical bias is based on the gender of the candidate and not the voter, since men and women have shown little differences in their reported unwillingness to vote for a woman candidate.[15] In one study, women candidates were rated more intelligent and concerned about people, but men candidates were still perceived as more knowledgeable about politics and considered stronger.[16] A later study done in 1990 revealed that female candidates can win national office if they convince voters that they possess masculine traits and are competent on "male" policy issues. This study found that voters' gender stereotypes have potentially negative implications for women candidates, especially when running for national office.[17]

The disadvantage women experience in voter perceptions is stronger if they are in their childbearing years and are the mothers of small children.[18] Voter perceptions of candidate acceptability have affected the willingness of mothers of small children to become candidates. In another study, women with small children were found to be as politically active as women without small children except in running for public office. Politically active men with small children were equally as likely to be candidates as those without children.

Challenges to Voter Discrimination as the Explanation for the Political Paradox for Women

Various studies have questioned voter and contributor discrimination as an explanation of the political paradox for women, including challenges to the supposition that female candidate attractiveness can be negative, that voters and party leaders react negatively to female candidates, and that gender rather than incumbency is the primary handicap confronting women candidates.[19] Sigelman, Sigelman, and Fowler explored whether physical attractiveness contributes to voter stereotyping of female candidates.[20] They found complex and indirect effects of femininity and female candidate attractiveness on voters. While perceived attractiveness had no direct impact on voter willingness to support the female candidate, it was positively related to perceptions of dynamism and femininity, which in turn were positively related to voter willingness to vote for the woman candidate. Thus, voter stereotyping of women in domestic roles undercut their willingness to elect women, but perceptions of female candidates as dynamic and feminine enhanced their willingness to vote for women.

Other scholars have contradicted findings that women candidates are less successful than men candidates when confounding factors are controlled. In an analysis of five 1982 elections in which women ran as major-party candidates for high-level offices—governor in Vermont and Iowa, and U.S. senator in Missouri, New York, and New Jersey—Zipp and Plutzer found that the sex of the candidate had little impact on voting.[21] Another study of voters' perceptions and attitudes using data from the 1982 American National Election Survey suggests that female candidates are not at a disadvantage when controls for incumbency are considered. When incumbency was controlled, voters were more likely to have contact with female candidates; were about as likely to recognize their names; made somewhat more favorable references to female candidates; and were just as likely to vote for women.[22]

Nor are women inferior fund-raisers,[23] or forced by party leaders to run only in overwhelmingly "hopeless" races.[24] Women are more likely, however, to be challengers. The political opportunity structure for any political challenger tends to restrict the number of women elected to office, since incumbents tend to win re-election and most incumbents are men.[25]

INCREASING OPPORTUNITIES FOR WOMEN AT THE NATIONAL LEVEL?

1984 as a Watershed Symbol Only?

If challengers to the political paradox for women are correct, opportunities for and visibility of women at the national level should be increasing, especially in the recent past. In 1984, Democrat and former House member from New York Geraldine Ferraro achieved the status of becoming the first woman vice presidential candidate for either major political party. This historic event led some observers at the time to conclude that the elections in that year may represent a watershed for women in obtaining national political visibility. In 1984, an unprecedented sixty-five women, thirty-five Republicans and thirty Democrats, also obtained a major-party nomination for U.S. House races, an 18 percent increase over the fifty-five women who received major-party nominations for House races in 1982.[26]

With offers of assistance from the Women's Campaign Fund, the Women's Trust, the National Women's Political Caucus, and the National Organization for Women, female candidate campaign organizations began to tap additional sources for assistance and to increase in professionalism.[27] Concern over a portending "gender gap," with popular reports circulating that women were beginning to disproportionately favor Democratic candidates, led the Republican party to promise to fund women senatorial candidates at levels as high as possible. Democrats responded to such pledges with their own promises of support for national female candidates.

Yet despite increased potential for advances in national political power for women, the general election outcomes in 1984 were disappointing to advocates of women as elected officials. Election results only preserved the status quo in terms of number of women in the U.S. House. While all female House incumbents who ran were victorious, two incumbents did not run, including Ferraro, who ran for vice president instead. These Democratic losses in the number of women in the House were offset by Republican gains. Thus, only twenty-two women out of 435 members were elected to the 99th Congress, constituting only 5 percent of House membership, a figure unchanged from the number and percentage of women in the 94th Congress.[33]

A Worldwide Political Paradox for Women?

Nor is the percentage of women in Congress substantially different from the number of women in Parliament in Britain. In 1974, with women there as in the United States constituting over 50 percent of the electorate, 96 percent of all the members of the British Parliament were male. In 1976, the total number of British MPs (Members of Parliament) who were women was twenty-eight, a number roughly equivalent to the number in Congress. In the 1970s, the trend in British politics for female candidates appeared to be an increasing number of female candidates standing for election, but no significant gain in the number obtaining office.[28] Norris reports this trend continued into the late 1980s.[29]

A Decline in Stereotypical Assignments for Women Members of Congress

Despite their small numbers within Congress, by the 98th Congress, women who did succeed in getting elected were no longer linked along sex-stereotyped lines to health, education, and children.[30] Only one of the twenty-three women in Congress at that time held a committee assignment on the Education Committee, while two or more women were on Armed Services, Appropriations, Science and Technology, Commerce, Budget, Public Works, and Transportation. The only committee associated with traditional women's issues to which a proportionately large number of women were assigned (six women) was the Special Committee on Aging.

The 104th Congress did bring about an increase in women achieving committee chairs rarely given to women. Senator Nancy Kassebaum (R-KS) became the first female chair in the Senate since 1945 when she took over the leadership of the Senate Labor and Human Resources committee.[31] Barbara Mikulski of Maryland is the first and only woman thus far to chair a Senate Appropriations subcommittee, and no woman has yet chaired any other of the Senate's exclusive committees, or subcommittees, on Appropriations, Rules or Finance.[32] In 1995, Barbara F. Vucanovich, in her last term in Congress at age seventy-three, rose to chair the House Subcommittee on Military Construction for one term. To date, no woman has ever chaired the full House Appropriations Committee. Nor has any woman chaired the other two exclusive House Committees—Ways and Means (or any of its subcommittees) or Rules.[33]

Some stereotypes related to women still remain, founded somewhat in reality. In a study of women who served in the House between 1915 and 1976, Gehlen found that congruent with the stereotypical niceness and nurturing often associated with female roles, women members were more reluctant than their male colleagues to oppose programs that they did not support.[34]

A Shift to Solo Campaigning with Few Gains in Numbers until the "Year of the Woman"

By the early 1980s, the nature of congressional campaigns for female candidates had changed. With one exception, women elected in the 98th Congress entered the electoral race on their own and fought vigorous campaigns to achieve office, a shift in the prevailing pattern until recent years of women succeeding their deceased fathers and husbands.[35]

This shift from spouse succession to solo campaigning, however, has not resulted in a rise in the number of women becoming national representatives. The number of female House members and senators in the 101st Congress did not increase appreciably over previous years. With only 28 of 435 House members female, women constituted 6.2 percent of the House. With only two out of 100 senators female, women constituted a minuscule 2 percent of the U.S. Senate. Thus, of the total 535 national representatives, the 28 women serving were 5.2 percent in the 101st Congress. The 102nd Congress was made up of 6 percent women in the U.S. House and 4 percent female representation in the U.S. Senate. Even with the record gains made by women in 1992, 1994, and 1996, only forty-seven women served in the U.S. House in the 103rd and 104th Congress and only 59 women serve in the 105th Congress; seven women served in the U.S. Senate in the 103rd Congress, eight female senators served in the 104th Congress, and nine women senators serve in the 105th Congress. Of the fifty-nine women serving in Congress in 1997, sixteen or 26.3 percent are women of color—one African American woman in the Senate; ten African American women, one Asian American/Pacific Islander, and four Latinos in the House.[36]

DIFFERENCES BETWEEN MALE AND FEMALE MEMBERS OF CONGRESS: ARE THEIR CONGRESSIONAL CAREERS CONVERGING?

This essay examines differences between male and female members of Congress for both background characteristics and measures of congressional "success." If those who do not believe discrimination is the primary explanation for the small number of women in national office are correct, then the political career paths of men and women should become more similar across time as women enter the labor force with greater frequency and assume a variety of jobs previously held only by men. If, however, voter stereotyping and other discriminatory factors are still important, then the political career paths and measures of success for male and female members of Congress should still be different, and little convergence will occur.

Data and Methodology

The data used here are a merged set drawn from the roster of U.S. congressional officeholders and biographical characteristics of the U.S. Congress, 1789–1989, covering the 1st to the 101st Congress. The data set contains variables describing congressional service and background characteristics for each person who has served in the U.S. Congress from March 1789 through July 1989. A record exists for every Congress in which each individual has served, as well as for each chamber in which each individual has served, constituting 41,209 cases. Thus, statistics are reported here for both the total number of two-year congressional terms served by women, as well as for women as a percentage of the total number of individuals serving in Congress.

Prior to gaining the right to vote in the Nineteenth Amendment to the U.S. Constitution in 1920, women did not participate actively as a group in politics. This analysis begins after the 67th Congress, and covers the 68th through the 101st Congress. Women are compared here to men serving in Congress at the same time.

Number of Women in Congress, by Year

Tables 5.1 and 5.2 show that the number of women in Congress has always been small. In the 68th Congress, immediately after the ratification of the 1920 amendment, only one lonely woman was a national representative. Between the 68th and 101st Congresses, the percentage of women in both houses rose steadily, if slowly and not consistently, from 0.2 percent to 5.2 percent—again increasing to only 5.0 percent of the total membership of Congress in 66 years. At that average rate of increase in the number of women per 66 years, women will not achieve 50 percent of the representation in Congress until the year 2582—almost 600 years from now. By the 105th Congress, the percentage of women increased to 11 percent, a sizable increase but still below the 50 percent proportional representation by gender would entail.

Table 5.2 also differentiates between Congresses when the White House was occupied by a Republican and those when the president was Democratic. Despite the image that Democrats are more supportive of women's rights, plus the greater frequency with which Democratic Party platforms have adopted pro-women stances in recent years, the average percent of women per term serving in Congress under Republican presidents (3.41 percent) is slightly higher than the average percent of women per term serving under Democratic presidents (2.98 percent).

In part, this partisan equality reflects the increase in the number of women in recent years relative to the number in earlier years, and the fact that the presidency has been dominated by Republicans since 1968. Yet during the presidencies of Democrats Harry Truman, John Kennedy, and Jimmy Carter, the number and percentage of women in Congress fell, while during the presidencies of Republicans Eisenhower, Nixon, Reagan, and Bush, the number and percentage of women in Congress rose slightly. Perhaps, also, during the pro-women administrations of Democrats, pro-women voters become complacent about increasing representation, while during the less supportive administrations of Republican presidencies, pro-women voters become galvanized to work for and support women congressional candidates. Also, the number of women in Congress during the pro-family

TABLE 5.1 Number of Women in Congress, by Year

Election	Congress	President	President's Party	Number of Women in Congress	Percentage
1922	68	Warren G. Harding	R	1	0.2
1924	69	Calvin Coolidge	R	2	0.5
1926	70	Calvin Coolidge	R	5	0.9
1928	71	Herbert C. Hoover	R	9	1.6
1930	72	Herbert C. Hoover	R	8	1.5
1932	73	Franklin D. Roosevelt	D	8	1.5
1934	74	Franklin D. Roosevelt	D	8	1.5
1936	75	Franklin D. Roosevelt	D	9	1.6
1938	76	Franklin D. Roosevelt	D	9	1.6
1940	77	Franklin D. Roosevelt	D	10	1.8
1942	78	Franklin D. Roosevelt	D	9	1.6
1944	79	Franklin D. Roosevelt	D	11	1.9
1946	80	Franklin D. Roosevelt	D	8	1.4
1948	81	Harry S. Truman	D	9	1.6
1950	82	Harry S. Truman	D	9	1.6
1952	83	Dwight D. Eisenhower	R	13	2.3
1954	84	Dwight D. Eisenhower	R	16	3.0
1956	85	Dwight D. Eisenhower	R	15	2.8
1958	86	Dwight D. Eisenhower	R	19	3.4
1960	87	John F. Kennedy	D	20	3.6
1962	88	John F. Kennedy	D	14	2.5
1964	89	Lyndon B. Johnson	D	13	2.4
1966	90	Lyndon B. Johnson	D	12	2.2
1968	91	Richard M. Nixon	R	11	2.0
1970	92	Richard M. Nixon	R	15	2.7
1972	93	Richard M. Nixon	R	16	2.9
1974	94	Gerald R. Ford	R	19	3.5
1976	95	Jimmy Carter	D	19	3.5
1978	96	Jimmy Carter	D	17	3.1
1980	97	Ronald Reagan	R	24	4.4
1982	98	Ronald Reagan	R	25	4.4
1984	99	Ronald Reagan	R	25	4.6
1986	100	Ronald Reagan	R	26	4.8
1988	101	George Bush	R	28	5.2
1990	102	George Bush	R	32	6.0
1992	103	Bill Clinton	D	54	10.0
1994	104	Bill Clinton	D	55	10.4
1996	105	Bill Clinton	D	59	11.0

TABLE 5.2   Summary of Women in Congress

Congressional Terms Under:	# of Terms	# of Women in Congress	Average % of Members per Term Who Were Women
Democratic President	19	353	2.98
Republican President	19	309	3.41
Total	38	662	3.20

conservative years of the 1950s was slightly higher than in the activist, more liberal 1960s, a decade that saw the launching of the second major women's movement in the United States in the twentieth century.

Making Individual-Based Comparisons

Table 5.3 examines the differences between men and women in terms of numbers serving and background characteristics, looking at individuals as the basis for comparison. Since 1921, 3653 individuals have served in Congress—2993 in the House and 660 in the Senate. Woman have made up only 3.3 percent of those individuals. Throughout two centuries of U.S. history, women have had little role in national lawmaking, since only 107 women have served in the House and 14 women in the U.S. Senate. Despite the small number of women in the Senate, proportionately the number of women who have served in the House is not statistically significantly greater (probability of chi-square = .08). Nor do women differ significantly from men in the regions from which they are elected (probability = .34). While 62.0 percent of all women who have served in Congress have been Democrats, political party is also not significantly related to gender of the representative (probability = .29).

If women in Congress do not differ from their male counterparts in region, chamber to which they are elected, and political party, do they differ in background characteristics? Men and women are both equally likely to have attended public secondary school prior to entering college, but do differ in college background (significance = .03). Women are more likely to have attended private colleges (53.7 percent) than are men (44.0 percent), but men are more likely to have attended Ivy League colleges (13.7 percent) than are women (0.2 percent). A higher percentage of men (29.8 percent) attended state universities than women (25.6 percent), while a slightly higher percentage of women (14.9 percent) than men (12.5 percent) attended no college at all.

Women are now more likely to be elected to Congress on their own rather than as widows succeeding their deceased husbands. From 1916 to 1940, however, 56 percent of women elected to the House were widows of congressmen who had represented the same district. That proportion dropped to 40 percent in the

TABLE 5.3   Number of Men and Women in Congress, 68th to 101st Congress

	Men		Women		Total		Proba-bility of Chi-Square
	Number	Per-centage	Number	Per-centage	Number	Per-centage	
Individuals serving:	3,532	96.7	121	3.3	3,653		
By chamber:							.08
House	2,886	81.7	107	88.4	2,993	81.9	
Senate	646	18.3	14	11.6	660	18.1	
By region: (1M)							.34
Northeast	928	26.3	32	26.4	960	26.3	
Midwest	1,071	30.3	29	24.0	1,100	30.1	
South	996	28.2	36	29.8	1,032	28.3	
West	536	15.2	24	19.8	560	15.3	
By party: (1M)							.29
Democrat	1,898	53.7	75	62.0	1,973	54.0	
Republican	1,612	45.6	46	38.0	1,658	45.4	
Other	21	0.6	0	0.0	21	0.6	
By relatives in Congress: (1M)							.00**
None	3,278	92.8	80	66.1	3,358	91.9	
1 or more	253	7.2	41	33.9	294	8.1	
By secondary education: (6M)							.39
Unknown	137	3.9	7	5.8	144	3.9	
Public school	2,775	78.7	89	74.2	2,864	78.6	
Private school	614	17.4	24	20.0	638	17.5	
By college: (3M)							.03*
None	442	12.5	18	14.9	460	12.6	
State university	1,051	29.8	31	25.6	1,082	29.6	
Private college	1,552	44.0	65	53.7	1,617	44.3	
Ivy League	484	13.7	7	0.2	491	13.5	
By prior service: (3M)							.00**
None	590	16.7	39	32.2	629	17.2	
Local	1,639	46.4	56	46.3	1,695	46.4	
State	1,161	32.9	23	19.0	1,184	32.4	
Federal	139	3.9	3	2.5	142	3.9	

*Significant at the .05 level.   #M = number of male cases missing.

**Significant at the .01 level.   #W = number of female cases missing.

Percentages are adjusted for missing cases.

1941–1964 period and to 30 percent in the 1965–1974 period; it continued to decline to only 9 percent in the 1980 and 1982 elections.[37]

Despite the reduction in the number of women members of Congress replacing deceased fathers or husbands in recent years and the increase in the number of women engaging in solo campaigning, women differ significantly (probability of chi-square = .00) from men in having relatives in Congress. Among women, 33.9 percent had at least one relative who had served in Congress, but only 7.2 percent of men had at least one relative who had served in Congress.

Men and women also differed in prior service before entry into Congress (probability = .00). A much greater percentage of women (32.2 percent) than men (16.7 percent) had no prior government service. While similar proportions of men (46.4 percent) and women (46.3 percent) had local government experience previously, men (32.9 percent) were more likely to have gained state government experience than women (19.0 percent). Few members of either gender had previous federal experience.

Making Comparisons on the Basis of Two-Year Congressional Terms

Table 5.4 explores similar questions using total number of two-year terms in Congress served since 1922 (18,737) as the universe, rather than total number of individuals who served. In contrast to the proportion of women who served (3.3 percent) as a percentage of the total number of individuals in Congress during that study time span, the number of total terms served by women falls to 2.5 percent, indicating that those few women who are elected to Congress on average are serving fewer terms than their male counterparts.

When total number of terms rather than total individuals form the universe from which men and women in Congress are compared, both chamber and region are significantly related to gender at the .00 level. The number of terms women served in the House (90.9 percent) as a percentage of total terms served by women in both houses is significantly greater than the terms served by men in the House (80.7 percent) as a percentage of the total terms served by men in both houses. This contrasts with political party affiliation, where of the total terms served by men, the percentage served by men who are Democrats (57.4 percent) is virtually identical to terms served by Democratic women as a percentage of the total number of terms served by women (57.4 percent).

Women have fared considerably better in the Northeast and considerably worse in the South than have men in obtaining congressional office, relative to the performance of each gender in other regions. Women have fared marginally better in the West and marginally worse in the Midwest than men. The percentage of terms served by women who are elected from the Northeast (34.4 percent) is significantly greater than the percentage of terms served by men elected from the Northeast (25.0 percent). The percentage of terms served by women elected from the South (21.2 percent) is significantly less than the percentage of terms men served from the South (31.2 percent). Women were somewhat more

TABLE 5.4   Number of Two-Year Congressional Terms Served by Men and Women, 68th to 101st Congress

	Men		Women		Total		Proba-bility of Chi-Square
	Number	*Per-centage*	*Number*	*Per-centage*	*Number*	*Per-centage*	
Terms served by men and women:	18,275	97.5	462	2.5	18,737		
By chamber:							.00**
House	14,754	80.7	420	90.9	15,174	81.0	
Senate	3,521	19.3	42	9.1	3,563	19.0	
By region: (3M)							.00**
Northeast	4,561	25.0	159	34.4	4,720	25.2	
Midwest	5,214	28.5	116	25.1	5,330	28.5	
South	5,703	31.2	98	21.2	5,801	31.0	
West	2,794	15.3	89	19.3	2,883	15.4	
By party: (1M)							.62
Democrat	10,490	57.4	265	57.4	10,755	57.4	
Republican	7,716	42.2	197	42.6	7,913	42.2	
Other	68	0.4	0	0.0	68	0.4	
By relatives in Congress: (2M)							.00**
None	16,942	92.7	321	69.5	17,263	92.1	
One or more	1,331	7.3	141	30.5	1,472	7.9	
By secondary edcation: (16M, 1W)							.01**
Unknown	543	3.0	25	5.4	568	3.0	
Public school	14,607	80.0	353	76.6	14,960	79.9	
Private school	3,109	17.0	83	18.0	3,192	17.1	
By college: (5M, 1W)							.00*
None	1,989	10.9	66	14.3	2,055	11.0	
State university	5,720	31.3	113	24.5	5,833	31.1	
Private college	8,105	44.4	247	53.6	8,353	44.6	
Ivy League	2,456	13.4	35	7.6	2,491	13.3	
By prior service: (9M, 1W)							.00**
None	2,799	15.3	110	23.9	2,909	15.5	
Local	8,596	47.1	237	51.4	8,833	47.2	
State	6,057	33.2	93	20.2	6,150	32.8	
Federal	814	4.5	21	4.6	835	4.5	

*Significant at the .05 level.   #M = number of male cases missing.

**Significant at the .01 level.   #W = number of female cases missing.

Percentages are adjusted for missing cases.

likely to be from the West (19.3 percent) than were men (15.3 percent), and somewhat less likely to be from the Midwest (25.1 percent) than were men (28.5 percent).

Using terms served as the unit of analysis, similar patterns emerge for male–female differences in relatives in Congress, college attended, and prior government service to those that appeared when individuals served was the unit of analysis. Each of these variables continues to be significantly related to gender of the member of Congress. Women are more likely to have had at least one relative in Congress and to have attended private colleges, and are less likely to have served at the state level prior to entering Congress. Additionally, secondary education is significantly related to gender, with women slightly less likely (76.4 percent) than men (80.0 percent) to have attended public schools.

Measures of Congressional Success

Table 5.5 examines measures of congressional success for individuals by gender. The age at which the member first entered Congress, the total years served in Congress, and the member's reason for leaving Congress are all significantly related at the .00 level to the gender of the member. In each instance, women are less successful than men. Service after leaving Congress is not related to gender.

On average, women are older (49.3 years old) than men (45.4 years of age) when they first enter Congress. Women serve an average of 6.6 years, 4.2 years less than the average years (10.8) served by men. The most common reason women leave Congress is a decision to not seek reelection (40.0 percent), while only 20.2 percent of men leave Congress because they do not seek reelection. Men (11.9 percent) are far more likely than women (2.5 percent) to have died in office. Women (6.7 percent) are slightly less likely than men (10.4 percent) to have been defeated in a general election.

Comparing Congressional Careers across Time by Decade

Table 5.6 examines trends in national representation by gender across time. When terms served is the unit of analysis, the proportion of women holding congressional office has increased from 0.8 percent of total congressional membership in the 1920s to 4.7 percent in the 1980s. Female representation in the House went from 1.0 percent in the 1920s to 5.3 percent in the 1980s, while Senate membership rose from 0 to 2.0 percent across the same time span.

While some aspects of qualifications had previously divided men and women—whether the individual had a relative who had served in Congress and the type of precongressional service held—men and women are becoming more similar. In the 1920s, 88.7 percent of all men serving in Congress did not have a relative who had served in the same institution, but only 22.2 percent of all women in Congress had no relative who had served there. This reflects the fact that many women were widows of members who died in office. By the 1980s, however, 95.6 percent of all men in Congress had no relative there, while 90.6 percent of all

TABLE 5.5 One-Way ANOVA and Contingency Table Results for Congressional Success, by Sex

Congressional Success	Male		Female		Total		Probability
	Mean		Mean		Mean		of F
ANOVA: Age first in Congress	45.4		49.3		45.5		.00**
Total years served	10.8		6.6		10.7		.00**
Frequencies, percentages:	*Number*	*Percent-age*	*Number*	*Percent-age*	*Number*	*Percent-age*	*of Chi-Square*
Reason left Congress (2M, 1W)							.00**
Unknown, N.A.	992	28.1	18	15.0	1,010	27.7	
General election defeat	367	10.4	8	6.7	375	10.3	
Died in office	419	11.9	3	2.5	422	11.6	
Did not seek reelection	713	20.2	48	40.0	761	20.8	
Sought other elective office	249	7.1	12	10.0	261	7.2	
Accepted federal office	75	2.1	0	0.0	75	2.1	
Elected to other House	115	3.3	1	0.8	116	3.2	
Resigned, withdrew, expelled	92	2.6	2	1.7	94	2.6	
Still serving	508	14.4	28	23.3	536	14.7	
Number of levels after Congress (553M, 28W)							.84
None	2,207	74.1	70	75.3	2,277	74.1	
One	655	22.0	21	22.6	676	22.0	
Two	110	3.7	2	2.2	112	3.6	
Three	7	0.2	0	0.0	7	0.2	

*Significant at the .05 level.   #M = Number of male cases missing or dead.

**Significant at the .01 level.   #W = Number of female cases missing or dead.

TABLE 5.6   Men and Women, by Two-Year Term, by Decade

	Men		Women	
	Number	*Percentage*	*Number*	*Percentage*
Terms served by men and women:				
1920s	2,206	99.2	18	0.8
1930s	2,739	98.5	42	1.5
1940s	2,747	98.3	47	1.7
1950s	2,675	97.4	72	2.6
1960s	2,685	97.5	70	2.5
1970s	2,637	96.8	86	3.2
1980s	2,586	95.3	127	4.7
By chamber:				
House				
1920s	1,782	99.0	18	1.0
1930s	2,219	98.5	34	1.5
1940s	2,209	98.1	43	1.9
1950s	2,157	97.1	64	2.9
1960s	2,167	97.2	62	2.8
1970s	2,129	96.3	82	3.7
1980s	2,091	94.7	117	5.3
Senate:				
1920s	424	100.0	0	0.0
1930s	520	98.5	8	1.5
1940s	538	99.3	4	0.7
1950s	518	98.5	8	1.5
1960s	518	98.5	8	1.5
1970s	508	99.2	4	0.8
1980s	495	98.0	10	2.0
By relatives in Congress:				
None:				
1920s	1,957	88.7	4	22.2
1930s	2,464	90.0	20	47.6
1940s	2,522	91.8	23	48.9
1950s	2,498	93.4	36	50.0
1960s	2,530	94.2	44	62.9
1970s	2,499	94.8	79	91.9
1980s	2,472	95.6	115	90.6
By prior service:				
None:				
1920s	387	17.5	11	61.1
1930s	532	19.4	22	52.4
1940s	564	20.5	14	29.8
1950s	510	19.1	23	31.9
1960s	303	11.3	12	17.1
1970s	174	6.6	5	5.8
1980s	329	12.8	23	18.3

(continued)

TABLE 5.6 *Continued*

	Men		Women	
	Number	*Percentage*	*Number*	*Percentage*
Local:				
1920s	1,067	48.4	7	38.9
1930s	1,346	49.1	17	40.5
1940s	1,340	48.8	25	53.2
1950s	1,268	47.4	40	55.6
1960s	1,196	44.6	46	65.7
1970s	1,072	40.7	40	46.5
1980s	1,305	50.6	62	49.2
State:				
1920s	677	30.7	0	0.0
1930s	750	27.4	3	7.1
1940s	742	27.0	8	17.0
1950s	792	29.6	3	4.2
1960s	1,015	37.8	7	10.0
1970s	1,214	46.0	36	41.9
1980s	867	33.6	36	28.6

women also had no relative who had served in Congress. Plainly, women had reached almost the same percentage as men on this characteristic and were being elected in their own right, rather than on the name recognition and contacts of deceased husbands.

A similar picture emerges when the precongressional service for both genders is examined. In the 1920s, 61.1 percent of women in Congress, contrasted with only 17.5 percent of men there, had no prior government or political experience. By the 1980s, these two percentages had almost converged, so that only 12.8 percent of men and 18.3 percent of women in congress had no prior government experience. In the 1980s, half of men and half of women in Congress had local experience before entering Congress. A slightly higher percentage of men (33.6 percent) than women (28.6 percent) had previous state-level experience. Despite this difference, however, the gaps between the experiential backgrounds of men and women in Congress have narrowed significantly across the 66-year time span studied.

CONCLUSION

Much has been written about the inroads women have made in politics in gaining elected office in recent years, especially at the state and local levels. Greater political participation by women has been viewed as beneficial.[38] Women are said to have unique contributions to make based on their differential role socialization, their greater concern with group harmony, and their emphasis on caring for future generations. The full participation of women, as well as all disadvantaged groups, would implement democracy in its highest and purest form, producing regime legitimacy, and would expand the talent pool from which national leaders are selected.

Despite such rhetoric and a significant narrowing in the experiential backgrounds of men and women who serve in Congress, the reality is that women have played virtually no role in shaping the nation's laws. Women could not vote in most states prior to 1920, and since then have succeeded in achieving only token representation in Congress. Even though the number of women serving in the U.S. Congress roughly doubled with the 1992 election, many obstacles remain for women seeking congressional office. And, even once elected, by every measure examined here, they are less successful. The gap between democratic rhetoric and representational reality for women is great.

NOTES

1. Ronald D. Hedlund, Patricia K. Freeman, Keith E. Hamm, and Robert M. Stein, "The Electability of Women Candidates: The Effects of Sex Role Stereotypes," *Journal of Politics,* 41 (1–2) (1979), pp. 513–524; and Carol Nechemias, "Changes in the Election of Women to U.S. State Legislative Seats," *Legislative Studies Quarterly,* 12 (February 1987), pp. 125–142.

2. Center for the American Woman and Politics. Eagleton Institute of Politics (New Brunswick, NJ: 1997).

3. Irene Diamond, *Sex Roles in the State House* (New Haven, CT: Yale University Press,1977); Susan Welch, "Recruitment of Women to Public Office," *Western Political Quarterly,* 31 (September 1978), pp. 372–380; Susan Gluck Mezey, "The Effects of Sex on Recruitment: Local Connecticut Offices," in Debra Stewart (Ed.), *Women in Local Politics* (Metuchen, NJ: Scarecrow Press, 1980); Ruth Mandel, "The Image Campaign," in James David Barber and Barbara Kellerman (Eds.), *Women Leaders in American Politics* (Englewood Cliffs, NJ: Prentice-Hall, 1986), pp. 261–271; and Robert Darcy, Susan Welch, and Janet Clark, *Women, Elections, and Representation* (Lincoln: University of Nebraska Press, 1994).

4. Margery M. Ambrosius and Susan Welch, "Women and Politics at the Grassroots: Women Candidates for Office in Three States." Paper presented at the annual meeting of the Western Social Science Association, April 1981.

5. Diamond, *Sex Roles;* David B. Hill, "Political Culture and Female Political Representation," *Journal of Politics,* 43 (1–2) (1981), pp. 159–168.

6. Alice S. Rossi, "Beyond the Gender Gap: Women's Bid for Political Power," *Social Science Quarterly,* 64 (1983), pp. 718–733.

7. Hedlund et al., "Electability of Women Candidates."

8. Ruth Schwartz Cowan, "The Industrial Revolution in the Home: Household Technology and Social Change in the Twentieth Century," *Technology and Culture,* 17 (1976), pp. 1–23.

9. Marcia Manning Lee, "Why Few Women Hold Public Office: Democracy and Sex Roles," *Political Science Quarterly,* 91 (1–2) (1976), pp. 297–314; and Marcia Lynn Whicker and Jennie J. Kronenfeld, *Sex Roles: Technology, Politics, and Policy* (New York: Praeger, 1986).

10. Darcy et al., *Women, Elections, and Representation.*

11. Kovach, Barbara E. *Sex Roles and Personal Awareness* (Lanham; London: University Press of America, 1990); R. D. Hess and J. V. Torney, *The Development of Political Attitudes in Children* (Chicago: Aldine, 1967); J. Boles and H. Duriot "Stereotyping of Males and Females in Elected Office: The Implications of an Attitudinal Study." Paper presented at the annual meeting of the Midwest Political Science Association, April 1980; J. Boles and H. Duriot, "Political Woman and Superwoman: Sex Stereotyping of Females in Elected Office." Paper presented at the annual meeting of the Midwest Political Science Association meeting, April 1981; R. B. Deber, "The Fault Dear Brutus: Women as Congressional Candidates in Pennsylvania," *Journal of Politics,* 44 (1982), pp. 463–479; L. Ekstrand and W. Eckert, "The Impact of Candidate's Sex on Voter Choice,"

Western Political Quarterly, 34 (1981), pp. 78–87: Hedlund et al., "Electability of Women Candidates," Virginia Sapiro, "If U.S. Senator Baker Were a Woman: An Experimental Study of Candidates' Images," *Political Psychology,* 3 (1–2) (1981–1982), pp. 61–83; Lee Sigelman and Susan Welch, "Race, Gender, and Opinion toward Black and Female Presidential Candidates," *Public Opinion Quarterly,* 48 (1984), pp. 462–475; Nancy E. McGlen and Karen O'Connor, *Women, Politics, and American Society* (Englewood Cliffs, NJ: Prentice-Hall, 1998), pp. 60–102; and Janet Clark, "Getting There: Women in Political Office," in Marianne Githens, Pippa Norris, and Joni Lovenduskit (Eds.), *Different Roles, Different Voices: Women and Politics in the United States and Europe* (New York: HarperCollins, 1994), pp. 99–110.

12. F. L. Gehlen, "Women Members of Congress: A Distinctive role," in M. Githens and J. L. Prestage (Eds.), *A Portrait of Marginality: The Political Behavior of the American Woman* (New York: Longman, 1977), pp. 304–319; McGlen and O'Connor, *Women, Politics, and American Society,* pp. 82–84.

13. Elizabeth Holtzman and Shirley Williams, "Women in the Political World: Observations," *Daedalus,* 116 (1987), pp. 25–33; Leonie Huddy and Nayda Terkildsen, "Gender Stereotypes and the Perception of Male and Female Candidates," *American Journal of Political Science,* 37 (1993), pp. 119–147.

14. Marcia Lynn Whicker and Todd Areson, "The Maleness of the American Presidency," *Journal of Political Science,* 17 (Spring 1989), pp. 63–73; Mandel "The Image Campaign"; Linda Witt, Karen M. Paget, and Glenna Matthews, *Running as a Woman: Gender Power in American Politics* (New York: Free Press 1994), pp. 1–28.

15. Susan Welch and Lee Sigelman, "Changes in Public Attitudes toward Women in Politics," *Social Science Quarterly,* 62 (June 1982), pp. 312–322.

16. Margaret Mericle, S. Lenart, and K. Heilig, "Women Candidates: Even If All Things Are Equal, Will They Get Elected?" paper presented at the annual meeting of the Midwest Political Science Association, April 1989.

17. Leonie Hoddy and Nayda Terkildsen, "The Consequences of Gender Stereotypes for Women Candidates at Different Levels and Types of Office," *Political Research Quarterly,* 46 (3) (1993), pp. 503–525.

18. Hedlund, et al., "Electability of Women Candidates."

19. A. Karnig and B. O. Walter, "Election of Women to City Councils," *Social Science Quarterly,* 56 (1976), pp. 605–613; Ekstrand and Eckert, "The Impact of Candidate's Sex;" Robert Darcy and S. Schramm, "When Women Run Against Men," *Public Opinion Quarterly,* 41 (1977), pp. 1–12; and R. Bernstein, "Why Are There So Few Women in the House?" *Western Political Quarterly,* 39 (1986), pp. 155–163; Carole Chaney and Barbara Sinclair, "Women and the 1992 House Elections," in Elizabeth Adell Cook, Sue Thomas, and Clyde Wilcox, (Eds.), *The Year of the Woman: Myths and Realities* (Boulder, CO: Westview Press, 1994), pp. 125–127.

20. Lee Sigelman, Carol K. Sigelman, and Christopher Fowler, "A Bird of a Different Feather? An Experimental Investigation of Physical Attractiveness and the Electability of Female Candidates," *Social Psychology Quarterly,* 50 (1) (1987), pp. 32–43.

21. John F. Zipp and Eric Plutzer, "Gender Differences in Voting for Female Candidates: Evidence from the 1982 Election." *Public Opinion Quarterly,* 49 (1985), pp. 179–197.

22. Darcy, Welch, and Clark, "Women, Elections, and Representation," pp. 74–100.

23. Barbara C. Burrell, "Women's and Men's Campaigns for the U.S. House of Representatives, 1972–1982: A Finance Gap?" *American Politics Quarterly,* 13 (1985), pp. 251–272; Robert M. Darcy, M. Brewer, and C. Clay, "Women in the Oklahoma Political System: State Legislative Elections," *Social Science Journal,* 21 (January 1985), pp. 67–78; Candice J. Nelson, "Women's PACs in the Year of the Woman," in Elizabeth Adell Cook, Sue Thomas, and Clyde Wilcox, (Eds.), *The Year of the Woman: Myths and Realities* (Boulder, CO: Westview Press, 1994), pp. 181–195.

24. I. Gertzog and M. M. Simard, "Women and 'Hopeless' Congressional Candidacies: Nomination Frequencies, 1916–1978," *American Politics Quarterly,* 9 (1981), pp. 449–466; and Janet Clark, Robert Darcy, Susan Welch, and M. Ambrosius, "Women as Legislative Candidates in Six States," in J. A. Flammang (Ed.), *Political Women: Current Roles in State and Local Government* (Beverly Hills, CA: Sage, 1985).

25. Robert Darcy and James R. Choike, "A Formal Analysis of Legislative Turnover: Women Candidates and Legislative Representation." *American Journal of Political Science,* 30 (1) (1986), pp. 237–255.

26. Barbara C. Burrell, "The Political Opportunity of Women Candidates for the U.S. House of Representatives in 1984," *Women and Politics,* 8 (1988), pp. 51–68.

27. Susan Carroll, *Women as Candidates in American Politics,* 2nd ed. (Bloomington: Indiana University Press, 1994).

28. Elizabeth Vallance, *Women in the House: A Study of Women Members of Parliament* (Atlantic Highlands, NJ: Athlone Press, 1979).

29. Pippa Norris, "The Impact of the Electoral System on Election of Women to National Legislatures," in Marianne Githens, Pippa Norris, and Joni Lovenduski (Eds.), *Different Roles, Different Voices: Women and Politics in the United States and Europe* (New York: Harper-Collins, 1994), pp. 114–121.

30. Rossi, "Beyond the Gender Gap."

31. Curt Anderson, "Kansas Women Rise to Power in Congress," *Times-Picayune* (November 26, 1994), p. A8.

32. Rep. Marcy Kaptur, *Women of Congress* (Washington, DC: Congressional Quarterly, Inc., 1996), pp. 6–7.

33. *Ibid.*

34. Gehlen, "Women Members of Congress."

35. Irwin Gertzog, "Changing Patterns of Female Recruitment to the U.S. House of Representatives," *Legislative Studies Quarterly,* 4 (1979), pp. 429–445.

36. Center for the American Woman and Politics, Eagleton Institute of Politics (New Brunswick, NJ, 1997).

37. Darcy, Welch, and Clark, *Women, Elections, and Representation.*

38. *Ibid.*

FURTHER READINGS

Bingham, Clara. *Women on the Hill: Challenging the Culture of Congress.* New York: Times Books, 1997.

Burrell, Barbara. *A Women's Place is in the House.* Ann Arbor: University of Michigan Press, 1994.

Carroll, Susan J. *Women as Candidates in American Politics,* 2nd ed., Bloomington: Indiana University Press, 1994.

Carroll, Susan J., Debra L. Dodson, and Ruth B. Mandel. *The Impact of Women in Public Office: An Overview.* New Brunswick, NJ: Center for the American Woman and Politics, 1991.

Darcy, Robert, Susan Welch, and Janet Clark. *Women, Elections and Representation.* Lincoln: University of Nebraska Press, 1994.

Fowler, Linda L., and Robert D. McClure. *Political Ambition: Who Decides to Run for Congress.* New Haven, CT: Yale University Press, 1989.

Fox, Richard Logan. *Gender Dynamics in Congressional Elections.* Thousand Oaks, CA: Sage Publications, 1997.

Gertzog, Irwin N. *Congressional Women: Their Recruitment, Treatment and Behavior,* 2nd ed. New York: Praeger, 1995.

Kirkpatrick, Jeane J. *Political Woman.* New York: Basic Books, 1974.

Phillips, Anne. *Engendering Democracy.* University Park: Pennsylvania State University Press, 1991.

Witt, Linda, Karen M. Paget, and Glenna Matthews. *Running as a Women: Gender and Power in American Politics.* New York: Free Press, 1994.

Why Are More Women State Legislators?

Wilma Rule

The 1994 and 1996 elections marked the first major standstill in women's election to state legislatures in over twenty years. It was the first time that a large number of legislatures actually had declines in women members. What was going on here? Was this the end of women's advances toward equal legislative representation? Was the women's movement dead? Would this decline have negative consequences for women state leaders and members of Congress?

Women actually increased their percentages in twenty-five of the fifty legislatures over the previous election in 1994, while in six states they held their own. In 1996 they averaged 21 percent of state legislatures, whereas ten years earlier they were 12 percent and in 1974 only 6 percent.[1] Women legislators have increased proportions by 75 percent since 1984 but have slipped from a 100 percent increase over the past decade.

While some trends from 1974 to 1986 remained the same, the elections of 1994–1996 show that indeed there is much change—some for the better and most making women's recruitment to state legislatures a little worse for the next decade.

This chapter asks the following questions:

1. What were the reasons for women's steady advance from 1974 to 1984? What has changed in 1994–1996? (see Tables 5.7 and 5.10).
2. What are the factors that are more favorable in the 1980s than in the 1970s? How does 1994 compare to 1984?

Original article appeared in the *Western Political Quarterly*, vol. 43 (June 1990). This version, revised by the author, is reprinted with permission by the author and the University of Utah, copyright holder.

TABLE 5.7 Women in U.S. State Legislatures, 1974 and 1984

	State Senate			State House			
	Number of Senators	Number of Women		Number of Members	Number of Women		Percentage of Women in Both Houses*
State		1974	1984		1974	1984	1974	1984
Alabama	35	0	1	105	1	5	1	4
Alaska	20	1	2	40	6	4	12	10
Arizona	30	3	4	60	10	12	14	18
Arkansas	35	1	0	100	2	7	2	5
California	40	1	2	80	2	12	3	12
Colorado	35	3	6	65	5	19	8	25
Connecticut	36	3	8	151	17	33	10	21
Delaware	21	1	3	41	6	7	11	16
Florida	40	1	1	120	6	18	4	16
Georgia	56	0	2	180	2	17	1	8
Hawaii	25	1	3	51	3	12	5	20
Idaho	35	1	3	70	6	12	7	14
Illinois	59	3	8	118	8	18	5	11
Indiana	50	3	4	100	6	14	6	12
Iowa	50	4	1	100	7	13	7	9
Kansas	40	1	2	125	3	21	2	13
Kentucky	38	2	2	100	3	8	4	7
Louisiana	39	1	0	105	2	5	2	3
Maine	33	1	6	151	16	35	9	22
Maryland	47	4	2	141	8	33	6	19
Massachusetts	40	2	7	160	7	19	3	9
Michigan	38	0	1	110	6	12	4	9
Minnesota	67	0	8	134	6	18	3	13
Mississippi	52	1	0	122	5	3	3	2
Missouri	34	1	1	163	10	18	6	10
Montana	50	2	2	100	7	12	6	6
Nebraska**	49	1	7	—	—	—	2	14
Nevada	21	1	2	42	4	3	8	8
New Hampshire	24	2	5	400	83	111	—	27
New Jersey	40	3	2	80	6	8	8	8
New Mexico	42	2	1	70	0	6	2	6
New York	61	3	5	150	4	15	3	10
North Carolina	50	1	6	120	8	20	5	15
North Dakota	53	3	3	106	10	12	8	10
Ohio	33	3	0	99	5	12	6	9
Oklahoma	48	0	1	101	2	10	1	7
Oregon	30	2	6	60	9	13	12	21
Pennsylvania	50	1	1	203	6	8	3	4

(continued)

TABLE 5.7 *Continued*

State	Number of Senators	1974	1984	Number of Members	1974	1984	1974	1984
		Number of Women			*Number of Women*		*Percentage of Women in Both Houses**	
Rhode Island	50	1	5	100	3	13	3	12
South Carolina	46	0	2	124	5	10	3	7
South Dakota	35	1	4	70	5	10	6	13
Tennessee	33	0	1	99	4	9	3	8
Texas	31	1	0	150	5	11	3	6
Utah	29	0	1	75	6	6	6	7
Vermont	30	3	4	150	17	29	11	18
Virginia	40	0	2	100	6	11	4	9
Washington	49	1	8	98	12	19	9	18
West Virginia	34	1	2	100	9	12	7	10
Wisconsin	33	0	2	99	6	24	5	20
Wyoming	30	1	2	62	4	16	5	20
Average Percentage		3.8	8.1		7.1	13.7	5.7	12.1

*Percentages are computed on the basis of numbers of state senate and house members in 1974 and 1984. The numbers of senate and house members in this table are for 1984.

**Nebraska is unicameral.

Source: "Women State Legislators as of January, 1974" (New Brunswick, NJ: Center for the American Woman in Politics, Eagleton Institute of Politics, Rutgers, 1974) and Council of State Governments, *State Elective Officials and the Legislatures, 1983–1984* (Lexington, KY: Council of State Governments).

EXPLAINING WOMEN'S INCREASES IN THE 1980s

In order to arrive at an explanation of women's growing power in 1984, past research is replicated and then other variables are added in an effort to understand the changes that have occurred since the 1970s. We examine whether women are still likely to be elected in states with small populations and large legislatures, as was true in the 1960s and 1970s. We also ask whether one can predict women's increases in the 1980s from the proportions in individual states in the 1970s.[2] We expect that states favorable in past decades will continue to be so, while at the same time others are now providing new opportunities for women's election to legislatures.

We also examine the relationship of Democratic or Republican Party dominance and women's recruitment to state assemblies and senates.[3] Are Republican Party-dominated states (i.e., those with 60 percent or more Republican members in the legislature) still favorable grounds for women's election, as in the 1960s and 1970s? And are Democratic Party states still unfavorable? We expect that the legislative barriers to women in the Democratic Party, particularly in the northern states, came down in the 1980s. But we also anticipate that the Republican Party states remained favorable grounds for women's election in that decade.

Competitive states—those that are not dominated by one party or another—had no relationship to women's election in the 1970s. We expect that trend to continue. This is because those states varied in the money that was spent for social welfare in the 1970s. Low-social-welfare states usually are not favorable for women's election to state legislatures, while those that spend more for this purpose are.[4]

Several scholars have observed that women are likely to be recruited in states that have a "moral" political culture, and are unlikely to be elected in "traditional" and "individualistic" states.[5] In moral states—such as those in most of New England as well as Arizona, Oregon, and Washington—politics is everybody's business. Elected officials are expected to be selfless and committed to promoting the public's interest. In the "traditional" state politics of the southern states, by contrast, government is of, by, and for a privileged few, usually white males. And in the "individualistic" states of Illinois, Massachusetts, and New York, government is viewed as if it were a business serving various competing interests for the state officeholders whose career is politics. This study anticipates that states with moral cultures will continue to be favorable and that women's recruitment in traditional and individualistic states will increase over a decade earlier.

Recently attention has turned to a new question: Does it make a difference in women's recruitment if legislators are elected under different election procedures? Yes, several scholars found, it does make a considerable difference.[6] They discovered that when voters could choose two or more representatives for the legislature instead of one from each district, many more women got elected to their state houses.

We expect that the importance of multimember districts for women's election to state legislatures will be upheld in this study. Also, we expect that the single primary (in which the candidate with the most votes wins the nomination) will be favorable to women. The double or runoff primary in some southern states requires that a candidate achieve an absolute majority vote before she or he runs in the final election.[7] A majority of votes is more difficult to achieve for a woman legislative candidate than it is for a male contestant. In consequence, the author expects that fewer women will be elected to legislatures in double-primary states.

This essay also examines whether the legislature is still a dead end for women legislators, as it was in the 1970s when few were elected to Congress. Where large proportions of women were elected to legislatures in low-population states (such as New Hampshire), few were elected to Congress; also, where a small proportion was recruited to the legislatures in high-population states (such as California), only a small number also went on to Congress.[8] We hypothesize that this situation has changed in the 1980s, with more opportunity for women legislators to move up to Congress and to statewide offices such as governor and secretary of state.

Of considerable interest is whether the women's movement has played a significant role in this period of great change in women's legislative representation. We expect that with the growth of the women's movement, there has developed a reciprocal relationship among women at various levels of government that had not been present before. Specific women's organizations, such as the National Organization for Women, are also expected to have aided women's recruitment in the 1980s.[9] In turn, an important base of women's organizations has been women in the workforce and professional women. It is expected that these changes in women's work outside the home have had a favorable impact on women's legislative recruitment in the 1980s as in the 1970s.

The factors promoting or hindering women's recruitment to state senates have been given scarce research attention, perhaps because few women were elected to them. However, the percentage of women in state senates has doubled in the last decade and in 1984 reached 8 percent. Women's recruitment to state senates may be of interest not only because it will broaden the representativeness of those chambers but also because it will provide a future pool of experienced and credible women candidates for the U.S. House of Representatives, which in 1990 was about 94 percent male.

We suggest that women's recruitment to state senates has a time-lagged, two-tiered pattern. We expect that those states where women were first elected in large numbers to state assemblies in the 1960s and 1970s, such as many in New England, will now have the largest percentages of women state senators. This is likely because women who have served some terms in the assembly and who have become well known should have greater chances for state senate election than those without a legislative background.[10]

METHODOLOGY

Our analysis required the gathering of some eighty—sometimes overlapping—political and socioeconomic contextual variables. For example, we collected data on the extent of party dominance in each house of the fifty legislatures for 1974 and 1984, as well as the strength of parties at the local and state levels. The data were collected primarily from standard sources (see Table 5.8).

Numerous and different statistical tests on various sets and subsets were conducted. These included Pearsonian correlations, factor analysis, and stepwise multiple regressions. The bivariate correlational analysis included separate and combined sets of the percentages of women in the assemblies and senates for the 1974 and

---

TABLE 5.8 Sources for Variables

Council for State Governments. *The Book of the States,* 1972–1973, 1974–1975, 1983–1984, and 1985.

National Center for Educational Statistics. *Earned Degrees Conferred,* 1972–1973, 1973–1974, and 1979–1980.

National Organization for Women.

Official Catholic Directory. Wilmette, IL: National Register Publishing Company,1983.

U.S. Bureau of the Census. *Characteristics of the Population, 1980; General Social and Economic Characteristics, 1980; Statistical Abstract of the United States, 1981, 1984, 1985, 1986, 1988, 1989* (Washington, DC: U.S. Government Printing Office, 1986).

TABLE 5.9   Continuity and Change in Women's Recruitment to State Assemblies and Senates, 1974–1984 (Based on Pearsonian Correlations)

I. *Continuing favorable factors, 1974–1984*
    Republican party, dominance of legislatures***
    Moral state political culture***
    Higher AFDC payments**
    No second primary**

II. *Continuing unfavorable factors, 1974–1984*
    Democratic dominance of legislatures, especially in former Confederate states***
    Traditional southern culture***

III *Factors no longer unfavorable, 1984*
    Small assemblies in high-population states[‡]
    Low-income states[‡]

IV. *New contextual conditions aiding women's recruitment, 1984*
    Individualistic state culture***
    Multimember assembly districts*
    Women in U.S. Congress**
    Women in labor force***
    Professional women**
    National Organization for Women***

***Significant at the .001 level.
**Significant at the .01 level.
*Significant at the .02 level.
[‡]Not statistically significant.

1984 periods in all fifty states, and in forty non-Confederate states. From this analysis, the direct relationship between women's election to state legislatures and political and socioeconomic variables was determined. The results are presented in Table 5.9.

Then a rotated orthogonal factor analysis using all the variables was undertaken. One objective was to verify the interpretation of the correlation analysis by employing another test using the same data; another was to provide a basis for reducing the data set. The next step involved multiple regression analyses with the reduced set of thirty-nine significant variables. Of six run only two are presented here. One regression used the decade's percentage increases in both chambers. The results are found in the section "The New Wave: States with the Most Increases 1974–1984." Another regression presented in Table 5.10 used the 1984 percentage of women in both chambers.

FINDINGS

Continuity and Change in All Fifty States, 1974–1984

The contextual variables related to women's political recruitment in the last decade are summarized in Table 5.9. They are based on simple bivariate correlations. In section I of Table 5.9, the continuing favorable contextual factors from the 1970s

TABLE 5.10 Women State Legislators' Party Affiliation and Women's Legislative Representation, 1996

State	Total Number of State Legislators	Women's Party Affiliation		Women's Percentage in Both Houses	Percentage Decrease or Increase since 1992
		Democratic	*Republican*		
Alabama	140	5	0	4	−2
Alaska	60	6	7 (1 Ind.)	23	+1
Arizona	90	10	17	30	−3
Arkansas	135	14	3	13	+3
California	120	19	4 (1 Ind.)	20	−3
Colorado	100	17	16	33	−2
Connecticut	187	34	16	27	+2
Delaware	62	2	11	21	+7
Florida	160	23	8	19	+1
Georgia	236	29	14	18	+1
Hawaii	76	11	4	20	−4
Idaho	105	9	21	29	−1
Illinois	177	20	21	23	0
Indiana	150	13	20	22	+3
Iowa	150	11	16	18	+3
Kansas	165	15	31	28	−1
Kentucky	138	6	6	9	+4
Louisiana	144	13	2 (1 Ind.)	11	+3
Maine	186	29	18 (2 Ind.)	26	−6
Maryland	188	42	12	29	+5
Massachusetts	200	33	15	24	+1
Michigan	148	19	14	22	+4
Minnesota	201	30	21	25	−2
Mississippi	174	17	3	11	+1
Missouri	197	18	21	20	0
Montana	150	18	18	24	+4
Nebraska	49	Nonpartisan		24	+4
Nevada	63	11	11	35	+8
New Hampshire	424	48	78	30	−4
New Jersey	120	8	10	15	+3
New Mexico	112	15	8	20	+1
New York	211	29	9	18	0
North Carolina	170	10	18	16	−2
North Dakota	147	8	13	14	−2
Ohio	132	12	18 (1 Ind.)	24	+3
Oklahoma	149	11	5	11	+2

(continued)

TABLE 5.10　*Continued*

State	Total Number of State Legislators	Women's Party Affiliation		Women's Percentage in Both Houses	Percentage Decrease or Increase since 1992
		Democratic	*Republican*		
Oregon	90	16	11	30	+3
Pennsylvania	253	14	15	11	+2
Rhode Island	150	28	8	24	−1
South Carolina	170	9	12	12	−1
South Dakota	105	8	12	19	−1
Tennessee	132	13	5	14	+2
Texas	181	20	13	18	+2
Utah	104	5	10	14	0
Vermont	180	34	20	30	−4
Virginia	140	16	5	15	+3
Washington	147	34	24	40	0
West Virginia	134	14	7	16	0
Wisconsin	132	17	15	24	−3
Wyoming	90	7	12	21	−3
Average Percentage		55%	44%	21%	+.006%

Note: Percentages are rounded. One percent of women legislators is non-partisan or independent.

Source: Center for the American Woman and Politics, Fact Sheets, "Women in State Legislatures 1994," and 1996.

are presented. These are descriptive of Republican-dominated New England states. In section II are listed two continuing negative factors for women's recruitment— Democratic Party dominance of the assemblies and state senates and traditional culture. Although the negative correlation with Democratic Party dominance has declined in the last decade, it is still significant in the following ten former Confederate states: Alabama, Arkansas, Florida, Georgia, Louisiana, Mississippi, North Carolina, South Carolina, Texas, and Virginia.

In section III the previously unfavorable relationship of small assemblies in high-population states no longer is a negative contextual factor as, for example, in the California of 1984. Nor are states that have a low per capita income. In the following section, there are six new variables that have emerged as significant for women's recruitment during the ten-year period. These include individualistic state cultures, such as those in the Midwest, and states with multimember assembly districts.

The remaining four favorable variables relate in various ways to the growth of the women's movement. The first shows a relationship between the election of women in Congress to greater representation of women in the same state's legislatures. Women's labor force participation and the presence of a large proportion of women professionals are also significant. Finally, women's associations (as represented in our data set by ratios of chapters of the National Organization for Women to state population) are shown to be highly correlated with greater percentages of women in state legislatures.

THE 1994 AND 1996 ELECTIONS

Comparing 1994 with the earlier years, we find that Republican Party dominance has been modified somewhat as a favorable factor. This is due in part to Republican majorities in the lower houses in the Carolinas and the state senate in Florida. Fewer women were elected to the legislatures in the former, while in Florida's senate there was no change from the previous election. The traditional southern culture and Christian fundamentalism appear related to growing Southern Republicanism. Generally, it differs from the moderate Republicanism of New England on approaches to such issues as abortion, crime, education, and welfare.

In 1994–1996 Democratic dominance of state legislatures appeared to be less of a negative factor in the former "solid South." Democratic dominance has been waning in the 1980s. Republican inroads seem to have brought more Democratic women into office as a result of party competition.

Another factor has been the Voting Rights Act. Previously gerrymandered legislative districts were redistricted in the 1980s and 1990s to give Blacks and Latinos representation previously denied them. As seats opened up, Democratic women typically have filled 10 to 15 percent of them in southern, as well as other, states.

As a whole, however, women have been disadvantaged whenever legislative election methods were changed. Thus, in the 1980s and 1990s nine former multimember legislative districts were changed to single-member ones. The result were drastic declines in some state's women's representation. Florida's, Hawaii's, and Wyoming's declined from about the fifth highest (averaging 20 percent women in 1984) to around twenty-sixth in 1994 (still with about the same average percentage of women legislators). Among the remaining multimember states, Arizona, Maryland, New Hampshire, and Washington were also leaders in 1984. They averaged 32 percent women legislators in 1996 with Washington State highest in the nation at 40 percent (see Table 5.10).

The decline from 100 percent to 75 percent in the growth of women's representation from 1984 to 1996 is due in part to the election system change. Switching to a semiproportional or proportional representation system for state legislatures would have brought more political equity for majority and minority women (and men).

In summary, the major changes in the last decade for women's legislative representation are a slight decline in the *favorability* of the Republican Party; a slight decline in the *unfavorability* of the Democratic Party; the unfavorable impact on women's legislative recruitment in states changing to single-member districts; and the 25 percent decline in the decade's growth rate of women's representation. The favorable factors listed in Table 5.9 show continuity from 1974 to 1996.

THE NEW WAVES: STATES WITH THE MOST INCREASES 1974–1996

In 1984 40 percent of the states had increases of women legislators of 100 percent or more over the previous decade. Ten years later the record was almost as good, with 36 percent growing at a high rate. Those eighteen legislatures (except for Kansas)—like the ones before them with large increases—constituted new ground for growth in women's representation (see Tables 5.7 and 5.10). In 1994–1996 these gains were consolidated. However, the average growth rate for all fifty states was less than one percent in these two elections.

There was only one Republican-dominated state, Kansas, in the 1994 group. The remaining seventeen were politically competitive or tending in that direction, and were Democrat-dominant states: Alaska, Arkansas, Georgia, Idaho, Illinois, Louisiana, Massachusetts, Michigan, Mississippi, Missouri, Montana, New Mexico, Nevada, Ohio, Pennsylvania, Texas, and Washington.

The most significant and striking growth pattern is found in five southern states. In Mississippi women's representation advanced from 2 percent to 12 percent, equaling the northern state of Pennsylvania. In addition, Mississippi, like the others, had a small contingent of Republicans among its women legislators.

The inland western states of Nevada and Montana increased 300 percent, and four other state legislatures in that region saw large increases. Five midwestern states showed growth of 100 to 150 percent. Lastly, the two eastern states with large increases were Pennsylvania, which had growth of 200 percent, and Massachusetts, with 166 percent more women legislators than the decade before.

New wave states of 1984 with the highest growth in state assemblies continued to augment appreciably in 1994, except for Florida, Hawaii, and Wyoming, whose slowdown was explained previously. The high-growth states included California, Colorado, Kansas, Maine, Maryland, Rhode Island, and Wisconsin. They varied in political party and political culture, and all at least doubled the number of women state senators by 1994.

A significant factor for the past decade has been the continued promotion and support of women candidates by women's organizations. Of course, there still exists a tremendous range, from 3.6 percent women legislators in Alabama to 39.5 percent in Washington State. And women still averaged only one-fifth of the nation's state lawmakers in 1996, although women constitute over half of America's population.

Most Powerful Predictors of Recruitment, 1984 and 1994

Our final analysis ascertains the most powerful predictors of women's assembly and senate recruitment as of 1984. In the stepwise multiple regression in Table 5.10, each variable may be regarded as a separate dimension. Highly intercorrelated clusters of variables have been removed through the computer routine in order to provide a parsimonious list and to avoid complicating the results with multicolinearity. The percentage that each variable explains is given in the last column of the table, and the total explained by the nine variables is 76 percent.

Table 5.11 contains contextual factors that relate to the two 1984 trends the data have previously shown. The first trend is the continuance of the 1974 favorable contextual pattern for assemblies and senates, as in independent variables 1 (percentage women in 1974 assemblies), 5 and 6 (higher educational and Aid to Families with Dependent Children [AFDC] expenditures), and 7 (the single primary). These four variables explain 45 percent of the variance. The second trend is that of the "new wave" states now favorable to women's election to state legislatures. These new wave variables are 2 (percentage women in congressional delegation), 3 (more professional women), 4 (percentage women statewide officials), 8 (more NOW chapters per population), and 9 (multimember state senate districts). These five variables explain 31 percent of the variance in women's 1984 legislative recruitment. The two trends for 1984 set forth in Table 5.11 were still in place in 1995. The oldest trend is continued above-average growth in women's representation in the states that led in the 1970s, including Arizona, Connecticut, Oregon, and Vermont. These and others favorable to women twenty years ago generally were higher in expenditures for education and aid to dependent children.

The second trend is strengthened due to increases from 1984 to 1994 in the number of women in Congress (from 25 to 57 members) and in the number of female statewide executive officers. The single primary continues as a boon for

TABLE 5.11 **Most Powerful Predictors of Greater Women's Recruitment to State Assemblies and Senates, 1984 (Multiple Stepwise Regression) (N = 50)**

Independent Variables*	Multiple Correlation Coefficient (R)	Cumulative Percentage of Variance Explained (R^2)	Percentage Variance Explained by Each Variable
1. Percentage women in 1974 state assemblies	.61	37	37
2. Percentage women in state congressional delegation, 1974–1984	.72	52	15
3. Percentage women professionals	.76	58	6
4. Percentage women statewide officials	.80	64	6
5. State educational expenditures	.82	67	3
6. State AFDC expenditures	.83	69	2
7. Single primary	.85	72	3
8. National Organization for Women	.86	75	3
9. Multimember senate districts	.87	76	1

*The *F* ratio when each of the variables was entered into the equation was significant at less than the .001 level.
Sources: Refer to Table 5.8.

women candidates as do the remaining states with multimember districts. Women's groups in the previous and this decade, such as the National Organization of Women, the National Women's Political Caucus and their local branches, and Emily's List providing campaign finance, are of major importance.

CONCLUSION

This analysis shows that women's recruitment to state legislatures has almost tripled in the past twenty years. For the 1970s there was a building on the gains in the Republican-moralistic states most favorable to women in the 1960s. In the 1980s no political party or political culture was dominant in the states where women legislators had the most dramatic increases. Most states that led in the 1970s and 1980s continued to advance, with state senates at least doubling women members by the 1994 elections. The 1996 legislative contests revealed that gains remained in place, but there were no significant increases in women's representation.

In 1994 the South broke out of its mold as the "solid [Democratic] South" for the first time in some 100 years. Republicans won three legislative bodies that previously had been Democratic, but the number of women legislators decreased. Gone is the southern Democratic Party as a negative factor for women's election in five states where their proportions at least doubled. Although women legislators' numbers are growing fast, seven of the ten southern states still have the lowest proportions in the nation.

Republican Party dominance was modified as a favorable factor for women's recruitment. Contemporary southern Republicanism appears to differ from New England Republicanism in approaches to abortion, education, and welfare. Also, Democratic dominance in the South became less unfavorable for women's recruitment in 1994–1996, in part because of Republican competition. States that are competitive generally have been good grounds for women candidates in the 1980s to 1990s.

Turning to structural arrangements, the change of election procedures for nine states from multimember districts to single ones since 1980 adversely affected women's legislative recruitment and growth in 1994–1996. A semiproportional or proportional election system would produce a fairer result for majority and minority women and men. Some multimember assemblies remain, and in four of them women's recruitment is in the top ten nationally.

The data presented in Tables 5.9 and 5.11 further substantiate the observation by other writers, including Mandel and Carroll, that the women's movement has made considerable impact on women's election to political office.[11] In addition, the large increase in women state executives and members of Congress from 1984 to 1996 has helped women's recruitment to state legislatures, and vice versa. In turn, women's organizations have provided womanpower and campaign financing to assist women's success at the polls. As numbers of women legislators grow, legal gains can be made not only for women and children but also for protecting and promoting the state's environment, health, and a peacetime prosperity.[12]

NOTES

1. E. Werner, "Women in the State Legislatures," *Western Political Quarterly,* 19 (1968), pp. 40–50; I. Diamond *Sex Roles in the State House* (New Haven, CT: Yale University Press, 1977); C. Nechemias, "Changes in the Election of Women to U.S. State Legislative Seats," *Legislative Studies Quarterly,* 12 (1) (February 1987), pp. 125–142.

2. Diamond, *Sex Roles.*

3. W. Rule, "Why Women Don't Run: The Critical Contextual Factors in Women's Legislative Recruitment," *Western Political Quarterly,* 34 (March 1981), pp. 60–77.

4. *Ibid.*

5. See Diamond, *Sex Roles;* D. Hill, "Political Culture and Female Political Representation," *Journal of Politics,* 43 (1981), pp. 159–168.

6. R. Darcy, S. Welch, and J. Clark, *Women, Elections and Representation* (Lincoln: University of Nebraska Press, 1994), pp. 160–168; W. Rule, "Multi-member Districts, Minority and Anglo Women's and Men's Recruitment Opportunity," and subsequent chapters on Maryland and Arizona in W. Rule and J. Zimmerman (Eds.),

U.S. Electoral Systems: Their Impact on Women and Minorities (Westport, CT: Greenwood Press, 1992).

7. A. P. Lamis, "The Runoff Primary Controversy: Implications for Southern Politics." *PS,* 7 (1984), pp. 782–787.

8. See Rule, "Why Women Don't Run."

9. T. J. Volgy, J. E. Schwartz, and H. Gottlieb: "Female Representation and the Quest for Resources: Feminist Activism and Electoral Success," *Social Science Quarterly,* 66 (1986), pp. 156–168.

10. G. Jacobson, G. Kernell, and S. Kernell, *Strategy and Choice in Congressional Elections* (New Haven, CT: Yale University Press, 1981).

11. R. Mandel, *In the Running: The New Woman Candidate* (New York: Ticknor and Fields, 1981); S. J. Carroll, *Women as Candidates in American Politics* (Bloomington: University of Indiana Press, 1985.)

12. S. Thomas, *How Women Legislate* (New York: Oxford University Press, 1994), chapters 3, 4, and 6. See also B. Burrell, *A Woman's Place Is in the House* (Ann Arbor: University of Michigan Press, 1994).

FURTHER READINGS

Burrell, B. *A Woman's Place Is in the House* Ann Arbor: University of Michigan Press, 1994.

Darcy, R., S. Welch, and J. Clark. *Women, Elections and Representation.* Lincoln: University of Nebraska Press, 1994.

Rule, W., and J. Zimmerman (Eds.). *U.S. Electoral Systems: Their Impact on Women and Minorities.* Westport, CT: Greenwood Press, 1992.

Thomas, S. *How Women Legislate.* New York: Oxford University Press, 1994.

Women State Legislators: Three Decades of Gains in Representation and Diversity

LYNNE E. FORD AND KATHLEEN DOLAN

The representation of women in American political institutions has been characterized both as a puzzle and a problem.[1] It is a puzzle because, although women make up over half of the U.S. population, they constitute a considerably smaller proportion of elected representatives at all levels of government. Even in 1998, women do not approach parity at any level of public office. Is this because women are somehow prevented from seeking and winning election or is it because they have simply chosen not to enter electoral politics as candidates? Research suggests some combination of factors, but does not definitively solve the puzzle. The under-representation of women in legislatures is a problem because it runs counter to the ideals of representative democracy. Is a representative system legitimate when the minority is consistently called upon to speak for the interests of a majority of citizens? One theme in democratic theory "concerns the distribution of power in a political community: the degree to which people are free to share in making decisions about the community, and ultimately, themselves."[2] To the extent that women are included, government is more representative of society as a whole—both substantively and symbolically.[3] Will the gains made by women in the most recent elections, particularly at the state legislative level, resolve the puzzle and the problem?

In this chapter we use two different kinds of data in order to more fully understand the nature of representation by women state legislators today and to see whether the type of woman serving in the state legislature has changed over time. Using this approach, we are able to create a profile of change over time and offer a full description of contemporary women state legislators. The most striking aspect of the population of women legislators today is the diversity in their backgrounds, reasons for seeking office, and in the agendas they pursue once in office. In the aggregate, women serving today are a reflection of the constituency they serve and offer the promise that a variety of women can win a seat and serve in the state legislatures, thus enriching both the quantity of women's representation and the quality of representative democracy overall.

GAINS FOR WOMEN OVER THE LAST TWENTY YEARS: ALL THINGS ARE NOT EQUAL

State legislatures are historically important institutions for women and it is at the state level that women have made the greatest gains in striving for some level of proportionality (see Table 5.12). Consider that in 1970, women held just 4 percent of all available state legislative seats and until 1974, no woman had been elected governor of a state in her own right. By 1984, women had tripled their participation in the state legislatures, comprising 12 percent nationwide. In 1992, called by many the "Year of the Woman," women made the largest single net gain in any one election cycle winning 1526, or 20.4 percent, of the 7424 seats available.[4] Yet by 1997, women had increased their ranks by only 88 seats, raising the percentage of women serving to 21.6.[5]

In contrast, progress at the federal level has been much slower. In 1975, women represented only 4 percent of the membership in the U.S. Congress. Ten years later, their proportion had crept to 5 percent and to merely 6 percent (32 women) in 1991. Finally, the elections in 1996 increased women's presence to 11 percent of the institution—fifty seats in the House and nine in the Senate.[6]

At local levels, measuring progress is more difficult because of the sheer number and variation in the kinds of positions available. Between 1975 and 1988, women's representation in county elected office increased from 3 to 9 percent and from 4 to 14 percent of all municipal elected positions.[7] Most visible at the local level are female big city mayors and in 1994, women were mayors of 18 of the 100

TABLE 5.12   Women's Representation in Elective Office over Time, 1977–1997

Level of Office	1977	1979	1981	1983	1985	1987	1989	1991	1993	1995	1997
U.S. Congress	4%	3%	4%	4%	5%	5%	5%	6%	10%	10%	11%
Statewide Elective	10	11	11	11	14	14	14	18	22	26	26
State Legislature	9	10	12	13	15	16	17	18	21	21	22

Source: Center for the American Woman and Politics (CAWP), National Information Bank on Women in Public Office, Eagleton Institute of Politics, Rutgers University.

largest U.S. cities.[8] By 1997, that number has dropped to 12 among the 100 largest cities, and 202 (20.7%) of the mayors in cities with populations over 30,000.[9]

THE IMPORTANCE OF STATE LEGISLATURES
TO WOMEN'S REPRESENTATION

All in all, women enjoy the greatest electoral successes at the state legislative level and the majority of research on women candidates and elected officials concentrates on women serving in state houses.[10] As women won increasingly more seats during the 1970s, a robust research effort confirmed the importance of state legislatures to women's representation in politics for a number of reasons. First, evidence shows that service in the state legislature functions as a key entry point to higher office; the rate of gains for women at the state level has a direct impact on the number of women serving in the national legislature and executive positions nationwide.[11] Of the 48 women who held seats in the 103rd U.S. Congress, 21 served in their state legislatures prior to being elected to the national legislature.[12]

Additionally, state legislatures hold particular importance for women from a policy perspective; many of the issues of direct concern to women are decided at the state level. The Equal Rights Amendment, issues of pay equity, spousal retirement benefits, teen pregnancy, women's health concerns, maternity leave issues, and workplace climate concerns have all received direct attention at the state level.[13] Research finds that a higher percentage of women than men spend time promoting passage of "women's rights" bills and that women are more likely to list "women's distinctive concerns" (defined to include policy areas like health care, welfare, and education) when asked to name their top legislative priority.[14] To many interested in the promotion of women's rights, this suggests that as the number of women serving at all levels increases, the attention devoted to policy of direct concern to women will also increase. There is some initial evidence to support this contention. Thomas, for example, found that when the proportion of women in the legislature falls below 15 percent, women like other minority groups are constrained in their legislative behavior. In states where the proportion of women reached or surpassed 20 percent, women legislators gave priority to bills dealing with issues of women, children, and the family and were more successful in introducing, monitoring, and passing distinctive legislation than were their male colleagues.[15]

Although, on the whole, women have increased their presence in state legislatures nationwide, the proportions of women legislators varies considerably among the fifty states (Table 5.13). What might account for these differences? Research in this area is still inconclusive, but suggests several possibilities. One such explanation may lie in the political culture of individual states and regions of the United States.[16] Historically, the dominant national culture in America has proscribed women's active participation in politics, defining the competitive electoral

TABLE 5.13   Women in the State Legislatures, 1997

State	Senate	House	Total	% of Total	Rank by %
Alabama	2	4	6	4.3	50
Alaska	3	5	8	13.3	43
Arizona	8	26	34	37.8	2
Arkansas	1	22	23	17.0	35
California	7	20	27	22.5	24
Colorado	10	25	35	35.0	3
Connecticut	9	45	54	28.9	10
Delaware	7	9	13	25.8	15
Florida	6	32	38	23.8	19
Georgia	7	32	39	16.5	36
Hawaii	5	8	13	17.1	33
Idaho	6	19	25	23.8	18
Illinois	11	35	36	26.0	14
Indiana	14	14	28	18.7	28
Iowa	12	20	32	21.3	26
Kansas	14	35	49	29.7	9
Kentucky	2	11	13	9.4	49
Louisiana	2	15	17	11.8	47
Maine	13	35	48	25.8	15
Maryland	8	48	56	29.8	8
Massachusetts	7	39	46	23.0	22
Michigan	3	31	34	23.0	23
Minnesota	22	40	62	30.8	6
Mississippi	3	19	22	12.6	45
Missouri	3	39	42	21.3	27
Montana	9	26	35	23.3	21
Nebraska	13	unicameral legislature	13	26.5	12
Nevada	5	16	21	33.3	4
New Hampshire	8	122	130	30.7	7
New Jersey	2	17	10	15.8	39
New Mexico	10	20	30	26.8	11
New York	8	31	39	18.5	29
North Carolina	6	23	29	17.1	34
North Dakota	6	18	24	16.3	38
Ohio	8	21	29	22.0	25
Oklahoma	6	9	15	10.1	48
Oregon	9	14	23	25.6	17
Pennsylvania	6	25	31	12.3	46
Rhode Island	11	28	39	26.0	13
South Carolina	3	19	22	12.9	44
South Dakota	5	13	18	17.1	32

TABLE 5.13 *Continued*

State	Senate	House	Total	% of Total	Rank by %
Tennessee	3	15	18	13.6	42
Texas	3	30	33	18.2	30
Utah	1	16	17	16.3	37
Vermont	12	48	60	33.3	4
Virginia	7	14	21	15.0	40
Washington	23	25	58	39.5	1
West Virginia	4	16	20	14.9	41
Wisconsin	9	22	31	23.5	20
Wyoming	4	12	16	17.8	31
United States	366	1,238	1,604	21.6	

Note: States with the exact same percentages are ranked the same; since there is a tie, no state is ranked 5th or 16th.

Source: CAWP, National Bank on Women in Public Office, Eagleton Institute of Politics, Rutgers University.

arena as most appropriate for men.[17] However, the considerable variation in the proportions of female representation across the states implies that some state environments may foster women's participation at both the mass and elite levels, while others do not.[18] In the South for example, women held only 13 percent of the seats in the region in 1994 compared with 20.4 percent nationwide.[19] In 1997, of the five states with the lowest percentage of women, three are from the old Confederacy. Irene Diamond found that "moralistic" cultures encourage a political environment "potentially receptive to the values and style that have traditionally been associated with women—concern with public welfare rather than personal enrichment and so forth" while "traditionalistic" cultures defined politics as an exercise in maintaining the status quo largely excluding the participation and interests of women.[20] In addition, the size of the legislative district, whether legislatures meet on a full or part-time basis, is characterized as professional or non-professional, and the level of pay has been found to exert some influence on the number of women elected.[21]

CHANGING PROFILES: THE "TRADITIONAL" VERSUS THE "CONTEMPORARY" WOMAN STATE LEGISLATOR

When scholars first began to study women elected to the legislatures, they compared their characteristics, motivations for seeking the office, and legislative behaviors to those of their male legislative colleagues.[22] They found that women elected through the early 1970s were less well educated and older than their male colleagues, less likely to be married with small children at home, unlikely to have pursued a professional career outside the legislature, more likely to be motivated to seek public office by civic concerns and the desire to make life better for others, unlikely to have been tapped for the seat by their local party elites (even though they may have worked for years within the party ranks), and have little expressed desire to pursue higher office or a full-time career in politics.[23] These early women legislators were forced to follow a rather passive path to office, dependent on political ties to others and situational factors beyond their control, one characterized by a vicarious status mediated by those with more direct access to political power and leadership structures.

More recently, as career paths and socioeconomic characteristics of men and women have converged, the number of women elected to office has increased. Many of the differences between male and female candidates found previously have largely decreased in importance for women seeking office in the 1980s and beyond.[24] Educational and occupational opportunities for women have expanded greatly, leading to ever-increasing numbers of women pursuing higher education and employment outside the home, often in areas that were previously considered nontraditional careers.[25] Similar changes have been occurring in politics. Recent research finds that as educational, occupational, and financial doors have been opened for women in the last twenty years, their political opportunity has expanded as well.[26]

The recent changes in women's social and political lives raise two main questions. First, are the women elected to office in the 1990s different from their predecessors of the 1970s and 1980s? In other words, have more recently elected women been able to combine politics, work, and family in ways not possible for an earlier generation of women legislators? Are they capitalizing on educational and professional occupational networks in an effort to increase their chances of being elected to political office? Second, if women state legislators are changing, what are they like today? What new characteristics and abilities do they bring to the state legislatures and what are the implications for the representation of women?

INDICATORS OF TRANSITION: THE EMERGENCE OF THE NEW-STYLE WOMAN LEGISLATOR OVER TIME

While others have asked a similar question, "Is there a new type of woman in office?" the dominant research approach continues to focus on examining differences between men and women currently holding political office.[27] Having found that women still differ from men in a number of areas, some researchers have concluded that women legislators have not changed. In our view, this approach doesn't completely address the question. Simply confirming that male and female legislators do not yet resemble one another on some number of indicators does not preclude the possibility of significant changes taking place among women themselves. In order to determine whether women have changed over time in relation to those who came before them, women need to be the primary focus of the inquiry. To undertake this examination, we collected demographic, political, and legislative data on all women serving in the legislatures of fifteen states in 1972, 1982, and 1992.[28] The states were selected to capture geographic diversity, political culture, the proportion of women in the legislatures, and the level of professionalism of the legislatures.[29] A total of 706 women who served in these state legislatures during the time periods under analysis.[30]

In comparing the demographic and personal characteristics of women serving across the three points in time, we were interested in whether women's preparation for office, work life, and family life had changed. For comparison, we selected occupation prior to entering the legislature as well as personal factors such as marital status, number of children, level of education, and age at the time of their first election. We expected that, like many women today, legislators of the 1990s would have taken advantage of expanding social and economic opportunities and therefore be more likely to have worked outside the home before serving in the legislature, have at least a college degree if not professional training, and be married.

Table 5.14 presents the comparative analysis results.[31] Women elected most recently are significantly more likely to be younger, married, and a member of a racial minority group than women serving in 1972 or 1982. Further, women in 1992 were more likely to be employed in business or professional positions and less likely to be homemakers prior to entering the legislature. In looking at levels of education, the likelihood that a woman serving in the legislature has a college degree is quite consistent over the twenty year period (33 percent in 1972 and 37 percent in 1992). The biggest change is in post-graduate education, where the number of women completing degrees beyond the B.A. more than doubles from 7 percent in 1972 to 17 percent in 1992.

In looking at women's preparation to run for political office, we focused on several political variables. In the past, women followed a path to the state legislature that required them to gain substantial political experience along the way through a series of elected or appointed offices most often beginning with the school board. These same women often devoted substantial time to service in the political party. The traditional image of women as a part of the "lick-em and stick-em" brigade of party workers is a familiar one in American politics and proved to be one of the only ways for women to attract the attention of party elites recruiting candidates for office. Since women were less credentialed than men at the time, party service and recognition increased their viability. This is not as necessary for women in the 1990s since their political portfolio is now more likely to include professional degrees and occupations as well as the financial backing gained through professional and occupational networks.

Table 5.14 compares women's previous political office experience and their service to the party, defined in this case as having held party office. There is no significant difference among women in having held elected or appointed offices prior to election to the legislature (41 percent in 1972 and 37 percent in 1992). There is, however, a significant difference in the type and level of previous office. Women in 1992 were three times more likely to enter the state legislature from a position on the town or city council (9 percent to 3 percent in 1972). Women in 1972 were twice as likely to have served on a state board or commission, usually in

TABLE 5.14   Difference of Means Analysis for Women State Legislators 1972–1992: Demographic, Political, and Legislative Variables—Means (percent) for Measures at Three Points in Time

	1972	1982	1992
Total Legislators (N)	87	241	378
Occupation			
Lawyer	11	10	9
Educator	25	22	19
Homemaker	25	20	8**
Business/Professional	11	16	22*
Support Personnel	11	9	8
Education			
College Graduage	33	35	37
Post College	7	13	17*
Law School	9	10	9
Age			
At first election	49	44	46**
Marital Status			
Married	68	77	81*
Race			
White	96	91	86*
Previous Political Office			
Any Office	41	32	37
Town/City Council	3	5	10*
County Council	3	5	6
Mayor/Deputy Mayor	1	2	2
State Board/Committee	15	9	7*
School Board	13	9	9
Committee Assignments			
Education	22	23	29
Health and Welfare	23	24	26
Appropriations	5	8	13*
Finance	12	12	16
Industry and Commerce	8	14	19*
Agriculture	6	8	13*
Committee Leadership			
Any Position	18	30	34*
Chair/Vice Chair	15	22	26*
Ranking Member	—	3	7*

*p<.05
**p<.01

an appointed position (15 percent to 7 percent in 1992). Political party service reflects the same trends, but the largest differences are found between 1982 and 1992. Forty-four percent of women in 1982 held party office compared with only 30 percent serving in 1992. This may mean that women no longer need the party in order to be recognized as viable candidates. It could also mean that political parties are casting a wider net in recruiting women to run for office and looking beyond the rather small pool of local party leadership. Alternatively, it may be a reflection the general trend away from involvement with parties seen nationally among candidates, public officials, and the electorate.

Finally, in looking at women's legislative activities inside the institution, we focused on committee service and leadership activities. Previous research found women serving on committees dealing with traditional "women's issues" defined as education and health and welfare.[32] It is not clear whether women were relegated by assignment to "women's" committees based on sex role stereotypes or whether women specifically chose these committees in order to concentrate their legislative impact.[33] Given that women's social and professional opportunities have expanded into nontraditional occupations over time, we might expect that women recently elected, if given the choice, would select a wider range of committee assignments including Finance, Appropriations, Industry and Commerce, Transportation, Energy, Agriculture, and Judiciary. In order to further expand their influence within the chamber, we expected that women serving in 1992 would be more likely to gain positions of leadership both on committees and in the chamber.

Table 5.14 shows that women in 1992 are not moving away from "women's issue" committees. There is no significant difference in service on education or health and welfare committees between women legislators in the three time periods. There is a difference, however, in service on the nontraditional committees. Women in 1992 are more than twice as likely to serve on Appropriations, Industry and Commerce, Transportation, and Agriculture committees than their 1972 predecessors. Rather than entirely abandoning issues most directly affecting women, families and children, women legislators appear to be expanding the scope of their influence to include financial and business concerns. In the process, they may also be expanding the definition of "women's issues." In the area of leadership, we found women in 1992 more likely to hold both committee and chamber leadership positions. In 1972, 18 percent of the women held a committee position and 2 percent held a leadership office in the institution. In 1992, 34 percent led committees and 8 percent were part of the chamber leadership.

In each of the areas we examined—personal and demographic characteristics, preparation for political office and legislative activity once elected—women in 1992 were significantly different from women serving in 1972 and 1982. The sum of the differences creates a portrait of contemporary legislators that resembles that of many modern professional women outside of politics. The contemporary woman legislator is likely to be married with children, have prepared for a career by earning a college or advanced degree, and entered the legislature from an occupation outside the home. These changes are important in relation to the representation of women. First, these changes signal political opportunities for all kinds of women—not just those who come from political dynasties or choose politics instead of a family life. Young women can decide that they want to prepare to seek political office and construct an educational and financial path that will allow them to do so. Once elected, they will share the characteristics and lifestyles of their peer group outside of politics. Symbolically this is important. Once inside the state legislature, women have moved to expand their range of interests beyond, but not instead of, the traditional issues of women, children, and the family. This will likely make them more viable candidates for higher office since they can broaden their legislative expertise in the process.

CONTEMPORARY WOMEN STATE LEGISLATORS: A DIVERSE GROUP WITH DIVERSE AGENDAS

Having seen that the characteristics and interests of women legislators have, in fact, changed over time, we turn to our second question: What are women legislators like today? In order to answer this question, we have to move beyond the information gathered through State Legislative Manuals. These sources do not give any information on motivations for seeking office, political aspirations, or issue priorities of the legislators; they focus almost exclusively on background characteristics and legislative assignments once in office. To get an idea of what women legislators are like in the 1990s, we needed to collect additional data from the women state legislators themselves. The data used to create a portrait of the contemporary woman state legislator come from an original mail survey of the 1373 women serving as U.S. state legislators in all 50 states during the 1992 legislative session.[34] The survey asked women legislators for more detailed information about their political, professional, and legislative careers. Surveys were returned from all 50 states and the number of surveys received from each state is strongly related to the number of women legislators serving in that state (r = .95). There were 627 surveys returned, for a response rate of 46 percent.

The women state legislators who responded to the survey closely match the entire population of women state legislators on such characteristics as political party, chamber of service, and race. For example, the political party identification distribution of all women state legislators in 1992 was 60 percent Democrat, 39 percent Republican, and 1 percent Independent. For our sample, the distribution is 59 percent Democrat, 40 percent Republican, and 1 percent Independent. Seventy-eight percent of all women legislators served in their state's lower chamber and 22 in the upper chamber. For our sample, 74 percent served in their lower house and 26 percent in the Senate. Finally, in terms of race, 88 percent of the legislators serving in 1992 were Caucasian, 9 percent were African American, and 3 percent were other races. In our sample, 92 percent of respondents were Caucasian, 5 percent were African American, and 3 percent were other races. Because the women who responded to the survey resemble the population from which they were selected, we feel confident about drawing an accurate portrait of the contemporary woman state legislator from our information.

In creating a more detailed portrait of women currently serving, we have focused our attention on women legislators' professional, political, and legislative attitudes and attributes. The trends suggested in the previous section are confirmed here: The current woman state legislator is decidedly different from the traditional women characterized by much of the earlier research.

PROFESSIONAL AND PERSONAL CHARACTERISTICS

In the area of demographic characteristics, we found that women serving in state legislatures in 1992 are a diverse group who have achieved a range of educational and occupational success far above that of women state legislators in the past. A survey of women state legislators done in 1977 found that 63 percent of these women had at least a college degree. Of this group, 26 percent had gone on to earn advanced degrees.[35] In 1992, fully 77 percent of the women in our sample had earned a college education, and another 18 percent had some college education. Further, 36 percent of the respondents held master's, PhDs, or law degrees. Clearly, these women are taking advantage of the greater educational opportunities available to women in the United States over the last twenty years.

Women have put their education to use by pursuing professional occupations outside the home. The women legislators in our survey were involved in an impressive array of careers, including law, education, journalism, business, and the health professions. In earlier times, women state legislators tended to be employed in clerical and sales positions, or not employed at all. Indeed, a 1977 survey found that 46 percent of women state legislators described themselves as housewives.[36] In our 1992 group, housewives comprised only 16 percent of the sample. This change in educational and occupational preparation for political office may prove important in determining what these women will do once they are in office.

Another important set of demographic variables to consider is that involving age and family life. In our sample, the women tended to be older, married women with children. While there was significant diversity in the age ranges of our sample (the youngest respondent was 26 and the oldest 83), the median age was 54 years old. That women state legislators tend to be middle aged is likely due to the number of years that they devote to educational, occupational, and family pursuits prior to their involvement in politics. In our sample, 73 percent of the respondents were married, 21 percent had been married but were presently widowed or divorced, and only 7 percent had never been married. The vast majority of these women were mothers (83 percent), and a fairly large group, 20 percent, had children who were under the age of 18. This data seem to illustrate that contemporary women state legislators are balancing family and professional obligations, much like the vast majority of women as a whole.

POLITICAL BACKGROUND

In examining the relatively slow pace of women's integration into political office in the United States, some researchers have suggested that women lack the political ambition and experience necessary for success. Previous research found that women traditionally entered public life through civic and volunteer activities, usually motivated by a sense of civic duty and a desire to make their community a better place. Having accomplished the specific change they sought, many of these women returned to private life without seeking additional office. Does this traditional portrait still apply to the contemporary woman state legislator? If state legislative seats are going to act as "feeder systems" for higher office, women need to develop attitudes and experiences that can propel them to progressively higher offices.

The women legislators in our sample possess significant office-holding experience prior to their election to the state legislature. In fact, only 33 percent of our respondents reported having no prior political office experience at all and 36 percent of them have held two or more previous offices. This confirms the pattern that others have found: Women state legislators tend to come to that office after having paid their political dues in a series of other offices.[37] Further, more of them came to the legislature having previously held elected office rather than appointed office, which means that they have the campaign experience necessary to successfully seek an office in the state legislature and presumably beyond.

Familiar patterns regarding women state legislators' paths to office are confirmed again when we examine the past offices that our respondents have held. The three most common previously elected positions are city or town council, county council, or local school board. Additionally, 17 percent have served as appointed members of various state boards and commissions. While numerous women had held elected or appointed office at the county and state level, the majority of women in our sample (56 percent) earned their political experience in local politics.

Turning to an examination of the attitudes women state legislators hold about politics and their position, we see considerable diversity among our respondents. For example, when we examine their motivations for entering politics, we see that the conventional image of the civic-minded woman legislator may no longer be applicable. A vast majority of the women in our sample (75 percent) expressed motivations for seeking office that could be characterized as ambition or opportunity-based motivations (such as they were recruited to run, wanted to enter politics, or had previous political experience), while only 32 percent expressed more traditional civic-oriented reasons (wanted to help community, liked idea of public service). Clearly, these data show that a significant portion of the sample exhibits some degree of political ambition.

On the issue of how committed our respondents are to the office of legislator and political office more broadly, the evidence is mixed. When we asked our respondents if they consider themselves to be full-time legislators, 54 percent reported that they do. This finding is especially interesting given that only 14 percent of our respondents serve in legislatures that could be considered full-time. Clearly these women are expressing a level of commitment to their position that is largely unrelated to the constitutional responsibilities and resources of their legislatures. Yet, respondents were pretty evenly split on whether they considered politics and public office a career. Forty-six percent indicated that they do not think of politics as a career, 40 percent said that they do, and 14 percent were unsure at this point. If we are correct in our assumption that considering politics as a career is related to progressive ambition for higher office, this 40 percent, while not a majority, still creates a substantial pool of candidates for the future.

In response to our question about their interest in seeking an office other than the one they now hold, 38 percent indicated that they definitely or probably will run for additional office, while 42 percent said no and 20 percent were unsure. Why don't more women say that they want to seek an additional office? The most common response to our inquiry into why these women do not intend to seek other office is satisfaction with the office of state legislator. This is followed by health concerns (which is not so surprising when you consider that the average age of our respondents is 54), a feeling of being burned out by politics, and a desire to have more time for self and family.

For those women who express ambitions for future political offices, where are they headed? Our survey asked respondents to indicate which elected office beyond the legislature they intended to seek. Since respondents were allowed to list more than one office, 235 women listed a total of 409 positions to which they aspired. The most frequently mentioned office (26 percent of all offices mentioned) was that of state senator, indicating that, for lower chamber legislators, the upper chamber is seen as desirable and possibly a path to other offices as well. The second and third most frequently mentioned offices were U.S. Representative and U.S. Senator. Together these offices accounted for 20 percent of the offices mentioned. Statewide elective office was less frequently mentioned than legislative office; the governorship was mentioned 14 percent of the time and the lieutenant governor's office 10 percent.

LEGISLATIVE ACTIVITIES

The final aspect to consider in portraying contemporary women state legislators is their legislative activity within the institution. Much of the recent research done on women state legislators suggests that women approach their legislative activities from a distinct perspective, a perspective shaped and influenced by their experiences as women.[38] For many researchers, this evidence suggests that women are concerned about issues having an impact on the lives of women and on areas of traditional concern to women, such as children, welfare, and education. To examine the role of these issue concerns in the legislative career of our respondents, we focus on their committee assignments, stated legislative priorities, and concerns about the problems facing women in the United States.

In looking at committee assignments, we see that our respondents are indeed focusing much of their legislative activity on these issues, but not to the exclusion of all other policy areas. Fifty-one percent of the women in our sample sat on at least one committee related to women's issues and about 20 percent of this group sat on at least two. Further, 40 percent of respondents sat on a health and welfare committee and 35 percent served on committees handling education policy. Yet, 46 percent were members of committees such as Appropriations, Banking, Finance, and Industry and Labor.

Finally, do women today list women's issues high on their legislative priority list? We asked our respondents to identify their top three legislative priorities during the most recent legislative session. Thirty-eight percent of the sample identified a legislative priority that we classified as being related to women's interests. Among the most frequently offered of these priorities were issues related to child care, families, and women's health. Yet, alongside these priorities, respondents listed concerns about economic development, substance abuse, labor issues, and agricultural and environmental issues. The data on committee assignments and legislative priorities indicate that these women legislators are sensitive to the needs of women and that they pay considerable attention to the so-called women's issues. It would be misleading, however, to portray contemporary women state legislators as a group solely devoted to the needs of their descriptive constituencies to the neglect of broader issues.

CONCLUSIONS

We began this chapter with a puzzle and a problem related to women's representation in American political institutions. Why has the increase in women's representation come so slowly, and now that women are present in greater numbers, what will it mean? From the earliest debates over suffrage to women's celebrated representation on the Senate Judiciary Committee, the assumption has been that an influx of women into the political process in significant numbers would radically alter the course of public life. The precise nature of this change, however, has been a matter for speculation and study. Would women act as agents of reform, pushing for legislative action to improve the lives of women and children; and in general, bring a distinctive "woman's" focus to their legislative work born out of their unique experiences in the private sphere? Often implied, but sometimes explicitly stated, is the underlying premise that women are women; one homogeneous body of actors sharing attitudes, agendas, and policy preferences. Very little research has been done to directly examine the diversity among women representatives and how who they are might affect what they are inclined to do as legislators.

Over the past twenty years, women in the United States have sought and won increased access to elective office at all levels of government. Nowhere has that success been more clearly documented than in the state legislatures. The 1990s, as a period of tremendous gain for women in state legislatures, present a significant opportunity to put some of these earlier assumptions about women state legislators to the test. Our examination of women state legislators, both over time and during the contemporary period, leads us to reject the earlier notions of women as a relatively homogeneous group. Indeed, our data illustrate the diversity of experience and interests these women bring to politics. As a group, women state legislators serving in the 1990s exhibit greater educational, occupational, political, and legislative diversity than the women who served in the past. Precisely how this diversity among the women themselves and in their political agendas will be reflected in the character of the legislatures in which they serve as we move into the next century remains to be seen.

NOTES

1. R. Darcy, Susan Welch, and Janet Clark, *Women, Elections, and Representation,* 2nd ed. (Lincoln, NE: University of Nebraska Press, 1994).

2. Virginia Sapiro. *Women in American Society: An Introduction to Women's Studies,* 3rd ed. (Mountain View, CA: Mayfield Publishing Company, 1994), p. 279.

3. Sue Thomas. *How Women Legislate* (New York: Oxford University Press, 1994).

4. CAWP Fact Sheet. (New Brunswick, NJ: Center for the American Woman and Politics, 1993).

5. CAWP Fact Sheet. (New Brunswick, NJ: Center for the American Woman and Politics, 1997).

6. CAWP Fact Sheet, 1997.

7. Jo Freeman. *Women: A Feminist Perspective,* 5th ed. (Mountain View, CA: Mayfield Publishing Company, 1995).

8. Freeman, *Women: A Feminist Perspective,* p. 415.

9. CAWP, Fact Sheet. (New Brunswick, NJ: Center for the American Woman and Politics, 1997).

10. See for example: Jeane Kirkpatrick, *Political Woman* (New York: Basic Books, 1974); Irene Diamond. *Sex Roles in the State House* (New Haven, CT: Yale University Press, 1977); Susan J. Carroll. *Women as Candidates in American Politics* (Bloomington, IN: Indiana University Press, 1985) and Thomas, *How Women Legislate.*

11. Darcy, Welch, and Clark, *Women, Elections, and Representation.*

12. CAWP Fact Sheet, 1993.

13. Darcy, Welch, and Clark, *Women, Elections, and Representation.*

14. Ruth Mandel and Debra Dodson. "Do Women Officeholders Make a Difference?" ed Sara E. Rix, *The American Woman* (New York: W. W. Norton, 1992; Sue Thomas and Susan Welch. 1991. "The Impact of Gender on Activities and Priorities of State Legislators." *Western Political Quarterly,* (1991) 44: 445–456.

15. Thomas, *How Women Legislate;* Rosabeth Kanter. "Some Effects of Proportion on Group Life: Skewed Sex Ratios and Response to Token Women." *American Journal of Sociology* (1977), 82: 965–90.

16. Daniel Elazar. *American Federalism: A View from the States,* 3rd ed. (New York: Harper and Row, 1984); Marjorie R. Hershey. "The Politics of Androgyny: Sex Roles and Attitudes Toward Women in Politics." *American Politics Quarterly* (1977), 5: 261–287; David B. Hill. "Political Culture and Female Political Representation." *Journal of Politics* (1981), 43: 157–168; Diamond, *Sex Roles in the State House.*

17. Kirkpatrick, *Political Woman;* Virginia Sapiro. *The Political Integration of Women* (Urbana, IL: University of Illinois Press, 1983).

18. Diamond, *Sex Roles in the State House;* Hill, "Political Culture and Female Political Representation"; Marjorie Spruill Wheeler. *New Women of the New South: The Leaders of the Woman Suffrage Movement in the Southern States* (New York: Oxford University Press 1993); and Darcy, Welch, and Clark, *Women, Elections, and Representation.*

19. CAWP Fact Sheet, 1993.

20. Diamond, *Sex Roles in the State House,* p. 22.

21. Sue Thomas. "Women in State Legislatures: One Step at a Time." in *The Year of the Woman: Myths and Realities,* ed. Elizabeth Adell Cook, Sue Thomas, Clyde Wilcox (Boulder, CO: Westview Press, 1994), pp. 141–159; Barbara Burrell. "The Presence of Women Candidates and the Role of Gender in Campaigns for State Legislature in an Urban Setting: The Case of Massachusetts." *Women and Politics* (1990), 10(3): 85–102.

22. Emmy E. Werner. "Women in the State Legislatures," *Western Political Quarterly* (1968), 21: 40–50.

23. See, for example: Carol Nechemias. "Changes in the Election of Women to U.S. State Legislative Seats." *Legislative Studies Quarterly* (1987), XII, 1: 125–142; Carol Nechemias. "Geographic Mobility and Women's Access to State Legislatures." *Western Political Quarterly* (1985), 38: 119–131; Wilma Rule. "Why Women Don't Run: The Contextual Factors in Women's Legislative Recruitment." *Western Political Quarterly* (1981), 34: 60–74.

24. Joan Hulse Thompson. "Career Convergence: Election of Women and Men to the House of Representatives." *Women and Politics* (1985), 5(1): 69–90; Darcy, Welch and Clark, *Women, Elections, and Representation.*

25. Sara Rix. *The American Woman.* (New York: W. W. Norton, 1992).

26. Barbara C. Burrell. "The Political Opportunity of Women Candidates for the U.S. House of Representa-

tives in 1984." *Women and Politics* (1988), 8(1): 51–69.

27. A question most recently posed by Patricia Freeman and William Lyons. "Female Legislators: Is There a New Type of Woman in Office?" ed. Gary Moncrief and Joel Thompson, *Changing Patterns in State Legislative Careers* (Ann Arbor, MI: University of Michigan Press, 1992).

28. The 15 states included in the sample are California, Georgia, Idaho, Illinois, Iowa, Nevada, New Jersey, Oklahoma, Oregon, Pennsylvania, South Carolina, South Dakota, Vermont, Virginia, and Wisconsin.

29. The 15 states represent all three classifications of legislatures formulated by the National Council of State Legislatures. California, Illinois, New Jersey, Pennsylvania, and Wisconsin are considered full-time, professional legislatures. Iowa, Oklahoma, Oregon, South Carolina, and Virginia are classified as transitional legislatures, moving from amateur to professional status. Georgia, Idaho, Nevada, South Dakota, and Vermont are considered part-time, amateur legislatures.

30. There may be missing data on some variables (committee assignments, year of birth, race, and marital status) for some women because of variation in information reported in state legislative manuals.

31. To test the hypotheses regarding changes among women state legislators over time, we conducted difference of means tests for the several dependent variables by the time period of service (1972, 1982, 1992).

32. Diamond, *Sex Roles in the State House;* Thomas and Welch, "The Impact of Gender Activities and Priorities of State Legislators."

33. Marylin Johnson and Susan Carroll. *Profile of Women Holding Office II* (New Brunswick, NJ: Center for the American Woman and Politics, 1978); Susan Carroll and Ella Taylor. "Gender Differences in the Committee Assignment of State Legislators: Preferences or Discrimination?" Paper presented at the annual meeting of the Midwest Political Science Association, Chicago, IL, 1989.

34. The mail survey was administered during July and August of 1992. We used a two-wave mailing procedure with a reminder postcard sent between survey mailings. The mailings occurred approximately 4 weeks apart.

35. Diamond, *Sex Roles in the State House.*

36. *Ibid.*

37. Alice Rossi. "Beyond the Gender Gap: Women's Bid for Political Power." *Social Science Quarterly* (1983), 58: 671–682.

38. Beth Reingold.. "Concepts of Representation Among Female and Male State Legislators" Paper presented at the annual meeting of the American Political Science Association, Washington, DC 1991; Michelle A. Saint-Germain. "Does Their Difference Make a Difference? The Impact of Women on Public Policy in the Arizona Legislature." *Social Science Quarterly* (1989), 70: 956–968; Thomas, *How Women Legislate.*

FURTHER READINGS

Barrett, Edith. 1997. "Gender and Race in the Statehouse: The Legislative Experience." *The Social Science Journal,* 34:2.

Considine, Mark, & Iva Ellen Deutchman. 1996. "Instituting Gender: State Legislatures in Australia and the US." *Women and Politics,* 16:4.

Darcy, Robert. 1996. "Women in the State Legislative Power Structure: Committee Chairs." *Social Science Quarterly,* 17.

Kathlene, Lyn. 1995. "Alternative Views of Crime: Legislative Policymaking in Gendered Terms." *Journal of Politics,* 57:3.

Reingold, Beth. 1996. "Conflict and Cooperation: Legislative Strategies and Concepts of Power Among Female and Male State Legislators." *Journal of Politics,* 58:2.

Richardson, Lilliard, & Patricia Freeman. 1995. "Gender Differences in Constituent Service Among State Legislators." *Political Research Quarterly,* 48:1.

Rosenthal, Cindy Simon, 1995. "The Role of Gender in Descriptive Representation." *Political Research Quarterly,* 48:3.

6

THE EXECUTIVE BRANCH: WOMEN AND LEADERSHIP

A growing list of nations in this century have selected female heads. These have included Great Britain, the Philippines, Argentina, Israel, Iceland, and India. However, the United States has not yet succeeded in electing a woman as our chief executive. The U.S. presidency has remained a bastion of maleness. Marcia Lynn Whicker and Hedy Leonie Isaacs have investigated the reasons for this and find four factors that account for the unlevel presidential "playing field" the women candidates face: (1) the presidential system itself, which relies more closely on direct, popular elections than does the parliamentary system, which elects its prime minister from among fellow party members; (2) the paucity of women gaining experience in the presidential "launching roles" of the vice presidency, the U.S. Senate, and governorships; (3) the difficulty women face in securing campaign funding for national and subnational races; and (4) long-standing public images of a conflict for women—and not for men—between familial and political roles. Is the lack of female presence in high elective office an issue that should be addressed by our government? If not the government, who? How can the role of women in high elective office be increased?

When, who, and how will Americans finally elect our first female president? Will the route to this office be as Diane Kincaid describes in her article, "Over His Dead Body: A Positive Perspective on Widows in the U.S. Congress," *Western Political Quarterly,* March 1978, pp. 96–104. That is, will the route to the White House for women be similar to that of women who first gained entrance to the Congress—widows of congressmen who had served in that district? These widows had campaign advantages often associated with an incumbent candidate, such as name recognition and campaign experience because many had campaigned with their husbands. Will a first lady who gains the public eye by being the wife of the president end up being our first female president? The first lady is a prominent figure in American political life. Barbara C. Burrell examines the first lady's role as a policy adviser to the President, which is now both recognized and problematic. Public opinion and the legal system have influenced and conditioned her participation in public policy development within the White House. This article brings together the legal conditioning of her formal governmental status with public perspectives on her roles. It considers the gendered nature of our response to the first lady as an actor in the White House advisory system and critiques limitations on her involvement as inconsistent with liberal political traditions. Laws, court decisions, and public opinion polls provide the "data" upon which this piece is built. This research brings together executive branch studies and issues evolving around the political equality of women in consideration of the presidential advisory system and the role of first lady. It shows that the first lady has been given a "quasi-governmental" status and that the public is ambivalent about her role in public policy making and her individualism.

Sara J. Weir focuses on the growing importance of the governorship in U.S. politics. She explores a new area of scholarly inquiry—women as governors. From the 1925 election of Nellie Taylor Ross (D-Wyoming) to the 1997 re-election of Christine Todd Whitman (R-New Jersey), fifteen women (twelve Democrats and three Republicans) have served as governors. While these numbers are small—as compared with the proportion of women elected to statewide offices or with men elected as governors—a growing number of women are running for and winning in gubernatorial contests and others are positioning themselves to run for governor by serving in other statewide elective offices. This article expands the study of gender and leadership to include the examination of the careers of the women who have served as governors, providing comparisons of their candidacies and administrations. Although the governorship has not served as the same avenue to the presidency for women as it has for men, the changing character of political ambition among women and the increased acceptance of women in high political office may change this.

The Maleness of the American Presidency

Marcia Lynn Whicker
Hedy Leonie Isaacs

INTRODUCTION

The U.S. presidency has historically been a bastion of maleness despite comments during the early Clinton administration that First Lady Hillary Rodham Clinton would be a "copresident." Aside from being first lady, the closest a woman has come to presidential power was the 1984 Democratic vice presidential nomination of Geraldine Ferraro. The earlier 1972 presidential candidacy of Democrat Shirley Chisholm, a Black woman from New York, was discounted by both the press and the public on sexual and racial grounds. In the 1988 primaries, Democratic U.S. Representative Pat Schroeder from Colorado briefly considered running for president but was unable to raise the necessary funds.

Yet women in more socially conservative societies, where fewer advances for women might be expected, have served as the chief executives of their countries. Throughout the decade of the 1980s, Conservative Party leader Margaret Thatcher was prime minister of Britain. In 1990 Mary Robinson became president of Ireland, which is governed through a parliamentary system. Indira Gandhi was prime minister of India from 1966 until her assassination in 1984 by religiously motivated Sikh extremists. Golda Meir, a former schoolteacher from Milwaukee, served as the prime minister of Israel during the late 1960s and early 1970s.

Isabel Perón, the second wife of Argentine leader General Juan Perón, was elected president of that country in 1974, becoming the first woman head of state in the Western Hemisphere. In 1962 Sirimavo Bandaranaike was elected prime minister of her native Sri Lanka, following the 1959 assassination of the former prime minister, her husband. And, with the fall of Ferdinand Marcos in the Philippines in 1986, Corazon Aquino was elected president there in a bitter and contentious campaign.

Why are women becoming chief executives in countries more socially traditional than the United States while still being excluded from the White House in all but secondary roles? The purpose of this essay is to explore this crucial political—and no longer merely academic—question.

THE PARLIAMENTARY SYSTEM VERSUS THE U.S. PRESIDENTIAL SYSTEM

Many of the female leaders cited here—with the exceptions of Perón and Aquino, who succeeded to leadership roles after the deaths of politically prominent husbands—achieved their power in parliamentary systems. Table 6.1 presents a listing of women national leaders from other countries, showing slightly more have obtained national leadership positions in parliamentary than in presidential systems. Prime ministers are not elected directly by the people but are chosen by their fellow party members, since the prime minister is the leader of the dominant party in parliament.[1] Party members and long-term colleagues likely have less traditional bias against women as political leaders than does the general electorate.[2]

In aspiring to leadership of a political party, parliamentary members start with an equality recognized legitimacy: All have been elected from their districts or in national elections, depending on whether single-member districts or proportional representation is the electoral basis. Party members seem to operate on a rough merit system, which provides rewards of power and leadership based on political and legislative performances.[3] Both male and female party members, once elected, have similar opportunities to excel in the tasks of creating national agenda, developing legislation, and shepherding proposals around or over legislative hurdles. In this arena, paying one's professional dues is important, recognized, and generally rewarded.

Only since 1980 have women come to be elected national chief executives in nationwide popular elections. In June 1980 Vigdis Finnbogadottir became the world's first popularly elected head of state in Iceland. In April 1990 Violetta Barrios de Chamorro was elected president of Nicaragua. (Michel Rocard, who became prime minister of the French Republic in June 1988, was appointed to that office by President Mitterand rather than elected.)

In the United States as well as in the various parliamentary systems, women active in party politics have become more similar to the men who are active. Table 6.2 shows that women national leaders were more likely to have obtained extensive political experience in parliamentary than presidential systems. Of women presidents, only 1 (14%) had extensive political experience compared with 5 (72%)

TABLE 6.1   Non-U.S. Women National Leaders

Name	Country	Years of Rule	Type of Government	Political Experience
Aquino, Maria Corazon	Phillippines	1986–1992	Presidential	None
Bandaranalke, Sirimavo	Sir Lanka	1960–1965, 1970–1977, 1994–	Parliamentary	None
Bhutto, Benazir	Pakistan	1988–1990, 1993–1996	Parliamentary	Limited
Brundtland, Gro Harlem	Norway	1981, 1986–1989, 1990–1996	Parliamentary	Extensive
Chamorro, Violetta	Nicaragua	1990–1997	Presidential	Limited
Charles, Mary Eugenia	Dominica	1966–1977, 1980–1995	Parliamentary	Extensive
Finnbogadottir, Vigdis	Iceland	1980–1996	Presidential head of state in a parliamentary system*	Limited
Gandhi, Indira	India	1966–1977, 1980–1984	Parliamentary	Extensive
McAleese, Mary	Ireland	1997–	Presidential head of state in a parliamentary system*	None
Meir, Golda	Israel	1969–1974	Parliamentary	Extensive
Pascale-Trouillot, Ertha	Haiti	1990–1991	Presidential	Extensive
Peron, Isabel	Argentina	1974–1976	Presidential	Limited
Robinson, Mary	Ireland	1990–1997	Presidential head of state in a parliamentary system*	Limited
Thatcher, Margaret	England	1979–1990	Parliamentary	Extensive

*These leaders were elected nationwide to the office of president which serves as head of state in parliamentary systems where the prime minister serves as head of government.

Source: Michael Genovese, "Women National Leaders: What Do we Know?" In Michael A. Genovese (Ed.), *Women National Leaders* (Newbury Park, CA: Sage, 1993), pp. 211–218.

female prime ministers. Between 1964 and 1976, the differences between male and female political elites in terms of social background, political status, political careers, and perceptions of the political process—all factors affecting one's potential for leadership—were decreasing. During that period, issue orientations were predominantly a matter of party agenda rather than of gender, with the exception of issues dealing directly with gender roles.[4] A 1990 study also confirms the narrow-

TABLE 6.2   Non-U.S. Women National Leaders by Experience and Type of Government

Type of Experience	Office Held		
	President	Prime Minister	Total
None	2 (29%)	1 (14%)	3
Limited	4 (57%)	1 (14%)	5
Extensive	1 (14%)	5 (72%)	6
Total	7	7	14

For the purposes of this analysis, Iceland and Irish presidential heads of state in parliamentary systems where the prime minister served as head of government were counted as presidents.

ing of the gap between men and women in "political ambition," the pursuit of public office for personal self-enhancement.[5] Across a twenty-two-year period (1964–1986), women exhibited a marked increase in political ambition not matched by similar increases for men.

The United States differs from countries with parliamentary systems in that the national political leader (the president) is elected by the people through the electoral college system. Despite concern over the biases this system causes,[6] the electoral college rarely fails to confirm the popular vote.[7] In practice, U.S. presidential outcomes may be based less on political and legislative merit than on effective media exposure and communications, levels of campaign funding, and the personal appeal of the candidate.[8]

Although party identification does affect outcomes in U.S. elections, the role and influence of U.S. political parties have diminished steadily in recent decades as candidates have opted to build their own campaign organizations.[9] In parliamentary systems, by contrast, party discipline has remained crucial to national political leadership: Parties control the nominating process and, through the selection of leaders, reward individuals who have provided loyal party service.

Women, while becoming leaders in political systems based more directly on merit, have fared less well in arenas where public opinion dominates.[10] In the United States, the antidiscrimination legislation has been a relatively recent occurrence, dating to the 1960s. Usually changes in legislation, whether antidiscriminatory or otherwise, are influenced and supported by the pace of change in public opinion. Thus, women only achieved the right to vote in 1920, with state ratification of the Nineteenth Amendment to the Constitution.[11]

In other areas, especially in employment, where advancement for women was previously predicated on changes in public opinion, social legislation has been necessary for female gains. The Equal Pay Act of 1963, requiring equal pay for equal work by men and women, was the first federal law against sex discrimination in employment. In 1972 and again in 1974, two major expansions of that act extended coverage to executive, administrative, and professional employees and to most federal, state, and local government employees.[12]

It was the 1964 Civil Rights Act (Title VII) that safeguarded equal opportunity for women in employment in both hiring and advancement. Originally intended to protect blacks and other racial minorities, the 1964 act included equal opportunity for women as an amendment—a political miscalculation by opponents of the act. Intending to kill the act by including coverage of women, opponents were surprised when the amended act passed. Title VII also covers sexual harassment on the job.[13] The Pregnancy Disability Act of 1978, an amendment to Title VII, provides pregnancy protections for female employees.[14]

Social legislation has also been necessary to protect women from discrimination in nonemployment areas. Federal legislation has prohibited discrimination by institutions receiving federal funds. In marriage and divorce, it has taken a combination of both court suits and legislation to diverge from the English common-law assumption that husband and wife are one, with reciprocal and unequal rights.[15] Only in 1974, with the passage of the Equal Credit Opportunity Act, was sex discrimination in credit approval banned.[16]

Popular biases against women, partially overcome through social legislation, still exist in politics and can be expressed more directly in U.S. presidential electoral politics than in parliamentary selection of prime ministers. As Madison feared, majority rather than elite rule—a founding principle of the nation and one to which most citizens readily adhere—can sometimes be used as an instrument of bias and prejudice.

AN ABSENCE OF APPROPRIATE POLITICAL EXPERIENCE

A survey of the previous political experience of presidents and party nominees for president since 1960 indicates that three backgrounds emerge as the dominant training grounds for those who would be president—the offices of vice president, U.S. senator, and governor.

John F. Kennedy, the first president born and elected in this century, was a Democratic U.S. senator from Massachusetts when he ran for the presidency in 1960. Democrat Lyndon Johnson, his successor, wielded great power for years as U.S. Senate majority leader before accepting the vice presidency in 1960 after a failed presidential bid. Had he not become president as a result of Kennedy's assassination, Johnson likely would have run again for the White House.

The necessity of first being tested in these presidential proving grounds has not been limited to Democrats, of course. Republican Richard Nixon served in the U.S. Senate and as vice president prior to his unsuccessful 1960 presidential bid against Senator John Kennedy and his successful 1968 bid against Vice President Hubert Humphrey.

The pattern holds even with the one "accidental" president in recent years, Republican Gerald Ford. Ford was catapulted to the vice presidency through the resignation of Nixon's corrupt vice president, Spiro Agnew. Within a few months, Nixon's own resignation, brought about by impeachable charges of obstruction of justice in the Watergate affair, propelled Ford into the presidency in August 1974.

In recent presidential history—1976, 1980, 1984, and 1992—candidates with gubernatorial experience have captured the presidency. Democrat Jimmy Carter, elected in 1976, served as governor of Georgia before making his surprising successful bid for the White House as a Washington outsider. In both 1980 and 1984, former Republican California Governor Ronald Reagan easily defeated his Democratic opponent. In 1992, Bill Clinton, governor of Arkansas, captured the White House.

Even unsuccessful presidential nominees have acquired their political experience in the U.S. Senate, the vice presidency, and the presidency. Former Vice President Nixon, who opposed Senator Kennedy in 1960, fits this pattern. In 1964, Republican Senator Barry Goldwater ran unsuccessfully against Vice President Johnson. Former Democratic Senator from Minnesota and incumbent Vice President Hubert Humphrey was defeated by former Vice President Nixon in 1968. In 1972, President Nixon defeated South Dakota Democratic Senator George McGovern.

In 1976, former Governor Jimmy Carter defeated incumbent President Gerald Ford and, in turn, former Governor Ronald Reagan defeated incumbent President Jimmy Carter in 1980. In 1984, President Reagan's unsuccessful Democratic opponent, Walter Mondale, had been both a Democratic senator from Minnesota and Carter's vice president.

This pattern of formative political experience in the U.S. Senate, a governorship, or the vice presidency continued to hold in 1988. All but one of the presidential and vice-presidential candidates fit the pattern, the exception being Jesse Jackson, a black Democratic candidate for president. Although Jackson ran in 1984 and again in 1988 before his candidacy was taken seriously, he did not attain his party's nomination for president or vice president.

On the Republican side, the major contenders early in the 1988 race were Vice President George Bush and U.S. Senate Majority Leader Robert Dole. Eventually, Bush gained the nomination and appointed Indiana Senator Daniel Quayle as his vice presidential running mate. All fit the pattern.

Early in the 1988 presidential primaries, the Democratic picture was more chaotic. By the date of the so-called Super Tuesday primaries in March, the three major contenders were Massachusetts Governor Michael Dukakis, the Reverend Jesse Jackson, and Tennessee Senator Albert Gore. Only Jackson, the first black to contend seriously for the White House, deviates from the norm.

Traditionally, blacks in the United States have been excluded from the highest echelons of elected office and political leadership. The sole exceptions have been former U.S. Senator Edward Brooke of Massachusetts and former Governor Douglas Wilder of Virginia. Jesse Jackson compensated for this exclusion by pursuing those avenues of political power open to him, including leadership in the black church and in the civil rights movement.

Before the close of the 1988 primaries, Governor Dukakis had secured enough votes to gain the Democratic nomination, and appointed an established

TABLE 6.3 Political Backgrounds of Recent Presidential Contenders

Year	Winner	Background	Loser	Background
1960	Kennedy	Senator	Nixon	Senator Vice president
1964	Johnson	Senator Vice president President	Goldwater	Senator
1968	Nixon	Senator Vice president	Humphrey	Senator Vice president
1972	Nixon	Senator Vice president President	McGovern	Senator
1976	Carter	Governor	Ford	Vice president President
1980	Reagan	Governor	Carter	Governor President
1984	Reagan	Governor President	Mondale	Senator Vice president
1988	Bush	Vice president	Dukakis	Governor
1992	Clinton	Governor	Bush	Vice president President

political insider, Texas Senator Lloyd Bentsen, as his running mate: In 1992, Clinton defeated incumbent George Bush, continuing the pattern of extensive political training in "launching roles" for both winners and losers in presidential elections (see Table 6.3).

Candidates with other political backgrounds, including experience as a U.S. representative, traditionally have been unsuccessful in capturing their party's presidential nomination. Democratic Representative Morris Udall from Arizona in 1976 and Republican Representative John Anderson from Illinois in 1980 were unsuccessful presidential candidates. In 1988, the campaigns of both Democratic Representative Richard Gephardt from Missouri and Republican Representative Jack Kemp from New York faltered.

Paradoxically, five recent presidents have served in the U.S. House of Representatives—Kennedy, Johnson, Nixon, Ford; and Bush. Yet their service in the House has been coupled, *in each case,* with later experience in the Senate or the vice presidency, two of the presidential "launching roles." Although five of the last seven presidents started in the House of Representatives, House experience in itself has not been sufficient to support a successful presidential nomination. The presidential candidacies of Morris Udall (Democrat), John Anderson (Independent),

Jack Kemp (Republican), and Richard Gephardt (Democrat), all of whom had held no public office higher than the House, failed.

Nor can it be stated that the three traditional political backgrounds are irrelevant to or an improper proving ground for the presidency. Each provides an opportunity to develop the qualities and skills that presidents need. The first of these characteristics is high political visibility, combined with tempered experience in the exercise of power. The second is broad legislative experience; senators, vice presidents, and governors all must sell their policies and programs to national and state legislatures as well as to the public at large.

Third, all three backgrounds require a working knowledge of national political issues and of the intricate intergovernmental balance between federal and state governments in achieving national domestic policy goals. One final advantage these backgrounds provide is rigorous practice in analyzing, staking out, communicating, and defending positions in a visible, public, and adversarial arena—not unlike what the presidential campaign trail requires.

Because few women have served in these presidential launching roles, the selection pool for female presidential candidates has been minimal. For example, in 1994 only 8 out of 100 U.S. senators and 1 out of fifty governors were women. No women have been elected vice president. Only 11 percent of the seats in the House were held by women. With such a disproportionately small pool of women presidential candidates, the odds of women achieving the presidency in the near term are statistically negligible. History shows that aspirants to the presidency usually enter politics at subnational levels through either state or local elective office. But entering politics at any level presents barriers to groups that have been excluded, including the major barrier of fund-raising.

CAMPAIGN FUNDING AND PAC POWER

Elections drive home the basic principle of politics: Money buys access to power. Political action committees (PACs), long guided by this principle, have grown in clout and number in recent years. Yet, women trying to enter politics at all levels have had difficulty raising money, especially from PACs. This is in part because they are more typically nonincumbents and in part simply because they are women.[17]

In politics as elsewhere, nothing succeeds like success. This produces a political catch-22 for would-be female candidates: PACs are more likely to support proven winners—that is, incumbents. As for nonincumbents, PACs give more freely to those perceived as more likely to win, typically white males. With lower budgets for their campaigns resulting from difficulties in fund-raising, women often cannot take full advantage of modern campaign techniques, including use of the mass media, especially television, and of political pollsters. These handicaps reduce the likelihood of female challengers being elected.

Given their difficulty in fund-raising from interest groups and especially from PACs, female candidates would benefit disproportionately from reforms in campaign financing. Public financing for presidential general elections has existed since the adoption of the Revenue Act of 1971, which provided the first-time income tax checkoff as a federal subsidy.[18] Although presidential candidates receiving public financing are limited in their total expenditures, their expenditures may be supplemented by independent spending—by PACs, for example. The Federal Election Campaign Act of 1971 established procedures for the public disclosure of contributions and expenditures of $200 or more. This law also set ceilings on the amount of contributions that presidential and vice-presidential candidates and their families could contribute, as well as on the amount spent for media advertising.[19]

Because women have been considerably less successful historically in reaching the traditional presidential launching roles, they have benefited less from public financing for the presidency. Further, public financing has not been adopted for other national and subnational offices, including the U.S. Congress and major state offices, where women might compete both more steadily and more successfully. Some members of Congress fear that public subsidies would encourage opponents by equalizing the resources available to incumbents and nonincumbents. Others believe, however, that the ceilings on total campaign spending that would necessarily accompany such additional public financing would further bias elections toward incumbents, who already have a proven track record and greater name recognition.

Despite such criticisms, proponents argue that the nation as a whole, not just female candidates, would benefit from the enactment of public financing legislation for Congress and other levels of government. These reforms would not only allow greater diversity in the pool of candidates for elective offices but also reduce the pressure on officials, once elected, to conform to special interests at the expense of national and constituents' interests.

THE IMAGE OF FEMALE CANDIDATES

Women have experienced additional handicaps to election to higher political office, in part because of the public image of women as candidates. Women are still viewed societally in terms of domestic roles, whereas men are viewed in terms of occupational roles. Female politicians are viewed as interlopers in the political arena who should function behind the scenes rather than out front as candidates.[20]

Female candidates, then, must convince the electorate that their home responsibilities are not too demanding to permit them to make the commitment required by political officeholding. Former Princeton, New Jersey, mayor Barbara Boggs Sigmund has referred to this as "the bind of your femininity."[21] A 1978 study of men's and women's campaigns found that women were asked more often how they would manage their family responsibilities if elected and whether their husbands and children approved of their political activity.[22] Men were not asked whether their wives and children approved of their political activity. Rather, familial approval of male political participation was assumed. In one poignant example of this double standard from the mid-1970s, U.S. Representative Martha Keys of Kansas married fellow Representative Andrew Jacobs of Indiana. They had met while serving on the House Ways and Means Committee. When each sought re-election in their districts, the political marriage became a campaign issue for Keys but not for Jacobs.[23]

Because of the political liability regarding family responsibilities that people associate with women, many female politicians are either single or widowed, or do not become active in politics until after their children are adults.[24] For example, Kathryn Whitmire, mayor of Houston, was a widow when she sought and was elected to political office. Barbara Jordan, former U.S. Representative from Texas and spokesperson for the Democratic Party, never married. Nor did Elizabeth Holtzman, a Harvard lawyer and former U.S. representative from New York, who played a highly visible role in the Watergate hearings in the early 1970s. Geraldine Ferraro, the Democratic vice presidential nominee in 1984, had older children by the time she gained national attention.

The public perception that married female candidates in their childbearing years will neglect their familial duties if they run for and hold elective office affects the likelihood of women achieving the presidency in two ways. First, it reduces the pool of available female candidates acceptable to the public. Second, it delays the entry into elective politics of those women who choose to marry and have children. Many female candidates never recoup this lost ground. During the period when women are bearing and raising children, their male counterparts who aspire to the presidency are gaining formative experience at the subnational and national levels. Men gain access to the requisite presidential launching roles on a schedule compatible with career advancement, whereas women face a substantially telescoped time frame, among other handicaps, for their advancement.

The negative image of women as candidates, especially those still in their childbearing years, continues to present a significant handicap. Election to political office requires the overt approval of over 50 percent of the electorate, in most cases. There is still a proportion of voters who will not support female candidates simply because they *are* women.[25] In highly competitive races and in races where an incumbent is being challenged—the typical races that women face—a successful candidate cannot afford to lose even a small fraction of that electorate automatically. Although the proportion of the electorate opposed to women on gender alone has been diminishing, this diminution is a slow process. Further, equality of opportunity in politics cannot be regulated or mandated given that it depends instead on shifts in public opinion. Some of the changes in political opportunities and electoral success for women, then, depend to a large extent on the pace of social change.

Birth control has played a helpful role in increasing the number of women in politics by allowing women to control the number and timing of their offspring. This control is crucial for those who contemplate a political career, especially while public perceptions continue to make it difficult for women with small children to engage in high-level elective politics.

CONCLUSION

We have discussed four factors that, traditionally, have diminished the opportunity for women to compete for the presidency:

1. The presidential system itself, which relies more closely on direct, popular election than does the parliamentary system, which elects its prime minister from among fellow party members
2. The paucity of women gaining experience in the presidential "launching roles" of the vice presidency, the U.S. Senate, and governorships—roles that men have traditionally attained before competing, successfully or unsuccessfully, for the presidency
3. The difficulty women have experienced in securing PAC and other campaign funding for national and subnational races
4. Long-standing public perceptions that the traditional childbearing and child-rearing roles of women conflict with simultaneous participation in high-level elective politics.

Equality of opportunity has not been legislated in presidential politics or, for that matter, in elective politics at any level. Reforms that encourage female participation at subnational levels, such as public financing and other campaign reforms, will certainly contribute to the available pool of female presidential candidates. Ultimately, shifts in public opinion must also occur—including a recognition that political roles no more conflict with familial roles for women than they do for men—in order to level the "playing field" of U.S. presidential politics for women.

Although legislation has not been used in the United States in the past to increase female presence in high elective office, legislation to make equal representation a major goal has a recent precedent. The actions of the European Parliament can serve as an example of how the role of women in national politics may be enhanced and sustained. In the fall of 1988, the European Parliament, which represents the twelve countries in the Common Market, passed a resolution endorsing a quota and affirmative action system calling for equal numbers of men and women in the elected bodies of its member countries. Not only did this resolution pass the European Parliament, but also at least ten of the twelve member countries have adopted rules on quotas as well as timetables for increasing female representation in their national parliaments. Similar resolve to place women in the United States in equal numbers in presidential launching roles, as well as in appropriate subnational political roles in state legislatures and local governments, could well be legislated.

NOTES

1. Jean Blondel, *Government Ministers in the Contemporary World* (Beverly Hills, CA: Sage, 1985).

2. Marcia Lynn Whicker and Jennie Jacobs Kronenfeld, *Sex Role Changes: Technology, Politics, and Policy* (New York: Praeger, 1986).

3. Richard Rose, "Government against Sub-Governments: A European Perspective on Washington," in Richard Rose and Ezra N. Suleiman (Eds.), *Presidents and Prime Ministers* (Washington, DC: American Enterprise Institute, 1980), pp. 284–347.

4. M. Kent Jennings and Barbara G. Farah, "Social Roles and Political Resources: An Overtime Study of Men and Women in Party Elites." *American Journal of Political Science,* 25 (1981), pp. 462–482.

5. Edmond Constantini, "Political Women and Political Ambition: Closing the Gender Gap." *American Journal of Political Science,* 34 (3) (August 1990), pp. 741–770.

6. John H. Yunker and Lawrence D. Longley, "The Biases of the Electoral College: Who Is Really Advantaged?" in Donald R. Matthews (Ed.), *Perspectives on Presidential Selection* (Washington, DC: Brookings Institution, 1973), pp. 172–203. Also see Nelson W. Polsby and Aaron Wildavsky, *Presidential Elections: Strategies of American Electoral Politics,* 6th ed. (New York: Charles Scribner's Sons, 1984).

7. Max S. Power, "Logic and Legitimacy: On Understanding the Electoral College Controversy," in Donald R. Matthews (Ed.), *Perspectives on Presidential Selection* (Washington, DC: Brookings Institution, 1973), pp. 204–238.

8. Stephen Hess, *The Presidential Campaign,* 3rd ed. (Washington, DC: Brookings Institution, 1988). Also see Stephen J. Wayne, *The Road to the White House: The Politics of Presidential Elections,* 3rd ed. (New York: St. Martin's Press, 1988).

9. Frank J. Sorauf, *Party Politics in America,* 5th ed. (Boston: Little, Brown, 1984), pp. 425–429.

10. Ronna Romney and Beppie Harrison, *Momentum: Women in American Politics Now* (New York: Crown, 1988).

11. William Henry Clark, "What Votes Can Win?" in James David Barber and Barbara Kellerman (Eds.), *Women Leaders in American Politics* (Englewood Cliffs, NJ: Prentice-Hall, 1986), pp. 218–234.

12. J. E. Buckley, "Equal Pay in America," in Barrie O. Pettman (Ed.), *Equal Pay for Women: Progress and Problems in Seven Countries* (West Yorkshire, England: MCB Books, 1975).

13. U.S. Department of Labor, Bureau of Labor Statistics, *1981 Weekly Earnings of Men and Women Compared in 100 Occupations* (Washington, DC: U.S. Government Printing Office, 1982).

14. Sheila B. Kamerman, Alfred J. Kahn, and Paul Kingston, *Maternity Politics and Working Women* (New York: Columbia University Press, 1983).

15. Susan Deller Ross and Ann Barcher, *The Rights of Women: The Basic ACLU Guide to a Woman's Rights,* rev. ed. (New York: Bantam, 1983).

16. Joyce Gelb and Marian Lief Palley, *Women and Public Policies* (Princeton, NJ: Princeton University Press, 1982).

17. Whicker and Kronenfeld, *Sex Role Changes,* pp. 162–163.

18. Stephen J. Wayne, *The Road to the White House: The Politics of Presidential Elections,* 3rd ed. (New York: St. Martin's Press, 1988), pp. 36–41.

19. *Ibid.*

20. Ruth Mandel, "The Image Campaign," in James David Barber and Barbara Kellerman (Eds.), *Women Leaders in American Politics* (Englewood Cliffs, NJ: Prentice-Hall, 1986), pp. 261–271.

21. Lisa W. Foderaro, "Women Winning Locally, but Higher Office Is Elusive." *New York Times,* April 1, 1989, pp. 29, 32.

22. Susan Gluck Mezy, "Does Sex Make a Difference? A Case Study of Women in Politics." *Western Political Quarterly,* 31 (1978), pp. 492–501.

23. Virginia Sapiro, *Women: Political Action and Political Participation* (Washington, DC: American Political Science Association, 1983).

24. Cynthia Fuchs Epstein, "Women and Power: The Role of Women in Politics in the United States," in Cynthia Fuchs Epstein and Rose Laub Coser (Eds.), *Access to Power: Cross-National Studies of Women and Elites* (London: George Allen and Unwin, 1981).

25. Whicker and Kronenfeld, *Sex Role Changes,* p. 165.

FURTHER READINGS

Barber, James David, and Barbara Kellerman (Eds.). *Women Leaders in American Politics.* Englewood Cliffs, NJ: Prentice-Hall, 1986.

Costello, Cynthia and Anne J. Stone. *The American Woman 1994–95: Where We Stand.* New York: Norton, 1994.

Darcy, R., Susan Welch, and Janet Clark. *Women, Elections, and Representation,* 2nd ed., revised. Lincoln: University of Nebraska Press, 1994.

Genovese, Michael A. (Ed.). *Women as National Leaders.* Newbury Park, CA: Sage, 1993.

Kelber, Mim (Ed.) *Women and Government: New Ways to Political Power.* Westport, CT: Praeger, 1994.

Mayer, William G. (Ed.). *In Pursuit of the White House: How We Choose Our Presidential Nominees.* Chatham, NJ: Chatham House, 1996.

Poisby, Nelson W., & Aaron Wildavsky. *Presidential Elections.* 9th ed. Chatham, NJ: Chatham House, 1996.

Rose, Gary L. (Ed.). *Controversial Issues in Presidential Selection.* 2nd ed. Albany, New York: State University of New York Press, 1994.

Thomas, Sue, and Clyde Wilcox. (Eds.) *Woman and Elective Office: Past, Present, and Future.* New York: Oxford University Press, 1998.

The Governmental Status of the First Lady in Law and in Public Perception

Barbara C. Burrell

> *I don't have a job. I don't get paid for doing anything. I don't have a formal role. That is not what this position gives you an opportunity to do.*

> Hillary Rodham Clinton, CBS interview
> January 19, 1997

In contemporary times both the legal system and the public have had to grapple with the idea of a presidential spouse serving publicly as a presidential assistant and policy adviser to the president. This activity has clashed with traditional beliefs about the role of the presidential spouse. Historically she was thought of as an icon of "womanhood" emphasizing wifehood, motherhood, and being a helpmate.[1] But "the traditional interpretation of the role reinforces the customary gender power differential: Men have considerable and broad power, women have limited and highly circumscribed power."[2] In this research I examine the governmental status of the first lady and public perspectives on her role.

The first lady's role in governance has become an important subject for scholarly research for two main reasons. First, her involvement raises issues for the contemporary women's rights movement and equality for women. She is viewed as a political leader and seemingly as a powerful person. Often she is described in the media as the second most powerful person in Washington. But she has no formal role or position, and her involvement in the policy domain of the White House has been controversial and viewed with suspicion conditioned by general attitudes toward women in politics and her seemingly nongovernmental position. It is necessary to reflect upon the sexism involved in responses to her participation in substantive governmental decision making.

Second, the emergence of the president as the key public figure in American politics and the growth in the staffing of the White House demands that we explore the advisory system around him.[3] The first lady and her staff have become part of that system as we will see. The research presented here brings together executive branch studies and women and politics studies in consideration of the presidential advisory system and the role of the first lady. My purpose is to examine the contemporary reality of the person serving as first lady. I first address her governmental status and then second consider public perspectives on what the first lady should be about. These two perspectives—the legal and the political—provide a context for presenting a philosophical assessment of this position within a liberal democratic tradition.

SEXUAL AND GENDER POLITICS AND THE FIRST LADY

A focus on the first lady as a policy adviser is especially problematic in examining equality for women in public life and contemporary feminism. One reason for this is we are not asking for a woman to be considered as an individual with certain credentials for political leadership who may happen to be a wife and mother (or not), but rather attribute political influence to her because of her private connection to a public official. The role of first lady presents a challenge to feminism. It mixes the private and the public in confusing ways, making sexual politics an issue. (Some have even suggested in disparagement and frustration that 1992 was the "year of the wife" rather than the "year of the woman.") Karlyn Kohrs Campbell has captured the problem: ". . . presidential wives raise the more problematic issue of the relationship between women, *sexuality,* and power. That is, spouses exert their power by virtue of their sexual and marital relationship to the president; their influence is indirect and intimate, a subtle intrusion of the private into the public, political sphere."[4] But should a person be constrained in her ability to act in the public sphere because of her private relations? Would we put a man in that position? Sexual politics frame ideas about the involvement of the first lady in White House policy-making activities. How does she differ from other White House advisers? Gender politics adds to this framing.

Gender politics involves the social construction of biological sex that gives rise to behaviors, roles, and ways of being, knowing, and doing within organizations and institutions.[5] Gender is "a set of practices, a performance, something we 'do.'"[6] Gender politics implies that activities are viewed differently when performed by men and when performed by women, and that masculinity and femininity pervade organizational behaviors. Gender power relations have effectively excluded women from government. Women have been largely absent from images of political leaders as well as from the set of practices involved with leadership and governance.[7]

A vivid example of the impact of gender politics in considerations of White House governance and the role of the presidential spouse in it occurred with Hillary Rodham Clinton's role as head of the Health Care Reform Task Force. Her presence as head of that task force placed her in a position of power and leadership usually accessible only to men. A contradiction was perceived between the "wifely" role of the first lady and the power of her position as chair of the Health Care Reform Task Force. As Guy[8] has pointed out, "By taking the lead in the Clinton administration's health reform effort, Hillary Rodham Clinton transformed the gender power of the post. . . . Hillary and her policy performance consciously and explicitly challenge the dominance and deference pattern evident in masculinity/femininity, husbands/wives, doctors/nurses, leader/followers."

THE PRESIDENTIAL ADVISORY SYSTEM AND THE FIRST LADY

Presidents need assistants to help them perform their duties and responsibilities. Not only has the staff grown in the twentieth-century but increasingly, policy making has been centralized in the White House: ". . . rather than delegating policy authority to executive agencies and departments, presidents since FDR have internalized policy expertise so as to exercise greater control over the policy making process. Given the expansive role of the federal government in the post-New Deal era, White House staffers have stepped in to perform integral and influential roles in both presidential policy making and politics."[9]

Since the Kennedy–Johnson administrations, senior presidential aides have become principal policy advisers.[10] The establishment of continuing functions within the presidential domain have institutionalized subunits within the White House and the Executive Office of the President.[11] White House staff dominate the policy-making process within the Executive Branch, having achieved supremacy over the Cabinet.[12] "Presidential staff have become powerful because they are functionally an extension of the president himself and because the functions they perform place them in a strategically commanding position relative to other actors in the political process."[13]

Members of the White House staff are often people who have worked on the presidential campaign or had staff positions when the president held other offices. They are especially valuable to the president because of their loyalty. For example, "FDR surrounded himself with New York political operatives and his more intellectual 'brain trust'; Jimmy Carter brought several Georgians to the White House with him; and Ronald Reagan initially surrounded himself with fellow Californians. . . ."[14] Women have mainly been absent from this circle of power. Rarely have they served as principal advisers to the president. According to Tenpas, who has examined the presence and positions of women in the White House staff through 1994, "women have made substantial gains in terms of both sheer numbers and seniority. . . . Despite such progress, there nevertheless appears to be a glass ceiling that prevents women from obtaining access to the president's inner circle. Thus, although the gender gap within the White House has narrowed, at the most senior level women remain on the periphery, much as they do in the private sector. . . . Whereas women may have obtained the most senior titles and a greater degree of access to the president, they are rarely as influential as their male counterparts who possess similar titles."[15]

Often the first lady has been the only woman close to the president in an advisory capacity. Many first ladies have served as political and policy advisers to their husbands but usually in private and behind the scenes, while in public preserving the facade of a traditional domestic "helpmate" whose main concern is being the nation's hostess. Those who have been more visible in their advising have met with a great deal of criticism, most notably First Ladies Abigail Adams, Edith Wilson, Eleanor Roosevelt, and Rosalynn Carter. Hillary Rodham Clinton has encountered that same tradition.

In *Presidential Leadership: Politics and Policy Making*, Edwards and Wayne provide an illustration of the principal structural units of the contemporary White House. At the top of their figure are three units. The president is in the center and to either side is the vice president and his staff and the first lady and her staff.[16] Pfiffner, in *The Modern Presidency*,[17] presents a figure descriptive of the "Ring of Power" in the White House Office, which includes in the top tier of rings the first lady and her office along with the president and the vice president.[18] These figures suggest the first lady occupies a structurally significant position in the White House. Also, White House organizational charts since the Carter administration have included the Office of First Lady. Yet few presidential texts have considered or discussed the first lady and her office as part of the presidential advisory system.

THE GOVERNMENTAL STATUS OF THE FIRST LADY

No one has elected her, as critics of an activist first lady have so often pointed out, but the presidential spouse has been given some governmental status. Two laws—the White House Personnel Authorization-Employment Act and the Postal Revenue and Federal Salary Act of 1967—and a 1993 judicial decision affect and condition the governmental status of the first lady. In 1978, Congress passed the White House Personnel Authorization-Employment Act. The main purpose of the law was to curb the appropriation of funds for unauthorized positions in the White House Office. Prior to passage of this law, Congress had authorized the president to have only six administrative assistants and eight other secretaries. But Congress had routinely appropriated funds for a much larger number of White House personnel without proper legislative authorization for those positions. The 1978 law provided authorization for more White House personnel in line with actual White House staffing.

This law also indirectly addressed the governmental status of the first lady. Section 105(e) authorized "assistance and services . . . to be provided to the spouse of the president in connection with assistance provided by such spouse to the president in discharge of the president's duties and responsibilities." Congress may have meant this authorization to focus on the ceremonial duties of the president, as the first lady had long acted as White House hostess, but nothing in the law suggests that limitation. Further, the law was written during the Carter administration in which First Lady Rosalynn Carter had been serving in a more formal public advisory role than any other first lady, perhaps with the exception of Eleanor Roosevelt. Rosalynn Carter had stirred controversy by sitting in on cabinet meetings and by serving as the President's ambassador to South American nations. Her actions as the "President's Partner,"[19] suggest that Congress recognized a larger conception of the first lady's role as an assistant to the president in formally acknowledging her status in this law.

As summarized in *Congressional Quarterly Almanac,* the legislative history of this bill made no mention of any particular controversy over the inclusion of authorization for funding of the first lady's office. (Authorization for funding of a staff for the wife of the vice president was also included.) In the debate on the floor of the Senate, it was mentioned that the White House had proposed including the presidential and vice-presidential spouses in the authorizations. In the only mention of this section of the proposed bill in floor debates, Senator Dole noted "'Authorization for the spouse is supposed to be in connection with their official duties,' a committee staffer said. But no one knows where their official duties end. Recently, questions have been raised about the fact that Rosalynn Carter, the President's wife, has at least seventeen persons on her staff, none of whom is covered by specific authorization legislation. Similarly, the Vice President's wife, Joan Mondale, who is involved in arts programs, has at least four aides paid out of government funds."[20]

Section 105(e) of the White House Personnel Authorization-Employment Act took on legal importance in January 1993, when immediately following his inauguration, President Bill Clinton appointed his wife, Hillary Rodham Clinton, to head his Health Care Reform Task Force. The Task Force established a number of working groups. Its own meetings and those of the working groups were held in private and its documents were not made public.

The Association of American Physicians and Surgeons brought suit against the Task Force to gain access to its meetings and documents. The Association argued that the Health Care Task Force chaired by the first lady was an advisory committee subject to the Federal Advisory Committee Act (FACA), which had been enacted in 1972 "to control the growth and operation of the 'numerous committees, boards, commissions, councils, and similar groups which have been established to advise officers and agencies in the executive branch of the Federal Government.'"[21] The act requires that any committee established to give advice to the President that includes members who are not governmental employees must follow open meeting laws. The law, however, exempts any committee composed wholly of full-time officers or employees of the federal government. In this case, the government argued that the Health Care Task Force was made up solely of government officials and therefore, exempt from FACA. The appellants argued, in contrast, that the Task Force was subject to FACA because its chair, the first lady, was not an officer or employee of the Federal Government.[22] The government argued that she was a functional equivalent of a federal employee.

At issue was the definition of an officer or employee of the federal government. FACA provided no definition, thus the appellants argued (and the lower district court had agreed) that the definition of an officer or employee in Title 5 of the U.S. Code applied. According to this section of the U.S. Code, an officer or employee must be, among other things, appointed to the civil service. Hillary Rodham Clinton had not been appointed to the Civil Service, thus she was not an officer or employee of the federal government. Therefore, the Task Force did not consist solely of government employees and must comply with the provisions of FACA.

In a June 22, 1993 judgment, the U.S. court of Appeals for the District of Columbia ruled that the first lady could be viewed as a "de facto officer or employee" of the federal government.[23] The Appeals Court determined that Title 1 of the U.S. Code provided "that a federal officer 'includes any person authorized by law to perform the duties of the office.' That definition could cover a situation in which Congress authorizes someone who is not formally an officer (such as the President's spouse) to perform federal duties." The Appeals Court noted that "Congress itself has recognized that the Presidential spouse acts as the functional equivalent of an assistant to the president" by its inclusion of the spouse in the White House Authorization-Employment Act. The Appeals Court stated that Section 105(e) of that Act "neither limits the particular kind of 'assistance' rendered to the president, nor circumscribes the types of presidential duties and responsibilities that are to be aided." The Court saw "no reason why a President could not use his or her spouse to carry out a task that the President might delegate to one of his White House aides. . . . It is reasonable, therefore, to construe Section 105(e) as treating the presidential spouse as a de facto officer or employee of the federal government. Otherwise, if the president's spouse routinely attended, and participated in, Cabinet meetings, he or she would convert an all-government group, established or used by the President, into a FACA advisory committee." The Appeals Court also noted in reference to the White House Authorization-Employement Act that "It may well be, as appellees argue, that many in Congress had in mind 'ceremonial duties,' but we do not think the presidency can be so easily divided between its substantive political and ceremonial functions."

But how can the first lady be a de facto officer or employee of the federal government? The Postal Revenue and Federal Salary Act of 1967 states that "a public official may not appoint, employ, promote [or] advance" a relative in an agency "in which he is serving or over which he exercises jurisdiction or control."[24] According to its legislative history, this is "to prevent a public official from appointing a relative to a . . . position . . . in the agency in which the public official serves or over which he exercises supervision." The law applied to all agencies in the executive, legislative, and judicial branches and specifically covered the president and vice president. Thus, for example, the president cannot appoint a spouse to a cabinet position (nor can he appoint a brother, sister, aunt, uncle, cousin, niece, nephew, an in-law, a step relative, or a half-brother or half-sister).

But a question remains concerning how far this prohibition extends through the executive branch. Does it include boards and commissions? What about service as a presidential assistant in the White House? The U.S. Appeals Court addressed this issue in its 1993 opinion. The Court said "we doubt that Congress intended to include the White House or the Executive Office of the President" as an executive agency. The Court went on to say that "The anti-nepotism statute, . . . may well bar appointment only to *paid* positions in government. . . . Thus, even if it would prevent the President from putting his spouse on the federal payroll, it does not preclude his spouse from aiding the President in the performance of his duties."[25] But if, as the Court suggested, Congress did not intend to include the White House or Executive Office of the President in the Postal Revenue and Federal Salary Act of 1967, then this should imply that a presidential relative could be paid for his or her service in an advisory capacity in one of these units.

Hillary Rodham Clinton was not paid as head of the Health Care Reform Task Force, nor is she paid for performing other duties as first lady. According to the Anti-Nepotism law, it is believed that she cannot be paid. But if, as the Appeals Court stated, Congress did not intend to include the White House or Executive Office in the Anti-Nepotism Act, then it should not be illegal to pay presidential spouses for their work as Presidential advisers. They cannot be appointed to a Cabinet position or oversee an executive agency, but they could serve in the White House in an official advisory capacity and be remunerated for that work. (This interpretation of the Court's ruling would affect other presidential relatives as well.)

Further, while she seemingly cannot receive a salary, the presidential spouse can hire a paid staff to work for her and she can serve as an unpaid assistant advising the president on public policy matters. This puts the first lady in a very peculiar position regarding her governmental status. It is especially problematic in contemporary times, when presidential spouses are quite likely to bring political and professional credentials to the White House that, if they were not a spouse, would make them candidates for top level positions throughout the executive branch as well as in the White House. For example, commentators at the beginning of the Clinton administration noted that in another Democratic administration Hillary Clinton would have been qualified for a presidential appointment.[26]

Perhaps even a more relevant example is Elizabeth Dole, wife of 1996 Republican presidential nominee Bob Dole, who not only has held two cabinet positions but has also been mentioned as a possible vice-presidential or presidential candidate. Bob and Elizabeth Dole confused the situation regarding the first lady as policy adviser in the 1996 presidential campaign when they "announced" that Elizabeth would not participate in White House policymaking.

As the spouse of the Republican nominee for president, Elizabeth Dole said she would not serve as a presidential adviser even though she had much experience in the executive branch. She and the nominee implied that that would be inappropriate. That seemingly necessary strategy in their campaign, clearly aimed at Hillary Rodham Clinton, was a not so subtle put-down of women and certainly complicated thinking about the first lady. As pointed out in a *Time* magazine piece on Hillary and Elizabeth, ". . . Dole has called Elizabeth his 'secret weapon,' his 'Southern strategy,' all the while making it clear that he is old-fashioned about the

East Wing, that Elizabeth won't be sitting in on cabinet meetings and serving as the unofficial Minister of Health Care. This is all the more ironic, given the fact that Elizabeth Dole, at 59 the only woman ever to serve in two different Cabinet posts for two different Presidents, has probably attended more Cabinet meetings than either Bob Dole or Bill Clinton."[27] Was she momentarily not qualified to advise the President because of her personal relationship to him, while being qualified both before and after his administration and even considered a possible candidate for president herself? If the roles were reversed and Elizabeth became president, would we expect former Senator Dole not to use his years of governmental experience in some advisory capacity? Sexual and gender politics predominated here.

The 1996 Dole strategy points to the importance not only of legal considerations conditioning actions of the first lady but also of public perspectives on her role. It is one thing for there to be a legal basis for the first lady's claim to governmental status, but public acceptance of a more engaged first lady in the policy-making apparatus of the White House must also be considered for a fuller assessment of the philosophical implications of a person in this role. Thus, the next section supplements our consideration of governmental status questions with an examination of public response to the involvement of the first lady in governance.

PUBLIC PERCEPTIONS

Hillary Rodham Clinton, after a frustrating first four years in the White House, commented that "In our country we expect so much from the woman who is married to the President—but we don't really know what it is we expect."[28] She also noted that she might be better off if she never expressed any opinions and "kept a bag over your head, or somehow make it clear that you have no opinions and no ideas about anything—and never express them, publicly or privately."[29] Earlier she had asked whether she was supposed to check her brain at the door of the White House.[30]

Eleanor Roosevelt broke the mold for first ladies in terms of her outspokenness and public activism. She was highly regarded, controversial, but quite popular. The Gallup Poll conducted the first national systematic public opinion poll on the popularity of the first lady in 1939. It found "Mrs. Roosevelt More Popular Than President," to quote the headline in the *Washington Post*.[31] Sixty-seven percent said they "approved of the way Mrs. Roosevelt has conducted herself as 'First Lady,'" while 33 percent did not approve.[32] Eighty-one percent of Democrats, and 43 percent of Republicans approved. Women were more supportive than men—73 percent to 62 percent approval.[33]

Prior to Hillary Rodham Clinton's tenure in the White House we have only a few systematic measures of what role or roles Americans preferred that first ladies perform. Nor has the public ever been asked whether we should even have a "first lady."

A few surveys in the late 1980s have explored aspects of this issue. In 1987, *USA Today* commissioned a national poll that asked "In the past, some first ladies have been more active than others in their husband's administration. Generally speaking, which do you think is the most important for a presidential spouse? Should the spouse: be involved in important administration decisions, support a national program, serve as a hostess of social events, stay in the background?"[34] Listed below are the responses:

15%—active in important administration decisions
32%—support a national program
29%—be a hostess for social events
18%—stay in the background

The *Ladies' Home Journal* in May 1988 commissioned a national survey of adult women that posed a similar question. They asked their respondents to "look at [a] list of activities and tell . . . which one best describes how you think a First Lady should spend the majority of her time—Pursuing special interests and causes, such as drug abuse, AIDS education, the homeless; remaining behind the scenes, supporting and being a "helpmate" to the president, serving as the President's representative at ceremonial functions, entertaining dignitaries, holding receptions and dinners, etc.; involving herself in government affairs (attending cabinet meetings, advising the President on policies and personnel, etc.). The majority opted for the First Lady being involved in special interests and causes (58 percent), while only 5 percent favored "involving herself in government affairs." Fourteen percent chose the ceremonial role, and 17 percent thought she should confine her activities to the "helpmate" role.[35] Clearly these polls do not show a public advocating the presidential advisory role for the First Lady. But neither do they directly ask whether the general public opposes such involvement. Rather they show that the public generally opts for those roles with which they have become familiar and which fit more traditional thinking about women's roles.

Hillary Rodham Clinton's role in the 1992 presidential campaign stimulated a new round of questions about the public's perception of what the first lady should be and what the person who occupies this role should do. Some poll questions suggested an openness about a First Lady being a presidential adviser. While 67 percent disapproved of "Hillary Clinton having a major post in her husband's administration" in April of 1992,[36] in a July 1992 poll, 58 percent said they approved of "having a First Lady who is involved in the President's policy decisions and the day-to-day operations of the White House staff."[37]

Reflecting on the Carter administration when Rosalynn Carter sat in on Cabinet meetings, the press quizzed President-elect Clinton in 1992 about Hillary attending and participating in cabinet meetings in his administration. He indicated that she would attend such meetings whenever she wanted.[38] This activity received little public support, however. Only 20 percent of a national sample in a *Los Ange-*

les Times poll thought "Hillary Clinton should sit in on the president's cabinet meetings while 68 percent were opposed,"[39] while a CBS/*New York Times* poll found 40 percent approving such an activity and 53 percent disapproving.

U.S. News & World Report queried a national sample of American adults about their support or opposition to Hillary Clinton undertaking a variety of activities at the time of Bill Clinton's inauguration. The results show continued preference for the more traditional roles than policy activism except for advocacy of the type of noncontroversial issues associated with contemporary first ladies. Do you favor or oppose these roles for Hillary Clinton?

	Favor	Oppose
Sitting in on cabinet meetings	37%	58%
Being a traditional first lady	70	21
Being an advocate for policies and programs to benefit children	90	7
Being a major advisor on appointments and policy	34	59
Testifying before Congress on issues that concern her	71	22

Hillary's tenure has sustained pollsters' interest in the role of the first lady. Thus, for example, *Redbook* in 1996 posed the question, "What kind of first lady would Americans *really* like to have in the White House?" To examine that question, *Redbook* commissioned a national poll asking "people to tell [them] what professional and personal traits would make, in their opinion, the ideal first lady." Their conclusion was

> a loving wife, a mom, a working woman, a spokesperson for domestic causes. While Americans can clearly respect their first lady as a woman who speaks her mind, our poll showed that they feel the job has definite boundaries: Though 58 percent say it is appropriate for the first lady to counsel her husband on issues, only 5 percent think her role should be that of official adviser. And 70 percent say it would be inappropriate for her to attend cabinet meetings.[40]

We should note however, that what *Redbook* asked their respondents was, "Think now about your ideal first lady, rather than a specific first lady in history. Do you prefer a first lady who primarily plays the traditional role of hostess, or one who is primarily more publicly involved in issues facing the country? Thirty-one percent opted for the traditional hostess, while 62 percent favored her being involved in issues.[41]

In addition to general questions about the role of the first lady, pollsters have also been interested in how the public rates the incumbent going back to Gallup's 1939 inquiry about Eleanor Roosevelt described earlier. Until Hillary became first lady, however, the public's perception of the person in the position had only been obtained on a sporadic basis.[42] And occasionally, the question has been posed in terms of approval or disapproval of the "job" the individual was doing as first lady (however that job might be defined). For example, in January 1997 CBS/NYT poll,

65 percent of a national sample said they approved "of the way Hillary Rodham Clinton [was] handling her job as first lady."[43]

Although they may have opted for a traditional first lady when asked about that role in the abstract, Americans have actually tended to approve when first ladies have taken on a task as a public policy assistant to the President. The popularity of Eleanor Roosevelt supports this idea, and reaction to activities of Rosalynn Carter and Hillary Rodham Clinton further illustrate this point.

In 1977, President Jimmy Carter sent his wife Rosalynn as his representative on a tour of Latin American countries to meet with their heads of state. This presidential action created a great deal of controversy in its planning stages.[44] After her return from Latin America, the Roper Organization asked a national sample of American adults two questions about their views on her trip. First, Roper asked the public how they would evaluate the job she had done. "Regardless of how you feel about what the role of a first lady should be, is it your impression that on her tour of Latin America Rosalynn Carter did an excellent job as a representative of the United States, a good job, not too good a job, or a poor job?" Seventeen percent gave her an excellent rating and 51 percent said she had done a good job, while nine percent said it was not too good a job, and three percent said she had done a poor job. (Nineteen percent responded that they did not know.)[45]

Second, Roper wanted to know if this is a role the first lady should play. Respondents were asked, "[d]uring June, Rosalynn Carter went on a visit to meet with government leaders in seven Latin and Caribbean nations as a representative of the United States to discuss matters of mutual interest to their countries and ours. Some people have said such a trip is not appropriate for a first lady, and that only elected officials or professional diplomats should represent the United States abroad. Others have said it is perfectly appropriate for a first lady to be sent on such a trip if the President wishes it. How do you feel—that a first lady should or should not officially represent the United States in talks with other countries? Fifty-five percent responded that she should, and 33 percent said she should not. Seven percent volunteered that it depended on who the first lady was, and 5 percent said that they did not know.[46] Thus, although she did not again undertake such a task during her husband's administration, Rosalynn Carter won much more approval than disapproval from the public for her venture."[47]

When President Clinton appointed Hillary head of his Health Care Reform Task Force, his action met with public approval. Numerous polls queried the public regarding their response to this presidential action. The polls showed early support for her taking on this appointment. Approximately six out of ten Americans either approved, supported, or thought it was appropriate for the president to name her as head of the Health Care Task Force, while about three in ten either opposed, disapproved, or thought it was inappropriate to have made this appointment. For example, Gallup, immediately after the appointment was announced, asked a national sample of adults "As you may know, President Clinton has appointed Hillary to head his task force on health care reform. In your opinion, is this an appropriate position for a first lady, or not?" Fifty-nine percent said "yes," and 37 percent said "no."[48] They also expressed early confidence in her "ability to handle her role in health-care policy and other domestic issues." In a March 1993 *Time* magazine poll, 33 percent said they had "a lot" of confidence, 49 percent said they had "some" confidence, and 16 percent said they had "none." Support for her leadership on this issue fell in 1994 as the Clintons' faltered in trying to win approval for their health care initiative in Congress.

A CAREER OUTSIDE THE WHITE HOUSE

My focus to this point has been on the question of a spouse serving on the President's official advisory staff. Another aspect of what a first lady is to do is the issue of a spouse having her own career outside of the White House. Freeing the spouse of cultural constraints to pursue her own career, while important in its own right, is also significant because it could result in her being treated as an individual by the public. This in turn might create greater acceptance of one of those career options being advisor to the president.

In contemporary times, as women have become a major part of the work force, the issue of the President's spouse having a career of her own while living in the White House has taken on meaning. The option was first presented to the public in the 1988 *Ladies Home Journal* poll cited above of a national sample of adult women. Respondents were asked "Suppose we were to elect a President whose wife has had an active and independent career. Do you think she should continue to work at her full-time job, or give up her career and devote full time to her duties as First Lady?" A plurality opted for being a full-time first lady—49 percent, while 41 percent thought she should continue to work at a career.[49]

The *Washington Post* asked a national sample in October 1996, "Do you think it is a good idea or a bad idea for the wife of the president of the United States to hold a full-time job in addition to her duties as first lady?" Forty-five percent believed it was a good idea and 38 percent thought it was a bad idea.[50] Thus, the American public appears to still be in conflict over this option. Younger individuals, women, Democrats, and independents were more supportive of this idea than people over 50, men, and Republicans.[51]

However, one finds more support for an independent career when the question is posed in terms of a specific individual with a particular job. For example, when asked whether Hillary Clinton should quit her job (as a partner in the Little Rock Arkansas law firm) in 1992 if Bill Clinton were elected president, 62 percent said no, while only 29 percent said yes.[52] And asked in the 1996 election campaign whether Elizabeth Dole should resume her job as president of the American Red Cross should Bob Dole be elected president, 75 percent of a national sample said yes, while only 20 percent said no.[53] Thus, we have an ambivalent public concerning their perspectives on what the role of the first lady should be and whether she should pursue her own career.

CONCLUSION

Where are we left then regarding the role of first lady, given her "governmental status" and public perspectives of her position that I presented here? Can the president's spouse be treated as an individual with the same ambitions and equality of opportunity as other political actors? Can the system be altered so she can become personally independent and achieve through merit? Should the spouse of the president be precluded from being a public policy adviser? The problem is how to treat the spouse of the president as an individual, to free her from the cultural constraints that have been imposed on this role. Constraints that have been placed on the presidential spouse's acting in the public sphere contradict the liberal tradition of individualism that has characterized American social and political culture. The individual is at the center of liberal democracy but patriarchy has limited woman's opportunities. Drawing on Susan Okin, Campbell has noted that ". . . despite contemporary commitments to individualism, there is a long tradition that brings the family and woman's traditional role in it into conflict with individual rights."[54] Behind the individual rhetoric of liberal philosophers, "it is clear that the family and not the adult human individual is the basic political unit."[55] Because of her position in the family, the first lady is not able to act as an independent individual. She may be credited with political influence, but it is an influence hidden behind a mask of domesticity and treated with considerable suspicion.

Liberal feminism is based upon the premise "that women are individuals possessed of reason, that as such they are entitled to full human rights, and that they should therefore be free to choose their role in life and explore their full potential in equal competition with men."[56] Freeing the first lady from cultural constraints to pursue her own career means not only an ability to work outside the White House but the opportunity to serve as a presidential adviser if that is the job she desires and can lay some claim to professionally as Hillary Rodham Clinton has done.

Adopting this activity or job should not be considered any differently from her taking on other professional positions. We cannot just talk about the presidential spouse being able to pursue a career outside the White House. She must also be able to have a career inside it, too, if we want to achieve equality, especially if we consider the context in which others have become presidential advisers. Clearly the presidential spouse is privileged in the advisory system because of the nature of her personal relationship to the president, but at the same time her activities receive closer scrutiny, especially when they are done publicly, than do those of other advisers. She even becomes more accountable because of the media spotlight that is upon her. Her own place in history is clearly related and dependent upon the job her spouse does.[57] In reflecting upon the puzzle of presidential spousal politics, we have to take into account the sexual and gender biases that influence our thinking and consider the presidential advisory system as a whole. We have to place that individual in the context of a quest for equal rights for women and their equal involvement in the public life of the nation. In the end, to argue against the president's spouse being able to take on a policy making role is to constrain women from playing an equal role in the political domain.

NOTES

1. Many first ladies have been engaged in their husband's political careers and been their advisers in the White House although often behind the scenes. It is the public nature of the involvement of contemporary first ladies that is the issue here. Those who have engaged publicly in policy making have usually been criticized.

2. Mary Ellen Guy, "Hillary, Health Care, and Gender Power," in Georgia Duerst-Lahti and Rita Mae Kelly (Eds.), *Gender Power, Leadership, and Governance* (Ann Arbor: University of Michigan Press, 1995), p. 239.

3. See for example, Charles Walcott and Karen Hult, *Governing the White House* (Lawrence: University of Kansas Press, 1995).

4. Karlyn Kohrs Campbell, "The First Lady: Public Symbol." Unpublished paper.

5. See among others Georgia Duerst-Lahti and Rita Mae Kelly (Eds.), *Gender Power, Leadership, and Governance.*

6. Georgia Duerst-Lahti, "Reconceiving Theories of Power: Consequences of Masculinism in the Executive Branch," in Mary Anne Borrelli and Janet Martin (Eds.) *The Other Elites: Women, Politics, and Power in the Executive Branch* (New York: St. Martin's Press, 1997), pp. 11–32.

7. See among others Georgia Duerst-Lahti and Rita Mae Kelly (Eds.), *Gender Power, Leadership, and Governance* and Sally J. Kenney, "New Research on Gendered Political Institutions," *Political Research Quarterly,* 49, pp. 445–466.

8. Mary Ellen Guy, "Hillary, Health Care, and Gender Power."

9. See Katie Tenpas, "Women on the White House Staff: A Longitudinal Analysis (1939–1994)," in Mary Anne Borrelli and Janet Martin (Eds.), *The Other Elites: Women, Politics, and Power in the Executive Branch,* pp. 91–106.

10. George Edwards and Stephen J. Wayne, *Presidential Leadership,* 2nd Edition (New York: St. Martins, Press, 1990), p. 175.

11. James P. Pfiffner, *The Modern Presidency* (New York: St. Martin's Press), p. 92.

12. See among others John Hart, *The Presidential Branch* (New York: Pergamon Press, 1987).

13. *Ibid.*

14. Karen O'Connor and Larry J. Sabato, *American Government: Roots and Reform* (New York: MacMillan Publishing, 1993), p. 257. See also Barbara Kellerman, *All the President's Kin* (New York: The Free Press, 1981) for a discussion of the president's kin.

15. Katie Tenpas, "Women on the White House Staff: A Longitudinal Analysis (1939–1994) in Mary Anne Borrelli and Janet Martin (Eds.), *The Other Elites: Women,*

Politics, and Power in the Executive Branch, pp. 92–93 and p. 95.

16. Edwards and Wayne, *Presidential Leadership,* 2nd Edition, p. 179 and George Edwards and Stephen J. Wayne, *Presidential Leadership,* 3rd Edition (New York: St. Martins Press, 1994), p. 186.

17. James P. Pfiffner, *The Modern Presidency.*

18. *Ibid,* p. 94.

19. Tom Morganthau, "The President's Partner," *Newsweek,* November 5, 1979, pp. 36–47.

20. Congressional Record, 1978, p. 20901.

21. Association of American Physicians and Surgeons, Inc., et al., Appellees v. Hillary Rodham Clinton, et al.

22. This point was only one of the issues in the case.

23. Association of American Physicians and Surgeons, Inc., et al., Appellees v. Hillary Rodham Clinton et al.

24. This law is often referred to as the Bobby Kennedy Law because it was promoted by Lyndon Johnson as President in response to President John Kennedy's appointment of his brother Robert to be Attorney General. Johnson intensely disliked Bobby Kennedy.

25. Emphasis is the author's.

26. See for example Joan Beck, "Hillary: Powerhouse or White Housewife?" *Chicago Tribune,* November 19, 1992, p. 21 and Eleanor Clift and Mark Miller, "Hillary: Behind the Scenes," *Newsweek,* December 28, 1992, pp. 23–25.

27. Nancy Gibbus and Michael Duffy, "Hillary vs. Liddy: Who would be the better First Lady?" *Time,* July 1, 1996, pp. 24–27.

28. Eric Pooley, "Reinventing Hillary," *Time,* December 2, 1996, p. 37.

29. *Ibid.*

30. Deirdre McMurdy, "The Political Wife: Hillary Clinton Redefines Her Role," *MacLean's,* July 1992, p. 34.

31. George Gallup, "Mrs. Roosevelt More Popular Than President, Survey Finds," *Washington Post,* January 25, 1939, Section 3, p. 1.

32. Roper Center Public Opinion Online Accession Number 0172124, Question Number 001.

33. Franklin Roosevelt received a 58 percent approval rating as president.

34. Roper Center Public Opinion Online Accession Number 0184209, Question Number 069.

35. From Roper Center Public Opinion Online, Accession Number 0209197, Question Number 001.

36. Mimi Hall, "Public rejects giving first lady a job." *USA Today,* April 2, 1992, p. 3A.

37. *Time*/CNN, July 23, *Public Opinion Index,* p. 3A.

38. Martha Sherrill, "A Clinton in the Cabinet?" *Washington Post,* December 19, 1992, p. D1.

39. *Los Angeles Times,* Poll, January 20, Public Opinion Index.

40. Lee Lusardi Connor, "The First Lady Americans Really Want," *Redbook,* October 1996, pp. 85–87.

41. These data were provided by Lee Lusardi Connor of *Redbook.*

42. See Barbara Burrell, *Public Opinion, The First Ladyship and Hillary Rodham Clinton,* (New York: Garland Publishing, 1997).

43. Roper Center Public Opinion Online, Accession Number 0271160, Question Number 032.

44. See Burrell, *Public Opinion, The First Ladyship and Hillary Rodham Clinton.*

45. Roper Center Public Opinion Online Accession Number 0115859, Question Number 021.

46. Roper Center Public Opinion Online Accession Number 0115860, Question Number 021.

47. It would have been enlightening had Roper's second question been asked prior to her trip also.

48. See Barbara C. Burrell, *Public Opinion, The First Ladyship, and Hillary Rodham Clinton,* 1997 for a full listing of the questions asked about Hillary's role as head of the Task Force.

49. From Roper Center Public Opinion Online, Accession Number 0209197, Question Number 001.

50. Roper Center Public Opinion Online Accession Number 0268922, Question Number 005.

51. Forty-eight percent of women, 52 percent of Democrats, 50 percent of independents, 53 percent of those between the ages of 18 and 34, 51 percent of those between 35 and 49 thought it was a good idea compared with 44 percent of men, 39 percent of Republicans, and 41 percent of those 50 and older. Mario Brossard of *The Washington Post* provided the data for this analysis.

52. Carol J. Castaneda and Brian O'Connell, "Women, Young Rate Hillary Clinton Highest," *USA Today,* March 24, 1992, p. 6A.

53. Gallup Poll for CNN/*USA Today,* Roper Center Public Opinion Online, Accession Number 0257333, Question Number 059.

54. See Karlyn Kohns Campbell, "The First Lady: Public Symbol," Unpublished paper, 1995 and Susan Okin, *Women in Western Political Thought* (Princeton, New Jersey: Princeton University Press, 1979).

55. Okin, *Women in Western Political Thought,* p. 282.

56. Valerie Bryson, *Feminist Political Theory* (New York: Paragon House, 1992), p. 159.

57. See Burrell 1997 for a more detailed discussion of the issue of accountability.

FURTHER READINGS

Barbara Burrell. *Public Opinion, The First Ladyship, and Hillary Rodham Clinton.* New York: Garland Publishing, 1997.

Betty Boyd Caroli. *First Ladies.* New York: Oxford University Press, 1995.

Ann Grimes. *Running Mates: The Making of the First Ladies.* New York: Morrow Publishing, 1990.

"Hillary Rodham Clinton's Image: Content, Control, and Cultural Politics." *Political Communication Symposium* (1997), 14(2).

The Feminist Face of State Executive Leadership: Women as Governors

Sara J. Weir

INTRODUCTION

The growing importance of state governance in the U.S. political system and of governors both as initiators and administrators of large annual budgets and major public programs like welfare make the study of state governorship increasingly important in the fields of public administration and executive leadership. The governorship is also politically significant because it is so often an avenue for aspiring presidential candidates. Given the increased focus on national budgets and deficit reduction, it can be argued that governors, especially of large states, possess the necessary qualifications to serve as president.

Of the five most recent U.S. presidents, three gained their political experience and national reputations by serving as governors. The case for governors as national executives is further strengthened by the experience that many governors have dealing directly with international trading partners—states such as New Jersey, Texas, and Washington depend on such trade for jobs as well as for tax revenues.

While much has been written about gubernatorial races and of governors as central figures in sub-national governance, an entirely new area of scholarly inquiry now explores women as governors.

THE STUDY OF WOMEN AS GOVERNORS

Very few studies of the governorship have focused on women as governors. However, from the 1925 election of Nellie Tayloe Ross (D-Wyoming) to the 1997 re-election of Christine Todd Whitman (R-New Jersey), fifteen women (twelve Democrats and three Republicans) have served as governors. While these numbers are small when compared with the proportion of women elected to statewide offices or with men elected as governors, a growing number of women are running for and winning in gubernatorial contests and others are positioning themselves to run for governor by serving in other statewide elective offices.

This article expands the study of gender and leadership to include the examination of the careers of the women who have served as governors, providing comparisons of their candidacies and administrations. While there are not enough cases to draw generalizable conclusions, patterns do emerge.

For example, what do we know about the women who have served as governors? Do patterns emerge in the candidacy and election of women governors, and, if so, what do recent elections tell us about the future prospects for women seeking to serve as governors? We begin with a review of the literature and then address the questions posed.

REVIEW OF THE LITERATURE

The inclusion of the study of women as state executives expands our understanding both of gender as a political variable and of the politics of executive leadership. This combination of realms of inquiry is, according to Virginia Sapiro, common in the study of women and politics.[1] When women such as Jeanne Shaheen or Christine Todd Whitman achieve top executive positions, they allow examination and force attention to socially defined gender roles.[2]

The careers of the women who have served as governors help us to determine if expectations about the impact of gender roles and stereotypes, and the political relevance of gender differences found in studies of women as legislators, also apply to state executives.[3]

Although the literature on women governors continues to be more journalistic than scholarly, recent books like former governor Madeleine Kunin's autobiography, *Living a Political Life,* are rich sources of information about gender and the exercise of power and leadership. Other autobiographical and biographical works include former Texas governor Ann Richards' *Straight from the Heart* and *Growing up Republican,* the story of the personal life and career of New Jersey governor, Christine Todd Whitman.[4] Although many details of their careers and lives are different, all three were (and are) longtime political party activists. Each describes efforts to overcome gender stereotypes and, at the same time, balance the demands that women face as parents—demands that are still far less of an issue for male candidates and office holders.

Beyond these biographical works, the literature focuses on particular gubernatorial races involving women,[5] and comparative case studies of the campaigns of women running for governor.[6] All of the books are very readable, and each provides important insight into both the personal lives and the campaigns of their subjects. But to begin studying this topic more systemically, one must look beyond these studies to the existing research on women and leadership.

Leadership refers to more than simply holding office: According to Genovese and Thompson, it ". . . is a complex phenomenon revolving around *influence*—the ability to move others in desired directions."[7] Like other chief executives, state governors are judged on their ability to exercise leadership within the confines of the political culture and institutional structure of their states. Governors also vary in the personal skills they bring to the job. The style, character, and personal attributes they possess determine how successful they will be as state executives.[8]

Like the presidency, the governorship is a highly gendered office. Executive leadership has been (and to a great extent continues to be) viewed as a traditionally masculine attribute. According to political pollster Celinda Lake, the qualities that make a good governor—toughness and executive ability—are most often associated by voters with men.[9] Should the women who seek the governorship attempt to redefine executive leadership or do they need to find ways to navigate politically by being as tough and decisive as their male counterparts?

The answer to this query is not easy or straightforward: Women candidates must work against the *soft* image put upon them by the media. For example, during the 1986 gubernatorial race in Nebraska between Kay Orr and Helen Boosalis, the candidates struggled to overcome the national media's unwillingness to view the race in conventional political terms. Although both candidates had extensive experience in state and local elective positions and although they debated the hard issues, such as taxes and the economy, it was mid-September before national newspapers were able to stop talking about the "historic race" between two women.[10] This focus on gender prompted Kay Orr to comment that the contest was "no bake-off."[11]

HISTORICAL OVERVIEW

The Surrogate Governors

The 1974 election of Ella Grasso (D-Connecticut) marked the beginning of an era for women as gubernatorial candidates—but three women had served as state governors prior to Grasso's election. Acting initially as replacements or "surrogates" for their husbands, all three were appointed or elected because their husbands were governors who could not, for one reason or another, hold office any longer. Two of the three women, Nellie Tayloe Ross (D) of Wyoming and Miriam Ferguson (D) of Texas, took office in 1925.

Nellie Tayloe Ross was elected to the governorship in a special election following the death of her husband and she served the remaining years of his term. Ross was then the Democratic party candidate for re-election in 1926, but was defeated by her Republican challenger in a close race (35,651 votes to 34,286 votes). She remained active in Democratic Party politics—at one point she served as Vice-Chair of the Democratic National Committee and in 1933 newly elected President Franklin D. Roosevelt appointed her to the position of Director of the Mint.

First appointed to the governorship when her husband resigned under threat of impeachment, Miriam Ferguson went on to be active in Texas politics for two decades. During that time she ran for governor five times and won twice, serving as governor from 1925–1927 and again from 1933–1935.

Both Ross and Ferguson first held office because their husbands were governor, but each went on to serve in appointed and elected positions based solely on their own ability. Their lifelong careers as public servants have many elements that are similar to the careers of later women governors. This is not the case with the third woman surrogate governor, Lurleen Wallace (D-Alabama).

Wallace succeeded her husband George Wallace in 1967, when Alabama state law barred him from succeeding himself. Lurleen was ill at the time of her election and she died while in office in May, 1968. There is little evidence that Lurleen Wallace exercised independent decision making authority during her years in office.

The Independently Elected Governors

Ella Grasso, a Democrat, was the fourth woman governor. Unlike her three predecessors, her rise to prominence in politics was not dependent on her husband. In 1974 Grasso defeated her Republican challenger, Robert Steele, in an open-seat contest, receiving 59 percent of the vote. She was reelected to a second four-year term in 1978, and although she again received 59 percent of the vote, it was a hotly contested primary and general election campaign.

Grasso was a fiscal conservative and a social moderate who imposed austerity programs during her first term and used her opposition to a state income tax as a major focus of both of her gubernatorial campaigns. She had gained some of her political experience working with John Baily, national chairman of the Democratic Party under President John F. Kennedy. Her status as a long-time party activist and elected official helped Grasso to avoid the *soft* image that other women governors, like Martha Layne Collins (D-Kentucky), struggled against. The late Governor Grasso stepped down for health reasons in the middle of her second term.[12]

Grasso was followed by other independently elected governors, including Dixie Lee Ray (D-Washington) in 1976, Martha Layne Collins (D-Kentucky) in 1983, and Madeleine Kunin (D-Vermont) in 1984.

Madeleine Kunin first ran for governor in 1982. She was defeated by the incumbent Republican governor Richard Snelling, but she came back to win the gubernatorial race in 1984, defeating the Republican candidate for the open seat in a very close race. She went on to be reelected to two additional two-year terms. In 1986 she won in a race that pitted her against Peter Smith, the Republican challenger, and the former mayor of Burlington, Bernie Sanders, a Socialist running as an Independent in the election.

The 1986 election of Kay Orr as governor of Nebraska marked two firsts in gubernatorial races involving women. Orr had served as state treasurer before running for governor and not only was she the first Republican woman to be elected governor of any state, but her 1986 race was the first gubernatorial contest between two women candidates of major political parties. This landmark race was not, however, a feminist contest.

Orr was "opposed to legalized abortion in all instances," while her opponent Helen Boosalis said she was personally opposed to abortion except in the case of "rape, incest or to save a mother's life."[13] Both candidates called for limits on tax increases, with Orr labeling herself as a "fiscal conservative." The race drew national attention because both candidates were female, but beyond this the candidates took similar positions on many issues. Orr won with 53 percent of the vote "in a state where Republicans outnumber Democrats by 75,000 registered voters."[14]

In 1990, Joan Finney (D-Kansas) became the first female gubernatorial candidate to defeat an incumbent governor. Barbara Roberts (D-Oregon) and Ann Richards (D-Texas) were also elected in 1990.

Roberts is the most politically liberal of all the women elected governor. She was the first woman elected governor of Oregon, but she "follows in the footsteps of Democrat Betty Roberts, who ran for governor in 1974, and Republican Norma Paulus, who ran in 1986."[15] A longtime activist in the Democratic Party, Barbara Roberts served two terms in the state house of representatives. In 1984 she was elected to the office of secretary of state. Roberts was open about her support for women's issues and her opposition to state initiatives aimed at limiting the rights and protections accorded homosexuals—in 1988 she opposed Measure 8, which repealed Democratic Governor Neil Goldsmith's executive order banning discrimination against homosexuals working in state government.[16]

The third woman elected to the governorship in 1990 was Ann Richards of Texas. Richards first received national attention when she addressed the Democratic National Convention in 1988. Her "poor George" comments were repeated throughout the campaign, but in Texas she was already well-known. Having served eight years as state treasurer, Richards modernized the state financial system and gained a reputation as a good administrator and a smart politician. She defeated Clayton Williams in an open-seat contest in 1990. Her victory was due, at least in part, to Williams' anti-woman comments during the campaign.

A liberal feminist, Richards made appointments that served notice that in the "New Texas" she had promised, state government would no longer be the preserve of white men. Her choices were 20 percent Hispanic, 15 percent black, 2 percent Asian, and an eye-opening 46 percent female; there were even two openly gay appointees.[17] Campaigning as a reformer, Richards introduced measures to stabilize insurance rates and attempted to address the unresolved question of "how to equalize financing among school districts that vary widely in their ability to raise money from property taxes."[18]

Although she campaigned against a state income tax, the Democrat-controlled state legislature adopted a $2.7 billion tax increase that included a revision of the state's major tax on businesses. According to Roberto Suro, "Although the levy is not strictly an income tax, businesses that used to pay taxes only on their capital assets now pay on assets or income, whichever is greater."[19]

Barbara Roberts and Joan Finney chose not to seek reelection in 1994. Richards ran for reelection, but the gender gap in voting that favored Richards in 1990 did not materialize in 1994—Richards was defeated by George W. Bush, a more moderate Republican than Williams.

In 1993, Christine Todd Whitman (R-New Jersey) ran against incumbent governor James Florio. Whitman campaigned on a promise of a 30 percent tax cut. Characterized by her detractors as "naive" and "aristocratic," Whitman defeated Florio in a very close race. The victory was tainted by allegations that Whitman's campaign "may have attempted to 'suppress' the black vote by essentially bribing black ministers not to rally their congregations for the Democrats."[20] Whitman survived the controversy and received high marks for integrity and compassion in a May 1994 poll conducted by the Asbury Park Press.

Whitman has made her reputation as a fiscal conservative and a social moderate. In January 1995 she announced a timetable for completing her promised 30 percent tax cut, yet, according to Dean Armandroff, executive director of the New Jersey Republican State Committee, she is not reflexively anti-government. "She really believes that there are legitimate roles for government."[21] For example, even with major cuts in state spending, she continues to strongly support social service programs.

Like Ann Richards, Whitman has appointed many women to leadership positions, including the first women to serve as attorney general, chief of staff, and executive director of the New York/New Jersey Port Authority. According to the National Leadership Conference of Women Executives in State Government, "Women also represent 248 out of 700 appointments to New Jersey's Boards and Commissions."[22]

Whitman has also urged the Republican Party to take a more moderate stance on the issue of abortion. The governor commented that "abortion was a deeply personal, not political, decision" and urged the GOP "to remove the anti-abortion plank from its 1996 platform."[23] Her stand on abortion probably explains why she was not seriously considered for the Republican vice-presidential nomination in 1996. It also contributed to her near defeat in her bid for reelection in 1997. After Whitman refused to sign a state bill outlawing "partial birth" abortion, the Christian Coalition shifted its support from Mrs. Whitman to a pro-life third-party candidate, Murray Sabrin.[24] Sabrin received nearly 114,000 votes, "virtually all of them at Mrs. Whitman's expense."[25]

Whitman was reelected to a second term as governor in 1997. Like her narrow victory over the incumbent governor in 1993, she defeated her Democratic party challenger Jim McGreevey by only one percent (27,000 votes).[26] While the abortion issue drew support of social conservatives away from Whitman, the major issue her Democratic challenger capitalized on was citizen anger over auto insurance rates in the state. In the end Whitman was able to mobilize support to form a winning coalition with 47 percent of the total vote. The impact of her close victory remains to be seen. Early predictions reflect partisan and ideological differences, more than actual knowledge of the impact of a close race on Whitman's ability to govern.

In 1996 Jeanne Shaheen was elected governor of New Hampshire in an open-seat contest. A three-term State Senator prior to her election, Shaheen and her husband Bill have been active in the New Hampshire Democratic Party for a number of years. According to Cary Goldberg, "Mr. Shaheen—who is called Billie, as his wife is called Jeannie—helped lead Jimmy Carter's come-from-behind New Hampshire campaign in the 1976 season, and Mrs. Shaheen performed similar magic for Gary Hart in the state in 1984."[27]

Even with a Republican-controlled state legislature, Shaheen has been quite successful with policy initiatives, including increased funding for kindergartens and health care reform. Her approval ratings are high and she is expected seek a second term in 1998.

Finally, for the second time in recent years a woman has been appointed to the governorship of Arizona following the resignation or impeachment of the elected governor. Former Secretary of State Jane Dee Hull replaced Fife Symington as governor in September 1997. Symington was convicted of federal fraud charges. Although not taking office with a well-formed policy agenda, Hull stated that education would be a priority.[28]

PATTERNS IN THE CANDIDACY OF WOMEN GOVERNORS

Types of Contests

As Table 6.4 shows, between 1974 and 1997, women ran in elections 44 times as major-party candidates for governor, winning in 14 races. In 1994 alone, nine women ran for governor; all were defeated. Women candidates are most successful in *open-seat* contests, with eight of fourteen victories in races with no incumbent (see Table 6.5). But what about the cases that do not fit this pattern?

Table 6.5 shows that two women governors, Ella Grasso (D-Connecticut) and Madeleine Kunin (D-Vermont), were first elected in open-seat contests and were reelected for a second, and in Kunin's case a third, term. More recently Joan Finney (D-Kansas) and Christine Todd Whitman (R-New Jersey) defeated incumbents in their successful gubernatorial races, and Whitman later went on to win reelection as an incumbent. The other race that varied from the common pattern of election was that 1986 Nebraska gubernatorial race between Republican candidate Kay Orr and her Democratic opponent Helen Boosalis. Not only was this the first race between two women candidates of the major political parties, but with her victory Orr became the first Republican woman to be elected to the governorship. In 1990 Orr was defeated in her bid for a second term by her Democratic challenger, Ben Nelson.

Previous Political Experience

Most women running for governor have held other state or local elected positions. For example, Ella Grasso was elected secretary of state in Connecticut in 1958. She went on to serve two terms as a U.S. representative before her election as governor in 1974. Madeleine Kunin, who served as lieutenant governor of Vermont, was defeated by incumbent governor Richard Snelling in the 1982 gubernatorial contest. She came back to defeat Republican John Easton in an open-seat contest in 1984. Her victory in a state known as a "bastion of Republicanism" was due in part to her high name recognition and past service in state government. Both Kay Orr and Helen Boosalis were well known in Nebraska electoral politics, with Orr serving as state treasurer and Boosalis as mayor of Lincoln. Ann Richards gained political experience serving two terms as state treasurer. First elected to the position in 1982,

TABLE 6.4 Women Candidates for Governor, 1974–1997 Major Party Nominees

Year	State	Women Candidates	Opponents	Seat	Results*
1997	NJ	Christine Todd Whitman-R	Jim McGreevey-D	incumbent	won 47%
1996	NH	Jeanne Shaheen-D	Bill Zeliff-R	open	won
1994	CA	Kathleen Brown-D	Pete Wilson-R	challenger	lost 40%
1994	CT	Eunice Strong Groark-ACP	John Rowland-R Bill Curry-D Tom Scott-I	open	lost 19%
1994	HI	Patricia "Pat" Saiki-R	Ben Cayetano-D and Frank Fast-I	open	lost 29%
1994	IA	Bonnie J. Campbell-D	Terry E. Bradstad-R	challenger	lost 42%
1994	IL	Dawn Clark Netsch-D	Jim Edgar-R	challenger	lost 34%
1994	MD	Ellen R. Sauerbrey-R	Parris N. Glendening-D	open	lost 50%
1994	ME	Susan M. Collins-R	Angus King-I Joseph Brennan-D Jonathan Carter-I	open	lost 23%
1994	RI	Myrth York-D	Lincoln C. Almond (R)	open	lost 44%
1994	TX	Ann Richards-D	George W. Bush (R)	incumbent	lost 46%
1994	WY	Kathy Karpan-D	Jim Geringer (R)	open	lost 40%
1993	NJ	Christine Todd Whitman-R	Jim Florio-D	challenger	won
1993	VA	Mary Sue Terry-D	George Allen-R	open	lost
1992	MT	Dorothy Bradley-D	Mark Racicot-R	open	lost 49%
1992	NH	Deborah Arnie Arneson-D	Steve Merrill-R	open	lost 38%
1992	RI	Elizabeth Ann Leonard-R	Bruce Sundlun-D	challenger	lost 34%
1990	NE	Kay Orr-R	Ben Nelson-D	incumbent	lost 49%
1990	OR	Barbara Roberts-D	Dave Frohnmayer-R	open	won 46%
1990	PA	Barbara Hafer-R	Bob Casey-D	challenger	lost 32%
1990	TX	Ann Richards-D	Clayton Williams-R	open	won 50%
1990	WY	Mary Mead-R	Michael Sullivan-D	challenger	lost 35%
1988	MO	Betty Hearnes-D	John Ashcroft-R	challenger	lost 35%
1988	VT	Madeleine Kunin-D	Michael Bernhardt-R	incumbent	won 55%
1986	AK	Arliss Sturgulewski-R	Steve Coper-D and Joe Vogler-I	open	lost 43%
1986	AZ	Carolyn Warner-D	Evan Mecham-R and Bill Schultz-I	open	lost 34%
1986	CT	Julie Belaga-R	William O'Neill-D	challenger	lost 41%
1986	NE	Kay Orr-R	Helen Boosalis-D	open	won 53%
1986	NE	Helen Boosalis-D	Kay Orr-R	open	lost 47%
1986	NV	Patty Cafferata-R	Richard Bryan-D	challenger	lost 25%
1986	OR	Norma Paulus-R	Neil Goldschmidt-D	open	lost 48%
1986	VT	Madeleine Kunin-D	Peter Smith-R and Bernard Sanders-I	incumbent	won 47%
1984	VT	Madeleine Kunin-D	John Easton-R	open	won 50%
1983	KY	Martha Layne Collins-D	Jim Bunning-R	open	won 54%
1982	IA	Roxanne Conlin-D	Terry Brandstad-R	open	lost 47%
1982	VT	Madeleine Kunin-D	Richard Snelling-R	challenger	lost 44%
1978	CT	Ella Grasso-D	Ronald Sarasin-R	incumbent	won 59%
1976	VT	Stella Hackel-D	Richard Snelling-R	open	lost 40%
1976	WA	Dixie Lee Ray-D	John Spellman-R	open	won 53%
1974	CT	Ella Grasso-D	Robert Steele-R	open	won 59%
1974	MD	Louise Gore-R	Marvin Mandel-D	challenger	lost 37%
1974	NV	Shirley Crumpler-R	Mike O'Callaghan-D	challenger	lost 17%

*Percentage of the vote received by women candidates according to *The Almanac of American Politics,* except in 1990 and 1992; 1990 and 1992 figures are from secretaries of state offices.

Source: Center for the American Women and Politics (CAWP), National Information Bank on Women in Public Office, Eagleton Institute of Politics, Rutgers University.

TABLE 6.5   Type of Electoral Contest in Which Women Governors Were Elected: 1974–1997

Open Seat	Challenger	Incumbent
Grasso (D) 1974	Finney (D) 1990	Grasso (D) 1978
Ray (D) 1976	Whitman (R) 1993	Kunin (D) 1986
Collins (D) 1983		Kunin (D) 1988
Kunin (D) 1984		Whitman (R) 1997
Orr (R) 1986		
Richards (D) 1990		
Roberts (D) 1990		
Shaheen (D) 1996		

Source: Center for the American Woman and Politics (CAWP), National Information Bank on Women in Public Office, Eagleton Institute of Politics, Rutgers University.

she became the first woman in Texas to hold statewide elected office since the days of Miriam Ferguson.[29]

In sum, holding other statewide elective office gives women the experience, partisan connections, and name recognition necessary to seek the governorship. Current New Jersey Governor Christine Todd Whitman is an exception to this pattern, gaining the experience necessary to seek the governorship by virtue of her family background, years of political involvement, and near defeat of incumbent Senator Bill Bradley in the 1990 senatorial race.

WOMEN GOVERNORS: THE 1990s AND BEYOND

Nineteen-ninety-four was definitely *not* "The Year of the Woman Governor." Nine women ran for state governor in the 36 gubernatorial contests held—none were elected. The race in Maryland was the closest and most hotly contested. In that race the Republican candidate, Ellen Sauerbrey, continues to dispute the victory of her Democratic opponent, Paris Glendening. Losing by only 5993 votes out of 1.4 million votes cast, she took the matter to the Maryland State Court. In her suit, Ms. Sauerbrey said she "had been cheated through votes cast by dead people, prison inmates and unregistered voters."[30] On January 13 a state judge ruled that Sauerbrey did not have enough evidence to overturn the election. Glendening and his running mate for lieutenant governor, Kathleen Kennedy Townsend, took office in mid-January.

In California, Kathleen Brown came into the race with the right family background, high name recognition, and previous political experience. However, like Dianne Feinstein in 1990, she was no match for Governor Pete Wilson. Feinstein recently announced she would not seek the governorship again in 1998, stating her desire to remain in the U.S. Senate. The growing importance of the governorship is illustrated by the national attention already being paid to an electoral contest that is still over a year away. Welfare reform, immigrant rights, and affirmative action—all policy issues that would have been primarily federal in scope—are now being decided at the state level and in no state are they more contestable than California.

CONCLUSION

Fifteen women have served as state governors. Today three women hold the office of governor, but eighteen women are currently lieutenant governors. According to the Center for the American Woman and Politics, women have been elected and appointed to statewide executive offices in all but two of the fifty states. Many more hold offices such as secretary of state or state treasurer—offices that have given most of the women discussed here the experience and recognition necessary to be elected governor.

How do we evaluate this record? What predictions can be made about the future of women as governors or the governorship as an avenue of mobility to the presidency for women? The progress made in the election of women governors is mixed, but there are several positive developments.

First, more women are running for and holding statewide elected positions—putting themselves in the "experience pool." If this trend continues, we should see many qualified female candidates in gubernatorial contests in 1998 and beyond.

Second, female candidates are beginning to defeat incumbents, showing their strength as candidates and their ability to raise money as challengers. Only Finney and Whitman have defeated incumbents, but many women now holding other statewide elected positions are poised to mount challenges in the upcoming electoral period. Republican state officeholders have received campaign support and advice from Christine Todd Whitman—currently the model for many Republican women seeking state elected office.

Third, Whitman and former governors Ann Richards and Madeleine Kunin are highly visible in their respective political parties. Whitman presented the Republican Party's response to President Clinton's 1995 State of the Union Address and Kunin currently holds a high-ranking position in the Clinton administration. Still, the picture remains less than perfect.

Although the governorship has not served as the same avenue to the presidency for women as it has for men, the changing character of political ambition among women and the increased acceptance of women in high political office may change this.

Throughout the history of the United States, only fifteen women have held the position of governor. No more than four women have served as governor simultaneously. All nine of the female candidates for governor in the November 1994 elections were defeated. With the growing importance of the governorship in U.S. politics, full political equality will not be achieved until more women are elected as state chief executives.

From Nellie Tayloe Ross, the first woman governor, to the women currently holding office, the governorship has been both a continuation of public service and a precursor to further political activity—their time as governor is just one part of their political lives.

The careers of women governors past and present continue to suggest ways in which women can reshape state executive governance. The fifteen women who have served as their state's chief executive officer serve as important role models for other women seeking statewide—and in the future, nationwide—elected office.

In conclusion, this article only begins to explore the subject of female governors. Closer examination of patterns of support for female gubernatorial candidates and analysis focusing more broadly on women holding other statewide elective offices will increase our understanding of state executive leadership. Further research on these and other related topics is clearly called for.

NOTES

1. Virginia Sapiro, *The Political Integration of Women: Roles, Socialization, and Politics* (Urbana: University of Illinois Press, 1983).

2. Margaret Conaway, Jill K. Conway, Susan C. Bourquet, and Joan W. Scott, *Learning about Women: Gender Politics and Power* (Ann Arbor: University of Michigan Press, 1987).

3. Susan Welch, "Are Women More Liberal than Men in the U.S. Congress?" *Legislative Studies Quarterly,* 10 (February 1985), pp. 125–134; Sue Thomas and Susan Welch, "The Impact of Gender on Activities and Priorities of State Legislators." *Western Political Quarterly,* 44 (June 1991), pp. 445–456; Barbara Burrell, *A Woman's Place Is In The House: Campaigning for Congress in the Feminist Era* (Ann Arbor: University of Michigan Press, 1994).

4. Madeleine Kunin, *Living a Political Life* (New York: Vintage, 1995); Ann Richards, *Straight from the Heart* (New York: Simon and Schuster, 1989); and Patricia Beard, *Growing up Republican, Christie Whitman: The Politics of Character* (New York: HarperCollins Publishers, 1996).

5. John Barrette (Ed.), *Prairie Politics: Kay Orr vs. Helen Boosalis, The Historic 1986 Gubernatorial Race* (Lincoln, Nebraska: Media Publishing and Marketing, 1987).

6. Celia Morris, *Storming the Statehouse: Running for Governor with Ann Richards and Dianne Feinstein* (New York: Simon and Schuster, 1992).

7. Genovese and Thompson, in *Women as National Leaders,* Genovese (Ed.) (Thousand Oaks, California: Sage, 1993), p. 1.

8. Genovese and Thompson, *Ibid.,* p. 2.

9. Celinda Lake, as cited in Eleanor Clift, "Not the Year of the Woman," *Newsweek,* October 25, 1993, p. 31.

10. Barrette, *Prairie Politics,* Chapter Three.

11. Interview, *New York Times Magazine,* September 22, 1986, as cited in Barrette, *op. cit.*

12. Center for the American Woman and Politics (CAWP), National Information Bank on Women in Public Office, Eagleton Institute of Politics, Rutgers University.

13. *New York Times,* as cited in Barrette, *op. cit.,* p. 95.

14. *Ibid.,* p. 155.

15. Jeff Mapes, *The Oregonian,* December 8, 1990, p. A7.

16. *Ibid.,* p. A12.

17. Alison Cook, "Lone Star," *New York Times Magazine,* February 7, 1993, p. 42.

18. Roberto Suro, "Texas Governor Proves Adept in Her First Year," *New York Times,* January 19, 1992, p. A16.

19. *Ibid.,* p. 16.

20. Gloria Berger and Matthew Cooper (with Scott Minerbrook and Michael Barone), "New Jersey: An Election Controversy." *U.S. News and World Report,* November 22, 1993, p. 30.

21. Dean Armandroff, as cited in Joe Donohue, "Whitman on Cutting (Tax) Edge of Stardom," *New Jersey Star-Ledger,* March 20, 1994, p. D3.

22. National Leadership Conference of Women Executives in State Government, letter of nomination for WESG "Breaking the Glass Ceiling" Awards, 1995.

23. Governor Christine Todd Whitman, as cited in "Whitman Condemns GOP Abortion Stance," *Philadelphia Inquirer,* July 13, 1994, p. 6.

24. Frank Rich, "Whitman's 1% Blowout" *New York Times,* November 10, 1997.

25. *Ibid.*

26. *Ibid.*

27. Carey Goldberg, "Women at The Helm of New Hampshire Politics" *New York Times,* Tuesday, Oct. 7, 1997, p. A8.

28. "Power Quietly Shifts Hands After Arizona Governor's Conviction," *New York Times,* Sunday, September 7, 1997, A25.

29. Ferguson served as surrogate for her husband, who could not run for reelection.

30. *New York Times,* January 14, 1995, p. A11.

FURTHER READINGS

Barrette, John (ed.). *Prairie Politics: Kay Orr vs. Helen Boosalis, The Historic 1986 Gubernatorial Race.* Lincoln, Nebraska: Media Publishing and Marketing, 1987.

Beard, Patricia. *Growing Up Republican, Christie Whitman: The Politics of Character.* New York: HarperCollins, 1996.

Burrell, Barbara C. *A Woman's Place Is in the House: Campaigning for Congress in the Feminist Era.* Ann Arbor: University of Michigan Press, 1994.

Dodson, Debra (ed.). *Gender and Policymaking: Studies of Women in Office.* New Brunswick, New Jersey: Center for the American Woman in Politics, 1991.

Genovese, Michael A. (ed.). *Women as National Leaders.* Thousand Oaks, California: Sage, 1993.

Githens, Marianne, et al. (eds.). *Different Roles, Different Voices: Women and Politics in the United States and Europe.* New York: HarperCollins, 1994.

Kunin, Madeleine M. *Living a Political Life.* New York: Vintage, 1994.

Morris, Celia. *Storming the Statehouse: Running for Governor with Ann Richards and Dianne Feinstein.* New York: Scribner's, 1992.

Richards, Ann, with Peter Knobler. *Straight from the Heart.* New York: Simon and Schuster, 1989.

Thomas, Sue. *How Women Legislate.* New York: Oxford University Press, 1994.

THE COURTS:
WOMEN AND DECISIONS

Does gender make a difference when it comes to the judicial branch? Karen O'Connor and Patricia Clark trace the intertwined quest for expanded rights for women and the U.S. Supreme Court's responses to those actions. They begin with an overview of the colonial period, move to the Civil War years, address the suffrage movement litigation, review the press for state laws and for the Supreme Court to address the issue of gender, and explore the legal status of women at the workplace as well as more contemporary attempts to expand women's rights. They find that fewer and fewer constitutional cases involving sex discrimination are coming before the Supreme Court each year—perhaps because women's rights groups are using their time and money to fend off challenges to a series of decisions adverse to abortion rights. Also, the author maintains that most of the "easy" constitutional cases have been decided, and there is fairly uniform application of the intermediate standard of review in the lower courts. Thus, most gender cases that the Supreme Court now chooses to hear involve employment discrimination and the scope of bona fide occupational qualifications permissible under Title VII of the 1964 Civil Rights Act. The authors conclude that, as the last decade of the 1900s draws to a close, the Supreme Court is expected to hand down decisions involving various kinds of sexual harassment. These decisions will be watched closely, given Paula Jones' charges against Bill Clinton as well as the debate over Bill Clinton's relationship with White House intern, Monica Lewinsky. Thus, as most state practices that discriminate against women are found unconstitutional by lower courts applying recent Supreme Court decisions, the Court has largely moved on to deciding thornier issues of employment discrimination, especially, sexual harassment.

If we had more female judges, could we expect to see more judicial decisions favorable to women? Elaine Martin investigates gender roles and judicial roles. It has been even more difficult for women to attain judicial office than to attain other public office, but indications are that the rate of increase of women judges is on the rise. This article first presents data on the increase from 1976 to 1997 in the number of women judges, or numerical representation, and considers the eligible pool theory as an explanation for that increase. It then examines the potential impact of the increase in women judges on the diversification of gender perspectives on the judicial bench, or interest representation. Results from studies done in the 1970s and early 1980s suggested that men's and women's similar legal training and socialization as lawyers minimized any potential gender differences in judicial behavior. However, more recent studies indicate that, as women's numbers move beyond the token stage and as younger females educated after the women's movement become judges, differences based on gender emerge more clearly. Research on this new generation of women judges suggests that these gender-based differences in experience may contribute to a widening gap between the behavior of men and women judges with respect to decisions in cases raising issues of gender or minority discrimination, with respect to leadership of courtroom personnel, and with respect to judicial role conceptions of "acting for" women's perspectives.

Women's Rights and Legal Wrongs: The U.S. Supreme Court and Sex Discrimination

Karen O'Connor and Patricia Clark

As early as March 31, 1776, Abigail Adams wrote to her husband, John, who was attending the Second Continental Congress:

> In the new Code of Laws . . . I desire you would Remember the Ladies, and be more generous and favourable to them than your ancestors. Do not put such unlimited power into the hands of the Husbands. Remember all men would be tyrants if they could. If particular care and attention is not paid to the Laidies [*sic*] we are determined to foment a Rebelion [*sic*], and will not hold ourselves bound by any Laws in which we have no voice, or Representation.[1]

Adams's admonitions to her husband had little impact on either the Articles of Confederation or, later, the Constitution. It was not until 1920 that the Nineteenth Amendment was added to the Constitution, offering women that most basic element of citizenship—suffrage. And, in the 1990s, despite long years of a concerted drive by women's rights groups to gain ratification of an amendment guaranteeing equal rights, the Constitution continues to afford women less protection from discrimination than men.

This article traces the intertwined quest for expanded rights by women and the U.S. Supreme Court's responses to these actions. Often, the Supreme Court is looked upon as ahead of its time, or at least that of public opinion, in the expansion of rights to minorities. This has not been the case with the expansion or guarantee of rights to women. Instead, as a general rule, the Supreme Court—the final interpreter of the Constitution—has lagged behind societal mores and realities when it has dealt with issues of concern to women. Thus, this article is an account of the efforts of heroic women and women's groups and the political reaction to those demands for full and equal rights under the Constitution and the Court's responses to those efforts.

THE COLONIAL PERIOD TO THE CIVIL WAR

During the colonial period, suffrage was largely determined by local custom and usage. While there are few records of women voting, it is clear some did, especially large landowners. Once individual states began to draft written constitutions, however, female suffrage evaporated. Women were also excluded by the shift from gender-neutral property-owning requirements to near-universal male suffrage. This emphasis on male suffrage also fostered the codification of many of the practices Abigail Adams denounced as contributing to the second-class citizenship of women.

Recognition and Reaction

Recognition of their own inferior legal status, however, did not come to women overnight. In 1848, in what is widely hailed as the first major step toward female equality under the Constitution, a women's rights convention was held in Seneca Falls, New York.

Eight years earlier, in 1840, two women active in the American abolitionist movement—Lucretia Mott and Elizabeth Cady Stanton—had traveled to London, for the annual meeting of the International Anti-Slavery Society. After a long and arduous journey, they were denied seating on the floor of the convention solely because they were women. Forced to take seating in the rear of the balcony, they could not help but begin to see parallels between their status and that of the slaves they were trying to free. They resolved to call a meeting to discuss women's second-class status, but their involvement in the anti-slavery movement and issues in their own lives kept them from calling a meeting in Seneca Falls until 1848.

At what is often called the Seneca Falls Convention and at a later meeting held in Rochester, New York, a series of resolutions and a Declaration of Sentiments were drafted, calling for expanded rights for women in all walks of life. Both documents reflected dissatisfaction with contemporary moral codes, divorce and criminal laws, and the limited opportunities for women to obtain an education, participate in the church, and to enter careers in medicine, law, and politics. While these issues continue to dominate the field of sex discrimination law today, none of the participants at the Seneca Falls Convention or subsequent conventions for women's rights saw the Constitution as a source of potential rights for women. Women's rights activists did, however, eventually see the need to amend the Constitution to achieve the right to vote.

While women continued to press for changes in state laws to ameliorate their inferior legal status, they also continued to be very active in the abolitionist movement.[2] During the Civil War (1861–1865), most women's rights activists set aside the cause of women's rights to concentrate on the war effort and abolition. Many who had been present at Seneca Falls or active in subsequent efforts for women's rights joined the American Equal Rights Association (AERA), an association dedicated to the abolition of slavery and woman suffrage. AERA members saw the issues of slavery and women's rights as inextricably intertwined, believing that woman suffrage would be granted when the franchise was extended to newly freed slaves.

The Fourteenth and Fifteenth Amendments

Even the AERA, however, soon abandoned the cause of woman suffrage with its support of the proposed Fourteenth Amendment to the Constitution. When a majority of its members agreed that "now is the Negro's hour," key women's rights activists, including Stanton and Susan B. Anthony, were outraged. They were particularly incensed by the text of the proposed amendment, which would introduce the word *male* into the Constitution for the first time. Although Article II of the Constitution does refer to the president as "he," the use of the word *male* was infuriating to many women.

Not only did Stanton and Anthony argue that women should not be left out of any attempt to secure fuller rights for freed slaves, they were also concerned that the text of the proposed amendment would necessitate the passage of an additional amendment to enfranchise women. How right they were. Soon after passage of the Fourteenth Amendment, the Fifteenth Amendment was added to the Constitution specifically to enfranchise black males previously ineligible to vote. Feverish efforts to have the word *sex* included to the amendment's list of race, color, or previous condition of servitude as improper limits on voting were unsuccessful. Women once again were told that the rights of blacks must come first.

Passage of the Fifteenth Amendment, and the AERA's support of it, led Anthony and Stanton to found the National Woman Suffrage Association (NWSA) in 1869. The NWSA's relatively radical demands for family and standards of dress reform, as well as its support of a well-known proponent of free love, Victoria Woodhull, led many to deride its more conservative demand for suffrage via a national constitutional amendment.

LITIGATING FOR SUFFRAGE

The NWSA's advocacy of controversial reforms led to a severe image problem for both the association and its goals. In 1869, to lend credibility to its cause as well as to short-circuit the possibility of a long battle for a universal suffrage amendment, Francis Minor, the husband of Virginia Minor, a prominent NWSA member, put forth his belief that women, as citizens, were entitled to vote under the existing provisions of the Fourteenth Amendment.[3] Minor saw the NWSA's possible resort to the courts as a means to gain favorable publicity for the organization.

Victoria Woodhull's presentation to Congress in January 1871, urging it to pass enabling legislation to give women the right to vote under the Fourteenth Amendment, provided the impetus for a concerted effort to test the logic of Minor's arguments. The day after her congressional appearance, Woodhull addressed the NWSA's annual meeting, infusing the association with a new sense of purpose and enthusiasm for the suffrage battle.

Francis Minor, along with Susan B. Anthony, quickly moved to seize upon the enthusiasm that Woodhull's suggestions created. Minor urged that test cases quickly be brought to determine if the courts would obviate the need for additional legislative action. A number of legal scholars and judges had publicly agreed with Minor's arguments; moreover, in rejecting Woodhull's request for enabling legislation, the House of Representatives had noted that if the right to vote was "vested by the Constitution . . . without regard to sex, that right can be established in the courts without further legislation."[4] And, more importantly, the newly appointed chief justice of the Supreme Court, Salmon P. Chase, had suggested that women test the parameters of the Constitution to determine whether they already were enfranchised by its provisions.

Despite Chase's encouragement, prior references to women by the Supreme Court had generally accepted only limited options for women. In *Dredd Scott v. Sandford* (1857),[5] for example, Scott's lawyer had argued that one need not have "first-class" citizenship to vote. After all, he pointed out, women were citizens yet uniformly were denied the franchise. In response, Justice Taney noted:

> Undoubtedly, a person may be a citizen, that is, a member of the community who form the sovereignty, although he exercises no share of the political power, and is incapacitated for holding particular offices. Women and minors, who form a part of the political family, cannot vote. . . .[6]

Despite this discouraging language, the NWSA initiated several test cases, hoping to have at least one case heard by the Supreme Court. Somewhat fittingly, the only one to reach the Supreme Court was *Minor v. Happersett,*[7] which involved Virginia Minor and her husband, Francis, as coplaintiffs, since married women had no legal right to sue in their own names.

Women, the Legal Profession, and the Supreme Court

Unfortunately for the NWSA, before *Minor* could be appealed to the Supreme Court, the justices heard another case involving gender discrimination under the Fourteenth Amendment. *Bradwell v. Illinois* (1873)[8] involved a challenge to the Illinois Supreme Court's refusal to admit Myra Bradwell to the practice of law solely because she was a woman. Bradwell's lawyer based her claim to practice law on the amendment's clause concerning privileges and immunities. Because Bradwell's lawyer was aware of the pending suffrage test cases, in his argument he rejected the notion that women were enfranchised under the same provisions. He carefully differentiated the practice of a chosen profession from the right to vote, putting the Court on notice that not even all women were in agreement over the scope and reach of the Fourteenth Amendment. And, despite the care he took to disassociate his client from the NWSA's tactics, the Court ruled 8 to 1 against Bradwell's petition.

The majority opinion—the first pronouncement from the Supreme Court on the issue of gender—was based on two grounds. First, because Bradwell was suing as a citizen of Illinois, the Privileges or Immunities Clause of Article IV, section 2, of the Constitution was held inapplicable to her claim and was held to apply only to matters involving U.S. citizenship. Second, since admission to the bar of any state was not one of the privileges or immunities of U.S. citizenship, the Fourteenth Amendment did not secure that right.

Far more damaging to the cause of women's rights, however, was a concurrence written by Justice Joseph P. Bradley, which is often referred to as his promulgation of the "Divine Law of the Creator." Writing for himself and two other justices, Bradley chose to base his decision on much broader grounds:

> The civil law, as well as nature herself, has always recognized a wide difference in the respective sphere and destinies of man and woman. Man is, or should be, woman's protector and defender. The natural and proper timidity and delicacy . . . (of) the female sex evidently unfits it for many of the occupations of civil life. The constitution of the family organization, which is founded in the divine ordinance, as well as in the nature of things, indicates the domestic sphere as that which properly belongs to the domain and functions of womanhood. . . . So firmly fixed was this sentiment in the founders of the common law that it became a maxim of the system of jurisprudence that a woman had no legal existence separate from her husband. . . . This very incapacity was one circumstance which the Supreme Court of Illinois deemed important in rendering a married woman incompetent fully to perform the duties and trusts that belong to the office of an attorney.
>   . . . The paramount destiny and mission of woman are to fulfill the noble and benign offices of wife and mother. This is the law of the Creator.[9]

Other Gender-Based Claims

Two years later, in *Minor v. Happersett* (1875), the Court again ruled against a claim for expanded women's rights. After the Minors filed suit against a St. Louis voting registrar who refused to accept Virginia Minor's application to vote, the Missouri Supreme Court ruled that states had the authority to bar women from registering to vote and that the Fourteenth Amendment had no impact on that right. On appeal, in rejecting Virginia Minor's claims that the judiciary was empowered to read into the Fourteenth Amendment the right of suffrage as a natural privilege and immunity of citizenship, the newly appointed Chief Justice Morrison R. Waite, writing for a unanimous Court, argued that the states were not inhibited by the Constitution from committing "that important trust to men alone." Nevertheless, the Court stressed that women were "persons" and may even be "citizens" within the meaning of the Fourteenth Amendment.[10]

Thus, by 1875, it was clear that women could not expect constitutional protections from discrimination from the Supreme Court. And, as the NWSA lost members and vigor, it saw little reason to bring other cases to the obviously unreceptive Court.

All of the gender-based discrimination cases heard by the Supreme Court during this era involved construction of the Privileges or Immunities Clause and not the Due Process or Equal Protection Clauses of the Fourteenth Amendment. In the *Slaughterhouse Cases* (1873),[11] argued and decided shortly after *Bradwell,* the Supreme Court had meticulously examined the scope of the Fourteenth Amendment. In addition to limiting the constitutional significance of the Privileges or Immunities Clause, the Court concluded that the Equal Protection Clause "is so clearly a provision for [the Negro] that a strong case would be necessary for its application to any other."[12] Although the Fourteenth Amendment would be revived as a potential tool for women's rights soon after the beginning of the twentieth century, at the end of the nineteenth century women had yet to win a favorable decision against sex discrimination from the Supreme Court. While women were gaining greater rights within the family through passage of married women's property acts in various states and were beginning to gain entry into institutions of higher learning, the Court stuck rigidly to its interpretation that the Equal Protection Clause of the Fourteenth Amendment was intended primarily to protect African Americans (i.e., African American males) from discrimination, and it held fast to traditional notions concerning women's proper role in society.

LITIGATING TO PROTECT WOMEN

Although the *Slaughterhouse Cases* did not provide a useful precedent for women seeking to practice law or to vote, the Court's opinion planted the seeds for judicial adoption of a very broad state police power to enact laws to protect the public health, welfare, safety, and morals. This view was accepted in several subsequent cases. In 1887, for example, in sustaining a law prohibiting the sale of intoxicating beverages, the Court built on the *Slaughterhouse* dissents of Justices Bradley and Stephen Field, announcing that it was ready to examine the *substantive* reasonableness of such state legislation. According to the Court, when state laws involving "the public morals, the public health, or the public safety" were at issue, the Court would "look to the substance of things" so as not to be "misled by mere pretenses."[13] Ten years later, in 1897, the Court for the first time invalidated a state statute on substantive due process grounds.[14] And, in 1905, in *Lochner v. New York,* the Court similarly invalidated a law regulating the work hours of bakers.[15]

Until then, the Court had rarely looked to the substance of legislation in addressing its validity. The Court's earlier readings of the Due Process Clause of the Fourteenth Amendment (or of the Fifth Amendment when federal legislation was involved) only guaranteed that legislation be passed in a fair manner, even though it might have an arbitrary or discriminatory impact. In *Lochner,* however, state laws would fail *unless* the provisions at issue were reasonable under "common knowledge." Thus, the Court refused to accept New York's claim that a *ten-hour maximum-hour* law for bakers was reasonable to ensure the health of the bakers. Instead, the Court found that it unreasonably interfered with the employers' and employees' freedom of contract protected by the Fourteenth Amendment, and found no common knowledge to justify such actions by New York.

The importance of common knowledge cannot be understated in chronicling the Court's treatment of gender. Often, "common knowledge" has substituted for the personal views of the individual justices. As Justice Bradley's "Divine Law of the Creator" opinion made quite clear, that view could easily lead to restrictions on the rights of women.

In the early 1900s, however, concern about the public health, welfare, and morals of women led women's rights activists, particularly those closely allied with the suffrage movement, to press for state laws to upgrade the status of working women.

At the turn of the century, although large numbers of women were entering the labor force, they were doing so by necessity—if single, to support themselves; if married, to add to their families' meager wages. Most women were confined to low-paying jobs in horribly substandard conditions, a circumstance highlighted by the 1911 Triangle Shirtwaist Factory fire in New York City, in which many young female workers lost their lives. Even before that time, however, some women had begun to work to improve the working conditions of women and children. And, whether out of civic concern or moral outrage, beginning in the 1890s, resolutions were adopted annually at suffrage conventions calling for improved conditions for women workers.

The National Consumers' League and Protective Legislation

The organization most responsible for change and for the Court's again addressing issues of gender was the National Consumers' League (NCL). The NCL grew out of a meeting of retail shop girls in New York City in 1890 who wanted to publicize their long hours and deplorable working conditions. Soon they were joined in their efforts by numerous upper-class women who became the guiding forces in the organization. Although the NCL initially attempted to use moral suasion, it soon became clear that legislation would be imperative to begin to remedy some of the most outrageous conditions unearthed by its members. By 1907, through the hard work of its national staff and numerous affiliates, the NCL had secured various sorts of maximum-hour or total restriction on night work for women in eighteen states.[16] Its leaders, therefore, immediately recognized how much they had at stake when the Supreme Court decided to review *Muller v. Oregon* (1908), a case challenging the constitutionality of an Oregon statute that prohibited the employment of women for more than ten hours a day. (Muller, the owner of a small laundry, had been convicted of violating the statute.) When *Muller* was accepted for review and oral argument, the NCL went to work immediately. Its general secretary quickly asked Louis D. Brandeis, the well-known attorney brother-in-law of one of its most active members, to take the case. Brandeis did so under one condition—that he have sole control of the litigation—a condition to which Oregon gladly acceded, thus allowing the NCL to represent it in court.

Numerous state court decisions involving protective legislation for women, as well as the Supreme Court's recent decision in *Lochner,* made it clear to Brandeis that a victory could be forthcoming only by presenting information, or "common knowledge," that could persuade the Court that the dangers to women working more than ten hours a day made them more deserving of state protection than the bakers in *Lochner,* and proving that there was something different about women that justified an exception to the freedom of contract doctrine enuciated by the Court in *Lochner.* Brandeis and the NCL would not challenge the Supreme Court's right, under substantive due process, to make that judgment.

NCL researchers compiled information about the possible detrimental effects of long hours of work on women's health and morals, as well as on the health and welfare of their children, including their unborn children. Brandeis stressed women's differences and the reasonableness of the state's legislation. In fact, his brief had but three pages of strictly legal argument, as against 110 pages of sociological data culled largely from European studies of the negative affects of long hours of work on women's health and their reproductive capabilities. The information presented by Brandeis was not all that different (except in quantity) from that presented on behalf of New York in *Lochner,* yet the Court appears to have been keenly persuaded by the contents of what has come to be called the Brandeis Brief.

In holding that the Oregon law was constitutionally permissible, the Court unanimously concluded "that woman's physical structure and the performance of maternal functions place her at a disadvantage in the struggle for substinence." Continued the Court:

> This is especially true when the burdens of motherhood are upon her. Even when they are not, by abundant testimony of the medical fraternity continuance for a long time on her feet at work . . . tends to injurious effects on her body, and as healthy mothers are essential to vigorous offspring, the physical well-being of woman becomes an object of public interest and care in order to preserve the strength and vigor of the race.[17]

The impact of *Muller* was immediate. State courts began to hold other forms of protective legislation for women constitutional, whether or not they involved the kind of ten-hour maximums at issue in *Muller*. Thus, eight-hour maximum-work laws in a variety of professions, outright bans on night work for women, and minimum-wage laws for women were routinely upheld under the *Muller* rationale. Much of this Court-sanctioned governmental protection, however, worked to keep women out of high-paying evening jobs or positions that they desperately needed to support their families.

The NCL's efforts to protect women from unscrupulous employers were victorious in the Supreme Court in several additional cases, but they ran into trouble in the early 1920s, ironically right around the time of the ratification of the Nineteenth Amendment. In *Stettler v. O'Hara* (1917), a lower court decision upholding Oregon's minimum-wage law for women was appealed to the Supreme Court. Forces opposed to governmental interference in contractual rights feared that a decision supporting additional protective legislation would open the floodgates of governmental regulation. Stettler's lawyers argued that a labor agreement between an employer and an employee could not be disturbed by the government. Because the Fourteenth Amendment forbade the state from denying any individual of liberty without due process of law, they argued that freedom of contract was protected by the amendment. The Court had once been amenable to this kind of argument, as attested by its decision in *Lochner*.

Building on the Court's far-ranging discussion of women and their physical, social, and legal differences from men, Brandeis, again presenting the state's case, structured his arguments similarly to those offered in *Muller,* arguing the importance of a living wage to the health, welfare, and morals of women. Before the Court could decide the case, however, a vacancy occurred on the Court and Brandeis was appointed to fill it. *Stettler* was then reargued in 1917; with Justice Brandeis not participating, the Court divided 4 to 4, thus sustaining the lower court's decision.[18]

Another NCL-sponsored case, *Bunting v. Oregon* (1917), also attracted a significant amount of attention.[19] Felix Frankfurter, Brandeis' handpicked successor as counsel for the NCL, used the same kind of arguments Brandeis had used in *Muller* and *Stettler.* In a 5-to-3 decision (with Brandeis again not participating), the Court extended *Muller* to uphold the constitutionality of the Oregon statute that established maximum hours for all factory and mill workers.

Differing Views about Protective Legislation

Although the NCL was victorious in these two cases, it had not anticipated the impact that the controversy within the suffrage movement over protective legislation would have on pending litigation. During the early twentieth century, women had come together to lobby for passage and then ratification of the Nineteenth Amendment. Once it was ratified, attempts were made to secure other rights for women. Women in the more radical branch of the suffrage movement, represented by the National Woman's Party (NWP), proposed the addition of an Equal Rights Amendment (ERA) to the Constitution. Progressives and NCL members were horrified because they perceived that an ERA would immediately invalidate the protective legislation they had lobbied so hard to enact.

When *Adkins v. Children's Hospital* (1923)[20] came to the Court, the NWP was ready. *Adkins* involved the constitutionality of a Washington, DC, minimum-wage law for women. The NWP filed an amicus curiae brief urging the Court to rule that, in light of the Nineteenth Amendment, women should be viewed on a truly equal footing with men. The division among women concerning equal rights and protective legislation was now exposed to public view. It was a debate that was to be resurrected again and again, both in the Court and in public discourse to the present day.

In *Adkins* the Court ruled 5 to 4 that minimum-wage laws for women were unconstitutional, thus resurrecting *Lochner,* which most observers thought had been overruled *sub subsilentio* in *Bunting.* The Court was unwilling to overrule *Muller* and thus simply distinguished it because it involved maximum hours and not wages. Nevertheless, the justices clearly believed that the Nineteenth Amendment conferred more rights on women than just the right to vote. In noting the newly emancipated status of women brought on by the amendment, the Court undoubtedly was responding at last in part to the proequality arguments offered by the NWP.

Adkins, unlike *Muller,* was decided by the narrowest of majorities. But it stood as valid law and as a ringing endorsement of the doctrine of freedom of contract regarding minimum-wage laws for women until 1937 (although the Court continued to uphold state maximum-hour provisions). In *West Coast Hotel v. Parrish* (1937), the Court finally abandoned its endorsement of substantive due process, explicitly overruled *Adkins,* and upheld Washington State's minimum-wage law for women.[21] By *United States v. Darby Lumber* (1941), the Court had completely abandoned substantive due process (and an equally insidious and excessively narrow view of the power of Congress under the Commerce Clause) when it unanimously upheld the validity of the federal Fair labor Standards Act, which prescribed maximum hours and minimum wages for all workers.[22] In hammering the last nail in the coffin of substantive due process, the Court also appeared to be escaping from the constitutional need to establish a difference between men and women.

While the Court was enunciating a view that men and women were equal as permissible objects of regulation, clearly they were not. Most states continued to bar or limit night work for women. And while a separate minimum wage for women could no longer be valid, employer practices of clustering women into certain positions at far lower wages than those paid to men continued to exist.

No new cases involving women's rights came to the Supreme Court until 1948. The NCL had obtained what it wanted, and the coalition of women's groups that had pressed for suffrage had largely disintegrated. Women were urged to support the war effort, and, after the war ended, to return home—to their traditional roles as wives and mothers. Thus, few groups were left to press for women's rights either in the legislatures or through the courts. The NWP did continue to press for equal rights and, in fact, was able to get a proposed ERA introduced into every session of Congress after 1923, but it chose to stay out of litigation until the 1970s.

NEW ATTEMPTS TO EXPAND RIGHTS

In *Goesaert v. Cleary* (1948)[23] and *Hoyt v. Florida* (1961),[24] the Court again made it clear that women were not guaranteed additional rights under the Fourteenth Amendment or elsewhere in the Constitution. Although the Fourteenth Amendment is a pledge of protection against state discrimination, over the years the Court has generally applied a two-tiered level of analysis to claims advanced under its provisions. Classifications based on race or national origin are considered suspect classifications and are entitled to be judged by the severe test of strict scrutiny. As such they are presumed invalid unless the government can show that they are "necessary to a compelling state interest" and that there are not less restrictive alternative ways to achieve those goals. In contrast, when the Court applies the less stringent level of ordinary scrutiny, which until 1976 included all other legislative classifications, a state must show only a conceivable or reasonable basis for its action.

Until 1971, the Court routinely applied this minimal rationality test to claims involving discrimination against women. In *Goesaert,* for example, it sustained a statute that prohibited women from dispensing alcoholic drinks from behind a bar unless they were the wives or daughters of male bar owners. Thus, forty years after *Muller,* the Court once again justified differential treatment of women by deferring to the state's special interest in women's social and "moral" problems. Under the reasonableness test, all that needed to be shown by the state was some rational basis for the law.

In *Hoyt* the Supreme Court accepted sex-role stereotypes as sufficient reason to uphold a Florida statute that required men to serve on juries while women could merely volunteer for jury service. When Hoyt was convicted by an all-male jury of second-degree murder for killing her husband with a baseball bat, she argued that the conviction violated her rights to equal protection of the laws and her Sixth Amendment right to be judged by a jury of her peers. The Supreme Court disagreed, holding that the Florida statute was not an arbitrary or systematic exclusion of women. Justice John M. Harlan concluded:

> Despite the enlightened emancipation of women from the restrictions and protections of bygone years, and their entry into many parts of community life formerly considered to be reserved to men, woman is still regarded as the center of home and family life.[25]

It was not until the dawn of the current women's movement that judicial perspectives on what constitutes reasonable discrimination began to change. In 1966 the National Organization for Women (NOW) was founded. Soon after, a plethora of other women's rights groups was created. Most of these groups renewed the call for passage of an ERA to the Constitution. While significant lobbying was carried out on that front, some groups, aware of the successes the National Association for the Advancement of Colored People (NAACP) had in securing additional rights for African Americans through the courts, began to explore the feasibility of a litigation strategy designed to seek a more expansive interpretation of the Fourteenth Amendment. Although prior forays into the courts had ended unfavorably, some women believed that the times had changed enough for the justices (or some of the justices) to recognize that sex-based differential treatment of women was unconstitutional. Many believed that the status of women and the climate for change were sufficiently positive to convince even a conservative Court that some change was necessary.

The American Civil Liberties Union (ACLU), long a key player in the expansion of constitutional rights and liberties, led the planning for a comprehensive strategy to elevate sex to suspect-classification status. Its first case was *Reed v. Reed* (1971).[26] Ruth Bader Ginsburg, a member of the ACLU board, argued the case before the Supreme Court. (Ironically, like the NCL's Louis Brandeis and Felix Frankfurter before her, Ginsburg, too, was ultimately to sit on the U.S. Supreme Court.) Her enthusiasm and interest in the expansion of women's rights via constitutional interpretation led the ACLU to found the Women's Rights Project (WRP).

At issue in *Reed* was the constitutionality of an Idaho statute that required that males be preferred to otherwise equally qualified females as administrators of estates for those who died. NOW, the National Federation of Business and Professional Women, and the Women's Equity Action League all filed amicus curiae briefs urging the Court to interpret the Fourteenth Amendment as prohibiting discrimination against women on account of sex. Democratic Senator Birch Bayh of Indiana, a major sponsor of the ERA, wrote one of the briefs, in which he attempted to apprise the Court of the glaring legal inequities faced by women and to link those inequities, at least in part, to the Court's own persistent refusal to expand the reach of the Equal Protection Clause to gender discrimination. Judicial decisions such as *Goesaert* and *Hoyt,* which allowed states to discriminate against women on minimally rational grounds, had made it clear to women's rights activists that a constitutional amendment was necessary if women were ever to enjoy full citizenship under the Constitution. But *Reed* was a critical first step.

Chief Justice Warren Burger, writing for a unanimous Court in *Reed,* held that the Idaho statute that provided "different treatment . . . to the applicants on the basis of their sex . . . establishes a classification subject to scrutiny under the Equal Protection Clause."[27] With these simple words, the Supreme Court for the first time concluded that sex-based differentials were entitled to some sort of scrutiny under the Fourteenth Amendment. But what type of scrutiny? According to Burger, who quoted an earlier 1920 case, the test was whether the differential treatment was "reasonable, not arbitrary" and rested "upon some ground of difference having a fair and substantial relation to the object of the legislation, so that all persons similarly circumstanced will be treated alike." The Court then found that the state's objective of reducing the workload of probate judges was insufficient justification to warrant this kind of sex-based statute. In fact, according to the Court, this was "the very kind of arbitrary legislative choice forbidden by the Equal Protection Clause."[28]

OTHER ATTEMPTS TO EXPAND RIGHTS

This major breakthrough heartened women's rights activists. It also encouraged the WRP to launch a full-blown test case strategy like that pursued by the NAACP Legal Defense and Education Fund that had culminated successfully in *Brown v. Board of Education* (1954).[29] WRP attorneys jumped at the opportunity to assist the Southern Poverty Law Center of Alabama with the next major sex-discrimination case to come before the Supreme Court, *Frontiero v. Richardson* (1973).[30] At issue in *Frontiero* was the constitutionality of a federal statute that, for the purpose of computing allowances and fringe benefits, required female members of the armed forces to prove that they contributed more than 50 percent of their dependent husbands' support. Men were not required to make any such showing about their wives.

By an 8-to-1 vote, the Court struck down the statute, which gave male members of the armed forces potentially greater benefits than females. More importantly, though, only a plurality of four justices voted to make sex a suspect classification entitled to the strict scrutiny standard of review. While four other justices agreed that the statute violated the Equal Protection Clause, they did not agree that sex should be made a suspect classification. In fact, three of them specifically noted the pending ratification of the ERA as a reason to wait—to allow the political process to guide judicial interpretation. This was to be the high-water mark of efforts to include sex, along with race, in the category of suspect classifications.

In *Craig v. Boren* (1976), Justice William J. Brennan Jr., author of the plurality opinion in *Frontiero,* formulated a different test, known as *intermediate* or *heightened scrutiny,* to apply to sex-discrimination cases.[31] The case involved a challenge to an Oklahoma law that prohibited the sale of 3.2 percent beer to males under the age of twenty-one and females under the age of eighteen. In determining whether this kind of gender-based differential violated the Equal Protection Clause, Brennan wrote that "classifications by gender must serve important governmental objectives and must be substantially related to achievement of those objectives."[32] He also specifically identified two governmental interests that would not justify sex discrimination: neither administrative convenience nor "fostering 'old' notions of role typing" would any longer be considered constitutionally adequate rationalizations of sex classifications.[33] Shedding many of the stereotypes that had been at the core of *Muller, Hoyt,* and *Goesaert,* the Court specifically noted that there was no more place for "increasingly outdated misconceptions concerning the role of females in the home rather than in the 'marketplace and world of ideas.'"[34] This new intermediate standard of review was subsequently used to invalidate a wide range of discriminatory practices, including some Social Security, welfare, and workers' compensation programs, alimony laws, age of majority statutes, and jury service exemptions that discriminated based on gender.

This is not to say that stereotypes do not still exert influence on the Court. In *Rostker v. Goldberg* (1981), for example, the Court considered congressional combat restrictions sufficient to rationalize the exclusion of women from the new draft registration requirements of the Military Selective Service Act.[35] A majority of the Court accepted the government's position that the statutory exclusion of women from combat positions combined with the need for combat-ready troops were sufficiently important justifications to meet the burden of the intermediate standard of review. The Court did not bother to consider the validity of the combat restrictions themselves. And, in *Michael M. v. Superior Court of Sonoma County* (1981), the Court held that California's statutory rape law, which applied only to males, did not violate the Equal Protection Clause.[36] Justice William H. Rehnquist noted that the state's concern about teenage pregnancy was a sufficiently strong state interest to justify the statute. Moreover, Rehnquist's opinion pointedly did not apply the intermediate scrutiny standard of review.

In late 1981 the Court was joined by its first female member, Sandra Day O'Connor. It was not long before she and the other justices were faced with another sex-based claim made under the Fourteenth Amendment. *Mississippi University for Women v. Hogan* (1982) involved a state policy that restricted enrollment in one state-supported nursing school to females. Writing for a five-member majority, O'Connor noted that when the purpose of a statute was to "exclude or 'protect' members of one gender because they are presumed to suffer from an inherent handicap or to be innately inferior, the objective itself is illegitimate."[37] As one commentator noted, "She out-Brennaned Justice Brennan." For example, O'Connor went even further than Brennan (long the Court's foremost liberal) by suggesting in a footnote that sex might best be treated by the Court as a suspect classification.

O'Connor's strong opinion in *Hogan* again brought to four the number of justices on the Court who apparently favored some sort of strict standard of review for sex-based classifications. But that number was quickly diminished with the elevation of William H. Rehnquist to chief justice and the appointments of Justices Antonin Scalia, Anthony Kennedy, David Souter, and Clarence Thomas to the Court by Republican presidents Ronald Reagan and George Bush. A change of but one justice in *Hogan* would have allowed Mississippi to continue its maintenance of an all-female nursing school.

The Court's slow evolution of its approach to gender-based discrimination claims quickened slightly with President Bill Clinton's appointments of long-time women's rights lawyer Ruth Bader Ginsburg, and then Stephen Breyer. Decisions since the arrival of these two newest justices clearly have solidified the Court majority that frowns on blatant sex discrimination, and, as some would argue, have set the stage for the Court to adopt a higher level of scrutiny to use in gender-based discrimination cases in the future.

In *J.E.B. v. Alabama ex. rel. T.B.* (1994), the Supreme Court considered the constitutionality of gender-based preemptory challenges made at the petitioner's paternity and child support trial after the state used nine of ten challenges to remove male jurors, which resulted in the seating of an all-female jury faced with determining whether the male petitioner had failed to make proper payments. Justice Harry Blackmun, writing for the Court, reaffirmed that "intentional discrimination on the basis of gender by state actors violates the equal protection clause, particularly where, as here, the discrimination serves to ratify and perpetuate invidious, archaic, and over broad stereotypes about the relative abilities of men and women." In what some members of the Court regarded as a departure from the traditional intermediate standard of review, Justice Blackmun noted that gender-based classifications require "an exceedingly persuasive justification." Finding no such justification, the Court extended an earlier holding in which it invalidated the use of preemptory challenges based on race to prohibit gender-based challenges. Interestingly, the Court expressly declined to decide whether classifications based on gender are inherently suspect. Instead, it noted that gender-based preemptory challenges are not substantially related to an important government objective.[38]

The importance of this language was highlighted two years later in *United States v. Virginia* (1996), where the Court was asked to consider the constitutionality of the exclusively male admissions policy of the state-supported Virginia Military Institute (VMI).[39] Virginia had long maintained VMI as a male-only college. When the U.S. government challenged the constitutionality of this practice, Virginia created the Virginia Women's Institute for Leadership (VWIL) at a nearby private women's school, Mary Baldwin College. The U.S. government argued that the VWIL program was not equal to the VMI experience and that Virginia's refusal to offer military-type training to women at VMI violated the equal protection clause of the Fourteenth Amendment of the U.S. Constitution.

A majority of the Court agreed with the U.S. government. Writing for the Court, Justice Ruth Bader Ginsburg applied the "exceedingly persuasive justification" standard earlier articulated by Justice Blackmun in *J.E.B.* She concluded that VMI's exclusion of women violated the equal protection clause and that the creation of VWIL was insufficient to remedy this continued constitutional infringement. While the Court in *United States v. Virginia* again declined to adopt the strict scrutiny standard of review for gender-based discrimination cases, both the concurring and dissenting opinions, written by Chief Justice William Rehnquist and Justice Antonin Scalia respectively, criticized the majority for apparently heightening the intermediate standard of review.

CONCLUSION

This possibility that the Court will use this new standard of review in assessing constitutional claims of sex discrimination may send women's rights activists looking for good new cases to bring to the Court to solidify or even heighten this standard. Since the late 1980s, however, the number of constitutional cases involving claims of gender-based discrimination have declined—at least at the level of the U.S. Supreme Court—due in part to the fairly uniform application of the traditional intermediate standard of review in the lower courts. In fact, the majority of the sex discrimination cases heard by the Court in the early 1990s involved employment discrimination and the scope of bona fide occupational qualifications permissible under Title VII of the Civil Rights Act of 1964.[40]

As the last decade of the 1900s draws to a close, the Supreme Court's docket is almost surprisingly reflective of headlines of the day. In its 1997 term, which spans from October 1997 to July 1998, the Court is expected to hand down decisions in four cases involving various kinds of sexual harassment.[41] In the wake of first the Senate nomination hearings of Clarence Thomas to the Supreme Court, record numbers of sexual harassment claims were filed all over the country. After lengthy litigation in the lower federal courts, the Court's attention has now turned to the myriad issues of sexual harassment that subsequently arose in the context of so much new litigation, including the proper construction and application of federal laws barring sexual harassment in the workplace or in educational settings— decisions that will be watched all the closer given Paula Jones' charges against Bill Clinton, as well as the debate over Bill Clinton's relationship with White House intern, Monica Lewinsky. Thus, as most state practices that discriminate against women are found unconstitutional by lower courts applying recent Supreme Court decisions, the Court has largely moved on to deciding thornier issues of employment discrimination, especially, sex harassment. How long the Court's attention will stay riveted to this narrow issue, however, is unclear.

NOTES

1. Quoted in L. H. Butterfield, Marc Friedlander, and Mary-Jo Kline (Eds.), *Book of Abigail and John* (Cambridge, MA: Harvard University Press, 1975), p. 21.

2. Much of this discussion comes from Nancy E. McGlen and Karen O'Connor, *Women, Politics, and*

American Society (Englewood Cliffs, NJ: Prentice-Hall, 1995), chap. 1.

3. Karen O'Connor, *Women's Organizations' Use of the Courts* (Lexington, MA: Lexington Books, 1980), chap. 3.

4. H. R. Report No. 22, 41st Congress, 3rd Sess., 1871.

5. 60 U.S. 393 (1857).

6. 60 U.S. 393 at 422.

7. 88 U.S. 162 (1875).

8. 16 Wall. (83 U.S.) 130 (1873).

9. 83 U.S. 130 at 141–142 (1873).

10. 88 U.S. 162 (1875).

11. 16 Wall. 36 (1873).

12. 16 Wall. 36 at 81.

13. *Mugler v. Kansas,* 123 U.S. 623 at 661 (1887).

14. *Allgeyer v. Louisiana,* 165 U.S. 578 (1897).

15. 198 U.S. 45 (1905).

16. Clement E. Vose, "The National Consumers' League and the Brandeis Brief." *Midwest Journal of Political Science,* 1 (November 1957), pp. 267–290.

17. *Muller v. Oregon,* 208 U.S. 412 at 421 (1908).

18. 69 Ore. 519, aff'd 243 U.S. 629 (1917).

19. 243 U.S. 426 (1917).

20. 261 U.S. 525 (1923).

21. 300 U.S. 379 (1937).

22. 312 U.S. 100 (1941).

23. 335 U.S. 466 (1948).

24. 368 U.S. 57 (1961).

25. 368 U.S. 57 at 61–62.

26. 404 U.S. 71 (1971).

27. 404 U.S. 71 at 75.

28. 404 U.S. 71 at 76.

29. Richard Kluger, *Simple Justice: The History of Brown v. Board of Education and Black America's Struggle for Equality* (New York: Alfred A. Knopf, 1976).

30. 411 U.S. 677 (1973).

31. 429 U.S. 190 (1976).

32. 429 U.S. 190 at 197.

33. 429 U.S. 190 at 198.

34. 429 U.S. 190 at 198–199.

35. 453 U.S. 57 (1981).

36. 450 U.S. 464 (1981).

37. 458 U.S. 718 at 725.

38. 511 U.S. 127 (1994).

39. 116 S.Ct. 2264 (1996).

40. See *International Union, UAW v. Johnson Controls,* 111 S. Ct. 2238 (1991), for example. Johnson involved a company's fetal protection policy that required women in certain hazardous positions to be sterilized as a condition of their employment. The Court ruled unanimously that the company's policies were not permissible exceptions to the scope of Title VII, which prohibits discrimination based on sex in terms or conditions of employment.

41. Joan Biskupic, "Supreme Court May Clarify Grounds for Sexual Harassment Suits," *The Washington Post,* January 24, 1998, p A4.

FURTHER READINGS

Babcock, Barbara Allen et al. *Sex Discrimination and the Law: History, Practice, and Theory.* Boston: Little, Brown, 1996.

Baer, Judith. *Chains of Protection: The Judicial Response to Women's Labor Legislation.* Westview, CT: Greenwood Press, 1978.

———. *Women in American Law.* New York: Holmes and Meier, 1991.

Boles, Janet. *The Politics of the Equal Rights Amendment: Conflict and the Decision Process.* New York: Longman, 1979.

Ginsburg, Ruth Bader. "Sexual Equality under the Fourteenth and Equal Rights Amendments." *Washington University Law Quarterly,* 161 (Winter 1979), pp. 161–201.

Goldstein, Leslie Friedman *Contemporary Cases in Women's Rights.* Madison: University of Wisconsin Press, 1994.

Kay, Herma Hill and Martha S. West. *Sex-Based Dis-crimination: Texts, Cases and Materials.* 4th ed. St. Paul, MN: West Publishing, 1988.

Kenney, Sally K. *For Whose Protection? Reproductive Hazards and Exclusionary Policies in the United States and Great Britain.* Ann Arbor: University of Michigan Press, 1993.

Levit, Nancy. *The Gender Line: Men, Women and the Law.* New York: New York University Press, 1998.

McGlen, Nancy E., and Karen O'Connor. *Women, Politics, and American Society,* 2nd ed., Upper Saddle River, NJ: Prentice-Hall, 1998.

Mezey, Susan Gluck. *In Pursuit of Equality: Women, Public Policy, and the Federal Courts.* New York: St. Martin's Press, 1992.

O'Connor, Karen. *Women's Organizations' Use of the Courts.* Lexington, MA: Lexington Books, 1980.

Rhode, Deborah L. *Justice and Gender: Sex Discrimination and the Law.* Cambridge, MA: Harvard University Press, 1989.

Women Judges: The New Generation

Elaine Martin

It has always been, and remains, difficult for women to succeed in attaining and retaining high political office in the United States. It has been even more difficult for women to attain judicial office than other public office for several reasons, two of which are particularly important. First, women judges must meet high standards of education and experience to be eligible for judicial office. Aspirants must have graduate law degrees, often successful candidates must also have at least five to ten years or more of trial experience. Second, judges are selected in complicated ways that make women judicial candidates dependent on their ability to build strong professional and personal reputations in the mostly male, and often conservative, legal circles that influence judicial selections. For example, the American Bar Association Committee on Federal Judiciary plays an important role in federal judicial selection by ranking nominees into three categories: Well Qualified, Qualified, and Not Qualified. There is ample evidence to suggest that such evaluators prefer the career patterns more closely associated with male lawyers.[1]

There are two major interrelated issues relevant to any discussion of women as judges: Why has the increase in the number of women judges been so slow, and do women judges behave any differently than men judges? Both are important. If the slow rate of increase in the number of women judges is due to gender discrimination, it may cast doubt on the legitimacy of our justice system. If women judges decide cases or administer their courts differently from men, their increasing numbers may create profound changes in our justice system.

These issues are often discussed in terms of whether women judges merely "stand for" other women in the numerical sense or whether they "act for" women.[2] In these terms, all women judges would necessarily "stand for" other women merely because they are also women. Women judges would not, however, necessarily "act for" other women. That is, although they would symbolically represent women, they might or might not act in a manner to further the interests and perspectives of other women. There seems to be a clear consensus that simple fairness requires numerical representation for women in political office (standing for). It is not so clear that such an increase will result in an increase in the representation of women's interests (acting for).

This article will first present data on the increase from 1976 to 1997 in the number of women judges, or numerical representation, and consider the eligible pool theory as an explanation for that increase. It will then examine the potential impact of the increase in women judges on the diversification of gender perspectives on the judicial bench, or interest representation. It will be demonstrated that the rate of increase in the number of women judges has accelerated in recent years and that this "new generation" of women judges will contribute to a growing diversification of perspectives on the American bench.

THE INCREASE IN WOMEN JUDGES

"Times are changing. The president made that clear by appointing me, and just last week, naming five other women to Article III courts." Ruth Bader Ginsberg made these remarks on August 20, 1993, following her inauguration as an associate justice and as the second woman member of the U.S. Supreme Court. Times, indeed, are changing. The president, William Jefferson Clinton, who appointed Justice Ginsberg broke all previous records to appoint 60 other women to federal district and appeals courts in his first term of office, giving over 30 percent of his nominations to women.[3] The number of women holding judicial positions on state courts of general jurisdiction increased 54 percent from 1987 to 1994, from a total of 483 to 746 women.[4] From 1992 to 1997, the number of women who held seats on their state's supreme court increased from 39 to 71, an 80 percent increase.[5] Two states, Minnesota and Michigan, for a time, had a female majority on their state supreme courts.

Yet, despite these increases, the proportion of women judges lags far behind the proportion of women lawyers. Judicial office in the United States has long been dominated by white, middle-class male lawyers with strong local connections. Because of the high visibility of U.S. Supreme Court Justices Sandra Day O'Connor and Ruth Bader Ginsberg, many people don't realize that there are proportionately far fewer women judges than other kinds of women politicians. Although there are many thousands of judges in the United States, only in the last twenty years have there been more than a few women judges in office at any given time, regardless of the level of government. An increase in the eligible pool of women lawyers from which judges are drawn and changing attitudes on the part of those who are influential in selecting judges has fueled the recent acceleration of the numbers of women judges.

THE ELIGIBLE POOL THEORY

The eligible pool theory holds that because relatively few women possess the requisite educational, political, and career credentials to be judges, they are unable to compete successfully for office. This theory essentially provides a gender-neutral explanation for the dearth of women judges. However, the lack of a sizable pool of qualified women lawyers does not fully account for the low representation of women on the bench or the wide range from state to state in the gender composition of their courts. Martin[6] concludes that the real key to explaining the variation among states in the number of women judges is the ability of women to capture a significant percentage of newly created judgeships. Cook[7] concludes that one major barrier to increased numbers of women judges is the resistance of those who control access to career opportunities that traditionally pave the way to the bench. These two notions—that womens' best chances for judgeships are newly created seats and that women lawyers are less likely to have the career opportunities that men do—help us see that the eligible pool theory does not operate in a gender-neutral manner.

Judges are drawn exclusively from the legal profession, and historically that profession has been overwhelmingly white and male. However, since the 1980s, there have been important changes in the gender composition of the legal profession, and therefore in the pool of lawyers from which judges are drawn. More women have gone to law school and more women have become lawyers and lower court judges. In 1980 only 8 percent of lawyers were women, by 1992 that figure had risen to 19 percent and by 1997 estimates were that 25 percent of lawyers were women.[8] Thus, in seventeen years the eligible pool of women lawyers has more than tripled. This increase in the proportion of women lawyers has not been matched by an increase in the proportion of women judges.

Table 7.1 compares the percentage of women judges on different kinds of courts in relation to the percentage of women receiving law degrees and the percentage of lawyers who are women.

Darcy, Welch, and Clark[9] have demonstrated the importance of the role of incumbency in discouraging qualified women legislative candidates from running for election or in succeeding in gaining office if they do run. A similar impact is at work in judicial selection. Federal judges serve lifetime terms. Vacancies, or opportunities for newcomers, occur only through death, resignation, or Congressional creation of new judgeships. Incumbent state court judges are extremely likely to be reelected, sometimes even running without opponents. Realistically speaking, a woman's best opportunity to become a judge is either to run for an open seat (no incumbent running) or to run for a newly created seat (no incumbent). Because of

TABLE 7.1   Percentage of Female Judges, Percentage of Women Receiving Law Degrees, and Percentage of Female Lawyers

Women	1980	1987	1993	1997
Federal Judges	5.4%	7.0%	11.1%	17.4%
State Supreme	3.6	6.5	11.2	20.0
State Trial	2.4	7.3	8.5	9.0*
Lawyers	8.0	13.0	19.0	25.0*
Law Degrees	30.0	40.0	45.0	47.0*

*Estimates

Sources: Elaine Martin, "State Court Political Opportunity Structures: Implications for the Representation of Women," presented at the American Political Association meeting, Washington, D.C., 1988; Elaine Martin, "Glass Ceiling or Skylight: Women State Supreme Court Justices," presented at the Southern Political Science Association meeting, Norfolk, Va., 1997; David Allen and Diane Wall, "Role Orientations and Women State Supreme Court Justices," *Judicature 77* (1993), pp. 156–165; and Nancy McGlen and Karen O'Connor, *Women, Politics and American Society, 2nd ed.,* Upper Saddle River, NJ: Prentice Hall, (1998), p. 183.

the increase in litigation in the United States, it is not uncommon for new judge-ships to be created at both the state and federal levels. These new judgeships offer an opportunity for women deemed eligible. Another problem, however, lies in the definition of eligibility.

It seems that a major impediment to women's attaining judgeships is an em-phasis on male career patterns as a standard for judging eligibility. It is quite clear that the attorneys who are ultimately selected as judges tend to have the same gen-eral characteristics over time and across the different selection systems, with some minor variations by state or region. These general characteristics point to a rela-tively narrow political-legal career path, as well as a very restricted socioeconomic pool from which state court jurists are selected.[10] For example, in 1986 the typical state supreme court justice was a white, male, attorney who became a justice at age 53, with possibly some prosecutorial or state legislative experience and with a high likelihood of previous experience as a trial court or intermediate appellate court judge. These successful candidates were also highly likely to have been born in their state and to have attended their state's law school.[11]

Although the number of women lawyers is increasing rapidly, there is still a time lag for those in the pool to acquire the professional experience and maturity traditionally considered necessary to judicial office. For example, in 1995, the aver-age state general trial court judge (usually a white male) was 46 years of age on first attaining office.[12] Thus, if the male pattern for judgeships prevails with respect to age, the pool of women lawyers eligible for state judgeships in 1995 would have been the number of women lawyers in the state twenty years previously, an obvi-ously small number. Yet, there is no particular reason, other than past history with white males, to assume that state trial court judges should be 46 years old instead of 36, thereby substantially decreasing the number of eligible women.

In addition, there is substantial evidence that women lawyers do not follow the same career patterns that men lawyers do. This may be, as Cook suggests,[3] be-cause women lawyers do not have the same range of opportunities as men lawyers. Women lawyers are clustered in the lower prestige ranks of their profes-sion, such as public sector employment, making less money, having less opportu-nity for advancement, and often subjected to varying degrees of gender bias.[14] Githens asserts that a major deciding factor in the selection of women as state court judges is often the lack of interest in the relatively poorly paid positions by more "successful" male attorneys.[15]

CHANGING ATTITUDES IN SELECTING JUDGES

It appears likely that one important reason for the recent rate of increase in the num-ber of women judges is a broader definition of eligibility for judicial office, because of changing gender-based attitudes on the part of those influential in the judicial se-lection process. One way to test this theory is to examine the career backgrounds of women selected as judges. If women's characteristics differ from the typical male ca-reer patterns depicted above, it is strong evidence of changing attitudes.

The United States does not have just one judicial system but a federal system and fifty different state court systems. One of the ways in which these diverse court systems vary is the manner in which they select their judges. All federal court judges, whether trial court or supreme court members are appointed by the president and confirmed by the Senate for life. The states use several different systems to select their judges and may use different methods for higher courts than for lower courts.

Federal Judges

In 1976, when President Carter took office, there were only five women judges out of over 500 federal district and appellate court judges. Carter announced publicly his intention of appointing more women judges and modified the selection process to be more inclusive. This explicit affirmative action program initiated by President Carter designed to appoint more women to the federal bench added forty new U.S. district court and appeals court judges.[16] Subsequent Republican presidents did not equal Carter's efforts, but their appointments of women judges far outnumbered all of their predecessors' except Carter. Pursuant to a campaign promise designed to capture the women's vote, President Reagan appointed the first woman ever to the United State Supreme Court. Thus, by 1992 when the next Democratic president took office, women constituted 11 percent of the federal bench. President Clinton launched a new affirmative action initiative that broke even Carter's records. Clinton, in his first term of office, appointed 169 federal district court judges, 51 of whom were women, and 29 appeals court judges, 9 of whom were women. Overall, less than half of Clinton's judges were white males, an amazing break with historical precedent. Nevertheless, over 70 percent of federal judges in active service in 1997 were white males. By the end of 1996, over 17 percent of federal judges in active service were women.[17]

Table 7.2 shows the number of women judges appointed by our last four presidents and indicates the percentage of their judicial appointments that were women.

TABLE 7.2   Women Federal Court Appointments by President

Court Level	Clinton 1992–96		Bush 1988–92		Reagan 1980–88		Carter 1976–80	
	%	N	%	N	%	N	%	N
District Court	30.2	51	19.6	29	8.3	24	14.4	29
Appeals Court	31.0	9	18.9	7	5.1	4	19.6	11
Supreme Court	50.0	1	-0-*		25.0	1	-0-**	

*Bush made 2 male appointments to the Supreme Court and no women.

**Carter made no appointments to the Supreme Court.

Source: Derived from Goldman and Slotnick 1997, tables 3 and 6

The backgrounds of women appointed to the federal bench from 1976 to 1996 by both Democratic and Republican presidents show remarkable similarity in several respects: They were younger, less likely to have been in private law practice when appointed and more likely to have had judicial experience than men appointees.[18] They also share another similarity. As a group, along with other nontraditional appointees (primarily African Americans), they have received generally lower merit ratings from the American Bar Association. Evidence suggests strongly that these generally lower ratings accorded to women and minority candidates are not an accurate reflection of genuinely lower qualifications for judicial offices.[19] It is argued that because of women's relatively recent entry into the field of law, they necessarily have fewer years of trial experience, and because of gender bias in the legal profession are more likely to obtain public service jobs. It is also argued that the ABA Committee on Federal Judiciary favors older, well-to-do, business-oriented corporation attorneys. Thus, the respective records on women appointments by the four presidents are also an indication of their willingness to break with tradition and broaden the definition of the eligible pool.

State Judges

In 1976, the same year that President Carter broke historical precedent in seeking women to appoint to the federal bench, twenty states had no women general jurisdiction trial court judges whatsoever, even though there were nearly 16,000 state and local judges in the United States. In fact, it was not until 1979 that every state had at least one woman serving as a judge.[20] The next decade saw significant change, however, with women more than doubling their numbers on state courts of general jurisdiction. This sizable increase in numbers led to only a 1.2 percent increase in the overall share of state benches held by women. This poor showing is due to a 16.4 percent increase in the total number of state judicial seats. Little is known about the career backgrounds of these new women judges. However, it is clear that women made their greatest gains in states that increased their numbers of judges, and that the ratio of increased numbers of women judges to the increased number of judicial seats is 22.6 percent.[21] This suggests that changing attitudes on the part of voters permitted women to capture a relatively high proportion of the new, open seats.

Evidence of changing attitudes is clearer with respect to state supreme courts. In 1987, only 6 percent of state supreme court positions were held by women[22] and twenty states had never had a woman state supreme court justice.[23] By September 1997, seventy-one women justices sat in forty-three states, and only seven states had no women justices.[24] Twenty-two states had one woman justice, fourteen states had two women justices, and seven states had three women justices.

Table 7.3 indicates the number of women justices on the supreme court in each state in the United States in 1997.

There are a number of differences between the career patterns of women justices sitting on state supreme courts in 1987 and those sitting ten years later. The more recent additions to the bench are younger (by four years), less likely to have

TABLE 7.3   States with Women State Supreme Court Justices, 1997

STATES: With no women	With one woman	With two women	With three women
Arizona	Alabama	Colorado	California
Florida	Alaska	Connecticut	Louisiana
Maine	Arkansas	Georgia	Michigan
Nebraska	Delaware	Idaho	Minnesota
New Hampshire	Hawaii	Iowa	Ohio
South Dakota	Illinois	Massachusetts	Virginia
Wyoming	Indiana	New Jersey	Wisconsin
	Kansas	New York	
	Kentucky	Oklahoma	
	Maryland	Rhode Island	
	Missouri	Texas	
	New Mexico	Vermont	
	Mississippi	Washington	
	Montana	West Virginia	
	Nevada		
	North Carolina		
	North Dakota		
	Oregon		
	Pennsylvania		
	South Carolina		
	Tennessee		
	Utah		

attended an in-state law school, more often drawn directly from a lower court, and almost three times as likely to have had prior experience as prosecutors.[25] These figures suggest two things. First, they indicate that the definition of the eligible pool has been broadened in many states in the last ten years to include career patterns more typical of women lawyers, thereby contributing to the increase in the number of women justices selected. They also suggest that women lawyers have established a successful judicial career ladder, considerably different from that of men, moving from experience as government prosecutors to trial court judges to appellate court judges to Supreme Court justices. Interestingly, there is some indication from a study of federal court judges' backgrounds that a similar career ladder has been followed by minority judges.[26] It may be that extensive judicial experience persuades judicial selectors that non-traditional candidates are capable, despite the dissimilarity in their legal careers to more traditional white, male candidates.

REPRESENTATION OF WOMEN'S PERSPECTIVES

The official, approved image of a judge is that of a person who is impartial and one who does not prejudge the merits of a case before hearing the evidence. What this means in a nutshell is that a good judge is supposed to put aside her or his personal feelings and values when donning the robe. The robe and all its trappings are designed to hide individual physical characteristics, and in so doing, also symbolically represent the impersonal nature of the act of judging. The formal rules of the judicial game reinforce these basic expectations. The law itself, statutes and precedents, the facts of the case, the requirements of evidence, the possibility of being overturned on appeal, even the nature of the adversarial system, all restrict the freedom of judicial discretion.

Yet, political scientists continue to study judicial characteristics in the assumption that personal, social, political and economic background characteristics may have an important impact on the way judges do their jobs. The strongest evidence to support this assumption comes from studies of the United States Supreme Court. For example, such features as the justices' partisan affiliations, prior career patterns, and religion have been shown to be important in judicial decisionmaking.[27] To the extent that the new generation of women judges brings to the bench backgrounds that are different from those of men judges, the women judges' impact on policymaking should be different.

A more controversial and feminist stream of scholarship takes the view that women's potential behavioral differences from men are rooted in gender role differences in behavior patterns, either biological or culturally induced. In this literature the focus is on gender differences as expressed in styles of personal interaction rather than voting patterns. Men are characterized as more "instrumental" and women as more "contextual" in their modes of thinking and feeling.[28] It is suggested that pervasive changes in institutional norms, values and processes may occur as women achieve numerical representation due to a uniquely feminine perspective.[29] The relatively new field of feminist jurisprudence argues that a significant number of female lawyers and judges will have a profound impact on the law.[30] These scholars contend that females, because of their experience as women in this society, will bring a different perspective to the law, will employ different legal reasoning, and will seek different results from the legal process.

Research on this new generation of women judges suggests that behavioral differences between men and women judges may emerge more clearly in the future. These differences may be expressed in the way men and women judges decide cases, in the way they run their courts, and in the way they view their judicial roles.

The largest body of evidence about potential gender differences in judicial behavior concerns decisions on court cases or sentencing in criminal cases. Studies of gender and judicial behavior conducted in the 1970s and studies conducted in the 1990s came up with different results. The handful of studies conducted in the 1970s and early 1980s concluded that there were no significant differences between men and women judges in their courtroom behavior.[31] These researchers explained their findings by suggesting that the common socialization that men and women received via law school training and legal experience prior to their judgeships made them more alike than different.

More recent studies conducted in the 1990s[32] contradict these early findings. For example, Allen and Wall[33] found that women on state supreme courts are more likely than men to be the most pro-female members of their court on women's issues. A study in Florida found that in contested custody appeals, all-male appellate panels were more likely to rule in favor of fathers than mothers, but mixed-gender panels showed no favoritism for either parent.[34] A study of Clinton's first-term appointees found that both women and black judges were more supportive of minority claims than were men or white judges.[35] It seems likely that some of the differences in findings can be attributed to differences in the types of women who were drawn to judicial office during the two time periods.

Judges are ordinarily the leaders of the employees of their courthouses. There is convincing evidence that gender bias is pervasive in court personnel administration, especially with respect to occupational segregation and a glass ceiling.[36] There is both anecdotal and survey evidence that suggests that women judges make a special effort to provide equity in hiring, promoting, and compensating practices for courtroom personnel.[37] There is some evidence that women judges may have different leadership styles, incorporating more emphasis on interpersonal relations than men judges.[38]

McGlen and O'Connor[39] contend that gender differences would be even greater if it were not that the very presence of women colleagues on the bench appears to make male jurists more sensitive to problems of gender bias. This contention is buttressed by a survey of women judges that found that the most frequently mentioned type of behavior that women felt "made a difference" had to do with woman's efforts to raise the consciousness of their male colleagues. Other responses to the survey made it clear that some women judges have a strong sense that part of their judicial role is to "act for" the interests of other women.[40]

A study done in the late 1980s gives some idea how judicial gender and feminist ideology may impact judicial decisions in court cases raising issues of gender bias.

Hypothetical Cases

In 1987, using hypothetical cases, this author conducted a large national survey of male and female state court judges to determine if male and female judges decide cases involving possible sex discrimination differently. Questionnaires were sent to all 483 female general jurisdiction trial court judges sitting in 1987 and to a random sample of 647 male judges stratified by court location. The response rate was 46 percent for the male sample and 61 percent for the women. Because it is reasonable to assume that holding feminist views influences judges' perceptions on women's rights cases, respondents were asked to indicate if they considered themselves feminists.

The five hypothetical cases raised issues of maternity leave rights, battered women's rights, abortion rights for minors, property rights for divorcing homemakers, and protection from sexual harassment on the job. Judges were asked to choose in favor of one party: the female claimants or the opposing party (private corporations, law enforcement officials, parents or spouses). All cases were drawn from newspaper accounts of actual decisions by state court judges. A description of the cases and the judges' hypothetical votes follows. Table 7.4 summarizes the judges' votes, using four groups: women feminists, women nonfeminists, men feminists, and men nonfeminists.

Property Rights for Divorcing Homemakers.

A fifty-five-year old woman is sued for divorce after thirty-seven years of marriage to a successful businessman. Her four children are grown. She is willing to accept a 50–50 split on community property and requests no alimony, but she demands 50 percent of the spouse's substantial retirement income at age sixty-five. She did not work outside the home during her marriage, but now has a job as a salesclerk. The job pays enough for her immediate needs, but the organization has no pension plan. Her husband is willing to pay her a portion of the face value of his annuities, but he refuses to share his income.

The female litigant in this case got her greatest amount of support from women, both feminist (94 percent) and nonfeminist (92 percent), and feminist men (91 percent). Male nonfeminists were less likely to award the woman her request for half of her spouse's retirement income (82 percent).

Maternity Leave.

A state law requires companies to give women four months' maternity leave and to reinstate them in the same or similar job. No provision is made for paternity leave. A woman sues because she is told no position is available when she attempts to return to work after taking her maternity leave. The company claims the law illegally discriminates against men and nonpregnant women and is too costly.

Women nonfeminist judges were the least generous of all judges in awarding this female litigant maternity leave. Ninety-three percent of female feminists, 91 percent of male feminists, and 85 percent of male nonfeminists were in favor of the woman's claim. It may be that female nonfeminists were fearful of "protective" legislation that might make it more difficult for women of childbearing age to get jobs. Be-

TABLE 7.4 Hypothetical Cases

Case	Women		Men	
	Feminists	*Nonfeminists*	*Feminists*	*Nonfeminists*
Divorce	94%	92%	91%	82%
Leave	93	77	91	85
Harassment	93	90	86	75
Abortion	92	81	85	71
Battered	67	59	48	43

fore the women's movement, such protective legislation was often used as an excuse for employment discrimination against women. It remains a controversial issue.

Protection from Sexual Harassment.
Two women are hired in a traditionally male-dominated occupation after a private company is ordered to end its sexually discriminatory hiring practices. Within six months, one woman resigns, refusing to discuss her reasons for doing so; the other woman files suit against the company for sexual harassment. She claims that her male coworkers created a climate of intimidation through sexually suggestive remarks, jokes, anonymous notes and cartoons, and boisterous requests for sexual favors. Despite her complaints to management, no action was taken. The company claims she is overreacting to normal male camaraderie, needs to develop a sense of humor, and is trying to cover up for her own ability to adjust to a new work environment. It would like to replace her. She wants monetary damages and wants to continue in her job with company protection from harassment.

Women, both feminists and nonfeminists, were more likely than men, both feminists and nonfeminists, to favor the female litigant in this case. The biggest difference was between women feminists (93 percent) and male nonfeminists (75 percent).

Abortion Rights for Minors.
A woman's boyfriend impregnates her 11-year-old daughter. Evidence indicates he has also sexually abused her 9-year-old daughter. The two girls are removed from the home by the Department of Social Services, which requests a court-ordered abortion for the older girl. The girl says she wants the abortion, but her mother protests that abortion is against her personal beliefs.

This case engendered its strongest pro-choice support from feminists and its least support from nonfeminists. Within feminists and nonfeminist categories, however, women were clearly more supportive of abortion rights. Although 92 percent of the female feminists and 85 percent of the male feminists would have granted the abortion, only 81 percent of female nonfeminists and 71 percent of male nonfeminists would do so.

Battered Women's Rights.
A class action suit is filed against a metropolitan police department by a group of battered women claiming a lack of law enforcement for crimes of domestic violence. They request that the court impose new rules of intervention to replace the individual discretion of police officers and to require officer training in the new methods. The police chief objects to the possible erosion of officer discretion and the increased likelihood of suits for false arrest.

The battered women in this case got far less support in their claim than female litigants in any of the other four cases. The most dramatic drop was in the support from nonfeminist men—only 43 percent "voted" for the battered women. Forty-eight percent of feminist men showed considerably less support than the 59 percent of nonfeminist women. Although feminist women showed the most support (67 percent), they also dropped dramatically from their usual over 90 percent support rate in the other cases. This case is different because support of the female litigants requires active judicial intervention in the established procedures of a law enforcement agency. It is on the cutting edge of *new* law and creates *new* rights.

All Five Cases. Female feminists were the most likely to decide in favor of female litigants in each of the five hypothetical cases; male nonfeminists were the least likely to decide in favor of female litigants in four of the five cases. In two cases, maternity leave and abortion rights for minors, male feminists were more likely to decide for the females than were female nonfeminists. In the cases of property rights for divorcing homemakers, male feminists and female nonfeminists expressed comparable views. However, female nonfeminists were more likely than feminist men to side with female litigants in the sexual harassment and battered women's rights cases. They also dropped dramatically from their usual over 90 percent support rate in the other cases.

Assuming that their responses to these hypothetical cases are an accurate portrayal of how these judges might behave in real-life cases, it seems that feminist female judges are the most willing to break new ground in cutting-edge cases like the battered women's rights case. Furthermore, although in general there were no big differences between nonfeminist women and feminist men, in the particularly difficult cases of sexual harassment and battered women, nonfeminist women were more willing than feminist men to reach for new law.

CONCLUSION

Although the percentages of female judges have yet to meet those of female lawyers, their numbers show a significant increase in the last decade. The numbers of females enrolling in law school and a definition of judicial eligibility more inclusive of women's unique legal careers suggests that we may expect even greater increases in the eligible pool of women judicial candidates in years to come. As more women judges take office, we may expect that this new generation of judges will have careers and personal backgrounds that reflect the unique career patterns of women lawyers more closely than did earlier women judges.

Results from studies done in the 1970s and early 1980s suggested that men's and women's similar legal training and socialization as lawyers minimized any potential gender differences in judicial behavior. However, more recent studies indicate that, as women's numbers move beyond the token stage and as younger females educated after the women's movement become judges, differences based on gender emerge more clearly. Research on this new generation of women judges suggests that these gender-based differences in experience may contribute to a widening gap between the behavior of men and women judges with respect to decisions in cases raising issues of gender or minority discrimination, with respect to leadership of courtroom personnel, and with respect to judicial role conceptions of 'acting for' women's unique perspectives.

NOTES

1. Marianne Githens, "Getting Appointed to the State Court: The Gender Dimension," *Women and Politics,* 15 (1995), pp. 1–23.

2. Hannah Pitkin, *The Concept of Representation* (Berkeley: University of California Press, 1967), p. 60.

3. Sheldon Goldman and Elliot Slotnick, "Clinton's First Term Judiciary: Many Bridges to Cross." *Judicature* 80 (1997), pp. 254–273.

4. Elaine Martin, "Here Come the Judges: An Analysis of State-Based Influences on the Selection of Women as Judges," presented at the Midwest Political Science Association Meeting, Chicago, IL., 1996.

5. Elaine Martin, "Glass Ceiling or Skylight: Women State Supreme Court Justices," presented at the Southern Political Science Association Meeting, Norfolk, VA, 1997.

6. Martin, "Here Come the Judges."

7. Beverly Cook, "Women Judges: The End of Tokenism," in Laura Crites and Winnifred Hepperle (Eds.), *Women, the Courts, and Equality* (Newbury Park, CA: Sage, 1978), pp. 84–105.

8. Nancy McGlen, and Karen O'Connor, *Women, Politics and American Society,* 2nd ed. (Upper Saddle River, NJ: Prentice Hall, 1998), p. 183.

9. Robert Darcy, Susan Welch, and Janet Clark, *Women, Elections and Representation,* 2nd ed. (Lincoln: University of Nebraska Press, 1994).

10. Harry Stumpf, *American Judicial Politics,* 2nd ed. (Upper Saddle River, NJ: Prentice Hall, 1997), p. 153.

11. Henry Glick and Craig Emmert, "Selection Systems and Judicial Characteristics: The Recruitment of State Supreme Court Judges," *Judicature* 71 (1987), pp. 228–235.

12. Robert Carp, and Ronald Stidham, *Judicial Process in America,* 3rd ed. (Washington, DC: CQ Press, 1996), p. 245.

13. Cook, "Women Judges."

14. Phyllis Coontz, "Gender Bias in the Legal Profession: Women "see" it, Men Don't," *Women and Politics* 15 (1995), pp. 1–22.

15. Githens, "Getting Appointed to the Supreme Court."

16. Elaine Martin, "Gender and Judicial Selection: A Comparison of the Reagan and Carter Administrations," *Judicature* 71 (1987) pp. 136–142.

17. Goldman and Slotnik, "Clinton's First Term Judiciary."

18. Martin, "Gender and Judicial Selection;" Goldman and Slotnick, "Clinton's First Term Judiciary."

19. Elliot Slotnik, "Lowering the Bench or Raising it Higher? Affirmative Action and Judicial Selection During the Carter Administration," *Yale Law and Policy Review* 270 (1983), p. 271.

20. Larry Berkson, "Women on the Bench: A Brief History," *Judicature* 65 (1982), pp. 286–293.

21. Martin, "Here Come the Judges."

22. Elaine Martin, "State Court Political Opportunity Structures: Implications for the Representation of Women," paper presented at the annual meeting of the American Political Science Association, Washington, DC, 1988.

23. David Allen and Diane Wall, "Role Orientations and Women State Supreme Court Justices," *Judicature* 77 (1993), pp. 156–165.

24. Martin, "Glass Ceiling or Skylight."

25. *Ibid.*

26. Goldman and Slotnick, "Clinton's First Term Judiciary."

27. C. Neal Tate, "Personal Attribute Models of Voting Behavior of U.S. Supreme Court Justices," *American Political Science Review* 75 (1981), pp. 355–367; Jeffrey Segal and Harold Spaeth, *The Supreme Court and the Attitudinal Model* (New York: Cambridge University Press, 1993).

28. Carol Gilligan, *In a Different Voice* (Cambridge: Harvard University Press, 1982); Sara Ruddick, "Maternal Thinking," *Feminist Studies,* 6 (1980), pp. 342–356.

29. Judith Resnik, "On the Bias: Feminist Reconsiderations of the Aspirations of our Judges," *Southern California Law Review* 61 (1988), p. 1877; Lyn Kathlene, "Power and Influence in State Legislative Policymaking: The Interaction of Gender and Position in Committee Hearing Debates," *American Political Science Review* 88 (1994) pp. 560–576.

30. See among others Leslie Goldstein, *Feminist Jurisprudence: The Difference Debate* (New York: Rowman and Littlefield, 1992).

31. Herbert Kritzer and Thomas Uhlman, "Sisterhood in the Courtroom: Sex of Judge and Defendant in Criminal Case Disposition," *Social Science Journal* 14 (1977), pp. 77–88; John Gruhl, Cassia Spohn, and Susan Welch, "Women as Policy Makers: The Case of Trial Judges," *American Journal of Political Science* 25 (1981), pp. 308–322; Thomas Walker and Deborah Barrow, "The Diversification of the Federal Bench: Policy and Process Ramifications," *Journal of Politics* 47 (1985), pp. 596–616.

32. Sue Davis, Susan Haire, and Donald Songer, "Voting Behavior and Gender on the U.S. Courts of Appeal," *Judicature* 77 (1993), pp. 156–165; Allen and Wall, "Role Orientations and Women State Supreme Court Justices;" *Florida Supreme Court Gender Bias Study* (1990; available from Florida Supreme Court).

33. Allen and Wall, "Role Orientations and Women State Supreme Court Justices."

34. Vicki Jackson, "What Judges Can Learn from Gender Bias Task Force Studies," *Judicature* 81 (1998), pp. 15–21.

35. Jennifer Segal, "The Decision Making of Clinton's Nontraditional Judicial Appointees," *Judicature* 80 (1997), p. 279.

36. Richard Kearney and Holly Sellers, "Gender Bias in Court Personnel Administration," *Judicature* 81 (1998), pp. 8–14.

37. Martin, "The Representative Role of Women Judges;" Martin, "Personnel Practices of Women Judges."

38. Martin, "Personnel Practices of Women Judges."

39. McGlen and O'Connor, *Women, Politics and American Society,* p. 93.

40. Martin, "The Representative Role of Women Judges."

FURTHER READINGS

Cook, Beverly, Leslie Goldstein, Karen O'Connor, & Susan Talrico, (Eds). *Women in the Judiciary Process.* Washington, DC: American Political Science Association, 1988.

Crites, Laura, & Winfred Hepperle (Eds). *Women, the Courts, and Equality.* Newbury Park, CA: Sage, 1987.

Epstein, Cynthia Fuchs. *Women in Law,* 2nd ed. Urbana: University of Illinois Press, 1993.

Goldstein, Leslie. *Feminist Jurisprudence: The Difference Debate.* Savage, MD: Rowman and Littlefield, 1992.

Martin, Elaine (Ed.). "Women on the Bench: A Different Voice?" Symposium issue, *Judicature* (1993), 77 (3).

"Proceedings of the National Association of Women Judges 1990 Annual Meeting." *Women's Rights Law Reporter* (Spring 1991), 13 (1) Spring.

PUBLIC POLICY:
THE FEMINIST PERSPECTIVE

Public policy in this country significantly influences the lives of American women. Diane D. Blair's article deals with the politics of reproduction and the implications for women as policy makers determine what is personal and what is political for women. Blair compares Margaret Atwood's novel *The Handmaid's Tale* (1986) and Ben Wattenberg's book *The Birth Dearth* (1987). Both works deal with the politics of reproduction, but from completely different perspectives. Atwood, writing from a feminist perspective, describes an imaginary future of total misery and wretchedness for women, one in which women have been reduced to the function of breeders. On the other hand, Wattenberg, writing from what Blair describes as a "nationalistic perspective," deplores the current American "birth dearth," blaming it primarily on "working women" and proposing a variety of pro-natalist remedies. Both books use a simple style to convey a complex message. Blair argues that among the significant implications of these two books, especially when they are read in tandem, are the following:

1. That pro-natalism, justified by the United States' relatively low fertility rate, has climbed high on many conservative agendas.
2. That this movement seriously jeopardizes many of the gains achieved by feminists in recent years.
3. That the contemporary pro-natalist drive has long and powerful historical precedents.

Joan Hulse Thompson examines the history of the Family and Medical Leave Act (FMLA) from initial draft through congressional enactment to executive and judicial interpretation. This legislation was passed by the House and Senate in 1990 and again in 1992, but President Bush vetoed the bill both times and Congress was unable to override. Both chambers passed the bill again early in 1993, and President Clinton signed it as his first major legislative accomplishment. The author describes the influence of the Congressional Caucus for Women's Issues (CCWI) in developing this legislation, building a bipartisan coalition across committee jurisdictions, and coordinating the efforts of outside advocacy groups. After the Republican victory in 1994, CCWI was able to survive only in a diminished, largely defensive role, but the FMLA represents a concrete achievement of the feminist movement for the benefit of working families.

Although numerous laws have been passed prohibiting sex discrimination in a variety of public policy areas, Ruth Bamberger finds the insurance industry has retained the practice of discriminating by sex in determining prices of its products. The industry argues its position on cost-efficiency and actuarial grounds. Women's rights and civil rights groups have criticized such discrimination on grounds of fairness and prevailing social policy. Although they have pursued their cause through multiple channels of government, the Supreme Court is perceived to be a primary agent of policy change. The Court has signaled that sex may be at risk as an insurance classification, but its role as shaper of public policy on this issue has been incremental at best.

Challenged from all sides, Roberta Ann Johnson argues affirmative action, nevertheless, continues to live on as a highly charged issue. This article (1) defines affirmative action, (2) details the development of federal affirmative action guidelines, (3) describes Supreme Court decisions and congressional responses to affirmative action, (4) describes how the states and the lower courts have become battlegrounds on the issue of affirmative action, (5) considers the ways in which affirmative action is a woman's issue, and (6) considers the future of affirmative action.

The Handmaid's Tale and *The Birth Dearth:* Prophecy, Prescription, and Public Policy

DIANE D. BLAIR

> *Six children [are] the minimum number for people of "normal" stock; those of better stock should have more.*
>
> THEODORE ROOSEVELT, 1907

> *As that great author and scientist, Mr. Brisbane, has pointed out, what every woman ought to do is have six children.*
>
> SINCLAIR LEWIS, 1935

> *There is nothing to compare to the joy of having six children. If every American family did that, we'd certainly have the greatest nation in the world.*
>
> PHYLLIS SCHLAFLY, 1987[1]

This article looks at two recent works on the politics of reproduction: *The Handmaid's Tale,* by Margaret Atwood, and *The Birth Dearth,* by Ben Wattenberg.[2] Since the former is an imaginative work by a popular novelist and the latter is a research report by a senior fellow at the American Enterprise Institute, one might assume that they would have little in common. In fact, however, these two books provide some direct, and often disturbing, points of comparison.

Both, for example, open with a selection from the Book of Genesis. Wattenberg's choice is from Book 1, Chapter 28: "Be fruitful and multiply, and replenish the earth. . . ." Wattenberg does not dwell upon this specific scriptural imperative, but human reproduction, and the need for much more of it in the contemporary United States, is the theme of his book. *The Birth Dearth* consists of three major parts, all laden with demographic and other data. In the first part, Wattenberg documents (and deplores) what he calls the United States' "fertility free-fall," a recent sharp decline in the total fertility rate (TFR) to below the population replacement rate of 2.1 children per woman. In the second part, Wattenberg offers his explanations for this "birth dearth" and outlines what he considers to be its most alarming economic, geopolitical, and personal consequences. Finally, Wattenberg suggests a long list of possible pro-natalist remedies for this present-day problem and impending crisis.

Atwood's scriptural epigram is both longer and more specifically woven into her novel. Indeed, the following biblical episode becomes both raison d'être and central ritual in the twenty-first-century political system she posits:

> And when Rachel saw that she bare Jacob no children, Rachel envied her sister; and said unto Jacob, Give me children or else I die. And Jacob's anger was kindled against Rachel; and he said, Am I in God's stead, who hath withheld from thee the fruit of the womb? And she said, Behold my maid Bilhah, go in unto her; and she shall bear upon my knees, that I may also have children by her (Genesis 30:1–3).

As the novel opens, fundamentalists, justifying their coup primarily on the grounds of an acute birth dearth, have seized power and established the Republic (actually the monotheocracy) of Gilead. The governing patriarchy, known as Commanders, has forced all women into rigidly stratified, socially useful functions. There are Wives, physically sterile but socially prominent women, who serve their Commander husbands as hostesses and household managers; Marthas, who do the cooking and cleaning; and Aunts, who run the Rachel and Leah Reeducation Centers in which women who have viable ovaries (that is, those who have given birth previously) and are "available" (divorced women, those married to divorced men, widows, and those deliberately widowed by the state) are trained to become proper Handmaids.

Handmaids, like the novel's narrator Offred (literally "of Fred," the name of the Commander to whom she is assigned) have only one function: to reproduce. As Offred wryly notes, she and her sister Handmaids are women of "reduced circumstances" (p. 8)—reduced, that is, to being nothing more than "two-legged wombs" (p. 136). Because their fecundity is so vital to natural survival, the Handmaids are well fed, relieved of all arduous work, and protected from physical danger. They are also, however, "protected" from many other ordinary activities that Offred, too late, realizes had been central to her previous happiness: reading, paid work, discussions of current events, privacy (as opposed to solitude), friendship (as opposed to a sterile "sisterhood"), and love (as opposed to enforced breeding).

During a Handmaid's period of maximum fertility, she is "serviced" by her Commander while lying between the spread legs of the Commander's Wife, a peculiar but strangely nonsexual arrangement. If sperm meets seed, there is an elaborate birthing ceremony nine months later in which the Handmaid delivers upon the Wife's welcoming knees. If repeated attempts at conception are unsuccessful, or if the resulting children are repeatedly born dead or deformed, the Handmaid is eventually exiled to a Third World colony to clean up toxic waste. In Gilead, a literal interpretation has been given to Rachel's "Give me children, or else I die."

THE SIMILARITY OF THE TWO WORKS

Other than their genesis in Genesis, their central premise of a population shortfall, and their popularity (*The Handmaid's Tale* ran thirty-six weeks on the *New York Times* best-seller list, and a shortened and serialized version of *The Birth Dearth* was syndicated in many U.S. newspapers), what do these two works have in common? First, both books are didactic; that is, they were designed to be instructive. Wattenberg acknowledges at the outset that his book is both "a speculation and a provocation" (p. 1). It is his genuine fear about the consequences of the birth dearth that has propelled him, a self-described optimist, into writing this "alarmist tract" (p. 10). According to Wattenberg, the very survival of Western civilization is at stake, and he chastises both liberals and conservatives for their failure to come right out and say what Wattenberg thinks urgently needs to be said: American women should be having more babies.

Atwood is somewhat more reticent in acknowledging the instrumentality of her intentions. "This book won't tell you who to vote for," she has said. "I do not have a political agenda of that kind."[3] Atwood, however, has long used her fiction for social criticism, and with specific reference to *The Handmaid's Tale* has observed: "Speculative fiction is a logical extension of where we are now. I think this particular genre is a walking along of a potential road, and the reader as well as the writer can then decide if that is the road they wish to go on. Whether we go that way or not is going to be up to us."[4]

This leads to the second point of clear comparability between the two works. Both are projectionist: They are grounded in present events and trends that are at least suggestive of a possible future. Wattenberg's projections are based on data and interpretations of data gathered from an impressive array of sources. Wherever he looks he finds evidence that in the "modern, industrial, free" nations (the United States, Canada, the nations of Western Europe, Japan, Australia, and Israel), the TFR is well below replacement rates. Most alarming to Wattenberg, despite a "heartening" decline in Third World fertility, is that we are now

> awash in the fruit of those TFR's in the six-plus range from a generation ago. Today there are 1.1 billion women of child-bearing age in the less-developed world! Even if those women reduce their fertility as the U.N. projects, there will be a flood of Third World babies, a real flood. Third World population, which is now 3.7 *billion* persons, is slated to rise to over 8 *billion* people in the middle of the next century! (p. 44)

What concerns Wattenberg most deeply is that, if present reproductive trends continue, by 2025 the Westernized nations will constitute only 9 percent of the world's population, down from 22 percent in 1950 and 15 percent in the 1990s; and that 9 percent will not be enough to spread democratic values, technological advances, and economic benefits. Wattenberg ruefully notes, " 'Manifest destiny' was not the cry of a no-growth continent of old people" (p. 71).

Atwood's novel contains no charts and graphs. It is obvious, however, that she, like Wattenberg, is a very close follower of current events, from which she has gleaned a number of happenings and ideas, which she has woven into a grim dystopia. In the contemporary United States, for example, abortion clinics have frequently been bombed and burned. In Romania, doctors performing abortions until recently were subject to twenty-five years' imprisonment or even death.[5] In Atwood's imagined Gilead, abortionists are executed and their bodies hung from hooks on "The Wall," as a deterrent, or else they are dismembered in gruesome "particicution" ceremonies. In the United States, homosexuals are often subject to legal and social penalties; in Gilead, "gender treachery," being nonproductive, is a capital offense. In the last few years, courts in at least eleven U.S. states have ordered women, against their wishes, to submit to cesarean section surgery when doctors decided that conventional childbirth could harm the fetus, and there have been increasing instances of litigation by the state in behalf of "fetus patients" against the bearing mothers; in Gilead, Handmaids are nothing but fetus-bearing vessels and must sacrifice all personal choice and pleasure in the fetus's behalf.[6] As in Gilead, so in the United States today, many major companies bar women under forty-five from certain jobs that might diminish their fertility or damage a fetus; toxic wastes are increasingly being shipped to Third World nations; "pro-life" forces have frequently held symbolic "funerals" for fetuses; and at least one state legislature has now required "dignified" burial or disposal of fetal remains.[7]

As Atwood has emphasized, although her novel is futuristic, it is not utterly fantastic. "There are no spaceships, no Martians, nothing like that," she has pointed out. In fact, when asked if Gilead could possibly happen here, she responds that some of it "is happening now," and that, "There is nothing in *The Handmaid's Tale,* with the exception of one scene, that has not happened at some point in history."[8]

Obviously, both Wattenberg and Atwood have looked closely at certain contemporary events and circumstances, have extrapolated these events into a highly undesirable future, and have written their books to alert readers to the dangers the authors see ahead. Since in some ways the "solutions" Wattenberg advocates are related to the dangers Atwood warns against, it is somewhat surprising to find as much agreement as there is between the two regarding the major factors that have depressed present birth rates.

FACTORS PRODUCING THE BIRTH DEARTH

Both Wattenberg, with long lists and charts, and Atwood, by indirection throughout the novel and in a "scholarly" appendix at the novel's end, suggest that among the factors producing the "baby bust" have been better contraceptive techniques, more education and higher income for females, delayed marriage, more frequent divorce, more abortions due to legalization, increased infertility and more open homosexuality. Most interesting, however, is that both writers—Wattenberg centrally, Atwood peripherally—implicate the women's liberation movement as possibly pushing us into undesirable futures.

For Wattenberg, the cause-and-effect relationship is very clear and entirely adverse. According to his analysis, "One clear root thought of the original [women's liberation] movement was this: Marriage, raising a family, or a large family, was no longer necessarily considered to be the single most important thing in a woman's life" (p. 127). As he has written elsewhere,

> About twenty years ago, corresponding almost exactly with the Birth Dearth—many women began to forge a new economic contract for themselves. They exchanged what anthropologists tell us was the original female contract—trading childbearing capabilities for economic sustenance in the home—for a version of the male practice—trading physical and mental labor for economic sustenance in the market.[9]

Hence, women's liberation led to women's presence in the workforce; and "working women," according to Wattenberg, are "probably the single most important factor" causing the birth dearth.[10]

Such generalizations may disturb at least some of Wattenberg's readers, and certainly his feminist ones. Especially when the policy implications of Wattenberg's philosophy are being considered, however, it is good that he has made his central premises so plain. Wattenberg insists, for example, that he wants pro-natalist policies that will expand rather than limit women's choices, and he suggests scores of possibilities. If "working women" are the "single greatest cause" of the birth dearth, however, it seems obvious that all solutions will be partial until women leave the workforce and resume their "original contracts."

For Atwood, the line between contemporary women's liberation and future Gileadean oppression is much more circuitous. In the "old times" (which, of course, are our times), Offred was sufficiently "liberated" to have had a college degree, a job, and a lover who eventually became her husband. Although she chose to have a child, many of her friends—working women who did not want the economic and other burdens of children, or who feared the fragility of the environment or the inevitability of nuclear catastrophe—did not. Others, because of the fertility-depressing and abortifacient effects of environmental pollutants, nuclear radiation, and toxic wastes, could not conceive or bear a healthy child. Furthermore, the sexual freedom and excesses of the "old times" produced not only fertility-impeding sexually transmitted diseases but also an escalating atmosphere of contempt for and violence against women. Hence, among the chief demands of women's liberationists were increased respect for women and improved physical protection. Offred's own mother, she recalls, marched in demonstrations to "take back the night," enthusiastically participated in pornographic-book burnings, and often mouthed antimale slogans such as "A man is just a woman's strategy for making other women."

Society was "dying of too much choice," Offred recalls (p. 25):

> Women were not protected then. . . . Now we walk along the same street, in red pairs, and no man shouts obscenities at us, speaks to us, desires us. . . . There is more than one kind of freedom, said Aunt Lydia. Freedom to and freedom from. In the days of anarchy it was freedom to. Now you are being given freedom from. Don't underrate it (p. 24).

Following an emotional birthing ceremony from which all males, all doctors, and all anesthetics have been excluded, Offred utters one of the book's most poignant lines:

"Mother, I think: Wherever you may be. Can you hear me? You wanted a woman's culture. Well, now there is one. It isn't what you meant, but it exists" (p. 127).

Atwood is a feminist, and the oppressions she describes can be much more clearly traced to the religious right than to the feminist left. Atwood's warning signals, however, are flashed at radical feminism as well as religious fundamentalism. Please remember, she seems to be saying, that the "protection" of women has always been the major justification for their oppression, and sometimes, however unfortunately, one must choose between freedom *from* and freedom *to*. Or, as Offred's Commander reminds her, "Better never means better for everyone. It always means worse for some" (p. 211).

As should be obvious by now, these two authors have written "message" books in order to convey diametrically different messages. Before further discussing those differences, however, one final similarity should be noted: Both authors employ a very simple style to clothe a highly complex message.

For many readers and book reviewers, it is the prosaic, unemotional tone with which Offred relates the most degrading and horrifying arrangements that makes the book so deeply disturbing. Leaving a particicution ceremony, where the Handmaids have been emotionally stampeded into tearing an accused rapist apart with their bare hands, they wish each other the conventional "You have a nice day" (p. 281). Thoughts can quickly turn from death to dinner, from bodies hanging on The Wall to sundresses and ice cream cones.

Oddly, while the novelist is presenting her grim forecast with restrained but imaginative force, it is the research fellow who hammers the reader with tones of breathless, desperate urgency. As the material already quoted indicates, Wattenberg's voice is shrill, overwrought, semihysterical. His favorite punctuation mark is the exclamation point. And in his determination to persuade the widest possible audience, his words and sentences often go beyond the simple to the simplistic. In outlining possible economic incentives to produce additional offspring, for example, Wattenberg holds out the promise of "a nice green check" (p. 154), "a green federal check" (p. 157), "a green Social Security check" (p. 157), and "real green cash money" (p. 158). "In a nonfree country," he lectures his apparently unsophisticated readers, "the ruler, or rulers, can sit down around a big table and make policy" (p. 143). One of his pieces of pictorial persuasion is a python (the United States) swallowing a pig (the post–World War II baby boom). Should the pictures not be sufficiently clear, Wattenberg supplies the sound effects: "Gobble, gobble, suck, suck" (p. 34).

DIFFERENCES BETWEEN THE TWO WORKS

The following short excerpts, the first from Atwood, the second from Wattenberg, illustrate not only the unadorned style employed by each author but also the profoundly different assumptions and values they bring to their work. In *The Handmaid's Tale*, Offred has been taken by her Commander to an illegal nightclub where the women are dressed in everything from chorus girls' shifts to old cheerleading costumes. Offred is dumbfounded, amused, and wildly curious, but any display of emotions could be fatal. Hence, she warns herself, "All you have to do, I tell myself, is keep your mouth shut and look stupid. It shouldn't be that hard" (p. 236). In the penultimate paragraph of *The Birth Dearth,* Wattenberg summarizes his solution to the impending crisis as follows: "After all, it's not such a big deal. All it involves is having another baby" (p. 169).

The reader quickly realizes that Atwood's "all" reverberates with the irony of centuries. In two simple lines, the author has captured the conventional wisdom passed down to women, and keeping them down, through the ages: Feign ignorance; don't ask questions; accept your lot; suffer in silence; what you don't know can't hurt you. In contrast, Wattenberg seems oblivious to the irony, and revolutionary implications, of his "all." Because women not only bear children but generally have had the major responsibility for nurturing and raising them to adulthood, the ability to control one's reproductive choices is the sine qua non of woman's ability to live in relative freedom. Almost all the advances of recent decades have recognized the centrality of reproductive freedom to any other meaningful kind of economic, political, or personal freedom for women. Yet Wattenberg, with offhand ease, is apparently ready to jettison these hard-won achievements, and to do so with no apparent recognition of the magnitude of what he is advocating.

To be fair, Wattenberg rejects any overtly coercive solutions to the birth dearth. He opposes outlawing either contraception or abortion, and suggests that enthusiastically pro-natalist public education (using three-children-each Jeane Kirkpatrick and Sandra Day O'Connor as prominent role models, for example) could be effective when coupled with some lucrative economic incentives. Among the many possibilities he suggests are much more extensive and less expensive day care, very profitable tax incentives, forgiveness of college loans to child-producing couples, and reorganizing Social Security in recognition of the fact that people who have no children or even one child are "cheating": They are "free riders" who "end up drawing full pensions paid for by children who were raised and reared—at a large expense—by children of other people" (p. 154). Wattenberg suggests everything from personal ads in the *New York Times* (to destigmatize these possible paths to marriage and children) to kibbutz-style collectives in the suburbs, without ever advocating anything even approaching the Gileadean model of society.

His perspective, however, is a nationalistic one. His goal, he says, is to preserve and promote precious political and economic freedoms that can only survive if the "free world" remains stronger than the authoritarian world and than the less developed nations, which are only beginning to absorb the values and benefits of the Western model. If some individuals must sacrifice a little bit of liberty to secure the future of freedom, so be it.

Atwood is also centrally concerned with freedom; how easily it is undervalued (Offred wistfully remembers going to a laundromat with her own dirty garments and her own money in her own jeans pocket, or checking into a hotel room); how quickly it can be taken away (shortly after the coup, all Compucounts [credit cards] coded female are canceled, rendering all women economically dependent in a noncash economy); and above all, how important it is to watch, as

Offred regrets she has not, as Atwood hopes her readers will, for signs of its endangerment.

Here especially *The Handmaid's Tale* brilliantly demonstrates the relevance of good social science fiction to politics. By taking a few parts of contemporary reality, exaggerating them, and extrapolating them into a possible future, Atwood makes her readers see the present more clearly, and recognize the possible dangers in what may otherwise appear beneficent, or at least benign.

IMPLICATIONS OF THE TWO WORKS

Read by itself, *The Handmaid's Tale* provides a fresh and interesting, sometimes alarming and sometimes amusing perspective on contemporary events and policies. When it is read in tandem with *The Birth Dearth,* three implications seem especially noteworthy.

First, the mere fact that the "birth dearth" has climbed high on at least some conservative agendas is important for all political observers and policy makers to recognize. Pat Robertson's attempt in the October 1987 televised Republican presidential debate to propose a prohibition on abortion as the best way to "ensure the fiscal stability of the Social Security system" was widely dismissed as an isolated bit of idiocy; but references, following Wattenberg, to child-free families as "freeloaders" on Social Security are becoming increasingly common. As further examples of the rising popularity of strategic demography, Jack Kemp has been warning that "no nation can long remain a world power when its most precious resource (i.e., its population) is a shrinking resource"; Gary Bauer, when serving as President Reagan's domestic policy adviser, noted "a lot of very worrying evidence on the population decline"; Allan Carlson of the Rockford Institute has taken up the cause of pro-natalism; and Phyllis Schlafly, as quoted at the outset, is proselytizing the need for and joys of much larger families.[11]

Thus far, these seem to be only sentiments, but could the increased popularity of strategic demography help to explain the explosive sudden popularity of day care?[12] Does it not seem surprising that federal child care legislation, vetoed so vehemently by President Nixon in 1971 for its family-weakening implications, denounced so thoroughly over the decades by the political right for its communal overtones, had emerged by 1988 as Senator Orrin Hatch's "number one policy issue"?[13] In *The Birth Dearth,* published in 1987, Wattenberg pointed out the strategic value of an issue like day care with the potential for uniting feminists and pronatalists. Even earlier, in a 1986 interview on the meanings in *The Handmaid's Tale,* Atwood pointed out that:

> Any power structure will co-opt the views of its opponents, to sugarcoat the pill. The regime gives women some of the things the women's movement says they want—control over birth, no pornography—but there is a price. . . . Anyone who wants power will try to manipulate you by appealing to your desires and fears, and some-

times your best instincts. Women have to be a little cautious about that kind of appeal to them. What are we being asked to give up?[14]

Presumably, nothing must be "given up" to get good day care legislation. If it is easier for women to work and to have children, women can work more comfortably, possibly at better jobs, and also have more children. Still, does it make a difference that at least some recent converts to day care advocacy may be less concerned with the welfare of working women than with the number of their progeny? Should a beneficial public policy be rejected simply because the motives of at least some of its advocates may be distasteful? Probably not—but certainly one should be aware of these purposes and be alert to attempts to advance them.

Especially after reading *The Handmaid's Tale,* reading Wattenberg can seem a bit like being parachuted behind enemy lines—an infuriating experience, but also highly instructive. Senator Orrin Hatch's proposed day care bill, much like Wattenberg's suggested scheme, has no income test and emphasizes the free enterprise and corporate sector. It does not authorize even greater federal funding for women who stay home and have three or four or more children as Wattenberg suggests would be even more expeditious (since even working women with day care will probably stop at one or two children). Others on the right, however, are beginning to suggest that this would be not only the most equitable but also the most progeny-producing policy.[15] How will feminists respond to those who say that *they* are pro-woman and only want to provide equal treatment for those who choose the "traditional" female functions? If feminists want greater economic opportunities for women, can economic opportunities be denied to those who want to be Wives, or even Handmaids?

The debate over surrogate motherhood has just begun, and has already sharply divided feminists.[16] At least some, however, would argue for the legality of an arrangement under which a woman who desperately wanted her husband's child could freely contract with a willing surrogate, who might find surrogacy much more pleasant and profitable than her other employment options. However, what if surrogacy, and in vitro fertilization, gained legal status primarily as part of a national pro-natal policy? If it is acceptable to countenance using a woman's womb to produce children for potential parents who want them, is it more or less acceptable to use modern technology to increase a nation's population count?

Wattenberg frets that fewer children will mean fewer housing starts, fewer consumers, fewer soldiers, and a weaker national defense: "At an estimated cost of approximately $300 billion, it [he is referring to the Strategic Defense Initiative] could be put together only by amortizing it over a large population."[17] Are housing starts and aircraft carriers less or more valid reasons for surrogate motherhood than personal satisfaction? And if women want their unique reproductive function recognized and subsidized by a grateful nation, does the public good have more or fewer claims on private reproductive choices? With the Wattenberg thesis fresh in mind, it is somewhat alarming to note economist Sylvia Hewlett approvingly quoting Charles de Gaulle to the effect that "having a child for a woman is a little like doing military service for a man. Both are essential for the welfare of the nation, and we should support both activities with public monies."[18]

This leads to a second important implication of these two works: The line between what is personal and what is political is a very fragile one, and it must be constantly patrolled. With the contemporary Supreme Court edging ever closer to what had come to be considered clear constitutional zones of privacy, this is surely a timely reminder, and one that feminists in particular may wish to ponder.

One of the earliest and most formidable obstacles that contemporary feminism encountered was a definition of politics so narrow as to exclude many of the issues and concerns of most importance to many women. There was a political sphere, which involved such matters as the gross national product and international spheres of influence and partisan realignment, and there was a personal sphere, which included such items as childbirth and child care. Policy makers, the media, even political scientists, did not "do" the politics of the family, or of rape, or of pornography, or of reproduction. Feminists have worked hard, and successfully, to get certain subjects into the public domain. It is largely because of their efforts that presidential candidates must now seriously address a whole range of "family" issues, that members of the U.S. Congress now regularly debate everything from teenage pregnancy to premenstrual syndrome, and that political scientists now schedule panels and sections on gender politics. What these two books suggest, however, is that once "women's" issues are in the public domain, they can become fair game for those who are not sympathetic to feminist aspirations. Feminists may see as obvious the legitimacy of demands for state entry into family affairs to prohibit and punish spouse abuse versus the nonlegitimacy of state regulation of maternal treatment of the fetus. Nonfeminists, however, may not recognize such a distinction.

Finally, these two predictive works, while focusing on the future, strongly suggest the advisability of remembering the past. There is absolutely nothing new about the concept of pro-natalism. Most of the world's cultures are now, and have always been, pro-natalist, and this specifically includes the United States. As the epigrams at the outset were selected to suggest, American women have periodically attempted to reduce and limit the size of their families only to be rebuked for their shameful lack of maternal and patriotic sentiments. The shame-sayers in the past were also nativist, jingoist, and ethnocentric. And, as in the past, white middle-class women are the favored scapegoats.

In the late nineteenth and early twentieth centuries, the political establishment, which of course was white and male, alarmed over the large families of recent immigrants as compared with the smaller families of earlier settlers, warned of "race suicide." Socialists countercharged that the call for large families was merely cloaking the capitalists' desire to fill their factories and armies.[19] Charlotte Perkins Gilman stormed at male hypocrisy:

> All this for and against babies is by men. One would think the men bore the babies, nursed the babies, reared the babies. . . . The women bear and rear the children. The men kill them. Then they say: We are running short of children—make some more. . . .[20]

Despite these and other protests, however, proponents of large families succeeded, temporarily at least, in idealizing them—and they could succeed again. As often as women have watched the hard-earned gains of periodic feminism swept back in succeeding waves of familialism, it is still easy to become time-bound, easy to assume that the contemporary women's movement is some kind of irreversible culmination of long centuries of progress. But the pro-natalist observations of strategic demographers have become a regular feature of the influential *Atlantic Monthly*.[21] And there is no small irony in the fact that one of the last issues of *Ms.* magazine styled itself a "Special Mother's Issue"; featured on the front a classic, cover-girl mother and serene child; and, in an article on "Careers and Kids," highlighted three-child Justice Sandra Day O'Connor and five-child Judge Patricia Wald, both of whom temporarily dropped out of the labor force when their children were small. The pro-natal message is everywhere.[22]

Wattenberg himself seems genuinely insistent that coercive solutions to the birth dearth are unacceptable. Never, however, does he explicitly acknowledge what he tacitly assumes: the coercive potential of public opinion. Nor, of course, can he guarantee that those whom he persuades of the birth dearth's dire nature will be as observant of privacy and choice as he would prefer them to be.

It is often assumed that the biggest barrier to smaller families in years past, and still around the world today, has been the lack of efficient contraceptive methods. In fact, however, "Birth control has always been primarily an issue of politics, not of technology."[23] As demographers have documented at length, contraceptive methods are, and always have been, less significant than attitudes in shaping women's reproductive choices.[24] It is these attitudes that Wattenberg very much hopes to change, and that Atwood warns may be very, very malleable.

NOTES

1. Theodore Roosevelt quoted in Linda Gordon, *Women's Body, Women's Right* (New York: Grossman, 1976), p. 141. Sinclair Lewis quote from *It Can't Happen Here* (New American Library, 1970), p. 19. Phyllis Schlafly's remarks from address to the Arkansas Governor's School for the Gifted and Talented, quoted in *Arkansas Democrat,* June 24, 1987.

2. Margaret Atwood, *The Handmaid's Tale* (Boston: Houghton Mifflin, 1986); Ben J. Wattenberg, *The Birth Dearth* (New York: Pharos Books, 1987).

3. Qutoed in Caryn James, "The Lady Was Not for Hanging," *New York Times Book Review,* February 9, 1986, p. 35.

4. Cathy N. Davidson, "A Feminist 1984," *Ms.,* February 1986, pp. 24–26, esp. p. 26.

5. For an analysis of thirty reported abortion clinic bombings between May 1982 and January 1985, see David C. Nice, "Abortion Clinic Bombings as Political Violence," *American Journal of Political Science,* 32 (February 1988), pp. 178–195. Romanian pro-natal policies are described in Dirk J. van de Kaa, "Europe's Second Demographic Transition," *Population Bulletin,* 42 (1987), pp. 3–57, esp. p. 30.

6. See Janet Gallagher, "Fetal Personhood and Women's Policy," in Virginia Sapiro (Ed.), *Women, Biology and Public Policy* (Beverly Hills, CA: Sage, 1985), pp. 91–116; Lisa M. Krieger, "Fetus Definitions Create Medical, Legal Inconsistencies," *Arkansas Democrat,* January 27, 1988, p. 7A; and Eve W. Paul, "Amicus Brief in Forced Caesarean Case," *Insider,* February 1988, p. 2.

7. On workplace restrictions, see Cynthia Ganney, "The Fine Line between Fetal Protection and Female Discrimination," *Washington Post National Weekly Edition,* August 24, 1987, p. 11. On toxic wastes, see "Toxic Shipments to Third World Likely to Increase," *Springdale (Arkansas) News,* April 26, 1987. On Minnesota act requiring burial of fetal remains, see "Judge Blocks Forced Fetal Burial," *Arkansas Democrat,* August 22, 1987.

8. Quoted in Davidson, "A Feminist 1984," p. 24.

9. Ben J. Wattenberg and Karl Zinsmeister, "The Birth Dearth: The Geopolitical Consequences," *Public Opinion,* 8 (December–January 1986), pp. 7–13, esp. p. 13.

10. Wattenberg, *The Birth Dearth,* p. 120.

11. Pat Robertson's formula is as follows: "By the year 2000 we will have aborted 40 million children in this country. Their work product by the year 2020 will amount to $1.4 trillion, the taxes from them would amount to $330 billion and they could ensure the fiscal stability of the Social Security System." Quoted and criticized by Charles Krauthammer, "Win, Place, Show Ridiculous in Politics," *Arkansas Democrat,* February 21, 1988. "The child-free families of today are the freeloaders on social security tomorrow," according to George Gilder, "Children and Politics," *Public Opinion,* 10 (March–April 1988), pp. 10–11, esp. p. 11. Jack Kemp and Gary Bauer, quoted in Allan L. Otten, "Birth Dearth," *Wall Street Journal,* June 18, 1987. Allan Carlson's views in "High-Tech Societies Don't Have High Enough Birthrates," *Washington Post National Weekly Edition,* April 28, 1986, pp. 23–24, and "What to Do, Part I," *Public Opinion,* 10 (March–April 1988), pp. 4–6. On Schlafly, see n. 1.

12. On the recent popularity of day care, see Barbara Kantrowitz with Pat Wingert. "The Clamor to Save the Family," *Newsweek,* February 29, 1988, pp. 60–61; and Cindy Skrzycki and Frank Swoboda, "Congress Has Discovered a New Problem: Child Care," *Washington Post National Weekly Edition,* February 29–March 6, 1988, p. 33.

13. On President Nixon's veto and past conservative opposition to day care legislation, see Jill Norgren, "In Search of a National Child-Care Policy: Background and Prospects," in Ellen Boneparth (Ed.), *Women, Power and Policy* (Elmsford, NY: Pergamon Press, 1982), pp. 124–139. Senator Orrin Hatch statement made on *The McNeil-Lehrer News Hour,* January 7, 1988.

14. Quoted in James, "The Lady Was Not for Hanging," p. 35.

15. Carlson, "What to Do, Part I," p. 5. Mrs. Pat Robertson quoted to this effect in *Arkansas Democrat,* March 2, 1988.

16. See Robyn Rowland, "Technology and Motherhood: Reproductive Choice Reconsidered," *Signs,* 12 (Spring 1987), pp. 512–528.

17. Wattenberg and Zinsmeister, "The Birth Dearth," pp. 9–10.

18. Sylvia Hewlett, "What to Do, Part II," *Public Opinion,* 10 (March–April 1988), p. 7.

19. Gordon, *Women's Body, Women's Right,* pp. 140–145.

20. Quoted in ibid., p. 145.

21. See R. J. Hernstein, "IQ and Falling Birth Rates," *Atlantic Monthly,* May 1989, pp. 73–79, and Jonathan Rauch, "Kids as Capital," *Atlantic Monthly,* August 1989, pp. 56–61.

22. See Edith Fierst, "Careers and Kids," *Ms.,* May 1988, pp. 62–64.

23. Gordon, *Women's Body, Women's Right,* p. xii.

24. Richard L. Clinton, "Population, Politics and Political Science," in Richard L. Clinton (Ed.), *Population and Politics* (Lexington, MA: Lexington Books, 1973), pp. 51–71, esp. pp. 54–55.

FURTHER READINGS

Chesler, Ellen. "Stop Coercing Women." *New York Times Magazine,* February 6, 1994, pp. 31, 33.

Daniels, Cynthia R. *At Women's Expense: State Power and the Politics of Fetal Rights.* Cambridge, MA: Harvard University Press, 1993.

DeGama, Katherine. "A Brave New World? Rights Discourse and the Politics of Reproductive Anatomy." *Journal of Law and Society,* 21 (Spring 1993), pp. 114–130.

Dixon-Mueller, Ruth. *Population Policy and Women's Rights.* Westport, CT: Praeger, 1993.

Elshtain, Jean Bethke. "If You're An Addict, It's Now A Crime to Give Brith." *The Progressive* 54 (December 1990), pp. 26–28.

Gallagher, Janet. "Prenatal Invasions and Interventions: What's Wrong with Fetal Rights." *Harvard Women's Law Journal,* 10 (1987), pp. 9–58.

Hartmann, Betsey. *Reproductive Rights and Wrongs.* New York: Harper and Row, 1987.

Kent, Bonnie. "Protecting Children, Born and Unborn." *Report from the Institute for Philosophy and Public Policy,* 11 (Winter 1991), pp. 13–15.

"The Politics of Pregnancy: Policy Dilemmas in the Maternal-Fetal Relationship." *Women and Politics,* 13 (3 and 4) (1993), entire issue.

Roberts, Dorothy E. "The Future of Reproductive Choice for Poor Women and Women of Color." *Women's Rights Law Reporter,* 14 (Spring/Fall 1992), pp. 305–314.

Williams, Joy. "The Case Against Babies," in Ian Frazier (Ed.) *The Best American Essays, 1997* (Boston: Houghton Mifflin, 1997), pp. 203–212.

The Family and Medical Leave Act: A Policy for Families

Joan Hulse Thompson

> My name is Liberia Johnson. In 1978, I was employed by a retail store in Charleston, South Carolina. . . . I became pregnant. . . . I tried to work because the income was so important to my family. My doctor told me that I was hypertensive and I had a thyroid problem. . . . If I did not stop working I would have a miscarriage. . . . The store manager . . . told me my job would be there after my baby was born. . . . I left at three months pregnant. I had a difficult pregnancy. I was in the hospital three times because I almost lost my baby. When I had my baby, I went and got my six weeks check up and the same day I went back to the store and asked for my job. . . . There was a new manager and he told me I don't have a job.[1]

On October 17, 1985, Ms. Johnson, married and the mother of five children, told her story to a joint oversight hearing on Disability and Parental Leave chaired by Congresswoman Patricia Schroeder (D-CO). Mary Rose Oakar (D-OH) and nine congressmen, six Democrats and three Republicans, attended part of the three-hour hearing that featured medical and academic experts, corporate and union representatives, and a local government official as well as another public witness, a single mother with an adopted daughter.

An oversight hearing is designed to attract attention from members of Congress, the press, and the public to an issue in hopes of gathering support for government action. Public witnesses like Liberia Johnson can play a brief, but significant, role. According to a veteran committee staff member, anecdotes are "the only thing that move people. A good public witness draws the rapt attention of the members."[2] They convince members of Congress in a very personal way that legislation is needed to remedy an injustice. The more heart-wrenching their stories, the better.

How did a black woman, who formerly worked a cash register and became a baker at a small hospital, get to tell her story to Congress? Public witnesses are usually located and coached by interest groups and subcommittee staff, but in this case the Congressional Caucus for Women's Issues (CCWI) was responsible along with the feminist National Women's Law Center (NWLC) and a subcommittee staff member. Several CCWI members, the CCWI staff, and a few interested attorneys led by the NWLC had been working on parental leave since early 1984. This issue illustrates the role of congresswomen and their caucus in developing and promoting a policy proposal to respond to the economic needs of women.

The House and Senate passed the FMLA in 1990 and again in 1992, but President Bush vetoed the bill both times and the Congress was unable to override either veto. Both chambers passed the bill again on February 4, 1993 and President Clinton signed it the next day, making it effective six months later (see Table 8–1). The 1992 election, hailed as the "Year of the Woman," made the difference for FMLA. The votes of women were crucial to Clinton's victory and the number of women in the House increased from twenty-nine to forty-eight and in the Senate from two to seven. Despite the Republican Congressional victory of 1994, when nine Democratic women lost, the 104th Congress number forty-seven women in the House and eight in the Senate. The 1996 election resulted in a net gain of three women in the House.

TABLE 8.1   Provisions of the Family and Medical Leave Act (PL 103-3) Signed by President Clinton on February 5, 1993

1. Family leave—Employees may take up to 12 weeks of unpaid leave per year for the care of a newborn, newly adopted, or newly placed foster child, or for the care of a seriously ill child, parent, or spouse.

2. Medical leave—Employees may take up to 12 weeks of unpaid leave per year for their own serious medical condition. When medically necessary, employers must permit intermittent leave for treatment, but workers may be required to temporarily transfer to another equivalent position.

3. Exemption—Employers with fewer than 50 employees within 75 miles of a work site are exempt. Approximately 5 percent of all employers are covered and about 45 percent of all employees.

4. Coverage—Employees must have worked at least 12 months and at least 1,250 hours (an average of 25 hours per week) during the previous year to be eligible for leave. Highly paid workers (top 10 percent) in a firm may be denied reinstatement, if they received timely notice and the employer can demonstrate substantial and grievous economic injury would occur. Other eligible workers are entitled to the same or equivalent positions upon their return to work.

5. Conditions—Health insurance, if it is provided by the employer, must be continued on the same basis during the period of the leave. Employees are not entitled to more than 12 weeks leave in one year regardless of circumstances. Employees are required to give 30 days' notice when the need for leave is foreseeable. Employers may require that a health care provider certify the serious health condition of the employee or their family member in order to qualify for leave and reinstatement.

6. Paid leave—Workers may choose to substitute accrued paid vacation, personal or family leave for unpaid family leave mandated by the FMLA. Employers are not required to permit workers to take paid sick leave for the care of a new or ill family member. However, employers may require workers to substitute any paid leave they have accrued for all or part of their unpaid FMLA leave.

7. Enforcement—Administrative and civil procedures are available for enforcement under the supervision of the Wage and Hours Division of the Department of Labor. Violators are liable for lost wages, benefits and other compensation, or actual monetary losses sustained by the employee up to the equivalent of 12 weeks pay. If employers can demonstrate a good-faith effort to comply with the law, they will not be assessed an additional monetary penalty as punishment for the violation.

8. Federal employees—Federal government workers are also entitled to 12 weeks of family or medical leave after 12 months of employment. The Office of Personnel Management is responsible for enforcement.

9. Congressional employees—Employees of the House of Representatives and the Senate are eligible for 12 weeks of family or medical leave, the same as private employees. Previous employee rights bills have usually exempted congressional employees.

While the numbers of women changed little, the speakership of Newt Gingrich brought big changes to the House of Representatives, including new rules that permitted the CCWI to survive only in a diminished role. The congresswomen retain the organizational name and can share some staff resources as a congressional member organization, but the full-time CCWI staff had to move out of its office in the Rayburn House Office Building, organize as Women's Policy, Inc. (WPI), sell subscriptions to its information services and solicit private financial support. WPI publishes a weekly newsletter, quarterly legislative status reports, and briefing papers on issues before Congress. Its supporters include members of Congress, both women and men.

WOMEN IN CONGRESS AND THEIR CAUCUS

Since the first woman entered the House of Representatives in 1917, congresswomen have been outsiders. Until the 1980s, none were invited to join either party's powerful yet informal social and political groups, such as Democratic Speaker Rayburn's Board of Education or the Republican Chowder and Marching Society founded by Richard Nixon and Gerald Ford. Even in the 1990s, congresswomen are still excluded from gym cliques of congressmen who play basketball and racquetball regularly.[3] As women politicians, they have been isolated from the social network of male politicians and from that of more traditional women outside of politics.

The congresswomen needed a support group. A congresswoman explained the significance of such social groups, as follows:

> Members who don't or can't participate in them are like the kid in college who has no one to study with; no one to exchange ideas with to get a broader idea of what's going on in the class; no one to work with to get the right kind of "vibes" about the course and the teacher. It takes longer for that kid to understand what is going on and often that student is never as good as he or she could be.[4]

The Congresswomen's Caucus, founded in 1977 by Elizabeth Holtzman (D-NY), Margaret Heckler (R-MA), and Shirley Chisholm (D-NY), had both social and policy goals. All the members were committed to the Equal Rights Amendment and to increasing the number of women in public office. Frequent meetings provided an opportunity for "conviviality, affection, and good feelings."[5] Bipartisanship strengthened the organization's claim to speak for women nationally.

The Congresswomen's Caucus was not the first such organization, although its focus on member, rather than constituency, characteristics was unusual. Paralleling the growth of special interest groups in the larger society, caucuses have flourished in the House. The Democratic Study Group was first in 1959. There were thirteen caucuses in 1974, over 100 in 1990, and, despite the rules change, about 130 in 1996.[6] Caucuses are voluntary associations of House members formed to help fulfill goals of representation, personal power, policy promotion, and reelection. Members from constituencies dependent upon the maritime industry formed the Port Caucus, those with steel mills joined the Steel Caucus, and so forth. Caucuses gather and distribute information, seek to influence congressional agendas and may attempt to build policy coalitions. Speaker Gingrich rose to power in the House as leader of a caucus, the Conservative Opportunity Society, founded in 1983.

Whether congresswomen initially felt that they should represent women nationally, most soon realized that if they did not speak for women no one else would.[7] However, not all congresswomen believe that the problems of women could best be addressed at the national level. Because they favored state, local, or private initiatives, most Republican congresswomen and some Democrats were out of step with the underlying liberal perspective of the caucus. Steps taken to convince all the women to join prevented the Congresswomen's Caucus from taking positions on issues important to its most active members. But requiring greater policy agreement threatened to make the Caucus a tiny, exclusively Democratic group with little hope of fulfilling its policy goals, especially in the conservative atmosphere of the early 1980s.[8]

A COED CAUCUS EXPANDS ITS INFLUENCE

Recurrent financial problems, a House rules change, the election of President Reagan, and a desire to be more effective on women's issues led the members of the Congresswomen's Caucus to invite congressmen to join their organization late in 1981. The following year the organization took on its new name, the Congressional Caucus for Women's Issues, and established an executive committee of congresswomen to set policy. The group grew from a membership of 10 to 150 by 1994 with 42 congresswomen and 108 congressmen. Although some congresswomen did not belong,[9] CCWI leaders were in a far better position with their expanded membership to command the attention of the media and the public, and pursue policy change in an institution where men hold the power positions.

Congresswomen do sit on the most powerful committees, but no woman chaired a committee in 1994[10] and the five subcommittees they chaired were not among the most powerful. Women have been part of the leadership structure in both parties, but not yet as high as the party leader or the party whip.[11] The concerns of other caucuses, such as the Congressional Black Caucus, won greater recognition as their members gained positions within the formal power structure. But due to electoral defeats, retirements, and attempts for higher office, that path has not worked very well for women.

Expanding the women's caucus to include supportive congressmen proved to be a shortcut. By 1985, the male members of CCWI included the Speaker, Majority Whip, nine committee chairs including Rules and three select committee chairmen. Although only about a dozen Republicans belonged, they included ranking members of four committees. In 1993–1994, male members of CCWI chaired 14 House committees and 44 subcommittees with ranking positions on 3 committees and 2 subcommittees. Having men in CCWI in the 103rd Congress had the effect of increasing its representation on the five committees that form an oligarchy of power in Congress from 15 seats to 66 seats.[12] When Family and Medical Leave passed the House, CCWI male membership included the Speaker, Majority Leader, Majority Whip, Democratic Caucus Chairman, and the Chairman of the Rules Committee. Although neither party leaders nor committee chairs can assure congressional passage, it did help women's issues to have publicly committed supporters in high places.

POLICY DEVELOPMENT BY THE CAUCUS

Attempts by the Congresswomen's Caucus to build coalitions or "to fashion and implement legislative strategies were . . . infrequent and superficial."[13] The expanded CCWI could do more. The same year the Caucus invited men to join, it also became the House coordinator for the Economic Equity Act, a package of bills initiated by Senator David Durenberger (R-MN) in response to the fate of the Equal Rights Amendment. The 98th Congress (1983–1984) was a very productive one for CCWI, largely because of the much publicized gender gap. Public opinion polls showed President Reagan to be much less popular with women than with men. Republican congressmen feared the women's vote and Democrats in Congress were anxious to exploit their potential advantage. Child support enforcement and pension reform legislation, both included in the Economic Equity Act, were enacted before the 1984 election.[14]

After President Reagan's landslide reelection victory over Walter Mondale and Caucus leader Geraldine Ferraro (D-NY), a CCWI staff member reflected "feminists are just poison"[15] now on the Hill. Then CCWI Director, Anne Radigan, explained:

> On Capitol Hill, legislators reacted negatively to the failure of the Democratic presidential ticket and its feminist adherents. Where only a few weeks earlier politicians had beaten a path to their doors, now feminist women's groups found themselves and their agenda held at a cool and measured distance.[16]

In order to advance women's economic issues in the 99th Congress, the CCWI adopted a new strategy of describing legislative proposals as "pro-family" rather than for women. The plan was to seize the politically popular label from conservatives and the religious right. The FMLA even bridged the politically divisive abortion issue by making it more economically feasible for women to continue an unplanned pregnancy. By the 1988 presidential election, both Republican George Bush and Democratic nominee Michael Dukakis were talking about family policy proposals, including both parental leave and child care.

During the Bush administration, the FMLA was joined on the House agenda by new women's equity legislation developed through CCWI. The Women's Health Equity Act, first introduced in July 1990 and enacted under Clinton in June 1993, increased research efforts on breast and ovarian cancer, menopause, osteoporosis, contraception, and infertility. The Economic Equity Act package was redesigned under CCWI leadership with thirty bills divided into sections on workplace fairness, economic opportunity, work and family, and economic self-sufficiency for women. The Violence Against Women Act, first introduced in 1990 and enacted with the Crime bill in 1994, expanded rape shield laws, created federal offenses for interstate spousal abuse, and provided funds for rape crisis shelters, additional police, prosecutors, and victim advocates.

Although abortion has been the driving issue for most feminist groups since the mid-1980s, CCWI had primarily an informational, rather than advocacy, role on abortion rights until January 1993. The 1992 elections added twenty-two new pro-choice women to the Executive Committee while two pro-life caucus congress-women did not return to the House. The new Executive Committee voted over-whelmingly to support the Freedom of Choice bill to codify the *Roe v. Wade* Supreme Court decision. In the 103rd Congress, CCWI was committed to removing restrictions on abortion funding and including abortion services in health care reform.[17] FMLA was a priority for CCWI from 1985 until its enactment, but certainly not its only concern.

PROS AND CONS OF GENDER NEUTRALITY

According to Anne Radigan, the caucus has long been committed to supporting gender neutral legislation. Therefore, a bill for parental, not maternity, leave was introduced. Protective laws, such as weight-lifting restrictions, have been used to keep women out of higher paying, non-traditional jobs. Mandatory maternity leave, by treating pregnancy as a special condition, could well lead to further workplace discrimination against women, such as a reluctance to hire or promote a woman who might become pregnant.

The Pregnancy Discrimination Act (PDA), an amendment to Title VII of the Civil Rights Act of 1964, was enacted in 1978 in response to a 1976 U.S. Supreme Court decision. The decision, *General Electric Co. v. Gilbert* (429 US 124), interpreted the previous statute as permitting employers to treat pregnancy differently from other medical conditions with respect to health insurance and leave policies. Under the PDA, women unable to work due to pregnancy or childbirth would have to be treated the same as other employees unable to work for medical reasons. The statute was gender neutral, but it left millions of women unprotected because their employers provided no health insurance or disability benefits. It also ignored the bonding needs of newborn infants and their families.

Also in 1978, the California legislature enacted a mandatory maternity leave program covering all employers in the state. However, the law was challenged in 1983 by a private employer who claimed that the state statute was reverse discrimination against males and violated the federal mandate for gender neutrality. In 1984, this argument was successful in federal district court, but it was reversed on appeal in 1985 and defeated again in a 1987 U.S. Supreme Court decision, *California Federal Savings and Loan v. Guerra* (479 U.S. 272).

While the issue was before the courts, Representative Howard Berman (D-CA), who had sponsored the state law while a member of the California legisla-

ture, considered sponsoring a bill at the national level that would mandate maternity and some paternity leave. He had the support of many California feminists
who believed that "since women alone bear children they are at an indisputable
disadvantage compared to working men and require an edge to help them remain
competitive in the workplace."[18]

Also in 1984, a small drafting group of lawyers who had fought for PDA and
a caucus staff attorney began to look for a way to respond to the initial federal
court decision—a manner in which to fill the coverage gap and recognize the
needs of women and their families, without abandoning the principle of gender
neutrality. Their solution was to frame a broad policy mandating parental leave for
both parents and medical disability leave for all workers. Congressman Berman
agreed to abandon his efforts in favor of this approach favored by the feminist organizations, including CCWI.

A more narrowly drawn bill for pregnant women with a small paternity leave,
to encourage a greater role for fathers in the care of newborns, would have had an
easier time gaining support. Making parental leave optional for either parent enabled opponents to score points with such remarks as, "This is ludicrous in the extreme. I don't need 18 weeks off if my wife has a baby."[19] Including all those temporarily medically disabled increased the cost of the bill to employers and,
therefore, their resolve to oppose it. Republican Senator Durenberger, usually a dependable ally on women's issues, expressed concern in 1990 that the costs of temporary medical leaves and leaves for the care of sick family members were "virtually untested in the private sector"[20] and therefore very difficult to predict.

CHARGES OF ELITISM AND DAMAGING REGULATION

Choosing to make the mandated leave unpaid kept the cost down and made the
policy self-policing, but at the price of raising difficult issues of social class.
Women's groups, like most interest groups, are composed primarily of members
from the middle class and above. They are potentially vulnerable to charges of in-
sensitivity to the real problems of working class women when their organizations
engage in conflicts over abstract principles of equality. That was why both the public witnesses at the October 1985 oversight hearing were African American. One of
Pat Schroeder's concluding remarks expressed her pleasure that, while "The bill
looks like it is for 'Yuppies,'" the hearing had demonstrated that "It's for everyone."
Demonstrating universality was clearly one of the goals of the congresswomen, the
caucus staff, and the women's groups when they planned the initial hearing.

Nevertheless, opponents described the women's groups as "powerful special-
interest groups" seeking to dictate policy against the best interests of both employers and the very employees whose interests they claimed to represent. Testimony
from the U.S. Chamber of Commerce at subsequent legislative hearings included
references to the fact that, "All employees . . . will be subject to a uniform parental
leave law, . . . whether they can afford to take advantage of it or not."[21] Furthermore, the business community argued that, "any mandated benefit is likely to re-

place other, sometimes more preferable, employee benefits . . . (such as) flextime, child-care, dental or liberalized leave benefits."[22] In 1989, a Texas Republican expressed the view that only the upper classes would be able to take the leaves while all workers would share the costs. He described the bill as "'Yuppie' welfare—a perverse redistribution of income."[23]

The mandatory nature of the legislation was critical for both sides and could not be compromised. Supporters proclaimed that the proposal "breaks new ground in labor law"[24] and, of course, business groups opposed it for exactly that reason. Proponents could and did compromise the number of weeks of leave and the number of employees a company must have to be covered; however, eliminating the mandatory nature of the regulation would have left nothing of substance. For business interests and their supporters in Congress, "Such legislation results in a loss of freedom of choice—the hallmark of our economic system."[25]

Government already regulates wages and working conditions. Further intrusions must be fought, according to the U.S. Chamber of Commerce, for the sake of maintaining the nation's international competitiveness and high rate of economic growth. Figures for employee benefit costs as a percentage of the payroll for Korea, Japan, and Taiwan were cited and shown to put U.S. industry at a disadvantage. European nations that grant paid family leaves were praised by supporters, but criticized by the Chamber of Commerce for rates of job creation below that of the United States. The Chamber argued that the costs of mandated family leave would devastate small businesses. It might lead to discrimination in hiring, making it difficult for women of childbearing age to even find employment.

To opponents, family leave was another well intentioned but misguided intervention in the employer-employee relationship. They argued that it would not serve the interests of the nation or even those of working women. To proponents, family leave was the next step toward a more humane society, just as child labor and minimum wage laws were fifty years before. In response to complaints about cost, prime sponsor Senator Christopher Dodd (D-CT), declared "It's mortifying that we can't offer a benefit like this that is a minimum standard of human decency."[26] Normal family life adjusts to adult employment schedules on a daily basis. Family and medical leave is for times of transition and crisis, when accommodating the business needs of employers would cause great harm to the family.

BUILDING SUPPORT FOR THE FMLA

According to then CCWI staff director, Anne Radigan, the legislative strategy for the Family and Medical Leave Act (FMLA) assumed compromise would be necessary for success. She described the CCWI plan in 1985 as follows: "At first, try to be as all-encompassing as possible, then go for as much as you can (realistically hope for), and finally get what you can."[27] Members of Congress tend to be pragmatic, because they want accomplishments to claim credit for back home.

Because public support is essential to win congressional support, the initial hearing and every subsequent hearing was planned with the media in mind. The first hearing had a star witness, Dr. T. Berry Brazelton, who has the charisma of a cable television star and the authority of a noted pediatrician and author. His testimony gave the bill the advantage of backing in the medical community. As hoped, he drew a feature story in *The Washington Post*. Subsequent hearings heard from a retail manager who recovered from cancer but was unemployed for two years, and a daughter who lost her job when she was absent caring for her father during the last weeks of his life.

After the first hearing the caucus staff monitored the media coverage and were both encouraged and discouraged. Both the AP and UPI wire services carried the story but both talked about maternity leave. "What did we do wrong?" lamented Anne Radigan. "How was that connection, the language . . . misunderstood? We are talking so very clearly about parents, mothers *and fathers*." On the other hand, there was good coverage and an opportunity to build support before opposition surfaced. Reflecting on media strategy three years later, Anne Radigan recalled that "most reporters covering the issue gave the bill a favorable spin."[28]

By 1989, *Congressional Quarterly* was referring to the FMLA as "a key item on the agenda . . . of organized labor."[29] At the first hearing in 1985, this point was made by a coal miner who prefaced his remarks with the question, "What's an official of a macho male coal miners union doing in a place like this?" He then described the parental leave proposal that the coal companies refused to accept in national contract talks in 1984, the growing number of women in coal mining, the changing family patterns in mining communities, and the special hardships facing rural families when their children are seriously ill. Medical treatment for cancer, for instance, is available only in major cities, requiring time off from work for travel to hospitals as far as 200 miles away.

Although his stories were emotionally compelling, the United Mine Workers spokesman made it clear that he was coming to Congress because the union had been unable to get parental leave through in contract negotiations. In a sense, he was asking Congress to circumvent the collective bargaining process. Unions want mandatory benefits so that their bargaining can focus on other issues.

Representative William Clay (D-MO), a black congressman and union ally, called the FMLA "preventive medicine, (because it) . . . goes to the heart of what is causing families to struggle."[30] As a cosponsor, Clay, the chairman of the Labor Management Subcommittee of the House Education and Labor Committee, proved valuable. However, his advocacy may also have strengthened the resolve of the business community. Clay is known for angry rhetoric, but not for legislative effectiveness beyond his own committee.

Furthermore, Education and Labor[31] was perceived as a partisan, ideological committee where liberals could win bills that would not pass in the more moderate House chamber or in the Senate. Opponents are more interested in compromise when they fear that without it they may suffer total defeat than when they can realistically anticipate eventual victory. Union support, while necessary for committee approval, was less important for enactment than the media coverage that would build support within the general public and therefore in the full chamber.

EXPANDING THE FMLA COALITION

In 1985, Schroeder's original bill provided for disability leaves, defining disability as "a total inability to perform a job, a notion of disability that the disabled rights advocates had been struggling for years to overcome."[32] Substituting "medical leave" resolved the objections of the disabled and gained the support of five organizations, including the Disability Rights Education and Defense Fund.

At the suggestion of Congresswoman Roukema (R-NJ), ranking minority member of Clay's subcommittee, the proposal was expanded in 1987 from parental to family leave by including leave to care for seriously ill, elderly parents. This inclusion brought the politically powerful American Association of Retired Persons and another group into the coalition.

Advocates recognized that women with difficult pregnancies and those who could not afford to risk losing their jobs might choose to have an abortion for financial reasons. Mary Rose Oakar, a Roman Catholic and pro-life CCWI member, said at the initial hearing that "nothing is more sacred than children in their formative weeks," making parental leave "a real, positive, minimum response." She also pledged, in her role as chair of the subcommittee responsible for federal employee benefits, that the federal government would be a model employer. Dale Kildee (D-MI), also a devout Roman Catholic, added that the bill promised to be "a real vehicle for making this government pro-family." Other pro-life members, including Republican Henry Hyde of Illinois and the U.S. Catholic Conference, supported the bill. However, anti-abortion forces could not develop a maximum lobbying effort for anything other than a prohibition of abortion.

In March 1989, the House Education and Labor Committee approved amendments to add a title including congressional employees among covered workers and a section outlining special rules for instructional personnel at public and private schools. The rules for educators were negotiated by the National School Board Association, professional unions representing teachers and other education organizations to provide employee coverage even at small schools and prevent undue disruption in classroom instruction from intermittent leaves or teachers returning at the very end of the term.

Businesses would be paying the cost of FMLA, so members of Congress wanted to see evidence of business support. After questioning ten major companies about their leave provisions, a caucus staff member invited General Foods Corporation to testify at the first hearing in 1985. The company has a policy of *paid* disability and child-care leaves as part of its plan to "meet contemporary and future needs of employees," explained its representative. Male employees had been reluctant to ask for leave, she continued, but recently a "very highly placed executive" had taken parental leave to be with his new baby and "he's being looked at as the domino."

Such a company had an incentive to support the FMLA. The governmental mandate would require its competitors to pay the cost of a minimal benefit, while its benefit package would remain attractive to prospective employees. At a subsequent hearing, Southern New England Telephone testified that parental leave enabled them to retain trained employees.

While the U.S. Chamber of Commerce, the National Federation of Independent Business, and the American Society for Personnel Administration testified against the bill, congressional staff found some small business representatives to argue for the bill. These included the National Federation of Business and Professional Women's Clubs and the National Association of Women Business Owners. Pat Schroeder said that from small business owners in her district she heard that "parental leave policies save employers the cost of hiring and training new employees. Most of all these policies help attract the best and the brightest, and retain a valued and trusted work force."[33]

The co-sponsorship of the four subcommittee chairs with jurisdiction was sufficient for success at that stage in the legislative process. The primary focus during full committee consideration was the cost for business, especially small business, to continue health insurance coverage of workers on leave and to hire temporary replacements. The original bill applied to employers with five or more workers, repeated concessions raised that number to 50, provided a legal means to deny some highly paid employees reinstatement, shortened the number of weeks of leave, restricted workers to either family or medical leave during a twelve-month period, and raised the number of weeks worked to be eligible. The bill still covered some part-time as well as full-time workers, intermittent as well as continuous leave, mandated continued health benefits if offered, and provided job guarantees for family and medical leaves. Since 95 percent of all private employers have less than 50 workers, only about 5 percent of companies and 45 percent of the private sector workforce is covered by the FMLA mandate.

CREATING A FMLA STUDY COMMISSION

Released in early 1987, the original annual cost estimate from the Chamber of Commerce for family leave alone was $16 billion; but this figure was based on the faulty assumptions that all workers would be replaced and that replacements would be paid more than regular workers. Under pressure, the Chamber reduced the estimated cost to $2.6 billion. After initial compromises, the nonpartisan Government Accounting Office estimated that the new bill would cost $188 million annually.[34] Based upon these figures, supporters estimated that the FMLA would cost employers only $6.50 per year per eligible worker. A report, produced by the CCWI research arm and the Women's Legal Defense Fund, found that unemployment resulting from the absence of parental leave costs American families at least $607 million a year and costs taxpayers about $108 million a year for government assistance programs.[35]

While the Caucus saw the FMLA as a first step in a new and desirable direction, opposition groups feared more costly encroachments if the bill succeeded in any form. Marian Wright Edelman of the Children's Defense Fund published a book in 1987 urging a comprehensive family policy. Her program, just as business anticipated, went beyond FMLA with calls for private and public funding for about six months of paid maternity and paternity leave. She also urged a reduction in the number of hours in a normal work week, an increase in the minimum wage, and more flexible scheduling of work time.[36]

Academic specialists, comparing the United States with other Western democracies in Europe and with Canada, have pointed out that in those countries payments are available to compensate for lost wages after childbirth. Realizing that such a proposal was too costly to win passage, successive versions of the FMLA provided for a study commission. This group would recommend means to provide salary replacement for employees taking parental and medical leaves. Those who wanted paid leaves were thus partially satisfied, since a study commission could improve prospects for a future program of leaves paid for by employers, Social Security, or some other means.

The final version of the FMLA Commission mandate focused on examining the administrative and implementation costs business groups feared from the law as enacted. Issues of productivity, alternative benefits, job creation, federal enforcement, and economic growth by sector had been added to the commission mandate in response to business criticism, and the examination of paid leave provisions was greatly reduced in importance. Consideration of the needs of employees who had been covered by the original proposal, but are not eligible for mandatory leaves under the new law were also added to the commission's charge. The commission report, submitted in April 1996 to a Congress dominated by FMLA opponents, reflected the fact that its bipartisan members were appointed before the 1994 Republican victory and therefore a majority were advocates of the FMLA.

CONTINUED CONFLICT OVER BUSINESS REGULATION

More ominous to the business community than the FMLA itself was the prospect that once one benefit became mandatory others would follow. Employers could be required to offer not only paid parental and medical leaves, but also health insurance to all employees and their families. In an era of tight federal budgets, the tendency has been to shift social welfare costs, borne by the national government in many countries, to private business in order to avoid calling for higher tax revenues.

The implications of enacting Family and Medical Leave then went beyond the narrow domain of women's issues. Opting for a gender neutral policy meant that passage, if accomplished, would be a major precedent for both governmental regulation of business and passing costs of social welfare programs on to private industry. Although this made passage more difficult, it also helped supporters attract a broader coalition than they could have for a narrowly drawn maternity leave bill.

President Clinton's health care reform proposal, introduced in November 1993, did include an employer mandate to cover 80 percent of the cost of health insurance for employees and their families, with government subsidies for small employers. The mandate was criticized by the U.S. Chamber of Commerce and other business representatives with the familiar argument that more governmental regulation would cost jobs in the private sector. According to opponents, FMLA, like health care reform, was "yet another Democratic effort to regulate industry, increase the bureaucracy and set the stage for costly litigation."[37]

At first, it seemed that no one wanted to be against universal health insurance coverage any more than they had wanted to position themselves against family leave, but Clinton's health reform lost public support after the insurance industry advertisements raised fears that those currently insured would have to pay more for less coverage. Nancy Johnson of Connecticut, a moderate Republican member of CCWI, "rose to prominence when Republicans recognized that they had a health care expert in their midst."[38] Congressional Democrats, however, were unable to either unite around one proposal in a partisan coalition or work with Republicans, such as Johnson, to develop a bipartisan proposal that could pass. "From the Republican point of view, Democrats had turned a deaf ear to their longstanding warnings that a big bill could never gain broad support because there would always be more risks associated with passing it then clear gains."[39]

The 103rd Congress began with the easy passage of FMLA, which unlike health reform had bipartisan support, limited direct impact, and an incremental approach, putting off paid leave and universal coverage to the future. While health reform dominated the agenda of the entire 103rd Congress, compromise efforts by the Democrats came too little and too late to save their majority status.[40]

THE POLITICS OF CONGRESSIONAL PASSAGE

With its strong public appeal, Family and Medical Leave was viewed as a potentially powerful political issue throughout its consideration. Although not at the top of the congressional agenda until 1993, it attracted and sustained public support from 1985 until its enactment. The story of its approval by Congress in 1990, 1992, and 1993 demonstrates that party politics and media strategies were decisive on FMLA.

The bill did not reach the floor of the House until 1990, but it was debated on the Senate floor in 1988. Just before the presidential and congressional elections, Democratic Senators brought minimum wage increases, parental leave, and child care to the floor "in an openly partisan fashion," according to *Congressional Quarterly Almanac*. "While the Senate waited for conference reports on fiscal 1989 appropriations bills, Democrats used their power as the majority party to put on the floor all the labor and social legislation they wanted to highlight in the closing weeks before the November 8 elections."[41] No vote was taken on the bills due to a Republican filibuster.

In 1989, Schroeder said, "the worst rumor we hear up here is that the (Republican) administration will ask us to schedule the bill (for floor action) around Mother's Day and then take men out of the bill."[42] Instead, the Democratic Speaker arranged for FMLA to pass the House, with its gender neutrality and governmental mandate intact, just in time for Mother's Day 1990. As the supporters of the FMLA celebrated its first ever passage in the House, opponents declared it dead.

A lobbyist for the National Association of Wholesaler-Distributors, Mary Tavenner, reported that, "I had John Sununu (White House Chief of Staff) look me straight in the eye and say that the president would veto it."[43] After refusing to meet with Republican supporters of the bill, President Bush vetoed the FMLA on the last Friday afternoon before the July 4th holiday; a time when the media and the public would be least attentive.

The vetoed bill was a substitute proposal, negotiated just prior to House floor consideration. It eliminated the possibility that the same worker would be eligible for both family and medical leave, totalling 25 weeks, in one year. The cap would be 12 weeks for either or both and the small employer exemption was modified as well. Such changes made the law less burdensome for business and therefore picked up support. This revised 1990 version, which for the first time included care of a seriously ill spouse, was supported by 198 Democrats and 39 Republicans while 54 Democrats and 133 Republicans opposed it. Three planned amendments were actually withdrawn by Republicans at the request of the White House, because their passage might have made the bill more attractive and made a veto more difficult to sustain.

One-third of the Senators faced reelection in 1990. Those who opposed the FMLA were not anxious to participate in another filibuster or take a recorded vote on the bill. Senate Majority Leader, George Mitchell, a Democrat, worked out a deal with Senator Robert Dole, the Republican leader, to permit the FMLA to pass on a voice vote on the condition that Mitchell would schedule a vote on a constitutional amendment to make flag desecration a crime. Thus each party was able to advance an issue it hoped would work to its advantage in the coming congressional elections.

While the 1990 Bush veto killed the bill for that session, the issue remained for the fall congressional campaign, the next Congress and the 1992 election. In a national public opinion survey taken in June 1990, 74 percent favored a law guaranteeing up to 12 weeks of unpaid parental leave.[44] One columnist predicted that the 1990 veto of FMLA, veto number 13 for Bush, would turn out to be unlucky for the President.[45] Although hardly decisive, the issue did contribute to the defeat of President Bush in 1992.

In 1991, Senator Christopher Dodd, the prime Senate sponsor, negotiated an additional compromise with Republican Senators Bond of Missouri and Coates of Indiana, who wanted to be responsive to business and also support pro-family legislation. This version added a provision allowing employers to deny reinstatement to their highest paid employees, if necessary to avoid "substantial and grievous economic injury to the operations of the employer" (Public Law 103-3). The bill passed both the House and the Senate in the fall of 1991, but no conference committee met until August 1992.

During the summer and fall of 1992, then Senator and Vice Presidential candidate, Al Gore, spoke movingly "of how fortunate he had been to take time off from work when his young son lay critically ill in the hospital after he was hit by a car."[46] The Senate passed the conference committee bill by unanimous consent on August 11 and the House followed suit by a vote of 241 to 161 on September 10,

1992. Advocating a new proposal to grant a tax credit to small and mid-sized companies who voluntarily granted family leave, President Bush sided with opponents who would not accept any form of mandatory leave. His veto was overridden in the Senate 68 to 31, but the House failed to attain the two-thirds vote necessary, voting 258 to 169.

The new Congress in 1993 moved quickly through the reconsideration of FMLA with hearings in January highlighting administration support and House and Senate passage early in February. On the final vote, FMLA was supported by 224 Democrats and 40 Republicans with 29 Democrats and 134 Republicans opposed. Although an amendment, negotiated with the Clinton administration, was added in the Senate calling for a full review of policy on homosexuals in the military, FMLA became President Clinton's first legislative victory. At the signing ceremony, he declared that "America's families . . . have beaten the gridlock in Washington to pass family leave."

IMPLEMENTATION OF FMLA

Despite President Bush's vetoes, the concept of family leave entered the agenda of the state governments during the years it was debated in Washington. Eighteen states, Puerto Rico, and the District of Columbia have some form of job protection for at least some workers who need family leave. A few of these measures are more generous than the FMLA; the others are the same or less comprehensive. Laws in ten states provide only maternity leave, but the newer statutes tend to be gender neutral.[47]

Experience with family and medical leave laws at the state level provided information on actual costs and benefits that was used to argue for the national approach. When finally enacted, FMLA did not supersede any provision of state law or local ordinances that provided more generous family or medical leave rights. If a state law provides for sixteen weeks of leave every two years, an eligible worker could, if family circumstances dictated, take sixteen weeks of leave one year under state law and twelve weeks the next year under FMLA. Corporations with worksites in more than one state would have preferred one federal requirement, but after the long delay in enactment, Congress refused to override benefits granted in the meantime by state legislatures. Some employers are therefore faced with both state and national standards to reconcile with guidance from the rules and regulations issued by the Department of Labor.

In the first year of implementation, the Labor Department received more than 125,000 requests for information about FMLA from employers and employees. Of the 3833 complaints it received during the first two years, over 90 percent were resolved quickly, often with just a phone call. In about 60 percent of the cases the employer was violating the act and in about 30 percent the employer was not violating the act. Less than 200 cases were pending at the end of the second year, and the department had filed eight lawsuits against employers by March 1996.[48]

Private lawsuits were also filed and they led to one definitive appellant ruling in 1995. The interim regulations issued by the Department of Labor included a section on employee notification when leave is unforeseeable that was ambiguous about whether the employee had to specifically mention the FMLA to be protected by it. Given the U.S. Chamber of Commerce's concern during Congressional passage about FMLA being a "yuppie" benefit, it is ironic that an employer pressed the courts to limit the benefits of FMLA to those who could articulate them. June Manuel, an employee of Westlake Polymers Corporation, lost her initial case, but won her job back in a Federal Appeals Court decision that quoted a floor statement by Congresswoman Roukema (R-NJ), a CCWI member and a key supporter of FMLA (*Manuel v. Westlake Polymers,* 66 Federal Reporter, at 762). The requirement for employer notification was clarified in the final Labor Department regulations to protect workers who are eligible for FMLA coverage, even if they are not aware of the law.

Advocates for women, such as the Women's Legal Defense Fund, have urged that the Labor Department take steps to publicize FMLA more widely and that Congress expand its reach to more workers and seek a means of partial wage replacement. The U.S. Chamber of Commerce continues to oppose employer mandates. It argues that "the FMLA does not expand the range of benefits available to employees; it simply locks one benefit into the package, thereby reducing the ability of employees to negotiate for other benefits they need more."[49]

Although some members of the House and Senate sought to represent business interests, the U.S. Chamber of Commerce and other employer interest groups were never part of the process of negotiating the provisions of the FMLA. As long as President Bush guaranteed a veto, they had nothing to fear and declined to participate in the talks that resulted in various compromise provisions. Once Clinton was elected and anxious to sign the FMLA, it was too late to expect supporters to listen to their concerns about specific provisions. "There were lots and lots of things they could have raised," reflected Donna Lenhoff of the Women's Legal Defense Fund, but by maintaining their adamant opposition they lost the opportunity to shape the final statute.[50]

Interest groups on both sides submitted comments to the Labor Department on implementation. Now the courts are deciding what terms such as "serious health condition" will mean in individual circumstances within the context of the regulations, the statute, and its legislative history. There have been no Supreme Court decisions and nothing definitive at the appellant level either. Trial court decisions indicate that working parents will be protected under FMLA, if they are needed to care for a child who is sick enough to meet the guidelines set in the regulations.

Congressional hearings focused on newborns and children with cancer, but the statute was inevitably ambiguous and the regulations are more inclusive. As long as the ill or injured child is under medical care and unable to participate in normal activities for more than three days (or would be without medical treatment), job protection will likely be available, even if paid sick leave is not. As the women's interest groups hoped, the FMLA represents a concrete accomplishment of the feminist movement for working families, especially to the extent common ill-nesses are covered.

Fear of a controversy about abortion that would have killed the bill kept advocates from seeking more explicit language on serious health conditions during congressional consideration.[51] Employer advocates did not discuss or defend absentee policies, which set specific standards for attendance *regardless* of medical excuses. While sick leave can be abused and employers do need a dependable workforce, requiring 98 percent attendance results in the termination of people facing real family hardship. It is these policies that have been the primary cause of litigation (see *Seidle v. Provident Mutual Life,* 871 Fed. Supp. 238, and *Brannon v. Oshkosh B'Gosh, Inc.,* 897 Fed. Supp. 1028).

FMLA was presented as a means to assure that employees faced with a family crisis would be able to keep their jobs and avoid welfare and Medicaid. Employer advocates never discussed or defended no-excuse attendance policies that allow workers with serious health conditions to be fired and become the taxpayers' responsibility. The FMLA does not require that employers allow workers to take paid sick leave to care for family members, because the primary focus was on job security and maintaining health care benefits. Issues of pay during leave were avoided deliberately as dictated by pragmatic politics.

CONCLUSION

Whether or not one hails FMLA as a first step toward creating a new national business culture that is friendly to families, its passage illustrated the role of the Caucus for Women's Issues in developing legislation, building a bipartisan coalition across committee jurisdictions, and coordinating the efforts of outside advocacy groups. Having leaned heavily on CCWI staff in the early stages, committee and personal staffs gradually took over staff responsibilities once the bill was launched. The CCWI presence was continued through its information services and represented by its members, especially the congresswomen and their legislative assistants for women's issues. Then director Lesley Primmer, once a legislative assistant to Olympia Snowe (R-ME), observed "moving legislation is done by personal and committee staff primarily, with the caucus serving in an intermediate role."[52]

The CCWI symbolizes what has been called the "second stage" of the women's movement, because it is a partnership of congresswomen and congressmen.[53] Anne Radigan once explained their goal, as follows:

> To get across to the public at large that women's issues are everybody's issues. Women don't live in a vacuum, they don't exist alone, and they certainly don't exist in a "we against them" adversary relationship. Women are wives who are dependent, women are wives who are working, women are daughters who are going to school, women are elderly parents who are vulnerable. . . . This is a family sort of prerogative. . . . Women's issues affect everyone.[54]

Women's issues, such as FMLA, were a priority after the 1992 election, but after the 1994 election the very survival of the CCWI was in doubt. Despite the 1996 reelection of President Clinton, the Republicans remain in control of Congress. CCWI is, therefore, primarily in a defensive position. Although Representative Schroeder introduced a bill in 1996 to expand the FMLA, she had no power to organize committee hearings to promote it and retired from the House at the end of the session.

While CCWI did introduce new Women's Health Equity and Economic Equity packages in 1996, it decided, under the new leadership of Nancy Johnson (R-CT) and Eleanor Holmes Norton (D-DC delegate), against introducing omnibus bills in the 105th Congress (1997–1998). At the end of 1997, CCWI numbered 50 congresswomen, 37 Democrats and 13 Republicans, and had adapted to working within a Republican-dominated environment by establishing bipartisan teams of congresswomen to protect their concerns within the committees.[55] In 1997, the caucus began to sponsor its own hearings on issues such as early childhood education and women business owners, but it no longer endorses legislation. With Republicans in control of the committee structure and CCWI divided from its support staff at WPI, the caucus cannot perform the role it did for the FMLA. As long as the Republican majority lasts, the early years of the 1990s will be the pinnacle of influence for the Congressional Caucus for Women's Issues.[56]

NOTES

1. Liberia Johnson, Joint Hearing on Disability and Parental Leave, 2261 Rayburn House Office Building, October 17, 1985, tape recorded by the author. Subsequent quotations from testimony at the same hearing will not be footnoted.

2. Anonymous staff interview with the author for a case study of pension reform legislation, Washington, DC, July 19, 1984.

3. Irwin N. Gertzog, *Congressional Women: Their Recruitment, Integration, and Behavior,* 2nd ed. (Westport, CT: Praeger Publishers, 1995), pp. 89–97.

4. *Ibid.,* p. 89.

5. *Ibid.,* p. 197.

6. Susan Webb Hammond, "Congressional Caucuses in the 104th Congress," in *Congress Reconsidered,* 6th ed., eds. Lawrence C. Dodd and Bruce I. Oppenheimer (Washington, DC: C.Q. Press, 1997), pp. 275–6, and Roger H. Davidson and Walter Oleszek, *Congress and Its Members,* 6th ed. (Washington, DC: C.Q. Press, 1998), pp. 340–2.

7. Joan Hulse Thompson, "Role Perceptions of Women in the Ninety-fourth Congress," *Political Science Quarterly,* 95 (Spring 1980), p. 73.

8. After the Republican takeover of the House, the Caucus faced a similar dilemma and, by 1997, had cho-

sen to seek more Republican congresswomen as members. Therefore, it focused on amendments and committee work, rather than promoting major legislative initiatives in the 105th Congress. The new CCWI is analogous to the Executive Committee of the old CCWI with the congressional subscribers to the WPI corresponding to the coed membership of the old CCWI.

9. Marge Roukema (R-NJ), a supporter of the FMLA since 1987, joined CCWI in mid-1993. There were 55 women in the 103rd Congress, 48 in the House and 7 in the Senate. In the House, 42 women belonged to the Caucus Executive Committee and 3 women senators were among the 10 senators who subscribed to the CCWI newsletter. There were 35 Democrats and 7 Republicans on the Executive Committee in 1994. After CCWI was defunded by the new Republican leadership, only one new Republican woman choose to join CCWI. Most of the Republican women who are coming to Congress now were recruited by Speaker Gingrich and are not feminists. CCWI had to change its approach to attract more Republicans.

10. Pat Schroeder was expected to become chair of the Education and Labor Committee in the 104th Congress. Since the Republicans won control of the House, she was ranking minority member rather than chair. Instead CCWI member Jan Meyers (R-KS) of the Small

Business Committee became the first woman to chair a House committee in twenty years. In the Senate, Republican Nancy Kassebaum, also of Kansas, took over as chair of the Labor and Human Resources Committee as a result of her party's victory. Both Meyers and Kassebaum voted no on final passage of the FMLA. All three women retired from Congress before the 1996 election.

11. After the 1994 elections, the diminished number of House Democrats reelected Barbara Kennelly (CT) over fellow CCWI member Louise Slaughter (NY) to the party post of Democratic Caucus Vice Chairman by a vote of 93 to 90. The Minority Leader, Minority Whip, and Caucus Chair are the three highest ranking minority party leadership positions. Jennifer Dunn (WA) is Republican Conference (caucus) Vice Chairman.

12. The most powerful committees were: Appropriations, Budget, Ways and Means, Rules, and Energy and Commerce. See Lawrence C. Dodd and Bruce I. Oppenheimer, "Consolidating Power in the House: The Rise of a New Oligarchy," in *Congress Reconsidered,* 4th ed., (Washington, DC: C.Q. Press, 1989) pp. 48–50.

13. Gertzog, *Congressional Women,* 1st ed., 1984, p. 202.

14. Joan Hulse Thompson, "The Women's Rights Lobby in the Gender Gap Congress, 1983–84," *Commonwealth,* 2 (1988), pp. 19–35. The other side of the gender gap, higher support among men for Republican candidates, played a major role in Democratic defeats in 1994. Richard L. Berke, "Defections Among Men to G.O.P. Helped Insure Rout of Democrats," *New York Times,* November 11, 1994, sec A, p. 1.

15. Anonymous staff interview with author, October 1985.

16. Anne L. Radigan, *Concept and Compromise: The Evolution of Family Leave Legislation in the U.S. Congress* (Washington, DC: Women's Research and Educational Institute, 1988), p. 12.

17. In the 105th Congress, abortion rights is still a priority for many, primarily Democratic, congresswomen, but efforts to attract Republican congresswomen required that it cease to be a priority for the CCWI.

18. Radigan, *Concept and Compromise,* p. 8.

19. Macon Morehouse, "Parental, Medical Leave Bill Gets Markup in Senate," *Congressional Quarterly Weekly Report,* 47 (April 22, 1989), p. 892.

20. Morehouse, "Markup in Senate," p. 892.

21. Christine A. Russell, Director of the Small Business Center, U.S. Chamber of Commerce, "America's Small Businesses Cannot Afford Mandated Leave," public information release, no date, pp. 1–2 (obtained from its author, 1/90).

22. *Ibid.*

23. Brian Nutting, "Parental-Leave Bill Passed by Panel," *Congressional Quarterly,* 47 (March 11, 1989), 519.

24. Radigan, *Concept and Compromise,* p. 2.

25. Russell, "America's Small Businesses . . .," p. 2. One precedent does exist. The Veterans' Reemployment Rights Act (1940) mandates up to four years of leave with job security for workers called to active military duty.

26. Morehouse, "Markup in Senate," p. 892.

27. Anne Radigan, Executive Director, Congressional Caucus for Women's Issues, personal interview with author, Washington, DC, October 18, 1985.

28. Radigan, *Concept and Compromise,* p. 15. Indeed, Ms. Radigan notes that some of the reporters had a special interest in the story, because they were dissatisfied with the parental leave policies of their own employers.

29. Nutting, "Passed by Panel," p. 519.

30. "Family and Medical Leave Act of 1987 Introduced," *Update,* (former newsletter of the CCWI) February 27, 1987, p. 13.

31. The Republicans changed the name of the committee; in the 105th Congress it was Education and the Workforce. Clay was ranking minority member.

32. Radigan, *Concept and Compromise,* p. 16.

33. "Family and Medical Leave Hearings in D.C. and on West Coast," *Update,* August 7, 1987, np.

34. "Capitol Boxscore," *Congressional Quarterly,* 47 (February 4, 1989), p. 243.

35. Roberta Spalter, Heidi Hartmann, and Sheila Gibbs, *Unnecessary Losses: Costs to Workers in the States of the Lack of Family and Medical Leave* (Washington, DC: Institute for Women's Policy Research, 1989), p. 3.

36. Marian Wright Edelman, *Families in Peril: An Agenda for Social Change* (Cambridge: Harvard University Press, 1987).

37. "Family Leave Waits for Clinton," *Congressional Quarterly Almanac,* (1992), p. 355.

38. Alissa Rubin, "Demise of Health Care Overhaul Produced Big Winners and Losers," *Congressional Quarterly,* 52 (October 1, 1994), p. 2799.

39. Alissa Rubin, "Overhaul Issue Unlikely to Rest in Peace," *Congressional Quarterly,* 52 (October 1, 1994), p. 2800.

40. Despite Republican congressional dominance, proposals for regulation of one segment of the health care industry, health maintenance organizations, returned to the political agenda in 1996. As with FMLA, advocates focused on the needs of mothers and newborns and Congress responded with a rule setting minimum hospital stays after childbirth. Further regulation seems likely.

41. "Democrats Stymied on Parental-Leave Bill," *Congressional Quarterly Almanac,* 1988, p. 263.

42. "Parental-Leave Bill Moves Forward," *Congressional Quarterly,* 47 (April 15, 1989), p. 815.

43. Alyson Pytte, "House Passes Parental Leave; White House Promises Veto," *Congressional Quarterly,* 48 (May 12, 1990), p. 1471.

44. A Louis Harris Associates poll of 1254 with a margin of error of plus or minus 3%. The other results were: opposed to such a law 24% and 2% unsure. Cited in *New York Times,* July 26, 1990.

45. Ellen Goodman, "Ambushing Bush on Family Leave," *Philadelphia Inquirer,* August 1, 1990, sec. A, p. 9.

46. "Clinton Signs Family Leave Act," *Congressional Quarterly Almanac* (1993), p. 389.

47. Donna Lenhoff and Sharon Stoneback, "Review of State Legislation Guaranteeing Jobs for Family or Medical Leaves," Women's Legal Defense Fund, August 1989, pp. 5–6; *New York Times,* July 27, 1990, p. A8; and "Family and Medical Leave Legislation in the States," Women's Legal Defense Fund, June 1991.

48. Commission on Family and Medical Leave, "A Workable Balance: Report to Congress on Family and Medical Leaves," April 1996, p. 85.

49. "Comments of The United States Chamber of Commerce Regarding the Interim Regulations Implementing the Family and Medical Leave Act of 1993," provided by Nancy Reed Fulco, Human Resources Attorney, U.S. Chamber of Commerce.

50. Donna Lenhoff, General Counsel, Women's Legal Defense Fund, August 12, 1997, telephone interview.

51. As a practical matter, it is very difficult to define serious illness. Even terminally ill patients may not be bedridden and advocates were very reluctant to create a definite list of covered conditions that would inevitably be incomplete.

52. Primmer interview, July 28, 1989.

53. Betty Friedan, *The Second Stage* (New York: Summit, 1981), pp. 250–55.

54. Radigan interview, October 18, 1985.

55. The 14 Legislative Teams are: Expanding the Violence Against Women Act, Preventive Health Services for Women, Educational Child Care and School Readiness, Job Training and Vocational Education, Title IX Anniversary Activities, Health Care Insurance Reform, Juvenile Justice, Women in the Military, Pensions and Retirement Benefits, Teen Pregnancy, Higher Education Act, Women-Owned Businesses, HIV/AIDS, and International Women's Rights.

56. In October 1997, the CCWI celebrated its twentieth anniversary with a gala attended by President Clinton and Secretary of State Madeleine Albright. Ten of the fifteen founding members were present as well as former co-chairs Patricia Schroeder and Senator Olympia Snowe.

FURTHER READINGS

Burrell, Barbara C. *A Woman's Place Is in the House: Campaigning for Congress in the Feminist Era.* Ann Arbor: University of Michigan Press, 1994.

Carroll, Susan J. *Women as Candidates in American Politics.* 2nd ed. Bloomington: Indiana University Press, 1994.

Conway, M. Margaret, David W. Ahern, and Gertrude A. Steuernagel. *Women and Public Policy: A Revolution in Progress.* Washington, DC: Congressional Quarterly, 1995.

Costain, Anne N. *Inviting Women's Rebellion: A Political Process Interpretation of the Women's Movement.* Baltimore: Johns Hopkins University Press, 1992.

Elving, Ronald D. *Conflict and Compromise: How Congress Makes the Law.* New York: Simon and Schuster, 1995.

Gelb, Joyce, and Marian Lief Palley. *Women and Public Policies.* 2nd ed. Princeton, NJ: Princeton University Press, 1987.

Gertzog, Irwin N. *Congressional Women: Their Recruitment, Treatment and Behavior.* 2nd ed. Westport, CT: Praeger, 1995.

Haas, Linda. *Equal Parenthood and Social Policy: A Study of Parental Leave in Sweden.* Albany: New York State University Press, 1992.

Klein, Ethel. *Gender Politics: From Consciousness to Mass Politics.* Cambridge, MA: Harvard University Press, 1984.

Margolies-Mezvinsky, Marjorie. *A Woman's Place: The Freshmen Women Who Changed the Face of Congress.* Southbridge, MA: Crown, 1994.

Mezey, Susan Gluck. *In Pursuit of Equality: Women, Public Policy, and the Federal Courts.* New York: St. Martin's Press, 1992.

Norris, Pippa. (Ed.), *Women, Media and Politics.* New York: Oxford University Press, 1997.

Stetson, Dorothy McBride. *Women's Rights in the U.S.A.: Policy Debates and Gender Roles.* Pacific Grove, CA: Brooks/Cole, 1991.

Thomas, Sue. *How Women Legislate.* New York: Oxford University Press, 1994.

Women's Research and Education Institute. *The American Woman: A Status Report.* New York: Norton, 1986, 1988, 1990, 1992, 1994, 1996.

Sex at Risk in Insurance Classifications? The Supreme Court as Shaper of Public Policy

RUTH BAMBERGER

Since the onset of the women's movement in the late 1960s, the private insurance industry has been confronted by civil rights groups, particularly feminist organizations, and government agencies over the treatment of insurance consumers whose risk potential is determined in part by sex classification. Numerous studies by congressional committees, state insurance commissions, and feminist ad hoc groups revealed practices whereby women in the same occupation, age, and health categories as men were subjected to demeaning underwriting criteria, denied equal access to coverage and benefits, particularly in health and disability insurance, and charged higher prices. Sex-based prices also appeared to affect men adversely, particularly in life and in auto insurance (for young men), with higher prices charged than for women.

As a result of political pressures, almost half of the fifty states have adopted insurance regulations nominally prohibiting differential treatment in coverage and benefits of men and women.[1] But sex is still widely used as a classification in setting prices for individual health, life, disability, auto, and retirement insurance. Only one state, Montana, prohibits by law the use of the sex classification for any purpose, including pricing.[2] Five other states ban the sex classification only in auto insurance, where it is seen to disadvantage men.[3] Selective prohibition of sex discrimination and inattention to the disparate economic impact of sex-divided pricing on women by the insurance industry are presently legally defensible in the absence of a constitutional presumption that sex classification violates women's right to equal protection of the law.

The insurance industry's reluctance to forego the sex classification is a direct consequence of insurance marketing methods that use classification to exclude some customers and price-compete for others. Actuarial tables demonstrate that women and men have different morbidity and mortality experience, though some studies conclude otherwise.[4] The sex classification, selectively used, promotes the impression that classifications are impelled by costs, not selling strategies. Most companies charge women higher prices for health, disability, and retirement plans, while men pay higher prices for life insurance and young men pay more for auto insurance. These price differences originated as sales discounts and continue to serve that function. In auto insurance, for example, women's discounts cease around age 25, although men at every age average more accidents than women, because their average annual mileage is higher than women's.

CRITIQUE OF INSURERS' USE OF THE SEX CLASSIFICATION

Criticisms of the insurance industry's use of the sex classification are numerous. The most basic is its acceptance of sex as an *a priori* differential. Simply stated, sex is used to justify using sex. What actuarial data tell us, then, is something about the average woman or man, but applications of these averages to individuals grossly distort the reality, with unequal treatment the result.[5] Stated another way, emphasis on the sex classification allows other meaningful risk factors to be overlooked.

Critics also argue that continued use of the sex classification perpetuates traditional stereotypes of men and women. For example, underwriting manuals well into the 1970s labeled women as ". . . malingerers, marginal employees working mainly for convenience, and delicately balanced machines eagerly awaiting a breakdown. . . . If a woman has disability coverage, the temptation exists to replace her earnings with an insurance income once work loses its attractiveness."[6]

Finally, insurers should not use a classification scheme over which the insured have no control. Sex, like race, is an immutable characteristic, and therefore, should not be used as a basis for determining costs and coverage of insurance policies. Critics document insurance practices prior to the civil rights movement where race was casually employed as a classification. More important for insurers, the practice was actuarially justified because blacks have higher morbidity and mortality rates. However, race, because it was recognized as a repugnant classification placing a badge of inferiority on blacks, ceased to be used as a classification. The same constraint should apply to the sex classification, critics argue, though in some respects, racial discrimination has been more invidious than sex discrimination.[7]

FEDERAL COURTS AND SEX DISCRIMINATION IN INSURANCE

Even though the campaign to eliminate sex discrimination in insurance has been waged largely at the state level, where the insurance industry is regulated, a major vehicle for challenging industry practice has been the federal courts via Title VII of the Civil Rights Act of 1964. The law states that it is an unlawful employment practice for an employer ". . . to fail or refuse to hire or to discharge any individual, or otherwise to discriminate against any individual with respect to compensation, terms, conditions, or privileges of employment, because of such individual's race, color, religion, sex, or national origin. . . ."[8] The Equal Employment Opportunity Act of 1972 broadened Title VII to include in the definition of employer government agencies at the state and local levels.

Since many companies and government agencies provide compensation by way of insurance benefits to their employees (over 80 percent of all Americans are enrolled in employer-sponsored health, disability, and pension plans), sex-based insurance plans became a viable target for calling into question the common practice of classification by sex. Civil rights and feminist groups surmised that if the federal courts would strike down sex-based employer plans that affected large numbers of people, this would have a spillover effect on the insurance industry. A careful examination of Supreme Court opinions in key cases provides clues about the direction of public policy in the controversy over the sex classification in insurance.

WOMEN AND THE SEX CLASSIFICATION IN DISABILITY AND RETIREMENT INSURANCE

Beginning with the 1970s, the Supreme Court decided several cases that have played a major role in defining the parameters of sex classification schemes in disability and retirement insurance. The disability cases, *Geduldig v. Aiello* (1974) and *General Electric v. Gilbert* (1976), raised the question of whether employer sponsored disability plans excluding pregnancy constituted unlawful sex discrimination.[9] In both cases, the majority of the Court upheld the plans, arguing that the pregnancy exclusion was not a sex-based classification, but a classification of "pregnant . . . and non-pregnant persons."[10]

Geduldig and *Gilbert* demonstrated the unwillingness of the Court to undo established insurance practice. The insurance industry has never considered normal pregnancy a disability; moreover, it argued in *Gilbert* that if pregnancy were included in an employee group plan, it would significantly drive up employers' costs.[11] Public reaction after the *Gilbert* decision was so great that in 1978 Congress passed the Pregnancy Discrimination Act as an amendment to Title VII, requiring employers with disability plans to include pregnancy benefits.[12]

In 1978, the Supreme Court considered the validity of a sex differential in an employee retirement plan in *Los Angeles Department of Water and Power v. Manhart*.[13] The case involved a pension program of the LA Department whereby women made larger contributions from their salaries to the pension fund than men, on the basis that women as a class live longer than men. The Department had calculated, from a study of mortality tables and its own employee experience, that women should contribute 14.84% more per monthly pay check than men, since they would draw more monthly payments from the fund over their average life span. The Court struck down the plan on a 6–2 vote. The central argument of the majority opinion, written by Justice Stevens, was that Title VII specifically prohibits discrimination against any *individual* on the basis of sex, and therefore it is illegal to treat one gender group differently from the other.

Although it appears that Stevens was attacking the common insurance practice of classifying by sex, he tempered the majority opinion by stating that Title VII was not intended to "revolutionize" the insurance industry:

> All that is at issue today is a requirement that men and women make unequal contributions to an employer-sponsored pension fund. Nothing in our holding implies that it would be unlawful for an employer to set aside equal retirement contributions for each employee and let each retiree purchase the largest benefit which his or her accumulated contributions could command in the open market. Nor does it call into question the insurance industry practice of considering the composition of an employer's work force in determining the probable cost of a retirement or death benefit plan.[14]

In 1983, the Supreme Court reaffirmed *Manhart* in *Arizona Governing Committee v. Norris,* though by a narrower margin, 5–4.[15] The state of Arizona's retirement plan differed from the Los Angeles plan, in that employee contributions were not determined by sex, but upon retirement, women's monthly payments were lower because of their longer life expectancy. The plan provided employees three options at retirement—a lump sum benefit, a fixed monthly payment over a fixed number of years, or a lifetime annuity. Women's benefits under the first two options were the same as men's, but the lifetime annuity option gave women a smaller monthly payment than men. The litigant in the case, Natalie Norris, in opting for the lifetime annuity, would be paid $320 per month at age 65, while a man in an identical situation would collect $354 a month.

Justice Marshall, who wrote the majority opinion, reaffirmed the Court's position in *Manhart:* "We have no hesitation in holding, . . . that the classification of employees on the basis of sex is no more permissible at the payout stage of a retirement plan than at the pay-in stage."[16]

In defending the retirement plan, the state of Arizona contended that Title VII was not applicable in its case, since retirement options were being offered through a third party (an insurance company) whose policies were comparable to what was available in the open market. The Court rebutted this argument by noting that when the state entered into such an agreement, it was the responsible agent for employee pension plans, and hence subject to Title VII requirements.

It should be noted that Justice Powell, who voted with the majority in *Manhart,* was on the minority side in *Norris,* precisely because the Arizona plan was provided by a third party insurer. He argued that striking down such a plan, where the insurer used actuarially sound sex-based mortality tables, amounted to revolutionizing the insurance and pension industries, which *Manhart* went out of its way to avoid.[17]

MEN AND THE SEX CLASSIFICATION IN RETIREMENT INSURANCE

The Supreme Court decisions in *Manhart* and *Norris* ended discriminatory treatment for women in a prospective manner, but they did not get retroactive relief of any kind, and the Court grandfathered into the future unequal payments to women already retired. Two years before the *Manhart* decision, however, the Supreme Court was more generous with men in the settlement of a dispute over a retirement plan for state employees of Connecticut. The case, *Fitzpatrick v. Bitzer* (1976), was brought by current and retired men employees of the state on the allegation that the statutory retirement plan discriminated against them on the basis of their sex.[18] The Connecticut plan allowed women employees with over twenty-five years of service to the state to retire at age fifty with full retirement benefits, while men were not eligible until age fifty-five. Reduced retirement benefits were also available to employees who left state employment before they were eligible to retire. The plan adversely affected men, who, if they left at age fifty-five, would receive less than a woman of similar age, who could already be drawing full benefits after age fifty. The Court not only struck down the retirement plan on Title VII grounds, but concluded that all retirees and their survivors were entitled, under protection of the Fourteenth Amendment, to retroactive payments dating back to the adoption of the pension program in 1939.

Surprisingly, the Supreme Court did not cite the *Fitzpatrick* decision in either *Manhart* or *Norris.* All three cases involved violations of Title VII of the Civil Rights Act of 1964, as amended in 1972. The awarding of back pay to men employees in the *Fitzpatrick* decision was rendered on Fourteenth Amendment grounds, namely, that Congress could require states to correct sex discrimination practices, even if the costs were significant.[19]

FITZPATRICK, MANHART, NORRIS AND THEIR AFTERMATH

The Supreme Court's decisions on sex discrimination in group retirement plans have had a wide impact on employer-sponsored pension plans. The TIAA-CREF retirement plan for college teachers is a case in point. The system of unequal payments to men and women retirees had been in the federal court pipeline for several years prior to *Norris* in 1983. On the same day that the Supreme Court handed down its decision in *Norris,* it remanded to the appellate courts two cases challenging the TIAA-CREF plan.[20] As a result, all TIAA-CREF participants now receive unisex benefits on annuity income payments made after May 1, 1980.[21]

On the question of retroactive payments to employees, the Supreme Court, on a 9–0 vote, granted relief to all men retirees and their survivors in *Fitzpatrick,* but was less kindly disposed to women retirees in *Manhart* and *Norris.* In *Manhart,* seven justices argued against retroactive pay. Justice Stevens, speaking for the majority, alluded to a precedent in *Albemarle Paper Co. v. Moody,* where the Court established generous guidelines for awarding back pay for violations of Title VII, but that it was not to be given automatically in every case.[22] Granting retroactivity in a case like *Manhart* would not be practical, according to Stevens, as pension plans could be jeopardized by drastic changes in the rules.[23] It was enough of a blow to employers to adapt to the Court's decision requiring equal contributions from men and women.

In *Norris,* the number of justices arguing against retroactive payments was reduced to five, while four supported some kind of retroactive relief. Justice O'Connor, whose vote was crucial in the 5–4 vote striking down the Arizona plan, did not go along with the four justices who thought that relief should apply to all benefit payments made after the federal district court's judgment in *Norris.* O'Connor maintained, as did Stevens in *Manhart,* that the magnitude of a decision awarding retroactive relief would have the effect of disrupting current pension plans.[24] In contrast, retroactive relief for men employees in *Fitzpatrick* was awarded. The Supreme Court granted men equal protection of the law in *Fitzpatrick,* but denied this protection to women in *Manhart* and *Norris.*

PROSPECTS FOR ELIMINATION OF THE SEX CLASSIFICATION IN INSURANCE

One immediate consequence of the *Manhart* and *Norris* decisions was the introduction of bills in Congress in the late 1970s and early 1980s to prohibit insurance companies nationwide from using the sex classification in determining coverage, benefits, and prices. Known as the Non-Discrimination in Insurance Act in the House and the Fair Insurance Practices Act in the Senate,[25] the bills were introduced under Congress's prerogative in the McCarran-Ferguson Act[26] and its authority to regulate interstate commerce and to legislate in matters of civil rights. While the legislation received wide support from women's groups and organizations such as the American Association of University Professors, the American Association of Retired Persons, and the Leadership Conference on Civil Rights, the insurance industry waged an expensive lobby campaign to kill the legislation and was successful.[27]

Thus far, most state Equal Rights Amendments and equal protection provisions have failed to protect women against sex discrimination in insurance. The insurance industry continues to use sex as a price classification, despite the numerous efforts of women's organizations to reverse public policy.[28]

THE SUPREME COURT AND PROSPECTS FOR ELIMINATING THE SEX CLASSIFICATION IN INSURANCE

It would be an overstatement to say that the Supreme Court has been the primary mover and shaker in shaping public policy on sex discrimination in the insurance industry. But one could cogently argue that in the American constellation of political decision makers, it has been a strategic actor. The Court's decisions in *Fitzpatrick, Manhart,* and *Norris* served notice to the insurance industry that sex discrimination in insurance merits heightened scrutiny. But the Court has also made it clear that it will not definitively reject sex discrimination.

Women's rights and civil rights organizations must look beyond the judiciary to eliminate the practice of insurance sex discrimination. One possible avenue is a reintroduced federal Equal Rights Amendment that incorporates a legislative history clearly articulating that the scope of equal rights for women and men extends to insurance practices. Sex, just like race, would be excluded as a price classification in insurance, because it would be unconstitutional. Only when gendered human beings have constitutional protection under an ERA will the Supreme Court, as guardian of the Constitution, speak out clearly against sex discrimination in insurance.

NOTES

1. Primary regulation of the insurance industry rests with the fifty states. This arrangement dates back to the mid-nineteenth century, when individual states legislated regulatory agencies to oversee the growing business of insurance. The McCarran-Ferguson Act, passed by Congress in 1945, reaffirmed state regulation, though not exclusively. Congress reserved for itself the authority to enact insurance legislation under the following clause in McCarran: "No Act of Congress shall be construed to invalidate, impair, or supersede any law enacted by any State for the purpose of regulating the business of insurance . . . unless such Act specifically relates to the business of insurance." 15 U.S.C. 1012 (b) (1982).

2. Montana Code Ann. 49-2-309 (1983).

3. Hawaii, Massachusetts, Michigan, North Carolina, Pennsylvania. For pathbreaking work on automobile insurance sex discrimination, see Patrick Butler, Twiss Butler, and Laurie Williams, "Sex-Divided Mileage, Accident, and Insurance Cost Data Show That Auto Insurers Overcharge Most Women," *Journal of Insurance Regulation.*, 6, 243–284 (Part I), 373–420 (Part II), 1988.

4. See U.S., Congress, Joint Economic Committee, *Hearings, Economic Problems of Women,* 93rd Cong., 1st Sess., 1973, pp. 151–220; "The Weaker Sex," *Life Notes,* National Association of Life Underwriters, April, 1974; California Commission on the Status of Women, *Women and Insurance,* 1975.

5. An excellent example is the sex differential used in dental and vision care insurance. No medical explanations are available to verify differences in men and women. Yet the insurance industry uses the sex classification anyway, and indeed has established such a differential, with the result that women pay higher rates. Robert Randall, "Risk Classification and Actuarial Tables as They Affect Insurance Pricing for Women and Minorities," in *Discrimination Against Minorities and Women in Pensions and Health, Life, and Disability Insurance.* Vol. I. U.S. Commission on Civil Rights, 1978, pp. 568, 576.
To further illustrate, studies of mortality differences by sex show a considerable overlap between men and women with respect to the age at which death occurs. For over 80 percent of males, one can find a matching female who died at approximately the same time. Sex is not a reliable predictor of mortality, so it would be misleading even to talk about an average man or average woman. For references to the debate over overlapping death rates of men and women, see Spencer Kimball, "Reverse Sex Discrimination: *Manhart,*" 83 *Amer. Bar Foun. Res. Jour.* 120–23 (1979), and Lea Brilmayer et al., "Sex Discrimination in Employer-Sponsored Insurance Plans: A Legal and Demographic Analysis," *University of Chicago Law Review,* 47, 530–31 (1980).

6. Quoted in Suzanne Stoiber, "Insured: Except in Case of War, Suicide, and Organs Peculiar to Females," *Ms.* (June 1973), 114.

7. Anne C. Cicero, "Strategies for the Elimination of Sex Discrimination in Insurance," 20 *Harv. Civ. Rts.-Civ. Lib. L. Rev.* 211 (1985); Brilmayer et al., "Sex Discrimination," 526–29; Jill Gaulding, "Race, Sex, and Genetic Discrimination in Insurance: What's Fair?" 80 *Cornell Law Review* 1682 (1995).

8. 42 U.S.C. 2000e-2(a) (1).

9. *Geduldig v. Aiello,* 417 U.S. 484 (1974). This case, challenging a California state disability plan, was argued on 14th Amendment equal protection grounds. With the exception of *Fitzpatrick v. Bitzer,* 427 U.S. 445 (1976), *infra* 17, which was argued on both Title VII and 14th Amendment grounds, other federal court cases referred to in this study were argued on Title VII grounds only; *General Electric v. Gilbert,* 429 U.S. 125 (1976).

10. 417 U.S. at 496–97 n.20.

11. 429 U.S. at 131.

12. Pregnancy Discrimination Act as codified at 42 U.S.C. 2000e (k) (1982).

13. *Los Angeles Department of Water and Power v. Manhart,* 435 U.S. 702 (1978).

14. *Ibid.,* at 717–18.

15. *Arizona Governing Committee v. Norris,* 463 U.S. 1073 (1983).

16. *Ibid.,* at 1081.

17. *Ibid.,* at 1099.

18. *Fitzpatrick v. Bitzer,* 427 U.S. 445 (1976). The significance of the 1976 *Fitzpatrick* decision was first described by Ruth Weyand, who was a senior attorney with the federal Equal Employment Opportunity Commission. See the *14th National Conference on Women and the Law Sourcebook* at 303–304 for Weyand's list of Title VII pension cases that ended early retirement pay discrimination against men with back pay before the retirement pay discrimination against women was ended without back pay.

19. A U.S. District Court's opinion on attorney's fees stated that the *Fitzpatrick* settlement would eventually cost Connecticut almost $400 million over forty years. 445 F. Supp. 1338, 1343 (D. Conn., 1978).

20. *Teachers Insurance and Annuity Association v. Spirt* and *Long Island University v. Spirt,* 691 F. 2d 1054, 463 U.S. 1223 (1983); *Peters v. Wayne State University,* 691 F. 2d 235, 463 U.S. 1223 (1983).

21. For a complete summary of TIAA-CREF action after *Norris,* see *News from TIAA-CREF,* October 9, 1984.

22. *Albermarle Paper Co. v. Moody,* 422 U.S. 405 (1975).

23. 435 U.S. at 718–23.

24. 463 U.S. at 1109–11. Five years after *Norris,* the Supreme Court ruled that the state of Florida did not have to pay $43.6 million in retroactive payments to male state employees whose spouses shared in their pension plans prior to *Norris.* At dispute in this case was a plan where male employees with spouses were paid less than female employees with spouses, on the basis that female spouses lived longer than the male spouses of female employees. *Florida v. Hughlan Long,* 56 *U.S. Law Week,* 4718–25 (1988).

25. For the House version of this legislation, see *Non-Discrimination in Insurance Act of 1983: Hearings on H.R. 100 Before the Subcommittee on Commerce, Transportation, and Tourism of the Committee on Energy and Commerce,* 98th Cong., 1st Sess. 1–15 (1983). H.R. 100 was significantly weakened through the adoption of an amendment that would exempt sex discrimination in individual private insurance contracts. For the Senate version of this legislation, see *Fair Insurance Practices Act: Hearings on S. 372 Before the Committee on Commerce, Science, and Transportation,* 98th Cong., 1st Sess., 2–16 (1983).

26. *Supra,* 1.

27. The campaign cost the industry almost $2 million. A group called the Committee for Fair Insurance Rates was financed by 33 companies for the express purpose of "educating" the public about the adverse consequences of H.R. 100 and S. 372. Common Cause *NEWS,* Sept. 21, 1983; *National Underwriter* (Life and Health Edition), Oct. 1, 1983, p. 2.

28. The National Organization for Women maintains an office in Washington, DC committed to eliminating insurance sex discrimination. I am indebted to Dr. Patrick Butler, Director of the NOW Insurance Project, for current information about action at the federal and state levels on sex discrimination in insurance.

FURTHER READINGS

Abraham, Kenneth S. *Distributing Risk: Insurance, Legal Theory, and Public Policy.* New Haven, CT: Yale University Press, 1986.

Benston, George J. "The Economics of Gender Discrimination in Employee Fringe Benefits: *Manhart* Revisited." *University of Chicago Law Review,* 49 (1982), 489–542.

Benston, George J. "Discrimination and Economic Efficiency in Employee Fringe Benefits: A Clarification of Issues and a Response to Professors Brilmayer, Laycock, and Sullivan"; Brilmayer, Lea, Douglas Laycock, and Teresa Sullivan. "The Efficient Use of Group Averages as Nondiscrimination: A Rejoinder to Professor Benston." *University of Chicago Law Review,* 50 (1983), 222–279.

Brilmayer, Lea, Richard Hekeler, Douglas Laycock, and Teresa Sullivan. "Sex Discrimination in Employer-Sponsored Insurance Plans: A Legal and Demographic Analysis." *University of Chicago Law Review* 47 (1980), 505–560.

Butler, Patrick, Twiss Butler, & Laurie Williams. "Sex-Divided Mileage, Accident, and Insurance Cost Data Show That Auto Insurers Overcharge Most Women." *Journal of Insurance Regulation,* 6 (1988), 243–284, 373–420.

Cicero, Anne C. "Strategies for the Elimination of Sex Discrimination in Insurance." *Harvard Civil Rights-Civil Liberties Review,* 20 (1985), 211–267.

Comptroller General of the United States. *Economic Implications of the Fair Insurance Practices Act.* Report to Sen. Orrin G. Hatch et al., GAO/OCE-84-1, April 6, 1984.

Gaulding, Jill. "Race, Sex, and Genetic Discrimination in Insurance: What's Fair?" *Cornell Law Review,* 80 (1995), 1646–1694.

Jerry, Robert H. II. "Gender and Insurance." In Conway, M. Margaret et al., *Women and Public Policy.* Washington, DC: Congressional Quarterly Press, 1994, pp. 102–123.

Kimball, Spencer L. "Reverse Sex Discrimination: *Manhart.*" *American Bar Foundation Research Journal* (1979), 85–139.

U.S. Commission on Civil Rights. *Discrimination Against Women and Minorities in Pensions and Health, Life, and Disability Insurance.* Vol. I, 1978.

Affirmative Action and Women

ROBERTA ANN JOHNSON

Challenged from all sides, affirmative action, nevertheless, continues to live on as a highly charged issue. Debate about affirmative action has often been heated and emotional. It has generated discussions about "merit";[1] it has buried academics in Department of Labor statistics;[2] it has absorbed lawyers and historians in interpretation of congressional intent;[3] it has bogged down the public policy experts with implementation matters;[4] and it has stimulated hotly debated referenda.[5]

In what ways has a policy of affirmative action assisted women to become more fully integrated into schools, training programs, and jobs? We will explore that question by examining the history and future of affirmative action policy. This article will (1) define affirmative action, (2) detail the development of federal affirmative action guidelines, (3) describe Supreme Court decisions and congressional responses to affirmative action, (4) describe how the states and the lower courts have become battlegrounds on the issue of affirmative action, (5) consider the ways in which affirmative action is a woman's issue, and (6) consider the future of affirmative action.

AFFIRMATIVE ACTION DEFINED

Affirmative action is a generic term for programs that take some kind of initiative, either voluntarily or under the compulsion of law, to increase, maintain, or rearrange the number or status of certain group members, usually defined by race or gender, within a larger group. When these programs are characterized by race or gender preference, "especially when coupled with rigorously pursued 'goals,' [they] are highly controversial because race and gender are generally thought to be 'irrelevant' to employment and admissions decisions" and are "immutable characteristics over which individuals lack control."[6]

This is a revised version of an article that appeared in the *Journal of Political Science,* vol. 17, Nos. 1 and 2 (Spring 1989). Reprinted with permission.

The author would like to acknowledge Megan Andesha and Bethany Aseltine, students at the University of San Francisco, for their assistance.

AFFIRMATIVE ACTION AND FEDERAL GUIDELINES

Significant moves to prohibit discrimination in the public sector began in the late 1930s and early 1940s, according to David Rosenbloom, who describes a series of executive orders, starting with the Roosevelt administration, that called for a policy of nondiscrimination in employment.[7] However, it is President John F. Kennedy's executive order, issued March 16, 1961, that is usually seen as representing the real roots of present-day affirmative action policy.[8] Executive Order 10,925 required government contractors to take affirmative action and established specific sanctions for noncompliance.[9] Nevertheless, even the order's principal draftsperson admitted that the enforcement process led to a great deal of complainant frustration.[10]

Before another executive order would be issued, civil rights exploded onto the public agenda. A march on Washington held on August 28, 1963, brought 200,000 black and white supporters of civil rights to the Capitol. In response to this and other demonstrations, and as a result of shifting public sentiment, President Kennedy sent a civil rights bill to Congress; it was passed in 1964, after his assassination. The Civil Rights Act of 1964 included in its provisions Title VI, which prohibited discrimination on the basis of race, color, or national origin by all recipients of federal funds, including schools, and Title VII, which made it unlawful for any employer or labor union to discriminate in employment on the basis of race, color, religion, sex, or national origin. Title VII also created the Equal Employment Opportunity Commission (EEOC) for enforcement in the private sector.

The following year, 1965, President Lyndon B. Johnson issued Executive Order 11,246 barring discrimination on the basis of race, color, religion, or national origin by federal contractors and subcontractors.[11] On October 13, 1967, it was amended by Executive Order 11,375 to expand its coverage to women. One major innovation of the order was to shift enforcement to the secretary of labor by creating an Office of Federal Contract Compliance (OFCC). Starting in 1968, the government established the enforceability of the executive order with legal action[12] and, for the first time, issued notices of proposed debarment (contract cancellation) using its administrative process.[13]

Prodded to be more specific about its standards, the OFCC began to spell out exactly what affirmative action meant in the context of the construction industry, and that became a model for all affirmative action programs.[14] During this period, President Richard Nixon played the role of champion of affirmative action, saving LBJ's executive order.

In 1968 the OFCC focused on blacks in the construction industry. The result was the Philadelphia Plan, which was developed in three stages. First, the OFCC required preaward affirmative action plans from low bidders in some labor market areas, like Philadelphia. But because there were no guidelines for acceptability, the industry pressured Congress, which stimulated an opinion from the comptroller general, who recommended that the OFCC provide minimum requirements and standards by which programs would be judged. The second or revised Philadelphia Plan was then developed. It required that contractors submit a statement of "goals" of minority employment together with their bids, which took into account the minority participation and availability in the trade, as well as the need for training programs. On September 23, 1969, the Labor Department issued its third and final set of guidelines for the Philadelphia Plan after having determined the degree to which there was discrimination in construction crafts. This final plan established ranges within which the contractor's goals had to fall and recommended filling vacancies and new jobs approximately on the basis of one minority craftsman for each nonminority craftsman.

The comptroller general found the revised plan illegal on the ground that it set up quotas. But the attorney general issued an opinion declaring the plan to be legal and advised the secretary of labor to ignore the comptroller general's opinion. The comptroller general then urged the Senate Subcommittee on Deficiencies and Supplementals to attach a rider onto its appropriations bill prohibiting the use of funds to pay for efforts to achieve specific minority employment goals. The Nixon administration lobbied hard in the House and succeeded in eliminating the rider. On reconsideration, the Senate also defeated the rider, and the Philadelphia Plan was saved.

In 1971 the Department of Labor issued general guidelines that had the same features as the Philadelphia Plan, making it clear that "goals and timetables" were meant to "increase materially the utilization of minorities and women," with underutilization being spelled out as "having fewer minorities or women in a particular job classification than would reasonably be expected by their availability. . . ."[15] The 1971 Department of Labor guidelines, called Revised Order 4, were to govern employment practices by government contractors and subcontractors in industry and higher education.

Hole and Levine, in *Rebirth of Feminism,* document the initial exclusion of women from the guidelines. In 1970 Secretary of Labor Hodgson even publicly remarked that he had "no intention of applying literally exactly the same approach for women" as was applied to eliminate discrimination against minorities.[16] However, because of publicity and pressure by women's groups, by April 1973 women were finally included as full beneficiaries in the Revised Order 4.

What is important about the Philadelphia Plan and the Department of Labor guidelines is that they established not only the principle but also the guidelines for the practice of affirmative action that other civil rights enforcement agencies and even the courts would follow.

During the 1970s, administrative changes strengthened affirmative action. The Office of Management and Budget enlarged and refined the definition of *minority group* and, under President Carter, affirmative action efforts were consolidated. By executive order on October 5, 1978, the OFCC went from overview responsibility, whereby each department had responsibility for the compliance of its own contractors (with uneven results), to consolidated contract compliance, whereby the OFCC was given enforcement responsibility over all contractors;[17] overnight, 1600 people who had been working for other departments were now working for Labor. The expanded program now was called the Office of Federal Contract Compliance Programs (OFCCP).

During the 1980s, there were attempts to weaken affirmative action. The Reagan administration publicly and continually criticized goals and timetables, calling them quotas.[18] By 1982 the OFCCP's budget and number of workers were significantly reduced. By 1983, while President Reagan used attitudes toward affirmative action as a litmus test to successfully reorganize the U.S. Commission on Civil Rights, his attempt to rescind or revise Executive Order 11,246 by specifically prohibiting numerical hiring goals was successfully stopped by opposition from within his own administration.[19] Nevertheless, during these years, the administration whittled away at the policy. In 1983 it instituted changes within the OFCCP that affected the agency's case determinations and remedies, although by January 1987 some of these changes were rescinded. On January 21, 1987, Joseph N. Cooper, director of the OFCCP, quit his job in protest. In an interview, he spoke candidly about the "number of officials in the Labor Department and elsewhere in the Administration who were intent on destroying the contract compliance program."[20]

While President George Bush, during his four-year term, was no friend to affirmative action, he seemed to oppose it for tactical political reasons rather than because of strident political ideology. Even Democratic President Bill Clinton, at first, seemed gun-shy when it came to affirmative action. Clinton abandoned Lani Guinier, his choice for director of the Civil Rights Division of the Justice Department, when she was portrayed by the media as the "quota queen." Although this characterization was untrue, Clinton quickly disassociated himself from Guinier and withdrew his nomination in the interest of maintaining his own centrist image.

Clinton seemed to have a change of heart during his second term in office. Affirmative action became a "friend of Bill's" by the end of 1997. This gave the issue and the president a lot of publicity. For example, when President Clinton hosted the first in a series of Town Hall meetings on race relations in Akron, Ohio, he created what newspaper reporters called "the most dramatic moment of the meeting" when he engaged in a heated exchange with the only outspoken opponent of affirmative action at that meeting. After the session, the Akron audience, consisting of college students, civic leaders, and business executives, was criticized for not including more divergent opinions on affirmative action. Within weeks, the president arranged for an official and well publicized White House meeting with some well known opponents of affirmative action. Another example of Clinton's well publicized support of affirmative action was his engagement with the issue at his long year-end presidential press conference on December 16, 1997. Accordingly, affirmative action continues to be a much discussed public policy issue for Americans partially because the president is publicizing and spinning it.[21]

THE BAKKE *DECISION AND OTHER COURT DECISIONS*

Affirmative action policy for student admissions has a very different history. Its source is Title VI of the Civil Rights Act of 1964 and Title IX of the Educational Amendments of 1972, not Executive Order 11,246. Title VI *requires* affirmative action steps to be taken in admissions *only as a remedy* for past discrimination. However, most minority affirmative action admission programs were self-imposed.[22] Title IX (subpart B, section 106.17) of the Educational Amendments of 1972, which prohibits *sex* discrimination, also calls for affirmative steps to be taken to remedy "past exclusion." A case having to do with minority affirmative action in admissions became the most well known and celebrated test of the principle of affirmative action.

Justice Lewis Powell announced the *Bakke v. University of California* Supreme Court decision to a hushed courtroom on the morning of June 28, 1978. He said, "We speak today with notable lack of unanimity." In fact, the 154 pages of judicial text presented *six* separate opinions and *two* separate majorities.[23]

Allan Bakke wanted to be a medical doctor. In 1973, at age thirty-three, while employed as a full-time engineer, he applied to a dozen medical schools, one of which was the University of California–Davis, and was turned down by all of them. The next year, after a second rejection from the twelve medical schools, Bakke sued the University of California in the California Court system, claiming that Davis's use of racial quotas was what had excluded him from medical school.

The *Bakke* case was not a strong one for those who supported affirmative action. On trial was an admissions program that reserved 16 of its 100 places for minority students (Blacks, Hispanics, and Asians), which looked like an admissions "quota" system. Furthermore, the Davis Medical School was founded in 1968, so the school could not claim that affirmative action was a remedy for past years of discrimination.

In this case, fifty-eight amicus curiae briefs were filled, and "The Court seemed less a judicial sanctum than a tug of war among contesting lobbyists.[24] When the dust cleared, the Court found a way both to admit Allan Bakke, now age thirty-eight, to the Davis Medical School and to defend the practice of affirmative action. By a 5–4 margin, the Court rejected the Davis program with a fixed number of seats for minorities; but also, by a different 5–4 margin, the Court accepted race-conscious admissions as being consistent with the Constitution and with Title VI.[25]

OTHER COURT DECISIONS AFTER BAKKE

Two cases that followed *Bakke, Weber* in 1979 and *Fullilove* in 1980, helped clarify the legal picture on affirmative action. In a 5–2 decision in *Weber* (two Supreme Court members did not participate), it was ruled permissible under Title VII for the private sector voluntarily to apply a compensatory racial preference for employment.

Brian Weber was an unskilled laboratory employee at the Gramercy, Louisiana, plant of the Kaiser Aluminum and Chemical Corporation. In 1974, while blacks made up 39 percent of Gramercy's general labor force, at the Kaiser plant, only 2 percent of the 273 skilled craft workers were black. Kaiser instituted a training program for its unskilled workers, earmarking half the trainee openings for blacks until the percentage of black craftspeople corresponded to their proportion in the labor force. Weber had more seniority than some of the blacks chosen for the program. The Court, however, argued that Kaiser's affirmative action program was a reasonable response to the need to break down old patterns of segregation.

The following year, in *Fullilove,* the Supreme Court decided, 6–3, that a congressional affirmative action program, a 10 percent set-aside of federal funds for minority business people, provided in the Public Works Employment Act of 1977, was also permissible under the Constitution.

Fullilove v. Klutznick was decided during the summer of 1980.[26] Chief Justice Burger wrote the majority opinion, which found the "limited use of racial and ethnic criteria" constitutionally permissible when its purpose was to remedy the present effects of past racial discrimination. With this case, Father Mooney suggests that, with certain qualifications, the Supreme Court legitimized affirmative action as a policy for U.S. society.[27] But not so when it came to layoffs.

In 1984, when layoffs were concerned, the Court shifted from its permissive view on classwide "race conscious remedies." On June 12, 1984, the Supreme Court issued its decision in *Firefighters Local Union No. 1784 v. Stotts,* which focused on the extent to which seniority systems may be overridden as part of court-ordered relief to remedy discrimination in employment. It was a 6–3 decision.

Carl Stotts was a black firefighter in the Memphis, Tennessee, Fire Department. He brought a class action lawsuit into federal district court in 1977, alleging discriminatory hiring and promotion practices in the department. This resulted in a consent decree in 1980 requiring that the percentage of black employees in each job classification be increased to the proportion of blacks in the local labor force.

The next year, because of budget problems, the city began to make plans to lay off firefighters on a seniority basis (last hired, first fired). "Black firefighters asked the court to prohibit the layoff of black employees. The court ordered the city not to apply its seniority policy in a manner that would reduce the percentage of blacks in the department. The case was appealed to the Supreme Court."[28]

The Supreme Court said that the seniority system could not be disregarded in laying people off and that although there was protection for actual victims of discrimination, "mere membership in the disadvantaged class was an insufficient basis for judicial relief."[29] In other words, a seniority system could be used to lay people off even though many blacks would be the first to go. The same was true in *Wygant v. Jackson Board of Education,* which was decided May 19, 1986.

In *Wygant,* nonminority teachers in Jackson, Michigan, challenged their terminations under a collective bargaining agreement requiring layoffs in reverse order of seniority unless it resulted in more minority layoffs than the current percentage employed. This layoff provision was adopted by the Jackson Board of Education in 1972 because of racial tension in the community that extended to its schools. In a 5–4 decision, the court said that this system of layoffs violated the rights of the nonminority teachers even though (unlike the case of *Stotts*) it was a part of their collective bargaining agreement. Powell, writing for the Court, argued that he could not find enough to justify the use of racial classifications.[30] Affirmative action was not as important as seniority when it came to layoffs.

Nevertheless, the "principle" of affirmative action actually survived in the majority's opinion in *Wygant.* The Court again affirmed that under certain circumstances policies using race-based classifications were justified. It was just that, for the majority, these were not the right circumstances. Marshall's words written in his dissenting opinion ring true: "Despite the Court's inability to agree on a route, we have reached a common destination in sustaining affirmative action against constitutional attack."[31] His assessment was to be proved correct in the February 25, 1987, case *US v. Paradise*, and in the March 25, 1987, case *Johnson v. Transportation Agency, Santa Clara County*.

In a 5–4 decision, in the *Paradise* case, the Court upheld a federal district court judge's order requiring Alabama to promote one black state police trooper for each white trooper from a pool of qualified candidates. Justice Brennan wrote the plurality opinion justifying the affirmative action program because of the "egregious" nature of previous bias against blacks. Justice Powell, in a concurring opinion, emphasized that the "quota" did not disrupt seriously the lives of innocent individuals; Justice Stevens's concurring opinion emphasized that the Court-imposed plans fell within the bounds of reasonableness, whereas the dissenters emphasized the undue burden the plan placed on the white troopers.

In the *Johnson* case, six of the nine Supreme Court Justices approved of Santa Clara county's affirmative action program. In 1978 Santa Clara's transit district's board of supervisors adopted a goal of a workforce whose proportion of women, minorities, and the disabled equaled the percentage of the county's labor force at all job levels. Women constituted 36.4 percent of the relevant labor market, and although women made up 22.4 percent of the district workers, they were mostly in clerical positions, with none in the 238 skilled jobs. In 1979 Diane Joyce and Paul Johnson competed, along with five others who were all deemed "well qualified," for the job of dispatcher, a skilled position. They had all scored over 70, the passing grade, in an oral examination conducted by a two-person panel. Johnson tied for second with a score of 75, and Joyce ranked third with 73. After a second interview, first Johnson was chosen, but then, because of affirmative action considerations, Joyce got the job. Johnson sued, contending that he was better qualified. In 1982 a judge ruled that Johnson had been a "victim of discrimination." The Reagan administration joined attorneys for Johnson and appealed to the Supreme Court.[32]

Justice William Brennan, in writing for the Court, put its stamp of approval on voluntary employer action designed to break down old patterns of race and sex segregation. "'Given the obvious imbalance in the skilled craft category' in favor of men against women, Brennan said, 'it was plainly not unreasonable . . . to consider the sex of Ms. Joyce in making the promotion decision.'" Brennan called the affirmative action plan "a moderate, flexible case by case approach to effecting a gradual improvement in the representation of minorities and women in the agency's work force."[33] Justice Antonin Scalia responded with a scathing dissent, emphasizing the burden that falls on the "Johnsons of the country," whom he called "the only losers in the process."[34]

THE COURT AND THE PUBLIC ARE DIVIDED ON AFFIRMATIVE ACTION

The Supreme Court remained divided on affirmative action, and by a bare majority the Court supported affirmative action for purposes of hiring and promotion, but not to determine layoff lists. A Gallup Poll conducted in June 1987 following the

Johnson decision showed that the public also continued to be divided on the issue of affirmative action and that the majority of those polled continued to be opposed (see Table 8.2).

Eight years in the White House allowed President Reagan to accomplish, with judicial appointments, what he was not able to do with judicial arguments. When Supreme Court justices retired, he used his power of appointment to add conservatives Sandra Day O'Connor and Antonin Scalia to the bench—and he appointed conservative William H. Rehnquist to be chief justice. Even so, as we have seen, affirmative action programs continued to win majority Court approval through 1987. Then, however, when Justice Powell, the "swing" vote, retired, and Reagan replaced him with conservative Anthony M. Kennedy, the Court was packed for the next affirmative action case.

On January 24, 1989, the Supreme Court announced its decision on the *Richmond v. Croson* case. The Court ruled, 6–3, that a 1983 Richmond, Virginia, ordinance that channeled 30 percent of public works funds to minority-owned construction companies violated the Constitution. Justice O'Connor, who wrote the majority opinion, argued that "laws favoring blacks over whites must be judged by the same constitutional test that applies to laws favoring whites over blacks"—namely, that classifications based on race are suspect and have to be scrutinized very carefully.

In scrutinizing this case, O'Connor did not see the necessary evidence of past discrimination that would justify using race-based measures. Black people made up 50 percent of the Richmond population, she noted, and although there was a "gross statistical disparity" between "the number of prime contracts awarded to minority firms and the minority population of the city of Richmond," still, she argued, this case does not "constitute a prima facie proof of a pattern of practice of discrimination." The appropriate pool for comparison is not the general population but the "number of minorities qualified to undertake the task," and O'Connor pointed

TABLE 8.2   Affirmative Action Ruling

	Approved	Disapproved	No Opinion
National	29%	63%	8%
Democrats	37	54	9
Republicans	22	74	4
Independents	27	64	9
Men	26`	66	8
Women	32	59	9
Whites	25	67	8
Blacks	56	34	10
Hispanics	46	47	7

Source: George Gallup Jr., "Little Support for High Court Ruling on Hiring," *San Francisco Chronicle,* June 15, 1987.

out that the city did not know exactly how many minority business enterprises (MBEs) there were in the relevant market that were qualified to undertake prime or subcontracting work in public construction projects. Even if there were a low number of MBEs, she argued, maybe it was not because of discrimination but because of "black career and entrepreneurial choices." "Blacks may be disproportionately attracted to industries other than construction."[35]

Justice Thurgood Marshall, in his dissent, found it "deeply ironic" that the majority did not find sufficient evidence of past discrimination in Richmond, Virginia, the former capital of the Confederacy. "Richmond knows what racial discrimination is; a century of decisions by this and other Federal courts has richly documented the city's disgraceful history . . . ," he wrote, and Marshall defended, again, the use of race-conscious measures to redress the effects of prior discrimination.[36]

The *Richmond* case did not end the debate, but perpetuated the uncertainty surrounding affirmative action plans. Now such plans could stand only if they could survive strict judicial scrutiny—for example, if they were adopted to eliminate "patently obvious, egregious discrimination that can be linked to the deliberate acts of identifiable parties." Mere numerical disparities would not be enough. Experts predicted that the lower courts would be flooded with challenges to affirmative action by white plaintiffs.[37]

OTHER CASES THAT INFLUENCED AFFIRMATIVE ACTION

On June 5, 1989, the court again decided a case that would affect affirmative action policy. In *Wards Cove Packing v. Atonia,* the court ruled, 5–4, that plaintiffs who are not employers have the burden of proving whether a job requirement that is shown statistically to screen out minorities or women is a "business necessity." The case redrew the ground rules unanimously established by the Court in 1971, which prohibited not only employment practices *intended* to discriminate but also practices that had discriminatory *impact.*

The plaintiffs in this case were non-whites—Filipino and Alaskan native cannery workers who were channeled into lower-paid unskilled jobs. Noncannery jobs were filled by the company with predominantly white workers who were hired in Washington and Oregon. With these statistics showing disparate impact, and consistent with precedent, the lower court asked the salmon canneries to justify, on grounds of "business necessity," the business practice of flying in whites for managerial jobs and hiring local non-whites to work in the cannery. Justice Byron White, writing for the majority, overturned eighteen years of precedent. He said that the cannery business did not have to prove anything. It was up to the non-white cannery workers to disprove the company's claim that there was no discrimination.

Justice John Paul Stevens, in his dissent, called the decision "the latest sojourn into judicial activism," accusing the majority of "[t]urning a blind eye to the meaning and purpose of Title VII. . . ."[38]

One week after the *Wards Cove* decision, the court dealt an even more lethal blow to affirmative action. In *Martin v. Wilks,* five members of the court ruled that whites may bring reverse discrimination claims against judge-approved affirmative action plans. This meant that consent decrees, which settle many discrimination suits and had been thought to be immune from subsequent legal attack, were now fair game.

The *Martin v. Wilks* case had its roots in the early 1970s, when a local chapter of the National Association for the Advancement of Colored People (NAACP), supported by the federal government, sued the city of Birmingham, Alabama, on the grounds that blacks were being discriminated against in hiring and promotion in the city's fire department. Several years later a settlement was reached, although the union representing the "almost all white work force" objected to the settlement at the hearing.[39] The Federal District Court "approved the settlement and entered a consent decree under which blacks and whites would be hired and promoted in equal number until the number of black firefighters approximated the proportion of blacks in the civilian labor force." A few months later, fifty white firefighters sued the city, claiming discrimination. The Federal District Court dismissed the suit. In 1987 the Eleventh Circuit Court overturned that dismissal, a decision inconsistent with those of every other circuit court, and reinstated the white firefighters in the city of Birmingham; a group of black firefighters appealed to the Supreme Court.

Chief Justice William Rehnquist wrote the majority opinion, in which he agreed with the Eleventh Circuit Court, arguing that a decree could be binding only on parties who had been part of the original lawsuit. "Outside groups" could not be required to join such a suit, and if they were not bound by the decree, they could sue. Justice Stevens's dissent pointed out that the Court's decision "would subject large employers who seek to comply with the law by remedying past discrimination to a never-ending stream of litigation and potential liability. He called the results 'unfathomable' and 'counterproductive.' "[40]

The next year, the Court rendered a decision supporting affirmative action. By a bare majority, the Supreme Court supported an affirmative action program in *Metro Broadcasting Inc. v. Federal Communications Commissions,* defending Congress' right to provide affirmative action for minorities and women in issuing broadcasting licenses. But, the composition of the Supreme Court was changing through retirements. Five years later, of the five justices favoring affirmative action in this case, only one, Justice John Paul Stevens, was still on the Court.

RESPONSES TO THE COURT DECISIONS

These decisions of the Court stimulated two important responses during the early 1990s. First, across the country, lawsuits were filed by white male workers who now had standing in the Court to allege that they had suffered reverse discrimination because of affirmative action programs, even programs that were court-imposed or that resulted from full trials. The effects were felt from San Francisco[41] to Birmingham.[42] The second important response to the Court's decisions came from Congress.

For six months, civil rights organizations and their congressional allies worked together to prepare legislation that would basically reverse three of the Supreme Court decisions, two that related to affirmative action, the *Wards Cove* case, "in which the Court ruled that . . . the plaintiff has the burden of proving that an employer had no business reason for a practice with discriminatory effects," and the *Martin v. Wilks* case, "in which the Court held that Court-approved affirmative action plans can be challenged as reverse discrimination. . . ."[43] The proposed legislation would also reverse another civil rights (but non–affirmative action) case, *Paterson v. McClean Credit Union,* "in which the Court ruled that an 1866 law prohibiting racial discrimination in contracts applies only to hiring agreements, not to on-the-job discrimination."[44]

The civil rights bill's sponsors, Senator Edward Kennedy (D-MA) and Representative Augustus Hawkins (D-CA), were confident about getting the majority necessary to pass the law. The challenge, which kept them negotiating behind closed doors, was to line up the sixty Senate cloture votes needed to shut off debate and to get the sixty-seven votes to guarantee override of a possible presidential veto. This civil rights bill, because it dealt with more subtle issues like "burden of proof" and "right to sue," was not as "sexy" as, for example, the Voting Rights Act, and the fear was that the supporting public might be less attentive to its fate.[45] Nevertheless, the White House watched closely.

At the end of May 1990, reporters were describing the "tough test" faced by the Bush administration. Although the president originally had warned he would veto the civil rights bill, by spring he was backing off from his threat. There seemed to be two reasons for his change of heart. First, it appeared that many Republicans in the Senate were ready to break with the White House to support the bill. The president's veto might not be sustained. The second reason for the president to look for compromise was his concern about his reelection. President Bush was eager to court the African American vote in 1992; in mid-1990, he had a 56 percent black approval rating and was the most popular Republican president among blacks since Dwight Eisenhower.[46] A compromise on the civil rights bill seemed likely. Thus, in 1990 it appeared that a committed pro–civil rights core in Congress and a pragmatic White House would help important elements of affirmative action to survive. But in the fall of 1990 President Bush vetoed the civil rights bill, and Congress was unable to override his veto. That December, Robert Allen, chairman of AT&T, arranged a private dinner between top business and civil rights leaders. A coalition of 200 top CEOs, the so-called Business Roundtable, voted to continue these talks, and both sides agreed to have lawyers meet to try to "hammer out their differences." Saving affirmative action and the civil rights bill now seemed probable.

The Bush administration, however, was unhappy with the prospect of such a compromise. Preparing for the presidential campaign of 1992, GOP strategists believed that a Republican anti–affirmative action position would be very effective and that a compromise bill would dilute the Republican political advantage on the quota issue. Therefore, the White House proceeded to destroy the business civil rights negotiations. Roundtable members were warned that their talks undermined business support for the president's version of a civil rights bill, and Chief of Staff John Sununu personally drummed up opposition among smaller companies. The White House campaign was blunt and vicious. Even Robert Allen came under personal attack from conservative columnist Pal Gigot in the *Wall Street Journal* because of his involvement. The participants who had seemed so hopeful buckled under the political pressure.[47] Then, a turn of events that no one could have predicted, made the passage of the congressional act virtually inevitable.

In Louisiana, an avowed racist and self-described Klan member, David Duke, became the Republican candidate for Senate. This represented a serious problem for the Republican party, which wanted desperately to disassociate themselves from him. Continuing with an anti–civil rights position, therefore, became problematic for Bush because such a position would seem too similar to Duke's position. Bush reversed himself on the civil rights bill; by the end of 1991, President Bush was on record supporting the civil rights legislation, and he signed it into law.

The Republican Party sought and failed to make affirmative action a *decisive* election issue in 1996. After the election, however, the issue continued to divide the two parties and exacerbate the problems inherent in the United States system of divided government. In 1997, President Clinton nominated Bill Lann Lee, a California attorney who supports affirmative action, to head the Justice Department's Civil Rights Division. For months, Senator Orrin Hatch (R-Utah), Senate Judiciary Committee Chair, and other Republican senators who objected to Lee's affirmative action position were successful in blocking a Senate confirmation vote. President Clinton circumvented their actions by nominating Lee as "Acting" Head of the Civil Rights Division after the Senate had recessed. But the controversy continued. "Lee's nomination, which was hardly seen as controversial when it was made . . . evolved into a high profile clash over affirmative action, as well as an epic Washington power struggle between the Democratic White House and the Republican Senate."[48]

Meanwhile, the Supreme Court continued to make decisions that struck down affirmative action programs; nevertheless, the Court never struck down the *principle* of affirmative action. In 1995, in *Adarand v. Pena,* the High Court overturned its *Metro Broadcasting* decision. In *Adarand,* the Court decided on the validity of a program that benefitted minority- and women-owned highway construction businesses. The court held differential treatment because of racial or ethnic origin inherently suspect, and said that the government can adopt affirmative action programs only when it can demonstrate that they correct real and present discrimination.

In November 1997, the Supreme Court was prevented from deciding a case scheduled on their docket to be argued just six weeks later. The case originated in Piscataway, New Jersey. Eight years earlier, in a move to reduce the number of business school teachers, the Piscataway School District laid off on the basis of race Sharon Taxman, a white teacher, instead of Debra Williams, a black teacher who they deemed to be equivalent. Civil rights advocates worried that this was not a strong case for affirmative action. In fact, they feared that the Supreme Court might use it as a vehicle to declare affirmative action unconstitutional. In a surprising move, the Piscataway School District paid Taxman $430,000 to settle her case and thus avoid its being heard by the Supreme Court. Civil rights groups contributed most of the settlement money. Like the *Wygant* case described earlier, in Piscataway, women teachers were pitted against each other when the operative affirmative action basis was race.[49]

LOWER COURT CHALLENGES TO AFFIRMATIVE ACTION

The educational system has been especially hard hit by anti affirmative action law suits. In 1996, the Supreme Court left intact a ruling that threatens affirmative action programs at state run colleges in three states, Texas, Louisiana, and Mississippi. Although the Clinton administration, nine states, and the District of Columbia all filed amicus briefs supporting affirmative action in the case of *Texas v. Hopwood,* the Supreme Court let stand the lower court's decision, which effectively reversed the *Bakke* decision in those three states.

Affirmative action programs in school districts across the country are also being challenged in Court. In San Francisco, a 1982 Court supervised consent decree limiting the student enrollment of any ethnic group in each San Francisco school to 40 percent, is being challenged by Chinese American parents. The parents claim the policy denies their children admission to the kindergarten of their choice as well as to prestigious Lowell High School. In addition, in Boston, parents have sued the oldest American public school, Boston Latin, because of the school's affirmative action policy guaranteeing a certain number of Latino and black seats; in Arlington Virginia, the lower court has already ruled that using racial preferences to admit preschoolers to three magnet schools violated the Constitution; and in Houston, Texas, parents are suing the school district because their children were denied admission to a magnet school, Lanier Middle School, due to racial caps on enrollment.[50] Just as the lower courts are a central arena for affirmative action policy, states are also making policy.

State Action

Much of the current public conversation, legislative debate, and referenda activities on affirmative action are taking place in the states. While the Supreme Court has never rejected affirmative action principles, some states have tried and succeeded in outlawing affirmative action. California's successful attempt via a referendum, has been the most well publicized. In November 1996, 54 percent of the California electorate voted in favor of proposition 209, what the proponents called the California Civil Rights Initiative. The Proposition prohibited the implementation of race- and gender-conscious affirmative action programs. As a result of the passage of "Prop 209," state-required affirmative action programs are now banned in California. However, in 1997, opponents of affirmative action in Houston, Texas failed to get the same results. In November, a referendum simply asked voters if they wanted to end the city's affirmative action programs. Decisively, voters said "No".

Of course, the Texas vote did not put the issue to rest in other states. By January 1998, the state of Washington's opponents of affirmative action collected more than enough signatures to put the affirmative action issue on their November, 1998 ballot. Their "Initiative 200" was modeled after California's Proposition 209. It is likely that many of the future changes in affirmative action will continue to be made at the state level.

AFFIRMATIVE ACTION: A WOMAN'S ISSUE

In only three of the major Supreme Court decisions were women the beneficiaries of the affirmative action programs in question. The *Johnson* case was specifically about the promotion of a woman in a program that provided affirmative action for women and minorities and the *Metro Broadcasting* case, and the *Adarand* case that overturned it, concerned programs whose beneficiaries were both women and minorities. All the other major Supreme Court cases concerned only minorities as beneficiaries. Not surprisingly therefore, the public is more likely to connect affirmative action to racial and ethnic minorities than to women. But affirmative action very clearly relates to women, in fact, women's very inclusion as beneficiaries came as a result of the efforts of women in politics.

In the beginning stages of affirmative action, women's rights organizations, such as the National Organization for Women (NOW) succeeded in getting women to be included as affirmative action beneficiaries. In 1967, when President Johnson amended the affirmative action Executive Order to include women, he did so as a response to their successful lobbying efforts; and in the early 1970s, when the rules of affirmative action were first being developed by the Department of Labor, it was only after women's groups effectively challenged and lobbied Labor that women, in 1973, became fully included in government guidelines.

However, the aim of affirmative action is the redistribution of benefits and opportunities. Has the program benefited women? Even with the Department of Labor guidelines, there is no guarantee that women as a protected class will be included in affirmative action pools, which are up to each employer to define.

As beneficiaries, industrywide figures consistently have painted a mixed picture for employed women under affirmative action. For example, Goldstein and Smith analyzed minority and female employment changes in over 74,000 separate companies between 1970 and 1972. They compared contractor and noncontractor companies with a presumption that federal contractors are more likely to conform to affirmative action goals. What they found surprised them.

Although, as expected, black males did economically better in employment in contractor companies between 1970 and 1972, so did *white males*. The big losers during these years were white women. Between 1970 and 1972, before the OFCC revised guidelines included women, white women not only showed no employment gains, they showed significant employment losses. In fact, white women's losses were equal in magnitude to the significant gains made by white males.[51]

Under the revised guidelines, it appears that the effect of including women in the federal affirmative action program, as a protected class, is mixed. From 1967 to 1980, for white women, "Rough stability prevailed over this period in their wages relative to white men," according to Smith and Welch. Sociologist Paul Burstein suggests an interesting explanation, rarely considered by economists, to account for why white women have not experienced a large wage advance under the 1972 guidelines. As a group, their "seeming decline" in income is probably due to the steady influx of relatively inexperienced female workers into the labor force. Women as a group are better off, but their average income drops.[52] The story on wages for black women is different. Between 1967 and 1980 the largest wage advances were achieved by black women, who went from earning 74 percent of the wage of similarly employed white women in 1967 to almost complete racial parity in 1980.[53] It has been suggested that "part of the reason for nonwhite women's gains . . . may be their having been so badly off initially that their jobs and incomes could improve considerably without posing any real threat to the normal workings of the economy."[54]

In a National Bureau of Economic Research paper, Jonathan Leonard studied the effectiveness of affirmative action for the employment of minorities and women.[55] Focusing on the period between 1974 and 1980, he also compared *contractor and noncontractor* establishments. Leonard compared the mean employment share of targeted groups and controlled for establishment size, growth, region, industry, occupation, and corporate structure. He found that members of protected groups grew faster in contractor than in noncontractor establishments, 3.8 percent faster for black males, 7.9 percent faster for other minority males, 2.8 percent for white females, and 12.3 percent for black females.[56] This suggests that affirmative action programs benefit black women and tend to help white women, though not as much as they benefit minorities.

When Leonard focused on the effect of compliance reviews—that is, the role they played over and above that of contractor status—he found that they advanced black males by 7.9 percent, other minority males by 15.2 percent, and black females by 6.1 percent. It *retarded* the employment growth of whites (including white women). Thus, he concluded, *"with the exception of white females,* compliance reviews have had an additional positive impact on protected group employment beyond the contractor effect."[57] His data also show that white women were not benefiting from affirmative action when it came to promotions.[58]

Leonard suggests an explanation for why white women's position in contractor companies has not improved significantly compared with noncontractor companies. It is that these women have so flooded the employment market that they have been hired in *both* contractor and noncontractor companies. As he says, "female [employment] share" has "increase[d] at all establishments because of the supply shift. . . ." Thus, his comparison of contractor and noncontractor hiring does not show the general large increase in white women hired. His explanation seems plausible considering the clear increase in the number of women employed, which is reflected by Bureau of the Census data for the period between 1970 and 1980.[59]

Although it appears that not all women have benefited directly from affirmative action, there are many specific cases where women (including white women) have directly benefited from an affirmative action approach. Affirmative action, with its emphasis on numbers and parity, can indirectly benefit women (including white women) because it inevitably shifts our focus from rhetoric to results. Thus, in some areas, such as academic admissions (which falls under Title IX protection), public scrutiny was all that was necessary to make possible a large redistribution of places to all women. Quoting McGeorge Bundy, Wilkinson wrote, "Since 1968 the number of women entering medical schools has risen from 8 percent to 25 percent of the total. A parallel increase has occurred in law schools. No constitutional issue is raised by this dramatic change, . . . the women admitted have had generally competitive records on the conventional measures."[60]

Even though they score competitively, I am arguing that affirmative action has helped these women get admitted to professional schools by focusing public attention on admissions criteria and admission results. In this context let us remember a Charlotte Perkins Gilman line in a poem that focuses on Socialist change. "A lifted world lifts women up," she wrote.

Thus, there is a mixed answer to the question "Does affirmative action benefit women?" Nonwhite women seem to have most clearly benefited directly from the program, but all women may be benefiting indirectly. Might affirmative action be a women's issue for reasons other than women's benefits?

Perhaps affirmative action could be seen as a woman's issue, in the tradition of social feminism, because it calls for a fairer distribution of social benefits. Of course, I am not suggesting that women be insensitive to the catalog of arguments, some of them practical, that have been made against affirmative action.[61] What I would suggest is that women (and men) be wary of falling into the trap of characterizing affirmative action as the "opposite" of a merit system. It is not. After all, proportionality is used even to select justices on the Supreme Court, where there may be a Jewish seat, a southern seat, a black seat, and now seats for two women.[62]

The major issue raised by affirmative action is not merit but redistribution. Allan Bakke's arguments were made against a special program benefiting minorities. Over and over he raised the flag of "fair competition," but Davis Medical School had another special program, which Bakke did not complain about—the dean's special admissions program "under which white children of politically well-connected university supporters or substantial financial contributors have been admitted in spite of being less qualified than other applicants, including Bakke."[63] Thus, the Bakke issue is not, and never was, special programs. The issue is who will be benefiting from these special programs—and that is a matter not of merit but of politics. And the country remains divided over this political question.

THE FUTURE OF AFFIRMATIVE ACTION

At a time when the judicial system and state initiatives seem to be chopping away at the legal status of affirmative action, the public remains divided on the issue, and the national debate over affirmative has only intensified.

In December, 1997, the *New York Times*/CBS News conducted a survey, asking virtually the same questions about affirmative action that they had been asking the public for over a decade. Since 1985, their surveys showed an erosion of support for "preferences" with a big drop in support in the late 1980s. Respondent's views on preferences for women were just as negative as their views on preferences for blacks. For example, in response to the question on preferential treatment, "Do you believe where there has been job discrimination in the past, preferences, in hiring and promotion should be given?" the response relating to blacks was almost the same strong negative one as the one relating to women; 37 percent respondents were for preference for women, 35 percent were for preferences for blacks; 51 percent were against preferences for women, 52 percent were against preferences for blacks.

How can affirmative action have a future given such strong opposition to affirmative action preferences? While the *New York Times*/CBS NEWS poll revealed strong opposition to preferential treatment, the survey also showed a public very much committed to diversity and the goals of affirmative action.

The polls revealed that a vast majority of the public does not want to see affirmative action abruptly ended. Only 12 percent want to see it "ended now" while 40 percent want it "phased out over the next few years" and 41 percent want affirmative action continued for the foreseeable future.

Furthermore, a large majority want special efforts to continue. Fully 63 percent favor "special education programs to assist minorities in competing for college admissions," and 69 percent favor "government financing for job training for minorities to help them get ahead in industries where they are underrepresented." As the *New York Times* summarizes it, "Asked what society should do with 'affirmative action programs giving preference to some minorities,' people were much more inclined to say that they should be maintained or revised than they were to say that they should be abolished."[64] Americans seem to want to level the playing field. Fully 69 percent polled favor the continuation of anti-discrimination laws. Thus, it is clear that the majority of Americans want some elements of affirmative action to continue as a part of public policy. However, the public debate will likely focus more on black and Latino men and women and less on white women.

NOTES

1. See Allan P. Sindler, *Equal Opportunity: On the Policy and Politics of Compensatory Minority Preferences* (Washington, DC: American Enterprise Institute for Public Policy Research, 1983).

2. See Jonathan S. Leonard, "The Effectiveness of Equal Employment Law and the Affirmative Action Regulation," Working Paper No. 1745, NBER Working Paper Series, National Bureau of Economic Research, November 1985 (unpublished).

3. See Thomas Sowell, *Civil Rights: Rhetoric or Reality?* (New York: William Morrow, 1984); and James E. Jones Jr., "The Bugaboo of Employment Quotas," *Wisconsin Law Review,* 5 (1970) p. 341.

4. Daniel C. Maguire provides the most complete compendium of practical "problems" in *A New American Justice* (New York: Doubleday, 1980).

5. The most widely discussed state initiative on the affirmative action issue is California's Proposition 209, passed by the electorate November 5, 1996.

6. Arval A. Morris, "Affirmative Action and 'Quota' Systems," Commentary, 26 Ed. *Law Report,* 1985.

7. David H. Rosenbloom, *Federal Equal Employment Opportunity Politics and Public Personnel Administration* (New York: Praeger, 1977), p. 60; see also James E. Jones, "Twenty-one Years of Affirmative Action: The Maturation of the Administrative Enforcement Process under the Executive Order 11,246 as Amended." *Chicago Kent Law Review,* 59 (Winter 1982); pp. 66–122; Paul Burstein, *Discrimination, Jobs, and Politics* (Chicago: University of Chicago Press, 1985), pp. 8, 13.

8. U.S., Federal Register, March 6, 1961, 26, pt. 2: 1977.

9. Rosenbloom, *Federal Equal Employment Opportunity Politics,* pp. 67–69.

10. Jones, "Twenty-one Years," p.f. 72.

11. *U.S. Federal Register,* 30, pt. 10: 12319.

12. In *U.S. v. Local 189,* United Papermakers and Paper-workers, 290F2d 368, and Crown Zellerbach Corp., 282F Supp. 39 (E. D. La. 1968) "the government sought an injunction against the union's interference with the company's contractual obligations under Executive Order 11,246. . . ." *Ibid.,* p. 83.

13. There are many who criticize the way affirmative action has been implemented. For an overview, see Leonard, Working Paper No. 1745, and Leonard, "Affirmative Action as Earnings Redistribution: The Targeting of Compliance Reviews," *Journal of Labor Economics,* 3 (3) (July 1985), pp. 380–384; see also James P. Smith and Finis Welch, "Affirmative Action and Labor Markets," *Journal of Labor Economics,* 2 (April 1984), pp. 285–286, 298

14. Leonard, Working Paper No. 1745, p. 4.

15. Sowell, *Civil Rights,* p. 41.

16. Judith Hole and Ellen Levine, *Rebirth of Feminism* (New York: New York Times Book Company, 1971), p. 46; see also Morris Goldstein and Robert Smith, "The Estimated Impact of the Antidiscrimination Program Aimed at Federal Contractors," *Industrial and Labor Relations Review,* 29 (4) (July 1976), pp. 523–543.

17. Interview with Joseph Hodges, assistant regional director, Office of Federal Contract Compliance, U.S. Department of Labor, Region IX, February 6, 1987.

18. See, for example, Joann S. Lublin and Andy Pasztor, "Tentative Affirmative Action Accord Is Reached by Top Reagan Officials," *Wall Street Journal,* December 11, 1985, p. 4; and Robert Pear, "Rights Chief Assails Hiring Goals as Failure," *New York Times,* November 1, 1985, p. 19.

19. Lublin and Pasztor, "Tentative Affirmative Action Accord."

20. Kenneth B. Noble, "Labor Dept. Aide Quits in Protest Over 'Lip Service' to Jobs Rights," *New York Times,* January 21, 1987; see also "Job-Bias Official Quits Labor Post," *Washington Post,* January 21, 1987.

21. Peter Baker, Michael A. Fletcher, "Clinton Runs a Town Hall Talk on Race," *San Francisco Chronicle,* December 4, 1997, pp. 1, 17; Marc Sandalow, "Focus on Race as Clinton Meets Press," *San Francisco Chronicle,* December 17, 1997, pp. 1, 19.

22. Interview with Paul Grossman, head of the Attorney's Division, Office for Civil Rights, U.S. Department of Education, Region IX, February 6, 1987.

23. Christopher F. Mooney, S.J., *Inequality and the American Conscience* (New York: Paulist Press, 1982), p. 5.

24. J. Harvey Wilkinson III, *From Brown to Bakke: The Supreme Court and School Integration* (New York: Oxford University Press, 1979), p. 255.

25. *Ibid.,* p. 301. Since Justice Powell was the "swing" vote, "An irony of Bakke, wrote Washington attorney and civil rights activist Joseph Rauh, was that 'Affirmative action was saved by a conservative Southern justice.'"

26. Mooney, *Inequality,* p. 101.

27. *Ibid.,* p. 103.

28. United States Commission on Civil Rights, *Toward an Understanding of Stotts,* Clearinghouse Publication 85, January 1985, p. 2.

29. *Ibid.*

30. Wygant v. Jackson Board of Education in *United States Law Week,* 54 (45) (May 20, 1986), pp. 4480f.

31. *Ibid.,* p. 4489.

32. David G. Savage, "Landmark Ruling Upholds Job Preferences for Women," *Los Angeles Times,* March 2, 1987, pp. 10, 22.

33. *Ibid.,* p. 22. See also "Caveats Reversed in Workplace Equality," Insight, *Washington Times,* April 27, 1987, pp. 8–12.

34. *Ibid.,* "Caveats Reversed."

35. Linda Greenhouse, "Court Bars Plan Set up to Provide Jobs to Minorities," *New York Times,* January 24, 1989, pp. 1, A12; Sandra Day O'Connor, "Excerpts from Court Opinions in Voiding of Richmond's Contracting Plan," *New York Times,* January 24, 1989, p. A12.

36. Thurgood Marshall, "Excerpts," *Ibid.,* p. A12.

37. Linda Greenhouse, "Signal on Job Rights," *New York Times,* January 25, 1989, pp. 1, A9.

38. Linda Greenhouse, "Court, Ruling 5 to 4, Eases Burden on Employers in Some Bias Suits," *New York Times,* June 6, 1989, pp. 1, A24; "Excerpts from Court

Opinions about Job Rights," *New York Times,* June 6, 1989, p. A24.

39. Linda Greenhouse, "Court 5–4, Affirms a Right to Reopen Bias Settlements," *New York Times,* June 13, 1989, p. A7.

40. *Ibid.*

41. Martin Halstuk, "White Cops' Suit Alleges Bias in S.F. Promotions," *San Francisco Chronicle,* September 26, 1989, p. 1.

42. Ronald Smothers, "Ruling on Firefighter Is Debated in Alabama," *New York Times,* June 14, 1989, p. A18.

43. Susan Rasky, "Rights Groups Work on Measure to Reverse Court's Bias Rulings," *New York Times,* December 30, 1989, p. A11.

44. *Ibid.*

45. *Ibid.*

46. Larry Martz, Ann McDaniel, and Bill Turque, "Bush's Pledge: 'I Want to Do the Right Thing,'" *Newsweek,* May 28, 1990, pp. 20, 21.

47. Bob Cohn and Thomas M. DeFrank, "A White House Torpedo," *Newsweek,* April 29, 1991, p. 35.

48. Marc Sandalow, "Lee Gets Acting Rights Position," *San Francisco Chronicle,* December 12, 1997, pp. 1, 11; "Senators Suggest Lee Must Leave in 120 Days," *San Francisco Chronicle,* December 20, 1997, p. 3.

49. Louis Freedberg, "Settlement Scuttles Test of Affirmative Action," *San Francisco Chronicle,* November 22, 1997, pp. 1, 12; Barry Bearak, "Civil Rights Groups Criticized for Avoiding a Decision," *San Francisco Chronicle,* November 22, 1997, p. 12.

50. Louis Freedberg, "Oldest School Faces Modern Controversy," *San Francisco Chronicle,* December 11, 1997, pp. 1, 12.

51. Goldstein and Smith, "Estimated Impact."

52. Burstein, *Discrimination,* p. 148.

53. James P. Smith and Finis Welch, "Affirmative Action and Labor Markets," *Journal of Labor Economics,* 2 (2) (April 1984).

54. Burstein, *Discrimination,* p. 150.

55. Leonard, Working Paper No. 1745.

56. *Ibid.,* p. 10.

57. *Ibid.,* p. 11.

58. *Ibid.,* p. 17.

59. See, for example, a study by Cynthia M. Taeuber and Victor Valdisera, *Women in the American Economy,* Current Population Reports, Special Studies Series P-23, No. 146, U.S. Department of Commerce, Bureau of the Census, p. 23, which focuses on occupations with major employment gains for women and shows that in many of the male-dominated fields, the percentage of women employed rose sharply.

60. Wilkinson, *From Brown to Bakke,* pp. 262–263.

61. The best list of arguments against affirmative action is in Maguire, *A New American Justice,* pp. 31–39.

62. Wilkinson, *From Brown to Bakke,* p. 269.

63. Charles Lawrence III, "The Bakke Case: Are Racial Quotas Defensible?" *Saturday Review,* October 15, 1977, p. 14.

64. Sam Howe Verhovek, "In Poll, Americans Reject Means But Not Ends of Racial Diversity," *The New York Times,* December 14, 1997, p. 18.

FURTHER READINGS

Cahn, Steven M. *Affirmative Action and the University: A Philosophical Inquiry.* Philadelphia: Temple University Press, 1993.

Greene, Kathanne W. *Affirmative Action and Principles of Justice.* New York: Greenwood Press, 1989.

Jones, James E., Jr. "The Bugaboo of Employment Quotas," *Wisonconsin Law Review,* 5 (1970), p. 341.

Maguire, Daniel C. *A New American Justice.* New York: Doubleday, 1980.

Mooney, Christopher F., S.J. *Inequality and the American Conscience.* New York: Paulist Press, 1982.

Orlans, Harold, and June O'Neill. "Affirmative Action Revisited," *Annals of the American Academy of Political and Social Science,* 523 (September 1992), pp. 144–158.

Rosenfeld, Michel. *Affirmative Action and Justice: A Philosophical and Constitutional Inquiry.* New Haven, CT: Yale University Press, 1991.

Sindler, Allan P. *Equal Opportunity: On the Policy and Politics of Compensatory Minority Preferences.* Washington, DC: American Enterprise Institute for Public Policy Research, 1983.

Sowell, Thomas. *Civil Rights: Rhetoric or Reality?* New York: William Morrow, 1984.

Thernstrom, Stephan, and Abigail Thernstrom, *America in Black and White: One Nation, Indivisible.* New York: Simon & Schuster, 1997.

United States Commission on Civil Rights. *Toward an Understanding of Stotts.* Clearinghouse Publication 85, January 1985, p. 2.

Wilkinson, Harvey J. III. *From Brown to Bakke: The Supreme Court and School Integration.* New York: Oxford University Press, 1979.

WOMEN, EMPOWERMENT, AND CULTURAL EXPRESSION

We have explored the issue of women in politics. We began with a theoretical component; moved to political attitudes, voting, and elections; looked at women and government; and continued with an analysis of women and national policy. We began with theory and conclude this volume with practice. In our concluding chapter, we look at two essays that deal with a feminist framework for organizations and the relationship between coffee, coffeehouse cultures, political discourse, and gender.

In her essay Kathleen P. Iannello identifies a modified consensual structure in which routine decisions are made by a few and critical decisions are made by the entire group membership. Other important characteristics of these model organizations include the following: (1) recognition of ability or expertise rather than rank or position, (2) the notion of power as the ability to accomplish or achieve goals (as opposed to the idea of power as domination), and (3) clarity of goals, which are arrived at through a consensual process. The author uses a case study of the governing body of one women's studies program at a small liberal arts college to illustrate the challenges and benefits of organizing consensually. The implications for women in this structure include experiences in an environment of trust and support as opposed to the more traditional hierarchical organizations in which only those at the top (all too often male figures) make critical policy with varying degrees of input from lower levels.

Our final article examines the often complex relationships between coffee, coffeehouse cultures, and gender, along with how these relationships have shifted historically. Elizabeth A. Kelly concludes with a look at the countercultural institutions that have emerged in the last two decades that draw on the traditions of free speech and cultural and political criticisms that were integral to the coffeehouse cultures of centuries past. The author describes the feminist community organizing and the cultural work since the late 1960s that has often centered around coffeehouses, sometimes in tandem with feminist bookstores and other forms of cultural expression. She describes two feminist coffeehouses and the political struggles attached to building alternative social and cultural institutions that prioritize women and their concerns or needs. Let us further examine female activism and how female attitudes and tactics can bring about change.

Anarchist Feminism and Student Power: Is This Any Way to Run a Women's Studies Program?

KATHLEEN P. IANNELLO

Since 1970, when the first women's studies program was established at San Diego State University, women's studies programs have flourished at colleges and universities in America as well as throughout the world. Recent data show there are now between 650 and 700 women's studies programs in the United States alone.[1] As these programs have evolved, women on college campuses, like their sisters in the larger social and political arena, have striven to organize "differently." This difference has meant attempts at building consensual organization and decision making rather than hierarchical organization based on parliamentary process according to that well-worn "road map" of procedure: *Robert's Rules*. While nearly everyone has had experience with centralized, hierarchical decision-making structures, signified by the typical "executive board" that makes decisions for the rest of the group, few have experienced the consensual approach. Within consensual organization, power is shared and the concept of an executive or management level of the structure is completely nonexistent.

This means that in order to build consensual structures, people often have to *learn* to *participate* in organizations in different ways than they have in the past. This "new process" is often a challenge for those who encounter it for the first time. For students involved in the governing organizations of women's studies programs, the challenge is even greater when they discover that consensual decision making means they have as much power over their own course of study as do faculty, staff, and administrators. However, shared power also means shared responsibility, which can seem quite overwhelming to those who are unaccustomed to it.

Faculty, administrators and students *are* sharing power. Is this any way to run a women's studies program? A case study of the governing body of one women's studies program, called the Women's Studies Program Advisory Council (WSPAC), sheds some light on the specific challenges as well as benefits of organizing consensually in an academic environment. The study also raises important questions regarding student participation. But first, in order to consider what might be unique to the academic setting in developing consensual organization, an overview of the history and evolution of feminist consensual structure in the nonacademic setting is useful for those who are unfamiliar with it.

ANARCHIST FEMINISTS AND CONSENSUAL STRUCTURE

By now students of feminist theory recognize that feminism is not a monolith. Variations of liberal, Marxist, socialist, radical, multicultural, and postmodern feminism abound (to name a few!). What these differing theories have most in common is their goal of reducing or eliminating male domination or patriarchy from society. Of these feminist frameworks, anarchist feminism, sometimes viewed as a part of radical feminism, focuses most specifically on the relationship between patriarchy and hierarchy. Anarchist feminists examine forms of organization that provide unequal access to economic, political, and social resources.[2] They argue that power, defined as domination, "originates in, and is transmitted through" these organizational structures, which they define as centralized, hierarchical forms.[3]

The way to begin the task of eliminating this power, they argue, is to build "alternative forms of organization alongside the institutions of the larger society."[4] By alternative forms of organization, they mean groups in which leadership positions are rotated and responsibility is shared among group members. In doing so, they attempt to "eradicate all the structural factors that create and maintain leaders and followers."[5] This is something that must be practiced on a daily basis, they argue, and not put off while waiting for larger social change. "For social anarchists . . . the revolution is a process, not a point in time; and how one lives one's daily life is very important. People don't learn that they can live without leadership elites by accepting socialist ones; they do not end power relationships by creating new ones."[6] Instead, there must be a redefinition of power—a qualitative change. This means a change from *power as domination* to *power as the ability to accomplish or achieve goals:* empowerment.

The women's consciousness-raising groups of the 1960s and early 1970s represent an attempt to build alternative organizations. According to Jo Freeman's account of their experiences, they succeeded in raising consciousness but not in operating in nonhierarchical ways. As Freeman indicates, there was a kind of "tyranny of structurelessness," in that lack of structure gave way to the development of informal leaders—individuals who gained power due to media attention or personal characteristics.[7] Such leaders were not chosen by the group and thus could not be removed by the group. Lack of a leadership "process" created a kind of tyranny—unaccountable leadership.

Since then, many women's groups have come to learn that nonhierarchy does not mean nonstructure. Combining the concept of nonhierarchical *structure* with theories of empowerment, anarchist feminists have developed what some call a modified consensual model of organization. What does this modified consensual *structure* look like? What follows are two examples. Both organizations exist in the same small New England city and are similar in size but differ in services performed and explicit goals. They are referred to here by fictitious names: the feminist peace group and the women's health collective.[8]

Feminist Peace Group

This organization describes itself as a group of feminist activists working for disarmament and social justice in its immediate community and the world. It is part of a larger women's peace organization that has branches in nations around the world. The local branch formed in the spring of 1983. The members describe themselves as

> feminist activists who were seeking a diverse, effective and explicitly feminist women's peace group. . . . (We) embrace feminism as the most effective and comprehensive analysis of our political, economic, social, and military institutions. We see the rule of men over women as the model for other forms of dominance and oppression. And we strive for a radically different society which values cooperation, non-violence, nurturance and spiritual integrity.[9]

The organization, which has a mailing list of over 100, relies on three categories of members: (1) active members who participate in project groups and retreats, (2) supporting members who attend events and participate in telephone trees, and (3) sponsoring members who provide financial support for projects and actions. The approximately fifteen active members meet once a month; they also divide into a number of project groups, which they say "allow us to divide responsibility and to work easily with new people."[10] The project groups offer a way for the organization to involve and assimilate new members. They view the project groups as a way of dealing with a growing membership—the groups allow them to maintain a system of shared decision-making and leadership roles. All group decisions are made through consensus, which means that all members present at meetings must agree on, or at least not object to, decisions being made. Meetings are "facilitated" by members, on a rotating basis. Both the meeting agenda and the decision about who will "facilitate" are determined in the first few minutes of every full meeting.

The three groups of members mentioned earlier provide a network of communication and support that hinges on each member's ability to contribute to the organization—whether that contribution is simply monetary, communicative, or time invested. Within the "active" group, ability and interest are recognized through the various project groups. An example is a media project called "redirection." This group designed a series of radio ads against the development and sale of war toys. They also developed a follow-up telephone survey to attempt to measure the influence of the ads on the local community. Some of the project groups have been in existence since the beginning of the organization, while new ones have been created and old ones dissolved. The membership of the project groups changes with the shifting interests and abilities of the overall group membership. The organization has also recruited new members simply by sparking interest in the community through specific projects such as the media project described previously.

One difficulty for this organization has been related to what it called the "housekeeping" chores, which include the collection of member dues, distribution of other monies raised through grants, keeping of membership lists and organization files, and preparation of two yearly social and informational public events. In the past these tasks simply fell to those interested and willing to do them. However, those falling into this category have numbered fewer as member interests and energies have been more focused toward the project groups.

It was decided by the active membership that a project group would be formed to deal with these housekeeping tasks. Members who placed themselves within this group were those who did not want to make a larger time commitment to other project groups. In other words, the development of this group provided active members yet another option of participation that best reflected their abilities at the time. That housekeeping became a problem for this group underscores the fact that every organization has a number of tasks that must be tended to in order to keep the organization functioning. This is important in that some aspect of the organization's operating procedures must speak to this issue. This may be a reason why some collectivist groups fail: They lack the *structure* to deal with basic operating problems or needs.

The Women's Health Collective

This organization describes itself as a "modified collective," numbering approximately fifteen member–workers. The organization's focus is on women's reproductive health. It was formed in 1972 by community members, as a nonprofit organization, "in response to the need for safe, legal abortion services for . . . women." Its mission statement indicates the goals of the organization as follows:

> To provide high quality, cost-accessible, health care for and by women that includes but is not limited to gynecological and abortion services.
>
> To empower women by informing them medically and politically and by training women healthworkers.
>
> To be a woman-operated business striving for consensual power-sharing and equality of worker input in major policy decisions.
>
> To have our business structure be seen as a working model for other interested groups.[11]

In more than two decades, the health collective has gone through two major orga- nizational and structural changes. At the time of its inception, the organization was established with a staff that made decisions about the day-to-day operation of the clinic. There was a separate (outside) board composed of community members, which met with the staff every two weeks to make major policy decisions. As the staff members explain, "This was helpful in the beginning, as a broad range of ex- perience and opinions were needed."[12] However, by the end of the first two years, the board had become what the staff described as a "technical legality," and was dissolved.

At this point the full staff became the board as well, and all staff members participated in all decision making, according to consensus. The staff/board met weekly at that time and made all routine as well as critical policy decisions, includ- ing the hiring of staff and determination of salaries. At this point in their develop- ment, the staff decided that all salaries wold be the same for all members. In terms of jobs and tasks, as they explain, "The philosophy of the collectivity involves the idea that each staff member should ideally be trained to do any given task. Most staff members rotate positions of counselor, coordinator and phone counselor. Training programs are arranged for staff to learn more specialized tasks such as lab work, administrative skills and physician assistant skills."

After nearly ten years of operating in this fashion, the health collective once again changed or modified its structure. Members indicate that there were two major reasons for a change: (1) a need to make the "business" of the organization more efficient and (2) a need to recognize, through position and salary, the exper- tise of certain members. The structure that recently developed out of these needs is one in which there are currently three coordinators who have responsibility for areas such as personnel, medical, and business matters. These tasks have been del- egated to them by the full staff. The women in the organization describe how the coordinator positions evolved from the expertise certain women brought with them when they joined the clinic. For instance, one member, who had worked in an- other medical organization, brought with her knowledge of medical protocol. She eventually became the medical coordinator.

It is also important to note that when expertise is lost, through the departure of a member, the position the member held is dissolved. For example, a woman who brought "political and communication" skills to the organization became out- reach coordinator. When she left the organization, the outreach coordinator's posi- tion was dissolved. While coordinator positions do not rotate, coordinators do make an effort to share knowledge and information with the rest of the group. While this new structure brought with it some differentiation as to position and salary, the full staff still makes policy decisions in these areas. The full staff now meets once a month to consider critical policy questions, with routine decisions delegated to coordinators.

Within the women's health collective, individual members said they joined because they were looking for a female-managed business where they expected to find a supportive work environment, more flexible working hours, and coworkers who really understood the individual's needs both inside and outside the workplace. In short, these individuals expressed a commitment to a distinctly feminist ethic of care.[13] None of these women were opposed to the kind of structure the health collective utilizes. However, some of them were surprised, upon being hired, to find that they would need to learn about consensus decision making in order to work within this group.

Like the feminist peace group, one of the most significant aspects of the women's health collective is the recognition of ability or expertise within the membership without the creation of hierarchy. Coordinators are *delegated* responsibility from the entire staff. Yet they also have a responsibility to educate the remaining staff in a specific area of routine work such as medical protocol.

This is a model of nonhierarchy that demonstrates the concept of empowerment, in that organization members become enriched or gain personal power through the expertise of others. The development of expertise in the health collective may be more important than in the peace group because of the external constraints: the health collective is a business that must deal with external hierarchies of the marketplace, of the medical as well as political worlds. For this group, the development and sharing of expertise may be much more a matter of survival than it is for the peace group, which is a volunteer organization with fewer time-constrained goals.

Modified Consensual Structure

The most significant aspect of these organizations is their structure (see Figure 9.1). This is evident in the way the women of the peace group and health collective make decisions. First, they are keenly aware of the distinction between critical and routine decisions. Decisions that are "critical" have the potential for changing the direction of the organization. Those that are "routine" are important to the operation of the organization on a daily basis—but are not likely to raise significant questions about changes in overall policy.[14]

In both the peace group and the health collective, critical decisions are reserved for the entire membership of the organization, while routine decisions are delegated horizontally. For example, in the peace group the project groups make routine decisions. In the health collective, it is the coordinators and their respective committees who make decisions about problems they are close to and have information about. It is recognized that routine decisions have the potential for becoming critical. In the event that they do, they are reconsidered by the entire group.

What is unique about the structure of these anarchist feminist groups is that everyone is involved in making critical policy. In hierarchical organizations, only those at the top, with varying degrees of input from lower levels, make critical policy. Additionally, in the anarchist groups, routine decisions are delegated horizontally to those who have an interest in making them. While such delegation can involve additional responsibility, authority, and expertise, it does not result in a superordinate–subordinate relationship.

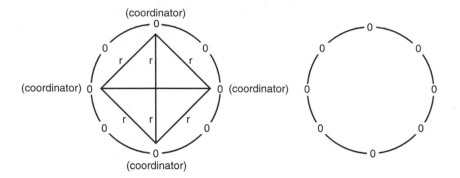

Modified Consensual Organization
Routine decisions are made inside
the circle, critical decisions are
made on the circle.

Consensual Organization
All decisions, critical and
routine, are made on the circle.

Key: 0 = organization members
        r = routine decisions
Lines on the circles and within the circle
represent paths of communication
within the organization.

FIGURE 9.1   Consensual and Modified Consensual Organization.

In the peace group, some rotation of members according to tasks helps to ensure that hierarchy does not develop. Because it is a volunteer organization, the peace group can afford the organizational costs involved in retraining members in new areas. The health collective decided that it could not afford those costs and therefore relied more on the "process" of the organization, including trust among members, to avoid the development of hierarchy.

Thus, while the most important defining element of these structures is the reserving of critical decisions for the entire membership, and the outward delegation of routine decisions to the few, other aspects of the internal environment are important to the maintenance of nonhierarchial structure. These aspects are best described by the term *process*. This includes the concepts of consensus, empowerment, and emerging leadership. Without the trust among members that is fostered through consensus decision making and the conscious effort to avoid domination, hierarchy would be difficult to avoid. In this way, the political ideals of the members and the ideological commitment to nonhierarchy are vitally important.

From the study of these two anarchist feminist groups, a modified consensual structure has been identified. Again, the most important defining element is the *outward,* not downward, delegation of routine decisions to the few and the reserving of critical decisions for the entire membership. Other important elements of the model include (1) recognition of ability or expertise rather than rank or position, (2) the notion of empowerment as a basis of consensual "process" and (3) clarity of goals that are arrived at *through* this consensual process.

IS THIS ANY WAY TO RUIN A WOMEN'S STUDIES PROGRAM?

Keeping in mind what has been learned about modified consensual structure through the examples of the peace group and health collective, we can return to the question: Is this any way to run a women's studies program? A case study of one program at a small liberal arts college serves as a starting point for this discussion.

In 1987 the Women's Studies Program Advisory Council (WSPAC) was established as the governing body for the women's studies program at Gettysburg College. While first consisting of seven faculty members, the organization soon expanded to include anyone on campus who wished to be a member. Today the council is composed of thirty-one members, with fourteen faculty members, thirteen students, one support staff person, and three administrators. The WSPAC sets policy for the women's studies program, which supports both a major and a minor and also plans cocurricular, campuswide events.[15]

There is a women's studies coordinator who serves a five-year term and is considered the equivalent of a department chairperson. She oversees the daily administration of the program with the assistance of an administrative assistant and one or more student assistants. The coordinator is a tenured faculty member in an academic department receiving one course release each semester for her administrative responsibilities.

Despite the existence of a coordinator, the WSPAC makes decisions consensually. In fact, in this case, the coordinator's commitment to shared decision making has fostered an atmosphere in which consensual process is more likely to thrive. The group meets every other week during the academic year and is structured very similarly to the peace group and health collective discussed earlier.

Each meeting is facilitated by members, on a rotating basis. The agenda is reviewed by the entire membership and is efficiently discussed, with a specific amount of time allotted for each item. This time designation is important for moving discussion along. Meetings last an hour and a half, rarely exceeding the designated time.

Everyone is asked to "check in" at the beginning of the meeting; each member says something about herself or the business at hand. This has the effect of fostering an "ethic of care" and the importance of participation within the organization. Likewise at the end of each meeting, everyone is asked to "check out" by evaluating the meeting "process," and again making any more personal comments they wish to make. Students, in particular, seem to feel comfortable with this part of the process. They describe the meetings as "relaxing." "It doesn't feel like work," one student remarked. Another student said: "No one has ever asked me to do this before, it makes me feel important to the organization."

The WSPAC does recognize the difference between critical and routine decisions and delegates routine decisions outward to various smaller committees that bring major policy issues back to the entire group. It is clearly structured as a modified consensual model. However, there are factors unique to the WSPAC, but common to campus organizations, that pose additional challenges with regard to maintaining consensual process.

One is its changing membership. From year to year, and sometimes from semester to semester, WSPAC membership changes. There is a basic core of faculty and the women's studies coordinator and administrative assistant, most of whom were among the founders of the group, who are ongoing members. Some of the administrators are continual members, and some are not. As expected, the student members are the most changeable due to the fact that they are only on campus for four years and during that time may or may not be participants.

Like new members of the peace group and health collective, new WSPAC members are often unfamiliar with consensual process and have to *learn* how to participate. One WSPAC faculty member explained, "You don't simply 'attend' a WSPAC meeting, you 'participate' and that places a lot more responsibility on you as a member. When I go to other committee meetings on campus I know the chairperson will do most of the work. That's not the case in a consensual organization." Frequent membership changes make the WSPAC's time invested in teaching "process" even greater. Since the turnover in students is most significant, the WSPAC assigns mentors, who are experienced members, to help students learn the nature of consensus versus voting, that there are no "motions" moved to the floor, and that everyone is a guardian of the process.

Along with the issue of changing membership come questions of differing knowledge. For example, students tend to be less familiar with the tenure and promotion process that affects faculty in women's studies. They may also be less aware of the role of particular administrators on campus. Likewise, faculty and administrators may be totally unaware of students' experiences in particular courses or their needs on campus. Because of this, the organization's "process" must allow for each member's vantage point. This is difficult under the pressures to get things done, such as major curriculum decisions for the next year. While this is sometimes a problem for the other organizations described in this article, it is not as much of a concern because their memberships are more constant and homogeneous. Furthermore, their deadlines are not tied to the time frame of academic semesters.

For the WSPAC this also raises the question of membership balance. The health collective and peace group might think of balance in terms of race, age, or ethnicity. While these are questions for women's studies committees as well, a central question for these organizations is the faculty–student ratio. This year the WSPAC's faculty–student ratio is almost even. In past years there have been many more faculty members than students. When this was the case, the faculty members of the group were constantly worried that student voices were not being heard. This year members of the WSPAC were struck by the novelty of one member asking with regard to an issue: "Has the *faculty* perspective been heard?"

What would happen if there were many more students than faculty? Could the organization adjust to the shift in the base of knowledge? Does a shift in the base of knowledge mean a shift in the base of power? Would women's studies at Gettysburg College or on any campus, become a "student-run" program? These are just a few of the questions raised due to increased student participation.

If the organization is truly consensual, it would be impossible to say that it was "run" by students or faculty. This means that no matter what the exact membership is, the "process" of the organization maintains a balanced perspective. One of the greatest difficulties in developing a consensual women's studies organization is the immediate environment. Colleges and universities are hierarchies. WSPAC members automatically bring to the organization their "position" on campus whether it be student, faculty member, administrator, or support staff member. These are not identities that can be checked at the door like a coat or umbrella. This reality puts additional pressure on the "process" of the organization to place all members on common ground with equal decision-making capability. This is particularly difficult when faculty and students are obviously not "equal" in the classroom. It is hard to say whether working toward equality in the WSPAC requires more effort on the part of the faculty or the students.

There is excitement among WSPAC members about the increased level of student involvement in the organization. As one nonstudent member explained it, "The larger student presence on WSPAC makes us even more committed to a process that creates equality." Likewise, the students are energized. "It's great to spend time with the other 'resident feminists' on campus," one student remarked. "Our participation will bring more positive attention to women's studies here." Similarly, another student said, "This is a new way for us to be taken seriously on campus."

Along with this new sense of importance, students also expressed uncertainties about their increased role. "I'm sometimes intimidated by the decisions we are making," one student said with regard to discussion about the hiring of part-time faculty. "We are affecting people's careers." Note here that students are intimidated by the nature of the *decision*, not by the other members of the organization. However, in these discussions students indicated the tendency to look to the coordinator or other faculty or administrators for direction when they thought the issue at hand was "too overwhelming." "They're the experts," one student commented. "When you've been in that professor's class, you tend to look to her for 'the answer.'" Yet the same students thought that their expertise as students was a factor, too. "We were able to give faculty information about our experiences in courses that they wouldn't have gotten otherwise," one student noted. "There was a real exchange."

As with the health collective, the sharing of knowledge and expertise in WSPAC contributes to a sense of equality. The recognition and analysis of differences in perspectives within the group is an open, ongoing process. One nonstudent member of the group said, "The legitimacy to air these issues makes the inequalities easier to deal with. If we are not willing to discuss and disagree then the process is not working. When it is working we are able to accomplish so much in a rational, responsive and respectful way. That's how it feels this year."

Beyond the mechanics of the modified consensual structure, the element of mutual respect and trust are central to the effective operation of this primarily faculty–student organization. Faculty members, students, and other WSPAC members have a mutual commitment to the goal of administering a high-quality women's studies program. It is to the benefit of all involved to reach that goal.

Is this any way to run a women's studies program? The National Women's Studies Association's report to the profession suggests that places of "liberal learning" provide a context, or moments in which theory and experience work together to transform students' sense of self and their relation to the world. "Women's studies' central responsibility is to facilitate such moments of recognition and to follow them with moments of empowerment."[16] In light of this statement, it seems entirely appropriate that women's studies students experience empowerment through participation in consensual organizations designed to administer women's studies programs.

NOTES

1. National Women's Studies Association, current estimate.

2. Lydia Sargent, *Women and Revolution* (Boston: South End Press, 1981), p. 116.

3. *Ibid.*, p. 115.

4. *Ibid.*, p. 114.

5. *Ibid.*, p. 116.

6. *Ibid.*

7. See Jo Freeman, *The Politics of Women's Liberation* (White Plains, NY: Longman, 1975).

8. Methods used to study these organizations were qualitative. Information was gathered through two years of personal observation of organization meetings, including special committee meetings and special projects/events, interviews with a cross section of women from both organizations, and the reading and researching of documents related to the history and operation

of the organizations. Similar methods were used to gather data on the WSPAC.

9. Organization mission statement, feminist peace group, pp. 1–2.

10. *Ibid.*

11. Organization mission statement, women's health collective, p. 1.

12. From a history of the women's health collective.

13. See Carol Gilligan, *In a Different Voice* (Cambridge, MA: Harvard University Press, 1982).

14. For a discussion of critical and routine decisions in organizations, see Philip Selznick, *Leadership in Administration* (Evanston, IL: Harper and Row, 1957), p. 56.

15. From a history of the WSPAC included in the *Policies and Procedures* manual.

16. *Liberal Learning and the Women's Studies Major* (College Park: National Women's Studies Association, 1991), p. 1.

FURTHER READINGS

Building United Judgment. Madison, WI: Center for Conflict Resolution, 1981.

Eisenstein, Hester. *Gender Shock.* Boston: Beacon Press, 1991.

Ferguson, Kathy E. *The Feminist Case against Bureau-cracy*. Philadelphia: Temple University Press, 1984.

Ferree, Myra Maix and Patricia Yancey Martin. *Feminist Organizations*. Philadelphia: Temple University Press, 1995.

Gilligan, Carol. *In a Different Voice*. Cambridge, MA: Harvard University Press, 1982.

Gilligan, Carol, Nona P. Lyons, and Trudy J. Hanmer. *Making Connections*. Cambridge, MA: Harvard University Press, 1990.

Hartsock, Nancy. "Foucault on Power: A Theory for Women?" in Linda Nicholson (Ed.), *Feminism/Post-modernism* (New York: Routledge, 1990).

Hirschmann, Nancy J. *Rethinking Obligation*. Ithaca: NY: Cornell University Press, 1992.

Jones, Kathleen B. *Compassionate Authority*. New York: Routledge, 1993.

Iannello, Kathleen P. *Decisions without Hierarchy*. New York: Routledge, 1992.

Leidner, Robin. "Stretching the Boundaries of Liberal-ism: Democratic Innovation in a Feminist Organization," *Signs* 16 (2) (1991), pp. 263–289.

Liberal Learning and the Women's Studies Major. College Park: National Women's Studies Association, University of Maryland, 1991.

Love, Nancy. *Dogmas and Dreams*. Chatham, NJ: Chatham House, 1991.

Martin, Patricia Yancey. "Rethinking Feminist Organizations," *Gender and Society,* (June 1990), pp. 182–206.

Sargent, Lydia. *Women and Revolution*. Boston: South End Press, 1981.

Swerdlow, Amy. "Motherhood and the Subversion of the Military State: Women's Strike for Peace Confronts the House Committee on Un-American Activities," in Elshtain, Jean Bethke and Sheila Tobias (Eds.), *Women, Militarism and War*. Savage, MD: Rowman and Littlefield, 1990.

Tong, Rosemarie. *Feminist Thought*. Boulder, CO: Westview Press, 1989.

Grounds for Criticism: Coffee, Passion, and the Politics of Feminist Discourse

Elizabeth A. Kelly

More than one-third of the world's people drink coffee today, but coffee has never been merely a beverage. Three centuries or so have gone by since it became an overnight rage among the fashionable and witty in cities across Europe. Jürgen Habermas, among others, has drawn attention to the role played by coffeehouses in the formation of a bourgeois public sphere in the late eighteenth century. Indeed, the role of the coffeehouse as a bastion of free speech had far-reaching implications: Coffee and the establishments serving it played an integral role in the founding of the United States and continue to provide arenas where discourses of resistance and alternatives to established "politics as usual" may take place. The GI coffeehouse movement, for example, promoted resistance to U.S. involvement in the Vietnam Conflict; places like Chicago's Mountain Moving Coffeehouse, established over twenty years ago and still operating today, have been focal points for the development of a feminist "women's culture" and served as safe spaces for the articulation of feminist and lesbian–feminist political thought.

This paper will explore the relationship between coffee and political discourse, paying particular attention to the role of coffeehouses as alternative public spheres. It will also examine the often complex relationships between coffee, coffeehouse cultures, and gender, along with how these relationships have shifted his-

I am grateful to Uma Narayan, Jacqueline Taylor, and Linda Hillman for their careful readings, encouragement, and insights. Michael Forman, Carl Larsen, and John Martin also deserve thanks for reading and commenting on an earlier version of this article and for providing the moment of its "conception."

torically. Considered by turns as cure-all or the "devil's brew," the common people's drink or the liquor of the elite, object of disdain or cause for celebration, coffee has seldom failed to elicit one emotion that perhaps best explains its powerful political impact: passion. I will argue that such emotions, often overlooked by political theory, indeed stand at the center of a critical theory of coffee drinking.

ORIGINS OF COFFEE

The origins of coffee drinking are shrouded in mystery; legends abound, but there is little factual evidence to show precisely when people began to drink this seductive brew, let alone who first concocted it. Remarkably similar accounts from Arab chronicles credit either King Solomon or the Prophet Muhammad with first "discovering" coffee. As the story goes, the great man interrupts a journey to visit a town whose inhabitants suffer from a strange, unnamed illness. On command from the Angel Gabriel, he roasts coffee beans and prepares a beverage whose curative powers are truly miraculous; the townsfolk recover completely after taking only a few sips.[1] Another tale has the dreaming Prophet visited by an angel, who commands Muhammad to fetch a bowl of water to a nearby field. When the water stops moving, a sign from Allah will appear. The next morning, Muhammad carries out these instructions: When the water in the bowl is still, he kneels in prayer. A shrub appears before him, and a voice commands him to taste its fruit. Obeying, he experiences a great surge of energy and leaves the field refreshed. The fruit, of course, is the coffee bean.[2]

A variation on the "discovery" theme centers on the dervish Omar, who is awakened one midnight by a huge apparition, the spirit of his long-dead mentor, which guides him to a coffee tree. Omar and his disciples at first attempt to eat the berries; they then try to soften them in water. When this fails, they drink the liquid in which the berries have been boiled. Shortly thereafter, victims of an epidemic of itching rampant in Mocha come to consult with Omar and are cured after drinking the brew. Their gratitude allows Omar to enter Mocha with honors; he becomes the patron saint of coffee growers, owners of coffeehouses, and coffee drinkers alike.[3]

Perhaps the most commonly told story of coffee's origins is that of the "dancing goats." Here Kaldi, a young Ethiopian goatherd, is depressed. Weary of searching for greener pastures and faced with a flock of tired, hungry goats, he rests, unable to move on. The herd begins to nibble sweet red berries off nearby bushes; suddenly all the goats begin behaving very strangely. The oldest billy goat kicks up his heels, cavorting ecstatically; the others quickly join him in a manic dance. Startled, Kaldi, decides to try the berries himself. He, too, begins leaping giddily about the hillside, his troubles forgotten. A passing monk is astonished to see shepherd and flock dancing about the meadow; he samples the berries, and invites other monks to join in. That night during prayers, the monks all feel remarkably alert. They spread news of the amazing discovery throughout the religious community;

the fame of the coffee berries—and the beverage brewed from them—spreads throughout the land.[4]

It seems safe to say that whoever the first coffee drinkers may have been, they experienced sensations ranging from exhilaration to religious ecstasy. None of the serious histories of coffee I looked at in the course of preparing this essay contains any mention—whether couched in terms of legend or fact—of the possibility that a *woman* may very well have been the first to hit on the concept of roasting, grinding, and brewing coffee beans into a beverage. This is peculiar, because women have historically been responsible for roasting, brewing, stewing, and fermenting all sorts of substances in the course of preparing food and drink. Given the highly gender-specific ways in which coffee has been both utilized and symbolized—from the days of dervishes and dancing goats down through the present—it is perhaps not surprising.

EARLY HISTORY OF COFFEE AND COFFEE DRINKING

Once legends of origin are dispensed with, coffee's history becomes much more prosaic. The practice of roasting coffee beans probably began around the thirteenth century, when the drink appears to have become popular in connection with Sufi Muslim religious practices. It was first widely used in the Yemen, but soon spread to Mecca and Medina. References to the beverage are found in scientific literature, philosophical tracts, folklore, and religious texts. The eleventh-century physician and philosopher Avicenna wrote that coffee "fortifies the members, cleans the skin, dries up the humidities that are under it, and give an excellent smell to the body." Another Islamic physician claimed that "it is by experience found to conduce the drying of colds, persistent coughs and catarrh, and to unblock constipation and provoke urination; it allays high blood pressure, and is good against smallpox and measles." He added a cautionary note that adding milk to the brew might "bring one in danger of leprosy." By the end of the fifteenth century, Muslim pilgrims had extolled coffee's restorative powers throughout the Islamic world. While the beverage remained one of the crops of the nocturnal devotional services of the Sufi religious order, those who were less spiritually inclined found it a pleasant stimulus to talk and sociability. Here, the coffeehouse was born.[5]

COFFEEHOUSE CULTURE IN SIXTEENTH-CENTURY ISLAM

The story of how coffee drinking fueled a democratic fad for coffeehouse culture across Europe during the seventeenth and eighteenth centuries, especially in England, is familiar. It has often been told in relation to demands for freedom of speech and freedom of the press, which were central to the politics of an emergent bourgeois public sphere. However, the historical and political antecedents of European coffeehouses in sixteenth-century Islam are far less well known. The actual preparation of the beverage differed depending on the cultural context, but in fifteenth-century Mecca and Cairo coffee's popularity—along with its tendency to encourage people to speak freely as they gathered in public places—was not just noteworthy but highly politically charged and acutely gender-specific.

In the Arab world, coffeehouses were essentially Muslim establishments, whose clientele was therefore exclusively male. They served as practical alternatives to the proscribed taverns where wines and other alcoholic beverages were served. With wine and other fermented drinks forbidden under Islamic law, local water often scarce and brackish, and goat's milk barely palatable, coffee was a perfect thirst quencher. It was served and drunk hot, but generally savored slowly; this all but demanded stationary, relatively protected places of consumption, where patrons could take their time, and which in turn served as the perfect setting for talk and socializing with others. Gaming, dancing, music, and singing—activities frowned upon by the strictest followers of Islam—went on in the coffeehouses, along with freewheeling social, political, and religious discussions. All of this was viewed by the authorities with suspicion, and many Islamic officials saw coffee as subversive. It gathered people together; it sharpened their wits and loosened their tongues; it stimulated political arguments and, at least potentially, fomented revolts.

In 1511 an official in Mecca, whose office apparently combined aspects of consumer advocacy and protection with the enforcement procedures of a vice squad, put coffee on trial. He convened a meeting of religious scholars who heard evidence from physicians regarding the putatively detrimental effects of coffee drinking and from religious leaders and government officials regarding the immoral and impious behavior of coffeehouse denizens. For a brief time the sale and consumption of coffee were banned in the city. However, the sultan turned out to be a coffee aficionado; within a year the official who had instigated the ban had been removed from his post, and coffeehouses once again flourished. However, in 1525–1526 a more serious incident surrounding coffee took place in Mecca, where a distinguished jurist, Muhammad ibn al-'Arraq, succeeded in closing down the coffeehouses for nearly two years.[6]

A similar pattern of opposition to coffeehouses and coffee drinking emerged in Cairo, where attempts were made to ban all coffee in 1532–1533 and where rioting broke out in the streets on several occasions during 1534–1535 when authorities attempted to shut down the coffeehouses. Here, again, secular and religious leaders were suspicious of the potential threats to their authority symbolized by nocturnal gatherings where people spoke freely and critically on any and all issues. These fears were real and sometimes took substantive form. In Istanbul, in 1633, Sultan Marat IV ordered all coffeehouses torn down on the pretext of fire prevention; they remained closed, "desolate as the heart of the ignorant," until the last quarter of the century. Perhaps the most remarkable, and definitely the most savage, example of the sporadic attempts to prohibit coffee drinking was seen in Turkey, where the grand vizier banned coffee outright in 1656. For a first violation of the ban, the punishment was the cudgel; for a second, the offender would be sewn into a leather bag and thrown into the Bosphorus, where the straits claimed many souls.[7]

Attempts to curtail coffee drinking or coffeehouse culture proved futile, however, over the long run. Throughout the Arab world, social life had been permanently and irrevocably altered by the ever-growing use of coffee, for in cities, towns, and villages, a previously unknown *public* institution—the coffeehouse—had grown up around the production and sale of this commodity. Talk, whether in the form of casual banter or passionate literary disputes and political arguments, was central to the new institution, as was a certain egalitarian spirit. The traveler Pedro Teixeira reported that in Baghdad coffee was "prepared and sold in public houses built to that end; wherein all men who desire it meet to drink it, be they great or mean."[8] In place of newspapers or other public forums, coffeehouses had quickly become places where information of all kinds, from place gossip to the latest trades in the market, could be exchanged simply by word of mouth. At least one Islamic critic bemoaned the way in which coffeehouse patrons "really extend themselves in slander, defamation, and throwing doubt on the reputations of virtuous women. What they come up with are generally the most frightful fabrications, things without a grain of truth in them."[9] This complaint retains its resonance today, although the sports bar or health club locker room might come more readily to mind as places where tall tales of male sexual prowess or conquest may be routinely overheard.

INTRODUCTION OF COFFEE IN EUROPE

The introduction of coffee to Europe, most likely through Venice and other Italian port cities, recapitulated many of the patterns that had been set in Arab lands a century or so earlier. In Europe, as in Islam, coffee drinking initially had religious connotations; in both cases the practice quickly gave rise to the public institution of the coffeehouse, which was often viewed with suspicion by authorities, if not deemed downright subversive of the state. A relatively egalitarian ethic, free speech, and the exchange of news and information also prevailed as the fad for coffee caught on in areas where both the beverage and the institutions it encouraged had previously been unknown. At first European Christians were skeptical about what was seen as a "pagan brew." Italian priests attacked the beverage virulently and successfully petitioned Pope Clement VIII in the hope that he would place coffee under papal interdiction throughout Christendom. The priests argued that coffee was the drink of the devil. Satan, they reasoned, had forbidden the Muslim infidels the use of wine (central to the Christian sacrament of Holy Communion), supplying them instead with his "hellish black brew." The pope, however, found the pungent aroma of the cup of coffee brought before him as evidence of this diabolical intrigue to be utterly irresistible. After tasting the drink, he pronounced it delicious and declared that it would be dreadful to let the infidels have exclusive use of the beverage. Pope Clement turned the tables on Satan by baptizing coffee on the spot. Thus sanctified, coffee no longer required an apothecary's prescription; ordinary people flocked to try the drink, which was sold on street corners throughout Italy.[10]

With this incident, we see a striking connection to the legends surrounding coffee's origin; clearly, the perceptions of the beverage's magical or medicinal properties have something to do with how its advent, whether in the Arab world or some chamber deep within the Vatican, is culturally remembered. In both contexts, religion, spirituality, and much medical healing were clearly and emphatically defined as exclusively male preserves—even, in many cases, at the expense of long-standing traditions of female dominance in these realms.[11] Thus it is particularly interesting that when coffee makes its appearance in Europe, it does so only after receiving papal approbation—in essence, recapitulating the earlier Islamic legends. In both cases, spiritually enlightened males get the credit for discovering, sanctioning, or sanctifying coffee drinking.

In 1650 the first European coffee house opened in Oxford, England, "at the Angel in the parish of St.-Peter-in-the-East."[12] It took another ten years before coffeehouses became truly popular in the university town, but complaints about them grew as their popularity increased. Neither the university nor the coffeehouses springing up in its environs welcomed women, either as scholars or as customers. By 1661 Anthony Wood opined that scholarship was in decline, since "nothing but news, and the affaires of Christendom is discoursed off and that also generally at coffee houses."[13] Roger North held that "the Scholars are so Greedy after News (which is none of their business) that they neglect all for it . . . a vast loss of Time grown out of a pure Novelty; for who can apply close to a subject with his Head full of the din of a Coffee House?"[14] By 1677 the vice chancellor of the University was ordering coffee sellers not to open after evening prayers on Sundays, but he opined that "at five of the clock they flocked all the more" to their favorite haunts. Three years later, a Puritan mayor attempted to close the coffeehouses down entirely on Sundays, but it seems highly unlikely that this edict was ever enforced, let alone obeyed.[15]

POPULARITY OF COFFEEHOUSES IN LONDON

Nowhere were coffeehouses so popular as in London, where the first one had opened in 1652. By 1700 there were about 3000 coffeehouses in the city, which at the time had a population of around 600,000; this works out to an almost unbelievable ratio of one coffeehouse for every 200 people. Coffeehouses represented a spectrum of interests, ranging from commerce to politics and literature. They generally opened off the street and were rather crudely furnished, with tables and chairs scattered about a sanded floor. Eventually booths were added and the walls covered with broadsides and newspapers of all kinds, playbills, handbills, and posters. Macaulay described the company at the famous literary establishment, Wills,' as consisting of "earls in stars and garters, clergymen in cassocks, pert templars, sheepish lads from the Universities, translators and index-makers in ragged coats."[16] Here, classes mixed more freely than they might elsewhere; no one who could put a penny on the bar was excluded. All were welcome in these centers of male networking; all, that is, except women.

Coffeehouses arrived on the London scene along with Puritan rule; they were especially suited to the social climate of the day, offering an antidote to taverns and alcoholism. One approving entry into the pamphlet wars that raged shortly after the advent of coffeehouse culture praised "this coffee drink" for having "caused a greater sobriety among the Nations," and added, by way of explanation: "Whereas formerly Apprentices and clerks with others used to take the morning's draught in Ale, Beer, or Wine, which, by the dizziness they Cause in the Brain, made many unfit for business, they use now to play the Good-fellows in this wakeful and civil drink."[17] While tea and chocolate were also available in the coffeehouses, alcoholic drinks were not; sobriety and moderation were the order of the day, and rules governing the behavior of coffeehouse patrons were prominently displayed on the walls of these establishments. Manners mattered in these places, although it is doubtful that all of the posted regulations were followed to the letter.[18]

Even allowing for a gap between theory and practice when it came to rules and regulations, the democratic character of the English coffeehouse and the sobriety encouraged there were significant at a time when the bourgeoisie was newly organizing as a class. Progressive ideas were in the air, and the coffeehouse as a public space where such thoughts could be aired was as novel a concept as coffee was a beverage. Here, as Habermas and others have noted, *men,* not only could meet to talk over the issues of the day but also begin to articulate a critique of the theory and practice of absolutist domination. Eventually these expressions of "public opinion" legitimated by rational consensus among relatively equal citizens would take on a political dimension of their own, as the bourgeoisie deployed this new, critical public sphere as a revolutionary instrument of class emancipation. The public sphere, insofar as it served to build public opinion in support of values like free speech, democracy, or the rule of law, also served to protect individuals from arbitrary actions of the state, and to mediate between the state and civil society. New technologies allowed newspapers, journals, and books to be produced cheaply and quickly; these media became more widely available than ever before, facilitating lively political debate and opposition—much of which, of course, took place in coffeehouses. The bourgeois public sphere may thus be seen as an arena where democratic discourse was not only available—at least to a limited extent— but, especially as exemplified by English coffeehouse culture, could flourish.[19]

GENDER POLITICS OF COFFEEHOUSE CULTURE

Joan Landes's contention that Habermas's notion of the "bourgeois public sphere" was essentially, and not just contingently, masculinist, bears mention here. Landes takes Habermas to task for not paying adequate attention to the way in which the eighteenth-century public sphere, described in outline here, was shaped by gendered categories and overtly sexist strategies, such as Rousseau's ideology of republican motherhood. The equation of "men" and "citizens" is thus not generic, for the public sphere was just as exclusive of women as the coffeehouse—whether located in fifteenth-century Cairo or eighteenth-century London.[20]

Clear evidence of this was seen in 1674, when unhappy wives published *The Women's Petition against Coffee*. The authors of this pamphlet declared that it was unhealthy for men to be spending so much time away from their homes. Men who became addicted to coffee, they argued, were becoming "as unfruitful as the deserts, from where that unhappy berry is said to be brought." The women complained that they were being neglected by their husbands, whose enjoyment of coffeehouse society placed "the whole race . . . in danger of extinction."[21] Especially interesting here is the way in which women's resentment of coffeehouses would appear to stem less from their exclusion from these male preserves than from the way in which the coffeehouse drew husbands and fathers away from the home (and the marriage bed). Coffeehouses, like taverns, were comfortable retreats from the responsibilities of family life, where men could both reduce the time and attention spent on domestic affairs and fritter away scarce financial resources, leaving less available for family needs. Not only did these public spaces exclude women; they also competed with women and domestic life for the time and money of men. Thus an interest in politics and public life could often provide a convenient excuse for men to hang out in such places, shirking their family responsibilities.

The gender politics of coffeehouse culture allow us to ask whether the political "fraternity" encouraged within the bourgeois public sphere of the eighteenth century resulted from something more than the mere exclusion of women. In spending long hours at the coffeehouse discussing the affairs of the day, men were withdrawing from the demands of family life at a time when the family constituted the basic economic unit of society. Thus women's responsibilities for domestic affairs and the household economy were only increased in the absence of men. Perhaps the democratic discourse of the new public spaces was built not just on the exclusion of women and the creation of specifically gendered categories like "republican motherhood," but also at the cost of increased anxiety and family labor on the part of wives, mothers, and daughters.[22]

COFFEEHOUSES, POLITICAL DISCOURSE, AND REVOLUTION

The coffeehouse played an integral role in revolutionary politics on the North American continent as well as in Europe. European settlers brought coffee with them to the colonies throughout the seventeenth and early eighteenth centuries. Four years after the British took control of Dutch New Amsterdam in 1664, coffee had eclipsed beer as the preferred breakfast drink of New Yorkers. In Boston the Green Dragon Coffee House, founded in 1697, would in later years be named the "headquarters of the Revolution" by no less than Daniel Webster. At the Green Dragon John Adams, Paul Revere, and others reportedly planned the Boston Tea Party, which made coffee drinking a patriotic act. Another Boston coffeehouse, the Bunch of Grapes, provided the stage for the first public reading of the Declaration of Independence. New York's Merchants Coffee House, located at the southeast corner of Wall and Water Streets, served as another focal point for revolutionary politics. The Sons of Liberty met there on April 18, 1774, to repel a shipment of tea arriving on a British ship; a month later citizens gathered there to draft a letter calling for a "virtuous and spirited Union" of the colonies against Great Britain, along with a congress of deputies—which would become the First Continental Congress. After the Revolution, the coffeehouse continued to play a political role, most notably hosting a huge reception on April 23, 1789, in honor of President–elect George Washington. Coffee was thus bound up, in the early days of the Republic, with a revolutionary politics of liberty and critical public opinion.[23]

Women were, for the most part, excluded from this political community, despite the fact that prewar boycotts and the need to quarter and provision the revolutionary army had politicized household economies before and after independence was declared.[24] Indeed, women had mounted public actions to police local merchants who hoarded scarce commodities in Poughkeepsie, Philadelphia, and elsewhere. On at least one occasion, coffee played a central role in such activity. In July, 1778, Abigail Adams reported to her husband, John, that "a Number of Females, some say a hundred, some say more, assembled with a cart and trucks, marched down to the Ware House" of an "eminent, wealthy, stingy Merchant" who was believed to be hoarding coffee in Boston. When the merchant refused to deliver the keys, "one of them seazd him by his Neck and tossed him into the cart . . . he delivered the keys . . . they . . . opened the Warehouse. Hoisted out the Coffee themselves, put it into trucks and drove off. . . . A large concourse of Men stood amazed silent Spectators."[25] By the end of the war, however, such patriotic activity on the part of women would be deflected into benevolence, with service and reform societies directing women's energies back into the private world of home and family.

Much the same state of affairs prevailed in Europe, although in the case of the French Revolution, comparable women's riots were more desperate, frequent, and violent; the issue was bread, not the luxury of coffee or tea.[26] The historian Michelet described coffee as "the great event which created new customs, and even modified human temperaments," ascribing to the beverage the intangible and spontaneous flow of wit characteristic of the age of the philosophes—but this was entirely gender-specific. Coffeehouse culture flourished in France after the famous Café Procope opened its doors in 1689. Located across from the Comédie Francaise, this establishment attracted authors, actors, dramatists, and musicians, along with philosophers and politicians. Voltaire, who is rumored to have consumed over seventy cups of coffee a day, was a frequent patron. So were Rousseau, Diderot, Beaumarchais, and—during the days of the Revolution—Marat, Robespierre, and Danton. As in England, French coffeehouse culture emphasized temperance, luring customers away from the taverns and wine sellers.[27]

The café society central to the revolutionary public sphere remained relatively intact throughout the nineteenth and early twentieth centuries in France, but by the end of the eighteenth century coffeehouse culture in England had all but vanished. For the wealthier classes, select "gentlemen's clubs" became the preferred place to assemble in the company of one's social peers; the poorer and less exclusive establishments reverted to their earlier roles as taverns or chop houses, and a new fad for drinking tea eclipsed the coffee-drinking habit. As the public life of coffee declined in England, it found new favor on the domestic scene in Germany, as a breakfast and afternoon drink in middle-class homes.

Coffee was not unknown in Germany. Its use, however, had ambivalent connotations, notably the notion that coffee drinking made men and women sterile, which spared a movement aimed at preventing women from drinking the brew. In 1732 Johann Sebastian Bach composed a "Coffee Cantata," inspired by his love of the brew, which includes the aria "Ah! How sweet coffee tastes! Lovelier than a thousand kisses, sweeter far than muscatel wine! I must have my coffee." The fact that Bach had two wives and fathered twenty children also tended to give the lie to claims regarding coffee's putative links to sterility. We are left wondering, however, just what the mothers of these children might have felt about any of this.[28]

In 1777 Frederick the Great of Prussia attempted to ban coffee consumption by ordinary citizens. Annoyed with the large sums of cash that were flowing to foreign coffee merchants, he declared:

> It is disgusting to note the increase in the quantity of coffee used by my subjects and the amount of money that goes out of the country in consequence. Everybody is using coffee. If possible, this must be prevented. My people must drink beer. His Majesty was brought up on beer, and so were his officers. Many battles have been fought and won by soldiers nourished on beer; and the King does not believe that coffee-drinking soldiers can be depended upon to endure hardships or to beat his enemies in case of the occurrence of another war.[29]

Retired soldiers were recruited as "coffee smellers" to go about arresting anyone caught secretly roasting or brewing the beverage, while physicians were encouraged to tell their patients that drinking coffee would make them sterile. This move of Frederick's generated numerous expressions of passive and active resistance. The public's desire for coffee however, won out in the end. Yet in Germany, coffee drinking became a private, domestic activity; coffee replaced flour soup or beer at breakfast and took on a new, gender-specific dimension as the focus of socializing among women in the afternoons. Breakfast coffee retained vestiges of the public functions of the coffeehouse, marking the start of the working day. After a cup or two in the morning, people were alert and ready to face the business day. In the nineteenth century the newspaper, another émigré from the coffeehouse, was added to this ritual. But the real impetus for the spread of coffee's popularity in Germany came from women of the new burgher class.

WOMEN AND "COFFEE CIRCLES" CULTURE

Recently arrived from the countryside, freed from work in the fields, townswomen gathered to drink coffee in the afternoons at one another's homes. The *Kaffeekränzchen,* or "coffee party," (literally "coffee circle") was entirely a women's affair; it demanded the relative freedom and leisure attached to the bourgeois cult of domesticity. Amaranthes's *Frauenzimmerlexikon,* the "Woman's Lexicon," defined it as "a daily or weekly gathering of several closely acquainted women, each taking her turn as hostess, and in which the members divert and amuse themselves with drinking coffee and playing *Ombre* [a popular card game of the day]." One way to "read" the significance of these gatherings is to suggest that women approached them with a passion that must be seen as compensation for their exclusion from other, more public, domains. In many respects, afternoon coffee parties served as a sort of exclusively female parallel to the exclusively male socializing of coffeehouses and taverns, often becoming the objects of ridicule. Indeed, to this day the word *Kaffeeklatsch* ("ladies gossip circle") retains extremely pejorative—and heavily gendered—connotations.[30] An alternative interpretation, however, might focus on the fact that women might simply have found the company of other women more interesting and stimulating than mixed company.[31]

Without romanticizing the women's coffee parties, it is important to protest the prevailing portrait of them as venues for trivial (i.e., domestic) gossip, especially as contrasted to images of coffeehouses as places where important (i.e., public) speech and activity would prevail. This serves to obscure the reality of how much time spent in taverns or coffeehouses—male preserves of "publicity"—was likely devoted to forms of "male" gossip, or conversations about sports, sexual conquest, tall tales, and the like, instead of (or, more charitably, in addition to) the serious political discourse that is often spoken of by theorists of the bourgeois public sphere. Perhaps there is something threatening to men in the image of women getting together and talking among themselves. The language is, indeed, replete with pejorative synonyms for "girl talk": *gab, gossip, chat, chitchat, chatter, babble, prattle,* and *hen party* are only a few of the terms used to devalue women in their verbal interactions. But perhaps this is not so much a matter of male fear as it is a question of women's internalization of second-class status. As Deborah Cameron notes, "Men trivialize the talk of women not because they are afraid of such talk, but in order to make women themselves down-grade it. If women feel that all interaction with other women is a poor substitute for mixed interaction and trivial compared with the profundities of men's talk, their conversations will indeed be harmless."[32]

Even more is at stake here than the use of language—powerful though language may be as a cultural significator of power and power-structured relationships. Ambivalence and anxiety about women's leisure time seem to have accompanied the rise of the bourgeois family; derogative responses to women's coffee parties may have been one manifestation of bourgeois male concerns in this regard. On the one hand, a wife's leisure may be taken as a positive reflection of her husband's status and affluence. On the other, however, this newfound leisure might give rise to a whole new set of worries about what "mischief" women might get up to if they have too much free time on their hands. Such concerns would eventually be borne out when Betty Friedan's germinal analysis of a "feminine mystique" emerging among middle-class women was published in the United States—a century after women's coffee parties were all the rage among the German bourgeoisie.[33]

COFFEE'S CHANGING ROLE IN TWENTIETH CENTURY

The movement of coffee out of the public sphere and into the private realm of the bourgeois family and its imitators in nineteenth-century Germany was paralleled in the United States, where, by the start of the twentieth century, the beverage had been thoroughly domesticated. Indeed, its gendered connotations underwent a further transformation when coffee drinking was promoted by the Women's Christian Temperance Union (WCTU) as an alternative to the alcoholic beverages that were readily available in saloons across the nation. The American Public Health Association supported the WCTU, claiming that there was "a physiological antagonism between coffee and alcohol, as well as between coffee and opium," and designating coffee a healthy stimulant, "much favored by brain workers," as well as an anti-malarial agent.[34] Female reformers of the Progressive Era often suggested founding coffeehouses in the slums as a means of displacing saloons. They looked favorably on the popularity of coffeehouses among Jewish and Italian immigrants, whose sobriety was noteworthy compared with that of many other immigrant groups. In the early 1900s, Jane Addams praised these working-class cafés as the "Salons of the Ghetto" and cited them for "performing a function somewhat between the eighteenth century coffee house and the Parisian café."[35]

The public sphere of the coffeehouses—whether in medieval Islam or eighteenth-century London and New York—had been an exclusively male domain. Throughout the twentieth century in the United States the domestic use of coffee would become something of a feminized cultural icon, central to the spread of commodity goods and consumer capitalist culture. George Lipsetz analyzed coffee's changing role as a cultural icon in a case study of the women's roles in the CBS network television show *I Remember Mama,* which consistently ranked among the top ten programs during its eight-year run in the 1950s. Both this production and a 1948 feature film of the same name were inspired by a collection of short stories by Kathryn Forbes entitled *Mama's Bank Account,* as were a Broadway play and radio performance. The stories, and their various media interpretations, dealt with Norwegian immigrant life in the years before the Great Depression. Lipsetz contrasted the role of coffee drinking in the movie and the television series, which was (not incidentally) sponsored by Maxwell House Coffee.[36]

In the motion picture one of "Mama's" teenage daughters was permitted to join her parents in a cup of coffee after she proved herself as an adult by rejecting a showy dresser set and accepting a piece of family jewelry for her high school graduation gift. The young woman's rejection of consumer goods in favor of traditional values was seen by moviegoers as praiseworthy. However, this was turned upside down in the television series, where tradition served only to legitimate the purchase of more and more consumer goods, and the family story became a lure to bring the audience commercial messages from the program's sponsor. As Lipsetz put it, "The product becomes a member of the Hansen family, while tradition and emotional support become commodities to be secured through the purchase of Maxwell House coffee."[37]

Coffee was cast in the dramatic narratives of the show in a variety of ways. Mama and Papa drank it together in the kitchen; it served as a means of calming down rambunctious children, as a spark for women's conversations, or as an excuse for having company; it facilitated clear thinking and problem solving. Perhaps more importantly, its magical attributes served to draw viewers toward other commodities seen in an equally respectful, if not quite so consistently magical, light.[38] A fundamental connection was established between the warmth of these nostalgic scenes of idyllic family life and the impetus of a consumer capitalist economy toward ever-expanding commodity purchases. In the context of the television series, the domestication of coffee drinking stands in sharp relief as an example of the subsumption by the "culture industry" of the critical public sphere of political discourse formerly found in coffeehouse culture. This iconography demonstrates the extent to which the industry's attendant forms of "publicity" and "entertainment" have come to serve as stand-ins for free speech and cultural critique.

Indeed, contemporary coffee advertisements would seem to demonstrate that coffee today has moved almost totally out of the public sphere and into the realm of privacy and intimacy. Television commercials for Folger's Coffee, for instance, evoke "traditional" family values far more insistently (and effectively) than any of the speakers at the 1992 Republican National Convention. In a typical spot we see the young African American soldier returning home, duffle bag over his shoulder, to share a cup of coffee with Mom in the family kitchen along with an affectionate hug—and "masculine" toss of a football—with a kid brother. In another, a young white woman returns home after college, and, by taking over the chore of making morning coffee, demonstrates that for all her education she still aspires to be "just like mom." Every December the handsome young son returns, we know not from just where—perhaps an Ivy League college?—his arms filled with brightly wrapped packages. The presents get put under the Christmas tree before he awakens his delighted family with the aroma of a pot of freshly brewed Folger's. Images are, indeed, often more powerful than words!

In this context it is also important to think of the unfolding heterosexual romance portrayed in a recent, ongoing series of commercials for Taster's Choice instant coffee or the call to "celebrate the moments of our lives" by drinking General Foods International Coffees. The latter ads often display various forms of female bonding, with sisters or former college roommates drinking coffee while engaging in nostalgic conversation. These relationships between women are depicted as either emphatically asexual or prophetically heterosexual, as when college pals reminisce about the handsome waiter at a European café. They are indicative of the confinement of female discourse, and especially the "symbolic speech" of female sexuality, to domesticity within an overarching framework of compulsory heterosexuality.[39] Indeed, coffee drinking is often equated with women making time for themselves in the midst of competing demands: An instant cappuccino, one ad implies, can make the conflicting demands of children, housework, a profession, and caring for elderly relatives melt away to nothing—and in just "an instant." Only rarely do we see coffee advertised in more "public" settings, notably the Folger's commercials that show diners in fancy restaurants drinking instant coffee that's been "switched" for a freshly brewed beverage. And even then the domestic message is clear: "I'll serve this at home" is, explicitly or implicitly, the tag line spoken by these putatively surprised patrons.

It might seem, in the United States at least, as if the pendulum had swung entirely from one side to the other, from a heavily male (public) sphere of coffeehouses and coffee drinking to a specifically female (private) realm of idyllic domesticity where coffee is just one of many commodities to be purchased and consumed. Indeed, it would not be difficult to develop a wholly negative, one-sided critique in the style of Horkheimer and Adorno, where the golden (masculine) age of the coffeehouse is valorized at the expense of a debased (feminine) mode of domestic coffee drinking. But such a critique would ignore the ways in which vestiges of the older traditions not only remain in contemporary society but on occasion have been manipulated consciously by members of progressive social movements in ways that subvert both the established "culture industry" and the gendered distinctions of the "public" and "private" spheres.

COFFEE AND ALTERNATIVE SOCIAL AND CULTURAL INSTITUTIONS

Countercultural institutions have emerged in the last two decades that draw on the traditions of free speech and cultural and political criticism that were integral to the coffeehouse cultures of centuries past. Indeed, these institutions may be situated in a context of political discourse that includes the café societies of Bohemian Paris at the turn of the twentieth century and Weimar Germany after the First World War.[40] The GI coffeehouse movement was a focal point, on and around a number of military installations, for organizing against the Vietnam Conflict. By the early 1970s, some peace protestors had shifted their efforts away from college campuses to military bases around the country. At Mountain Home Air Force Base in Idaho, for example, peace workers "opened a coffeehouse for GIs in an abandoned theater downtown; they called it the Helping Hand. They had meetings that advised enlisted personnel how to assist the antiwar movement. They published an antiwar newspaper for the base, began counseling GIs on how to file for conscientious-objector status, and opened a small library of radical books."[41] Comparable efforts were made across the country, with coffeehouses springing up in the vicinity of almost every major military base. Over a hundred underground newspapers would be published, often in conjunction with coffeehouse activities. For a while there was even talk of unionizing the military. In at least some cases, these initiatives involved discussions of class relationships (between middle-class and working-class peace organizers and between civilians and GIs) and confrontations with feminist issues that sparked difficult and lively debates.[42]

Since the late 1960s, in cities and towns across the United States, feminist community organizing and cultural work has often centered around coffeehouses, sometimes in tandem with feminist bookstores and other forms of cultural expression. While some of these businesses have been relatively short-lived experiments in collectivity and other alternatives to capitalist organizations, others have survived and continue to do so despite an often hostile economic climate. In Chicago, for example, the Mountain Moving Coffeehouse celebrated its twenty-fifth anniversary in 1998. Its very name connotes the political struggles attached to building alternative social and cultural institutions—it is no easy task to "move the mountains" of entrenched sexism and homophobia that militate against feminist organizational agendas prioritizing women and their concerns or needs.

Technically speaking, Mountain Moving is set somewhat apart from the "tradition" of coffeehouse culture, not just in that it provides a space for feminist/lesbian cultural expression but also because this space is not permanently devoted to the consumption of coffee or any other comestibles. Rather, Mountain Moving Coffeehouse has met on Saturday nights in space made available by at least two Chicago churches. Coffee, tea, soda, and sweets are served at intermissions or before and after programs, and are somewhat incidental to the featured events. At large-drawing concerts, the bulk of the audience never leaves the sanctuary space of the church to visit the third floor of the building where the library and refreshments are available. Smaller events, such as a popular crafts fair held during the December holiday season, take place entirely on the third floor, and in these instances coffee is more integrated. In addition to sponsoring a variety of ongoing reading, discussion, and support groups for women and children, with an emphasis on lesbian political issues, Mountain Moving Coffeehouse has brought a wide range of cultural programming to Chicago's feminist community (at affordable prices). A typical month includes events ranging from comedy to folksingers to a jazz duo, along with showings of artwork by differently abled women.

Despite its departures from more conventional forms, the heart of traditional coffeehouse culture has been retained insofar as Mountain Moving's clientele sustains a lively alternative to more mainstream forms of information sharing, community support, and entertainment. The importance of countercultural institutions such as this should not be underestimated. In addition to providing safe spaces for critical discourse and cultural events, they are places where symbolic speech, represented by styles of dress, bodily presentation, and other nonverbal forms of behavior, may find free expression. For some women this freedom to "speak" symbolically is a luxury unavailable in other venues of everyday life.

A young woman who is a recent graduate of college where the author teaches poignantly expresses the importance of such symbolic speech and the need for places where it may be freely and safely articulated. She describes herself as "a walking stereotype of a young 'Generation X' lesbian" who is a "regular" at Mountain Moving events, saying, "I look like a twelve-year-old boy—short hair, no makeup, no dresses, no skirts, definitely no high heels; when people aren't sure, they assume I'm male." She is frequently the object of homophobic verbal assaults on the streets of Chicago, but at coffeehouse events she looks "like everyone else." At Mountain Moving there are no "gender police" to call her to account for transgressing standards of "feminine" appearance or behavior, so she can feel comfortable just being herself. Coffeehouse events serve to remind her that she is not "alone in the world"; she feels empowered "to know that there's a group of people trying to move the mountain together, and not just me." When she was first coming out as a lesbian in Chicago, "it was really affirming to be surrounded by other lesbians, given that there's so much homophobia in the 'real' world." She still sees the coffeehouse as a place where she is guaranteed community and conviviality: "It's as if I'm a battery that runs down in the real world, but I can go to Mountain Moving and get recharged."[43]

Lynette J. Eastland spent several months studying Twenty Rue Jacob, a feminist coffeehouse and bookstore in Salt Lake City, Utah. She described her experiences as a participant–observer in this ethnographic study, citing the importance of everyday relationships to the coffeehouse community:

> The days I liked the best were those heavily loaded with people. . . . Sometimes they purchased something, but most often these days were primarily socially oriented. We would sell a lot of cups of coffee, some lunches and maybe a record or two. The women would greet each other warmly with hugs and smiles and catch up on the news of each others' lives. Some would come in to check the bulletin board and posters for local activities . . . or to see who was there, but mostly they came to pass time with one another, to find a friendly face.[44]

Here, it would seem, the exclusively male atmosphere of the eighteenth-century coffeehouse has been irrevocably altered by the social and political needs of women "customers"; while the gender specificity may have been inverted, traditions of free speech, public information, and sociability have been retained.

Indeed, in some instances, the explicitly political connections have been positively exploited. Eastland recounts how a typical day at Twenty Rue Jacob might include a scene such as the following, which involved

> two young women who came in early afternoon and ordered two cups of coffee. They were obviously upset and isolated themselves from the few people gathered around the counter . . . they asked to speak to [the manager, who] pulled up a chair and sat down. The two women held hands across the table as they talked. Both appeared very young, very attractive and were wearing dresses and high heels. . . . They needed the name of a lawyer, they said, who would be sensitive to their problem. They were being threatened by the ex-husband of one of the women, who said he would take [her] child away if they continued to see each other. They were confused and afraid and needed help.

The manager of the coffeehouse supplied the women with the name and phone number of an attorney; while we do not know "the rest of the story," it is clear that Twenty Rue Jacob played an integral role in making available to patrons information that might otherwise be unavailable or difficult to obtain from "mainstream" sources. Once again, echoes of past traditions linger, though with a twist.[45]

Oppositional and progressive coffeehouse cultures such as the two described here represent viable alternatives to the commodity culture of the mass media and serve as reminders of how it may still be possible to create public spheres where critical political discourse may be sustained in troubled times. Perhaps more importantly, as the vitality of feminist coffeehouses today would tend to indicate, such publicly discursive moments can be recreated in ways that inform a new generation of citizens. Here the links between the passions stimulated by coffee drinking and free speech undertaken in public association not only reach back through time of medieval Islam or the Enlightenment but also stretch forward to an as yet unimagined future. For those who prize a good cup of coffee along with democracy and passionate critical discourse, there may yet be hope.

NOTES

1. Aytoun Ellis, *The Penny Universities: A History of the Coffee-Houses* (London: Secker and Warburg, 1956), p. 3; Ralph S. Hattox, *Coffee and Coffeehouses: The Origins of a Social Beverage in the Medieval Near East* (Seattle: University of Washington Press, 1985), p. 12.

2. Ellis, *The Penny Universities,* p. 17.

3. Claudia Roden, *Coffee* (New York: Penguin, 1977), p. 20; David Joel, and Karl Schapira, *The Book of Coffee and Tea* (New York: St. Martin's Press, 1982), pp. 5–6.

4. Sara Perry, *The Complete Coffee Book* (San Francisco: Chronicle Books, 1991), p. 7; Roden, *Coffee,* p. 20; Schapira, *The Book of Coffee and Tea,* p. 6.

5. Norman Kolpas, *A Cup of Coffee* (New York: Grove Press, 1993), p. 14; Hattox, *Coffee and Coffeehouses,* pp. 22–28; Perry, *The Complete Coffee Book,* p. 7; Roden, *Coffee* p. 20.

6. Hattox, *Coffee and Coffeehouses,* p. 37.

7. *Ibid.,* pp. 32–39; Roden, *Coffee,* p. 21.

8. Hattox, *Coffee and Coffeehouses,* p. 93.

9. *Ibid.,* p. 101.

10. Perry, *The Complete Coffee Book,* p. 8; Roden, *Coffee,* p. 21; Schapira, *The Book of Coffee and Tea,* p. 9.

11. David F. Noble, *A World without Women: The Christian Clerical Culture of Western Science* (New York: Knopf, 1992), esp. pp. 3–39.

12. Ellis, *The Penny Universities,* p. 19.

13. *Ibid.,* p. 24.

14. *Ibid.,* p. 27.

15. *Ibid.,* p. 24.

16. Quoted in Roden, *Coffee,* p. 28.

17. Quoted in Edward Robinson, *The Early English Coffee House, with an Account of the First Use of Coffee* (1893) (Christchurch, Hants.: Dolphin Press, 1972), p. 117.

18. *Ibid.,* pp. 109–110.

19. Jürgen Habermas, *The Structural Transformation of the Public Sphere: An Inquiry into a Category of Bourgeois Society,* trans. Thomas Burger with the assistance of Frederick Lawrence (Cambridge, MA: MIT Press, 1989).

20. See Joan B. Landes, *Women and the Public Sphere in the Age of the French Revolution* (Ithaca, NY: Cornell University Press, 1988), pp. 7, 129.

21. The Women's Petition Against Coffee, representing to publick consideration the grand inconveniences accruing to their sex from the excessive use of that drying, enfeebling liquor. Presented to the right honorable the keepers of the library of Venus by a wellwiller. London, 1674.

22. Thanks to Uma Narayan for this insight. On the family as an economic unit, see Laurel Thatcher Ulrich, *Good Wives: Image and Realty in Northern New England, 1650–1750* (New York: Oxford University Press, 1982).

23. Kolpas, *A Cup of Coffee,* p. 22.

24. Linda K. Kerber, *Women of the Republic: Intellect and Ideology in Revolutionary America* (New York: Norton, 1986), p. 35.

25. L. H. Butterfield (Ed.) Abigail Adams to John Adams, July 31, 1778, *Adams Family Correspondence* (Cambridge, MA: Belknap Press, 1963), II, p. 295, quoted in Kerber, *Women of the Republic,* p. 44.

26. *Ibid.,* p. 44.

27. Roden, *Coffee,* p. 25.

28. Perry, *The Complete Coffee Book,* p. 17; Josh Glenn, "Coffee Time," *Utne Reader,* November/December 1994, p. 62.

29. Roden, *Coffee,* p. 22.

30. Wolfgang Schivelbusch, *Tastes of Paradise: A Social History of Spices, Stimulants, and Intoxicants,* translated from the German by David Jacobson (New York: Vintage Books, 1993), p. 69.

31. See, for example, Carroll Smith-Rosenberg, "The Female World of Love and Ritual Relations between Women in Nineteenth-Century America," *Signs,* 1 (1) (1975), pp. 1–29.

32. Deborah Cameron, *Feminism and Linguistic Theory,* cited in Jane Mills, *Womanwords: A Dictionary of Words about Women* (New York: Free Press, 1989), p. 44. See also Dale Spender, *Man Made Language,* 2nd ed. (New York: Pandora, 1991), p. 106–108.

33. Betty Friedan, *The Feminine Mystique* (New York: Norton, 1963).

34. "The Abuse of Alcohol from a Sanitary Standpoint," *American Kitchen Magazine,* 5 (1) (April 1896), p. 33, quoted in Harvey A. Levenstein, *Revolution at the Table: The Transformation of the American Diet* (New York: Oxford University Press, 1988), p. 99.

35. Jane Addams, "Immigration: A Field Neglected by the Scholar," *The Commons,* January 1905, p. 16.

36. George Lipsetz, "Why Remember Mama? The Changing Face of a Women's Narrative," in *Time Passages: Collective Memory and American Popular Culture* (Minneapolis: University of Minnesota Press, 1990), pp. 77–96.

37. *Ibid.,* p. 89.

38. *Ibid.,* p. 90.

39. Adrienne Rich, "Compulsory Heterosexuality and Lesbian Existence," *Signs,* 5 (4) (1980), pp. 631–660.

40. See, for example, Georges Bernier, *Paris Cafes: Their Role in the Birth of Modern Art* (New York: Wildenstein, 1985); and Henry Pachter, "Expressionism and Café Culture," in *Weimar Etudes* (New York: Columbia University Press, 1982).

41. Randy Shilts, *Conduct Unbecoming: Gays and Lesbians in the U.S. Military* (New York: St. Martin's Press, 1993), p. 152.

42. See Ellen Willis, "Radical Feminism and Feminist Radicalism" in Sonya Sayres, et al (Eds.), *The 60s without Apology* (Minneapolis: University of Minnesota Press, in cooperation with Social Text, 1984), pp. 111–112.

43. Suzy Stanton, personal communication, October 20, 1994. Suzy is a 1994 graduate of De Paul University. At De Paul, she was instrumental in founding an organization for lesbian, gay, and bisexual students and for developing and administering a survey of homophobic attitudes on campus—no mean feats at a Catholic institution of higher education.

44. Lynette J. Eastland, *Communication, Organization and Change within a Feminist Context: A Participant Observation of a Feminist Collective* (Lewiston, NY: E. Mellen Press, 1991), p. 176.

45. *Ibid.,* pp. 184–185.

FURTHER READINGS

Eastland, Lynette J. *Communication, Organization and Change within a Feminist Context: A Participant Observation of a Feminist Collective.* Lewiston, NY: E. Mellen Press, 1991.

Kerber, Linda K. *Women of the Republic: Intellect and Ideology in Revolutionary America.* New York: Norton, 1986.

Landes, Joan B. *Women and the Public Sphere in the Age of the French Revolution.* Ithaca, NY: Cornell University Press, 1988.

Rich, Adrienne. "Compulsory Heterosexuality and Lesbian Existence," *Signs,* 5 (4) (1980), pp. 631–660.

Smith-Rosenberg, Carroll. "The Female World of Love and Ritual: Relations between Women in Nineteenth-Century America," *Signs,* 1 (1) (1975), pp. 1–29.

CONTRIBUTORS

Frances E. Akins is a doctoral candidate in political science at the University of Georgia and is currently a research associate with SDR Incorporated, a marketing analytics and consulting firm. She has published in *American Political Quarterly*.

Denise L. Baer is president of Strategic Research Concepts, a Washington, DC area consulting firm and a professional lecturer with the Graduate School of Political Management, George Washington University. She has worked as a consultant for numerous groups. She is the author of numerous reports, *The Year of the Woman Voter?* (1998); *African American Women in the 1996 Elections* (1997); *The Gender Gap at the Democratic and Republican Conventions* (1996); *The U.S. House Democratic Caucus: Two Hundred Years of Leadership in the People's House* (1996); co-author of two scholarly books, *Politics and Linkage* (1993) and *Elite Cadres and Party Coalitions* (1988), and has had articles published in *American Review of Politics, Political Research Quarterly, Women and Politics,* and *Political Behavior*. She is completing a book on political parties and social movements and beginning a book on *Feminism in Black and White* to be co-authored with C. DeLores Tucker.

Ruth Bamberger is professor of political science and chair of the Department of History and Political Science at Drury College, Springfield, MO. She has researched extensively in the area of sex discrimination in insurance since it became a major public policy issue in the mid-1970s. She has authored papers on the topic, which have been presented at the Midwest Political Science Association, Southern Political Science Association, and the Southwestern Social Science Association. In 1981 Dr. Bamberger was granted an honorary research fellowship at the University of Durham, England, where she researched sex discrimination in insurance in the British system.

Irene J. Barnett is a doctoral student in political science at Kent State University. Her interests are in comparative politics and women in politics.

Linda L. M. Bennett is professor and chair of political science at Northern Kentucky University. She is the author of *Symbolic State Politics: Education Funding in Ohio* (1984) and co-author of *Living with Leviathan: Americans Coming to Terms with Big Government* (1990). She has also authored or co-authored articles on American government and politics.

Stephen E. Bennett is professor of political science at the University of Cincinnati. He is the author of *Apathy in America, 1960–1984* (1986), co-author of *Living with Leviathan: Americans Coming to Terms with Big Government* (1990), and co-editor of *After the Boom: The Politics of Generation X* (1997). He is currently working on a study of the political knowledge and opinions of young Americans.

Diane D. Blair is professor emeritus at the University of Arkansas. She has written extensively on Arkansas politics and government, state politics, and women in politics. She currently serves as Chairman of the Corporation for Public Broadcasting.

Charles S. Bullock III is the Richard B. Russell Professor of Political Science at the University of Georgia. Among his co-authored or co-edited books are *Law and Social Change* (1972); *Implementation of Civil Rights Policy* (1984); *The New Politics of the Old South* (1988); and *Runoff Elections in the United States* (1992), which won the Southern Political Science Association's V. O. Key Book Award. He is a past president of the Southern Political Science Association and past chair of the American Political Science Association's Legislative Studies Group.

Barbara C. Burrell is a researcher and head of survey design at the University of Wisconsin Extension Survey Research Laboratory. She is the author of *Public Opinion, The First Ladyship, and Hillary Clinton* (1997) and *A Woman's Place Is in the House: Campaigning for Congress in the Feminist Era* (1994). She has also researched party politics and gender in the United States.

Nancie E. Caraway is a scholar and writer living in Honolulu and Washington, DC. In addition to her feminist research, she is completing a screenplay on the life of Petra Kelly, feminist founder of the German Green party.

Regan Checchio is a doctoral candidate at the University of Iowa. Her research interests include American politics and global democratization.

Cal Clark is a professor of political science at Auburn University. He is the author of *Taiwan's Development;* co-author of *Women in Taiwan Politics;* and *Comparing Development Patterns in Asia;* and co-editor of *Dependency Reversal; State and Development; The Evolving Pacific Basin,* and *Beyond the Developmental State.*

Janet Clark is professor and chair of political science at the State University of West Georgia. (She received her Ph.D. from the University of Illinois and taught at New Mexico State University and the University of Wyoming.) She is the co-author of *Women, Elections, and Representation; Women in Taiwan Politics;* and *Government and Politics in Wyoming*. She has served as president of the Western Social Science Association and the Women's Caucus for Political Science. She is currently the editor of *Women & Politics*.

Patricia Clark is a graduate student in the School of Public Affairs at American University. A graduate of Villanova Law School, she is interested in issues of law, justice, and society.

Elizabeth Adell Cook teaches in the Department of Government and Politics at the University of Maryland, College Park. She is the co-author of *Between Two Absolutes: Public Opinion and the Politics of Abortion* (1992) and co-editor of *The Year of the Woman: Myths and Realities* (1994). She has also published many scholarly articles on feminist consciousness and abortion politics.

Kathleen Dolan is assistant professor of political science, University of Wisconsin-Oshkosh. She has written several articles on women state legislators, attitudes toward women candidates, and voters' willingness to vote for female candidates. Her research interests include women and politics, electoral behavior, and legislative behavior.

Lynne E. Ford is associate professor of political science, College of Charleston, where she teaches courses on U.S. politics, political behavior, political psychology, women and politics, and comparative gender. Her research interests include women in elective office, citizenship through service learning, and the development of political attitudes in adolescents. She has written on women serving in state legislatures and on women in politics in South Carolina.

Joanne V. Hawks, director of Sarah Isom Center for Women's Studies, University of Mississippi, teaches courses on the history of southern and American women and the role of women in society. With Carolyn Ellis Staton she has researched and written articles on women in southern legislatures from the 1920s to the present.

Laura Jane Hoffman is a graduate student in the Political Science Department, University of Georgia.

Kathleen P. Iannello is associate professor and chair of the Political Science Department at Gettysburg College. She teaches courses in American politics and feminist theory. She is the author of *Decisions Without Hierarchy*.

Hedy Leonie Isaacs is a doctoral student in the Graduate Department of Public Administration at Rutgers University, Newark. She has held an adjunct faculty position at the University of the West Indies–Mona Campus. She has worked extensively with the public service in the area of human resource management.

Roberta Ann Johnson is professor of politics at the University of San Francisco. (She has a B.A. degree [magna cum laude, Phi Beta Kappa] from Brooklyn College and M.A. and Ph.D. from Harvard University.) She has served as a technical assistance specialist in the Office for Civil Rights, U.S. Dept. of Education. In 1992 she had a Fulbright Grant to teach American politics and women's studies at the University of Indonesia, Jakarta. In 1993–1994, she was the National Endowment for the Humanities Chair at the University of San Francisco. In 1994, she received federal funding through the Campus Compact program to develop a service-learning course on the homeless. She has published numerous articles on minorities, women, the disabled, and civil rights–related topics in journals such as *Western Political Quarterly, Policy, Revista/Review Inter Americana,* and *Policy and Politics*. She has also published a book, *Puerto Rico: Commonwealth or Colony?* (1980).

Elizabeth A. Kelly is associate professor of political science and director of women's studies at De Paul University in Chicago. She is the author of *Education, Public Knowledge, and Democracy* (1995) and is currently working on a book about Jane Addams's social and political thought. She enjoys a good cup of coffee.

Susan A. MacManus is professor of public administration and political science in the Department of Government and International Affairs at the University of South Florida, Tampa. She is past president of the Southern Political Science Association, and the Florida Political Science Association. She has published numerous articles on women in local politics in leading journals. Her most recent book is *Young v. Old: Generational Combat in the 21st Century,* Westview Press, 1996.

Elaine Martin is professor at Eastern Michigan University in Ypsilanti. She teaches courses in judicial politics, women in politics, and public administration. She has published extensively on the subject of gender and the judiciary and is now at work on a book: *Distinguished Women: Voices from the Bench*.

Arthur H. Miller is professor of political science and director of the Iowa Social Science Institute at the University of Iowa. He has established a national and international reputation for his research on citizen evaluations of government and factors influencing public decision making. He has published numerous articles in the leading professional journals of the United States and Europe. His most recent books include *Public Opinion and Regime Change* (1993), and *Presidential Campaigns and American Self-Images* (1994).

Adam Newmark completed his MA in American Politics in the Department of Government and International Affairs at the University of South Florida in 1998.

Maureen Rand Oakley is a doctoral student at Kent State University. Her current research is on comparative state fetal protection laws.

Karen O'Connor is professor and chair of government in the School of Public Affairs at American University. A past president of the Women's Caucus for Political Science, she is the author of several books and articles on women's issues, law and American politics including *Women, Politics & American Society,* 2nd ed. (with Nancy E. McGlen, 1998); *American Government: Continuity & Change* (with Larry Sabato, 1997), and *No Neutral Ground: Abortion Politics in an Age of Absolutes* (1996).

Jennifer Ring is director of women's studies and associate professor of political science at the University of Nevada, Reno. She received her doctorate from the University of California, Berkeley and is the author of *The Political Consequences of Thinking: Gender and Judaism in the Work of Hannah Arendt* (1997); *Modern Political Theory and Contemporary Feminism: A Dialectical Analysis* (1991); and articles and reviews on political theory, feminist theory and epistemology, and multicultural feminism, published in *Political Theory, American Journal of Political Science, Review of Politics,* and *Women and Politics.*

Wilma Rule is an adjunct professor of political science at the University of Nevada, Reno, and co-editor with Joseph F. Zimmerman of *U.S. Electoral Systems: Their Impact on Women and Minorities* (1992) and *Electoral Systems in Comparative Perspective: Their Impact on Women and Minorities* (1994). She is the author of numerous articles on women's recruitment to state and national legislatures.

Carolyn Ellis Staton is associate provost and associate vice chancellor for academic affairs and professor of law at the University of Mississippi Law School. (She received her undergraduate degree from Tulane University; her masters from Columbia University, and her juris doctorate from Yale Law School.) Formerly, she was in private practice in New York and was an assistant U.S. attorney in the District of New Jersey. She was also a Fulbright Fellow in Germany. Currently, Ms. Staton serves as reporter on evidence for the Mississippi Supreme Court Advisory Committee on Rules. She is the author of books and articles on evidence, criminal procedure, and sex discrimination. She teaches courses on evidence, sex discrimination, criminal procedure, and school law.

Gertrude A. Steuernagel is professor of political science at Kent State University. She is co-author of *Women and Public Policy: A Revolution in Progress* 1995; and *Women and Political Participation: Cultural Change in the Political Arena* 1997.

Joan Hulse Thompson is associate professor of political science at Beaver College, Glenside, PA, and has served as an American Association of University Women Education Foundation Fellow at the Congressional Caucus for Women's Issues in 1983–1984. She was an American Political Science Association Congressional Fellow in 1985–1986. She teaches courses on American politics and public law, including a course on Congress and another on gender roles and family policy.

Charles Tien is assistant professor at Hunter College, CUNY. His research interests include minorities and women in Congress, presidential elections, and political methodology.

Sara J. Weir is associate professor of political science at Western Washington University in Bellingham. She teaches courses in domestic policy analysis and women and politics. Her current research is in the area of women and leadership.

Marcia Lynn Whicker is professor and chair of the Graduate Department of Public Administration at Rutgers University, Newark. She has held faculty positions at Virginia Commonwealth University, University of South Carolina, Temple University and Wayne State University. She has worked for various government agencies, including the U.S. Senate Budget Committee and a U.S. House member as an APSA Congressional Fellow; the Department of Health, Education, and Welfare; the Tennessee Valley Authority; and the U.S. Comptroller as a national bank examiner. She has published fifteen books and numerous scholarly and journalistic articles in the areas of public policy, public administration, American national politics, and leadership.

Lois Duke Whitaker is professor and chair of the Department of Political Science, Georgia Southern University in Statesboro. She is the author of many pieces on women and politics and on U.S. national government, including a co-edited volume with James MacGregor Burns, William Crotty, and Lawrence Longley, *The Democrats Must Lead: The Case for a Progressive Democratic Party.* Her research interests also include mass media and politics, and state and local government. Currently, she is working on a manuscript featuring civil rights activists and their contributions to the civil rights movement in the Deep South. She has taught at the University of South Carolina, Columbia; the University of Alabama, Tuscaloosa; the University of San Francisco; Clemson University; and Auburn University, Montgomery. She is a past president of the Women's Caucus for Political Science: South; is a past president of the South Carolina Political Science Association, and is Program Vice-President for the League of Women Voters of South Carolina. She is the recipient of the Clemson University Chapter of the American Association of University Professors (AAUP) Award of Merit for distinctive contributions to the academic profession (May 1992).

Thomas E. Yatsco is a doctoral student at Kent State University. He is doing research on Medicaid reform and states' governing capacity.